THE TECHNICAL MASTERY OF

Bowling Progression

Path to Ultimate Motor Skills Acquisition

MOHAMED JANAHI

The Technical Mastery Of Bowling Progression
Copyright © 2024 by Mohamed Janahi

ISBNs
Hardback: 978-1-963351-03-3
Ebook: 978-1-963351-06-4
Paperback: 978-1-963351-02-6

Printed in the United States of America

I've poured my heart and soul into crafting this book, with an aspiration that it can light up the path for numerous nations to thrive in the world of bowling. This book is a testament to my unwavering dedication to our beloved sport. With unwavering resolve, let's unite to revive bowling to its former glory and forge an enduring legacy for generations to come.

MJ

CONTENTS

ABOUT THE AUTHOR

Mohamed is more than just a bowler; he is a coach, a researcher, and a remarkable example of a journey through the world of bowling that's laced with tenacity, hard work, and an insatiable quest for knowledge.

In the 1990s, Mohamed emerged as a bright star in the Gulf region's youth bowling scene. His journey was unique; he had no formal coach and a distinctive self-taught approach. As he set out on his quest for excellence, he explored the technical and psychological aspects of the sport in a way that sets him apart.

In the pursuit of excellence, Mohamed was a self-forged bowler, a solitary figure who, devoid of formal coaching, embarked on a personal odyssey to master the art of bowling. His journey was one of both a physical and psychological nature, constantly pushing the boundaries of his mental fortitude. His style, unique and idiosyncratic, evolved from the blend of traditional and contemporary power tactics, bearing witness to a keen mind always in search of the perfect equation. He was haunted by the enigma of the professional bowlers from the Professional Bowlers Association (PBA) and other luminaries of the sport, ceaselessly pondering what made them excel and how they managed to thrive in a game that demanded not just skill but profound mental resilience.

Yet, there's more to his story than just technique. His emotional connection to bowling is profound. Bowling became his lifeline, especially during his formative years. It was a bridge to break free from loneliness and establish social connections. The day he scored a remarkable 82 in his first game, a momentous transformation occurred. It was the first time he felt socially accepted, and bowling became more than just a sport; it became a means of connecting with others.

This journey wasn't without its trials. Mohamed's decision to use a 16-pound ball, the famous Faball Blue Hammer, as a 13-year-old was unconventional. The prevailing belief was that a heavier ball led to better results, but Mohamed defied norms and followed his instincts.

His ascent in the bowling community was remarkable, marked by victories at the GCC Singles Event in 1994 and 1995. However, despite offers to play for other countries, Mohamed chose a different path. He felt that other nations had better resources and support, and he was determined to carve his own way to success. This determination led him to tirelessly seek sponsorships, develop innovative training environments, and even modify equipment to improve his precision.

Mohamed's commitment to learning and mastering the sport is evident in his impressive collection of over 22 professional qualifications, including those in sport psychology, nutrition, conditioning, and more. He didn't just excel as a bowler; he also became a coach, inspiring the next generation of bowlers.

His story is a testament to unwavering dedication and a pursuit of excellence. It's a message to bowlers worldwide that with determination, resilience, and a hunger for knowledge, new heights in bowling can be reached.

Today, Mohamed's contributions to the bowling community extend beyond his playing days. He's deeply involved in scholarly and scientific research, striving to uncover the secrets of skill acquisition in bowling. His legacy is defined by a commitment to the psychological aspects of the game, transforming how bowlers approach their performance.

In his prime, Mohamed achieved remarkable success in the Asian Bowling Tour, consistently ranking among the top 7 bowlers from 2011 to 2016 out of a field of 500 Asian bowlers. His unwavering dedication to the sport was undeniable.

However, in 2017, a pivotal realization altered his course. He recognized that becoming a true professional bowler required a robust support system, superior coaching, and more resources than he currently possessed. Balancing international competition with his responsibilities as a banker, a father, a coach, an entrepreneur, and a part-time ABF tournament bowler was unsustainable.

This realization led him to shift his focus towards coaching. From 2017 to 2022, Mohamed dedicated himself to coaching in various nations, sharing his expertise as a head coach of Jordan, Saudi Arabia, Kuwait, Iran, and Bahrain. He organized an astounding 82 camps and clinics in Asia, the Middle East, and Europe. Despite his coaching success, a fundamental question continued to occupy his mind - what defines true bowling skill and how can one become a bowling prodigy?

To find answers, Mohamed embarked on a mission to obtain top coaching certifications, delving deep into the psychology of bowling. His pursuit of knowledge led him to pursue a bachelor's degree in sport psychology in England. At every juncture, he absorbed new techniques and perspectives to help bowlers unlock their full potential.

This journey wasn't without its challenges. Mohamed often wondered why the winning formula eluded him in his early years. In 2019, he reached out to the top 58 bowlers and 12 coaches from around the world, hungry for more insights. The result is this comprehensive manual, a collaborative effort of his friends and colleagues in the coaching community.

Mohamed's journey through the world of bowling is one of perseverance, unwavering commitment, and a deep love for the sport. His contributions have reshaped how bowlers approach their game, both technically and psychologically. His story continues to inspire and guide the bowling community towards new horizons in skill acquisition and performance.

DEDICATION

This book is dedicated to HH Sheikh Nasser bin Hamad Al Khalifa, Commander of Bahrain's Royal Guard, Deputy Chairman of the Higher Committee for Energy and Natural Resources, and the head of the government's Supreme Council for Youth and Sports.

I extend my heartfelt gratitude to HH Sheikh Nasser for his unwavering commitment to the advancement of sports development in the Kingdom of Bahrain. His visionary leadership, intellect, and innovative ideas have propelled our sport to new heights, establishing it as a dominant presence on the global stage.

Under the dedicated guidance of HH Sheikh Nasser, the youth and sports movement in the Kingdom of Bahrain has experienced a remarkable upsurge across various domains. His steadfast commitment to youth and sports has not only raised the bar but has also propelled Bahrain to a position of formidable competition on the international stage.

This book, "The Technical Mastery of Bowling Progression - Path to Ultimate Motor Skills Development," serves as a testament to the transformative power of visionary leadership, unwavering dedication, and an unrelenting pursuit of excellence. It mirrors our collective aspiration to reach the pinnacle of sporting achievement, much like the tireless efforts of HH Sheikh Nasser to enhance and cultivate optimal sport development in the Kingdom.

FOREWORD

We are all aware that, overall, athletics may not be of utmost importance. Although it provides entertainment and distraction, it does not control life or death. "Sports is the most important of the unimportant things in life." - Arrigo Sacchi, Famed football manager.

Beyond just being a form of exercise and pleasure, sports can help us better understand who we are. It lets us understand why some players succeed, even under pressure, but others struggle.

This book examines how we may all work to be the best versions of ourselves through a cutting-edge investigation of what I now refer to as sports science. The book takes us on a tour through the intriguing worlds of the human body and mind by first examining why younger siblings frequently outperform their older counterparts.

Sport has become a more important cultural institution recently, which is intriguing to observe. Few countries have escaped the accomplishments of outstanding bowlers, whether it be the imposing steps of Jason Belmonte or EJ Tackett on the PBA Tour, the resounding displays of Choi Bok or Park Jong in championship matches, or Anthony Simenson's capacity to use bowling as a medium for artistic expression. These players will continue to cherish the ever-evolving and inspiring field of bowling.

This sports science-focused book, offers a thorough examination of the elements that go into achieving peak performance. It provides insightful advice on how to reach our maximum potential in the game of bowling by drawing on a wide range of research, personal experiences, and interviews with elite bowlers and instructors from around the world.

You will investigate the complex interactions between physical prowess, mental toughness, tactical decision-making, and the psychology of game mastery as you set out on this instructive trip. You will obtain a greater grasp of what it takes to maximize your performance on the bowling alley through engrossing anecdotes, academic studies, and useful advice.

Also acknowledged in this book are the significant contributions of many people who kindly contributed their knowledge and experiences. This book's pages are enhanced by the insights and viewpoints of top bowlers like Parker Bohn as well as renowned coaches like Frank Buffa and Del Warren.

Finally, this book provides proof of the long-lasting influence of athletics in reshaping our lives and propelling us to new heights. "The Great Bowling Equation - Maximizing Performance with Optimal Psychological Transitions" is certain to leave a lasting impression on your path to bowling excellence, whether you are an aspiring bowler, an experienced professional, or simply someone with an interest in the psychology of success.

PROLOGUE:

As I immerse myself in the world of bowling, I see the top bowlers' extraordinary abilities and accomplishments every day. My desire to join their ranks is stoked by their astounding performances on television, in my social media feeds, and in the newspaper pages. What are my odds of doing the same? Even after spending quite a good amount of time on this subject, the resolution is equally depressing and perceptive.

One in 2000 high school bowlers has a chance of becoming a professional bowler. These probabilities are enormously increased, though, on the path to winning the sport. The International Bowling Federation (IBF) estimated that there were more than 100 million registered bowlers globally as of 2021. Jason Belmonte is the only bowler among them to have pulled off the incredible accomplishment of winning 15 major championships in the course of just 10 years. There are 67 million bowlers in the United States, yet only one, Walter Ray Williams Jr., has won more than 100 PBA and PBA regional titles combined.

I'm excited to announce that I've written a trilogy of books that explore the subject of peak performance and flow state in bowling. These publications are the result of my in-depth research and personal experiences, and they attempt to give thorough insights into all facets of bowling, whether they be technical, psychological, or the development of talent.

The first book in the trilogy is titled **"The Bowling Flow Blueprint: Nurturing Talent and Decoding the Science of Elitism."** This book discusses the critical function of identifying and developing bowling talent. It offers a guide for developing an atmosphere that promotes growth, skill development, and achieving the coveted flow state in bowling by drawing on the knowledge of great instructors and the most recent studies.

"The Neuro-Psych Mastery in Bowling" explores the complex connection between the mind and performance as we move on to the psychological aspect of bowling. This book provides bowlers with tools to harness the power of their brains and make seamless transitions toward their best performance on the lanes by examining subjects like mental toughness, focus, motivation, and managing pressure.

The Technical Mastery of Bowling Progression: Path to Ultimate Motor Skills Development," the third book in the series, is a comprehensive manual for learning how to develop superior motor skills when bowling. This book decodes the mysteries of technique, form, and precision through in-depth research and useful exercises, providing bowlers with useful tools to hone their abilities and reach their maximum potential.

These three volumes provide a thorough and all-encompassing analysis of bowling's art and science when taken together. This trilogy will be a priceless resource on your road to success in bowling. Whether you're an expert pro aiming to improve your techniques, a coach seeking to bring out the best in your athletes, or a passionate bowler longing to deepen your knowledge of the sport,

This book, "The Technical Mastery of Bowling: Progression Path to Ultimate Motor Skills Acquisition," is a comprehensive and illuminating book that takes a deep dive into the world of bowling. It goes beyond viewing bowling as a mere sport and explores its role as a way of life. In the following pages, you'll embark on an extensive exploration that dissects the significance of competition in athletics and demystifies the enigma of greatness, particularly within the context of bowling.

The journey begins with an in-depth examination of the sport through the lens of Piaget's esteemed 4 Stages of Cognitive Development. This perspective provides valuable insights into the intricate cognitive processes involved in developing the motor skills required for bowling. This foundational understanding sets the stage for a profound grasp of the complexities of bowling.

Moving forward, the book systematically dissects the stages of competence and skill acquisition in the sport. It offers a clear, step-by-step breakdown of the path that bowlers follow as they strive for mastery. This comprehensive exploration not only provides theoretical insights but also practical guidance for aspiring athletes and coaches.

One of the book's most noteworthy contributions is the introduction of my own Skill Acquisition Model called the Janahi FRI Model. This model challenges conventional skill acquisition frameworks, offering a fresh perspective on how bowlers can approach skill development within the sport. It opens up new possibilities for understanding and achieving mastery in bowling.

To complement its theoretical framework, the book provides readers with a meticulously crafted Optimal Development Plan. This plan isn't just a theoretical concept; it's a tangible and practical roadmap for aspiring bowlers. It serves as the key to unlocking the elusive state of flow, where peak performance becomes an attainable reality.

This book isn't confined to theory; it's enriched with practical strategies for enhancing skill acquisition. Throughout its pages, the book emphasizes the importance of prioritizing overall athletic development before honing specific bowling skills. This holistic approach is reinforced by the introduction of PEL (Performance Engaging Experience Learning) learning ratios, showcasing their application across all learning stages in bowling.

The book also engages in a detailed analysis of the ongoing debate between traditional training methods and transfer skill training in the context of bowling. It provides insights into the potential for transformative results through the strategic alteration of automated movement patterns. Readers are invited to explore various strategies that can lead to this transformative change.

In essence, whether you're an aspiring bowler looking to elevate your skills, a coach aiming to guide your athletes to excellence, or simply someone captivated by the world of athletics and competition, this book is a valuable resource. It offers profound insights into the nuanced world of skill development, competition, and the pursuit of excellence within the captivating realm of bowling.

This book dedicates a substantial section to the pivotal role of coaches in the world of bowling, delving deep into the qualities that define a top-notch bowling coach and highlighting the essential attributes that epitomize coaching excellence. Additionally, it unravels the transformative journey from being a player to becoming a coach, illuminating the pathways and experiences that guide bowlers toward becoming exceptional mentors. These pages also provide valuable insights into coaching within the framework of ecological dynamics, a dynamic approach that acknowledges the intricate and ever-evolving nature of coaching in the realm of bowling. This section serves as an invaluable resource, offering a comprehensive understanding of the coaching dimension for both aspiring coaches and players alike within this dynamic sport.

Within these pages, you'll discover the keys to technical mastery and gain the wisdom to redefine your approach to this dynamic and timeless sport. This book invites you to embark on a transformative journey, one that transcends the sport itself and offers profound insights into human achievement and the relentless pursuit of greatness through the art of bowling.

Let's now go out on this fascinating trip together, studying the fascinating world of professional bowling, solving the mystery of excellence, and learning about the amazing tales that motivate and stoke our passion. May bowlers of all skill levels find this book to be a source of knowledge and inspiration as it illuminates the road to excellence.

Turning each page will take us deeper into the bowling world, revealing its inner workings and illuminating the extraordinary people who influence the game. As you step onto the approach and strengthen your hold on the ball, let's discover the wonderful world of competitive bowling.

I am honored and appreciative of the chance to educate and enlighten the bowling community. My objective is that these publications will inspire and equip bowlers of all skill levels to achieve new levels of performance and fulfillment on the lanes, in addition to informing and educating them.

THANK YOU

First and foremost, I owe an immeasurable debt of gratitude to my beloved wife. Her unwavering encouragement, understanding, and unselfish support were the driving force behind my decision to embark on this writing journey once again. Throughout the process, she stood by my side, understanding that my commitment to this book, alongside two others, would mean less time for shared moments. Her belief that my career is our shared priority was a constant source of motivation, and her patience and understanding were unwavering. Thank you for being my rock and my biggest cheerleader.

And a heartfelt thank you to my brother, Yousif (Yoyo), who has been my unwavering support throughout the years. He's been there through the highs and lows of my career, pushing me to be better, even better than himself. His joy in my bowling achievements, be it titles or coaching milestones, has been a constant source of light in my darkest moments. When the path seemed uncertain, I could always turn to him to rekindle my self-belief and remind me of my true potential. You've been my guiding star, and for that, I'm eternally grateful.

I must also express my heartfelt appreciation to my mentors, Juha Maja, Patrick Henry, Mario Joseph, Ron Hoppe, and Tim Mack. Over the course of 25 years, these extraordinary individuals have been instrumental in shaping my understanding of the world of bowling. Their wisdom, guidance, and generosity in sharing their knowledge have been invaluable. They have not only been mentors but also friends and sources of inspiration, and for that, I am profoundly grateful.

To all those who have supported, encouraged, and contributed to the making of this book, your influence has been immeasurable. Your belief in this project and its potential impact on the world of bowling is deeply appreciated. This book stands as a testament to the power of collaboration and the unwavering support of loved ones and mentors alike.

SPORT AS A WAY OF LIFE: UNDERSTANDING THE SIGNIFICANCE OF COMPETITION IN ATHLETICS

Beyond the confines of time, culture, and location, sport has always had a substantial impact on human civilization. It becomes more than just something we do for fun; it becomes a lively representation of who we are. Sports have several facets that shape our civilization, including social, mental, emotional, and physical ones. This thorough investigation dives into the innate desire to compete and the underlying idea of sport as a way of life, drawing on research in psychology, sociology, anthropology, and sports sciences.

The heart of competition in sports

All sporting undertakings are fundamentally competitive, setting them apart from other physical activities. It increases excitement, fervor, and emotion in the realm of sports. In essence, competition entails people or groups going above and beyond to exceed one another while always aiming for success. Sports' competitive character fosters a dynamic and demanding environment that encourages participants to reach their full potential, push their physical and mental boundaries, and continuously develop their abilities.

Athletes compete in a variety of sports, from team sports like basketball, football, and soccer to individual sports like track and field, gymnastics, and swimming. Boxing and mixed martial arts are examples of combat sports that entail direct physical conflict. The criteria, scoring methods, rankings, and awards that are painstakingly created to choose winners and foster a sense of satisfaction and achievement make clear this natural competitiveness. However, sports competition extends beyond the physical sphere and enters the mental and emotional spheres as well. In order to overcome obstacles like pressure, setbacks, and uncertainty, athletes require unwavering mental toughness, resilience, and psychological knowledge. The emotional and mental challenges of competition can be just as difficult as the physical ones, necessitating the overcoming of adversity, fear, and self-doubt. This diverse aspect of rivalry makes sports a complex endeavor with many facets.

The irresistible allure of sport and competition

Sport is appealing not just because it is physical and entertaining but also because it embodies the fierce human spirit of competition, which has been a part of our existence since the dawn of time. The act of competition has had a lasting impact, reshaping cultures, societies, and individual lives, from the ancient Greek Olympic Games to contemporary professional sports. This essay sets out on an investigative trip, exploring the idea of sport as a way of life, revealing the significant role that competition plays in athletic undertakings, and exposing the profoundly embedded need for competition that exists in human nature.

We begin to understand sport's and competition's symbiotic relationship and the tremendous influence it has on our lives as we begin to unravel the tapestry of sport and competition. Understanding the importance of competition and accepting it as a necessary aspect of life helps us realize our full potential as athletes and as people traveling the complex road of life.

The drive to compete: ingrained by evolution

Our evolutionary history shows that competition developed as a survival strategy. Early on in the evolution of humans, finding food, shelter, and mates was of utmost importance. Competitors' success increased the likelihood that their genes would be passed on to succeeding generations, perpetuating their unique features. This competitive nature has been ingrained in us genetically through countless generations. Therefore, this ancestral urge motivates us to compete and succeed in a variety of spheres of life, including sports.

The nature of competition and our unrelenting quest for greatness are reflections of who we are as people. We all have an intrinsic urge to test our limits, outperform our past successes, and improve upon who we already are. Competition serves as a stimulus for advancement, self-discovery, and personal growth in the world of sports. Athletes take on difficulties, establish goals, and commit to constant practice and improvement. They want to outperform themselves and achieve new performance levels with every competition. This never-ending quest for greatness is fundamental to who we are as people.

Nurturing the competitive spirit: societal and cultural influences

Sports competition has an allure that is frequently heightened by social and cultural variables. Sports competitions are engrained in our traditions and customs in many countries. Athletes are given the esteem of heroes and role models, encouraging others to start their own athletic careers. People are motivated to compete because of the expectations, accolades, and incentives attached to sporting accomplishments. The competitive spirit thrives in this social and cultural context, giving people a sense of direction, drive, and community.

We can trace our innate need for competition to our evolutionary past. It is a system that has been formed by the struggles of reproduction, survival, and the unrelenting desire for success. Competition may have had a significant impact on early human history, according to evolutionary psychologists. Only those who prevailed in these struggles to survive the tough competition for scarce resources were able to carry on their genetic heritage. Humans developed a competitive instinct as a result of this selection process. Understanding this evolutionary viewpoint offers useful insights into our intrinsic desire to compete in other spheres, such as sports.

Psychological factors: unveiling the motivation

Numerous psychological elements have an impact on the inner motivation to participate in sports. According to McClelland's theory of needs, the need for achievement is one of these elements. Individuals are driven to aim for success, create goals, and take on difficulties by their urge to achieve. This urge for achievement manifests in sports as the desire to win, enhance performance, and top prior successes. Sports become an essential part of people's lives when they compete in them, giving them a sense of fulfillment, motivation, and purpose.

Another psychological aspect influencing the fundamental motivation to compete is shown by the self-determination hypothesis. Autonomy, competence, and relatedness are basic human needs. Athletes are more likely to be intrinsically driven in the setting of sports if they believe they are autonomous, competent, and socially connected within their sport. They take pleasure in the competition process and feel better overall. By addressing these self-determination demands in sports, we may advance the idea of sport as life, in which people compete in sports for the sake of self-expression, self-actualization, and self-improvement.

Self-esteem, or one's assessment of one's own value, is another psychological component that affects the intrinsic motivation to participate in sports. Through accomplishments and victories, sports tournaments give people the chance to prove their skills, gain recognition, and boost their self-esteem. Having high self-esteem can be a powerful motivation in sports, encouraging people to devote time, energy, and money to their hobby and regard it as a major part of their lives. Higher levels of motivation, performance, and happiness in their sport are frequently seen in athletes.

Here's a list of both intrinsic and extrinsic motivations for bowlers:

Intrinsic Motivations:

Enjoyment of the Game: *Many bowlers are intrinsically motivated because they simply enjoy bowling. The satisfaction derived from rolling a perfect strike or improving one's skills is a reward in itself.*

Personal Challenge: *Intrinsic motivation can come from the challenge of mastering the sport. Bowlers who enjoy pushing their limits and seeing their own progress are intrinsically motivated.*

Sense of Mastery: *The desire to master the art and technique of bowling is often an intrinsic motivation. The personal satisfaction of executing a perfect shot can be a powerful driver.*

Autonomy: *Some bowlers are motivated by the autonomy they have in choosing how they approach the sport. They value the freedom to develop their unique style and strategies.*

Intrinsic Reward of Improvement: *The process of self-improvement can be intrinsically rewarding. Each small step toward becoming a better bowler can be motivating.*

Flow State: *Achieving a flow state, where one is fully immersed and absorbed in the game, is often an intrinsic reward for bowlers. The joy of being "in the zone" motivates many to keep playing.*

Personal Fulfillment: *Bowling can provide a sense of personal fulfillment and purpose, which serves as a strong intrinsic motivation.*

Physical Activity: *Some bowlers are intrinsically motivated by the physical exercise and health benefits that come with the sport.*

Competence and Skill Development: *The process of developing competence and skills in bowling can be intrinsically motivating, as it leads to a sense of achievement.*

Intrinsic Passion: *Having a deep passion for the sport of bowling itself can be a psychological motivator that keeps bowlers engaged and motivated.*

Extrinsic Motivations:

Prize Money: *In professional and competitive bowling, prize money is a significant extrinsic motivator. The prospect of earning a financial reward for success drives many bowlers.*

Trophies and Awards: *Winning trophies, medals, and other awards is an extrinsic motivator, as it provides tangible recognition of achievement.*

Endorsements and Sponsorships: *Professional bowlers often seek extrinsic motivation in the form of endorsements and sponsorships, which can lead to financial gains.*

Scholarships: *For college and youth bowlers, scholarships provided by universities can be a compelling extrinsic motivator to perform well.*

Social Recognition: *The external recognition and social status that come with being a successful bowler are extrinsic motivators for some.*

Peer and Fan Support: *Bowlers may be motivated by the support and applause they receive from peers, family, and fans, which can boost their self-esteem.*

Team Success: *In team events, the desire to win for the sake of the team is an extrinsic motivator, as it's driven by the desire to contribute to collective success.*

Career Opportunities: *Success in bowling can lead to extrinsic motivators like coaching opportunities, television appearances, and involvement in the bowling industry.*

Public Attention: *For some bowlers, the attention they receive from the media and the public is an extrinsic motivator.*

The power of the surrounding environment: social and cultural factors

The inherent motivation to compete in sports is significantly shaped by the social environment. An individual's motivation and participation in sporting events are greatly influenced by his social network, which includes his coaches, teammates, and supporters. Athletes who experience more social support have been shown to be more motivated, self-assured, and satisfied with their sport. Athletes benefit from social support in terms of a sense of community, support, and reinforcement, which increases their innate motivation and desire to compete in sports. Additionally, the social connections and relationships made through athletics promote a sense of identity and community, where people feel part of a bigger community and find meaning and joy in their sport.

The State of Flow

Athletes frequently try to reach the flow state, also referred to as "being in the zone," in the world of sports, which is characterized by total immersion, unshakable attention, and peak performance. This psychological state has received a great deal of attention in sports psychology because it is so important in fostering the innate desire to compete and determining how people view athletics as a way of life.

Several essential characteristics that define the "flow state" in sports add to its attractiveness. Athletes who are in a flow state are focused on the current moment, have clear goals in mind, receive immediate feedback, experience a balance between obstacles and skills, feel in control, and lose self-consciousness. When athletes reach this stage, their abilities are well-matched to the obstacles they are facing, and they are completely immersed in the activity. They find themselves performing at their very best because they are driven to overcome challenges and accomplish their objectives. In addition to improving motivation, performance, and enjoyment, this state of flow has a positive effect on an athlete's physical and mental health.

LUCAS LUIS LEGNANI: PERSEVERANCE

There have been defining moments in my career where I've experienced an indescribable feeling—the kind that makes me believe that a higher power has intervened and guided me. These moments of flow and synchronicity, where my mind and body are perfectly aligned with the present, are rare and precious. They remind me of the magic that can happen in this sport and fuel my passion to continue pushing forward.

A mix of human and environmental factors is necessary to achieve flow state in sports. The nature of the sport itself, the competition atmosphere, and the degree of challenge all have an impact on an athlete's capacity to enter the flow state, even though criteria like skill level and motivation are important. Sports that provide quick input, like long-distance running, tend to be less conducive to experiencing flow state than sports that do, like golf or swimming. In addition, flow state is more likely to occur in sports that balance skills and difficulties while adjusting the level of difficulty to an athlete's capabilities. Finding that balance is essential since too simple or too difficult sports can interfere with the flow experience.

The setting of the competition has an additional impact on an athlete's capacity to enter flow state. There are many variables at play, including the degree of competitiveness, the number of viewers, and the performance pressure. Competitions with high stakes and high pressure can increase anxiety and self-consciousness, making it harder to enter the flow state. In contrast, a friendly and encouraging environment of competition that fosters autonomy, competence, and social relationships creates the ideal setting for athletes to experience flow state.

For athletes, being in a flow state while doing sports has many advantages. People who reach this state express greater levels of intrinsic motivation, happiness, and enjoyment in their sport. With increased concentration and intensity, their performance achieves its peak. Athletes' mental health and general well-being are benefited by the positive psychological state of flow, which is characterized by a loss of self-consciousness and a sensation of control.

In conclusion, sports cover more than just physical activity; for many people, they are a way of life. Individual traits like motivation, personality, and skill level, as well as social and cultural elements like social support and cultural norms, all have an impact on a person's intrinsic motivation to compete in sports. With its total immersion, unshakable attention, and peak performance, the concept of flow state in sports is essential for strengthening the innate urge to compete and defining the whole experience of sports as a way of life. Achieving flow state in sports has many advantages, including improved performance, contentment, and enjoyment. It is impacted by both individual and situational circumstances. Recognizing the innate motivation to compete in sports as well as the idea of flow state helps to explain why people are driven to sports as a way of life and why competition is a crucial component of the sporting world.

THE ENIGMA OF GREATNESS

What really qualifies as greatness and how can one get it? Does brilliance in bowlers like Walter Ray Williams, Earl Anthony, Jason Belmonte, Norm Duke, and Parker Bohn come naturally, or can it be attained through perseverance? These issues have sparked a variety of discussions, disputes, and viewpoints. Humans are inherently driven to strive for greatness, which motivates us to achieve in many facets of our culture. Understanding what greatness is and how it has changed over time has important ramifications for society, business, and education. Investigating the complex elements that lead to its formation is vital, for this reason.

Throughout history, there have been many different interpretations of what it means to be great. In former times, greatness had a spiritual connotation, and people who were considered geniuses were frequently thought of as being on par with the gods. As geniuses used their innate ability to create something original and exceptional, it was thought that talent was crucial in achieving greatness. It was believed that genius could not be taught because it was seen to be an innate talent. Because of this, wannabe bowlers without innate talent might only emulate it. The adage "Genius must be born and can never be taught" by John Dryden (Dryden, 1693/1885, p. 60) is quite true.

However, relying just on one's own intellect is insufficient. Regardless of having extraordinary skills, true development and refinement come through never-ending diligence. Consistent effort makes up for any weaknesses, even if one has ordinary ability. One can only succeed through perseverance, as the basis of all success is rigorous work. A philosophical study of the characteristics and processes of genius is outside the purview of this discussion. However, it is important to remember that consistent hard work and an unshakeable will to succeed lead to results that are equivalent to those that some bowlers ascribe to natural talent.

Although there were many different viewpoints on the topic, Francis Galton's book "Hereditary Genius," which was published in 1869, marked the beginning of the scientific investigation of this issue. Galton proposed that genius is mostly an inherited attribute based on his research of the families of famous people, motivated by the theories of his cousin Charles Darwin. Galton acknowledged the value of ardor, fervor, and persistence but argued that, regardless of their surroundings, people with great natural abilities will always ascend to the top (Galton, 1874). However, not everyone agreed with this viewpoint.

Famous scientists in Western civilization tended to do their finest work under particular political, economic, social, cultural, and religious circumstances, according to Alphonse de Candolle's research from 1873. This emphasized how crucial environmental influences are. De Candolle's results, however, only explained how environmental factors affected society as a whole and did not provide any new information about the variances that were seen among people living in the same group.

An all-encompassing strategy is needed to comprehend brilliance in the context of bowling. While innate skill undoubtedly plays a role in spectacular accomplishments, it is not the only factor. A bowler's path to success is shaped by the interaction of intrinsic abilities and environmental influences, as well as by unwavering determination and perseverance. The pursuit of greatness requires, among other things, cultivating a growth mindset, accepting difficulties, and constantly improving one's skills.

Even if this audacious claim is accurate, Watson was at least honest about the need for further data on this subject. With the rise of cognitive psychology, the emphasis turned to figuring out how people develop expertise, which has since emerged as the primary differentiator in elite performance. According to Nobel laureates William Chase and Herbert Simon, it takes a decade of devoted practice and study to master chess (Chase & Simon, 1973). This idea is known as "the 10-year rule." Using this research as a foundation, K. Anders Ericsson and his associates broadened the focus to include a variety of fields, including sports, music, professional writing, and the humanities and social sciences (Ericsson, Charness, Feltovich, & Hoffman, 2006). According to researchers who use the expertise performance framework, excellence primarily results from domain-specific knowledge that is learned through countless hours of deliberate practice, where people persistently seek feedback and work to push themselves beyond their comfort zones (Colvin, 2010; Coyle, 2009; Ericsson, Krampe, and Tesch-Romer, 1993; Syed, 2010).

Although careful practice is extremely important, it might not be the only deciding factor. More moderate and integrative opinions are likely to be more accurate, even if historical leaders who took extreme stances on important disputes of their era, such as the nature vs nurture argument, are frequently the most referenced and renowned philosophers and psychologists (Simonton, 1976, 2000a). Researchers from a variety of fields, such as behavioral genetics, neuroscience, developmental psychology, personality psychology, and positive psychology, have gathered a lot of evidence over the past 25 years that suggests the origins of greatness are much more complex than any one theory can account for (Marcus, 2012; Shenk, 2011; Kaufman, 2013). Sometimes things are not as simple as they first appear to be.

Let's investigate the practice-related viewpoint. Since participants without the necessary abilities have already been removed, many studies that concentrate on experts frequently have a small sample size. As a result, these abilities are no longer valid indicators of performance. What do we notice when we take a representative sample from the entire population? Although purposeful practice is a key component of becoming an expert, can anyone reach the top of his field with just deliberate practice alone? Unquestionably important—perhaps even more so than other personal characteristics—is deliberate practice. However, the majority of discrepancies cannot be explained by additional personal or environmental factors.

Finding more problems requires more investigation. What relationship does your DNA have to your initial motivation to become a practitioner? The essential ingredients of brilliance are passion and perseverance, but what gives rise to these traits? Researchers studying behavioral genetics have discovered that nearly all psychological qualities can be linked to genes. So, it stands to reason that hereditary characteristics, which constantly interact with environmental influences, influence motivation and the capacity to persevere through challenges. This isn't always the case, though.

Furthermore, the 10-year rule is not always applicable (Simonton, 1994, 2009a). For instance, far before the mandatory age of 10, prodigies and savants exhibit outstanding skills, even at an expert level. Some people appear to have natural talent without needing to train, like the savant who can sit at a piano and start playing tunes with ease.

It is now clear that the 10-year rule is an average with a sizable amount of fluctuation rather than a rigid rule. In fact, those who show to be the most productive and accomplished over the course of their lifetimes tend to need the least amount of time to gain the requisite information in specific artistic and scientific domains. However, there doesn't seem to be any early edge in being exceptional in fields like creative writing. In reality, greatness may not be attained for a further ten years on average after achieving a professional skill level. Furthermore, having too much knowledge could prevent excellence. According to research, specialists face the risk of becoming highly specialized and rigid thinkers. The dangers of overtraining can be avoided, though, by developing skills in a variety of different subjects.

Exploring these numerous facets makes it clear that the road to greatness is complex and nuanced. Despite being crucial, purposeful practice and domain-specific knowledge are not the only factors that determine success. Motivation and perseverance are influenced by genetic and environmental variables. The 10-year rule also acts as a basic guideline but is highly variable across various industries and people. Prodigies and savants demonstrate remarkable ability without a lot of work, challenging the idea that competence development follows a set course.

In the end, greatness is a complicated combination of factors that defies easy explanations. It necessitates a multidisciplinary approach that understands the complex interactions between heredity, environment, practice, passion, and adaptability. People who want to achieve greatness must take a balanced approach, using purposeful practice, embracing a variety of experiences, and remaining receptive to ongoing learning and progress.

Let's now explore the topic of talent in this argument. Many well-known writers in this sector frequently represent talent as if it indicates that certain people are born with completely formed skills. Although psychologists concur that a variety of attributes, including IQ, creativity, abilities, hobbies, and personality traits, contribute to brilliance, no smart scientist would assert that any of these traits are wholly deterministic. No feature is entirely developed at birth, which gives potential for late bloomers and prodigies who can quickly burn out, according to scientists. Furthermore, no wise scientist would claim that a trait is immutable just because it is impacted by DNA. It is still possible to change a trait, even if it has a high heritability coefficient. It turns out that the genetic component of brilliance is much more complex and fascinating than previously thought.

First off, qualities like creativity and leadership that contribute to greatness don't seem to function just by being together. Instead, they appear to depend on the proper fusion of numerous interacting genes in order to manifest. In addition, the road from genes to talent to greatness is frequently winding and full of unanticipated detours. Reputable behavioral geneticists support moving beyond determining how many traits are inherited. The study of epigenetics looks at the numerous ways that the many interconnected genes that make up a trait can be activated or silenced in response to environmental stimuli.

Genes tug us in different directions, sometimes gently and sometimes not so subtly, impacting our decisions and deeds. There are various ways that the "multiplier effect," which describes how minor genetic advantages add together to produce substantial observable differences, works. The selection of the taller youngster for the basketball team by elementary school students is an example of how the environment may amplify disparities. The slightly more gifted and driven musician, meanwhile, may also make a number of decisions over the course of his life that add up to significant differences over time.

In addition, it has been discovered that a lot of things that were once assumed to be influenced by the environment, such as parenting methods, have strong hereditary components. For instance, rather than being a direct result of parenting on their children's behavior, the perceived relationship between parental phenotype and offspring phenotype is frequently attributed to a shared genotype between parents and children. Undoubtedly, parenting is important. Water has a big impact on fish, even if it cannot explain why different species differ. Parenting has an impact on a child's growth, but not

CHOI BOK EUM: RESILIENCE

When I first started bowling, it was a thrilling and unforgettable experience. I was in the fifth grade, and one day, my parents took me to a bowling alley. I remember rolling that bowling ball for the first time and the exhilaration I felt when it hit the pins. From that moment on, I was hooked. For about a month, after finishing my school lessons every day, I would head to the bowling alley and play over 10 games by myself. It was my passion and a way for me to escape into a world of excitement and challenge.

As I reflect on the environment I grew up in, I realize how it has shaped the person I am today. Many people have supported and uplifted me throughout my journey. My parents, in particular, prayed for me every day and provided unwavering support. My fellow bowlers during that time also played a significant role in my development. The joy of playing the sport I loved gave me a sense of purpose and allowed me to envision a future centered around bowling. In middle school and high school, my mentor, who was also my coach on the high school bowling team, honed my skills and helped me pursue my dreams.

in the way you may think. Because parenting is subject to genetic influence, like all other behaviors, parenting is also influenced by genes. Teachers, friends, and parents all have a big impact on how a person's genes show up. When compared to higher-income homes, where genes account for a larger fraction of the diversity in cognitive capacity, low-income households make the relevance of environmental support particularly clear.

We come across a wide range of aspects when we investigate greatness across several fields. Depending on the particular field, different traits are present in varying ratios and combinations to make up greatness. Compared to thriving in academics or scientific endeavors, excelling in sports requires a different set of talents, attitudes, and mental capabilities. The criteria for obtaining greatness in art, performance, or entertainment are different for both types of brilliance. Diverse abilities and perspectives are crucial, even within the same domain. Consider how, while both being writers, poets, and science writers can seem to come from separate species.

There are also additional things to think about. By definition, only a small group of people can call themselves the finest in a given subject, and no two people's routes to greatness are alike. Some people even come up with their own original strategies for purposeful practice that others might use. Many questions arise when two people can arrive at the same result using radically different strategies. Is creativity the secret to success in every field? Can someone achieve greatness solely by winning the gold medal in the 100-meter sprint and outrunning everyone else? Similar to this, some fields, like mathematics, may require a higher level of talent specialized to the field, while others, like throwing darts, may rely more heavily on intensive practice. Is it necessary for every aspirant to have a lot of talent in order to succeed? Furthermore, it is not always easy to tell the difference between excellent performance and expert performance. What constitutes the limit? Is the 100-meter dash gold medalist the only one who possesses greatness, or is the runner-up also great?

The interaction between nature and nurture is far from simple as we learn more about the complexity of talent and brilliance. A wide range of genetic and environmental factors influence talent rather than being fixed and predestined at birth. The complex interplay of a person's genes, environment, and personal decisions determines his path to greatness. It is a dynamic process that calls for a complex comprehension of the various traits, abilities, and attitudes that contribute to excellence in particular fields.

The top of the iceberg in terms of brilliance is skill and effort. The motivation and passion that fuel outstanding accomplishments are shaped by a wide range of life experiences and early developmental contacts. But how can these encounters affect how ideas are formed? What effects on thinking and performance do mentality, stress, and stereotype threats have? Can people with mental illnesses, learning impairments, and other types of minds be considered valuable assets on the road to greatness? Let's not overlook the importance of luck and chance in the big picture either. How do these elements combine to produce greatness? Even if they are difficult, these inquiries are necessary to grasp brilliance from a scientific perspective.

Psychology's obsession with the study of greatness is profound, and many people from all areas of life can benefit from its lessons. As we learn more about this topic, it becomes clear that there is far more complexity, variety, and allure to greatness than any one viewpoint or model can fully capture. It is time to look beyond the limited parameters of talent and effort since brilliance covers a huge tapestry of components that weave together in extraordinary ways.

We need to explore the depths of human potential in order to fully understand the meaning of greatness and its enigmatic layers. We start to understand the enigmas surrounding brilliance through a thorough investigation of life experiences, cognitive processes, psychological states, and individual variances. Through this scientific journey, we gain priceless insights that illuminate the very nature of human excellence.

UNLOCKING BOWLING GREATNESS *By Rick Benoit*

World-famous bowling coach Rick Benoit discusses his life story and the little-known techniques for winning the game. Benoit underlines that while the path to greatness is not guaranteed, there is a common trait shared by people who succeed in it by drawing on their own experiences and observations. The fundamental difference between players lies in their mentality and attitude toward the game, even though physical talents and methods are crucial. In order to create champions, Benoit emphasizes the value of original thought, self-awareness, tenacity, self-assurance, motivation, communication, and work ethic. He emphasizes comprehensive growth with his ground-breaking "To Be Ready" approach, which includes mental, physical, skill, training, and competition readiness. Benoit helps athletes reach their maximum potential by accepting invisible obstacles and comprehending the constantly shifting elements of bowling.

Although I am originally from the United States and go by the name Rick Benoit, my bowling career has brought me all over the world. My father and other family members shared their love of bowling with me while the doors were locked and most people were asleep. I come from a bowling family and a time when keeping score and action bowling were commonplace in bowling centers. Even though I participated in other sports as a child, bowling was always a part of my life because of how committed my family was. I attribute a lot of my success to the knowledge and experience I gained while I was a spectator rather than a competitor. I appreciated every chance I got to share my brother's enthusiasm for his sport during the ten years I played softball. My elder brother pursued a career in professional bowling. Yes, I was a decent bowler, but I think my ability for coaching came from the lessons I acquired from watching and strategizing. A frustrating injury prevented me from following the route of an athlete when I decided to give up team sports, but it did pave the way for my coaching career. Since I came from a small town, I have found great delight in assisting people in achieving their lane success goals. My desire to be of service to others has driven me to become a better coach.

In my perspective, there is no set or guaranteed road to greatness, but those who succeed share a certain trait. Every road contains accidents and barricades; the path is never straight and is never beautiful. There is drama, disagreement, confusion, and frustration. That is sufficient to drive away a lot of gifted athletes and coaches.

In actuality, "untold secrets" are frequently not as spectacular as you may imagine. The greats have persevered despite several obstacles, and something kept them going. They persisted and never gave up. I have seen a lot of physical talent, skill, and potential vanish into obscurity. However, if we were to assemble all the greats in a single space, the energy there would illuminate the Empire State Building. Even though you wouldn't notice the same physical prowess or comprehend the same tactical message, you would still recognize them as champions.

Champions are typically obstinate and passionate, making them quite simple to spot. They have determination and attention. They might not concur with you because they have self-confidence. You must recognize and respect what it takes to achieve that level in order to collaborate with the best. You will need to establish your credibility in order to win their trust. The greats don't just follow others' leads mindlessly.

There is no one location to go if you're looking for the physical abilities necessary to be great. There is no single style to adopt. There are only two ways to succeed: either you are superior to everyone else or you are one of a kind. Our history is full of both, but the majority are unique, so here's a question for you: what program promotes individuality?

Athletes can be unique in a variety of ways, and frequently they aren't even aware of it. A great coach, like a great bowler, has an artistic perception of shapes and angles that science cannot account for. Our sport's greatness and challenge go hand in hand. The only sport that features an invisible course and ever-changing variables is bowling. Science is unquestionably involved; hence, the claim that it is unimportant is false. However, the equation is never the same because the variables are continuously shifting.

I've had the good fortune to exchange ideas with practically all of the Professional Bowlers Association (PBA)'s athletes, as well as several of the finest female athletes in history. I'm happy to relate a tale that a dear friend and fellow coach told me. This coach spent a number of years on Team USA's coaching staff, and he recalls the time when athletes first began traveling to Colorado Springs, Colorado, the official Olympic training facility.

The crew was informed that they would be tested on their ability to process information when they arrived. The testing's results, not their content, are what the article is about. The examiners revealed that the bowling athletes had received greater grades than the participants in the other sports. Untold secrets of the greats were revealed, nevertheless, when the same results repeated themselves three years in a row with different players on the team. It's no longer a mystery to me, and I believe that this is an important message to impart to people who are interested in learning the buried secrets of bowling champions.

The fundamental difference between them is not what they think, but rather how they think. I believe it is much simpler to modify athletes' physical game than it is to alter their mentality. But concentrating on both is necessary to make them champions. The "Essential Elements" and a "To Be Ready" program form the core of what I teach (BowlU). The fact that more than 75% of what we give is non-physical makes these programs special. There are countless ways to teach the physical game, but there are some universal lessons we can all share. Although I haven't read any of the athlete stories in this book, I am aware of them because there is no other road to the top, a healthy dosage of experience, as well as understanding of how to manage competitive feelings.

I respond that I don't have time to look back because I'm currently focusing on my current difficulty when the conversation turns to myself and what makes me "great." It's great if I've paved a route for others to follow, but that is not my main goal. I firmly believe in what I'm doing, and those who value the effort I've put in inspire me to keep going. I do not mindlessly follow others, unlike the great athlete, because I tried it and it never made sense to me. I am aware of my own distinctive thinking and don't care about what others may think or do. I am not a rebel or someone else's enemy. I completely accept the path that others follow, but when it comes time to discuss the issues, I am confident that I am correct. I am so knowledgeable about my subject that even if I say something incorrectly, others will still understand it.

It's not being smug or arrogant to say that; rather, it's expressing a shared success attribute. Like a great athlete, a great coach needs to be devoted to his beliefs. And in a sport with intangible obstacles, that's not simple. I've had a lot of career success by communicating with others in a way that helps them understand the sport, not just how I do. I'm attempting to help an athlete or coach achieve their best, not to prove them right or wrong. I make it a point to explain things in a way that the athlete or coach can grasp. As you can see, effective coaching calls for a unique set of communication abilities, and when speaking with outstanding athletes, it is more important to comprehend their perspectives. In the off-season, those of us who have the good fortune to work together frequently have a deeper understanding of one another.

Thinking, theory, comprehension, and investigation are all prevalent during the off-season. I employ a framework that I've refined via trial and error. My long career in the sport has helped me create a program that is unmatched. I definitely fit the "unique" description, then. "To Be Ready" is the program's motto, and it refers to both our personal and professional objectives.

- *Mind Ready*
- *Body Ready*
- *Skill Ready*
- *Training Ready*
- *Competition Ready*

The distinctive qualities I bring to the sport fall under these "Readiness" categories.

Since our sports history has shown that there is no right or wrong, I am less concerned with the physical aspect of the game while I am searching for excellence. I check for a champion's character qualities, which heavily rely on his "self-skills."

- *determination*
- *confidence*
- *motivation*
- *communication*
- *work ethic*

The conditions in which an athlete competes have a significant impact on his needs. Although there are many conditional superstars in our sport, the real icons are the ones that can perform at a high level anyplace. Even then, it could still take some time for them to adjust to a new environment and recognize it. At the elite level, changes in technology, competition formats, and the pool of athletes have a considerably greater impact than anything else. A great bowling instructor has his own physical game theory, but more significantly, a great coach develops an athlete's creative talents and unleashes their mental potential.

Rick Benoit, BowlU President and Lead Instructor

The emphasis of this enlightening article moves to the strategies underlying professional bowler Parker Bohn's enduring success. Parker examines the relevance of striking the right balance between strikes and spares, emphasizing the need to master spare conversions as a means to success. He discusses his own insights towards being mentally and physically prepared, putting a strong emphasis on the value of honesty and self-evaluation. Parker has refined his ability to repeat shots with consistency and control by streamlining his approach and keeping perfect timing. The article ends with insightful guidance on coping with the ups and downs of the game, advising bowlers to welcome challenges, maintain their fortitude, and treasure the important life lessons that bowling teaches.

THE ART OF BOWLING MASTERY: A SIMPLE APPROACH TO CONSISTENT SUCCESS *By Parker Bohn*

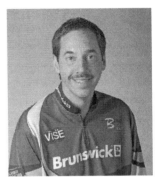

Identifying information Parker, often known as Butch, is a bowler whose career started when he was very young. His last name is Bohn. I became addicted to bowling after my mother took me there when I was eight years old. I would pull at her pant leg, pleading with her to let me return and feel the rush of busting pins.

I credit a lot of my success to my parents since they encouraged me in all I did. They supported me in following my interests and constantly underlined the value of pursuing excellence. "Second place is just the first loser," my father would frequently remark, inspiring in me a desire to succeed. They gave me the chance to participate in regional competitions, and as I grew older and saw success, I ventured further, even taking part in adult tournaments as a junior bowler.

However, as a left-handed bowler, I looked up to Earl Anthony, the finest bowler of his era, in addition to my parents, who served as my role models. But Dave Davis, who, along with his wife JoAnne, recognized my talent, took me under his wing and taught me how to hone and grow my game.

I've had a number of coaches and mentors who have helped shape my bowling abilities during my career. My first junior coach gave me direction in the beginning, but Dave Davis, Mark Roth, and Johnny Petraglia Sr. had a significant influence on my playing. Mark placed an emphasis on spare shooting and lane reading, while Dave stressed the value of developing a reliable and consistent game. The PBA tour, where the lane conditions are different from those at home, is where Johnny Petraglia Sr. taught me the nuances of playing the game. I am incredibly appreciative of the advice and knowledge these gentlemen gave me.

My goal when I was a teen was to play on the PBA tour and take home a single championship. I had no idea that this desire would propel me over a 30-year period to win 35 PBA championships, two Player of the Year awards, and a plethora of other honors. I make myself new goals with each success. Only a select few players have reached the milestone of making over $100,000 in a season, so that was my goal. After I attained that milestone, I aimed to continue performing at that level each year and eventually win the PBA Player of the Year award. I kept raising the bar for myself and worked hard to get better without putting my objectives out of reach.

The majority of my life has been devoted to my bowling hobby. I've been successful on the lanes thanks to my dedication and endless hours of practice. Nothing makes me happier than watching young bowlers' enthusiasm grow as they knock down pins, turn spares into strikes, and finally develop a true love for the sport. The priceless beauty of their smiles.

My capacity to take lessons from every experience, whether good or bad, was one of the major qualities that helped me reach an outstanding level. I learned a lot from each ball that was thrown down the lane, but it was also crucial to evaluate my attitude and strategy. I worked hard to improve my abilities while constantly imagining the ideal shot to seal a victory. Whether I won or lost, taking a step back and considering what happened helped me improve as a bowler. Unwavering self-belief and confidence have also been essential to my journey. Without self-assurance, it is difficult to win others' trust and support.

My game was shaped by growing up in a bowling center with lots of grease on the centers. It posed difficulties, but it also gave me a benefit when the lanes stopped working. Being able to adjust to various circumstances became a part of my skill set because we are all products of our environments. When the lanes started to transition, I was able to flourish despite having a minor disadvantage due to the limited amount of oil I could bowl on as a child on heavily oiled lanes. We should all recognize and build upon our individual strengths. To make their B, C, and D games as strong as possible, I always advise bowlers to focus on strengthening their weaker areas.

I started off participating in regional competitions as I advanced in my bowling career, and as I did so, I gradually broadened my horizons to include competitions farther away. My eyes were opened to the possibilities of achievement on a global scale by the success I had on the PBA Tour in America. The PBA Tour presents the ideal opportunity to test your bowling prowess against the best if you really want to compare yourself to the best.

I concentrated my practice sessions on the areas of my game that needed the most work. Our sport has traditionally depended heavily on spares. The top bowlers can regularly convert spares, which sets them apart from the competition. I committed myself to perfecting my outside shooting abilities as well as my poise and control at the foul line.

There will inevitably be highs and lows in every sport. You might be at the top of the world one day and at the bottom the next. It's imperative to enjoy the highs and keep riding the success wave as long as you can. But at trying times or slumps, taking a step back and taking a break can frequently bring clarity and help you get beyond challenges. A fresh viewpoint and insightful information can result from pausing to think things over and reconsider your strategy.

No matter how big the competition is, preparation is essential. It is vital to prepare yourself physically and emotionally. Additionally, it's critical to make sure your equipment is in excellent shape. Don't be the person who scrambles to put his things together at the last minute. Being well-prepared beforehand puts you in the lead and enables you to concentrate only on your performance as opposed to rushing to get everything together.

I would strongly advise the next generation of bowlers to accept and comprehend the truth that not every ball will result in a strike. When I was younger, hitting a double or triple was exciting. I discovered that there are strikes and spares in the game. It's useless to become upset over a nine-pin leave. Instead, concentrate on perfecting your spare shooting technique, because converting spares reliably will give you more chances to win titles.

We all have the same objective of bringing down 10 pins with one ball when I step into the lanes to compete against other bowlers. It's critical to be completely honest with yourself and determine whether you are at the top of your game, physically fit, mentally sharp, and prepared for the task at hand. Every day offers a fresh chance to perform at your peak and triumph.

My game is really straightforward, which is the key to my ability to repeat shots repeatedly. I get to the foul line with perfect timing, starting with my left foot and left hand at the same time. The control a golfer has when hitting a golf ball or a baseball player has when hitting a fastball are both mirrored in the stable release of the ball. The key is to be completely in control of your body when you release.

My lifetime passion has been bowling, and I am incredibly appreciative of the possibilities and experiences it has provided. It has molded who I am as a person and given me priceless life lessons. I am humbled by the talent and abilities of the next generation of bowlers as I continue on my quest. Their skill in controlling the ball is amazing. Even though I may soon be retired, I still get a great deal of satisfaction from watching new bowlers succeed. My pleasure never stops when I witness a beginner bowler knock down a few pins, convert a spare, or eventually accomplish a strike.

"We are all products of our environments" Parker Bohn

The capacity to take a step back and learn from any circumstance, no matter how positive or trying, was one of the qualities that helped me reach an outstanding level in bowling. It's important to seize those opportunities to learn from each ball that travels down the lane. A motivating factor is the desire to continuously improve oneself and pursue the dream of hitting the ideal shot to win a significant competition. Success might not always be assured, but taking a step back and considering each event enables growth and self-improvement. Furthermore, self-confidence is crucial. A bowler may go a long way with confidence because it is difficult to win others' confidence and support when one lacks self-belief.

My path has led me to the realization that my upbringing had an impact on how I played the game. The bowling center where I grew up had more oil on the lanes than most of the other centers in my neighborhood. Since we are all products of our environment, this particular situation had both benefits and drawbacks. On heavily oiled lanes, it first put me at a minor disadvantage, but it also gave me the resiliency and agility to succeed when the lanes started to fail. It's critical to understand and take advantage of each person's unique strengths and weaknesses. The pursuit of constantly raising one's weaker areas and attaining new heights has no limitations.

I continued to strive for greatness as I moved from regional competitions to international competitions. My primary goal was to win the PBA championship, but little did I know that it would start me on an unbelievable adventure. After thirty years, I can look back with pride on 35 PBA championships, two Player of the Year honors, and a plethora of other achievements. But as goals were achieved, new ones also appeared. My goal was to replicate the feat every year while pursuing the coveted PBA Player of the Year award once I hit the milestone of earning more than $100,000 in a season. The bar was always being raised, challenging me to go beyond my comfort zone while still remaining within my grasp. I have a great deal of respect for the talent and skill of the younger generation of bowlers now that I am beyond 50 years old. I accept the knowledge that my time in the sport is coming to an end because they have taken the sport to new heights.

For me, bowling is a passion that comes from the bottom of my heart rather than just a game. My long hours spent honing my skills have been rewarded with triumphant and joyous moments. The greatest thrill, though, comes from watching the upcoming bowlers set out on their own amazing journeys. The triumphant smiles on their cheeks serve as a constant reminder of the beauty and enduring force of this sport.

The value of readiness, in retrospect, has been one of the primary concepts that has guided me throughout my career. Being properly prepared was essential, whether it was for my physical, emotional, or technical well-being. Rushing through last-minute preparations is insignificant compared to the advantage of showing up fully prepared and competitive. It is a lesson that applies to every aspect of life: the need to be fully prepared and present at all times.

I provide the following advice to bowlers in the younger generation: Recognize that not all balls will result in strikes. In my early years, even if I left a pin standing, a double or triple made me happy. The ratio of strikes to spares is crucial to the sport of bowling. While a run of hits is unquestionably thrilling, it's important to keep in mind that success also depends on routinely turning spares into runs. Don't be discouraged if you leave one or two pins hanging; instead, concentrate on improving your spare shooting abilities. You'll have lots of chances to fight for championships and earn important points if you can master the art of spare conversion.

I recognize that my goal, to knock down 10 pins with a single ball, is the same as that of my fellow competitors when I step onto the lanes to compete. Assessing one's readiness for the task at hand requires being completely honest. Am I performing at my best? Am I physically and mentally ready? Is my equipment functioning at its best? Most importantly, can I handle the challenge mentally? These introspective exercises are essential for setting oneself up for success and winning on any given day or week.

I attribute my ability to regularly repeat shots to my game's simplicity. I achieve excellent timing as I approach the foul line by starting with my left foot and left hand at the same time. This method enables me to release with stability and control throughout, similar to how a golfer would strike a ball or a baseball player would hit a fastball. I aim for the same amount of control when delivering the bowling ball, just as they have total control of their body at the point of impact.

In conclusion, I want to underline how critical it is to embrace both the high points and low points that one experiences along the way. You might find yourself at the top of the globe one day, celebrating your victories. The peak can be lonely, though, as everyone is trying to push you down from your perch, so keep that in mind. On the other hand, when confronted with a slump or difficult circumstances, taking a step back and giving oneself time to reevaluate can frequently result in breakthroughs. Give yourself time to think and ponder in order to refocus and rekindle your enthusiasm for the game.

I find comfort in the idea that bowling is more than just a sport; it's a way of life, as I think back on my own career. It has instilled discipline in me, given me tremendous delight, and taught me priceless life lessons. It has been nothing short of amazing to go from being a kid bowler pulling at my mother's pant leg to becoming a decorated professional. I've had the good fortune to have amazing role models, mentors, and supporters along the way who encouraged me to be my best self.

My advice to all prospective bowlers is straightforward: Have ambitious goals, put in a lot of effort, have confidence in yourself, and never lose sight of how much fun bowling is. The bowling community is a thriving, diverse family that is eager to welcome new members who share their love for this appealing sport. So put on your shoes, take hold of the ball, and go out on your own remarkable bowling adventure. Your successful knockout of the pins is awaited, and your fellow bowlers' fellowship will help you get back up.

Parker Morse Bohn III, 35 PBA Titlist

THE JOURNEY TO GREATNESS IN BOWLING: ENDURING PAIN AND EMBRACING FAILURE

The dream of becoming a professional bowler is shared by people everywhere. Young people frequently desire to represent their country through sports, play in the elite PBA, or travel abroad. But the chances of these aspirations coming true are frequently slim, particularly in the world of bowling.

I've spent a lot of time seeing and talking to bowlers who want to compete in elite tournaments at the junior, collegiate, amateur, and professional levels. Surprisingly, very few bowlers who are looking to enhance their skills are familiar with the recognized scientific theories of long-term bowler growth. Because of this, many bowlers, along with their parents and coaches, unknowingly adhere to training, competition, coaching, and growth patterns that impede their ability to realize their potential and attain their goals.

Individuals with a sense of entitlement are not unfamiliar with competitive bowling, including players, parents, and coaches. Many frequently think that their success in the amateur, collegiate, or junior categories ensures future victories in the sport. Studies, however, have demonstrated that this idea is not at all accurate. In actuality, a sizable portion of age group winners who flourish as young teenagers do not continue to win titles as adults. In reality, many of these previous winners frequently give up playing when they meet adults, especially pros who compete for fame and money.

Even though the majority of parents, coaches, and bowling officials, as well as aspiring world-class bowlers and their parents, have the best of intentions, they frequently don't have a comprehensive understanding of the crucial elements and phases that result in the growth of world-class bowlers. One frequently underestimates the rarity and statistical impossibility of a top junior bowler making it to the PBA Tour, the highest level of professional bowling. As a result, a lot of bowlers and those who support them make dubious decisions regarding their future, skipping out on their schooling and making little preparation for life after the sport.

Bowlers constantly look for excuses for their ascent to greatness, much like other bowlers want championships. Having devoted over 25 years to bowling, from trying to play professionally to coaching players at the highest levels of competition, I have seen how the best bowlers have gotten better at handling discomfort than most.

The fundamentals of bowling—gripping the ball, approaching the foul line, and continuously shooting at the pins until they all fall—might appear straightforward at first. It's a concept that seems doable and uncomplicated. But because we are rational beings, we have found ways to improve our physical prowess and move more effectively. So begins our quest to raise our bowling averages. As bowling experts, we teach you, the bowler, the "fundamentals" of the sport in an effort to improve your performance. Some of you are so passionate about the game that you go above and beyond to compete at the top levels. Reaching the summit necessitates comprehension, a tolerance for suffering, and a passion for ongoing progress, but playing recreationally only requires a basic understanding and love of learning.

The Underestimated Challenge:

It's easy to think, "I can do that too," or "That shot doesn't seem too difficult," when we see the finest bowlers in the world win PBA Tour competitions on television. Making a shot may not be particularly difficult, in fact. A completely different situation arises when you must duplicate the same shot under pressure in a competition where your livelihood is on the line. The genuine difficulties of being a great bowler can be underestimated by even the most talented bowlers. Bowlers frequently overestimate their skills while underestimating the difficulties they confront. This is known by coaches as the skill-challenge ratio. Unfortunately, amateur bowlers frequently have this notion because they don't realize how difficult it is to be the best at something that seems easy. The quest for excellence in a variety of fields, including business, the arts, and other sports, follows this pattern. True greatness means enduring suffering, accepting failure, and adjusting to difficult situations with an emphasis on learning. Many of us have spent endless hours on assignments, reports, or bowling games only to come up short or be dissatisfied with the results. This may be the tipping point for some people, leaving them disappointed and perplexed by their perceived failure. However, it is precisely during these times—not when they are at their most successful—that champions are developed. The greatest bowlers frequently recount how they overcame hardship and disappointment and struggled to discover their genuine vocation. They experience more suffering than the ordinary bowler, businessperson, or performer, yet they accept failure as vital feedback. Disappointment is used as fuel by remarkable achievers, who use it to grow and learn along the way.

Exploring the X-Factor:

A select few bowlers participate on the illustrious PBA Tour and across the globe. These people have wowed the entire world with their exceptional abilities and unusual playing styles. Amateur bowlers frequently blame their success on innate skill or a unique gift, especially when considering how many victories they rack up. This makes us wonder about the elusive quality that distinguishes these bowlers from the competition.

The X-factor in bowling comes in many forms. Some bowlers have an uncanny ability to read lane conditions, adjusting their game effortlessly. Others possess innate rhythm and timing, making their throws seem effortless. These talents are honed through years of practice, resulting in a level of skill that sets them apart.

In the bowling world, legends like Earl Anthony, Walter Ray Williams Jr., and Norm Duke exemplify the X-factor. They weren't just bowlers; they were masters, each with their own unique style. Earl Anthony had pinpoint accuracy and poise under pressure. Walter Ray Williams Jr. was incredibly versatile and had an enduring career. Norm Duke could read lanes like no other, adapting seamlessly to changing conditions.

The X-factor in bowling isn't just about talent; it's about dedication to perfecting one's craft. It's a reminder that greatness often comes from relentless effort. Bowling provides a canvas for these exceptional individuals to showcase their talents. So, the next time you step onto a bowling alley, remember that greatness can be achieved with dedication, unlocking your own X-factor and making your mark on the sport.

PETE WEBER X-FACTOR

1. **Showmanship and Charisma**: Pete Weber is known for his charismatic and showman-like personality on the lanes, creating an electrifying atmosphere during his performances. His memorable catchphrases and gestures have made him a fan favorite.

2. **Pinpoint Accuracy**: Weber's pinpoint accuracy and precision in shot-making under pressure set him apart. He consistently hits his target, even in challenging conditions.

3. **Experience and Legacy**: With a rich family history in bowling and a Hall of Fame career, Weber's experience and knowledge of the sport contribute to his X-factor. He's regarded as a bowling legend.

4. **Poise Under Pressure**: Weber's ability to maintain composure in high-stress situations, particularly in major tournaments, underscores his mental resilience and competitive spirit. His calm demeanor when the stakes are high is a key component of his X-factor.

TOMMY JONES X-FACTOR

1. **Extensive Experience**: With a career spanning several decades, Tommy Jones has acquired a deep understanding of the sport, including the ability to read lane conditions and adapt his game effectively.

2. **Consistency**: Jones is known for his ability to deliver accurate shots consistently, even under challenging conditions, contributing to his sustained success in the sport.

3. **Competitive Spirit**: His fierce competitive spirit and determination enable him to thrive in high-pressure situations, leading to consistent performances in major tournaments.

4. **Confident Gaze**: Jones possesses a strong-looking face and a confident gaze that can have a psychological impact on his opponents. His mere presence on the lanes can make other bowlers feel the intensity of competition, causing them to become normal in comparison to his formidable demeanor.

5. **Versatility**: Jones' adaptability and the ability to adjust to different lane patterns have contributed to his success on both domestic and international bowling circuits.

DOM BARRETT X-FACTOR

1. **Technical Mastery**: Dominic Barrett's X-factor shines through his exceptional technical mastery of the sport. His in-depth understanding of bowling mechanics and the precision with which he executes each shot demonstrate his technical prowess.

2. **Quick Start and Repeatable Shots**: An integral part of Barrett's X-factor is his rapid start with no pause in his stance. This seamless, quick approach allows him to consistently repeat shots with remarkable accuracy, showcasing his unwavering technique.

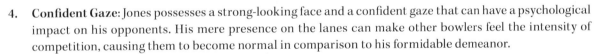

3. **International Success**: Dominic Barrett's X-factor extends to his extensive international success, where he has represented England. His accomplishments on the global stage highlight his competitive excellence and skill in diverse playing conditions.

4. **Versatility and Adaptability:** Beyond his technical prowess, Barrett's versatility and adaptability on the lanes are crucial components of his X-factor. He can adjust his game to various lane conditions and oil patterns, making him a well-rounded and formidable competitor. His versatility underlines that the X-factor in bowling encompasses technical skill, quick execution, and the ability to perform consistently on the international stage.

5. **Looks Easy:** What further distinguishes Barrett is his ability to make the situation look easy, maintaining a demeanor that remains unfazed and unemotional, in stark contrast to the visible frustrations or elations often displayed by other bowlers. This sense of in-control ease sets him apart as a cool and collected force in the world of bowling.

TIM MACK X-FACTOR

1. **Versatility and Adaptability:** Mack's versatility and adaptability on the lanes are integral components of his X-factor. He possesses the capability to adjust his game to various lane conditions and oil patterns, making him a well-rounded and formidable competitor in different playing environments.

2. **High-Powered Bowling Style:** Mack's X-factor is further defined by his high-powered and authoritative bowling style. His delivery exudes power and energy, adding an electrifying aspect to his presence on the lanes.

3. **Experience and Knowledge:** With a wealth of experience in professional bowling, Tim Mack's X-factor is reinforced by his profound knowledge of the sport. He has a deep understanding of bowling's intricacies, which contributes to his continued excellence and his role as a respected figure in the sport.

4. **Global Visionary and World Tour Pioneer:** Tim Mack holds a unique place in bowling history as one of the very first to envision and implement the concept of a world tour during the mid-'90s. His vision extended the reach of professional bowling far beyond traditional borders, as he traveled the world, spreading the concept of power bowling and cranking to diverse regions such as Korea, Australia, Singapore, Sweden, Norway, Finland, and many others. Mack's efforts were instrumental in globalizing the sport, fostering a more inclusive and interconnected community of bowlers, and leaving an indelible mark on the international landscape of professional bowling.

5. **Exceptional Leadership and Coaching:** Tim Mack's X-factor extends to his exceptional ability to lead a team, both as a captain and a coach. His unique blend of experience, innovation, knowledge, team spirit, and positivity makes him an invaluable asset to any team. Mack's leadership style is characterized by a motivating and collaborative approach, inspiring team members to reach their full potential. His coaching prowess goes beyond technical guidance, encompassing a holistic understanding of the mental and strategic aspects of the game. As a result, Mack's presence on a team is synonymous with unity, growth, and a winning mindset, creating an environment that any team would dream of having.

FRANÇOIS LAVOIE X-FACTOR

1. **Pinpoint Accuracy:** François Lavoie is known for his exceptional accuracy, consistently hitting his target, even in challenging lane conditions. His precision in shot-making sets him apart in the sport.

2. **Versatility and Adaptability:** Lavoie possesses the ability to adapt to different oil patterns and playing conditions, showcasing his technical versatility. He can adjust his game to suit a variety of scenarios, making him a formidable competitor.

3. **Calm Demeanor**: François Lavoie maintains composure under pressure, particularly in major tournaments, where he consistently performs well in high-stakes situations. His calm and collected attitude highlights his mental resilience.

4. **International Success**: His achievements in international competitions and his ability to excel in diverse playing conditions underscore the combination of technical skill, adaptability, and mental fortitude that make up his X-factor. Lavoie's continued success serves as a testament to his dedication and skill in the sport.

JAKOB BUTTURFF X-FACTOR

1. **Unique Wrist Position**: Jakob Butturff's X-factor is prominently characterized by his extraordinary wrist position, a key element of his bowling technique. His wrist's distinctive rotation allows him to create a unique and powerful rev rate, resulting in unparalleled pin action and hook potential on the lanes.

2. **Distinctive Bowling Style**: Butturff's unique two-handed, left-handed style sets him apart in the world of bowling. His unorthodox approach, combined with the exceptional wrist action, makes him instantly recognizable and a dynamic force in the sport.

3. **Fearless Confidence**: An integral part of Butturff's X-factor is his unwavering confidence on the lanes. He is known for taking calculated risks and making bold moves during competitions, particularly in high-pressure situations. His fearless approach to the sport contributes to his success and captivates the audience.

4. **Versatility and Adaptability**: Beyond his unique style and wrist position, Jakob Butturff also demonstrates the versatility to adapt to various lane conditions and oil patterns. This adaptability makes him a well-rounded and formidable competitor, showcasing that the X-factor in bowling encompasses technical skill, style, and the confidence to push boundaries.

JESPER SVENSSON X-FACTOR

1. **Ultimate Powerful Two-Handed Style**: Jesper Svensson's X-factor is defined by his awe-inspiring two-handed style, which generates the highest rev rate on the professional bowling tour. His immense power and revolutions result in explosive pin action and remarkable hook potential, setting him apart as one of the most dynamic and powerful bowlers in the game.

2. **Automatic Shot Repetition**: Another remarkable element of Svensson's X-factor is his remarkable ability to consistently repeat shots with precision. His uncanny consistency in delivering shots showcases his incredible control and unwavering technique.

3. **Fearless Demeanor**: Jesper Svensson's fearless face in high-pressure situations is a significant component of his X-factor. He fearlessly embraces challenges, taking calculated risks and making bold moves during competitions, particularly in clutch moments. His unwavering confidence contributes to his captivating and dynamic presence on the lanes.

TOM DAUGHERTY X-FACTOR

1. **Underdog Story:** Daugherty's remarkable underdog story, particularly his victory in the 2011 PBA Tournament of Champions, showcases his determination and ability to succeed against formidable opponents.

2. **Consistency Under Pressure:** He consistently maintains composure and delivers crucial shots under intense pressure, highlighting his mental resilience and ability to perform when it matters most.

3. **Determination:** Daugherty's determination to succeed in the face of adversity and prove his mettle on the lanes adds an inspiring element to his X-factor.

4. **Relentless Effort and Unconventional Style:** His continued pursuit of excellence and relentless work ethic reinforce the idea that greatness in bowling can be achieved through unwavering effort, resilience, and a memorable underdog spirit. What sets Daugherty apart is not just his story but his distinct and unconventional bowling style. His approach to the game is a rarity, a style that is not found in any educational book of training. Daugherty's unorthodox technique challenges traditional norms, making him a true original in the world of professional bowling. His ability to succeed with a style that defies convention adds an extra layer of intrigue to his X-factor, showcasing that greatness can emerge from unique and uncharted approaches to the game.

KRISTOPHER PRATHER X-FACTOR

1. **Spare Shooting Precision and Accuracy:** A defining aspect of Kristopher Prather's X-factor is his exceptional precision and accuracy in spare shooting. He consistently converts spares with remarkable consistency, showcasing his ability to maintain focus and reliability in clutch moments.

2. **Beautiful Balanced Bowling Style:** Prather's distinctive X-factor is reflected in his balanced and aesthetically pleasing bowling style. His smooth and graceful approach on the lanes is a testament to his technical mastery and control over his shots.

3. **Lane Manipulation Expertise:** Another component of Prather's X-factor is his keen understanding of lane conditions and his skill in manipulating them to his advantage. He can read the lanes and adapt his game effectively, making him a strategic and adaptable competitor.

SAM COOLEY X-FACTOR

1. **Power and Rev Rate:** Sam Cooley's X-factor is prominently defined by his exceptional power and rev rate. His remarkable ability to generate significant revolutions on the ball results in extraordinary pin action and hook potential, setting him apart as one of the most powerful bowlers on the professional tour.

2. **Cool Demeanor:** An integral aspect of Cooley's X-factor is his cool and composed demeanor while on the lanes. He maintains his calm under pressure, even in high-stakes situations, showcasing his mental resilience and ability to perform consistently.

3. **Poker Face:** One of Sam Cooley's X-Factors is his "poker face." He possesses a calm and expressionless demeanor during tournaments, which can be

advantageous in high-pressure and competitive situations. His ability to maintain a poker face allows him to conceal his emotions, stay focused, and perform consistently, making it difficult for opponents to gauge his mental state and intentions on the lanes.

4. **Unique Swing:** His X-factor also extends to his unique and recognizable swing style. Cooley's swing is distinctive and adds to his overall charm and character in the sport.

5. **Fearless Face:** Sam Cooley's fearless face in high-pressure situations is a significant component of his X-factor. He embraces challenges and takes calculated risks, making bold moves during competitions. His fearless attitude contributes to his captivating and dynamic presence in the world of bowling.

KYLE TROUP X-FACTOR

1. **Distinctive Appearance:** Kyle Troup's instantly recognizable Afro hairstyle and vibrant wardrobe make him stand out visually, adding an element of showmanship to his presence in the sport.

2. **Two-Handed Style:** Troup's unique two-handed bowling technique allows him to generate a high number of revolutions on the ball, creating extraordinary pin action and hook potential.

3. **Versatility:** He has demonstrated the ability to adapt to different lane conditions and oil patterns, showcasing his adaptability and versatility in the sport.

4. **Charismatic Personality:** Troup's charismatic personality and ability to engage the audience make him a fan favorite, creating an electrifying atmosphere during his performances.

TOM SMALLWOOD X-FACTOR

1. **Underdog Story:** Tom Smallwood's remarkable underdog story, particularly his victory in the 2009 PBA World Championship, highlights his determination and ability to succeed against significant odds, adding an inspiring element to his X-factor.

2. **Consistency Under Pressure:** Smallwood consistently maintains composure and delivers crucial shots under intense pressure, showcasing his mental resilience and ability to perform when it matters most.

3. **Dedication and Work Ethic:** His continued pursuit of excellence and unwavering work ethic reinforce the idea that greatness in bowling can be achieved through relentless effort, resilience, and a memorable underdog spirit.

Mike Fagan X-Factor:

1. **Strategic Decision-Making:** An integral aspect of Fagan's X-factor is his strategic decision-making on the lanes. Known for his ability to read oil patterns and make calculated adjustments, he consistently positions himself for success by making smart choices during competitions.

2. **Flawless Swing:** Fagan's X-factor is further highlighted by his flawless and aesthetically pleasing swing is often regarded as one of the most beautiful in the world of professional bowling.

3. **Emotionless Demeanor Under Pressure:** One of Mike Fagan's X-factors is his stoic and emotionless demeanor under pressure. Whether facing critical moments in a

match or competing in high-stakes tournaments, his face remains unchanged, enabling him to maintain focus, execute shots with consistency, and conceal his emotions from opponents.

4. **International Competence and Extreme Versatility:** Fagan's X-factor extends to his competence on the international stage. Representing the United States in various competitions, he has showcased his skills against top bowlers from around the world. His extreme versatility is evident in his ability to execute a wide range of shot shapes and angles, from playing a straight shot to generating as much hook as two-handers when needed during competitions.

RAFIQ ISMAIL X-FACTOR:

1. **Technical Skill and Precision:** Rafiq Ismail is known for his remarkable accuracy and the ability to consistently deliver precise shots, even under challenging lane conditions, showcasing his technical prowess.

2. **Experience and Knowledge:** His extensive experience in professional bowling has provided him with a deep understanding of the sport, including the ability to read lane conditions and adapt his game effectively.

3. **Consistency Under Pressure:** Rafiq Ismail maintains composure under high-pressure situations, consistently delivering crucial shots in major tournaments, highlighting his mental resilience and ability to perform when it matters most.

4. **Versatility:** His adaptability to different oil patterns and lane conditions underscores his technical versatility and mastery of the sport's intricacies.

SHAYNA NG'S X-FACTOR

1. **Technical Precision:** Shayna Ng is known for her technical precision in shot-making. Her ability to consistently hit her target, even under challenging lane conditions, showcases her skill and accuracy in the sport.

2. **Versatility and Adaptability:** Ng's adaptability to various oil patterns and playing conditions underscores her technical versatility. She can adjust her game to suit different scenarios, making her a well-rounded competitor.

3. **International Success:** Her accomplishments in international competitions, including representing Singapore, highlight her competitive excellence on a global scale. Ng's ability to perform in diverse playing conditions showcases her X-factor.

4. **Mental Toughness:** Shayna Ng's ability to maintain composure under pressure, especially in major tournaments, demonstrates her mental resilience and determination. Her calm demeanor in high-stakes situations is a key aspect of her X-factor.

Chris Barnes X-Factor:

1. **Precision and Accuracy:** Chris Barnes' X-factor is prominently defined by his exceptional precision and accuracy on the lanes. His ability to consistently hit target areas with pinpoint accuracy sets him apart as a bowler with remarkable control over the ball's trajectory and placement, making him a formidable competitor.

2. **Strategic Mindset:** An integral aspect of Barnes' X-factor is his strategic mindset during tournaments. He approaches each

game with a calculated and thoughtful strategy, adapting to lane conditions and opponents' styles. This strategic approach showcases his mental acuity and ability to make informed decisions under varying circumstances.

3. **Stoic Presence:** One of Chris Barnes' X-factors is his stoic presence on the lanes. He maintains a calm and composed demeanor, regardless of the situation. This stoicism allows him to stay focused, avoid distractions, and execute shots with consistency, creating a sense of reliability that adds to his competitive edge.

4. **Versatility in Ball Choices:** His X-factor also extends to his versatility in selecting and using different bowling balls effectively. Barnes possesses a deep understanding of equipment and lane conditions, allowing him to make optimal choices that maximize his performance across various scenarios.

5. **Mental Toughness:** Chris Barnes' mental toughness in high-pressure situations is a significant component of his X-factor. He thrives under challenging conditions, staying resilient and focused when the stakes are high. This mental fortitude contributes to his longevity and success in the competitive world of professional bowling.

Marshall Holman X-Factor:

1. **Aggressive Playing Style:** Marshall Holman's X-factor is prominently defined by his aggressive playing style on the lanes. Known for his powerful shots and attacking approach, Holman creates intense pin action and puts constant pressure on opponents, establishing himself as a dynamic and assertive force in the world of professional bowling.

2. **Emotionally Charged Performances:** An integral aspect of Holman's X-factor is his emotionally charged performances. He wears his emotions on his sleeve, expressing passion and intensity during competitions. This emotional energy fuels his competitive drive and adds a captivating dimension to his presence on the professional bowling tour.

3. **Fearless Lane Presence:** One of Marshall Holman's X-factors is his fearless lane presence. He embraces challenges and isn't afraid to take risks, making bold moves and decisions during matches. This fearless attitude contributes to his reputation as a competitor who can make clutch shots in critical moments.

4. **Unconventional Delivery:** His X-factor also extends to his unconventional delivery style. Holman's unique and recognizable bowling delivery adds flair and unpredictability to his game, making it challenging for opponents to anticipate his shots and adapt to his unorthodox approach.

5. **Showmanship:** Marshall Holman's showmanship is a significant component of his X-factor. He brings entertainment value to the sport with his animated reactions, celebratory gestures, and interactions with the audience. This showmanship not only engages fans but also adds a charismatic quality to his overall persona as a professional bowler.

Osku Palermaa X-Factor:

1. **Dominant Two-Handed Power:** Osku Palermaa's X-factor is prominently defined by his exceptionally powerful two-handed bowling style, surpassing many of his peers in terms of sheer force and energy. His ability to generate tremendous power and revolutions on the ball distinguishes him as one of the most forceful and impactful bowlers in the professional circuit, setting a standard for the two-handed technique.

2. **Unparalleled Flexibility:** One of Osku Palermaa's X-factors is his unparalleled flexibility in adapting to different lane conditions, leveraging his powerful two-handed style. His adept adjustments showcase a strategic approach that optimizes his performance based on the unique challenges posed by varying dynamics in the game.

3. **Ambidextrous Bowling Mastery:** His X-factor also extends to his mastery of ambidextrous bowling with the two-handed technique, showcasing not only power but also versatility. Palermaa's proficiency in using both hands adds a unique and strategic layer to his game, providing him with a distinct advantage over opponents.

4. **Ice-Cool Under Pressure:** Osku Palermaa's cool and composed demeanor under pressure is a significant component of his X-factor, especially notable given the sheer power of his two-handed style. Whether in high-stakes situations or critical moments in a match, his ability to stay calm enhances his decision-making and shot execution, reinforcing his status as a dominant force on the professional bowling tour.

Norm Duke X-Factor:

1. **Exceptional Spare Shooting:** Norm Duke's X-factor is prominently defined by his exceptional spare shooting ability. His precision and consistency in converting spares, even in challenging conditions, showcase a mastery of the fundamentals and contribute to his overall success as a professional bowler.

2. **Creative Shot-Making:** An integral aspect of Duke's X-factor is his creative shot-making on the lanes. Known for his ability to read lane conditions and adapt his game, he often employs inventive strategies and shot angles, keeping opponents guessing and demonstrating a high level of strategic intelligence.

3. **Mental Toughness:** One of Norm Duke's X-factors is his unwavering mental toughness. He maintains focus and composure in high-pressure situations, allowing him to make critical shots and strategic decisions with a calm and collected demeanor.

4. **Signature "Duuuuuke":** His X-factor also extends to his signature " Duuuuuke", a focused and intense gaze he directs towards the pins before releasing the ball. This ritual not only adds a psychological edge to his game but also reflects his deep concentration and mental preparation.

5. **Versatility:** Norm Duke's versatility is a significant component of his X-factor. He excels in various playing conditions, adapting his style to different oil patterns and lane surfaces. This adaptability makes him a well-rounded and consistently competitive force on the professional bowling circuit.

PIAGET'S 4 STAGES OF COGNITIVE DEVELOPMENT

The 4 Stages of Cognitive Development by Piaget are deeply entwined with the path to greatness in any subject, including bowling. The ground-breaking theory of Jean Piaget describes the essential phases that people go through as their cognitive capacities develop from childhood to adulthood. These phases—sensorimotor, preoperational, concrete operational, and formal operational—offer a thorough framework for comprehending a bowler's ideal growth.

The conceptual underpinning of developmental psychology is Jean Piaget's theory of cognitive development. This theory, which was created by Swiss scientist Jean Piaget in the middle of the 20th century, completely changed how we think about how children learn and what intelligence is. According to Piaget's theory, children move through various stages of cognitive development, each of which is distinguished by particular cognitive skills and modes of thought. The notion places a strong emphasis on how involved kids are in their own education. Piaget saw kids as inquisitive explorers who were often interacting with their surroundings, doing experiments, and observing things to try to make sense of what was going on. Children build their conceptual understanding and form mental images of the world through these encounters.

The conventional wisdom that children's thinking is just an adult's thinking with less development was contested by Piaget's idea. He showed that children's cognitive processes differ qualitatively from those of adults and go through major changes as they advance through the developmental stages.

Our knowledge of child development has been significantly impacted by Piaget's theory, which has also had an impact on a wide range of disciplines, including education, psychology, and neuroscience. It emphasizes how crucial it is to take children's developmental stage into account when developing instructional strategies and interventions.

According to Jean Piaget's theory of cognitive development, children go through four different learning stages as they develop. This theory strives to comprehend the true nature of intelligence as well as how children gain information. **The sensorimotor stage (birth to two years), preoperational stage (ages 2 to 7), concrete operational stage (ages 7 to 11), and formal operational stage (ages 12 and up) are among the stages that Piaget suggested.**

Children actively participate in learning, according to Piaget, acting like young scientists who conduct experiments, record observations, and investigate their surroundings. Children continually absorb new information through their interactions with their surroundings, add to their existing understanding, and modify their preconceived conceptions in order to take into account new information.

The Evolution of Piaget's Theory of Cognitive Development

At the juvenile age of 11, Swiss prodigy Jean Piaget, who was born in the late 1800s, displayed extraordinary intelligence by writing his first scientific work. Piaget first became interested in children's intellectual development while working with eminent psychologists Alfred Binet and Theodore Simon to standardize their renowned IQ test.

A Clash of Perspectives: Piaget vs. Vygotsky

The theories of Lev Vygotsky and Jean Piaget in the area of child development are very different from one another. Vygotsky emphasizes the influence of society and culture more than he does the importance of curiosity and active participation in learning. Contrarily, Piaget holds that development is primarily influenced by internal elements, with external influences like culture and interpersonal connections having less of an impact.

Nephews, Daughters, and the Unveiling of Child Cognition: Inspiration from Observation

Piaget's acute observations of his own nephew and daughter led to his curiosity about the cognitive development of children. These personal encounters supported his emerging theory that children's minds are not merely scaled-down versions of adults' thoughts. Children had generally been thought of up until that moment as little copies of grownups. But Piaget was one of the first to see how different children's and adults' mental processes were from one another.

The Growth Paradigm: From Quantitative to Qualitative Transformations

In his pioneering theory, Piaget proposed that intelligence develops and evolves across a number of developmental stages. There are both qualitative and quantitative differences in the ways that the two age groups think, suggesting that older children's cognitive talents are not just faster versions of those of their younger peers. Piaget made perceptive observations that led him to the conclusion that children do not have lower intelligence than adults by nature; rather, they simply have different ways of thinking. In fact, Piaget's discovery awed Albert Einstein, who said that it was an idea "so simple only a genius could have thought of it."

The Stage Theory Unveiled: Illuminating Children's Cognitive Development

The well-known stage theory of Piaget provides a thorough framework for comprehending how children's cognitive development occurs. The evolution of cognitive functions and skills over time is explained by this idea. According to Piaget, the majority of early cognitive development depends on action-based processes before progressing to include changes in mental operations. The development of a child's cognitive landscape is shaped by this dynamic interaction, laying the path for improved comprehension and reasoning skills. In terms of child psychology, Jean Piaget's theory of cognitive development constitutes a significant paradigm shift. He challenges the idea that children are just smaller versions of adults by highlighting the distinctive character of children's cognition through his rigorous observations and ground-breaking ideas. Piaget provides us with a profound insight into how young minds perceive, learn, and interact with their environment by illuminating the complex phases of cognitive development.

The Sensorimotor Stage: Exploring The World Through Senses And Actions
Birth to 2 Years: Unleashing the Athlete Within

Infants and toddlers embark on an exciting exploration of the world during the exuberant sensorimotor stage of cognitive development. These young athletes learn and advance in their comprehension of the world through their senses and physical interactions with their surroundings.

Mastering the Art of Movement: Key Characteristics and Developmental Milestones

1. Dynamic Exploration: They actively interact with their surroundings to learn about the world through their vivacious motions and thrilling interactions.

2. Learning Through Action: By doing simple yet effective activities like sucking, gripping, seeing, and listening, these future champions learn important facts about their surroundings.

3. The Mystery of Object Permanence: When they realize that objects continue to exist even after they are out of sight, a paradigm-shifting insight occurs. This fresh insight, known as object persistence, stimulates their cognitive development.

4. Self-Realization: This stage paves the way for a more profound sense of self-awareness as they start to identify themselves as separate creatures that are distinct from the people and things around them.

5. The Power of Cause and Effect: They experience a monumental epiphany when they realize that their activities can have genuine effects on the outside world, rekindling their sense of agency.

Young athletes are propelled into a frenzy of growth and exploration throughout the sensorimotor stage. Every contact they have with their surroundings leads to fresh insights about how the world really works. Their cognitive growth expands quickly throughout this very little period of time. Along with learning physical skills like crawling and walking, they also pick up language quirks from the coaches and teammates they come across. The master coach, Piaget, further divides this stage into sub-stages, with the development of early representational cognition emerging as the pinnacle.

The formation of the core idea of object permanence, according to Piaget, is a significant turning point in this period. In training, athletes are taught that things have autonomous lives that go beyond our senses. This insight enables children to give names and words to the things they come into contact with, laying the groundwork for efficient communication and cognitive development.

Examples

At 18 Months: A toddler at 18 months of age engages in active exploration of the world, including playing with colorful toys and objects. They touch, feel, and manipulate these items, learning about textures and cause-and-effect relationships. As they discover that knocking over a tower of blocks is the result of their actions, they are beginning to grasp the concept of cause and effect.

At 14 Months: A 14-month-old child is in the early stages of the sensorimotor phase. They eagerly participate in simple activities that involve handling objects like building blocks or soft toys. This hands-on exploration helps them develop their motor skills and an understanding of object permanence. They are starting to realize that objects continue to exist even when they can't see them.

At 20 Months: A toddler at 20 months is a curious explorer of their surroundings. They actively observe and interact with objects, watching how they move and listening to the sounds they make. This sensory exploration aids in their cognitive development as they learn about the world around them and how different elements are connected.

The Preoperational Stage: Embracing The Playful Spirit

2 to 7 Years: Unleashing the Power of Imagination and Language:

You've arrived at the thrilling preoperational stage of development, as young athletes plunge headfirst into the world of language and imagination. They now begin a fascinating voyage of symbolic thinking and communication, building on the foundation established in the earlier stage.

1. The Language Revolution: Unleashing the Power of Words and Pictures

Athletes start to think figuratively and appreciate the power of language and imagery at this exciting stage. They develop their capacity for thought expression and social interaction by using these potent tools to depict objects.

2. Wrestling with Egocentrism: The Battle to See Beyond the Self

Athletes are challenged to overcome the issue of viewing the world purely from their own perspective as egocentrism takes center stage during this period. As they traverse the complicated complexities of social interactions, it becomes tough for them to understand the perspectives of others.

3. The Concrete Frontier: Conquering the Realm of Tangible Thinking

Young athletes tend to think in concrete terms, even when their linguistic and cognitive abilities are developing. They are excellent at pretend play and enjoy immersing themselves in fanciful situations, but they have trouble understanding abstract ideas and using logic.

4. The Elusive Concept of Constancy: Decoding the Secrets of Stability

During this phase, consistency proves to be a perplexing mystery. Children learn a lot about the world through pretend play, but they have a hard time understanding constancy—the idea that things stay the same despite changes in appearance.

5. An Action-Packed Playtime: The Interplay Between Pretend and Reality

Children display their mastery of pretend play throughout this exciting time of development. However, their way of thinking is strongly grounded in the physical features of their environment. Consider a researcher presenting a lump of clay that has been separated into two equal pieces as an example. The child is next given the option of a tightly curled ball or a piece that has been flattened into a pancake form. The preoperational athlete has a tendency to be mesmerized by the sight of the flat shape, viewing it as larger even though the parts are the same size. This strikingly exemplifies their propensity for concrete thinking.

JENNY WEGNER: Concrete Operational Stage

I was a meticulous young bowler, meticulously counting each step: one, two, three, four, release! Every single shot during practice followed this ritual. At the tender age of six, I joined the only women's league team in our small hometown. It was a defining moment for me when, at just 10 years old, I secured a spot on the "A-team." I became the youngest player ever to compete alongside adults in the second-highest division. Playing alongside a former member of the Swedish National Team, I felt a burning desire to improve and prove myself as her equal, if not better.

Hypothetical examples

The Language Revolution in Bowling: A 4-year-old bowler named Timmy excitedly tells his coach about his bowling ball. He describes it as "super-duper fast" and "rainbow-colored." Timmy's ability to use vivid language to express his thoughts about the bowling ball showcases how young athletes in the preoperational stage unleash the power of words and imagery in their bowling adventures.

Wrestling with Egocentrism in Bowling: During a friendly bowling match, 6-year-old Emily becomes upset when her friend uses a different-colored bowling ball. She insists that her own ball is the best because it's her favorite color. Emily's difficulty in considering her friend's perspective illustrates the challenge of egocentrism that young bowlers may face as they learn to understand the preferences of others.

The Concrete Frontier in Bowling: David, a 5-year-old bowler, loves to engage in pretend play on the bowling lanes. He pretends that each pin is a different character and narrates elaborate stories as he rolls the ball. However, when his coach introduces the concept of scoring, David struggles to grasp the abstract idea of adding up points, preferring to stay in the world of tangible, imaginative bowling adventures.

The Elusive Concept of Constancy in Bowling: During a bowling practice, 7-year-old Sarah becomes puzzled when a pin gets knocked down and then set back up. She finds it hard to comprehend that the pin is still the same despite its momentary change in appearance. Sarah's struggle to grasp the constancy of objects in the bowling alley highlights the challenge young bowlers face in understanding this concept.

An Action-Packed Playtime in Bowling: In the midst of an action-packed bowling playtime, a 4-year-old bowler named Jake is presented with two equal-sized pieces of modeling clay. One is shaped into a ball, and the other is flattened into a pancake.

Jake is fascinated by the flattened shape and insists that it's bigger, even though both pieces have the same amount of clay. This example illustrates how young bowlers in the preoperational stage often focus on concrete, visual aspects of objects in their play.

Concrete Operational Stage: Unleashing The Power Of Logical Thinking
7 to 11 Years: Mastering the Art of Concrete Reasoning

As they go into the concrete operational stage, where their thinking significantly shifts toward logic and structure, get ready to see the development of young champions. Despite the fact that their thinking is firmly rooted in the material world, their capacity for logic and empathy grows.

1. The Logic Crusade: Unveiling the Power of Reasoning

Athletes start a fascinating voyage of logical thinking about actual occurrences during this breath-taking stage. They start to understand the laws that control the world around them more clearly as they start to solve the riddles of cause and effect.

2. Conquering Conservation: Embracing the Balance of Equivalence

The realization of conservation by athletes is a significant turning point. They now realize that a short, wide cup holds the same amount of liquid as a tall, thin glass. This realization demonstrates their developing capacity to evaluate and contrast various facets of their environment.

3. The Rise of Logical Warriors: Battling with Rigid Reasoning

The difficulty of rigidity may also present itself to the tangible operational champions as their thinking becomes more logical and structured. Their propensity for concrete cognition makes it challenging for them to understand abstract and speculative ideas, necessitating additional growth and development in this area.

4. The Inductive Voyage: Discovering Patterns and General Principles

The concrete operational athletes set out on a thrilling inductive logical voyage. With specific knowledge at hand, they deftly reason their way to identifying general truths, deepening their comprehension of the world and its complexities.

Hypothetical examples

The Logic Crusade in Bowling: At 10 years old, Emily, an aspiring bowler, starts to apply logical thinking to her bowling game. She begins to understand that adjusting her bowling approach can directly impact her scores. For instance, she realizes that using a different angle or speed can lead to different pin configurations after her throw. This newfound logical reasoning helps Emily improve her bowling strategy as she navigates the cause-and-effect relationships within the game.

Conquering Conservation in Bowling: During a junior bowling league, 9-year-old Daniel learns the concept of conservation. He observes that when his coach pours the same amount of soda from a wide, shallow cup into a tall, narrow cup, the amount of liquid remains the same. This realization of equivalence in quantity demonstrates Daniel's growing ability to compare and contrast different aspects of his bowling environment.

The Rise of Logical Warriors in Bowling: 11-year-old Mia is a talented young bowler, but she sometimes struggles with rigid reasoning. She finds it challenging to understand abstract bowling strategies discussed by her coach, as her thinking is strongly rooted in the concrete aspects of the game. Mia needs additional development to bridge the gap between her logical thinking and more abstract bowling concepts.

The Inductive Voyage in Bowling: In a bowling clinic, 8-year-old Alex notices a pattern in his bowling performance. After studying his scores over several games, he deduces that he tends to score higher when he focuses on his arm's consistency in each throw. This inductive reasoning allows Alex to identify a general principle for improving his bowling game, deepening his understanding of how to perform better in the sport.

In this transformational phase, athletes let go of the last vestiges of egocentrism and gain a fresh perspective on the feelings and opinions of others. They recognize that their own ideas and beliefs are distinctive and that not everyone shares them, opening the door to empathic interactions. These young champions' bodies are still developing and thriving as they go into the concrete operational stage. They see gains in strength, coordination, and balance every day, which equips them to succeed in a variety of physical activities. This stage sees a considerable improvement in fine motor skills, giving athletes more dexterity and precision. They are more equipped to overcome physical problems with grace and finesse thanks to their improved control over their motions. A series of physiological changes are triggered by the definite operational stage. Hormonal alterations lead to changes in body composition and increased muscle mass, which fuel the athletes' physical development and transformation.

In a nutshell, the stage of concrete operationalization is an exciting period in the cognitive development of young athletes. They master the power of reason, successfully overcoming actual events. Their comprehension of the universe expands as they discover the principles of conservation and explore inductive reasoning. They develop stronger relationships with others by letting go of egocentrism and embracing empathy. They develop their fine motor abilities while becoming physically stronger and more coordinated. The tangible operational stage is evidence of their growing capacities and lays the foundation for upcoming victories in the fields of reason and comprehension.

The Formal Operational Stage: Unleashing The Power Of Abstract Thinking
Age 12 and Up: Rising to the Challenge of Abstract Reasoning

As they go into the formal operational stage, where their cognitive powers reach unprecedented heights, get ready to see the emergence of intellectual warriors. Adolescents and young adults who possess the power of logic, deductive reasoning, and a grasp of abstract concepts can enter a world where many answers and scientific thinking are possible.

1. Embracing the Abstract: Expanding the Horizons of Thought

Champions travel a path of speculative problem-solving and abstract thought at this magnificent level. They explore ideas that go beyond the limitations of the material world as they explore unknown mental landscapes. They can deal with difficult moral, intellectual, ethical, social, and political problems that call for theoretical and abstract reasoning thanks to their improved cognitive powers.

2. Deductive Masterminds: Unlocking the Power of Reasoning

As these cerebral warriors advance, they master the art of deductive logic, a potent technique that enables them to connect abstract ideas to specific data. They carefully connect the dots and reach logical conclusions as they untangle the complex webs of knowledge.

3. Abstract Ideas Take Center Stage: The Hallmark of Formal Operational Thinking

The pinnacle of the formal operational stage emerges as the capacity to think abstractly about events and ideas. Champions go above the limitations of the physical world and embrace the world of ideas and theories. They are able to explore the complexities of hypothetical scenarios and picture numerous potential solutions to issues, seeing possibilities beyond the present reality.

4. Strategic Visionaries: Planning for the Future

These extraordinary minds display the capacity to methodically plan for the future with their newly discovered cognitive aptitude. They develop strategic plans to overcome the obstacles ahead using abstract reasoning. They can anticipate and plan for speculative scenarios thanks to their visionary perspective, which gives them the ability to make wise choices and control their future.

Champions see great improvements in strength and coordination throughout this period, which sees physical growth and development blossom. Their physical strength increases, giving them a strong base on which to build their cerebral victories. Their cognitive journey is accompanied by physiological changes. Their bodies are still being shaped by hormonal changes, which have led to additional compositional changes and gains in muscle mass. These changes enhance their physical potential and create the foundation for athletic success.

The formal operational stage is the apex of cognitive growth, and this is when champions truly reach their intellectual and abstract potential. They operate in a realm beyond the concrete with their ability to dive into speculative issues and take on abstract ideas. With a clear strategic vision and the capacity to make plans, they accept their intellectual destiny. They embody a harmonious fusion of cerebral and physical strength as their physical abilities continue to grow. Their full potential is released during the formal operational period, which drives them to greatness in both the intellectual and physical spheres.

Hypothetical examples:

Embracing the Abstract in Bowling: Sarah, a 14-year-old bowling prodigy, is no longer limited to thinking solely about the physical aspects of the game. She delves into the abstract world of bowling strategy, contemplating how factors like lane conditions, oil patterns, and mental focus can influence her performance. Sarah's ability to explore these abstract concepts allows her to tackle complex challenges in her bowling journey, such as adapting her approach to various lane conditions.

Deductive Masterminds in Bowling: In a high school bowling tournament, 16-year-old Alex demonstrates his deductive reasoning skills. He observes that on days when he practices his arm swing diligently and focuses on his release technique, his scores consistently improve. By connecting these specific observations to his overall performance, Alex deduces that refining his arm swing and release is a key factor in his success, showcasing his ability to use deductive logic in improving his bowling game.

Abstract Ideas Take Center Stage in Bowling: As part of a bowling club, 18-year-old Mia explores abstract ideas related to the sport. She engages in discussions about the future of bowling, considering how technology and changing social dynamics might impact the game. Mia and her fellow club members contemplate hypothetical scenarios and potential solutions to keep bowling relevant and vibrant. Their ability to think abstractly about the sport's future exemplifies the hallmark of formal operational thinking in bowling.

Strategic Visionaries in Bowling: Mark, a 20-year-old competitive bowler, possesses the ability to strategically plan for his bowling career. He envisions a path to success that involves not only improving his technical skills but also considering the financial and logistical aspects of pursuing bowling at a professional level. Mark's visionary perspective and abstract reasoning allow him to make informed choices, set realistic goals, and plan for the future of his bowling career with confidence.

Stage	Age Range	Psychological Aspects	Thought Process	Neurological Differences	Strengths	Weaknesses
Sensorimotor Stage	Birth to 2	Dynamic exploration, learning through action, self-realization, power of cause and effect	Understanding the world through senses and physical interaction	Developing object permanence	Rapid cognitive and physical growth	Limited ability to express with words
Preoperational Stage	2 to 7	Language development, egocentrism, concrete thinking, understanding constancy, pretend play	Developing symbolic thinking and language skills	Expanding cognitive abilities	Flourishing imagination, symbolic play	Difficulty in understanding others' perspectives
Concrete Operational Stage	7 to 11	Logical thinking, conservation, overcoming rigidity, inductive reasoning	Improved understanding of cause and effect, concrete problem-solving	Cognitive development progresses	Concrete reasoning, mastering logic	Struggles with abstract and speculative ideas
Formal Operational Stage	12 and up	Abstract thinking, deductive reasoning, handling abstract ideas, strategic planning	The ability to think abstractly, dealing with complex, hypothetical situations	Expanded cognitive capabilities	Intellectual growth, strategic vision	Can be less experienced in the physical realm

Table 1- These stages provide a general framework for understanding cognitive development and may vary from individual to individual.

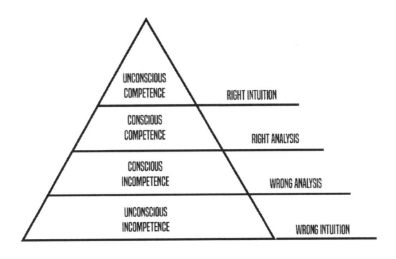

STAGES OF COMPETENCES

All bowlers start out at the very beginning and gradually hone the abilities and strategies necessary to excel in their chosen sport. The Conscious Competence Learning Matrix, a four-stage model illustrating the many phases of learning a bowler goes through to gain new skills, can be used to characterize this process.

This approach can be used by coaches to teach their bowlers new techniques, strategies, and plays while also guiding them through the learning process. Because coaches can ask themselves: "What stage is the bowler at and what is preventing the learning from progressing?" the Conscious Competence Learning Matrix is particularly helpful in resolving training barriers. In this approach, the conscious competence hypothesis aids coaches in better understanding challenges and how to best overcome them.

The concept also encourages the bowler to evaluate his own personal growth because the conscious competence theory forces analysis at an individual level.

Stage	Description	Characteristics
Unconscious Incompetence	In this stage, individuals are unaware of their lack of knowledge or skills in a particular area, such as bowling.	- Lack of awareness about the skill or knowledge required for bowling.
		- May exhibit overconfidence or underestimate the complexity of the task.
Conscious Incompetence	Individuals in this stage become aware of their lack of proficiency in bowling.	- Recognize the need for learning and skill development in bowling.
		- May feel frustrated or overwhelmed by the challenges they face in acquiring the necessary skills.

Stage	Description	Characteristics
Conscious Competence	In this stage, individuals actively learn and practice the skills required for bowling.	- Engage in deliberate practice and seek feedback to improve their bowling technique.
		- Develop a growing level of proficiency and accuracy in executing bowling movements.
Unconscious Competence	At this stage, individuals have acquired a high level of skill and can perform bowling techniques effortlessly.	- Perform bowling skills without conscious effort or active thinking.
		- Demonstrate consistency and precision in executing complex bowling movements.

Table 2: Stages of Competences

How the Conscious Competence Learning Matrix Works

Stage 1: Unconscious Incompetence

It's common for bowlers to embark on their journey without a clear understanding of the exact skills they need to master. This initial stage in the Conscious Competence Learning Matrix is often characterized by what we call "Unconscious Incompetence." In simpler terms, it means that bowlers may not even be aware of what they don't know.

As coaches, it's vital for us to acknowledge that no one, not even the most seasoned bowlers, possesses complete knowledge of every facet of this intricate sport. Just like how we might be utterly ignorant of the complexities of quantum physics, bowlers, especially beginners, might not fully comprehend the nuances of bowling technique. This awareness is the first step towards effective coaching.

However, as coaches, we stand on the other side of the spectrum. Our level of expertise and knowledge in bowling exceeds that of young and aspiring bowlers. It's our responsibility to guide and inform them. But we must not make the mistake of assuming that they possess the same level of knowledge as we do. Instead, our role is to put ourselves in their shoes, to remember how it felt when we were learning the skill, and to progressively introduce and develop the essential concepts over time.

The bowler isn't yet aware of his lack of bowling expertise or knowledge. He could not be knowledgeable about the best methods, plans, and tools for bowling. Additionally, He could be physically uncoordinated and weak to carry out the right form.

In other words, the young bowlers have no idea that they need to master the talent and are fully unaware of it, thus our role as coaches is to raise awareness.

Stage 2: Conscious Incompetence

Bowlers must first recognize their inability to do a new skill before moving on to stage 2 of the Conscious Competence Learning Matrix, also known as "Conscious Incompetence." This awareness is essential because it signals the start of the learning process. Bowlers begin experimenting with the technique through focused practice, gaining feedback, and further honing their proficiency. Depending on elements like motivation, the caliber of coaching feedback, the level of attention, and the presence of a supportive atmosphere, different levels of competency can be attained in different amounts of time.

At this point, the beginner bowler realizes how little He knows or can do in the sport. Although He may have begun to grasp some fundamental skills, He could find it difficult to consistently or correctly apply them. The bowler could feel frustrated or challenged as He tries to get better at his game at this point. However, with perseverance and dedication, students will start to see results and start to apply strategies more reliably.

Coaches and bowlers may find Stage 2 to be difficult. Although bowlers are now aware of the skill they need to develop, they still find it difficult to put it into practice. As individuals become more aware of their lack of experience with the new talent, they could feel frustrated. Many bowlers are aware of the enormous amount of information they still need to learn and the substantial work needed to succeed at a high level. Some bowlers might even consider quitting. As coaches, it is imperative that we offer unwavering support and encouragement while utilizing a motivating and encouraging coaching approach. Ideally, bowlers follow our advice and commit to learning and honing the new talent, moving on to stage 3: "Conscious Competence."

Hypothetical Examples

Sarah starts to become cognizant of her lack of ability. She acknowledges that she lacks the abilities and information necessary to regularly produce the desired outcomes in bowling. However, she is driven to get better and goes through the conscious incompetence stage by doing the following:

Awareness of Incompetence: *Sarah realizes how unprepared and uninformed she is for the game. She is aware of how erratic her play is and how difficult it is for her to consistently strike the pins accurately. She understands that in order to increase her bowling performance, she must continue to hone her abilities.*

Seeking Knowledge and Guidance: *Sarah proactively looks for information and direction to enhance her abilities. She begins by watching and analyzing more seasoned bowlers at her neighborhood lanes. To further understand the mechanics, tactics, and strategies of bowling, she also studies books, watches online courses, and consults with expert bowlers.*

Practice and Skill Development: *For Sarah to become a better bowler, careful practice is her main goal. She spends time honing her approach, release, and accuracy at the bowling center. To locate the bowling ball that fits her style the best, she experiments with various tactics and practices with several bowling balls. In order to improve her technique, she also pays close attention to her body alignment, arm swing, and follow-through.*

Embracing Feedback: *Sarah regularly solicits advice from skilled bowlers and her other competitors. She appreciates constructive feedback and grabs the chance to develop. Whether it's altering her grip, honing her footwork, or enhancing her timing, she recognizes her areas for development and tries to fix them. She is receptive to criticism and modifies her strategy as necessary.*

Setting Goals: *Sarah establishes clear objectives to track her development and maintain motivation. She establishes both short-term objectives, like raising her average score by a given number of pins or boosting her spare conversion rate, and long-term objectives, like participating in a neighborhood bowling tournament or hitting a particular bowling average. She routinely assesses her development and acknowledges her successes, which keeps her motivated and focused.*

Persistence and Patience: *Sarah is aware that progress requires time and effort. Even when she encounters obstacles or disappointments, she maintains her patience and persistence. She remains dedicated to her daily practice schedule and keeps looking for information and direction. She recognizes that making errors is a necessary aspect of learning and views them as chances to advance.*

Sarah slowly emerges from the stage of conscious incompetence and starts to observe improvement in her performance as she keeps practicing her bowling techniques carefully. Her overall bowling scores begin to increase as her pin-hitting precision and consistency increase. As her self-assurance grows, she advances to the following level of skill development.

Stage 3: Conscious Competence

A bowler enters the stage of conscious competence after moving past conscious ineptitude. The bowler has reached this stage after putting in the necessary time to practice and gain the essential skills. Effective use of these talents still necessitates intentional effort, though. When the bowler concentrates and focuses on his actions, He can perform effectively since He is fully aware of his talents. Let's examine the specifics and procedures of conscious competence in relation to bowling, using an example.

At this point, the bowler has a solid base of bowling abilities and a thorough awareness of the technical aspects of the sport. He is able to consciously use the right approaches and strategies to attain his desired objectives because He has recognized his own personal strengths and weaknesses. The bowler shows the ability to execute shots precisely, but continuing to perform at a high level consistently requires focus, effort, and concentration. Depending on the bowler's level of concentration and focus throughout each shot, performance may change.

Hypothetical Examples

Example: Think about Sarah, a bowler who has attained conscious competence. Sarah has developed her bowling abilities via years of training and practice, as well as a thorough comprehension of the sport. She is aware that her accuracy and capacity to gauge lane conditions are her strongest suit. To ensure consistent and accurate shots, Sarah intentionally applies her expertise and uses particular tactics during her approach and release. She does, however, admit that staying focused and concentrated is essential for maintaining her level of performance throughout the game. Sarah is aware that each shot demands her whole focus and effort to carry out correctly, producing good results.

Example: Let's take Alex, a bowler who has attained a level of conscious proficiency in the sport, as an example. Alex has dedicated a lot of effort to honing his bowling abilities. He is proficient in the grip, posture, approach, and release as well as other technical aspects of the sport. Alex is able to successfully employ his skills during competitions, but it takes focused effort and concentration. He is conscious of both his positive traits, such as accuracy, and negative traits, such as spare conversions. Alex works on developing mental skills to control his emotions and stay focused during contests by routinely practicing with purpose, asking his coach for feedback, and practicing these skills. He adjusts his equipment, pace, and line accordingly and aims for consistency in his performance. He is flexible to various lane circumstances.

The Process of Conscious Competence in Bowling

Step 1: Execution of Skill with Concentration and Focus Bowlers utilizes newly learned abilities and strategies with the utmost intensity and concentration when they reach the stage of conscious proficiency. They carefully monitor their form, approach, and release as they perform each shot. Bowlers increase their chances of succeeding by remaining focused throughout the entire game.

An experienced bowler practices newly learned techniques with intense focus, carefully monitoring form, approach, and release during each shot to increase the chances of success.

Step 2: Analysis and Modification Bowlers who are conscious of their performance continually evaluate their strikes and make the required corrections. To choose the best line and delivery, they consider the lane conditions, the position of the pin, and the behavior of the ball. Bowlers can improve their technique and adjust to the shifting game dynamics by analyzing the results of each shot.

A competitive bowler reviews performance after each game, consistently identifying areas for improvement. He adjusts his approach or delivery to address recurring challenges, such as leaving specific pins standing.

Step 3: Intentional Practice and Seeking Feedback Bowlers at the conscious competency stage put in intentional practice time to improve their game. They concentrate on honing their talents through repetitive drills and exercises and target particular areas for improvement. They also actively seek input from mentors, teammates, or video analysis to pinpoint their strong points and areas that still need improvement.

An aspiring professional dedicates several hours to focused practice each week, concentrating on honing specific skills. He actively seeks feedback from coaches and teammates to pinpoint strengths and weaknesses.

Step 4: Mental Preparation and Emotional Management Successful bowlers are aware of how crucial mental preparation is. They create techniques to

CHRISTOPHER SLOAN:
Intentional Practice and
Seeking Feedback

In those early days, Fergal McLoughlin, my first coach from Ireland, played a pivotal role in encouraging me to expand my horizons and compete beyond the borders of my homeland. Little did I know that this would lead me to the person who would shape my game into what it is today. One individual stands out among the many who have contributed to my journey—Brian Michael. He has been instrumental in transforming my perception of the game by introducing me to unique training methods that have had a profound impact on my development. We devoted countless hours to refining my physical game, meticulously aligning my steps and timing until a breakthrough occurred, forever etching a defining moment in my mind.

Beyond the physical aspects, Brian emphasized the mental fortitude required to compete at the highest level. He introduced me to a wealth of articles on mental toughness and designed specific drills to sharpen my focus and resilience. To this day, one particular drill continues to resonate with me and is ingrained in my practice routine as a reminder of the mental strength necessary for success. As I write this piece, I am compelled to revisit those articles Brian shared with me, seeking to sharpen my mental tools for the upcoming weeks of intense competition.

control their emotions and keep a clear head even in stressful circumstances. They use strategies like visualization, deep breathing, and encouraging self-talk to keep calm and in control throughout the game.

A skilled bowler prioritizes mental preparation, using techniques like visualization and positive self-talk to stay composed during competition and manage emotions effectively.

Step 5: Adaptability to Bowling Conditions Bowlers who are cognizant of their competence can adjust to different lane circumstances. They have the expertise and understanding to choose the right ball, modify their delivery, and alter their technique with confidence. Regardless of the bowling conditions, their versatility enables them to maximize their performance and produce beneficial outcomes.

A seasoned bowler competes in various tournaments with varying lane conditions. He confidently selects the right bowling ball, adjusts delivery, and modifies technique to adapt to changing conditions, optimizing performance.

Step 6: Consistency in Technique Consistency A key component of conscious competency in bowling is consistency. A repeatable, dependable approach that regularly produces accurate shots is something bowlers work to improve. They improve their chances of getting consistent results and reducing performance differences by concentrating on keeping a constant approach, release, and follow-through.

A dedicated bowler consistently practices his approach and release, striving for a repeatable, dependable technique that produces accurate shots consistently, minimizing performance variations during league play.

When a bowler reaches conscious competency, it means He has acquired the essential information and abilities through practice and education but still needs to make a conscious effort to use them successfully. A bowler can flourish at this stage of expertise in bowling variations by deliberately using skills, practicing with intention, working on mental preparation, being adaptable, and aiming for consistency.

Stage 4: Unconscious Competence: The Mastery of Unconscious Competence in Bowling

The highest point of bowlers' skill development is represented by the final step of the Conscious Competence Learning Matrix, which is referred to as "Unconscious Competence." Bowlers have reached a high degree of expertise at this point, where using tactics and strategies is effortless and instinctive. Let's be specific about what it means to achieve unconscious competency in bowling. Bowlers who have attained unconscious proficiency can use their techniques without making a conscious effort. They can execute the tactics and strategies they have perfected flawlessly because they are embedded in their muscle memory. The bowler makes motions that seem effortless and the technique appears as though it has come naturally to him. Bowlers who have reached the point of unconscious competence consistently provide strong performances. Precision, accuracy, and dependability define their shots. They constantly get high scores, successfully convert spares, and reach their targets. Their proficiency and capacity to consistently deliver outstanding performances are demonstrated by their level of consistency. Bowlers with unconscious skills are remarkably adaptable. They adapt to varying lane conditions, oil patterns, and equipment modifications with ease. They have an innate

YANNAPHON LARPAPHARAT
Unconscious Competence

On the other hand, there are moments when I need to push myself even harder. I dive into intense practice sessions, reminding myself of past successes and the feeling of delivering a flawless shot. I often revisit old videos of my games, analyzing my technique and pinpointing areas for improvement. This process of self-reflection helps me refine my skills and maintain a continuous upward trajectory. Preparing for major events requires a holistic approach. Physically, I focus on maintaining my fitness level and ensuring that my body is in optimal condition to endure the demands of competitive bowling. Mental preparation is equally vital. I engage in visualization exercises, picturing myself executing each shot flawlessly and feeling the rush of adrenaline as the pins topple one by one. I cultivate a strong mindset, building resilience to overcome any obstacles that may arise during the competition.

ability to read and comprehend the constantly shifting circumstances, which enables them to make the required modifications without having to think about it. Due to their ability to adapt, they can continue to compete at a high level despite the difficulties given by varied bowling venues. Bowlers who have reached the level of unconscious competence utilize their physical and mental abilities effectively. They bowl with fluidity and ease thanks to their deeply entrenched abilities and approaches. They make their movements as efficient as possible, saving energy and cutting back on pointless work. Their entire effectiveness on the lanes is maximized thanks to this efficiency, which translates into constant performance. Bowlers who are unconsciously competent have remarkable decision-making abilities. They have the ability to quickly make intuitive decisions based on experience and instinct. In response to the requirements of the situation or the particular lane conditions, they automatically modify their approach, speed, or equipment. Their intuitive and instinctive decision-making process enhances their total performance and enables them to master any bowling setting.

Bowlers who have attained unconscious competence radiate self-assurance. Their abilities have embedded themselves profoundly, giving them a strong sense of self-assurance. They perform well under duress, maintain cool under pressure, and are resilient. Their unwavering confidence in their talents strengthens their mental fortitude and helps explain their reliable performance.

Hypothetical example:

Consider John, a skilled bowler who has been competing at a high level for a number of years. John has spent many hours honing his skills and has attained a level of unconscious proficiency as a result. John can smoothly execute a variety of strokes, like as strikes and spares, during competitions without consciously considering his technique. He is able to make quick assessments of the shifting lane circumstances, modifications to his approach, pace, and equipment, and split-second decisions regarding changes in strategy. John consistently gives exceptional performances and does it with a high degree of accuracy and consistency. He emanates confidence in his skills and maintains his composure under pressure, which leads to exceptional performance in tournaments.

When bowlers reach the stage of unconscious competence, their abilities and techniques are instinctive, and they may throw strikes without exerting any conscious effort. Their movements become automatic and smooth as muscle memory takes over. The bowlers' attention moves from considering the game's mechanics to lane circumstances, picturing the shot, and planning. They immediately assess lane conditions, alter their equipment, speed, and line, and make split-second judgments on spare conversions or changes in strategy based on their experience and instinct. Bowlers routinely perform well without having to deliberately think about their technique. They have no trouble reproducing their performance in other settings and tournaments. Bowlers can react instinctively to various lane conditions and are highly versatile. They have a thorough comprehension of the game, a high level of skill mastery, and the experience and intuition necessary to bowl with assurance and calmness.

Hypothetical example:

Sarah is a bowler who has attained a level of unconscious expertise in the sport. For many years, Sarah has been bowling and has logged many hours practicing and competing. Her muscle memory is entrenched with the abilities and methods she has mastered. Sarah may execute shots throughout contests without consciously considering her technique. She has the ability to read the state of the lanes, intuitively alter her gear, speed, and line, and make split-second decisions regarding spare conversions or strategy changes. She routinely performs at a high level and has a natural knack for lane changes. Sarah is able to bowl with poise and assurance in any circumstance because she has a strong grasp of the game, a high level of skill mastery, and a high level of self-assurance in her abilities.

As bowlers advance from one step to the next, they frequently experience an awakening or a sense of success that lets them know they have entered the next phase of their educational journey. The same is true for "plateaus" where bowlers feel like they have not advanced.

Example

The model is particularly intriguing in this context. Imagine a bowler you train who is an outstanding performer but who struggles when pressured in competition. Commentators refer to this as choking. A bowler overthinks what He is doing at this point, and his normally fluid movement becomes mechanical, just like it did while He was still "learning" at stage 3.

The highest level of performance for bowlers is Stage 4 in the Conscious Competence Learning Matrix. It is essential to realize that Stage 3 is a stage of conscious competence rather than a performance stage. Bowlers must go back to the broad picture and concentrate on key triggers that cover all the necessary stages in order to advance to

Stage 4. Coaches are crucial in assisting bowlers in developing their key words so they may consistently perform at Stage 4. Let's talk about the significance of Stage 4 and how Stage 3 becomes Stage 4. Bowlers perform at the very best of their abilities. It is the stage of automaticity where using talents automatically comes naturally. At this stage, bowlers can rely on their muscle memory and experience to routinely deliver excellent results rather than consciously thinking about each particular phase. The secret to Stage 4 is using key words or cues to start the desired behaviors and responses.

Bowlers must change their attention from every little aspect of the procedure to the overall picture of performance in order to move from Stage 3 to Stage 4. Coaches are essential in assisting bowlers in developing their key phrases or triggers, which encompass all the actions required for outstanding results. The use of these key phrases serves as a mental shortcut that activates the required muscle memory and simplifies the implementation of tactics and strategies. For bowlers, key phrases act as strong cues and reminders to utilize their skills and deliver their best games. Each bowler's personal phrase should elicit the desired attitude and actions. They serve as a mental switch that enables bowlers to skip conscious cognition and access their unconscious competence in order to enter the performance zone. Key words are reinforced and repeated during practice and training to help establish their connection to peak performance. The difficult part for bowlers is to hang around Stage 4 throughout genuine performances. They can maintain the zone and continuously perform at their best by relying on their key words and triggers. It is crucial for bowlers to return to Stage 3 after the performance and conduct a careful analysis of their performance. They can evaluate what went well and where they need to make improvements thanks to this evaluation. In order to assist bowlers in improving their abilities and tactics, coaches play a critical role in enabling this evaluation process.

Stage	Example for Bowlers	Example for Coaches	Challenges	Strengths
Stage 1: Unconscious Incompetence	A beginner bowler who is unaware of the need to learn specific bowling techniques.	Introducing a novice bowler to the basic concepts and skills of bowling.	Lack of awareness about the need to learn, resistance to change.	Opportunity for growth and development, openness to learning new skills.
Stage 2: Conscious Incompetence	A bowler who recognizes the need to improve his skills but is still learning and not yet proficient.	Providing guidance and practice opportunities to help bowlers develop their skills.	Frustration and impatience, self-doubt, the challenge of breaking old habits.	Increased motivation, willingness to learn and improve.
Stage 3: Conscious Competence	A bowler who has developed a solid foundation of skills and can perform with focus and concentration.	Refining techniques, providing feedback, and guiding bowlers in applying strategies.	Maintaining consistency, managing distractions, adapting to different lane conditions.	Increased control and precision, ability to apply learned skills effectively.
Stage 4: Unconscious Competence	A highly skilled bowler who performs effortlessly and automatically without conscious effort.	Fine-tuning advanced techniques and strategies, helping bowlers maintain focus and confidence.	Complacency, plateauing, maintaining motivation and continuous improvement.	Effortless execution, ability to perform under pressure, automaticity in skills.

Table 3 - For bowlers and coaches alike, each stage of the Conscious Competence Learning Matrix is discussed along with pertinent examples. The difficulties that come with each stage are listed, including complacency, frustration, resistance to change, and distractions. However, each stage's benefits or strengths are also emphasized, including chances for development, elevated drive, enhanced command, and automaticity in performance.

This informational table offers a clear explanation of the Conscious Competence Learning Matrix's operation and aids in helping coaches and bowlers alike comprehend the many learning phases, their traits, and the techniques required to advance and reach greater levels of performance.

Moving between competences stages during tournament

Reaching Stage 4, the pinnacle of the Conscious Competence Learning Matrix, known as "Unconscious Competence," is the ultimate goal for professional bowlers. At this stage, bowlers achieve a remarkable level of mastery and proficiency in their game, allowing them to perform with unparalleled ease and consistency. However, even the most skilled bowlers can encounter challenges that force them to temporarily revert to a state of conscious competence.

Let's explore various scenarios and techniques for bowlers to regain their unconscious competence during both tournaments and practice:

Some examples of causes

Unfamiliar Technique: *Bowlers may find themselves having to use an unfamiliar technique during a tournament due to various reasons. This can occur when they encounter lane conditions that are drastically different from what they are used to, or if they are faced with challenging spares or splits that require an unconventional approach. In some cases, they might be experimenting with a new technique in a high-pressure situation.*

Mental Challenge: When faced with an unfamiliar technique, bowlers may experience anxiety and self-doubt because they lack confidence in executing it effectively.

Physical Challenge: Physically, the challenge lies in the execution of an unfamiliar technique, requiring conscious control over muscle movements.

Injury During Play: *Injuries can occur during a tournament for various reasons, such as accidents or overexertion. These injuries can force bowlers to adapt their approach and technique to minimize discomfort and prevent exacerbating the injury. In some cases, bowlers may choose to play through the pain in order to complete the tournament, which necessitates a conscious effort to control their movements.*

Mental Challenge: Dealing with an injury can lead to mental stress, affecting focus and potentially causing frustration. Bowlers may worry about their performance and recovery.

Physical Challenge: The primary physical challenge is managing the injury itself. However, consciously controlling movements to avoid further injury can lead to muscle strain or discomfort.

Tricky Lanes: *Tricky or unplayable lanes can emerge due to changes in oil patterns, lane conditions, or even the impact of other bowlers on the lane. These challenges can cause bowlers to question their usual approach and necessitate a shift in strategy. The uncertainty and frustration arising from these conditions can affect a bowler's game.*

Mental Challenge: Tricky lanes can be mentally challenging, causing self-doubt, frustration, and a loss of confidence. Bowlers may second-guess their decisions and struggle to adapt to the conditions.

Physical Challenge: Adapting to challenging lane conditions is physically demanding, potentially leading to muscle strain or discomfort as bowlers consciously adjust their approach and technique.

Fatigue During the Tournament: *Fatigue often sets in as tournaments involve multiple games, and bowlers may face physical exhaustion as a result. Extended play can lead to muscle fatigue, affecting the bowler's strength and coordination. As fatigue accumulates, bowlers may compensate by using more force to deliver the ball accurately.*

Mental Challenge: Fatigue can result in mental fatigue, leading to reduced focus, decision-making difficulties, and a lack of mental resilience. Bowlers may become more prone to self-doubt and frustration as a result.

Physical Challenge: Physical challenges during fatigue involve muscle tiredness and a loss of coordination. The bowler may exert extra force to compensate for diminished strength, leading to inconsistencies and an increased risk of injury.

MOTOR SKILLS DEVELOPMENT IN BOWLING

Bowling, a sport enjoyed by millions worldwide, is not only a game of precision and technique but also a fascinating domain for exploring the principles of motor development. Motor development in bowling encompasses the journey from a beginner, who is learning the fundamental mechanics of the game, to a seasoned professional, who executes strikes and spares with remarkable accuracy. This intricate process involves the acquisition and refinement of motor skills, the optimization of muscle memory, and the mastery of various bowling techniques. In this discussion, we will delve into the captivating world of motor development in bowling, exploring the stages, techniques, and factors that shape a bowler's journey from novice to expert, highlighting the significance of motor learning and skill acquisition in this dynamic sport.

Acquiring, honing, and using motor knowledge, experience, and programs are all parts of motor learning. It is closely linked to cognitive and conative traits, motor skills, foreknowledge, cognitive talents, and movement method principles. Running uses more than 80 muscle groups and 46 bones in the locomotor system, making it a fundamental expression of human motor ability. The best possible synchronization of motions is crucial for performing motor tasks accurately. Three stages can be distinguished in the motor learning process: the initial verbal-cognitive stage, in which a novel movement structure is recognized and understood; the associative stage, in which the movement structure's components are combined and modified to fit changing conditions; and the autonomous stage, in which movement becomes automatic with few mistakes. Beginners make needless movements, engage irrelevant muscles, and struggle to find balance during the first phase, which leads to inaccurate starting positions, inflexible posture, and improper movement rhythm. This stage usually lasts between 15 and 30 hours. Movement quality significantly improves during the second, associative phase, with softer, more relaxed motions as superfluous actions eventually decrease. During this period, which lasts for three to five months, a motor stereotype develops in the motor portion of the central nervous system. The autonomous phase, which follows the second and third phases, is characterized by movement automation and the best fusion of each kinematic and dynamic movement characteristic. This phase lasts for many years and is never fully finished. However, unexpected situations like acute exhaustion, great pressure, or high levels of stress may result in the breakdown of the motor stereotype.

Short-Term and Long-Term Programming

An appropriate motor program must exist in order to perform a certain movement successfully. A motor program, according to Schmidt (1977), is a set of instructions that are established before the movement is started and are transmitted from the central nervous system to the muscles. Both short-term and long-term motor memory contain motor programming. For immediate movement control, short-term motor memory, which records sensory input from the environment such as visual, auditory, and kinesthetic signals, is essential. It serves as a working memory and has a short lifespan of about 30 seconds. On the other hand, well-trained and automatic motor tasks are stored in long-term motor memory. During the early stages of learning, short-term memory is especially crucial, but both types of memory are essential for motor learning.

Comprehension and Sensory Shift in Bowling: Beginners in bowling may struggle to fully grasp the dynamics and timing of the sport. They often have a hazy and deficient understanding of bowling techniques. Distinguishing between vital and less important aspects of the game can be challenging. Visual aids, such as diagrams or videos, are frequently used to explain bowling concepts, with verbal instructions providing additional guidance.

Short-Term Memory examples in Bowling:

Adjusting to Lane Conditions: During a bowling competition, bowlers encounter a lane with an unusual oil pattern. To adapt to the changing conditions, they rely on their short-term memory. They observe how their ball reacts to the lane's surface and quickly make mental notes about necessary adjustments. This short-term memory allows them to fine-tune their approach and release for the current game.

Conversing with a Coach: In between frames, bowlers may have a brief conversation with their coach about their performance. The coach provides immediate feedback and suggestions for improvement. The bowler must rely on their short-term memory to retain and apply this feedback for the remainder of the game, making quick adjustments based on the coach's guidance.

Long-Term Memory examples in Bowling:

Automated Bowling Technique: Seasoned bowlers who have practiced for many years have developed an automated bowling technique stored in their long-term memory. This includes the precise mechanics of their approach, release, and targeting. They no longer need to consciously think about each step; their muscle memory takes over, allowing them to consistently deliver the ball with accuracy and power.

Past Tournament Success: Professional bowlers have a wealth of experiences stored in long-term memory. This includes memories of past tournament victories, strategies that worked well in specific conditions, and lessons learned from defeats. They draw on this long-term memory to make strategic decisions during high-pressure competitions, using past successes and failures to inform their choices.

The phases of motor learning: building the foundations

Three unique stages make up the motor learning process, each of which is essential to the growth of movement coordination. Let's examine these stages and how they affect our capacity for precise and adaptable athletic performance.

Phase 1: Movement Foundation

Beginners familiarize themselves with the basic concepts of movement during the first stage of motor learning. However, they can only carry out these movements under ideal circumstances and only with deliberate effort. Results are modest due to a lack of efficiency and technique. The comprehension of motion and motor experiences is hazy, deficient, and frequently out of sync with the ideal dynamics and timing of the desired motion. Beginners find it difficult to distinguish between vital and less important movement

Development of Bowling Motor Awareness: Developing motor awareness, including bowling-specific motor programs, is essential for improving technical aspects in bowling. Research suggests that there can be a transfer of motor skills and knowledge between related sports, which can aid bowlers in learning and adapting to new techniques.

components and stages. Usually, visual signals like illustrations, pictures, or videos are what people first understand. The main sensory signal system shifts to visual information, with verbal instructions from teachers serving as a backup. Beginners learn the fundamentals of movement and lay the foundation for execution with this combo.

As beginners begin to execute a movement, their central nervous system accesses the motor memory, which stores specific motor programming or foreknowledge. These programs are rather rare in motor memory during the early phases of learning more complex motor tasks like tennis, skiing, bowling, or gymnastics. As a result, first efforts might not be successful right away. It's critical to keep in mind that individual characteristics, including motor foreknowledge and experience, motor ability, mental attention, motivation, and effort, play a big influence. Progress is an individual journey.

Hypothetical Examples:

Example 1: A bowler who is just starting to acquire the fundamental motions and skills of the game. This person might have trouble performing the actions correctly and consistently, and might only be able to do so in ideal circumstances with consistent conscious concentration. He might not have a well-developed technique that is efficient, and He might not fully comprehend the motor sensations that are involved in the movement. To develop his fundamental understanding of movement and lay the groundwork for execution, He could rely largely on verbal instructions from his instructor as well as external sensory cues like sight.

Example 2: A bowler with some experience who is still acquiring more difficult motor skills including advanced methods and tactics. This person might comprehend the fundamental motions and methods of bowling better, but He might still find it difficult to execute more difficult motions consistently. Although He may have some motor foresight recorded in his memory, it is insufficient for him to successfully complete the more difficult tasks. To do better, He might need to keep honing his skills and putting in more practice while also emphasizing mental focus, drive, and general effort.

The development of motor awareness, often referred patterns as motor programs, is crucial for affecting the technical aspects of a given sport. Bernstein's research (in Latash, 1998) indicates that there is a significant transfer of motor skills and knowledge between related motor circumstances. For instance, knowledge of gymnastics, track and field, or tennis can help someone learn skiing, basketball, or football, and vice versa. A beginner's transition to learning new movement methods in other sports will go more smoothly the more motor knowledge, experience, and programs He has under his belt.

Integration of Kinesthetic Receptors in Bowling: Bowling motor programs become more precise as kinesthetic receptors are integrated during this stage. The sensory systems, including verbal, sensory, and kinesthetic signals, interact more effectively, resulting in a precise understanding of movement within spatial and temporal parameters.

Beginners frequently think they are performing a task correctly during this phase while, in fact, their performance is superficial or wholly erroneous. Their restricted range of motion is the main cause of this. They place a lot of emphasis on their visual perception system and see their eyes as the most crucial optical analyzers. Visual information alone is insufficient, though. Movement coordination is greatly aided by kinesthetic sensors found in tendons, ligaments, and joints. These sensory receptors keep an eye on muscle tension, joint angles, and body position. Since kinesthetic analysis depends on experience, previously learned motor programs and memory, it is not fully developed in novices. As a result, the flow of feedback information is insufficient, partial, inaccurate, and impatient. Beginners need visual training to help them understand verbal instructions. The main execution components should be highlighted, technical elements should be repeated if necessary at a slower rate, and instructors should give succinct explanations. It's critical to just give newcomers the knowledge they need in order to avoid depleting their drive and attention span.

The inability to discern between proper and improper movements, a lack of range of motion, stiffness, an inappropriate tempo, and poorly coordinated movements are all signs of this phase's rigidity of movement. According to Bernstein in Latash (1998), the fundamental reason is the phenomena of "irradiation" within the motor cortex of the central nervous system. Due to the unregulated activation of muscles that are not used in particular actions, this causes interference and obstruction between muscle groups. Additionally, practicing can wear bowlers out physically and mentally, making it harder for them to focus. The fear of failure might make learning even more difficult. Enthusiastic newcomers must be careful not to feel under pressure to meet improbable deadlines. Bowlers

Mitigating Factors in Bowling: Instructors working with beginner bowlers should consider mitigating factors such as muscle interference, physical and mental fatigue, and the fear of failure. Providing assistance, adjusting the pace of learning, and assessing individual bowling capabilities can promote early success in learning bowling.

should receive encouragement from the instructor, who should also focus on fixing key errors without overloading them with knowledge. In each attempt at a movement, a beginner can only successfully manage one or, at most, two aspects.

Instructors must take into account mitigating factors by providing assistance, changing pace or power, and assessing the player's technique based on their unique motor capabilities in order to promote early success in motor learning. Unsuitable motor skills are frequently to blame for mistakes. Last but not least, creating a solid basis for skill development requires a positive learning environment that is marked by respect, motivation, adequate surroundings, a good climate and temperature, and proper equipment.

Example 1: Bowlers who are still learning their motor skills may have trouble using the proper technique and separating important movement components from less important ones. They can believe they are carrying out the task well when, in fact, they are doing it carelessly or incorrectly. The teacher must assist the novice with ocular control and give clear explanations and examples of technical features while highlighting the crucial components of execution. To avoid overwhelming the novice with too much information, the instructor must also give good energy and encourage the bowler while only rectifying serious errors.

Example 2: Bowlers with greater expertise may have acquired motor foresight or motor programs that enhance their ability to quickly pick up new movement patterns in other sports, such as football or skiing. It becomes simpler for bowlers to master new movement techniques as they gain more motor knowledge, experience, and routines. However, bowlers may still feel stiffness in their motions, which may be seen in their inability to tell the difference between perfect and incorrect actions, their lack of suitable movement amplitude, stiffness, and tension, as well as their improper execution tempo and lackluster coordination of their movements. To ensure a good start in the learning process, the instructor must assess the bowler's playing technique in light of their unique motor talents and provide aid by reducing speed or power.

Phase 2: Movement Accuracy

A crucial turning point in the journey toward mastery is the stage of precise movement synchronization. Here, the bowler exhibits the capacity to carry out motions with extraordinary precision while attentively observing the ideal technique pattern. Errors may still happen, but they're less noticeable and happen less frequently. Bowlers noticeably improve with continued practice as their actions become more fluid and coordinated and exhibit finer coordination. However, development is not always linear, and people may experience brief developmental plateaus. Avoiding consolidation of errors is crucial because repeated incorrect motions over time can ingrain them in the bowler's motor memory. Due to their propensity to have incorrect ideas about movement and motor programs, people who self-taught themselves sports like tennis, skiing, swimming, or bowling are especially susceptible to this issue. As a result, interference between competing programs prevents approaches from being used effectively, emphasizing the significance of professional direction.

Avoiding Error Consolidation in Bowling: It's crucial to prevent the consolidation of errors during this phase because repeated incorrect movements can become ingrained in the bowler's motor memory. Self-taught bowlers, especially those without professional guidance, may be susceptible to this issue due to misconceptions about movement and motor programs.

As a result of the integration of kinesthetic receptors, motor programs display increased precision throughout this stage. The verbal, sensory, and kinesthetic signal systems interact more successfully, leading to a precise knowledge of movement in accordance with outside spatial and temporal parameters. Movement anticipation becomes better, utilizing both internal and external stimuli, while conscious control loses dominance. Movements are carried out effortlessly and appear to have been planned by the subconscious. The development of a cognitive and symbolic system becomes essential in addition to feedback, kinesthetic control, and sensory control. The bowler abstracts physical actions into ideas, words, or phrases to enable rational management and enhance communication with the coach. Bowlers get better at describing their own movements, distinct stages, and crucial times in great detail. Additionally, kinesthetic perceptions become more acute and sensitive to changes in the environment and equipment dynamics.

Automation of Bowling Techniques: During this phase, bowlers aim to automate their bowling techniques. They work to ensure that their movements become second nature, allowing for consistent and reliable performance in competitive settings.

Practice should concentrate on honing the technique under typical conditions throughout this period. Favorable circumstances frequently result in optimal outcomes. However, difficulties arise in unpredictable, dynamic, and unfavorable circumstances, which may lead to the approach failing and having long-term effects on the game. Therefore, perfect, consistent, and standard-condition execution of the technique is something that both the bowler and the instructor must work toward. By sticking to this objective, the bowler sets out on a path to proficiency, strengthened by improved movement coordination and a finely tuned comprehension of the nuances of the sport.

Rigidity of Movement in Bowling: Beginners in bowling may exhibit rigidity in their movements, characterized by an inability to discern between proper and improper bowling techniques, limited range of motion, stiffness, inappropriate tempo, and poorly coordinated movements. This rigidity can be influenced by factors within the motor cortex.

In this regard, a beginner bowler who has taken some training from a qualified instructor could serve as an example of a bowler. The bowler's performance and movement grow more synchronized as He repeats the motion. He can communicate with the instructor more effectively and transform thoughts into physical motions. However, He might still make mistakes, particularly in challenging and unpredictable conditions, which could have a long-term detrimental effect on his performance. The instructor's and the bowler's objective is to use the technique consistently, correctly, and under expected conditions.

Phase 3: Movement Solidify

In this advanced stage, a bowler demonstrates exceptional stability while using the best technique despite unpredictable and challenging conditions. Fully automated and unwavering behavior is achieved via the motor program. The bowler seamlessly combines verbal and sensory information with delicate kinesthetic feelings. The technique's ability to be used in a competitive setting is at its highest. The motor program is precisely adjusted to the bowler's special skills and traits, fostering movement anticipation and the capacity to make appropriate adjustments. In addition to consistency and

Training Under Demanding Conditions: Training under demanding and unpredictable conditions becomes crucial to ensure ongoing control and modification of techniques. High levels of movement coordination are achievable only if the program can adapt swiftly.

Repetition for Mastery: Experts suggest that 40,000 to 50,000 repetitions of a specific motor task are needed to completely stabilize and automate one's technique in bowling.

dependability, this sophisticated motor software easily adjusts to the unforeseen internal and external factors that emerge during play. Despite distractions like mental stress, physical or mental exhaustion, competitive stress, bad weather, and other environmental variables, the bowler can retain perfect technique. A method that cannot adapt to such changes is completely useless. As a result, the system places a focus on training under demanding and unpredictable conditions, ensuring ongoing control and modification. High levels of movement coordination can only be attained if the program is adaptable enough to quickly adjust to both internal and external changes. Only by using this method will the intended objectives be consistently attained. Experts have found that 40,000 to 50,000 repetitions of a particular motor task are needed to completely stabilize and automate one's technique (whether it be in tennis, skiing, or bowling). In this stage, the practice method transforms into a "training match," where the goal is to achieve the desired results through the simulation of competitive situations and strategic aspects.

One of the most important elements in learning and using the method in a competitive setting is concentration. The duration of the process can range from a few minutes to several hours. Bowlers must focus on making the motion and steer their thoughts in that direction. Ideomotor training, or repeatedly mentally practicing a movement pattern, strengthens motor memory and consolidates the

Concentration and Mental Training: Concentration is a key element in mastering bowling techniques. Bowlers undergo mental training to enhance their ability to focus during each attempt. Clearing the mind of distractions and maintaining intense concentration is essential for success.

motor scheme (Singer, 1981). It is essential to promote a culture of optimism and a positive perception of appropriate mobility. Past mistakes should be quickly erased from memory since they reduce bowlers' confidence in themselves and their skills. The bowler must focus on a single goal and push aside all other thoughts just before starting a motor task. One of the greatest professional bowlers in history, Bernhard Langer, famously said, "There is no future and no past, there is only the present and me." High levels of focus require a lot of mental energy, which is, to some extent, constrained by the bowler's level of fitness. Physically healthy people have an easier time maintaining intense concentration for extended periods of time (Glyn, 1992). To attain its full potential, concentration requires rigorous and organized training, just like any other talent.

A bowler must repeat his motor task up to 10,000 times before his technique is completely stabilized and automated. His movement gets more coordinated as He continues through the learning phases, and He constructs a flexible program that responds to both internal and external changes. In order to obtain the desired outcome, the bowler might practice his technique in a "training match" that simulates competition conditions and strategies.

LEARNING METHODS FOR MOTOR SKILLS DEVELOPMENT

The application of efficient learning strategies is necessary for the development of motor skills in order to acquire and improve knowledge. The exact motor task, the learner's age, and his level of motor learning are all taken into consideration while selecting these learning strategies. When choosing the best strategy, integrating different methodologies is a crucial consideration. The necessity of using synthetic and combination approaches increases with the degree of interdependence among the motor activity's constituent parts. A strategy that focuses on learning each component separately may be more suitable for people who have trouble with unfamiliar movement components.

1. The technique of teaching

Especially in the early phases of motor learning, verbal guidance is an essential component of human expression and communication. It entails presenting ideas, laws, and inferences, giving model definitions, and more. It also involves communicating information about the basic characteristics of movements. Open-ended discussions with unscripted questions and possible answers are one format for instruction. It may also include discussions or disputes in which various viewpoints, attitudes, arguments, and counterarguments are presented. Instructors should adhere to the progressive transition from simple to complicated, familiar to unfamiliar, and focus on pertinent and crucial material when imparting instructions. They should also present objective facts. For motor learning to be successful, instruction must be effective.

Motor skill development can be accelerated by implementing suitable instructional strategies and learning methodologies. These methods consider the particulars of the motor task, the learner's developmental stage, and the significance of explicit and progressive instruction.

*Here are some examples of the steps a bowler may take in the technique
of teaching motor skill development in bowling:*

Instruction: *The coach instructs students verbally and explains the grip, posture, approach, and release of each motor skill or technique that needs to be acquired. The lessons are simple, to the point, and founded on the fundamentals of proper bowling technique.*

Demonstration: *By teaching the bowler the correct form, movement, and timing, the instructor explains how the motor skill or technique should be applied. In order to emphasize important components of the skill, slow-motion or stop-action techniques may be used in the demonstration.*

Practice: *Under the direction of the coach, the bowler puts the motor skill or technique into practice, concentrating on following the directions and replicating the modeled form. The bowler practices the move numerous times to develop muscle memory and familiarity with the proper technique.*

Feedback: *The coach offers suggestions for enhancement and advice on how to make changes in response to the bowler's performance. The criticism is positive, detailed, and concentrated on coordinating the bowler's performance with the proper technique.*

Adjustment: *Based on the input given, the bowler modifies his technique, changing the grip, posture, or release. The bowler puts the new adjustments into practice while continuing to receive feedback, make adjustments, and practice.*

Reinforcement: *Positive reinforcement, encouragement, and acknowledgment of success are some of the ways the instructor encourages the proper technique. The bowler's accomplishments are applauded, while mistakes are pointed out in a motivational and encouraging way.*

Progression: *The instructor advances to more complex motor abilities or techniques as the bowler gains proficiency in his, building on the foundation of the previously mastered skills. As the bowler's ability level increases, the instruction becomes more complicated and difficult.*

Application: *In diverse bowling settings, that include various lane conditions, spare shots, or competitive gameplay, the bowler employs the gained motor abilities and tactics. The bowler keeps honing his techniques and applying them in various situations in order to improve performance overall.*

2. The technique of demonstrations

The sensory signal system, especially the visual information, is the basis of motor learning. Along with other teaching methods like vocal instructions, demonstrations are an essential part of the learning process. A demonstration ought to be precise, understandable, and suitable for the learner's age and developmental stage. In order to ensure that the demonstration is appropriate for the learner's cognitive and physical capacities and represents real-world applicability, the teacher must evaluate the demonstration's effectiveness and relevance. Showcasing a range of actions that fall within the normative range is crucial, keeping in mind the particular learner's constraints and distinctive qualities. A conceptual and visual comprehension of movement, as well as the use of cognitive processes and muscle activation, are necessary for effective motor learning. An important part of the right hemisphere of the brain is involved in how we think about motor tasks.

*Here are some examples of the steps a bowler may take in the technique
of demonstrations for motor skill development in bowling:*

Observation: *The bowler closely examines the form, movement, and timing while watching the teacher or coach demonstrate the motor skill or technique. The bowler closely observes the demonstration to comprehend how to execute the talent.*

Visualization: *The bowler creates a mental picture of the appropriate shape and movement by visualizing how the motor skill or technique should be used correctly. The bowler uses visualization to internalize the proper technique and get in the right frame of mind for the upcoming practice.*

Imitation: *The bowler resembles the exemplified shape and motion, making every effort to precisely imitate the proper technique. As the talent is mastered, the bowler may begin with slow-motion or partial replicas before moving on to full-speed imitations.*

Practice: *In order to develop muscle memory and familiarity with the proper technique, the bowler repeatedly performs the motor skill or technique utilizing the model shape and motion. The bowler concentrates on replicating the model's form and making improvements in response to criticism.*

Feedback: By comparing the bowler's performance to the modeled form and highlighting areas for development, the coach offers comments on the performance. The criticism is detailed, helpful, and concentrated on bringing the bowler's performance in line with the proper technique displayed in the example.

Adjustment: Based on the comments given, the bowler makes modifications to fit the exhibited form, such as changing the grip, posture, approach, or release. The bowler puts the new adjustments into practice while continuing to receive feedback, make adjustments, and practice.

Reinforcement: Positive reinforcement, encouragement, and acknowledgment of success are some of the ways the instructor encourages the proper technique. The bowler's accomplishments are applauded, while mistakes are pointed out in a motivational and encouraging way.

Application: In diverse bowling settings, such as various lane conditions, spare shots, or competitive gameplay, the bowler employs the gained motor abilities and tactics. The bowler keeps honing his techniques and applying them in various situations in order to improve performance overall.

3. Situational methodology (synthetic method) in motor learning

A popular and organic method of teaching motor skills, the situational methodology is frequently utilized for simpler actions. Beginners benefit the most from it since they are better able to understand movement as a whole rather than its individual parts, making it particularly appropriate and beneficial for them. However, as it does not immediately indicate mastery of complex movements, learning movement as a whole should not be understood literally. Each movement has vital and fundamental parts, yet not all movements are equally tough or composed. Beginners must learn these foundational skills as soon as possible. Athletes can exhibit their abilities and traits on two levels using the situational method. Replicating the whole motor task as it was demonstrated is required at the first level. The second level involves carrying out a condensed version of the assignment while still doing a comprehensive analysis of it. In both situations, the instructor must spot excessive flaws and improper movements. Minor mistakes may be accepted, however, speaking too much should be avoided. Novices acquire and process information in an undifferentiated and lower-level manner since their motor patterns are still developing. It is important to point out that focused practice causes stronger emotional reactions, which might be a deciding factor, particularly in the early learning stages. High levels of interest and propensity for physical activity have a good effect on pupils' focus and drive.

Beginner bowler: The situational methodology may be useful for teaching the fundamental motions and techniques of bowling to a novice player. To help the newbie watch and understand the movement as a whole, the instructor could first execute the proper stance, arm swing, and ball release. The novice could next attempt to perform the exercise exactly as shown. The instructor might then make the assignment easier and have the beginner resemble the movement while still studying it as a whole once the beginner has mastered this level. In this condensed version, you can use a lighter ball or concentrate on only one portion of the technique at once. The teacher would keep an eye out for incorrect movements or flaws and give feedback to fix any mistakes.

Advanced bowler: The situational methodology can help even experienced bowlers when they are learning a new technique or modifying an existing one. For instance, bowlers may utilize the situational methodology to dissect a technique into its basic elements if they are having trouble with their release and want to improve their backswing. Bowlers might first take in and absorb the entire motion before concentrating on imitating the backswing precisely as it was displayed. The assignment might then be made simpler and bowlers could focus on mimicking the movement while still studying it as a whole when they have mastered this level. In this condensed version, the backswing is given more attention by practicing with a lighter ball or taking it more slowly. Once more, the trainer would keep an eye out for any flaws or inappropriate movements and would give comments to fix them.

Here are some examples of the steps a bowler may take in the situational methodology for motor skill development in bowling:

Contextualization: Specific bowling scenarios, such as various lane conditions, spare shots, or competitive gameplay, are set up by the instructor to demand the usage of a variety of motor abilities and methods. Real-world situations are provided to the bowler that calls for the use of a variety of abilities and methods.

Analysis: In order to perform well in that setting, the bowler examines the particular bowling scenario and determines the motor abilities and techniques that are pertinent and essential. The bowler evaluates the situation's requirements and chooses the best abilities and strategies to use.

Integration: To attain the intended result in the particular bowling scenario, bowlers incorporate the pertinent motor skills and techniques into their performance. They do this by applying them in a coordinated manner. To master integrating several abilities and approaches in real-time, the bowler practices mixing them.

Feedback: The coach evaluates the efficiency of the used motor skills and techniques while providing feedback on the bowler's performance in the particular scenario. The focus of the feedback is on how skills and techniques are applied in the context of the circumstance, emphasizing areas that need work and praising effective execution.

Adjustment: Bowlers enhance the integration of motor abilities and techniques in a particular situation by making modifications based on the feedback they have received. To improve performance even further, the bowler practices using the modified abilities and strategies in both comparable and dissimilar circumstances.

Reinforcement: Through support, encouragement, and acknowledgment of progress, the instructor reinforces the proper use of motor skills and procedures in situational contexts. The bowler receives praise and reinforcement for successfully putting the acquired skills and strategies into practice.

Repetition: To improve proficiency and flexibility, the bowler repeatedly applies motor abilities and strategies in a variety of bowling scenarios. This process includes contextualization, analysis, integration, feedback, adjustment, and reinforcement.

Bowlers can learn and use abilities and techniques in pertinent and realistic scenarios thanks to the situational methodology in motor skill development, which improves their capacity to perform well during actual gameplay. It aids bowlers in acquiring the mental agility, judgment, and flexibility required for success in competitive bowling.

4. The analytical procedure

The analytical procedure is a methodology that entails dissecting a movement technique into smaller parts, teaching each part separately, and then progressively integrating them into the whole movement in the final phase. It is frequently employed for extremely complex movements that cannot be fully learned. This strategy faces difficulties, nevertheless, with regard to the long-term learning of discrete parts and the procedure for combining them into a coherent whole. Repeating isolated movements repeatedly can make them automatic and have a big impact on the overall movement pattern and rhythm. As a result, it is important to learn the components in the correct order. The core movement pattern must be maintained throughout the procedure. The various parts should be taught in the same order that they appear in the kinematic and dynamic structures of the basic method. The movement as a whole need not be mastered just because you have mastered a few individual sections. Usually, this method is used in conjunction with another strategy, with a preference for one over the other depending on the learner's development, skills, and the complexity of the activity. During the early phases of motor learning, the analytical method is typically used, and each mastered component is quickly incorporated into the basic action.

The analytical method can help a professional bowler perfect a challenging move like the 2-10 split (for right-handers). The movement would be divided into fractions, with each fraction being taught separately, before gradually integrating the taught fractions with the basic movement in the final phase.

A coach could instruct a beginner bowler in proper ball release technique using the analytical method. In order to keep the underlying movement plan throughout the process, He would divide the movement technique into fractions, teach each fraction separately, and then gradually integrate them with the fundamental movement in the final phase.

Here are some examples of the steps a bowler may take in the analytical procedure for motor skill development in bowling:

Identification: The bowler chooses a certain motor skill or technique, such as his approach, release, or targeting, that He wants to hone. The bowler chooses one specific area of his game that needs analysis and improvement.

Dissection: The bowler decides the specific motor skill or technique, such as approach, release, or targeting, He wishes to develop. The bowler picks one particular area of his game that needs examination and improvement.

Analysis: Each element of the bowler's motor ability or technique is carefully dissected, with an emphasis on body alignment, movement, timing, and coordination. The bowler evaluates each element's advantages and disadvantages to identify places where He can get better.

Practice: The bowler works on improving his movement, coordination, and timing by practicing each individual element of the motor skill or technique separately. The bowler practices each element repeatedly in order to develop muscle memory and enhance performance.

Integration: The bowler practices the entire motion while perfecting each individual component before reintegrating it into the overall motor skill or technique. The bowler concentrates on integrating the precise elements into a fluid and successful performance.

Feedback: A teacher, coach, or training partner provides feedback to the bowler on how well He executed the practiced motor skill or technique. The criticism focuses on the enhancements made to the individual components and the integrated performance's overall efficacy.

Adjustment: Based on the input given, the bowler adjusts, improving the coordinated use of the motor skill or technique. To further improve his skill and consistency, the bowler practices the modified performance.

Reinforcement: Positive reinforcement, encouragement, and acknowledgment of progress are used by the trainer, coach, or training partner to promote the proper application of the practiced motor skill or technique. The bowler's accomplishments in enhancing a particular motor ability or technique are praised and encouraged.

Repetition: The bowler repeats the identification, dissection, analysis, practice, integration, feedback, adjustment, and reinforcement processes for further motor abilities or techniques He wishes to hone, honing various facets of his performance in order to increase his overall skill development.

5. The complicated procedure

The situational and analytical learning approaches are combined in this method, resulting in a mutually beneficial interaction that improves the acquisition of motor skills. Individual skill components are first practiced individually, followed by training the entire approach gradually and eventually returning to specific components for improvement. The situational exercise, which serves as a supplemental element, is more important for beginner bowlers than the analytical exercise. Regardless of the strategy chosen, it is imperative to be vigilant during the process to avoid the consolidation of incorrect movement conceptions that might result in mistakes. To achieve quality movements, you must practice a lot. It's fundamental to remember that there isn't a single approach that works for everyone in all circumstances. The following factors should be taken into mind while using any learning strategy:

- When choosing a learning strategy, keep in mind things like biological and chronological age, past knowledge, movement experience, and details about the particular exercise.
- Rather than only addressing the effects of improper motions, attention should be given to determining the underlying causes.
- Inadequate motor skills (such as agility, strength, and coordination) and an unfavorable morphological constitution can all contribute to improper motions.
- It's imperative to fix significant mistakes first because they frequently cause minor ones to occur.
- Errors and shortcomings should be fixed in the order they were discovered.
- Instructions should correspond to how bowlers perceive their motions through their senses.
- The remedial procedure should not only point out flaws but also encourage optimistic thinking, advancement, and confidence.
- Instructions should be appropriate for the bowlers' age and level of maturity.
- To impact movement patterns, the instructor should use a variety of communication techniques, such as verbal cues, visual demonstrations, examples, and imitation exercises.
- Acknowledging and applauding effective technique use is crucial for inspiring and supporting bowlers.
- To ensure thorough comprehension and successful instruction, the educator should study the method from a variety of angles.
- When correcting mistakes, it's important to respect the bowlers' privacy and refrain from criticizing them in front of their teammates.

Bowlers can maximize their learning process and advance toward perfecting their skills in a helpful and efficient way by following these guidelines.

Example 1: The situational-analytical method is being used to train a novice bowler. The coach starts by emphasizing the replication of the motor activity while teaching the basic motion of the bowling action as a whole. The coach will then gradually split the movement into its component parts and teach each one independently using the analytical method. After that, the student is returned to situational exercises where He practices the full bowling motion once more while incorporating the different elements He previously learned. Finally, the coach concentrates on honing particular components until He is masterful. The coach closely observes the learner's motions and corrects any incorrect movement perceptions before they become errors.

Example 2: A skilled bowler is receiving coaching to improve a few minor technical flaws. The instructor examines the bowler's technique from a variety of angles and notices that there is a slight hitch in the backswing. The coach fixes the kink by dissecting each component of the action using the analytical method. He maintains the rest of his technique while concentrating on teaching the bowler to get rid of the hitch. The bowler is then returned to situational drills where He practices the whole bowling motion once more while incorporating the earlier modification. When the bowler effectively applies the method, the instructor provides encouraging feedback and praise. The bowler's privacy is also respected by the instructor, who never chastises him in front of other people.

Here are some examples of the steps a bowler may take in the complicated procedure for motor skill development in bowling:

Familiarization: *The bowler gains familiarity with several aspects of bowling, such as lane conditions, oil patterns, and pin placements. The bowler gains awareness of and ability to adjust to the difficulties offered by these various conditions.*

Analysis: *In order to alter his approach, targeting, speed, or ball choice to changing conditions, the bowler evaluates the particular obstacles offered by the complex situations. The bowler recognizes tactics and strategies that can be useful in the current circumstance.*

Practice: *Focusing on adjusting his motor skills to the unique obstacles provided by the changing conditions, the bowler practices employing the specified tactics and techniques in challenging situations. The repetition of the exercise in many challenging circumstances helps the bowler develop flexibility and versatility.*

Evaluation: *The bowler assesses his performance in challenging circumstances, considering his advantages, disadvantages, successes, and opportunities for development. To gain understanding and modify his approach and technique, the bowler asks for criticism from a trainer, coach, or training partner.*

Adjustment: *Based on the assessment and feedback, the bowler modifies his motor skills and tactics, improving his approach and technique to be more efficient in challenging conditions. To further cement the gains obtained, the bowler practices the altered performance.*

Reinforcement: *Through encouraging feedback, encouraging words, and acknowledging accomplishments, the trainer, coach, or training partner supports the proper application of sophisticated motor skills and procedures in challenging situations. The bowler's accomplishments in adjusting to the altering circumstances and utilizing practical tactics are appreciated and emphasized.*

Repetition: *The bowler practices and perfects his performance in a variety of scenarios to increase his adaptability and versatility in bowling. He repeats the process of familiarization, analysis, practice, assessment, adjustment, and reinforcement in many challenging situations.*

6. The ideomotor technique

The development of a thorough grasp of movement is the cornerstone of efficient motor learning. Novice bowlers frequently have imprecise, partial, and occasionally erroneous perceptions of movement that do not match the kinetic and temporal elements of correct technique. However, correct knowledge can be formed with the aid of educators. Beginners can quickly understand the fundamentals of movement by being given both verbal and visual instructions, which can later be reinforced by using motor programs that have been stored in their memory.

The ideomotor technique, which involves performing movements in the mind, is a prime example of the effectiveness of mental learning. Only the motor cortex, which is in charge of designing motor structures, is active during this process. Athletes "perform" the movement technique in their minds by concentrating on its key elements. This tactic can be used in a variety of circumstances. For instance, athletes can mentally recreate particular movement phases during the concentration phase, significantly improving their performance. The ideomotor technique can aid in the consolidation of the movement pattern through repeated conceptual repeats that outweigh real physical exercise. The memory traces before the subsequent repetition become more robust and current as a result, increasing the stability of the movement pattern.

Even when athletes are hurt, unable to physically exercise, or momentarily unable to execute the movement skill, the ideomotor training technique is still beneficial. It enables students to keep their attention and concentration at important performance times. In order to better position themselves for crucial competition moments, athletes might successfully "eliminate" tension and competitive pressure. Ideomotor training can help bowlers improve their mental imagery abilities, increase their performance, and sharpen their competitive mindset.

Example 1: Using the ideomotor approach may help a beginner bowler who is having trouble with his technique. Before performing the movement physically, students can visualize and mentally practice the proper movement pattern to have a basic grasp of it and work on solidifying it. He might be able to perform better in tournaments and refine his technique thanks to this.

Example 2: Employing the ideomotor approach may be advantageous for a professional bowler who is recuperating from an injury. When He is unable to physically train, He can still mentally practice the movement pattern, which can help him maintain his muscle memory and keep the movement pattern fresh in his mind. When He is able to, this can speed up his recuperation and let him return to physical activity more easily.

Here are some examples of the steps a bowler may take in the Ideomotor technique for motor skill development in bowling:

Mental Rehearsal: *The bowler practices and visualizes in his mind how to use the appropriate motor skills and methods. The bowler visualizes himself or herself flawlessly, accurately, and fluidly carrying out the required skills.*

Visualization: *The bowler visualizes every step of the bowling motion, including the approach, release, follow-through, and ideal trajectory of the ball. The bowler visualizes himself or herself confidently and competently carrying out each phase of the skill.*

Sensory Imagery: *The bowler uses sensory images, including visual, aural, and tactile signals, in his mental rehearsal. The bowler visualizes the sound of the ball striking the pins, the experience of holding the ball in his hand, and the feeling of his body moving naturally during approach and release.*

Emotion Regulation: *During the ideomotor technique, the bowler controls his emotions and mental state, staying focused and upbeat. The bowler develops a sense of composure, assurance, and tenacity while picturing success and reaching his objectives.*

Repetition: *As part of his regular practice regimen, the bowler regularly goes through the mental rehearsal and visualization process. In addition to physical practice, the bowler uses the ideomotor technique to strengthen his motor abilities and techniques through mental imaging and visualization.*

Transfer to Physical Practice: *The bowler incorporates mental rehearsal and visualization with the actual performance of the motor abilities and methods during his physical practice. The bowler attempts to duplicate the vivid mental image in his actual bowling style by using the mental rehearsal as a roadmap for his physical performance.*

Evaluation and Adjustment: *The bowler assesses his performance in light of the internal picture and modifies it as necessary. The bowler requests feedback from a teacher or coach to pinpoint areas that need work, and then He hones his motor skills and techniques in response to the criticism.*

7. The iterative procedure

In the world of bowling, the highly mechanized and adaptive movement phase is where the iterative technique shines. It is used primarily when athletes can consistently use ideal technique in a variety of settings. This technique entails a succession of motions that are repeated and separated by brief pauses. In the athlete's motor memory, each execution leaves a trace that paves the way for the development of other traces. The level of technique automation, the athlete's motor abilities, the intricacy of the movement, the number of repetitions, focus, and motivation are just a few of the variables that affect how effective this approach is.

Prioritizing the movement's proper execution is essential when using the iterative process. Otherwise, improper motions could become automatic, developing into bad habits. When the actions closely mirror the essential components of competitive technique, the strategy produces the best outcomes. The length of the breaks in between repeats is crucial during the repetition process. Athletes may become physically and mentally exhausted or even bored if the breaks are too short. Finding the ideal balance is crucial.

The iterative approach has the disadvantage of predominantly activating the left hemisphere of the brain, which may reduce drive and creativity. Feedback on the correct performance of the motor task becomes necessary at this phase in order to combat this. The coach must give the athletes a variety of standards so they can assess their own performance on their own. By doing this, the instructor gradually cedes control of movement execution to the athlete. Athletes who rely on their inner feelings and feedback information develop a greater sense of accuracy and control.

Athletes should contrast their subjective experiences with objective evidence of their skill, such as video footage. This enables people to match their perspective of their performance to the actual results. Only when there are significant movement faults should the instructor step in during this stage. Unexpected mistakes might occur as a result of things like weariness, a lack of focus, hidden injury, or general depletion from training. Therefore, educators need to have academic expertise, real-world experience, and analytical skills. Athletes must obtain timely and pertinent information from them so they may acquire the necessary instruction to improve their skills.

Hypothetical Examples

Example 1: John is a skilled bowler who is aware of the sport's core principles. Through the iterative process, he is working to improve his abilities and sharpen his talents. With small breaks in between, he repeats the motions of his bowling technique to establish a trace in his motor memory and become ready for the construction of a new trace. In order to avoid automating the incorrect actions, John uses this strategy while paying attention to the proper technical execution of each movement. In order to improve his feeling of execution precision, he also receives feedback information from his instructor on how to carry out the motor job properly.

Example 2: Sarah is a beginner bowler who is studying the fundamentals of the sport. She is using the ideomotor method to gain a basic comprehension of movement. With the aid of her instructor's visual and vocal cues, Sarah "performs" the bowling method movements in her head, focusing on the key elements of the technique. During the concentration phase, she appears to make a mental jump and complete particular movement stages. The ideomotor method might help Sarah strengthen her movement pattern and get ready for the crucial competitive moments. Sarah might switch to the iterative process to hone her skills and enhance her technique as she obtains more knowledge and proficiency with the method.

In bowling, the iterative procedure may involve the following steps:

Initial Attempt: An initial attempt is made by the bowler to execute a certain motor skill or technique, such as the approach, release, or follow-through. This effort might not be flawless and contain flaws or errors.

Feedback and Analysis: Based on observation and analysis of the bowler's initial attempt, the instructor or coach gives feedback and direction on areas for growth. The feedback could offer advice on the motor skill's technique, alignment, timing, or other facets.

Practice and Repetition: The bowler repeatedly practices the motor skill while incorporating the coach or instructor's input. The bowler concentrates on perfecting the technique, making changes in response to criticism, and practicing the skill repeatedly to ensure proper execution.

Evaluation and Adjustment: After each repetition, the bowler assesses his performance and compares it to the desired result and the input He has got. Based on his own evaluation of his own performance and the coach's or instructor's criticism, the bowler makes modifications and improvements.

Progressive Difficulty: The level of difficulty may be progressively raised as the bowler gains more mastery of the motor skill. This might entail introducing new varieties, boosting speed or accuracy, or including trickier parts of the talent.

Reflective Practice: Reflective practice is when a bowler takes the time to consider his performance, pinpoint his areas for development, and create goals for improvement. To further hone the motor skill, this may involve self-evaluation, self-feedback, and self-directed practice.

Continued Feedback and Refinement: The coach or instructor keeps giving the bowler feedback as the cycle of practice, assessment, and modification continues. The bowler looks for regular criticism and direction to improve his motion and technique.

BOWLERS' DIFFERENT LEARNING METHODS: VISUAL, AUDITORY, AND KINESTHETIC LEARNING STYLES

Based on individual learning preferences, including visual, auditory, and kinesthetic inclinations, the effectiveness of various learning approaches in the context of bowling training can vary. Each learning method reflects a different strategy for gaining knowledge and enhancing skills.

Visual

In the context of bowling, visual learners have a distinct set of traits and learning preferences that affect how they approach skill development. These people typically process and assimilate information through their sense of sight. Because of their innate preference for visual stimuli, they typically learn best when given visual aids, demonstrations, diagrams, and photographs. Visual learners are better able to mentally picture and represent concepts, activities, and things. They are highly spatially sensitive, which enables them to precisely notice and decipher movements and object placement on the bowling lane. They can comprehend the game's mechanics, such as the angles, trajectories, and spin of the bowling ball, thanks to their spatial awareness.

In addition to having a preference for well-organized and aesthetically pleasing learning materials, visual learners frequently demonstrate exceptional attention to detail. They are proficient at imitating seen strategies and adapting them to their own game, thus they flourish in circumstances where they can observe and understand the actions of skilled bowlers. When playing games, these people are frequently adept at spotting patterns and choosing their strategies based on visual cues.

The capacity of visual learners to quickly process visual information and turn it into useful knowledge is one of their significant advantages when it comes to bowling. They can effectively learn and incorporate new tactics into their repertoire by watching and visually analyzing the motions of seasoned bowlers. Because of their attention to detail, they are able to modify their approach, release, and targeting in response to visual feedback. Visual learners, who mainly rely on visual input for effective learning, may encounter difficulties in auditory or kinesthetic learning contexts. They could find it difficult to understand ideas or instructions that are just explained or physically demonstrated. Their attention to visual details might sometimes occasionally make it difficult for them to comprehend the big picture or to notice crucial auditory or kinesthetic cues.

Consider a visual learner who desires to get better at shooting spares in bowling as an example. He may learn something from watching how-to videos or seeing professional bowlers use various spare tactics. The visual learner can better understand the mechanics by observing the movements, foot positioning, and arm swing of these bowlers. He can then use this information to better his own game by modifying his strategy and objectives to increase the rate at which He converts spare resources.

Auditory

In the context of bowling, auditory learners have unique traits and learning preferences that center on their auditory senses. These people learn best through verbal communication, conversations, lectures, and listening to directions and criticism. They prefer aural stimulation. hearing learners have heightened hearing sensitivity and superior auditory memory. They are skilled at processing and remembering verbally delivered information and are able to quickly understand and retain cues, directions, and explanations. They can analyze and apply auditory information to their bowling technique thanks to their capacity for information absorption. Strong listening abilities and a predisposition to participate in conversations and group discussions are common characteristics of auditory learners. They do best in situations where they can actively engage in verbal conversations, such as when they may ask questions of coaches or deliberate on tactics with teammates. These people are excellent at taking in and understanding verbal input, which enables them to modify their bowling technique as needed at the moment. They learn best when they pay attention to spoken instructions and criticism. Demonstrations, coaching instructions, or conversations with seasoned bowlers can all help them learn new skills. They can recall and imitate the verbal signals they have heard thanks to their excellent auditory memory, which makes it easier for them to execute good bowling skills. However, auditory learners may have difficulties when given primarily visual learning tools or when the information is not verbally delivered. If there are no accompanying vocal explanations, they could find it difficult to comprehend and digest complex visual diagrams or demonstrations. Additionally, because they favor aural input, they could rely too much on spoken instructions and miss crucial kinesthetic or visual signs.

Think of a bowler who is attempting to develop his timing and rhythm as an auditory learner. The repetitive sound of the ball striking may be helpful to him. He can improve his sense of time and synchronization by learning to internalize the aural cues related to a smooth and consistent release. He might also benefit from conversing with trainers or seasoned bowlers who can offer vocal criticism and pointers on obtaining the appropriate time.

Kinesthetic

In the context of bowling, kinesthetic learners are those who favor active learning methods such as hands-on activities and physical movement. To process and remember information, they rely on their sense of touch, bodily awareness, and physical sensations. These students do best in a setting where they may actively use their bodies and senses to study. They are well-coordinated and have a great sense of bodily awareness. They are able to establish a strong connection between their actions and the intended outcomes in bowling thanks to their intrinsic capacity to comprehend and manage their bodily movements. These people have a keen awareness of the bodily feelings and feedback they encounter when using their bowling techniques. Kinesthetic learners learn best when they are actively involved in and manipulated physically. They favor active participation in the bowling game, hands-on training, and learning by doing. To absorb and hone their bowling technique, they use a combination of physical actions, muscle memory, and sensory feedback.

In bowling, kinesthetic learners' capacity to assimilate knowledge through active practice and repetition stands out as one of their significant advantages. They gain knowledge through physically practicing bowling techniques, experiencing the release and spin of the ball in their hand, and watching the trajectory that results from it. This practical method enables them to master the subtleties of their bowling technique and build a solid kinesthetic memory. Their biggest obstacle is when they are given learning strategies that are primarily theoretical or passive. Without the chance for direct experience and tactile exploration, they could find it difficult to understand abstract ideas. They might also rely less on oral instructions and visual examples, preferring instead to rely on their own bodily feelings and trial-and-error learning.

Think of a kinesthetic learner who is practicing his balance and body alignment throughout the approach to bowling. He might gain from frequently physically exercising his stance, footwork, and arm swing to build muscle memory and coordination. He can hone his technique and acquire more consistency in his delivery by consciously performing physical motions and sensitizing himself or herself to the feelings connected to appropriate balance and alignment.

Learning Method	Visual Learner	Auditory Learner	Kinesthetic Learner
The Technique of Teaching	Watches instructional videos demonstrating proper bowling technique	Listens to an audio recording of a coach explaining the steps	Physically practices bowling movements while receiving feedback
The Technique of Demonstrations	Observe a skilled bowler's hand position and approach visually	Listens to a coach describing the key elements of a good approach	Imitates the bowling technique by physically performing the movements
Situational Method (Synthetic Method)	Watches a video of professional bowlers executing different lane conditions	Listens to a coach narrating a scenario involving challenging lane conditions	Simulates bowling in various lane conditions, focusing on adapting their approach
The Analytical Procedure	Studies a diagram illustrating the correct arm swing and release position visually	Listens to an instructor explaining the timing and coordination of each movement	Practices the arm swing and release separately to refine each component
The Complicated Procedure	Examines a visual guide detailing different spare shooting techniques	Listens to an explanation of different spare shooting strategies	Practices different spare shooting techniques physically on the lanes
The Ideomotor Technique	Visualizes themselves executing a perfect strike before taking their shot	Mentally repeats the sound of the pins crashing after a strike	Physically rehearses their approach and release in their mind before executing it
The Iterative Procedure	Observes the footwork and body alignment of successful bowlers visually	Listens to verbal cues from a coach about footwork timing and positioning	Actively repeats the footwork patterns and focuses on muscle memory during practice

Table 4 - These examples illustrate how each learning method can be adapted to cater to the specific learning preferences and styles of visual, auditory, and kinesthetic learners in the context of bowling.

Learning Method	Visual Learners	Auditory Learners	Kinesthetic Learners
The Technique of Teaching	8	7	9
The Technique of Demonstrations	9	8	9
Situational Methodology	7	7	9
The Analytical Procedure	8	8	9
The Complicated Procedure	6	7	9
The Ideomotor Technique	7	8	8
The Iterative Procedure	8	7	9

Table 5 – Level of effectiveness is rated out of 10, with 10 being the highest effectiveness.

All of the learning strategies mentioned above are advantageous for bowlers with varied personality types since they are capable of adapting their learning preferences to various teaching approaches. However, depending on the learner's preferences and learning style, each method's efficacy may differ. The ratings in the table are arbitrary and predicated on common patterns. Actual efficacy may differ based on unique conditions and the bowler's particular needs.

It's crucial to remember that everyone has different preferences and learning styles, so it's advantageous to use a variety of approaches to meet everyone's demands. The table provides a broad picture, but it's crucial to take individual variances into account when creating a successful learning program for bowlers.

Below table listing 30 famous bowlers, their identified learning methods (visual, auditory, or kinesthetic), and evidence supporting these identifications:

Bowler	Learning Method	Evidence supporting these identifications
Mika Koivuniemi	Visual	Precision in targeting, benefits from visual aids.
Walter Ray Williams Jr.	Visual	Meticulous, likely uses diagrams and visuals for improvement.
Jesper Svensson	Auditory	Rhythm and timing suggest reliance on auditory cues.
Jason Belmonte	Auditory	Unique style may require verbal feedback.
Dominic Barrett	Kinesthetic	Smooth physical approach indicates kinesthetic learning.
Norm Duke	Kinesthetic	Emphasis on body control suggests kinesthetic approach.
Paeng Nepomuceno	Visual	Known for accuracy, likely benefits from visual feedback.
Pete Weber	Kinesthetic	Natural talent may align with kinesthetic learning.
Kelly Kulick	Auditory	Strong mental game indicates reliance on verbal strategies.
Chris Barnes	Auditory	Known for strategy, benefits from verbal instructions.
Liz Johnson	Visual	Consistency suggests reliance on visual feedback.
Osku Palermaa	Kinesthetic	Unconventional style may stem from kinesthetic experimentation.
Shannon O'Keefe	Auditory	Strong decision-making skills indicate auditory learning.
Marshall Holman	Kinesthetic	Aggressive style likely developed through physical practice.
Kim Yeau Jin	Kinesthetic	Agile movements suggest kinesthetic approach.
Carolyn Dorin-Ballard	Visual	Technical prowess indicates reliance on visual feedback.
Parker Bohn III	Kinesthetic	Agile movements suggest kinesthetic approach.
Clara Guerrero	Visual	Technical skills may be enhanced through visual aids.
Diandra Asbaty	Auditory	Mental strength and strategy suggest auditory learning.
Kim Terrell-Kearney	Visual	Technical excellence may come from visual feedback.
Brian Voss	Kinesthetic	Known for versatility, likely developed through physical practice.
Tannya Roumimper	Auditory	Decision-making skills may be influenced by auditory learning.
Shalin Zulkifli	Visual	Technical excellence may come from visual feedback.
Tore Torgersen	Visual	Technical skills may be enhanced through visual aids.
Rafiq Ismail	Kinesthetic	Athletic approach suggests kinesthetic preference.
Amleto Monacelli	Kinesthetic	Known for precise movements, likely kinesthetic learner.
Wu Siu Hong	Visual	Known for accuracy, benefits from visual feedback.
Marshall Kent	Visual	Known for power and accuracy, benefits from visual feedback.
Kelly Kulick	Kinesthetic	Athletic approach aligns with kinesthetic learning.
Shogo Wada	Kinesthetic	Agility and finesse suggest kinesthetic approach.
Jazreel Tan	Visual	Precision and consistency may come from visual feedback.
Anthony Simenson	Visual	Highly attentive to visual cues and patterns in the game. He often relies on visual aids and demonstrations to learn new skills and strategies in bowling.
Bill O'Neal	Auditory	Known for his active participation in verbal discussions and group conversations with coaches and teammates. He values verbal instructions and criticism to modify his bowling technique effectively.
Tommy Jones	Kinesthetic	Prefers hands-on training and active participation in the game. He frequently engages in physical drills and exercises to develop muscle memory and sensory feedback for his bowling technique.
Ildemaro Ruiz	Kinesthetic	Athletic approach suggests kinesthetic preference.
Aumi Guerra	Visual	Technical excellence may come from visual feedback.
Joonas Jehkinen	Auditory	Decision-making skills may be influenced by auditory learning.
Pontus Andersson	Kinesthetic	Known for physical approach, likely kinesthetic learner.
Caroline Lagrange	Visual	Precision and consistency may come from visual feedback.
Ahmed Shaheen	Kinesthetic	Athletic approach implies kinesthetic preference.
Sean Rash	Visual	Excels in observing and analyzing the movements of other bowlers. He frequently studies video footage of his own and other professional bowlers' performances to refine his technique.

Table 6 - listing 30 famous bowlers, their identified learning methods (visual, auditory, or kinesthetic), and evidence supporting these identifications.

Please note that these categorizations are speculative and based on the limited information available (Author's research) about these bowlers' learning preferences. Additionally, learning styles can vary among individuals, and many bowlers may employ a combination of visual, auditory, and kinesthetic learning methods in their training.

SKILL ACQUISITION ENHANCEMENT METHODS

Method 1 – Movement Freedom

What distinguishes professional bowlers like EJ Tackett, Anthony Simenson, and Walter Ray Williams from the rest? The secret is in their superb movement coordination, particularly in the way they coordinate their abilities with the bowling lane. The definition of movement coordination is "the alignment of body movements with the surrounding environmental objects and events." In plainer terms, it entails finding a balance between our limb movements and the particular situations in which we bowl. Timing, checkpoints, and release strategies must all be considered while making precise and sequential bodily motions to reach this level of coordination.

Despite what many people think, skilled bowlers don't just keep repeating the same move. Every shot gives a diverse scenario that necessitates a variety of movement patterns. Bowlers must adjust to and use a variety of movement patterns throughout a game in order to attain ideal coordination. Furthermore, it's critical to acknowledge that every person differs in terms of his anatomical structure, level of strength, and degree of flexibility. Therefore, the perfect coordination pattern for one bowler may not be the same for another.

Consequently, how can we gauge and evaluate coordination in bowling? Understanding how the bowler uses mechanical "degrees of freedom" is one method to do this. The various ways that joints and limbs can move are referred to as degrees of freedom. A bowler's body has several degrees of freedom, including various joints in the arm that provide movement in a variety of directions.

The process of changing the degrees of freedom present in a movement pattern is part of learning a bowling skill. For instance, beginners may initially have poor coordination, rotating their wrists only a little and barely rotating their trunks while swinging. They eventually develop the ability to relax particular muscles as they advance and practice, which allows them to make better use of the degrees of freedom at their disposal.

Complexity of Degrees of Freedom: Another pain point is the complexity of understanding and managing the degrees of freedom involved in bowling movements. Teaching beginners to unlock and utilize these degrees of freedom can be a challenging process, as it requires them to develop specific muscle control and relaxation techniques.

An increased use of the available degrees of freedom is a common feature of bowling technique development. Understanding the mechanics of bowling techniques and the parts involved in the movement is crucial when talking about freedom of motion. The execution of shots improves and becomes more reliable the more relaxed the muscles are during these actions.

Hypothetical Examples

Example 1: John is attempting to improve his coordination of movement as he trains to become a bowler. In order to comprehend how top bowlers like Walter Ray Williams and Anthony Simenson connect their abilities with the bowling lane, he closely studies them. John observes that they move their bodies in precise, sequential motions with a focus on timing, checkpoints, and release techniques. John is inspired by their methods and learns that, rather than just repeating the same shot, getting ideal coordination requires adapting to and using a variety of movement patterns throughout a bowling session. He concentrates on figuring out what works best for him because he is aware that his own anatomical structure, strength, and flexibility are important factors in creating his perfect co-ordination pattern.

Example 2: Emily, a novice in the realm of bowling, is eager to strengthen her ability to coordinate her movements. She is aware that improving at a sport entails changing the degrees of freedom that are present in her movement patterns. Emily initially had poor coordination, relying primarily on simple wrist rotation and little trunk rotation in her swing. However, Emily progressively learns to relax particular muscles and open the degrees of freedom that are available to her body with dedicated practice and supervision. Her technique improves as she starts to use more fluid motions, maximizing the range of motion in her shoulder, hip, and arm joints. Emily learns that the more relaxed her muscles are during these motions, the more consistently and successfully her shots are. This realization comes as she obtains a deeper understanding of the mechanics of bowling techniques.

Hypothetical Example

Task: Improve Swing and Release by Maximizing Degrees of Freedom

Scenario: *John understands the importance of adapting to various movement patterns and utilizing degrees of freedom in his body to enhance coordination. He wants to work on his swing and release to achieve a more consistent and effective performance.*

Cues and Concepts:

Swing and Release Coordination: *The swing and release are critical aspects of your game. You need to make the most of the degrees of freedom in your arm joints for a more fluid and adaptable motion.*

Training Plan:

Observation:

Task: *Watch videos of top bowlers, such as Walter Ray Williams and Anthony Simenson, paying particular attention to their arm swing and release. Notice how they adapt their arm movements to different lane conditions and pin placements.*

Self-Analysis:

Task: *Reflect on your own swing and release. Identify areas where you may be restricting your arm's degrees of freedom. Are you gripping the ball too tightly or tensing your muscles excessively during the swing?*

Experimentation:

Task: *During practice sessions, deliberately experiment with your arm swing and release. Loosen your grip slightly and focus on allowing your arm to move more freely. Try different release techniques to discover what feels most comfortable and effective.*

Mental Visualization:

Task: *Mentally visualize the ideal swing and release you want to achieve. Picture your arm moving smoothly and fluidly, adapting effortlessly to the lane conditions.*

Feedback and Adjustments:

Task: *Record your practice sessions and review your form. Seek feedback from a coach or experienced bowler. Make adjustments based on their recommendations to improve your swing and release.*

Outcome: *By consciously working on maximizing the degrees of freedom in his arm joints during the swing and release, John can achieve a more adaptable and consistent motion. This will result in improved coordination, allowing him to adapt to different scenarios, lane conditions, and pin placements, ultimately enhancing his overall bowling performance.*

Method 2 - Exploratory Actions

For bowlers, maintaining consistency is frequently the most difficult component of their game. While physically muscling the ball or swinging the bat is important, proper perception is just as important for attaining strong co-ordination. In order to achieve the intended result, perception entails accurately detecting critical information and creating a close association between this information, limb movements, and the bowling ball. The investigation and discovery of pertinent knowledge is a crucial part of the learning process.

We perform a substantial number of exploratory movements without even recognizing them, and they are crucial for acquiring the data required to lead a swing. Consider the pre-performance rituals that bowlers engage in before each shot. Observing the lanes, choosing the ball, wiping it, envisioning the lane and the ideal trajectory line, aligning the body, talking to yourself, taking deep breaths, and then making the shot are all steps in these routines. It has been discovered that these activities help the bowler focus on important information. Decisions like choosing a ball can be made through visual and non-visual investigation. After selecting a ball or making changes to the release, we keep continually investigating its characteristics. These ostensibly pointless movements are crucial because they facilitate perceptual search. On the basis of the information we learn from our investigations, we occasionally change our tactics or the ball we choose. It becomes obvious that by executing these exploratory motions, one learns to find the information required for well-coordinated bowling movements, which is a crucial element of becoming a skilled bowler.

The timing and balance of the entire body at the release stage, as well as how the ball is released, are crucial indicators. In this situation, it is vital to comprehend what constitutes the optimal technique's optimum point. Coaches and seasoned bowlers are aware that there is a significant amount of information other than visual cues that are used to direct bowling motions. One of bowling's main problems is resolved by combining visual and non-visual information.

Hypothetical Examples

Example 1: Bowler A's ability to explore and find pertinent information was found to be constrained in a bio-mechanical examination. His pre-performance practice lacked active non-visual and visual explorations, which hindered his ability to make decisions while playing. The coach suggested adding conscious exploratory actions, such as paying closer attention to the lanes, practicing visualization, and deliberately seeking tactile information when choosing a ball. Bowler A can obtain more pertinent information, develop his capacity for decision-making, and increase the consistency of his bowling performance by honing his exploratory behaviors.

Example 2: Bowler B demonstrated robust exploratory movements and a great sense of sensibility throughout the bio-mechanical study of his pre-performance routine. He keeps a close eye on the lanes, picks the right ball, and actively explores both the visual and non-visual realms to learn more. As a result, Bowler B was able to make wise choices, alter tactics, and choose the best ball depending on the information acquired. He displayed remarkable coordination between his upper and lower body technical skills and tactile sensibility. In order to increase his sensitivity to haptic input and continually improve his overall performance in bowling, the coach emphasized the need to sustain and further strengthen these exploratory motions throughout practice.

Example 3: The value of exploratory movements in improving a bowler's perception and overall performance was acknowledged by Coach A. To encourage bowlers to actively investigate visual and non-visual clues during their pre-performance routines, they introduced specialized drills and exercises into their training sessions. Coach A highlighted the value of paying attention to the lanes, picturing the desired trajectory, and using self-talk to focus the bowler on pertinent information. Additionally, He supported experimentation among bowlers by encouraging them to use various ball choices and release methods. This atmosphere fostered experimental actions and decision-making based on obtained data. Under Coach A's direction, bowlers improved their overall shot repeatability and gained heightened haptic sensitivity.

Scenario: Teaching Swing and Release Based on Exploratory Actions

Coach: Let's explore how to improve your swing and release by integrating exploratory actions into your practice routine. We'll focus on enhancing your perception and acquiring valuable information to optimize your bowling movements.

Cues and Concepts:

1. **Perception and Information Integration:** *Perception is essential for strong coordination. It involves accurately detecting critical information and creating a connection between this information, your limb movements, and the bowling ball.*

2. **Exploratory Actions:** *Many of the activities bowlers perform before each shot, such as observing the lanes, choosing the right ball, envisioning the lane, and aligning your body, are actually exploratory movements. They help you focus on crucial information, make decisions, and facilitate perceptual search.*

3. **Adaptive Decision-Making:** *Exploratory actions involve both visual and non-visual investigation. You continuously gather information about the ball's characteristics and adapt your tactics accordingly. These seemingly small movements are crucial in finding the information needed for well-coordinated bowling.*

Training Plan and Tasks:

1. Observation and Visualization:

Task: Observe experienced bowlers, focusing on their pre-performance rituals. Notice how they take time to choose the right ball and visualize their shots. Understand the importance of these actions in perceiving critical information.

2. Pre-Performance Routine:

Task: Incorporate a pre-performance routine into your practice. Start by observing the lanes, choosing your ball, wiping it, and envisioning your ideal trajectory line. Align your body and take deep breaths to prepare for your shot.

3. Exploratory Actions:

Task: While choosing your ball, consciously explore its characteristics, such as weight, grip, and texture. Make changes to your release technique and continually investigate its impact on your shots. Learn to use these exploratory movements to gather information.

4. Balancing Body and Release:

Task: Pay close attention to the timing and balance of your entire body at the release stage. Experiment with different release techniques, considering both visual cues and non-visual information like the feel and feedback from your hand.

5. Feedback and Adaptation:

Task: Record your practice sessions and review your pre-performance routine and release. Seek feedback from your coach or a more experienced bowler. Use this feedback to adapt and refine your exploratory actions.

Outcome: *By integrating exploratory actions into your practice, you'll enhance your perception and decision-making abilities. This will enable you to gather valuable information to optimize your swing and release. Over time, you'll develop a more well-coordinated and adaptable bowling technique, combining both visual and non-visual cues to improve your performance on the lanes.*

Method 3 - Movement-Related Feedback

The incapacity of beginner bowlers to completely absorb and pay attention to the multiple sources of information that direct their motions is one of the biggest problems they confront. Therefore, augmented feedback, which offers extra information to help players develop ideal skills including steps, swing, timed release, and body alignment, can be of tremendous use to novices. For instance, regular coaching input on the upper body's position throughout the bowling swing might hasten the acquisition of this talent. In this section, we'll talk about how augmented feedback can speed up the development of bowling skills.

Imitating the style of more accomplished bowlers during practice is a typical strategy among bowlers. Coaches frequently give advice on technique with the goal of helping bowlers create an ideal set of skills in their heads. However, as we already established, there isn't a single flawless technique. There are numerous skill modifications that can still produce the intended results for each person and environment they come across. For coaches, this idea has important ramifications on how to give and receive feedback during practice. In the motor learning literature, the use of movement-related feedback to enhance skill acquisition has been extensively investigated.

Videos of bowlers' practice sessions are one type of visual feedback that is becoming more and more common, especially in bowling. Bowlers can evaluate their accuracy in ball trajectory and how well it matches their technical proficiency with the use of this feedback.

Priority should be placed on giving the bowler some say in the timing of movement-related feedback. Allowing feedback to be self-regulated improves motivation and produces better learning strategies. There is a widespread

SHOGO WADA

Method 3 - Movement-related feedback

My early days in the sport were far from glamorous. My coach wasn't a renowned professional; instead, it was a picture of the Japan Cup that adorned the walls of my home. After returning from school each day, I would eagerly watch bowling videos, absorbing every detail and studying the techniques of the best in the game. It was my own version of training, a way to immerse myself in the world of bowling.

misperception that in order to "perfect" their technique, bowlers need to acquire as much input from their coach as possible. However, a moderate amount of movement-related input that only addresses the most crucial facets of the technique is most advantageous to the bowler. The "best" approach for each bowler to move will vary significantly because of his distinct physical and mental qualities. To attempt to bowl a ball exactly like a top bowler is therefore irrational for all bowlers. Feedback should be used to help bowlers develop the mechanically sound foundations of their movement patterns, such as creating angular momentum and maintaining correct body angles.

Bowlers can improve their abilities in a way that is suited to their unique abilities and styles by receiving focused and pertinent criticism. Coaches can speed up the learning process and assist bowlers in becoming more proficient in their sport by making appropriate use of movement-related feedback.

Hypothetical Examples

A coach who critiques a novice bowler's technique excessively, even for minor issues unrelated to his present level of expertise. The bowler could feel overburdened and disappointed as a result of his inability to implement all of the feedback at once. Instead, the coach could give advice that is concentrated on the skill's most important components, such as creating angular momentum or maintaining body parts' proper angles. The bowler is more likely to feel motivated and create efficient learning techniques if given some control over when and how much feedback is given and if it is suited to his current level of expertise.

Tenpin Coach Examples:

Example 1: Coach A realized the value of giving new bowlers augmented feedback to speed up the development of his skills. Coach A used video recordings of the bowlers' swings during practice sessions to give visual feedback. He assisted the bowlers in determining how precisely his ball trajectory matched up with his technical proficiency. Coach A concentrated on crucial elements including steps, swing, timing release, and body alignment while giving the bowlers detailed feedback to assist him in making the necessary corrections and enhancing his overall technique. Coach A enabled a more effective learning process for the bowlers, speeding up the development of his skills by employing movement-related feedback.

Example 2: Coach B was aware of the importance of personal variations and modifications in bowling approaches. Coach B tailored and pertinent feedback to each bowler based on his distinct physical and mental attributes rather than imposing a single "perfect" method. He concentrated on enhancing the basic mechanical concepts underlying movement patterns, such as producing angular momentum and upholding correct body angles. Coach B stressed feedback self-regulation, giving the bowlers authority over when input was given. This strategy improved the bowlers' motivation and aided in the creation of individualized, efficient learning plans. Coach B helped the bowlers develop higher skills in their game by employing movement-related feedback well.

Hypothetical Examples:

Example 1: Bowler X recognized the importance of movement-specific feedback for enhancing his bowling abilities. He actively looked for opportunities to get his coach's input during practice. Bowler X evaluated the accuracy of the ball's trajectory and alignment with the participants' technical abilities by watching video recordings of his swings. He paid close attention to his steps, swing, timing of release, and body alignment, and He adjusted as necessary in response to the input. Bowler X accepted the idea of personal adaptations and applied the criticism to improve his performance on the lanes and his technique.

Example 2: Bowler Y understood the value of utilizing movement-related feedback effectively throughout his skill-development process. He actively practiced self-regulation throughout practice sessions and discussed his preferences for feedback with his instructor. Bowler Y recognized that getting too much feedback might not be helpful and instead concentrated on getting focused, pertinent criticism on the most important elements of his technique. He used the feedback to make adjustments to the underlying mechanical principles guiding his movement patterns in an effort to provide the best possible angular momentum and preserve the correct body angles. Bowler Y improved his bowling abilities and became more skilled at the game thanks to his commitment and use of movement-related feedback.

Scenario: Teaching Swing and Release Using Movement-Related Feedback

Coach: *To improve your swing and release, we'll focus on using movement-related feedback as a tool to accelerate your skill development. Movement-related feedback will help you make adjustments in your steps, swing, timed release, and body alignment, leading to improved bowling skills.*

Cues and Concepts:

*1. **Augmented Feedback:** For beginners, absorbing and paying attention to multiple sources of information can be challenging. Augmented feedback provides additional information to help develop essential skills. In this case, we'll use feedback to improve your upper body's position during the bowling swing.*

2. ***Varied Skill Modifications:*** *There isn't a single flawless technique, and there are many ways to achieve desired results in bowling. Coaches must be aware that skill modifications can still lead to success, and feedback should address the most crucial aspects of the technique.*

3. ***Movement-Related Feedback:*** *We'll use feedback, such as video analysis, to help you assess your ball trajectory and its alignment with your technical proficiency.*

Training Plan and Tasks:

1. Video Analysis:

Task: Record your practice sessions, especially focusing on your swing and release. Use video analysis to evaluate your technique, looking for areas that need improvement.

2. Self-Evaluation:

Task: Watch the recorded videos and self-evaluate your performance. Pay attention to your upper body's position during the swing, your release timing, and the alignment of your body. Identify areas where you can make improvements.

3. Prioritizing Feedback:

Task: Focus on the most crucial aspects of your technique, such as creating angular momentum and maintaining proper body angles. Prioritize feedback that addresses these critical elements.

4. Self-Regulated Feedback:

Task: Give yourself control over the timing of movement-related feedback. When you feel ready to receive feedback or have questions about specific aspects of your technique, access the video analysis. This approach enhances motivation and allows you to tailor your learning strategies.

5. Coach's Input:

Task: Discuss your self-evaluation and video analysis with your coach. They can provide expert guidance on how to refine your technique based on your unique physical and mental qualities.

Outcome: *By incorporating movement-related feedback into your practice, you'll gain a better understanding of your swing and release, allowing you to make necessary adjustments. You'll learn to prioritize feedback on critical aspects of your technique and tailor your learning to your unique abilities and style. This approach accelerates your skill development and helps you become a more proficient bowler.*

An essential factor to take into account in the field of motor learning is how frequent and excessive feedback affects a bowler's capacity to learn and develop new skills. Bowlers' ability to learn may suffer if they receive an excessive amount of feedback. The fact that overwhelming feedback frequently prompts bowlers to talk to themselves while in the stance position is one cause of this interference. But critical self-analysis might divert the bowler's focus away from the task's main objective. It is crucial to keep a productive attentional focus and pay attention to the effects of the bowler's motions rather than the internal production of those movements in order to maximize skill improvement.

Bowlers can improve their motor learning process by changing their attentional focus to the repercussions of their movements on the outside world. Bowlers should focus on the results and effects of their actions rather than becoming fixated on the details of their technique. With an external focus, they can more clearly understand how their actions affect the bowling ball, the lane, and target accuracy.

As bowlers get into their "stance" posture to get ready to deliver the ball, it is very important to practice keeping an appropriate attentional concentration. Self-talk frequently appears during this stage as bowlers analyze and criticize their moves in their minds. Excessive self-talk, however, can lead to a mental burden that takes focus away from the current activity. To combat this, bowlers should work to make it a habit to focus on outside cues that are directly related to the intended results. This can be done by picturing the ball's trajectory, concentrating on the targeted goal, or paying attention to the ball's trajectory and pin carry.

Bowlers can access the power of their subconscious mind and allow the well-practiced movements to flow effortlessly by adopting an external attentional focus. This makes it possible to use the bowling method in a smoother and more fluid manner. In addition, because bowlers trust their muscle memory and rely on their innate abilities, it reduces the likelihood of overthinking and analytical paralysis.

Example

A coach regularly critiques a beginner bowler's posture, grip, and swing during practice. The bowler's coach instructs him to maintain balance, release the ball properly, and keep his elbow straight. However, the bowler starts to self-talk when in the stance position as a result of being overloaded with information. Instead of concentrating on the outcomes of his motions, such as hitting the target on the lane, He starts to consider all the many parts of his technique. The bowler finds it difficult to make consistent shots as a result of his attentional concentration being diverted from the task aim. Instead, if the instructor had provided more general instructions like "try to hit the target" or "aim for the center of the pins," the bowler may have focused on the impact of his motions on the outside and enhanced his performance.

GRIPS ADJUSTMENT FOR ENHACING THE FREEDOM OF MOTION: SUCCESS IS IN THE DETAILS *By Del Warren*

After reflecting upon my last 12 years at the Kegel Training Center, I realized that a fair share of my lessons involved very simple solutions to fix or improve the student's game. So for this article I wanted to focus on some of these observations which I hope will give you some insight and help guide you in a different but faster direction when looking to improve certain parts of your game.

Problem #1: Inconsistent release point, accuracy and/or lack of revolutions.

Ron Hoppe has always professed the importance of thumb timing. Bill Taylor first said that "The ball will let go of you." "You do not let go of the ball." Both coaches are stating that if the ball is fit properly, the thumb will exit at the proper time with minimal manipulation or grip pressure by the bowler. Proper thumb timing is essential for good bowling. If the grip does not produce this, it can cause all of the above challenges and more.

*Try some of the following ideas which I have seen produce immediate results. The first is a no brainer and is something the pros pay close attention to. **Clean and re-tape your thumb hole**. Having a clean thumb hole with new tape placed in the proper position for your thumb can produce amazing results. Used properly, tape can change the **overall size and shape** of the thumb hole. John Janawicz, who recently was inducted into the USBC Hall Of Fame, started with 15 pieces of tape **(Picture – Thumb with tapes)** placed in the front and back of the hole. At the end of the tournament, he was down to just 3 pieces. That is how much his hand changed during that grueling event. Each day he reassessed his thumb size and made sure that both the front and back tape was new and clean. Recently, I worked with a student who was sure they needed a completely new fit. When examining his thumb holes, the tape was so old that it was a green color. The holes were slick to the touch and the tape was placed in a random fashion. After cleaning and placing the tape carefully, we found that the fit was fine and the bowler's overall performance greatly improved.*

***Experiment with different types of tape, sizes, applications, shapes and textures**. Your individual skin texture plays a large role in assessing thumb timing. For example, dry skin tends to be slick. When combining a urethane thumb slug with dry skin, the ball can be very difficult to hang onto even when the overall fit is good. Consider looking for tape that has a bit more friction such as white or a cork insert. There is also a product that has a rubber insert that is extremely tacky. I have seen several women with smaller thumbs and drier skin use this product with great success.*

***Other options and findings.** To verify these findings, I searched the internet to see if there have been any studies on gripping forces vs. friction and skin texture. To my surprise there was. Here are some excerpts of the study.*

FRICTION, NOT TEXTURE, DICTATES GRIP FORCES USED DURING OBJECT MANIPULATION

G. Cadoret and A. M. Smith
Department de Physiologie, Universite de Montreal, Quebec, Canada.

*When strong adhesives increased the friction of the smooth surface compared with textured surfaces, **grip forces decreased as friction increased.** That is, friction appears to be a more important factor in determining the grip force than either texture or surface films at least for the range of textures and coatings examined in this study. This tells me the importance of not only the shape and tightness of your thumb hole, but the products you use inside the thumb hole as well as on the thumb. This may be the biggest difference in producing the best overall thumb timing. The most commonly used tape is white (textured) and black (smooth). There is a huge difference in friction between the two. If you have dry, slick skin, use white tape and stay away from black. Conversely, if your skin is on the tacky side, you may want to use more black than white.*

The other product I alluded to in the previous paragraph is thumb or fitting tape. This product is placed directly onto the bowlers thumb, changing the surface friction of the thumb. This can aid in reducing overall grip pressure and improve thumb timing. What I really love about this product is that it gives the pro shop and coach a tool to help fine tune the bowler's release point especially those with problem skin.

Finally, if these suggestions do not produce the results you would like, try getting refit by your pro shop professional and experiment with different grips. I believe everyone should have their grip checked twice per year anyway; your hand does change as you get older. The foundation of a good physical game starts with a grip that is comfortable and requires a minimum amount of grip pressure. After trying some of these suggestions, the best test I know is to have your customer/ student go back to their old grip after they have thrown the new one for 4 or 5 games. It is amazing to see folks drop the ball using their old faithful grip sometimes as early as the ball starting into the hinge.

Problem #2: Lack of balance, accuracy and consistent break point.

If I made the above statement to you, your first reaction for a solution may be to see a coach, get on video and change something in your physical game. The truth of the matter is that when this occurs, many bowlers need to just start by looking down at their feet to find the answer. I have to estimate approximately 30% of the players I work with need some kind of work on their bowling shoes to produce the proper slide. In fact, most bowlers start with a pair of shoes that will not match up to the synthetic approaches to produce a proper slide. The bowler then figures out a way to compensate getting to the foul line without falling down. This usually produces no slide. This leads to BAD MECHANICS simply because the shoes would not allow them to transfer the energy to the ball down the target line efficiently and consistently. The slide is critical in so many ways to good bowling. Here are just a few:

1. *The slide is the foundation of the body for balance especially since the body is in a constant state of motion or equilibrium.*

2. *The slide length and speed gives the ball time to come down from the top of the backswing. This smooth transition is a key to transferring energy to the ball efficiently and consistently.*

3. *An inconsistent slide can cause the ball to be off line because it can change the bowlers thumb timing, i.e. release point, as previously mentioned above. Releasing the ball early will cause the bowler to miss right or a late release will cause the bowler to miss left. This inconsistency can also cause the bowler to have little or no flat spot at the bottom of the swing. This is critical in controlling the break point and the overall shape of the shot. Without that, good ball reaction is difficult to obtain.*

4. *Injuries are more likely to occur if the body is not allowed to come to a gradual stop at the end of the bowler's shot. We often see knee, hip and lower back injuries due to the bowler sticking or stopping prematurely over and over again.*

The fact is that approach friction changes day to day just like lane conditions do. With that said, taking care of your shoes in order to deal with the change of approach friction is a key in all of the areas mentioned above. Synthetic approaches change more than wood. A bowler must manage these changes. Start by purchasing a good pair of shoes which allow you to change the soles and heels. These types of shoes are much more affordable today with more models to choose from. If this solution is not in your budget, get with your coach or pro shop operator to help you adjust your current shoes using a slip-on slide sole or even try different socks on the outside your shoes. My wife Dawn uses a sock to slide properly. If the approaches are a too slick, she takes the sock off.

Problem #3 Inconsistent Launch Angles

I've been blessed to have been able to coach and learn at the Kegel Training Center now for 12 years. I have used our C.A.T.S. System and now SPECTO to study why most bowlers are not as consistent and accurate as they should be. The conclusion may shock you and is as simple and elementary as any fundamental in the game of bowling. A conservative estimation is that 95% of all of our lessons revolve around bowlers standing too far to the inside of the intended target line which produces an arm swing and ball path not on the line of play. This causes all kinds of inconsistencies and compensations in the bowler's physical game. Some of the most common are missing in both directions, early turn at the release point, a late release, a spinning release or even a full roller, lack of ball speed or even lack of rev rate. Often you will see the ball behind the bowlers back with an inside out loop. Bowlers can hit their ankles or the opposite may occur where the ball gets trapped behind the body and have to move far away from the angle during the release. To start repairing this, you must educate the bowler about the importance of the line of play. At the Kegel Training Center, we use several tools like the Torch X, SPECTO and Lasers to help visualize the line. We can then re- position the bowler so that they start slightly to the outside of the line of play and with the correct footwork end up directly on the proper board. This concept is critical for consistency from the release point to the breakpoint. This will also help reduce the compensations in the physical game and the possibility of injury.

Finally, I wrote this article in an effort to help coaches and players improve faster. It is my hope that info will clear up some of the confusion that is so simple to fix and help everyone enjoy this wonderful game more!

Del Warren, Vice President Kegel Training Center

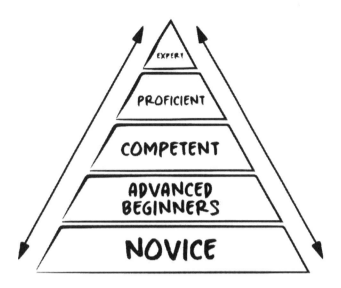

SKILL ACQUISITION STAGES

The scientific study of how bowlers learn and carry out motions in the game of bowling is known as skill acquisition, sometimes known as motor learning and control (Williams & Ford, 2009). It investigates the elements that affect how bowlers of all ability levels learn, use, and retain their bowling abilities. The cognitive stage, the associative stage, and the autonomous stage are frequently used to define skill acquisition even though it is a continuous and dynamic process without distinct stages (Fitts & Posner, 1967).

The process by which people improve their talents, strategies, and techniques in the sport of bowling is referred to as skill acquisition. It includes all of the skills necessary to develop as a skilled bowler, including physical coordination, mental focus, and tactical judgment. In order to become skilled in bowling, one must first learn the game's fundamentals, including footwork, arm swing, release, and targeting, as well as gain a thorough awareness of lane conditions, ball dynamics, and how to adapt to various oil patterns. It includes the ongoing hone and polishing of techniques by repetition, guidance, and experience. In order to improve your bowling skills, you must be committed, persistent, and open to new ideas and approaches. Gaining new skills is the key to realizing your full potential on the floor, whether you're a novice looking to learn the fundamentals or an expert bowler looking to step up your game.

The Stages of Learning

The First Stage: The Cognitive Stage

The "learning stages model," developed by Paul Fitts and Michael Posner in 1967, describes the many phases of skill development. This model's initial step is called the cognitive stage, where the bowler, also referred to as the "skilled-bowler," concentrates on comprehending the cerebral components of bowling, such as "what to do and how to do it." The bowler listens to the coach's directions during this phase and makes an effort to follow them. It's crucial to remember that during the early stages of learning, a lot of mistakes are to be expected because the bowler lacks the information and abilities needed to remedy them. In order to help the bowler in his endeavours, the coach must provide the bowler with constructive criticism. It's vital to understand that the bowler's performance throughout this phase cannot be constant due to the high variation in performances. To help the bowler achieve better consistency and superior performance, corrective input is therefore crucial. During this phase, it is also essential to create a welcoming, encouraging, and unique learning environment because doing so improves learning (Correia et al., 2019). Hall (2002) asserts that cognitive processes advance together with motor abilities. Coaches must therefore supply clear and correct information to aid learning during the cognitive stage. The long-term growth of the bowler might be hampered by inadequate or poor instruction. In other words, ineffective coaching and subsequent learning can seriously hinder a bowler's future development.

The Cognitive Stage of Learning in Bowling: The learning process for bowling starts with the cognitive stage. The bowler concentrates on learning the game's fundamentals at this stage. It is a phase in which deliberate work, focus, and attention to detail are essential. Every motion and action is deliberate and requires ongoing cognitive processing. The bowler makes an effort to comprehend the fundamental bowling mechanics, including the approach, release, and targeting. The bowler is also still working on the physical strength and coordination needed for a reliable bowling technique. At this stage, learning is focused on laying a firm foundation and gaining a thorough understanding of the game's essential components. For bowlers to advance in their game, their capacity to take in and digest information is essential. Bowlers steadily improve in their ability to execute critical bowling skills and tactics via diligent practice and coaching. The cognitive stage lays the foundation for future skill development and opens the door to moving on to the following learning stages.

AHMED SHAHEEN

The Autonomous Stage

In the late '90s and early 2000s, I experienced a state of flow—a period of remarkable success where I ranked first in the Asian bowling rankings and consistently placed in the top positions in various tournaments. It was a time when everything seemed to align, and I felt unstoppable.

To maintain consistency and hone my skills, I relied on one fundamental principle: simplicity. I focused on mastering the basics, repeating drills daily, and ensuring that my game remained uncomplicated. Alongside technical training, I delved into the mental aspects of bowling, finding comfort in the presence of an audience and developing a new perspective on the game.

Hypothetical Examples

Examples of Bowlers at the Cognitive Stage:

10-year-old Johnny recently started playing in a bowling league. Despite having no prior experience, he is eager to learn the game. Johnny is concentrating on comprehending the fundamental principles of bowling during the cognitive stage. He gains knowledge about optimal ball grip, foot placement on the approach, and pin-aiming technique. He moves slowly and deliberately as he considers each step of the procedure constantly. He trains frequently to develop his muscle memory and enhance his coordination, and he frequently looks to his coach for direction and feedback.

A young woman named Sarah recently started bowling as a pastime with her pals. She is in the cognitive learning stage and has never bowled before. Sarah reads books and watches online tutorials to study the fundamentals of bowling since she is keen to comprehend the game's mechanics. She concentrates on maintaining a straight arm, positioning her feet correctly, and hitting the pins. She continually assesses her posture and technique in light of her observations and input from her pals. She trains frequently to hone her abilities and increase her self-assurance as a bowler.

Mike is a middle-aged man who used to bowl occasionally when he was younger but has been away from the sport for a considerable amount of time. He just signed up for a bowling league and is currently relearning the game at the cognitive level. Although Mike is familiar with the fundamentals of bowling, he needs to review them and work on his technique. To restore his muscle memory, he starts by concentrating on his grip, stance, and approach. He concentrates on the targeting, release, and posture of his body. To improve his abilities and get back into the game's flow, he trains frequently and asks his teammates for comments.

The Second Stage: The Associative Stage

Bowlers reach the associative stage after putting in a lot of practice and making significant improvements to their bowling abilities. At this point, bowlers start to link environmental signals to the precise motions needed to meet their skill objectives. It's essential for coaches to let their players make errors so they may learn from them and improve. Due to their improved knowledge and comprehension, bowlers exhibit fewer and less noticeable faults as a result of honing these skills.

Refinement and Improvement in the Associative Stage: Fitts and Posner's (1964) model states that because there is still a possibility for development, this stage is frequently referred to as the refining stage. Bowlers primarily concentrate on executing the skill successfully and consistently throughout this period. Additionally, imagery can contribute to the development of a talent. When applying skills from one well-learned ability to a related one, mental imagery might be helpful (Hall, 2002). As a coach, you may help bowlers improve their confidence and technique by encouraging them to set goals and use imagery to picture these goals.

The Associative Stage of Learning in Bowling: Bowlers advance past the first cognitive stage during the associative stage, which is the second learning phase. Bowlers now turn their attention to improve their technique, coordination, and overall performance. Bowlers can now carry out their movements with more ease and efficiency because of the development of muscle memory and their fundamental understanding of the mechanics of bowling. Now, the focus is on honing their abilities and tactics to consistently produce better results.

Bowlers are better able to carry out their activities more automatically and with less effort in the associative stage. This enables students to learn more about the nuances of the game, analyze their motions, and make changes for improved accuracy and effectiveness. Bowlers work to improve their technique with each practice session, striving for a more accurate and consistent execution of their shots. They increase their awareness of environmental cues and how they affect performance, taking use of this knowledge.

It is imperative that you, as a coach, offer direction and encouragement during this phase of learning. Encouragement to develop objectives and use images to imagine accomplishment can help bowlers become more motivated and self-assured. Additionally, coaches are essential in establishing a supportive and demanding training environment that promotes skill development and ongoing progress. Coaches help bowlers develop as good and accomplished bowlers by fostering their development in the associative stage.

Hypothetical examples of Bowlers at the Associative Stage:

Lisa has been playing competitive bowling for a while and has progressed to the associative learning level. She is working on increasing her accuracy and targeting while maintaining a consistent approach, release, and follow-through. In order to perfect her performance, Lisa worked on tiny alterations to her body position, timing, and pace. She also observes the state of the lanes, records her ratings, and examines performance statistics to pinpoint areas that need work. In order to make modifications and continuously improve her technique and strategies to compete at a higher level, she asks her coach and fellow bowlers for comments.

Mark is an accomplished bowler with years of experience and a high degree of competence. He is currently working to increase his consistency and adaptability as he learns in the associative stage. Based on the various lane conditions and oil patterns, Mark is adept at modifying his approach, release, and targeting. To diversify his toolbox of abilities, he trains on various lane surfaces, works on various spare techniques, and experiments with various bowling balls. To always challenge himself and keep up his high level of performance, he constantly evaluates his performance, makes modifications, and sets precise targets.

Emily has been playing bowling for a few years for fun, and she has advanced to the associative stage of learning. She participates in neighborhood leagues and likes to bowl with friends. Emily is now working on honing her spare shooting and converting challenging splits after developing a consistent approach and release. She works on her spare targeting, performs spare drills, and asks guidance from more seasoned bowlers in order to master various spare approaches. To enhance her overall performance and contribute more to her team, she also works on reading lane circumstances, modifying her ball speed, and experimenting with various tools.

The Third Stage: The Autonomous Stage

The Fitts and Posner model identifies the autonomous stage as the last phase of skill development. As the skill has been automated, bowlers at this stage exhibit a high level of motor skill mastery with little conscious awareness. The autonomous stage relies on implicit learning, when the bowler uses the ability with little attention or purposeful thought, in contrast to the cognitive stage, which calls for deliberate and conscious effort (Hall, 2002). At this point, bowlers have a thorough understanding of the sport and make few mistakes. If a mistake is made, the bowler can identify it and make the necessary corrections. But it's crucial to remember that even at the autonomous stage, a coach's assistance may be beneficial. While bowlers can provide self-feedback, coaches with trained and observant eyes can spot subtle characteristics that the bowlers themselves would find difficult to notice.

Underpinning Factors for Autonomous Skill Execution Attaining the autonomous stage requires several key components: A) Quality of Instruction and Practice: For bowlers to gain the requisite abilities, the coach must provide effective and well-planned instruction and practice sessions. During this phase, instruction and criticism are received, which greatly aids in the development and mastery of the talent. B) Amount of Practice: To get to the autonomous stage, the bowlers must put in a significant amount of deliberate practice. Bowlers can improve their performance by strengthening their techniques, developing muscle memory, and practicing on a regular and organized basis. C) Bowlers' Motivation: Moving on to the autonomous level depends heavily on the bowlers' drive and motivation to succeed in their sport. The dedication required to train consistently and push oneself to higher levels of skill execution is fuelled by a strong desire to get better and a passion for the sport.

The Importance of Coaches in the Autonomous Stage Despite the fact that bowlers at the autonomous stage are capable of self-feedback, a skilled coach is still beneficial. Coaches enhance a bowler's performance by bringing knowledge, experience, and a new viewpoint. Their keen observations can spot small areas that need development and offer helpful advice to improve the bowler's execution. Coaches can also help bowlers improve their technique, address any lingering flaws, and maintain a high level of performance. Coaches act as dependable mentors, ensuring that bowlers continue to develop and advance their skills even at the independent stage.

Striving for Mastery: Attaining the Autonomous Stage For bowlers, achieving the autonomous stage—the highest level of skill execution—is a desirable objective. It denotes a degree of competence at which the ability becomes automatic. The level of instruction and practice, the quantity of purposeful practice, and the bowlers' constant motivation must all be present for them to reach this degree. The likelihood of reaching the autonomous stage considerably rises by using efficient coaching methods, offering insightful practice drills, and developing bowlers' passion and perseverance. As bowlers get to this level, they become accomplished athletes who are able to practice their craft with the dexterity, accuracy, and easy grace of real masters of the game.

Hypothetical examples of Bowlers at the Autonomous Stage:

Michael, a professional bowler, spent countless hours honing his skills and competing before reaching the autonomous stage of learning. He has honed his approach, release, and follow-through to the point that they are automatic. Based on the lane conditions and oil patterns, Michael may easily modify his ball speed, rev rate, and targeting. He can quickly and accurately make modifications to maintain high scores because he has a good feel of how to read the lanes. Michael also has a thorough awareness of equipment selection and ball motion, which enables him to select the ideal ball for various lane conditions and maximize his performance. He constantly competes at the highest level, earning top marks, and is praised for his extraordinary abilities and methodical approach to the game.

Sarah is a professional female bowler who, after many years of hard work and practice, has reached the independent stage of learning. She has honed a distinctive style and technique that are ideal for her physical characteristics and playing circumstances. Sarah shoots with great accuracy and precision, and she is practically flawless in her spare shooting. She is skilled in a variety of spare techniques and can swiftly adjust to diverse pin arrangements. In order to maintain her high level of performance, Sarah is a pro at analyzing the lane conditions and modifying her approach, release, and targeting. She is renowned for her dependability, adaptability, and mental toughness on the lanes and has won several competitions.

Senior bowler, John has been playing for years and has progressed to the stage of independent study. His actions are swift, effortless, and automatic, and he has a plethora of expertise and information regarding the game. John can regularly and accurately strike his targets because he has exceptional control over his ball speed, rotation, and targeting. He plays the game strategically, adapting his approach in response to the performance of his rivals and the lane circumstances. Because of his remarkable abilities, sportsmanship, and capacity to compete at a high level despite his age, John is well-liked in his bowling community.

Stage	Example on Bowlers	Example on Coaches' Way of Coaching	Steps/Strategies	Challenges	Strengths
Cognitive Stage	Bowler is new to bowling and learning the basics	Coach provides instructions and corrective feedback	- Focus on understanding the basic mechanics of bowling	- High error rate due to lack of knowledge and skills	- Opportunity for foundational learning
			- Concentrate on conscious effort and attention to detail	- Difficulty in performing consistently	- Building a strong foundation for skill development
Associative Stage	Bowler is refining technique and coordination	Coach allows bowler to make mistakes and uses environmental feedback	- Continuously practice and perform the skill	- Reducing errors and improving consistency	- Progressing towards skill refinement and consistency
Autonomous Stage	Bowler performs skills effortlessly and automatically	Coach's presence still valuable for astute observation	- Refine skills through imagery and goal-setting - Execute skills with minimal conscious awareness	- Focusing on specific cues for skill improvement - Maintaining skill proficiency without conscious effort	- Increasing skill refinement and coordination - Ability to self-correct errors and make precise adjustments
			- Coach provides feedback on subtle and convoluted elements that may go unnoticed by the bowler	- Striving for consistency and superior performance	- Demonstrating mastery and proficiency in skill execution

Table 7- Skill Acquisition Stages

Enhancing Skill Efficiency:

Bowlers frequently have a tendency to use more muscles than are required to carry out the intended movements when learning new skills. But as bowlers advance and improve their techniques, muscle recruitment becomes more effective and declines, while the coordination of muscle contractions gets better. This means that through practice, bowlers develop the ability to use only the muscles required for performing the skill, saving energy and obtaining higher levels of movement precision. For bowlers who are aiming to be the best in their sport, mastering skill efficiency is a major goal.

Bowlers frequently experience visual selective attention challenges in the early stages of developing their skills. This means that it is difficult for them to concentrate on particular parts of their performance and recognize mistakes that need to be fixed. However, bowlers gain the capacity to focus their attention on the key cues that support successful skill performance through persistent practice and experience. Bowlers are better able to improve their motor performance, recognize faults more clearly, and make the necessary corrections because of this improvement in visual selective attention.

Coaches should assist bowlers in reaching the autonomous stage, which is the highest level of skill mastery, according to the acclaimed Fitts and Posner model. At this stage, bowlers can use their motor abilities naturally without having to pay attention to them. It represents the highest level of skill development when the movements are automatic and ingrained. In order for bowlers to go through the cognitive and associative stages and achieve the highest degree of skill execution, coaches are essential.

Applying Skills to Different Motor Tasks Bowlers move on to the transfer phase after successfully completing each step of skill acquisition. The use of learned skills in various but related motor activities is referred to as transfer of learning. Bowlers can adjust their technique and competence to a variety of bowling conditions and obstacles because of this capacity to transfer talents. It is a crucial stage in the growth of a well-rounded and adaptable bowler.

In order to reach full potential as a bowler, skill efficiency needs to be refined. A bowler can advance through the levels of skill development and become a master of his sport by honing muscle recruitment, synchronizing muscle contractions, enhancing visual selective attention, and other related skills. He can achieve the autonomous level, where his abilities are completed effortlessly and flawlessly, with the assistance of coaches, who act as important advisers along the way. From there, the application of learning enables him to use his abilities in a variety of bowling situations, laying the groundwork for his continued development and success as a bowler. Accept the process, make a commitment to methodical practice, and observe as he develops his abilities and succeeds in the fascinating world of bowling.

Example

When learning how to deliver the ball, beginner bowlers frequently apply too much effort by holding the ball tightly, utilizing their arms too forcefully, and overextending their bodies. However, as players gain skill efficiency, they discover how to employ just the right amount of muscle recruitment required to throw the ball precisely and with the proper amount of power, decreasing superfluous muscular strain and enhancing their overall control and accuracy.

Beginner bowlers could experience difficulties with timing and coordination, resulting in jerky and erratic movements when delivering the ball. However, as they advance and increase skill effectiveness, they learn to smoothly coordinate their actions with better timing and rhythm. The outcome is a more fluid and effective delivery that enhances their effectiveness since they are able to activate the appropriate muscles at the appropriate time.

Novice bowlers sometimes display poor stability and balance, which results in unreliable shots and frequent stumbles or falls. They learn to have a more steady and balanced body stance throughout their approach, delivery, and follow-through as their skill efficiency increases. They can use their muscles more effectively and efficiently as a result, which enhances their balance, stability, and general control.

Due to irregular muscle contractions and poor coordination, beginner bowlers may struggle to control the pace and direction of the ball. However, as they advance and improve their skill efficiency, they discover how to precisely control their muscular contractions, which enables them to throw the ball with a constant rate of speed and precision. Ball deliveries become more effective and efficient because of enhanced muscle coordination.

Novice bowlers frequently deal with excessive muscle tension and tiredness, which lowers performance and raises the risk of injury. They learn to relax extraneous muscles and conserve energy as they improve their skill efficiency, which enables them to sustain their performance level for lengthy durations of play. They can deliver the ball with less effort and a lower chance of injury because of their greater muscular efficiency, which boosts their performance and endurance on the lanes.

THE TRANSFER OF SKILLS FROM ONE SPORT TO BOWLING

The transfer of learning

Applying what has been learned in one environment to another is the process of transfer of learning. It is essential to the growth of a bowler's ability across a range of motor skills. Bowlers must comprehend their lessons completely and be able to apply them in many contexts in order to achieve transfer. For instance, the body angles and movements necessary for bowling can be acquired from the motor patterns used in a golf swing. Positive, negative, and neural learning transfer are the three different forms.

Positive Transfer:

When teaching new skills, coaches work to generate positive transfer because it shows the bowler's growth is progressing. Positive transfer causes bowlers to permanently store the talent in their long-term memory. Coaches boost the possibility of positive transfer by assisting bowlers through the learning process, decreasing the likelihood of erroneous skill execution in game-like scenarios.

Coaches use practical tactics and procedures that improve skill integration in order to promote positive transfer. They put a lot of emphasis on drawing parallels and links between various skills so that bowlers may apply what they've learned to new situations. Coaches assist bowlers in identifying and putting to use the common components between talents by highlighting the fundamental principles and concepts, supporting positive transfer.

Examples

A bowler may benefit from positive transfer if He has good balance and coordination from other sports like basketball or golf. The body awareness and control learned in these activities can be transferred to bowling, enabling the bowler to swiftly pick up the new talent and show consistent performance and efficient motions.

A bowler who has prior experience playing a different ball sport, such as baseball or softball, may benefit from that experience in his bowling game. The ability to toss and release a ball accurately and powerfully can be transferred to the bowling delivery, assisting the bowler in quickly picking up on the ideas of timing, release, and follow-through and efficiently using his bowling technique.

A bowler may benefit from positive transfer if He has established good hand-eye coordination through activities like playing video games, darts, or table tennis. A bowler can enhance skill efficiency in delivering the ball more rapidly by improving accuracy and precision by being able to track moving objects, gauge distances, and coordinate hand movements.

When learning a new form of bowling, a bowler who has previously mastered another form of bowling, such as candlepin bowling or lawn bowling, may experience positive transfer. The core concepts of body mechanics, coordination, and accuracy can be transferred, helping the bowler to adapt his talents to the new type of bowling more rapidly, even though there may be some changes in the rules and practices of other kinds of bowling.

A bowler may benefit from positive transfer if He has received coaching or training in another activity that emphasizes similar physical characteristics, such as strength training, flexibility workouts, or core stability exercises. The physical conditioning and muscular growth from the prior training can transfer to bowling, strengthening the bowler's efficiency on the lanes and improving his total physical capabilities.

Positive Transfer With Walter Ray William

Walter Ray Williams Jr., a legendary figure in both horseshoe pitching and professional bowling, has undoubtedly demonstrated the concept of positive transfer of skills between these two seemingly different sports. Horseshoe pitching and bowling share certain fundamental elements that allowed Williams to excel in both disciplines. Firstly, the precision and accuracy required in horseshoe pitching, particularly in aiming and releasing the horseshoe to encircle a stake, directly translate to the accuracy needed in bowling to consistently hit specific pins. The ability to gauge distances and angles with precision, honed through years of horseshoe pitching, undoubtedly contributed to Williams' remarkable accuracy as a bowler.

Walter Ray Williams Jr.'s skills in horseshoe pitching positively transferred to bowling in terms of both biomechanical and neurological aspects.

Willaim's Biomechanical Factors:

a. **Muscle Memory:** Biomechanically, Williams developed exceptional muscle memory in his arms, wrists, and fingers from years of horseshoe pitching. This muscle memory allowed him to control the release of the horseshoe with precision. When he transitioned to bowling, this finely tuned muscle memory transferred seamlessly to controlling the release of the bowling ball. The intricate motor skills he honed while pitching horseshoes translated into a consistent and controlled release in bowling, which is critical for accuracy.

b. **Balance and Weight Transfer:** Both horseshoe pitching and bowling require a balanced and coordinated approach. The weight transfer from the backswing to the delivery is crucial in both sports. Williams' experience in controlling his body's balance and weight transfer in horseshoe pitching was directly applicable to bowling. This biomechanical understanding helped him maintain balance throughout his approach and execute accurate deliveries.

Neurological Factors:

a. **Hand-Eye Coordination:** Neurologically, Williams had developed exceptional hand-eye coordination through his years of horseshoe pitching. This neurological skill allowed him to precisely aim and release the horseshoe to encircle the stake. When transitioning to bowling, his finely tuned hand-eye coordination played a pivotal role in targeting specific pins. His brain's ability to process visual information and translate it into precise physical actions was a valuable asset in both sports.

b. **Reaction Time:** Reaction time is another neurological aspect that played a role in Williams' success in both sports. In horseshoe pitching, he needed to react quickly to adapt to the distance and angle of the stake. This ability to react swiftly and make adjustments was advantageous in bowling, particularly when dealing with changing lane conditions or making last-minute adjustments to his delivery.

c. **Mental Toughness:** Neurologically, Williams' experience in high-pressure situations in horseshoe pitching contributed to his mental toughness. The ability to stay focused, remain calm under pressure, and visualize successful outcomes are crucial neurological skills. These mental attributes positively impacted his performance in bowling, especially during competitive tournaments and televised matches.

Negative Transfer:

When bowlers have false beliefs about how a skill should be used, negative transfer can happen. For instance, some bowlers can erroneously feel that the right method to achieve a hook in bowling involves violently flicking their wrists. To avoid the learning process being hampered by negative transfer, coaches must recognize and dispel these myths. Negative transfer, however less often, can prevent bowlers from learning new abilities in various situations.

In resolving misconceptions and directing bowlers toward the right knowledge of skills, coaches play a significant role. Coaches assist bowlers in creating precise mental images of the required methods by giving explicit instructions and examples. To reach peak performance, they stress the significance of good body mechanics, alignment, and timing. Bowlers can replace false impressions with true ones through excellent coaching, reducing the possibility of negative transfer.

Coaches need to be alert for indications of poor transfer during practice. To spot any inconsistent motions or faulty tactics that result from misunderstandings, they watch bowlers' movements and assess how they are executed. When a problem is found, coaches

MOHAMED JANAHI "TARZAN"- THE BULKIEST BOWLER ON WORLD TOUR

During my teenage years in Wichita, Kansas, I was deeply involved in both academics and bowling. I also developed a passion for bodybuilding, working out twice a day and participating in local competitions. However, my dedication to bodybuilding led to unintended consequences. I gained dense muscle, particularly in my upper body, which restricted my arm swing and gripping pressure essential for bowling.

My muscular physique and increased body weight negatively impacted my bowling performance. Realizing this, I made the difficult decision to shift my focus away from competitive bodybuilding. Instead, I modified my workout routines to prioritize conditioning tailored specifically for bowling. This change allowed me to regain my free arm swing and grip control, striking a balance between strength and fluidity. It marked a turning point in my bowling career, where my dedication led to success on the lanes.

work quickly to help bowlers align their actions with the required skill levels by providing remedial feedback and direction. Coaches use a variety of tactics, such as breaking down difficult skills into smaller, more accessible parts, to prevent negative transfer. Coaches can more effectively remove misconceptions and direct bowlers toward accurate execution by focusing on and isolating particular facets of the technique. In order to identify any potential misunderstandings and facilitate their rectification, coaches also encourage bowlers to reflect on and evaluate their own performance. In order to reduce negative transfer, it is also crucial to provide a helpful and good learning environment. Bowlers feel at ease asking questions and getting explanations when coaches provide open channels of communication. Coaches encourage a growth mindset, which encourages a readiness to learn and adapt, lowering the possibility of persistent misconceptions preventing skill improvement.

Examples

It is possible for a bowler to have negative transfer while switching from cricket bowling to ten-pin bowling if He has learned and mastered his previous type of bowling. The bowler may need to unlearn or modify his prior techniques to adapt to the new style, which could cause initial difficulties and inconsistencies in his performance. The techniques, movements, and muscle memory developed in the alternative style of bowling might not be directly relevant to ten-pin bowling.

When learning to bowl, a bowler who has mastered a different ball sport, like baseball, could encounter unfavorable transfer. The bowler might initially struggle to adapt and develop the proper muscle memory for bowling, which could result in inconsistencies and errors in his bowling performance. The muscle memory and motor patterns developed in the other sport may not directly translate to the specific movements and techniques required in bowling.

A bowler who has received guidance or instruction in another sport or activity with dissimilar movements or body mechanics, such as martial arts, may experience unfavorable transfer in bowling. The bowler may need to intentionally unlearn or adjust his prior tactics because the muscle memory, motor patterns, and muscle recruitment utilized in the other sport or activity may not be appropriate for bowling. This could cause confusion and difficulty when bowling.

When trying to acquire a new and proper method, a bowler who has bad habits or improper skills from prior bowling experiences could experience unfavorable transfer. Unlearning and relearning can be difficult, and the bowler may initially struggle to break old habits and adjust to the new method, resulting in mistakes and inaccuracies in his bowling performance.

A bowler may experience unfavorable transfer if He has physical restrictions or injuries from past sports or activities. For instance, a bowler who has difficulty performing the required motions and skills in bowling owing to prior injuries or medical issues may find it challenging to improve skill efficiency and perform at his best.

When a previously acquired ability develops into a difficult-to-break habit, negative transfer may take place, leading to performance mistakes. This occurs when learning new talents becomes difficult due to coordinated movements shared by various skills or tasks. Coaches should distinguish similar movements and approaches explicitly to help bowlers avoid misunderstanding and enhance their learning outcomes in order to reduce the negative transfer effects.

It is crucial to understand that negative transfer is temporary and can be beaten with the proper coaching strategy, repetition, and persistence. Bowlers can more easily adapt to new approaches by spotting and treating negative transfer early on, which eventually leads to better performance.

Neutral Transfer: Unrelated Skills

Neutral transfer, on the other hand, happens when prior knowledge has no appreciable impact on learning a new ability. For instance, it is doubtful that a bowler's proficiency at chess will translate in any significant way to his ability to play bowling. There is simply no meaningful connection between the two processes in neutral transfer.

Sport	Transfer Type	Explanation	How it Affects Bowling Skills
Golf	Positive	Similar body mechanics, balance, and coordination	Improved control and precision in the bowling approach.
Baseball	Negative	Different ball-handling techniques	Potential interference due to conflicting ball-handling movements.
Table Tennis	Positive	Hand-eye coordination, reflexes	Improved accuracy and reaction time for hitting target areas.
Yoga	Positive	Flexibility, balance, body awareness	Better posture and positioning during the bowling delivery.
Weightlifting	Positive	Strength, power	Increased ability to generate speed and control in bowling.
Pool	Neutral	Hand-eye coordination, precision	Minor influence on overall bowling skills due to different mechanics.
Tennis	Neutral	Agility, hand-eye coordination	Limited impact on bowling skills as it focuses on different movements.
Basketball	Positive	Throwing skills and hand-eye coordination	Enhanced timing, release, and follow-through in bowling.
Darts	Positive	Hand-eye coordination, aiming	Improved control and precision in the bowling approach.
Gymnastics	Negative	Different body mechanics, focus on flexibility	Potential interference due to conflicting body movements.
Soccer	Neutral	Running, endurance	Limited direct transfer, but improved stamina can aid overall performance.
Swimming	Positive	Core stability, endurance	Improved balance and stamina for maintaining consistent delivery.
Martial Arts	Negative	Different body mechanics, focus on flexibility	Potential interference due to conflicting body movements.
Archery	Neutral	Concentration, aiming skills	Minor influence on bowling skills due to different techniques.
Track and Field	Neutral	Speed, agility, strength	Limited impact on bowling skills as it focuses on different movements.
Volleyball	Neutral	Hand-eye coordination, teamwork	Minimal direct transfer but can improve communication in team bowling.
Badminton	Neutral	Reflexes, agility	Limited influence on bowling skills due to distinct mechanics.
Skiing	Positive	Balance, lower body strength	Improved stability and lower body control during the bowling approach.
Cricket	Negative	Different ball-handling techniques	Potential interference due to conflicting ball-handling movements.
Ice Hockey	Neutral	Balance, coordination	Limited direct transfer, but enhanced coordination can aid overall control.

Table 8 – Examples of sports that have an impact on bowling

Promoting Positive Transfer: Creating Optimal Learning Conditions

According to research, certain engagement levels can promote effective learning transfer. First and first, bowlers need to be able to recognize and utilize the essential components of various situations. A foundation of mastered abilities that may be used in a variety of contexts or alongside other talents is necessary for this skill transferability. Before moving forward in the context of bowling, essential abilities including physical conditioning, balance, mobility, and flexibility must be mastered.

Along with teaching bowlers how to use methods, wise coaches also stress the significance of easily accessible self-monitoring of their own thought processes. Bowlers ought to be encouraged to examine their thought processes and keep an eye on their development. With the help of their self-awareness and metacognition, bowlers may evaluate their performance, pinpoint their areas for growth, and make the required adjustments to increase their skill acquisition.

It is important to provide bowlers the chance to practice their abilities in a variety of settings so they can adapt and use them in diverse circumstances to create an atmosphere that promotes positive transfer. Coaches can design practice sessions that force bowlers to use their knowledge in unfamiliar situations, improving their capacity to successfully generalize and apply what they have learned.

In order to assess the effectiveness of their movement and skill execution in various conditions, bowlers, for instance, can watch a filmed session of open and closed-circuit exercises. It is advantageous to understand how the environment impacts skill performance since it educates the bowler, aids in the positive transfer of learning, and encourages bowlers to perform on their own.

Bowlers must prioritize focus and practice mindfulness in addition to the previously mentioned characteristics in order to improve their skill growth. During practice sessions, bowlers must maintain mental focus and refrain from cognitive diversion. Coaching is less successful when bowlers are distracted with irrelevant ideas or distractions because their focus is split.

Bowlers occasionally might not even be aware that they are mentally preoccupied during practice. However, when bowlers repeatedly make mistakes and struggle to identify and remedy them, instructors can spot indicators of a lack of focus and attention. Here, coaches can play a crucial role in assisting bowlers in sharpening their focus and attentiveness.

Coaches might begin by discussing the importance of attention and purpose in practice with bowlers. Bowlers may better grasp the effects of interruptions on their performance if the value of mental engagement during practice sessions is emphasized. Coaches can assist bowlers in maintaining a focused and present state during practice, boosting their capacity for learning.

Additionally, coaches might teach particular methods and exercises to improve awareness and concentration. Exercises for breathing, concentration, and guided visualization are a few examples of these. Coaches can aid bowlers in gaining the capacity to maintain continuous focus, enhance attention to detail, and successfully execute their skills by adding such techniques into training sessions.

Coaches can establish an environment where bowlers can completely engage in the learning process by encouraging a focus and mindfulness-focused setting. This helps players maximize their practice sessions, accelerate the development of new skills, and eventually provide their best efforts in real-world bowling situations.

Sports and techniques that bowlers can use to enhance the beneficial transfer:

Playing sports like darts, pool, or table tennis that require good hand-eye coordination can assist bowlers in improving their accuracy and precision. Similar visual tracking, aiming, and hand-movement requirements to bowling are found in these games, which can benefit bowling and enhance a bowler's overall performance.

Bowlers can improve their physical strength and power by doing strength training exercises like weightlifting or resistance training. This can have a favorable impact on how well they bowl. Strengthening can help bowlers create more power in their delivery and enhance their overall performance on the lanes, as bowling demands a particular level of strength to release the ball with speed and control.

Bowlers' flexibility, balance, and body awareness can all be improved by the practice of yoga or other flexibility exercises, which will aid their bowling technique. Flexibility is essential for bowlers because it enables them to acquire the correct body positions and movements for a quick and accurate delivery. Increased flexibility can help bowlers keep their balance, reduce joint stress, and play at their best overall.

Playing various types of bowling, such as candlepin, duckpin, or lawn bowling, can assist bowlers in getting a deeper grasp of bowling principles and strategies that they can then apply to their main form of bowling. The basic concepts of body mechanics, coordination, and accuracy may be transferred, allowing bowlers to adapt their abilities and strategies to many bowling styles, even though there may be variances in the rules and techniques of various kinds of bowling.

Participating in core-stability-required activities like Pilates, gymnastics, or swimming can help you improve your bowling. Bowling requires core stability because it gives the body a solid platform for the delivery motion. Bowlers' ability to maintain balance, manage their motions, and release their ball with power can all be improved with increased core stability.

Participating in team sports, such as basketball, volleyball, or soccer, can assist bowlers to improve their communication, teamwork, and decision-making abilities. Bowling is a team sport in some configurations, as well as an individual activity in others. Bowlers may cooperate more effectively with colleagues, plan ahead, and perform better in team bowling competitions by developing their communication and teamwork abilities.

Bowlers' focus, concentration, and mental toughness can all be improved by engaging in mental exercises like meditation, visualization, or mindfulness. For accurate motions and smart judgments to be made during bowling, one must be mentally focused and concentrated. Bowlers can perform better on the lanes and remain composed under pressure with the aid of improved mental skills.

JANAHI'S FRI MODEL: REVOLUTIONIZING THE SKILL ACQUISITION FRAMEWORK IN BOWLING

Introducing The Fri Model: Enhancing Skill Acquisition In Bowling

Mohamed Janahi's new model, called FRI, was created with coaches, bowling federations, and players in mind. It aims to deliver the most recent research on skill learning in a usable and approachable manner. The FRI Model helps coaches successfully organize, monitor, and assess their coaching methods by providing a visual depiction of important principles and concepts. The Foundation, Refinement, and Implementation Model, or FRI Model, is a framework that emphasizes the value of focused practice, useful feedback, and progressive skill improvement.

Three essential parts make up the FRI Model:

FOUNDATION: Building a solid foundation of core abilities is the main goal of this stage. The fundamental methods and motions needed for each sport are learned and practiced by athletes. It entails breaking down difficult abilities into simpler parts and gradually enhancing them.

REFINEMENTS: Athletes focus on honing their abilities and expanding their knowledge of the sport during this phase. Deliberate practice is what they do, which is targeted training with particular objectives. Coaches provide athletes with constructive criticism, assisting them in identifying areas for development and guiding them toward peak performance.

IMPLEMENTATION: The FRI Model's last phase involves using newly gained abilities in competitive situations. Athletes take part in simulations of video games where they practice applying their skills to real-world conditions. This phase places a focus on flexibility, judgment, and the capacity to work under pressure.

The FRI Model is intended to develop into a trustworthy resource for coaches dealing with young bowlers, providing insightful information on skill acquisition and usage. Its goal is to offer coaches evidence-based advice that will help them better understand how to develop players' skills in the setting of young sports.

The FRI Model was created with the main purpose of providing coaches with an all-inclusive resource. The approach illustrates how fundamental ideas from the study of skill development can be transformed into useful coaching tactics by presenting key premises. Additionally, the FRI Model aids in the long-term development of young bowlers as well as the professional advancement of coaches.

FOUNDATION - Essential Qualities of Youth Bowlers:

a) Drive and Inspiration: In order to learn a talent, like bowling, motivation and drive are essential. According to repeated studies (Ericsson et al., 1993), motivated athletes are more likely to deliberate practice and persevere in their pursuit of skill improvement. Coaches should foster a motivating and encouraging practice atmosphere, provide tough but realistic goals, and offer opportunities for autonomy and choice during practice activities to inspire young bowlers.

Example: Youth bowlers can be encouraged by coaches to create personal goals, such as raising their strike rate or accuracy, and receive incentives or praise for reaching these goals. In order to increase motivation, they might also set up a lively and enjoyable practice environment with friendly competitions, challenges, and incentives.

b) Self-Determination Theory: Self-Determination Theory (SDT) states that when bowlers' core psychological demands for autonomy, competence, and relatedness are satisfied, they are more likely to be motivated, engaged, and persistent in their skill-acquisition journey. Coaches can build a healthy team culture where athletes feel encouraged and connected, encourage self-directed learning, acknowledge and reward their competence, and support young bowlers in this area.

Example: Youth bowlers can participate in the decision-making process by helping coaches choose practice drills, establish practice objectives, and plan practice sessions. To increase their sense of competence, they can also offer regular feedback on their performance, noting their strengths and areas for development. Youth bowlers might benefit from having a supportive team environment that values open communication, mutual respect, and common goals.

ARTURO QUINTERO – "EL NIÑO DE ORO"

Self-Determination Theory

As I honed my skills and dedicated countless hours to the sport, I quickly rose to the highest level of competition. By the time I turned 14, I was already competing among the best in the world. It was during this time that I earned the nickname "El Niño de Oro," which translates to "The Gold Kid." This moniker was bestowed upon me when I achieved a remarkable feat: bowling a perfect game in Arabia in 2001, which granted me the extraordinary prize of 1 kilogram of gold. That unforgettable moment solidified my place in the bowling world and fueled my passion even further.

c) Embracing Change: A key quality in developing athletic talents, notably in bowling, is adaptability. Youth bowlers are more likely to succeed in competitive situations if they can quickly modify their tactics and strategies in response to shifting task demands, such as shifting lane conditions or opponent plans. By including drills and activities that imitate a variety of task demands and fostering problem-solving and decision-making skills during practice, coaches can promote adaptability in young bowlers.

Example: Youth bowlers can learn to adapt their tactics and strategies by participating in practice sessions that imitate various lane conditions, such as dry or oily lanes. Additionally, they might encourage young bowlers to try out various tactics during practice to improve their adaptability to various circumstances, such as altering their approach angle or ball speed.

d) Performing under Pressure: Athletes in the sport of bowling must be able to perform under pressure, especially in competitive situations. Young bowlers who can remain composed, and focused, and perform at a high level under pressure are more likely to succeed. Youth bowlers' coaches can help them develop psychological strategies for performing under pressure, such as goal-setting, visualization, self-talk, and stress management methods.

Example: Youth bowlers can learn to control their emotions and perform well under pressure by participating in pressure circumstances during practice sessions, such as simulated contests or high-pressure scenarios. In order to help young bowlers manage stress and preserve the quality of their play, they can also offer mental skills training, such as relaxation techniques or constructive self-talk strategies.

Points	Example of Bowler	Example of Coach's Way of Coaching	Steps	Strategies	Challenges	Strengths
Drive and Inspiration	A bowler inspired to improve and achieve high scores in competitions.	Recognizing and reinforcing the bowler's intrinsic motivation by setting challenging goals.	Creating a positive and supportive training environment.	Encouraging the bowler to set personal goals and providing positive reinforcement for achievements.	Addressing external factors that may affect the bowler's motivation, such as pressure from parents or peers.	Fosters enthusiasm, dedication, and self-drive in the bowler.
Self-Determination Theory	Bowlers who take ownership of their learning, set goals, and seek opportunities to improve.	Encouraging the bowler's autonomy and providing opportunities for self-directed learning.	Promoting autonomy and self-directed learning.	Supporting the bowlers in setting personal goals and making decisions related to their training.	Fostering a team culture that values autonomy and self-motivation.	Enhances motivation, engagement, and sense of accomplishment in the bowler.
Embracing Change	Bowlers who can adjust their technique and strategy to different lane conditions and pin placements.	Incorporating drills and exercises that simulate various lane conditions and challenging pin placements.	Simulating different lane conditions and pin placements in practice sessions.	Encouraging the bowlers to analyze and adapt their technique and strategy based on changing conditions.	Adapting to different oil patterns, lane surfaces, and pin placements in competitions.	Enhances competitiveness and performance in various bowling environments.
Performing under Pressure	A bowler who maintains focus, composure, and high-performance quality during competitive matches.	Developing psychological skills for performing under pressure, such as visualization and stress management techniques.	Teaching stress management techniques and mental preparation strategies.	Creating a competitive training environment that includes simulated pressure situations.	Performing under pressure in tournaments or important matches.	Enables consistent performance and success in high-pressure situations.

Table 9 – Janahi FRI Model – Foundation Stage

REFINEMENT – BUILDING BLOCKS:

a) Mastering the Craft through Practice: The FRI Model emphasizes the value of efficient practice in developing skills. Activities that are particular to bowling skills and are demanding, concentrated, and deliberate constitute effective practice. Deliberate practice, which entails setting precise goals, obtaining feedback, and making appropriate adjustments based on input to continuously improve performance, goes beyond merely repeating drills or exercises. Coaches may guarantee that young bowlers practice effectively by planning organized practice sessions that are specific to each bowler's needs.

Example: Coaches can create drills that concentrate on certain parts of bowlers' technique, such as accuracy, speed, or targeting. They can provide each bowler with clear objectives, feedback on how He did, and encouragement to make changes as a result in order to advance his abilities. To improve the transfer of skills from practice to competition, they can also include game-like scenarios, such as simulated competitions or drills that mirror competitive conditions.

b) Learn to perform: The FRI Model acknowledges the difference between performance and learning. Performance is the actual application of abilities in certain circumstances, such as contests, while learning is the acquisition or improvement of skills. Instead of only concentrating on performance outcomes, coaches should place a higher priority on building a learning-oriented environment that prioritizes skill acquisition.

Example: Youth bowlers can practice without worrying about making errors or doing poorly if coaches give them the chance to try out new tactics, strategies, and approaches. Instead of just concentrating on winning or losing in competitions, they can highlight the process of learning and progress. Additionally, they can offer help and feedback that is focused on learning and skill development rather than just performance outcomes.

c) Embracing Individual Progression in Learning: The FRI Model illustrates that improving one's bowling abilities is a non-linear process and that different people advance at various rates. Some bowlers may improve quickly at first, while others may advance more slowly until they make unexpected breakthroughs. The unique learning pace of each bowler should be acknowledged and respected by coaches, who should act patiently and understandingly.

Example: Coaches can create practice sessions that are tailored to the specific requirements of bowlers, offering varying degrees of difficulty and progressions according to their skill level and rate of learning. Even if tiny advancements and breakthroughs come about at different periods for many bowlers, they can still be supportive and encouraging.

d) Errors as Pathways to Improvement: The FRI Model recognizes that mistakes are an essential part of learning and that they can offer insightful feedback for development. Errors might point to areas that need improvement or adjusting to improve performance. Coaches should promote a positive attitude toward mistakes and see them as chances for growth and learning.

Example: Coaches can foster an environment where mistakes are viewed as chances for growth and learning rather than as failures. They can offer constructive criticism on blunders, assisting young bowlers in identifying their weak points and offering advice on how to strengthen them. They can also inspire bowlers to think back on their performance and use their mistakes as learning opportunities to improve their technique.

e) Perfecting (Error-Free) the Learning Process: Coaches may create a culture where mistakes are seen as opportunities for development and learning rather than failures. They can help young bowlers discover their weak points and provide guidance on how to enhance them by providing constructive criticism on errors. Additionally, they can encourage bowlers to reflect on their performance and use their blunders as opportunities to learn and advance their craft.

Example: With an emphasis on proper technique and motions, coaches can begin with simple practice drills and build up complexity and difficulty as bowlers advance. To make sure bowlers comprehend the proper motions and approaches, they can give explicit instructions and demonstrations. During practice, they can also offer rapid feedback and correction to stop mistakes from becoming ingrained habits. This strategy can aid young bowlers in building a strong foundation of proper movements and techniques, which can enhance their long-term skill development.

f) Mindful Instructional Approach: The FRI Model places a strong emphasis on the value of applying guidance and coaching feedback thoughtfully and strategically. The way that instructions and comments are given, as well as when they are given, have a big impact on how well people learn. To be as effective as possible and to avoid overwhelming or demotivating bowlers, coaches should be aware of these aspects.

Example: When giving directions and comments, coaches can adopt a learner-centered approach by taking each bowler's unique needs and preferences into account. They can speak in an upbeat and motivating manner, highlighting certain areas that require development and making practical ideas for change. To accommodate various learning styles, they can also employ a number of feedback techniques, including verbal, visual, and kinesthetic. In addition, instructors can promote self-evaluation and self-reflection, enabling bowlers to take charge of their own learning.

Points	Example of Bowler	Example of Coach's Way of Coaching	Steps	Strategies	Challenges	Strengths
Mastering the Craft through Practice	A bowler who engages in deliberate and focused practice sessions, working on specific skills and techniques.	Designing practice sessions that target specific skills and provide clear objectives and feedback.	Setting clear practice goals and objectives.	Structuring practice sessions that focus on specific aspects of technique, strategy, or mental skills.	Creating a practice routine and maintaining discipline and focus during training.	Enhances skill development and improves overall performance in bowling.
Learn to perform	A bowler who prioritizes learning and skill acquisition over immediate performance outcomes.	Encouraging the bowler to focus on learning and growth rather than being solely results-oriented.	Emphasizing the importance of skill development.	Promoting a growth mindset and embracing challenges as learning opportunities.	Managing the bowler's expectations and dealing with potential frustration from temporary setbacks.	Fosters a long-term perspective, resilience, and continuous improvement in the bowler.

Points	Example of Bowler	Example of Coach's Way of Coaching	Steps	Strategies	Challenges	Strengths
Embracing Individual Progression in Learning	A bowler who experiences periods of rapid improvement, plateaus, and occasional setbacks during skill development.	Providing guidance and support to navigate through different phases of skill development.	Recognizing that skill acquisition is not always a linear process.	Encouraging persistence and effort during plateaus or setbacks.	Managing the bowlers' motivation and keeping them engaged during challenging periods.	Enhances adaptability, resilience, and understanding of the learning process in the bowler.
Errors as Pathways to Improvement	A bowler who views errors as valuable feedback and opportunities for improvement.	Creating a safe and supportive learning environment where errors are embraced and used for learning.	Encouraging bowlers to analyze and learn from their mistakes.	Providing constructive feedback and guidance to help the bowler learn from errors.	Cultivating a growth mindset and overcoming the fear of making mistakes.	Fosters a culture of continuous improvement, learning, and skill refinement in the bowler.
Perfecting (Error-Free) the Learning Process	A bowler who engages in practice tasks that gradually increase in difficulty, minimizing errors during skill acquisition.	Implementing a systematic approach where the bowler is guided to minimize errors during practice.	Breaking down skills into smaller components and gradually increasing task difficulty.	Providing demonstrations, modeling, and guidance to ensure correct execution and minimize errors.	Balancing challenge and skill level to prevent frustration or overload.	Promotes efficient skill acquisition and reduces the likelihood of developing incorrect techniques or habits.
Mindful Instructional Approach	Bowlers who receive timely and specific instructions and feedback that enhance their understanding and performance.	Delivering concise and clear instructions and feedback tailored to the bowler's needs and skill level.	Providing instructions and feedback that focus on key aspects of technique and strategy.	Using guided discovery approaches to encourage the bowler to reflect and problem-solve.	Tailoring instructions and feedback to individual learning styles and preferences.	Enhances the bowler's technical understanding, decision-making, and self-correction abilities.

Table 10 – Janahi FRI Model – Refinement Stage

IMPLEMENTATION - Mastering Design

a) Bowlers Factors: The FRI Model takes into account the distinct qualities, advantages, and room for development that each bowler or team possesses and how those things affect his performance. To enhance skill development and improve overall performance, coaches must take these elements into account when planning practices and competitions.

Example: Coaches can evaluate the bowlers or teams' physical, technical, tactical, mental, and emotional qualities and create practice programs that cater to their individual needs. For instance, instructors can create drills that concentrate on enhancing aiming abilities for a bowler who struggles with accuracy. Coaches can create team-based drills that encourage collaboration and cohesion if a team has trouble communicating and working together.

b) Meeting the Challenge: The FRI Model recognizes that factors related to the bowling job, including lane conditions, pin location, and scoring systems, have a big impact on performance. In order to promote efficient skill learning, coaches should consider these task demands when planning practice sessions and competitions. This will help them create a setting that is both realistic and challenging.

Example: By reproducing lane conditions, changing pin placements, and employing scoring systems that resemble real competitions, coaches can recreate competitive conditions during practice. This can improve bowlers' performance in actual contests by teaching them to be flexible and perform well under a variety of task restrictions.

c) Environmental Factors: The FRI Model recognizes that the training environment—which includes both physical and social factors—can have a significant impact on both the learning process and performance outcomes. Coaches should work to create a motivating, encouraging, and inclusive training atmosphere that stimulates learning, develops motivation, and fosters personal growth.

Example: Bowlers can feel encouraged, appreciated, and driven when they train in a friendly and inclusive environment created by coaches. They can foster friendly relationships, foster teamwork, and give bowlers chances to share knowledge with one another. Additionally, coaches can make sure that the training space is secure, well-equipped, and supportive of learning. This includes maintaining the space's lighting, ventilation, and equipment.

Points	Example of Bowler	Example of Coach's Way of Coaching	Steps	Strategies	Challenges	Strengths
Bowlers Factors	Bowlers who recognize and leverage their own strengths and weaknesses, as well as the strengths and weaknesses of their team members.	Helping bowlers identify their strengths and weaknesses and understand the team dynamics.	Conducting individual and team assessments.	Assigning roles and responsibilities based on individual and team capabilities.	Balancing individual goals with team goals.	Fosters collaboration, team cohesion, and the utilization of each team member's strengths.
Meeting the Challenge	Bowlers adjust their technique and strategy based on the specific demands of the bowling task, such as lane conditions, pin placement, and scoring system.	Coaching bowlers to analyze and adapt their techniques and strategies to match the task demands.	Familiarizing bowlers with different lane conditions and target patterns.	Teaching bowlers how to adjust their line, speed, and ball selection based on the task demands.	Helping bowlers manage task-related frustrations or difficulties.	Enhances adaptability, versatility, and performance in various bowling conditions.
Environmental Factors	Bowlers who acknowledge the impact of the training environment, including physical and social factors, on their learning and performance.	Creating a positive and supportive training environment that fosters motivation and growth.	Designing training spaces that are conducive to learning and skill development.	Encouraging social support and teamwork among bowlers.	Dealing with distractions or external pressures during training or competitions.	Provides a supportive and inclusive environment that enhances learning and performance in bowlers.

Table 11 – Janahi FRI Model – Implementation Stage

The FRI Model for bowling emphasizes the significance of developing positive character traits in young bowlers and embraces important ideas like high-quality practice, the distinction between learning and performance, the non-linear nature of skill acquisition, the value of mistakes as learning opportunities, and the wise application of instructions and feedback. The model also emphasizes crucial design elements, such as team dynamics, task needs, and environmental issues. Coaches can foster a learning environment that fosters skill growth, adaptability, and outstanding performance in young bowlers by implementing these ideas into their coaching procedures.

Furthermore, the FRI Model acknowledges that young bowlers may have various degrees of drive, self-reliance, adaptability, and pressure tolerance. Because of this, coaches should modify their methods to fit the special requirements and features of each bowler, promoting his personal development.

Example: Coaches can help young bowlers become more motivated and self-reliant by using motivational techniques including goal-setting, reinforcement, and positive reinforcement. By exposing bowlers to diverse lane conditions, pin placements, and tournament forms, they can also foster adaptation by offering a challenge for them to adapt and modify their strategy. Coaches can also employ pressure training methods like mental skills training and simulated competition scenarios to help bowlers become resilient and perform well under pressure.

The FRI Model also places a strong emphasis on the importance of high-quality practice above sheer volume. It acknowledges that purposeful, focused, and demanding practice outperforms rote repetition in terms of skill development. Coaches must plan practice sessions that are interesting, useful, and specific to each bowler's needs.

Example: With specified objectives, feedback mechanisms, and progressions, coaches can design practice exercises that focus on particular technical, tactical, mental, or emotional components of bowling. Additionally, they can include simulations of actual competitive circumstances to encourage bowlers to use their talents in a real-world setting. Additionally, instructors should encourage bowlers to engage in reflective practice by encouraging them to evaluate their performance, create goals, and monitor their development. This will result in a higher degree of learning.

The importance of high-quality practice above mere quantity is another point made by the FRI Model. In comparison to mindless repetition, thoughtful, focused, and challenging practice improves skill development, the article notes. Coaches should create practice sessions that are interesting, useful, and tailored to each bowler's individual needs.

Example: In order to highlight distinct practice focuses at different phases of skill development, coaches can employ periodization or phased training methodologies. Additionally, they can regularly check on the development of the bowlers and modify practice schedules as necessary to account for any variations in performance. Additionally, coaches should stress the value of encouraging bowlers to adopt a growth mindset by urging them to see setbacks or mistakes as chances for learning and improvement rather than as failures.

The FRI Model also recognizes that learning and performance do not follow a straight line. While honing their skills, bowlers may go through phases of quick improvement, plateaus, or brief setbacks. To help bowlers successfully move through these phases, coaches must comprehend and manage these performance changes while offering the right support and advice. The FRI Model acknowledges that mistakes are a necessary component of learning and can act as helpful building blocks for advancement. Bowlers should be allowed to make mistakes and learn from them without fear of repercussions or criticism if coaches can provide a safe and encouraging learning environment for them.

Example: Coaches can employ errorless learning strategies that gradually increase the level of difficulty while minimizing errors and keeping a high level of enthusiasm and involvement from the bowlers. They can also offer constructive criticism that emphasizes the process rather than the result, pointing out areas for improvement and offering solutions. Coaches can also motivate bowlers to think back on their mistakes, pinpoint the causes, and come up with remedies to avoid making the same errors again.

The FRI Model for bowling focuses on key ideas like high-quality practice, the distinction between learning and performance, the non-linear nature of skill acquisition, the value of errors as learning opportunities, and the prudent use of instructions and feedback. It also emphasizes the importance of desirable characteristics in young bowlers. Additionally, it emphasizes important design principles like team dynamics, task needs, and environmental issues. Coaches may create a supportive, interesting, and productive learning environment that promotes skill development, flexibility, and outstanding performance in young bowlers by implementing these principles into their coaching procedures.

Challenge Point Model (SPM)

In the area of motor learning and skill development, Mark Guadagnoli and Tim Lee created the Challenge Point Model (CPM), a theoretical framework. According to this paradigm, the perfect challenge point is reached when the level of difficulty of a practice activity matches the skill level of the learner. Learning may be hindered by tasks that are too simple or complex. The CPM is frequently used by coaches to create practice sessions that efficiently improve skill development in a variety of sports, including bowling.

The significance of identifying the ideal challenge point for each individual bowler is one of the CPM's core ideas. Practice exercises for beginner bowlers should be reasonably simple to let them concentrate on the core technique and form. For instance, trainers may set up short-range targets or utilize lighter balls to assist beginners in developing fundamental throwing and aiming techniques without overwhelming them with difficult tasks.

Example 1: Practice activities should be created to give an adequate amount of challenge that motivates intermediate bowlers—those who have mastered some fundamental techniques but may still have difficulty with accuracy and consistency—to enhance their performance. For instance, to provide intermediate bowlers with a challenge and aid in the development of their accuracy and decision-making abilities, coaches may set up intermediate-distance targets or utilize medium-weight balls in addition to varying the lane conditions or pin placements.

Example 2: Advanced bowlers who have mastered the fundamentals and are striving for high-performance levels require practice activities that are extremely difficult to push them beyond their comfort zones and encourage further skill development. To mimic the competitive situations that experienced bowlers could face in actual games, coaches may set up targets that are farther out, utilize heavier balls, or build more complicated lane conditions. As they seek to play at their best under challenging circumstances, advanced bowlers can use this to hone their technique, decision-making, and adaptation skills.

BALANCING CHALLENGES AND SKILLS FOR ENGAGING FLOW:

When the amount of challenge in the bowling game meets the player's skill level, a feeling of equilibrium results, and flow state develops. Elite athletes may exhibit this when they take part in competitive events or face opponents that challenge them to use their cutting-edge abilities and plans to succeed.

8% CHALLENGE (FLOW STATE) - BOWLING EXCELLENCE IN PRACTICE:

Practice Challenge: Skilled bowlers dedicate their practice sessions to challenging themselves by setting up lane conditions and targets that are precisely 8% harder than their current skill level. This slight increase in challenge during practice pushes them to focus and perform at their best, resulting in a flow state as they adapt to the elevated difficulty. These deliberate practice sessions help them sharpen their skills and maintain their excellence.

15% CHALLENGE (SLIGHTLY OVERWHELMED) - UPCOMING BOWLER'S TRAINING:

Training for Improvement: Young and aspiring bowlers undergoes training sessions that intentionally introduce challenges 15% greater than their current skills and abilities. These training sessions involve practicing on challenging lane conditions, facing opponents with higher skill levels, and working on advanced techniques. While they may initially feel slightly overwhelmed, these training sessions are designed to push them to improve, encouraging them to put in extra effort and learn from experienced bowlers to enhance their skills.

0% CHALLENGE (BOREDOM) - ROUTINE PRACTICE:

Routine Practice for an Experienced Bowler: Experienced bowlers engages in practice sessions that lack any additional challenge compared to their usual training routine. These routine practice sessions involve familiar drills, exercises, and lane conditions that do not stimulate their abilities or provide any new challenges. As a result, they may experience boredom and a lack of engagement during these practice sessions, highlighting the importance of introducing variety and challenges to keep their practice engaging and productive.

Challenge Point Model in the context of bowling:

Customizing practice tasks - The Challenge Point Model highlights the significance of tailoring practice assignments to offer bowlers the best possible challenge point. Tasks for newcomers or bowlers with lesser ability levels ought to get progressively harder as their abilities develop. Conversely, more experienced bowlers need practice exercises that push their limits and test their current skills while remaining at a manageable degree of difficulty.

For example, for bowlers who lack motivation, for instance, coaches can create practice activities that are entertaining, interesting, and compatible with their tastes and preferences. To increase motivation and involvement in practice, this can involve utilizing interactive games, drills with prizes, or introducing team competitions.

Promoting Adaptability: Practice drills should replicate various bowling environments that competitors might have. Variations in target designs, lane conditions, or bowling ball selection are examples of this. Bowlers can improve their capacity to modify their methods, decision-making, and strategies in response to shifting situations during gameplay by being exposed to a variety of conditions during practice.

For example, Coaches can design practice sessions that require bowlers to use a variety of lane conditions, including dry, greasy, or shifting lane patterns. Bowlers may be forced to adjust their technique, ball speed, and target alignment as a result, which may help them become more adaptable.

Managing Errors: According to the Challenge Point Model, mistakes are seen as worthwhile learning experiences. Coaches ought to create practice drills that let bowlers make mistakes and grow from them. These mistakes give bowlers feedback to assist them in pinpointing areas where they may improve, which promotes in-depth learning and skill development.

For example, Coaches may purposefully design drills that are just a little bit challenging for the bowlers' current ability level, which could result in some mistakes. This can force bowlers to think critically, evaluate their performance, and devise plans to fix their mistakes, which will advance their expertise.

Task Constraints and Environment Constraints: Designing practice activities that correspond with the ideal challenge point for bowlers requires taking into account task restrictions, such as distance, target patterns, and lane conditions, as well as environmental constraints, such as illumination, noise, and distractions.

For example, to test a bowler's accuracy, judgment, and adaptability, coaches can modify the lane conditions or the target's distance. In order to aid bowlers in better adjusting to in-game circumstances, coaches can also set up a practice environment that replicates competition settings, with comparable lighting and noise levels.

Feedback and Instruction: The Challenge Point Model's crucial components are instruction and feedback. Feedback from coaches should be immediate and precise, highlighting important areas of technique, strategy, and decision-making. Additionally, guided discovery methods can be used to help bowlers evaluate their performance and pinpoint their weak points. Instructions should be brief, understandable, and customized to the learning preferences and ability level of the bowlers.

For example, during practice sessions, instructors can give feedback that highlights the bowlers' technique, strategy, and decision-making strengths and areas for development. Additionally, they can employ guided discovery methods to assist bowlers in understanding their performance better, such as by posing open-ended questions or fostering self-reflection.

Points	Example of Bowler	Example of Coach's Way of Coaching	Steps	Strategies	Challenges	Strengths
Customizing Practice Tasks	Beginner bowlers gradually progressing from straight shots to hook shots as their skills improve.	Adjusting practice tasks to match the bowler's skill progression, gradually increasing the difficulty.	Assessing the bowler's current skill level.	Designing practice tasks that align with the bowler's skill progression.	Balancing the challenge level to ensure it is both stimulating and achievable for the bowler.	Promotes skill development and gradual improvement, preventing tasks from being too easy or too difficult.
Promoting Adaptability	Bowlers practicing on various lane conditions, such as dry or oily surfaces, to develop the ability to adjust their technique.	Introducing bowlers to different lane conditions during practice sessions.	Providing a variety of lane conditions and target patterns.	Encouraging bowlers to adapt their technique and strategy based on changing conditions.	Ensuring the practice conditions are representative of real-game scenarios.	Enhances bowler's adaptability and ability to perform well under different bowling conditions.
Managing Errors	Bowlers intentionally making mistakes during practice and analyzing them to improve their technique.	Creating practice tasks that allow bowlers to make errors and learn from them.	Encouraging bowlers to reflect on their performance and identify areas for improvement.	Providing constructive feedback on errors and guiding bowlers on how to correct them.	Creating a safe and supportive environment where bowlers feel comfortable making mistakes.	Helps bowlers learn from their mistakes, leading to skill improvement and increased self-awareness.
Task Constraints and Environment Constraints	Bowlers adjusting their speed, line, and ball selection based on the specific lane conditions and pin placement.	Manipulating task constraints, such as lane conditions and target patterns, to challenge the bowlers.	Modifying the lane conditions, pin placement, and target patterns during practice.	Creating distractions or variations in the practice environment to simulate real-game conditions.	Adapting the practice environment to align with the optimal challenge point for the bowlers.	Enhances bowlers' ability to perform well under different task and environmental constraints.

Points	Example of Bowler	Example of Coach's Way of Coaching	Steps	Strategies	Challenges	Strengths
Feedback and Instruction	Bowlers receiving timely and specific feedback on their technique, strategy, and decision-making during practice.	Providing feedback that focuses on key aspects of technique, strategy, and decision-making.	Offering constructive feedback based on observation and analysis.	Using guided discovery approaches to encourage self-reflection and problem-solving.	Delivering feedback and instructions that are tailored to the individual bowler's needs.	Facilitates skill development and promotes effective learning through targeted feedback and instruction.

Table 12 – Challenge Point Model for Bowling

The Challenge Point Model provides a thorough framework for planning bowling practice sessions, taking into account elements like the skill levels of bowlers, their motivation, adaptability, and the importance of mistakes in the learning process. Coaches can improve skill acquisition and foster performance excellence in bowlers by creating practice assignments, managing errors, taking into account task and environment limits, and offering effective feedback and guidance. It is vital to keep in mind that highly competent youth bowlers may lack motivation if the challenge is set too low, and low-skilled youth bowlers may have trouble staying motivated if the goal is set too high due to their limited success in reaching the training objectives.

THE OPTIMAL DEVELOPMENT
PLAN FOR BOWLING

Bowling is a much-liked sport that demands excellent talent, technique, and strategy to play well. The object of the game is to knock down as many pins as you can by rolling a ball down a path. Despite the fact that it may seem like a straightforward sport, mastering bowling takes extensive practice and commitment. Bowlers need a thorough growth plan that addresses all facets of their game if they want to improve to the level of a world champion. This introduction will discuss the requirements for producing a world-class bowler as well as the distinction between a development plan and the Long-Term Athlete Development (LTAD) model.

What it takes to reach world standard:

A bowler needs a blend of technical, physical, and mental qualities to attain global standards. Physical and technical skills both apply to the bowler's strength, speed, and flexibility. Technical skills are the ability to roll the ball consistently and accurately. Focus, concentration, and the capacity to handle stress are examples of mental skills, in contrast. A bowler requires an organized, thorough growth plan in order to improve these talents. All facets of the sport should be covered in this plan, including technical instruction, physical conditioning, mental preparation, and competition strategy. The strategy must be created to meet each bowler's specific requirements and to bring out the best in him.

The difference between a development plan and LTAD:

A development plan, while distinct from the LTAD model, is crucial for a bowler's growth and improvement. LTAD is a methodical, all-encompassing approach to athlete development that considers the special qualities of each stage of an athlete's growth. It acknowledges that athletes have various rates of physical, mental, and emotional development and that their training regimens must take this into account.

The long-term approach to athlete development, or LTAD, considers the athlete's entire lifespan. It begins with athletes' first exposure to the sport and lasts until they stop participating in competitive play. LTAD understands that as athletes' needs evolve, their training and competition schedules must also do the same.

It takes a lot of time, commitment, and work to develop into an elite-level bowler. It is a journey that starts with understanding the fundamentals and progressively moves on to more advanced abilities and techniques. Bowlers must create a thorough plan that emphasizes both physical and mental preparation, as well as strategic planning, in order to succeed. In this literature, we will look at the approaches taken to begin a bowler's journey from fundamentals to top level, the preparedness needed, and the perseverance needed to succeed. Bowlers must be physically prepared before they can start their trip to elite-level bowling. As a result, they must be proficient in the fundamentals of the sport, such as good stance, footwork, ball delivery, and targeting. In order to do these tasks regularly and successfully, they ought to have also acquired the requisite strength, stamina, and flexibility. Bowlers should participate in consistent training and conditioning regimens that emphasize enhancing their level of general fitness in order to be physically prepared. To enhance their performance, they should also focus on their particular weak points, such as grip power or balance. To avoid injury and keep performance at its highest level, it's also critical to maintain a healthy diet and receive enough rest and recuperation time.

Bowlers need to be mentally prepared for the trip to elite-level bowling in addition to being physically ready. This entails cultivating mental abilities including resilience, attention, concentration, and visualization. Additionally, bowlers need to be able to control their emotions and maintain their motivation despite defeats or difficulties. Bowlers should do regular mental exercises and visualization techniques to improve their mental toughness. They should also attempt to cultivate a growth mentality and encourage self-talk, which can aid them in overcoming challenges and failures. Bowlers can benefit from practicing mindfulness techniques like meditation or deep breathing to stay concentrated and composed under pressure.

Here is a brief explanation of each stage in relation to bowling:

- **PLAYFUL DEVELOPMENT:** In this phase, emphasis is placed on introducing young athletes to bowling in a friendly and secure setting. The focus is on fostering basic movement abilities via play and discovery, including balance, coordination, and agility.

- **STAGE 1 – FUN AND FITNESS PHASE:** The main emphasis is still on having fun and encouraging fitness while learning the fundamental technical and strategic aspects of bowling. Athletes pick up proper ball-throwing technique as well as the fundamentals of competition and scoring.

- **STAGE 2 - DEVELOPMENT PHASE:** Athletes now continue to refine their technical abilities while concentrating on enhancing their physical capabilities. They increase the amount of physical activity they do in their routines, including strength training and aerobic conditioning.

- **STAGE 3 - TRAIN TO PERFORM:** Athletes begin to specialize in a single area of the sport, such as strike shooting, spare shooting, or lane play, at this stage. They concentrate on mastering the techniques and methods of bowling. In order to perform better, they also endeavor to develop their mental faculties, such as concentration and focus.

- **STAGE 4 - DOMESTIC AND NATIONAL COMPETITIONS:** Athletes start competing at this point in local, regional, and national events to gain experience and hone their competitive abilities. They continue to hone their technical and tactical skills while also emphasizing their physical and psychological competitive preparation.

- **STAGE 5 - OPEN CHAMPIONSHIPS AND ZONE STANDARDS:** Athletes compete in open championships during this phase and seek to meet zone criteria, which are particular performance standards needed to compete at higher levels of competition. They put a lot of emphasis on competing against top athletes and expanding their international experience.

- **STAGE 6 - WORLD ELITE LEVEL:** Athletes compete at the Olympic Games and other top international competitions at this point because they are among the best in the world at what they do. To ensure their long-term success in the sport, they continue to hone their skills and talents while putting an emphasis on measures for injury prevention and recovery.

PHYSICAL DEVELOPMENT (MATURATION)

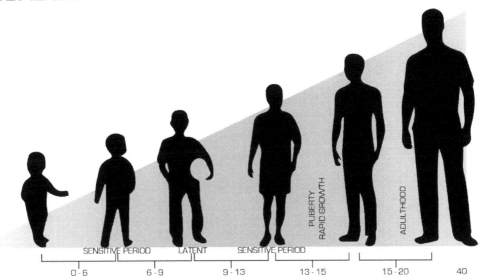

Different phases in a precise order can be found in individuals physical development but they happen in unique schedule. Development is not continuous but can stop at times and then jump to the next stage

PLAYFUL DEVELOPMENT

The primary goal of the PLAYFUL DEVELOPMENT stage is to foster a love of physical health in children by getting them involved in a variety of activities. Learning basic movement techniques and using them in a play-based context is the main objective. Children have the opportunity to be physically active every day through activities including scheduled classes and games, as well as unstructured play at home, school, childcare facilities, etc. Structured play should last at least 30 minutes per day for toddlers and 60 minutes per day for preschoolers. Every day, unstructured play might last anywhere from 60 minutes to several hours. The development of basic movement abilities like agility, balance, coordination, and walking should be promoted by involvement in a range of activities. While young children may enjoy bowling for entertainment at birthday parties or family outings, it is not advised for them to participate in an organized bowling program until they have passed Stage 1 of the program.

STAGE 1 – FUN & FITNESS PHASE

For kids, having fun and encouraging fitness remain the top priorities, along with developing the basic movement techniques necessary for sporting success. Children and youth bowlers should take part in a variety of sports to improve their general fitness because they are at a prime age for learning movement abilities.

Adult beginners who engage in other forms of exercise three or four times per week might also wish to give bowling a shot once or twice per week. These individuals will learn the fundamental abilities necessary to enjoy and play the game in their first year of bowling.

Bowlers with intellectual or physical limitations can need more time to develop specific technical skills and more opportunities to practice them. Given that bowlers with disabilities frequently fall into the "overweight" area on the Body Mass Index (BMI) scale, it is crucial to include exercise activities that may be done on the lanes or outside the bowling center to advance general health and wellness.

Roles Structure

Coaches are essential to the growth of bowlers, and they have a number of important duties to fulfill. First and foremost, coaches need to make sure the bowler is properly fitted for the ball. To play at their peak and avoid injuries, bowlers must have equipment that is well-suited. To maintain their coaching abilities and stay current with the most recent methods and ideas, coaches should also take part in coach education programs, such as the 5 or community initiation coach education as part of the National Coaching Certification Program.

If a bowler is having trouble with a specific talent, instructors should also incorporate drills and instructional strategies. They should be able to spot any places where a bowler could want extra aid and give focused teaching to assist in overcoming obstacles and enhancing performance.

Kids' growth is extremely important, and it is also influenced by their parents and their support system. They ought to be respectful of the coach's influence on their child's growth and advancement as a bowler. It's critical for parents to support their child's involvement in a bowling program by adhering to its guidelines, such as its attendance requirements, practice schedules, and restrictions.

The bowlers themselves should put fun and enjoyment of the game first. Since bowling is a recreational activity, having fun while playing the game should always come first. If bowlers need further coaching or instruction to advance their abilities, they should be proactive in asking for it through the bowling center.

The employees at the bowling centers can help bowlers progress as well. They should help bowlers choose their equipment to ensure a good fit, as well as offer the right programs and training to boost participation. The employees of bowling centers should be dedicated to the overall promotion of bowling for the future by keeping a professional and businesslike demeanor, offering encouragement to bowlers and instructors, and making sure that all lanes adhere to certification and sanctioning requirements for fair and safe play.

The following criteria can be used to determine when a bowler is prepared to advance to the Development Phase: finishing three games, hitting the head pin consistently (30% of the time), keeping the ball on the lane (30% of the time), and making 5-10% of spares. These clues point to the bowlers having reached a foundational level of proficiency and being prepared to advance to the next phase of their bowling development.

Cognitive And Psychological Changes:

In **Stage 1** - Cognitive and psychological aspects in a kid's brain are primarily focused on foundational development and building a positive attitude toward the sport. Here are the key changes and improvements in these aspects at this stage:

1. **Introduction to Bowling Knowledge:**
   - Kids acquire basic knowledge about the rules, equipment, and techniques of bowling. They become familiar with the terminology and scoring system.

2. **Interest and Curiosity:**
   - Kids develop an initial interest and curiosity about the sport. They are eager to learn and explore the game.

3. **Positive Attitude:**
   - Kids are encouraged to develop a positive attitude toward bowling. Coaches and mentors create a supportive and enjoyable environment, promoting a love for the sport.

4. **Basic Problem-Solving Skills:**
   - Kids begin to develop basic problem-solving skills related to executing shots and targeting pins. They learn to make simple adjustments based on their early experiences.

5. **Teamwork and Social Skills:**
   - Kids in group settings start to develop teamwork and social skills, which are essential for participation in recreational and competitive bowling.

6. **Attention and Focus:**
   - Attention span and focus are enhanced as kids learn to concentrate on their shots and observe the results.

7. **Goal Setting:**
   - Kids are introduced to the concept of goal setting, even if it's at a basic level. They may set goals related to improving their accuracy or achieving a specific score.

8. **Positive Reinforcement:**
   - Kids receive positive reinforcement from coaches and mentors, reinforcing their self-esteem and self-efficacy. This helps build confidence in their abilities.

9. **Emotional Regulation:**
   - Kids start learning how to manage emotions related to success and failure. They develop resilience to handle the ups and downs of the game.

10. **Self-Identity as a Bowler:**
    - Kids begin to form a self-identity as a bowler. They see themselves as part of the bowling community and identify with the sport.

11. **Introduction to Competition:**
    - Some kids may have their first experiences with friendly, low-pressure competitions. This introduction to competition can foster a sense of sportsmanship.

12. **Intrinsic Motivation:**
    - Kids may start to discover intrinsic motivation, finding enjoyment in the process of learning and playing rather than solely focusing on outcomes.

In Stage 1, the cognitive and psychological aspects are centered on building a strong foundation and fostering a love for the sport. Kids develop the basic skills and mindset necessary to continue their bowling journey. The emphasis is on creating a positive and supportive environment, encouraging curiosity and a sense of belonging to the bowling community. These early developments lay the groundwork for future stages of improvement and competition.

Neurological Development:

In **Stage 1** -, kids are primarily focused on having fun, encouraging fitness, and developing basic movement techniques. The neurological changes and improvements inside the athlete's body at this stage are more related to general motor development, spatial awareness, and the foundational skills necessary for bowling. Here are some key neurological aspects to consider:

1. **Motor Skills Development:**
   - Kid in this stage are still refining their motor skills, including balance, coordination, and fine motor control. These improvements lay the foundation for executing bowling techniques.

2. **Spatial Awareness:**
   - Spatial awareness is crucial for understanding the bowling lane, pin placement, and the trajectory of the bowling ball. Kids develop spatial intelligence as they practice their shots.

3. **Cognitive Skills:**
   - Cognitive development plays a role in understanding and following the rules of the game, tracking scores, and making basic strategic decisions.

4. **Visual Perception:**
   - Kids enhance their visual perception as they focus on aligning themselves with the target, identifying their bowling stance, and tracking the movement of the bowling ball.

5. **Sensory Integration:**
   - As they practice, bowlers integrate sensory information from their bodies and the environment. This includes feedback from their muscles, joints, and visual cues to refine their movements.

6. **Concentration and Attention:**
   - Learning to maintain focus during a game is essential for kids. This is an early development of attention control and concentration.

7. **Hand-Eye Coordination:**
   - Developing hand-eye coordination is fundamental for releasing the ball accurately. Kids improve their ability to synchronize their hand movements with their visual perception.

8. **Balance and Posture:**
   - Balance and posture are essential for maintaining a consistent approach and delivery. Improvements in these areas ensure a stable and controlled release of the bowling ball.

9. **Memory and Learning:**
   - Basic memory and learning processes are involved in remembering the rules and techniques of bowling, as well as recalling previous experiences to adjust their performance.

10. **Emotional Regulation:**

   - Learning to handle the emotional aspects of competition, such as stress, excitement, and disappointment, contributes to emotional regulation and resilience.

At this early stage, the neurological changes are foundational and serve as building blocks for the more advanced skills and techniques that will be developed in the later stages of a bowler's career. Kids build a strong neurological base, laying the groundwork for more complex neurological enhancements in the following stages.

Brain Regions And Cognitive Functions Development:

1. **Spatial Information:**

   - During this stage, kids are in the early phases of developing spatial awareness and sensory-motor coordination.

   - Basic spatial cues, such as lane orientation and the position of pins, are processed in the brain.

   - Bowlers learn to align themselves with the lane and develop a basic understanding of the physical aspects of the game.

2. **White Matter (WM):**

   - White matter tracts are in the early stages of forming connections related to sensory-motor integration and spatial perception.

   - Basic neural pathways are established for processing sensory input and initiating motor responses during bowling.

3. **Motor Cortex:**

   - The motor cortex is engaged in the foundational stages of motor skill development.

   - Kids are refining basic motor skills necessary for a bowling approach and release.

4. **Somatosensory Cortex:**

   - The somatosensory cortex processes basic tactile and proprioceptive feedback from the body's movements.

   - Kids are learning to interpret sensory input related to their body's positioning and balance during bowling.

5. **Superior Parietal Lobule (SPL):**

   - The SPL is involved in basic sensory integration and spatial orientation.

   - Kids are developing rudimentary spatial awareness and orientation within the bowling environment.

6. **Inferior Occipitofrontal Fasciculus (IOFF):**

   - IOFF pathways support the early stages of visual perception and cognitive functions relevant to bowling.

   - Kids are forming basic connections for visual processing related to the sport.

7. **Intraparietal Sulcus (IPS):**

   - The IPS plays a role in elementary spatial and numerical processing.

   - Kids are developing basic skills for perceiving spatial relationships and understanding simple numerical concepts relevant to bowling.

8. **Precuneus:**

   - The precuneus contributes to the early stages of self-awareness and visual imagery.

   - Kids are beginning to build self-awareness and visualize bowling actions.

During the **FUN & FITNESS PHASE**, the focus is on introducing kids to the basic elements of the sport, and their brain regions and cognitive functions are in the initial stages of development. As they progress through the subsequent stages, these neural circuits and cognitive skills will become more refined and specialized, contributing to their growth as bowlers.

Hormones Development:

During **Stage 1 (6-9 years old)**, kid are at an early developmental phase, and hormonal changes are relatively stable, with hormone levels within typical ranges for their age group. The focus during this stage is on physical growth and development, and kid are not experiencing significant hormonal changes related to puberty. Here's an overview of the key hormones and their characteristics during this stage:

1. **Testosterone and Estrogen**: At this stage, kid's testosterone and estrogen levels are at their baseline. These sex hormones are responsible for the development of male and female secondary sexual characteristics during puberty. Since kid in this age group haven't reached puberty, their levels of testosterone and estrogen are low.

2. **Cortisol**: Cortisol, often referred to as the "stress hormone," plays a role in regulating energy metabolism and responding to physical stress. While cortisol is produced in response to stress, exercise, and training, kid's cortisol levels are relatively stable and not significantly impacted by sports activities.

3. **Growth Hormone (GH)**: GH is crucial for tissue growth, repair, and recovery. During this stage, GH levels are primarily influenced by overall growth and development. GH plays a role in normal childhood growth, but it is not subject to significant fluctuations in response to exercise or sports training.

4. **Insulin**: Insulin regulates blood sugar levels and nutrient uptake by cells. While insulin is involved in energy metabolism, it operates within typical ranges for kid, and they generally do not experience significant fluctuations in insulin levels due to sports activities.

5. **Epinephrine (Adrenaline)** and **Norepinephrine**: These hormones are released in response to stress and exercise, increasing heart rate and preparing the body for physical activity. Kid experience small fluctuations in these hormones during exercise, but they are not at the same level of hormonal response seen in adults.

6. **Thyroid Hormones (T3 and T4)**: Thyroid hormones are important for regulating metabolism and energy production. In kid, thyroid hormone levels are relatively stable and primarily driven by normal growth and development.

7. **Insulin-like Growth Factor-1 (IGF-1)**: IGF-1 is produced in response to GH and is crucial for muscle growth and repair. During this stage, kid's IGF-1 levels are primarily influenced by overall growth, and exercise-related fluctuations are minor.

8. **Aldosterone**: Aldosterone regulates electrolyte balance. Kid generally have stable aldosterone levels not significantly influenced by sports activities.

9. **Adiponectin and Leptin**: Adiponectin and leptin play roles in fat metabolism and appetite regulation. These hormones function within normal ranges for kid, and exercise-induced changes are minor.

10. **Melatonin**: Melatonin is important for regulating sleep patterns, which is essential for recovery and development. At this stage, melatonin helps establish healthy sleep patterns necessary for growth.

During Stage 1 (6-9 years old), the primary focus is on overall physical growth, skill development, and fostering a love for sports. Hormonal changes related to sports activities are minimal, and fluctuations are within the typical ranges seen in kid of this age. The emphasis is on creating a supportive and enjoyable environment for young athletes.

Technical Skills - Main Checklist Of Stage 1 Bowlers

The sport of bowling calls for both physical and mental agility. Kids need to have a firm grasp of the game at this point, be able to use the right tactics, and have a reliable warm-up regimen in order to perform well. The bullet points and headlines pertaining to bowling techniques and skills are shown below.

In the early stages of learning, kids are introduced to a range of fundamental technical skills to build a strong foundation. The Bowling Approach Checklist ensures they start from the right position, understanding where to stand on the approach and the concept of walking towards the foul line. It emphasizes taking small, controlled steps to the target, building directional awareness, and instilling the basic approach process.

When it comes to the Swing Checklist, kids are taught to develop a gentle and controlled arm swing. The focus is on a straight, pendulum-like motion that enables them to guide the bowling ball effectively. As grip and posture are critical components, beginners learn the importance of a proper grip, basic hand positioning, and a relaxed grip to maintain control. For posture, the emphasis is on a simple stance with feet shoulder-width apart, ensuring balance throughout the approach.

The Ball Delivery Checklist focuses on controlled steps during the approach, aiming towards the pins, and gently releasing the ball while maintaining consistent delivery direction. This helps kids get accustomed to the mechanics of the actual delivery process. Stance plays a pivotal role in their development, where they are encouraged to adopt a starting stance that is comfortable and balanced, with an understanding of proper foot positioning and alignment.

Timing and Body Alignment are integrated into their skill set as well. Kids are guided towards understanding the timing of their approach and how it synchronizes with their swing. This introduces them to a basic rhythm in their bowling routine. In terms of body alignment, the focus is on facing the pins during the approach and aligning their body with the target. The goal is to keep this aspect simple, emphasizing alignment with the target area.

The Upper Body Checklist concentrates on maintaining a relaxed and steady upper body during the approach. Young kids also develop a basic pre-shot routine or setup. They grasp the guiding role of the upper body in the delivery process. As for the Lower Body Checklist, beginners work on taking small, controlled steps to ensure balance and stability in the lower body. Achieving a simple and balanced finish position at the foul line completes this checklist.

By covering these essential technical skills, kids in the early stages of bowling are given a structured and progressive approach to their development. The primary objective is to provide a positive and enjoyable learning experience while instilling the core skills necessary for a lifelong journey in the sport of bowling.

Bowling Technical Skills (Stage 1) Checklist:

Bowling Approach Checklist for Very Beginner Young Kids:

- **Step Placement:** Understand how to stand in a designated starting position.
- **Approach Awareness:** Learn the concept of walking towards the foul line.
- **Steady Steps:** Practice taking small and controlled steps during the approach.
- **Directional Awareness:** Begin to focus on walking towards the pins or target area.

Swing Checklist for Very Beginner Young Kids:

- **Gentle Swing:** Develop a gentle and controlled arm swing.
- **Straight Swing:** Understand the need for a straight and smooth swing motion.
- **Pendulum Motion:** Begin to mimic a pendulum-like swing.

Grip and Posture Checklist for Very Beginner Young Kids:

- **Proper Grip:** Learn to hold the bowling ball correctly.
- **Hand Positioning:** Understand basic hand positioning and ball grip.
- **Relaxed Grip:** Focus on maintaining a relaxed grip for control.
- **Basic Posture:** Begin to learn a basic stance with feet shoulder-width apart.
- **Balance:** Practice balance during the approach.

Ball Delivery Checklist for Very Beginner Young Kids:

- **Controlled Steps:** Learn to take small and controlled steps toward the foul line.
- **Aiming:** Understand the concept of aiming or targeting towards the pins.
- **Gentle Release:** Begin to learn to release the ball gently and smoothly.
- **Directional Consistency:** Practice consistent delivery direction.

Stance Checklist for Very Beginner Young Kids:

- **Starting Stance:** Develop a basic and comfortable starting stance.
- **Foot Position:** Understand the role of the feet in the stance.
- **Simple Stance:** Practice a simple and stable stance with feet parallel.

Timing Checklist for Very Beginner Young Kids:

- **Approach Timing:** Begin to understand the timing of the approach and the swing.
- **Synchronized Steps:** Focus on synchronizing steps with the arm swing.
- **Basic Rhythm:** Develop a basic rhythm and coordination in the approach and delivery.

Body Alignment Checklist for Very Beginner Young Kids:

- **Facing the Pins:** Learn to face the pins or target area during the approach.
- **Alignment Awareness:** Begin to understand the importance of aligning the body with the target.
- **Simplicity:** Emphasize simplicity and alignment with the target.

Upper Body Checklist for Very Beginner Young Kids:

- **Relaxed Upper Body:** Practice maintaining a relaxed and steady upper body during the approach.
- **Pre-Shot Routine:** Develop a simple pre-shot routine or setup.
- **Guiding Role:** Understand the role of the upper body in guiding the ball.

Lower Body Checklist for Very Beginner Young Kids:

- **Controlled Steps:** Work on taking small and controlled steps during the approach.
- **Balance and Stability:** Practice balance and stability in the lower body.
- **Finish Position:** Focus on achieving a simple and balanced finish position at the foul line.

This checklist is intended to provide young kids with a structured and progressive approach to developing their bowling skills. The emphasis should always be on creating a positive and enjoyable learning experience.

STAGE 2 – DEVELOPMENT PHASE

Depending on when they begin bowling, young teenagers in the learn-to-bowl stage might be of any age, from young children to adults. The main goal of this stage is to advance the fundamental abilities acquired in the stage before and to learn more advanced technical abilities and strategies as the young teenager gains experience. Additionally, young teenagers will learn about the psychological preparation needed for practice and participation in regional leagues. Adult bowlers can compete in events as well. As young teenagers advance through this level, they may decide to purchase their own equipment as they learn how to choose the best gear for comfort and game improvement.

Young teenagers in their teens who have not yet hit puberty are still in a great time to learn sports skills. In order to avoid becoming overly specialized in bowling, it is crucial for them to keep playing a range of sports. Adult bowlers should actively participate in league play and partake in additional off-lane physical activity including aerobic, strength, and flexibility training, or other sports. The choice between the competitive stream and Bowling for Life will need to be made by young teenagers at the conclusion of this phase.

Role Structure

Coaches are extremely important to the growth of young teenagers, so they should emphasize their education by taking part in coaching education and certification. Drills should be used to improve performance indicators by enhancing skills for greater consistency and proficiency. Coaches should also encourage frequent practice and involvement in league play, provide strength, flexibility, and stamina training that may be done at the bowling center, and offer advice to young teenagers on purchasing their own equipment. Encourage cross-training and involvement in other physical or sporting endeavors as well, putting more emphasis on the development process than just the young teenager's performance.

Young teenagers should recognize their coaches' contributions to their growth as bowlers and as members of their support systems. In addition to encouraging their child's participation, they should observe the program's rules and look for programs with trained coaches. It's crucial to keep a long-term perspective on the kid's bowling development and pay attention to the development process rather than just the result.

The bowlers themselves should make a commitment to enhancing their technical abilities and mental preparation during both league play and practice. It is advised to engage in consistent practice, which should include three non-scoring games for skill development per week and three league games. Year-round, they should do cross-training exercises to improve their strength, endurance, and flexibility, putting more of an emphasis on the development process than the final result.

For bowling-specific skill training, a ratio of one on-lane session to one league series is advised. Additionally, participating in another sport or physical activity four to six times per week for between thirty and sixty minutes can be good for overall development.

The employees at bowling centers should offer advice on choosing equipment to ensure that it fits bowlers properly, offer pertinent classes and programs to boost participation and promote bowling in a helpful and authoritative way. The overall health of bowlers can also be improved by providing healthy food options at the snack bar, such as fruits, vegetables, or low-fat yogurt. For a high standard of play to be maintained, it is crucial that all lanes adhere to certification and sanctioning requirements.

Having consistently struck the head pin 40% of the time, keeping the ball on the lane 60% of the time, finishing 6 games, making 15-20% of spares, and hitting a strike rate of 10% are all signs that a bowler is prepared to go to the Train to Perform stage.

National, provincial, and territorial bowling organizations ought to support initiatives like Goal to Bowl for school bowling, set and enforce minimum coaching standards for contestants in active leagues and tournament coaches, and collaborate with owners of bowling centers to encourage the employment of certified and experienced coaches.

Cognitive And Psychological Changes:

In **Stage 2** - Young teenagers continue to progress in their cognitive and psychological aspects, building upon the foundation established in Stage 1. At this stage, the focus shifts toward more advanced technical and strategic abilities, alongside mental preparation. Here are the changes and improvements in cognitive and psychological aspects in young teenagers at this stage:

1. **Advanced Bowling Knowledge:**

   - Young teenagers deepen their understanding of the sport, including advanced rules, lane conditions, and equipment. They become more knowledgeable about various strategies in bowling.

2. **Increased Passion and Dedication:**

   - Young teenagers develop a stronger passion for bowling and a higher level of dedication to improving their skills. They may spend more time practicing and engaging in the sport.

3. **Technical Skill Development:**

   - Young teenagers actively work on improving their bowling techniques, focusing on elements like hand placement, release, and lane adjustments. They develop a deeper understanding of lane conditions.

4. **Mental Preparation:**

   - Young teenagers learn about the psychological aspects of the game, including managing stress, concentration, and visualization techniques. Mental preparation becomes an integral part of their training.

5. **Strategic Thinking:**

   - Young teenagers begin to think strategically, considering lane patterns, adjustments, and their competition. They learn to make informed decisions during gameplay.

6. **Continued Team and Social Development:**

   - Young teenagers participating in team settings further develop teamwork and social skills. They bond with teammates and understand the importance of collaboration.

7. **Attention to Detail:**

   - Young teenagers pay closer attention to details in their game, such as targeting specific pins and achieving desired ball reactions. They refine their accuracy.

8. **Setting Ambitious Goals:**

    - Young teenagers start setting more ambitious goals related to their performance, such as achieving higher scores or competing in specific events.

9. **Self-Motivation:**

    - Young teenagers become more self-motivated and committed to their improvement. They take greater ownership of their progress and practice routines.

10. **Emotional Resilience:**

    - Young teenagers continue to build emotional resilience, learning to cope with the challenges and frustrations that come with the sport. They maintain a positive attitude in the face of setbacks.

11. **Individual Identity as a Bowler:**

    - Young teenagers solidify their identity as bowlers and may begin to identify themselves as athletes. Bowling becomes a significant part of their self-identity.

12. **Competitive Experience:**

    - Young teenagers often gain more competitive experience, participating in leagues and events. This exposure to competition contributes to their understanding of sportsmanship and the thrill of competing.

13. **Intrinsic Motivation and Passion:**

    - Many young teenagers develop a deep intrinsic motivation and passion for bowling, finding joy in the continuous pursuit of mastery and self-improvement.

In Stage 2, cognitive and psychological development takes on a more advanced and strategic nature. Young teenagers are dedicated to mastering technical skills, understanding the mental aspects of the game, and embracing the challenges of competition. They set higher goals, take greater responsibility for their development, and nurture their passion for the sport. These developments set the stage for further growth in subsequent stages of bowling.

Neurological Development:

In **Stage 2 - Development Phase**, young teenagers continue to advance their skills and techniques, and neurological improvements become more pronounced as they refine their abilities. Here are some of the key neurological changes and improvements that occur during this stage:

1. **Refined Motor Skills:**

    - Young teenagers in this stage improve their motor skills significantly. Their movements become smoother, more controlled, and more precise as they refine their techniques.

2. **Enhanced Spatial Awareness:**

    - Spatial intelligence continues to develop, with young teenagers gaining a deeper understanding of lane conditions, pin placements, and the nuances of different bowling environments.

3. **Advanced Cognitive Skills:**

    - Cognitive development progresses, allowing young teenagers to develop more advanced strategies, read lane patterns, and adapt their game based on changing conditions.

4. **Visual Perception and Depth Perception:**

    - Young teenagers improve their visual and depth perception as they become more accurate in targeting specific spots on the lane and understanding the ball's trajectory.

5. **Fine-Tuned Sensory Integration:**

    - Sensory integration becomes more refined, allowing young teenagers to better interpret feedback from their body and surroundings to make quick adjustments during a game.

6. **Concentration and Attention Control:**

   - Young teenagers work on honing their concentration and attention control, which are vital for maintaining focus during longer competitions and making accurate shots.

7. **Advanced Hand-Eye Coordination:**

   - Hand-eye coordination becomes more precise, allowing young teenagers to consistently hit their target and adjust for different lane conditions.

8. **Improved Balance and Posture:**

   - Balance and posture are further perfected, ensuring a stable and controlled delivery of the ball even in challenging conditions.

9. **Memory and Learning Enhancement:**

   - Memory and learning processes continue to develop, enabling young teenagers to remember complex lane patterns, adapt to different oil conditions, and apply past experiences to their performance.

10. **Emotional Regulation and Resilience:**

    - Young teenagers at this stage become more adept at managing their emotions during competitive play, developing resilience to handle the ups and downs of the sport.

11. **Tactical Decision-Making:**

    - With a deeper understanding of the game, young teenagers begin to make more tactical decisions, such as adjusting their equipment and techniques based on lane conditions.

12. **Multi-Sport Adaptability:**

    - For young bowlers transitioning into this stage, participation in other sports enhances their adaptability and cross-training capabilities, which can benefit their overall athleticism.

During Stage 2, neurological changes are more pronounced as young teenagers progress from basic skills to more advanced techniques and strategies. They build upon the foundational neurological improvements from Stage 1, and their development becomes more specialized as they gain experience and compete in various events. These neurological enhancements prepare them for the more demanding stages of their bowling career.

Brain Regions And Cognitive Functions Development:

1. **Spatial Information:**

   - In this stage, bowlers, both young and adult beginners, are advancing their spatial awareness and sensory-motor coordination.
   - They become more skilled at understanding lane geometry, pin positioning, and alignment techniques for improved accuracy.

2. **White Matter (WM):**

   - White matter tracts continue to form connections, enhancing sensory-motor integration and spatial perception.
   - Advanced neural pathways develop to process sensory input and execute precise motor responses during bowling.

3. **Motor Cortex:**

   - The motor cortex becomes more specialized as bowlers refine their motor skills, especially their approach, release, and accuracy.
   - The focus shifts towards perfecting the execution of bowling techniques.

4. **Somatosensory Cortex:**
   - The somatosensory cortex processes more complex tactile and proprioceptive feedback.
   - Bowlers develop a heightened sensitivity to their body's positioning and movement in relation to the bowling lane.

5. **Superior Parietal Lobule (SPL):**
   - The SPL becomes more engaged in sensory integration and advanced spatial orientation.
   - Bowlers refine their spatial awareness and orientation within the bowling environment, crucial for precise shots.

6. **Inferior Occipitofrontal Fasciculus (IOFF):**
   - IOFF pathways expand to support advanced visual perception and cognitive functions tailored to bowling.
   - Bowlers improve their visual processing skills, especially for reading lane conditions and pin locations.

7. **Intraparietal Sulcus (IPS):**
   - The IPS is involved in more sophisticated spatial and numerical processing.
   - Bowlers refine their ability to perceive complex spatial relationships and apply mathematical concepts to their strategies.

8. **Precuneus:**
   - The precuneus plays a greater role in self-awareness and visual imagery.
   - Bowlers enhance their self-awareness and can mentally visualize and plan their bowling actions.

Stage 2 (DEVELOPMENT PHASE) is characterized by the advancement of neural circuits and cognitive functions related to bowling. As bowlers gain experience and engage in league play, their brain regions become more specialized and efficient in processing the information required for improved performance. This stage marks a transition from basic skills to a more nuanced understanding of the sport, setting the stage for further development in the subsequent stages.

Hormones Development:

Stage 2 (9-12 years old) represents a phase where young teenagers are still pre-pubertal, and the focus is on continued physical and skill development. Hormonal changes at this stage are relatively stable, as puberty has not yet begun, but there can be some subtle shifts in hormone levels. Here's an overview of the key hormones and their characteristics during this stage:

1. **Testosterone and Estrogen:** Testosterone and estrogen levels remain low during this stage; as young teenager have not entered puberty. These sex hormones are responsible for the development of secondary sexual characteristics, which have not yet started to develop significantly.

2. **Cortisol:** Cortisol continues to play a role in regulating energy metabolism and responding to physical stress. While cortisol levels may vary in response to exercise and sports activities, these changes are relatively small compared to what is seen in adults.

3. **Growth Hormone (GH):** GH still plays a vital role in growth and development. During this stage, GH is primarily influenced by overall growth. Exercise and physical activity contribute to normal growth but do not lead to significant fluctuations in GH levels.

4. **Insulin:** Insulin remains important for regulating blood sugar levels and nutrient uptake by cells. Young teenager's insulin levels respond to dietary intake and energy metabolism, but significant changes in insulin levels due to sports activities are not typically observed.

5. **Epinephrine (Adrenaline) and Norepinephrine:** These hormones respond to stress and exercise, increasing heart rate and preparing the body for physical activity. While young teenager may experience some fluctuations during exercise, these changes are less dramatic compared to adults.

6. **Thyroid Hormones (T3 and T4):** Thyroid hormones continue to be crucial for metabolism and energy production. During this stage, they operate within typical ranges for young teenager, primarily influenced by normal growth and development.

7. **Insulin-like Growth Factor-1 (IGF-1):** IGF-1 is produced in response to GH and supports growth and muscle repair. Young teenager's IGF-1 levels continue to be primarily driven by overall growth, and exercise-related changes are relatively minor.

8. **Aldosterone:** Aldosterone continues to regulate electrolyte balance. Young teenager's aldosterone levels are stable and not significantly impacted by sports activities.

9. **Adiponectin and Leptin:** Adiponectin and leptin function within typical ranges for young teenager, influencing fat metabolism and appetite regulation. Exercise-related changes in these hormones are relatively small.

10. **Melatonin:** Melatonin remains essential for regulating sleep patterns. During this stage, it helps maintain healthy sleep patterns necessary for growth, recovery, and overall well-being.

In Stage 2 (9-12 years old), young teenager are still focused on skill development and enjoying sports. While hormonal changes are relatively minimal compared to later stages, regular physical activity continues to be important for overall health and growth. Puberty-related changes in hormone levels and physical development are on the horizon but have not yet fully manifested. The key is to provide a supportive and enjoyable environment for young athletes.

Technical Skills - Main Checklist Of Stage 2 Bowlers

At this stage, developing a structured and progressive approach is crucial to nurturing their potential as future competitive bowlers. The checklist for young teenagers encompasses various technical aspects, starting with the Bowling Approach. Young bowlers must now focus on more refined step placement, refined approach awareness, enhanced step control, and directional precision. This allows them to walk confidently toward the foul line, maintaining a consistent and reliable approach while optimizing their stance and body alignment for power and precision. It's essential to emphasize maintaining balance and control throughout the approach and achieving an advanced finish position for improved performance.

Moving on to the Swing, young teenagers should work on generating a forceful yet controlled arm swing, emphasizing precision in the swing path and mastering the dynamic pendulum motion. The Grip and Posture checklist encourages them to develop a good ball grip, perfect hand positioning, and maintain a relaxed yet purposeful grip to enhance control and power while embracing an advanced posture with shoulder-width feet for improved balance.

In the Ball Delivery category, Young teenagers need to achieve enhanced control over their steps and perfect their aiming skills for laser-like accuracy. They must also focus on achieving a smooth and polished ball release, which ensures consistency in their delivery direction. The Stance checklist emphasizes a more advanced starting stance, expert foot positioning, and strategic alignment to enhance comfort, power, and targeting precision.

Timely development of approach synchronization and efficient rhythm in the Timing section is essential for advanced performance. Their understanding of rhythm and coordination should reach a more in-depth level. The Body Alignment checklist sharpens their targeting skills, and they must exhibit heightened awareness when aligning their body accurately with the target, aiming for advanced targeting precision while maintaining a simplistic and effective alignment.

In the Upper Body section, Young teenagers should develop controlled upper body strength, which aids in guiding the ball with precision. Crafting a customized pre-shot routine that aligns with their unique style and enhances performance is also a priority, and they must master the role of the upper body in guiding the ball with precision.

Finally, in the Lower Body checklist, advanced step control, enhanced balance, stability, and a polished finish position at the foul line are essential. These aspects ensure that their steps are deliberate and controlled, their balance is maintained throughout the approach, and their finish position is not only balanced but also polished with precision and control at the forefront of their minds. This comprehensive checklist offers a structured and progressive approach to help young teenagers advance their bowling skills, guiding them toward becoming advanced and competitive bowlers in their age group. This approach ensures they develop advanced techniques and skills while maintaining a positive and enjoyable learning experience throughout their bowling journey.

Bowling Technical Skills (Stage 2) Checklist:

As young bowlers progress and advance into their teenage years, they require a more detailed and structured checklist to continue their development. The Bowling Approach Checklist for Young Teenagers provides a step-by-step guide for these budding athletes:

1. **Advanced Step Placement**: Building on their earlier understanding, young teenagers should now learn how to position themselves in a designated starting point precisely. This involves being aware of the optimal stance for their unique physique.

2. **Refined Approach Awareness**: Young teenagers should now master the concept of walking confidently towards the foul line with purpose and confidence. They should focus on maintaining a consistent and reliable approach.

3. **Enhanced Step Control**: Advancing from steady steps, Young teenagers should now work on refining their approach by gaining complete control over each step. This involves improving the smoothness and fluidity of their movement.

4. **Target-Oriented Direction**: As their skills progress, young teenagers must begin to sharpen their directional awareness. This involves walking deliberately towards their chosen target area, such as the pins or a specific board on the lane.

The Swing Checklist for Young Teenagers helps them develop a more sophisticated and consistent arm swing:

1. **Increased Swing Force**: Young teenagers should work on developing a more forceful yet controlled arm swing. This involves generating additional power without sacrificing accuracy.

2. **Precision in Swing Path**: Building on the concept of a straight swing, they should now aim for an even more precise and consistent swing path. This minimizes the chances of the ball veering off course.

3. **Dynamic Pendulum Motion**: Advanced bowlers understand that the pendulum motion should not only be mimicked but also executed dynamically. Young teenagers should work on mastering this dynamic pendulum-like swing for increased control and accuracy.

The Grip and Posture Checklist for Young Teenagers refines their understanding of these fundamental aspects:

1. **Sophisticated Ball Grip**: While maintaining a relaxed grip is essential, young teenagers should now develop a more sophisticated understanding of how to tailor their grip to suit their unique style and the lane conditions.

2. **Hand Position Mastery**: They should focus on perfecting their hand positioning and ball grip, ensuring that it enhances both control and power.

3. **Advanced Posture**: With a more mature stance, Young teenagers should strive to maintain an advanced posture, with feet shoulder-width apart and body balance that allows for more power and control.

The Ball Delivery Checklist for Young Teenagers builds on their existing skills:

1. **Enhanced Control**: Their small and controlled steps should become even more controlled and deliberate as they learn to dictate their pace.

2. **Precision Aiming**: Precision in aiming should be honed, allowing them to consistently target specific pins or boards with accuracy.

3. **Smooth Release**: Building on the concept of a gentle release, Young teenagers should focus on achieving an incredibly smooth and polished ball release.

4. **Laser-Like Direction:** Advanced bowlers understand that consistent directional delivery is key to success. Young teenagers should work on achieving a laser-like consistency in this aspect.

The Stance Checklist for Young Teenagers helps them refine their starting position:

1. **Advanced Starting Stance:** As they mature, their starting stance should evolve to be more comfortable, powerful, and precisely aligned with their target.

2. **Expert Foot Positioning:** They must master the art of positioning their feet correctly to optimize their balance and control.

3. **Strategic Stance Alignment:** Advanced alignment is crucial; Young teenagers should develop a stance that places their body in the perfect position for accurate targeting.

The Timing Checklist for Young Teenagers refines their sense of rhythm and coordination:

1. **Expert Approach Timing:** Young teenagers should now exhibit mastery in their approach timing, ensuring that the approach and swing are perfectly synchronized.

2. **Efficient Synchronization:** Building on basic rhythm, they must strive to synchronize their steps with their arm swing efficiently.

3. **In-Depth Rhythm Analysis:** A more in-depth understanding of rhythm and coordination is necessary at this stage.

The Body Alignment Checklist for Young Teenagers sharpens their alignment and focus:

1. **Advanced Target Focus:** While facing the pins was the goal earlier, now Young teenagers must work on their targeting skills with a deeper understanding of precision.

2. **Perfected Alignment Awareness:** They must have a heightened awareness of aligning their body accurately with the target.

3. **Sophisticated Simplicity:** The simplicity of alignment should be perfected, ensuring that the body's position is both simple and effective.

The Upper Body Checklist for Young Teenagers fosters a more advanced understanding of upper body mechanics:

1. **Controlled Upper Body Strength:** They should now develop controlled strength in the upper body, which aids in guiding the ball with precision.

2. **Customized Pre-Shot Routine:** As young teenager, they should be introduced to develop a basic a customized pre-shot routine that suits their unique style and enhances their performance.

3. **Mastery of Upper Body Control:** The upper body should be a tool for precise guidance, and they must master this aspect.

The Lower Body Checklist for Young Teenagers sharpens the stability and control of their lower body:

1. **Advanced Step Control:** Young teenagers should work on developing advanced step control during the approach, ensuring that their steps are deliberate and controlled.

2. **Enhanced Balance and Stability:** They must focus on maintaining a heightened level of balance and stability during their entire approach, from the first step to the final release.

3. **Polished Finish Position:** The finish position at the foul line should be not just balanced but also polished, with precision and control at the forefront of their minds.

This checklist provides young teenagers with a structured and progressive approach to developing their bowling skills, guiding them toward becoming advanced and competitive bowlers in their age group. It emphasizes the development of advanced techniques and skills while maintaining a positive and enjoyable learning experience.

By following this checklist, bowlers can ensure they have a strong foundation in bowling technique, posture, arm placement, footwork, and spare techniques, as well as proper equipment evaluation and athlete development.

STAGE 3 (TRAIN TO PERFORM)

The young athletes who have made the decision to "Train to Perform" are committed to striving for greatness and to putting in the necessary time and effort to complete the necessary training in order to compete at the provincial, national, international, or professional levels of bowling in the future. In this stage, there is a lot of dedication and drive to compete in leagues and regional competitions. The young athletes concentrate on both on-lane and off-lane training to make sure they are both physically and emotionally ready to excel in their game. In order to further develop their talents, young athletes are given more in-depth technical training at this point by a licensed coach.

The young athletes have improved their consistency in using the recognized bowling techniques. The development of the young athletes continues to be greatly influenced by training and practice. The primary goal at this stage is to exhibit consistent execution of the appropriate technical, tactical, psychological, and physical aspects of the sport, but competition and scoring are also significant. The young athletes' passion for the sport is still paramount during this period of growth, regardless of whether they compete or not.

Role Structure

Bowling coaches have a significant impact on their athletes' growth, thus they should constantly work to improve. In order to enhance and polish their skills for consistency and proficiency, they should take part in the coaching education program. Strength, flexibility, and stamina training regimens should be created, maintained, and improved for both inside and outside the bowling center practice. Advanced skills and drills listed on the bowling matrix should also be introduced. Coaches should also give young athletes advice on the acquisition of additional personal gear and urge them to practice unassisted without scoring in order to improve their skills. They should also encourage them to take part in cross-training exercises and other physical or sporting activities. Instead of the young athlete's score, the development process should be the main focus.

Parents and other supporters should respect the coach's contribution to their child's growth and development as a young athlete, look for programs with qualified coaches, encourage their child to participate in the program by abiding by its rules and keep a long-term perspective on their child's growth. They should also place more emphasis on the developing process than the grade.

Young athletes themselves should make a commitment to developing their technical abilities, practice imagery in both practice and league play, practice independently without scoring for skill development, engage in cross-training activities for strength, stamina, and flexibility, and concentrate on the process rather than the result. Their overall program should include aspects of health and wellness, such as proper eating and rest.

A ratio of two on-lane practices to one league series should be followed while practicing bowling-specific skills. Six to eight times a week, for 45 to 60 minutes each should be dedicated to other sports or physical activities.

To maintain participation and increase skills, bowling center employees should offer the proper programs and teaching. They should also conduct themselves professionally, do business as usual, and encourage the young athletes and coaches to advance the sport of bowling as a whole. To provide educational seminars, they should also collaborate with NSO, PSO, and TSO. It's also crucial to make sure that all lanes satisfy certification and sanctioning requirements.

A young athlete should complete six to eight games, keep the ball on the lane 90% of the time, hit the head pin 50% of the time, make 50% of spares, and have a strike rate of 20% to 30% before moving on to the Train to Compete stage.

Cognitive And Psychological Changes:

In **Stage 3 - Train to Perform,** players advance their cognitive and psychological aspects as they become more committed to achieving excellence in bowling and preparing for competitive success. Here are the changes and improvements in cognitive and psychological aspects in players at this stage:

1. **Enhanced Mental Resilience:**

   - Players further develop mental toughness and resilience, as they are dedicated to competing at higher levels. They learn to manage the pressures of competition effectively.

2. **Strategic Mastery:**

   - Players deepen their strategic understanding of the sport, focusing on lane patterns, lane breakdown, and opponent analysis. They become adept at adjusting their game in response to changing conditions.

3. **Advanced Technical Proficiency:**

   - Players refine their technical skills, with an emphasis on consistency and precision. They aim for higher levels of accuracy in their throws and master various release techniques.

4. **Competition Focus:**

   - Players place a strong emphasis on competition and consistently participating in leagues and regional tournaments. The competitive experience sharpens their focus on winning and achieving success.

5. **Setting Ambitious Goals:**

   - Players continue to set ambitious goals for their performance, such as winning regional or national championships. They create clear and measurable objectives to guide their training.

6. **Visualizing Success:**

   - Visualization techniques become a vital part of their mental preparation. Players regularly visualize successful shots, matches, and outcomes to enhance their performance.

7. **Time Management and Commitment:**

   - As their commitment to the sport grows, players improve their time management skills to balance training, competition, and other life responsibilities effectively.

8. **Focus on Consistency:**

   - Players prioritize consistency in their game, aiming for precision in each throw. They understand that consistent performance is essential for success.

9. **Emotional Control:**

   - Players continue to develop emotional control, maintaining composure during competition. They learn to handle both successes and setbacks with equanimity.

10. **Review and Analysis:**

    - Players engage in detailed post-game analysis to assess their performance. They review their decisions, execution, and outcomes to identify areas for improvement.

11. **Goal-Driven Motivation:**

    - Motivation becomes strongly goal-oriented. Players are driven by their aspirations to compete at higher levels, win titles, and gain recognition as accomplished young athletes.

12. **Self-Confidence:**

    - Confidence in their abilities grows, and players develop a strong belief in their potential to succeed at provincial, national, and international levels.

13. **Increased Competition Exposure:**

    - Players gain more experience competing at the regional and possibly national level, which contributes to their development as competitive young athletes.

14. **Team Collaboration:**

    - Team players continue to collaborate effectively with teammates, fostering camaraderie and teamwork while competing in league play and tournaments.

15. **Professional Support Utilization:**

    - Players understand the importance of professional support from coaches, physiologists, nutritionists, and sports psychologists. They proactively seek and use this support to optimize their performance.

16. **Staying Committed:**

    - Players remain highly committed to the sport, prioritizing their training, competition schedule, and continued development.

In Stage 3, players undergo significant psychological and cognitive growth as they intensify their commitment to becoming high-level competitive young athletes. They demonstrate enhanced focus, technical proficiency, and mental resilience. The pursuit of ambitious goals and the continuous quest for self-improvement drive their motivation and passion for the sport. This stage sets the foundation for further advancement and success in the sport of bowling.

Neurological Development:

In **Stage 3 - Train to Perform**, young athletes are committed to achieving excellence and are dedicated to the rigorous training needed to compete at provincial, national, international, or professional levels of bowling. At this stage, neurological changes and improvements continue to play a crucial role in enhancing a young athlete's performance. Here are the key neurological changes and improvements that happen during Stage 3:

1. **Refined Motor Control:**

    - Young athletes in this stage continue to refine their motor control, enabling them to make highly precise and controlled movements during their approach and delivery.

2. **Enhanced Proprioception:**

    - Proprioception, the awareness of one's body and its movements, improves. This heightened sense of body position helps young athletes maintain consistent deliveries and adjust to varying lane conditions.

3. **Improved Reaction Time:**

    - Reaction time becomes faster, allowing young athletes to respond quickly to lane conditions and make rapid adjustments during competitions.

4. **Advanced Muscle Memory:**
   - Muscle memory further develops, ensuring that young athletes can consistently reproduce their preferred shots with little variation.

5. **Cognitive Adaptability:**
   - Cognitive adaptability improves, enabling young athletes to strategize, change tactics, and problem-solve effectively during competitions, even under high-pressure situations.

6. **Emotion Regulation and Mental Resilience:**
   - Young athletes work on enhancing their emotional regulation and mental resilience, which are critical for staying composed and focused in competitive environments.

7. **Increased Concentration and Mental Endurance:**
   - Concentration becomes more intense, and mental endurance improves, allowing young athletes to maintain focus over longer periods during tournaments.

8. **Tactical Decision-Making:**
   - Young athletes develop more advanced tactical decision-making skills, such as selecting the right equipment and altering techniques to adapt to complex lane conditions.

9. **Visual Processing and Targeting Skills:**
   - Visual processing skills continue to improve, enabling young athletes to analyze lane patterns and make precise adjustments to their targeting based on real-time feedback.

10. **Improved Pattern Recognition:**
    - Young athletes become adept at recognizing recurring lane patterns and adjusting their game accordingly, ensuring consistent performance.

11. **Deepened Memory and Learning Capacity:**
    - Memory and learning capacity continue to evolve, allowing young athletes to accumulate knowledge and experience that can be applied to their game.

12. **Stress Management Skills:**
    - Young athletes develop better stress management skills, ensuring they can cope with the demands of competitive play and high-stakes situations.

13. **Enhanced Adaptability to Lane Conditions:**
    - Young athletes become more adaptable to varying lane conditions and are better equipped to assess and respond to changes in oil patterns.

In Stage 3, the neurological changes and improvements become more specialized and refined. Young athletes are prepared to excel at higher levels of competition, and their training focuses on both the physical and mental aspects of the game. The neurological enhancements during this stage help them perform consistently and optimally in competitive bowling scenarios, setting the stage for even more advanced development in subsequent stages.

Brain Regions And Cognitive Functions Development:

1. **Spatial Information:**
   - Spatial information processing becomes more refined as young athletes aim for greater precision in their shots.
   - They improve their ability to read and adapt to changing lane conditions.

2. **White Matter (WM):**
   - White matter connections strengthen, enabling faster transmission of sensory-motor information.

- Young athletes refine their neural pathways for quicker reaction times and improved decision-making.

3. **Motor Cortex:**
   - The motor cortex undergoes further specialization to accommodate advanced techniques and strategies.
   - Young athletes focus on consistent execution of complex motor patterns.

4. **Somatosensory Cortex:**
   - Enhanced proprioception and tactile feedback processing support more precise body movements.
   - Young athletes become acutely aware of their body's positioning and muscle control during play.

5. **Superior Parietal Lobule (SPL):**
   - The SPL is more actively engaged in sensory-motor integration and spatial orientation.
   - Young athletes fine-tune their spatial awareness for intricate adjustments in their game.

6. **Inferior Occipitofrontal Fasciculus (IOFF):**
   - Advanced visual processing skills continue to develop, crucial for reading lane conditions and adjusting strategies.
   - Young athletes become adept at recognizing and adapting to various lane patterns.

7. **Intraparietal Sulcus (IPS):**
   - The IPS is involved in complex spatial and numerical processing, particularly in strategy planning.
   - Young athletes excel in making data-driven decisions and executing calculated shots.

8. **Precuneus:**
   - The precuneus plays a vital role in self-awareness and mental imagery for planning shots.
   - Young athletes develop strong mental visualization and strategic planning skills.

In **Stage 3**, young athletes demonstrate dedication and drive in both on-lane and off-lane training, aiming for consistent execution of technical, tactical, psychological, and physical aspects of the sport. Their passion for the sport remains unwavering, whether they compete or not, and they continue to develop the cognitive functions and neural pathways needed to excel in the game. These improvements set the stage for even more advanced development in the subsequent stages of their bowling journey.

Hormones Development:

Stage 3 (12-15 years old) represents a phase where many young athletes enter puberty, and significant hormonal changes associated with growth and development occur. These hormonal shifts play a crucial role in physical and athletic progress. Here's an overview of the key hormones and their characteristics during this stage:

1. **Testosterone and Estrogen:** Puberty brings about a significant increase in sex hormone production. Testosterone levels rise in boys, leading to the development of secondary sexual characteristics like increased muscle mass and body hair. In girls, estrogen levels rise, contributing to the development of breast tissue and wider hips.

2. **Cortisol:** Cortisol continues to be released in response to physical stress, exercise, and training. Hormonal fluctuations related to exercise are more pronounced than in earlier stages.

3. **Growth Hormone (GH):** GH remains important for growth and development, but its effects become more pronounced during puberty. GH is crucial for increased muscle and bone growth.

4. **Insulin:** Insulin still regulates blood sugar levels and nutrient uptake by cells. Changes in insulin sensitivity may be observed due to growth and increased muscle mass.

5. **Epinephrine (Adrenaline) and Norepinephrine:** These hormones play a significant role in the body's response to stress and exercise. As athletes become more physically capable, their bodies can release more of these hormones to increase heart rate and direct blood flow to muscles during physical activity.

6. **Thyroid Hormones (T3 and T4):** Thyroid hormones continue to regulate metabolism and energy production. With increased growth and development, their role becomes more prominent.

7. **Insulin-like Growth Factor-1 (IGF-1):** IGF-1 levels continue to rise due to the influence of GH. IGF-1 promotes growth and muscle development.

8. **Aldosterone:** Aldosterone maintains electrolyte balance and fluid regulation. As physical activity levels increase, aldosterone levels may fluctuate due to changes in sweat and sodium balance.

9. **Adiponectin and Leptin:** These hormones remain involved in fat metabolism and appetite regulation. As athletes' bodies change and adapt, fluctuations in these hormones may impact body composition.

10. **Melatonin:** Melatonin continues to be important for regulating sleep patterns. Hormonal changes, combined with the demands of sports and school, may affect sleep and circadian rhythms.

In Stage 3 (12-15 years old), the onset of puberty triggers significant hormonal changes that drive physical development. Young athletes experience growth spurts, changes in body composition, and the development of secondary sexual characteristics. Hormones like testosterone and estrogen play pivotal roles in these processes. Proper nutrition, hydration, and structured training programs become more critical to support athletic development while ensuring overall health and well-being. Coaches, parents, and athletes need to be aware of the unique needs and challenges associated with this stage.

Technical Skills - Main Checklist Of Stage 3 Young Athletes

Mastering the technical skills essential for young athletes in stage 3 requires a meticulous focus on various elements during their development. Coaches play a pivotal role in structuring each skill separately, with particular emphasis on the critical starting posture and body angle. As young athletes progress through their training, they engage in drills designed to establish a natural five-step distance before initiating their approach. The significance of appropriate starting points becomes evident in preventing timing issues and unnecessary speed during the approach. This checklist addresses key aspects such as body angulation, swing timing steps, and the crucial release position, providing coaches with a comprehensive guide to nurturing accurate and consistent performances in young bowlers. Through a detailed exploration of the components involved, coaches can empower young athletes to cultivate precision and efficiency in their bowling techniques.

For teaching young athletes on technical stage , coaches must focus on structuring each skills separately. The starting posture and body angle are crucial. Young athletes should perform drills using standard steps to ascertain their natural five-step distance before beginning the approach. To prevent timing issues and needless speed, adjust the beginning point appropriately. The inside side of the shoe and the board it covers define the board where the young athlete stands.

Body angulation is essential throughout the approach to provide the space needed for the swing and the ball. At the conclusion of the third of five steps, the majority of top young athletes have a body angle of 45–65 degrees, which they hold until the end of their approach. The "release position" is what young athletes should have in place by the time they reach the third step's conclusion.

With the ball kept below the head, eye fatigue concerns that could affect targeting are minimized. Additionally, this position improves alignment, increases accuracy, and prepares the body for the release position.

Five steps make up the swing timing process. The non-bowling arm initiates the swing during the first step when the first step's sole touches the ground. The second step involves shifting weight from the non-bowling arm to the bowling arm at the peak of the swing to initiate a free-falling swing motion of the ball. The third step is a longer, faster step that brings the hip rotation to a close and increases body speed towards the direction of the foul line. The backswing stops briefly as it reaches the top of the fourth step, which is the shortest and fastest of all the steps. The fifth step is the longest and needs to be taken rather quickly to keep the body moving at a constant rate.

The shoulders should stop rotating throughout the follow-through as the swing continues to naturally travel forward. Towards the target, the follow-through could continue. A successful bowling shot depends on the beginning location, body angle, stance, and swing timing phases.

Depending on the young athlete's preference, follow-through may continue in either the right channel or the direction of the target. The right arm, on the other hand, must stay straight and pointed at the target. The fingers of the right hand should be placed so that the ball rotates in the proper direction during the release and follow-through.

A young athlete's accuracy and consistency on the lane can be greatly increased by learning and refining the right stance, body angle, and swing timing steps. Young athletes can prevent needless speed and timing issues by determining the natural 5-step distance and changing the starting point accordingly. Furthermore, maintaining a sufficient body angle throughout the approach and up until the release position can create the space needed for the swing and ball.

Young athletes may make sure that the ball is moving at the right times and angles to maximize accuracy and speed by having a firm understanding of the necessary swing timing steps. The swing should begin with the first step, and the ball should begin to move as soon as the first step's sole makes contact with the ground. When the heel of the second step contacts the floor, the non-bowling arm should transfer weight to the bowling arm and aim at the goal with the ball moving downward.

Establishing the release position with the upper body slanted forward and to the side to create room for the downswing, the third stride is longer and faster to complete the hip rotation and produce greater body speed toward the foul line. The downswing should begin when the last step is by the side of the fourth step, with the backswing reaching its peak and the ball stopping briefly. The fifth stride, which should be the longest and swiftest to maintain balance, should be taken into the body's balance line with the trailing foot angled at about 45 degrees upon release.

Developing good technique and practice habits is crucial for being a successful young athlete. Young athletes can enhance their accuracy, consistency, and performance on the lane by comprehending and using the right stance, body angle, and swing timing stages.

Bowling Technical Skills (Stage 3) Checklist:

1. Starting Posture and Body Angle:
- Position: Place your head above the little toe on your push-off foot.
- Aim: Establish a vertical balance plane for your body and ball trajectory.

2. Approach Timing and Positioning:
- Adjust starting point to prevent timing issues.
- Stand on board defined by inside side of shoe.
- Maintain body angulation throughout approach.
- Aim for body angle of 45-65 degrees by third step.
- Achieve release position by conclusion of third step.

3. Ball Position:
- Keep ball below head level.
- The ball is pushed over the bar into the motion in front of the body at second step.
- The ball is behind the head at fourth Step

4. Swing Timing Steps:
- First step: Non-bowling arm initiates swing.
- Second step: Shift weight from non-bowling to bowling arm.
- Third step: Longer, faster step to close hip rotation.

- Fourth step: Brief pause at top of backswing.
- Fifth step: Long and quick step for constant momentum.

5. Follow-Through and Targeting:

- Shoulders stop rotating in follow-through.
- Follow-through may continue towards target.
- Maintain straight right arm pointed at target.
- Proper finger placement for correct ball rotation.

6. Maximizing Accuracy and Consistency:

- Refine stance, body angle, and swing timing.
- Maintain sufficient body angle for swing and ball.

7. Understanding Swing Timing:

- Begin swing with first step.
- Ball movement starts with first step's sole contact.
- Transfer the ball weight to bowling arm by heel of second step.
- Start downswing as last step is by fourth step's side.

8. Release Position and Downswing:

- Establish release position with forward-slanted upper body.
- Third stride: Longer and faster for hip rotation.
- Begin downswing at fourth step's side with peak backswing.
- Fifth stride: Long and swift step for balance.

Example of Stage 3 Technical Skills worksheet

Skill	Objectives	Strategies	Duration	Assessment Examples	Reports/Exercises/Drills	KPIs
Footwork	1. Achieve optimal and consistent footwork.	- Maintain balance and posture throughout the approach.	6 months	- Assess balance and posture during practice.	Balance drills, ladder drills, foul line drills.	Consistent step pattern, proper posture.
	2. Develop controlled lateral movement on the approach.	- Focus on lateral weight transfer between steps.		- Record lateral movement and its impact on accuracy.	Lateral slide drills, lateral movement analysis.	Controlled and balanced approach.
Timing	1. Attain optimal and consistent timing.	- Develop a pre-shot routine and maintain step timing.	11 months	- Evaluate synchronization of steps and swing.	Metronome drills, video analysis, step-count drills.	Consistent timing, smooth transitions.
	2. Improve transition timing from backswing to release.	- Focus on a smoother transition at the release point.		- Assess the flow from backswing to release.	Transition drills, release point analysis.	Fluid and efficient transition.
Release	1. Master an optimal and consistent release point.	- Focus on a consistent hand position at the release.	12 months	- Track release point and accuracy.	Release point drills, hand position analysis.	Accurate release, minimal variations.
	2. Develop a versatile release for various lane conditions.	- Practice adjusting release for different oil patterns.		- Observe adaptation to lane conditions.	Oil pattern drills, release versatility exercises.	Adaptability to varying lane conditions.
Alignment	1. Achieve optimal and consistent body and target alignment.	- Establish a focal point and body alignment system.	6 months	- Analyze alignment and pin action.	Target drills, lane sight alignment, alignment checks.	Consistent alignment, targeted results.

kill	Objectives	Strategies	Duration	Assessment Examples	Reports/Exercises/Drills	KPIs
Swing	2. Enhance alignment adjustment skills for spares and strikes.	- Develop a spare system and alignment process.		- Assess alignment changes for different pin configurations.	Alignment for spares drills, pin configuration analysis.	Precise alignment for spares and strikes.
	1. Develop a smooth and controlled swing.	- Maintain balance and rhythm during the backswing.	4 months	- Evaluate the fluidity of the swing.	Swing rhythm drills, balance drills, pendulum exercises.	Fluid and controlled swing.
Lane Play	2. Improve swing versatility for varied lane conditions.	- Practice adjusting swing path for different oil patterns.		- Observe swing adaptability to lane conditions.	Swing adaptability drills, swing path analysis.	Adaptability to diverse lane conditions.
	1. Adapt to varying lane conditions and patterns optimally.	- Analyze lane conditions and make precise adjustments.	12 months	- Adjust strategies based on lane performance.	Lane pattern drills, lane breakdown analysis.	Effective adaptation to lane conditions.
	2. Develop advanced lane play strategies for different oil patterns.	- Create a strategy playbook for various oil patterns.		- Apply strategies in real-time to diverse patterns.	Pattern-specific drills, strategic planning exercises.	Effective execution of diverse strategies.
Spare Shooting	1. Improve spare shooting accuracy and consistency optimally.	- Develop a systematic spare shooting approach.	Ongoing	- Track spare conversion rate.	Spare system drills, spare shooting accuracy analysis.	High spare conversion rate.
	2. Enhance spare targeting precision for corner pin spares.	- Develop specific targeting techniques for corner pins.		- Assess targeting accuracy and conversion rate.	Corner pin targeting drills, corner pin accuracy checks.	Precise targeting for corner pin spares.
Mental Toughness	1. Enhance mental resilience optimally under pressure.	- Practice relaxation, visualization, and focus techniques.	Ongoing	- Evaluate composure during competitive scenarios.	Mindfulness exercises, pressure simulation, visualization.	Maintaining composure, handling pressure.
	2. Develop strategies for maintaining focus throughout a game.	- Establish mental routines for consistent focus.		- Observe focus maintenance during practice and play.	Focus maintenance drills, mental routines development.	Sustained and consistent focus.
Ball Speed	1. Control ball speed for different lane conditions optimally.	- Adjust approach and release for varying speeds.	6 months	- Measure ball speed variations.	Speed drills, approach speed adjustments.	Consistent ball speed for conditions.
	2. Improve ball speed adaptability for spares and strikes.	- Practice altering ball speed for different pin configurations.		- Assess ball speed adjustment for various spares.	Ball speed versatility drills, pin configuration analysis.	Precise ball speed for spares and strikes.

Table 13 – This table provides a more detailed approach to each skill, offering objectives and strategies to help young athletes in their development. The specified duration for each skill is 6 months, but individual progress may vary. Ongoing practice and dedication are essential for reaching the desired performance level.

Tactical Education

To develop their abilities and raise their chances of success on the lanes, these teenage bowlers must get a variety of tactical teaching. In order to regularly pick up single and multiple-pin spares, they must perform spare shooting drills. They must also be able to read the state of the lanes and alter their approach and ball choice through lane play. Knowing which ball to utilize depends on the lane circumstances and personal playing preferences. The ability to execute various shots with accuracy and consistency is also essential. To remain focused and confident under pressure, it's important to develop mental toughness. Finally, it's crucial to maintain a high level of physical fitness in order to prevent injuries and enhance performance in general. Bowling newbies can develop their abilities and be successful on the lanes by concentrating on these tactical instruction topics.

1. **Basic Game Understanding:**
   - Teach young bowlers the fundamental rules and scoring system of the game.

- Ensure they understand the concept of frames, strikes, spares, and open frames.
- Introduce them to the idea of a spare as a mark and a strike as two consecutive marks.

2. **Targeting and Pin Placement:**
   - Teach the concept of targeting specific pins, especially the head pin, to increase the chances of hitting the pocket.
   - Explain the importance of pin placement and how it can affect pin action and maximize the chances of striking.

3. **Lane Reading:**
   - Introduce the basics of lane reading, including oil patterns and lane conditions.
   - Teach them to adapt to different lane conditions by changing their line and targeting.

4. **Spare Shooting:**
   - Emphasize the importance of spare shooting, as spares can significantly impact scores.
   - Teach them specific techniques for converting common spares, such as the 7-10 split, 4-7-10 split, and single-pin spares.

5. **Strategic Shot Selection:**
   - Guide them in selecting the most appropriate shots based on pin positioning and the situation in the game.
   - Encourage them to assess their own strengths and weaknesses to make informed shot selections.

6. **Lane Management:**
   - Teach them how to manage the lane throughout a game, considering lane breakdown and transition.
   - Explain the importance of being proactive in adjusting their lines and targeting as the game progresses.

7. **Match Play Strategies:**
   - Introduce basic match play strategies, such as understanding the opponent's strengths and weaknesses.
   - Teach them to adapt their game plan based on the opponent's performance.

8. **Mental Game Tactics:**
   - Begin introducing mental strategies, such as maintaining focus, staying positive, and handling pressure.
   - Teach them how to regroup after a missed shot or challenging frame.

9. **Score Management:**
   - Help them understand the significance of score management and maintaining a consistent pace throughout the game.
   - Teach them basic score tracking techniques to assess their performance during the game.

10. **Team Play and Communication:**
    - For those involved in team play, emphasize effective communication with teammates.
    - Teach them how to strategize and collaborate with their team to achieve a common goal.

11. **Setting Personal Goals:**
    - Encourage bowlers to set achievable goals for each game, such as a target score, spare conversion rate, or a specific number of strikes.

- Teach them the value of self-assessment and goal adjustment as they progress.

12. **Game Plan Development:**

- Introduce the concept of creating a game plan before each competition.

- Teach them how to adapt the plan based on performance and lane conditions.

Tactical education in Stage 3 focuses on building a strong foundation in the strategic aspects of bowling. It's essential to tailor coaching and instruction to the individual needs and skill levels of young bowlers, gradually introducing more advanced tactics as they develop their understanding of the game.

STAGE 4 (DOMESTIC AND NATIONAL COMPETITIONS)

At provincial championships, bowlers who are training to compete consistently place in the top three. These bowlers practice with extreme care and adhere to a meticulously organized, periodized schedule, with the Provincial Championships serving as the year's most important competition.

These bowlers take part in training throughout the year that is specially created to improve their performance in the listed contests. They grow more dependable in their performance as they advance through this stage, and they can withstand the stress of competitive events. The Integrated Support Team (IST), which consists of physiologists, nutritionists, and sports psychologists, should be consulted by both the coaches and the bowlers to guarantee that the overall program planning and monitoring are supported by professional guidance.

Bowlers are able to practice and compete in a variety of settings, and their training plans are beginning to take an increasingly individualized approach based on performance evaluation and the identification of potential improvement areas. The "PHV" (Peak Height Velocity) stage of physical development should be passed by all bowlers, and physical training can be centered on yearly fitness testing and monitoring. The top-three finishes at the provincial level in tournaments are a reflection of the bowlers' consistently strong technical skill levels.

At this stage, bowlers are given comprehensive technical training by knowledgeable coaches. Another crucial step is the creation and implementation of a system for identifying and tracking potential bowlers of the highest caliber. The entire program's priority for training will determine the amount, frequency, and intensity of both training and competition. Bowlers will increase involvement in other physical and sporting activities during the regeneration phase of training to provide a mental break and promote recovery.

Role Structure

Staff and owners of bowling centers are essential in supporting bowlers' growth. They should make sure that customers have access to the right programs and opportunities so they can continue participating and develop their skills. Additionally, providing financial incentives to bowlers who need a lot of practice time can help them improve their game. It is crucial for bowling centers to provide an emphasis on healthy selections in their snack bar, encouraging bowlers to choose healthier options. The general development of bowlers can also be aided by working with National Sport Organization to provide educational seminars.

By imposing minimal coaching criteria or requirements for active league and tournament coaches, The National Sport Organization programs can further help the development of bowlers. Offering bowlers the chance to compete in local, regional, and provincial competitions can give them significant competitive experiences. Coaches can be guaranteed to have the most recent information and abilities by consistently providing and promoting chances for professional development. The National Sport Organization -hosted bowler skill development clinics can also help improve bowlers' skills. A framework for identifying and assessing talent can be developed collaboratively to aid in the identification and support of potential elite-level bowlers. Additionally, collaborating with owners of bowling centers to encourage the use of qualified and certified coaches can improve the standard of coaching in the sport as a whole.

There are a number of signs that a bowler is ready to advance to the (Train to Win) stage. These might include consistently finishing 10-15 games per week, making 60-70% of spares successfully, striking the head pin in 70% of tries, ensuring the ball stays in the lane in 90% of throws, and reaching a strike rate of 30%–40%. These signs may indicate that a bowler has established a strong base of abilities and is prepared to go to the following level of practice and competition.

Cognitive And Psychological Changes:

In **Stage 4 - Domestic and National Competitions**, bowlers continue to progress in their cognitive and psychological aspects, with a focus on competing at higher levels and maintaining consistent performance. Here are the changes and improvements in cognitive and psychological aspects in bowlers at this stage:

1. **Elite Competition Focus:**
    -   Bowlers at this stage place a primary focus on elite domestic and national competitions, such as provincial championships. Their motivation to excel and win in these events intensifies.

2. **Mental Resilience under Pressure:**
    -   Bowlers further enhance their mental resilience and coping strategies to deal with the stress and expectations of elite competitions. They develop the ability to perform under intense pressure.

3. **Strategic Expertise:**
    -   Bowlers deepen their strategic knowledge of the sport. They become adept at reading lane conditions, analyzing opponents' strengths and weaknesses, and developing game plans for specific competitions.

4. **Adaptability:**
    -   Adaptability becomes a key cognitive skill. Bowlers learn to adjust to varying lane conditions and competitive environments, ensuring that they can maintain high-level performance.

THE PEAK HEIGHT VELOCITY (PHV) stage is a crucial period in the physical development of individuals, particularly in the context of sports such as bowling. PHV is the point during adolescence when an individual experiences the most rapid growth in height. It is often associated with the onset of puberty.

For competitive bowlers, passing through the PHV stage is significant because it can influence various aspects of physical performance. During this stage, individuals undergo significant changes in body composition, muscle mass, and skeletal growth. These changes can affect coordination, balance, strength, and overall physical capabilities.

It's important to note that the exact timing of the PHV stage can vary among individuals. Generally, it occurs between the ages of 11 and 14 for girls and between 13 and 16 for boys. However, there can be considerable variability, and some individuals may experience their PHV earlier or later.

Coaches and trainers often consider the PHV stage when designing training programs for young athletes. It's a time when athletes may be more responsive to certain types of training and skill development. However, it's crucial to approach training holistically, considering not only physical development but also psychological and skill-related aspects.

For competitive bowlers, the PHV stage may be a time when they need to adapt their technique, equipment, and training to accommodate the changes in their bodies. This could involve adjustments in posture, strength training, and skill refinement to optimize performance.

5. **Goal Achievement:**

   - Bowlers set specific goals for their performance in national competitions and work systematically toward achieving them. Goal setting becomes an integral part of their training.

6. **Emotion Regulation:**

   - Emotion regulation becomes crucial, as bowlers aim to maintain composure and manage their emotions during competitive events. They learn to stay focused and avoid distractions.

7. **Self-Reflection and Analysis:**

   - Bowlers engage in rigorous self-analysis and performance review. They consistently evaluate their game, decisions, and strategies to identify areas for improvement.

8. **Strong Team Dynamics:**

   - Bowlers who compete as part of a team continue to foster strong team dynamics and collaboration. They work closely with teammates, supporting each other in pursuit of success.

9. **Advanced Visualization:**

   - Visualization techniques become more sophisticated. Bowlers regularly visualize complex scenarios, like entire matches or tournament progress, to prepare mentally.

10. **Coaching and Professional Support:**

    - Bowlers actively seek and value coaching and support from professionals, ensuring that their physical and mental preparation aligns with their competitive goals.

11. **Time Management and Prioritization:**

    - Bowlers further develop time management skills and prioritize training, competition, and recovery. Balancing these aspects of their lives becomes even more critical.

12. **Consistency and Reliability:**

    - Maintaining consistent, reliable performance is a top priority. Bowlers understand that reliability is essential for success in high-level competitions.

13. **Reviewing High-Pressure Scenarios:**

    - Bowlers expose themselves to high-pressure situations during training and mental preparation to build a strong resistance to stress and anxiety.

14. **Game Preparation:**

    - Bowlers engage in systematic game preparation, which includes studying opponents, analyzing lane conditions, and setting specific performance objectives.

15. **Commitment to Excellence:**

    - Commitment to achieving excellence in the sport remains unwavering. Bowlers are dedicated to fine-tuning their game and consistently striving for success at the national level.

16. **Learning from Losses:**

    - Bowlers gain valuable insights from losses and setbacks, using them as opportunities for growth and improvement.

In Stage 4, bowlers continue to refine their cognitive and psychological aspects as they transition to elite domestic and national competitions. They develop a keen sense of strategy, adaptability, and goal-driven motivation. High-pressure scenarios become part of their training to build mental resilience. These bowlers have a deep commitment to achieving excellence and are willing to put in the effort required to compete at the highest level. The skills and mindset they cultivate in this stage set the stage for further advancement in their bowling careers.

Neurological Development

In **Stage 4 - Domestic and National Competitions**, the neurological changes and improvements in bowlers are crucial for maintaining a high level of performance in competitive bowling. Here are the key neurological changes and improvements that happen during Stage 4:

1. **Enhanced Muscle Coordination:**
    - Bowlers continue to refine their muscle coordination and fine-tune their movements. This improvement ensures that their deliveries remain consistent and accurate.

2. **Precise Spatial Awareness:**
    - Spatial awareness becomes more precise, enabling bowlers to assess lane conditions and make precise adjustments to their shots, especially in challenging oil patterns.

3. **Optimized Proprioception:**
    - Proprioception reaches an advanced level, enhancing the bowler's awareness of their body's position and movements. This is essential for maintaining a consistent and repeatable delivery.

4. **Sharper Reaction Time:**
    - Reaction time becomes even quicker, allowing bowlers to adapt rapidly to changing lane conditions or unexpected situations during competitions.

5. **Advanced Muscle Memory and Kinesthetic Sensitivity:**
    - Bowlers further develop their muscle memory and kinesthetic sensitivity, making it easier to replicate their preferred shots and quickly identify any discrepancies.

6. **Improved Cognitive Flexibility:**
    - Cognitive flexibility improves, helping bowlers switch strategies and tactics seamlessly during competitions, making them more adaptable to different scenarios.

7. **Mental Toughness and Resilience:**
    - Bowlers work on building their mental toughness and resilience, which are essential for handling the stress and challenges associated with high-level competition.

8. **Heightened Focus and Concentration:**
    - Focus and concentration are sharpened, allowing bowlers to sustain their mental sharpness over extended periods of competitive play.

9. **Advanced Tactical Decision-Making:**
    - Bowlers make more advanced tactical decisions, such as equipment choices and shot adjustments, based on their understanding of lane conditions and the competitive environment.

10. **Refined Visual Processing and Targeting Skills:**
    - Visual processing and targeting skills become even more precise, helping bowlers analyze complex lane patterns and make micro-adjustments for consistent performance.

11. **Expert Pattern Recognition:**
    - Bowlers become experts at recognizing and interpreting various lane patterns, allowing them to anticipate and respond to changing conditions effectively.

12. **Deepened Memory and Learning Retention:**
    - Memory and learning capacity continue to improve, enabling bowlers to accumulate a wealth of knowledge and experience to apply to their game.

13. **Stress and Pressure Management:**

- Bowlers develop highly effective stress and pressure management skills, ensuring they can stay composed and focused in high-pressure competitive situations.

14. **Superior Adaptability to Lane Conditions:**
    - Bowlers become exceptionally adaptable to a wide range of lane conditions and are well-equipped to quickly assess and respond to evolving oil patterns.

In Stage 4, bowlers have reached a high level of neurological development, which allows them to excel in domestic and national competitions. Their training and experience have honed their skills to perform consistently and confidently in stressful tournament scenarios. These neurological enhancements provide them with a competitive edge, making them top contenders in their respective divisions.

Brain Regions And Cognitive Functions Development:

1. **Spatial Information:**
    - Spatial information processing becomes highly refined as bowlers aim for precise execution of shots in competitive environments.
    - They adapt rapidly to varying lane conditions and opponent strategies.

2. **White Matter (WM):**
    - White matter connections become more efficient to accommodate quick sensory-motor feedback and complex decision-making.
    - Bowlers refine their neural pathways for fast and accurate execution of strategies.

3. **Motor Cortex:**
    - The motor cortex experiences further specialization, focusing on the intricate motor patterns and shot adjustments needed for competitive success.
    - Bowlers develop the ability to execute under pressure and in high-stress situations.

4. **Somatosensory Cortex:**
    - Enhanced proprioception and tactile feedback processing allow for precise body control and shot adjustments.
    - Bowlers fine-tune their awareness of muscle control and body positioning in intense competition.

5. **Superior Parietal Lobule (SPL):**
    - The SPL is actively engaged in spatial orientation, tactical decision-making, and sensory-motor integration.
    - Bowlers refine their spatial awareness and decision-making skills under pressure.

6. **Inferior Occipitofrontal Fasciculus (IOFF):**
    - Visual processing skills are sharpened as bowlers adapt to different lane conditions and competing styles.
    - Bowlers become adept at reading and responding to the nuances of lane patterns.

7. **Intraparietal Sulcus (IPS):**
    - The IPS is increasingly involved in complex spatial and numerical processing, critical for strategic planning during competitions.
    - Bowlers excel in making quick, data-driven decisions in the heat of competition.

8. **Presumes:**
    - The precuneus continues to play a central role in self-awareness, mental imagery, and strategic planning.

- Bowlers refine their mental visualization and shot planning skills, vital for success in competitive scenarios.

In **Stage 4**, bowlers practice with extreme care, following meticulously organized schedules, and focusing on provincial and national championships as the most critical competitions. The cognitive functions and neural pathways developed during this stage enable them to excel in high-stress situations, and their ability to adapt to varying conditions and make precise decisions continues to improve. These developments pave the way for even higher levels of competition in the subsequent stages of their bowling journey.

Hormones Development:

Stage 4 (16-19 years old) is a period of continued growth, maturation, and hormonal changes in adolescent athletes. Hormones play a vital role in shaping physical development and athletic performance during this stage. Here are the key hormonal changes and developments in athletes aged 16-19:

1. **Testosterone and Estrogen:** In boys, testosterone levels continue to increase, leading to the development of muscle mass, strength, and the deepening of the voice. Girls also experience a rise in estrogen levels, which affects body fat distribution and the regulation of the menstrual cycle.

2. **Cortisol:** Cortisol levels may fluctuate in response to the increasing demands of competitive sports, academic stress, and other factors. Proper stress management techniques become essential for athletes.

3. **Growth Hormone (GH):** GH remains critical for tissue growth, repair, and recovery. During this stage, GH contributes to muscle development and repair, making it important for athletic performance.

4. **Insulin:** Insulin sensitivity may change due to shifts in body composition, muscle development, and energy expenditure during intense training and competition.

5. **Epinephrine (Adrenaline) and Norepinephrine:** These stress hormones continue to be essential for the body's "fight or flight" response. They play a role in increasing heart rate, blood flow to muscles, and focus during athletic events.

6. **Thyroid Hormones (T3 and T4):** Thyroid hormones maintain their role in regulating metabolism and energy production. They help athletes sustain energy levels during strenuous activities.

7. **Insulin-like Growth Factor-1 (IGF-1):** IGF-1 remains important for muscle growth and recovery. It works in synergy with GH to promote muscle development, repair, and adaptation to training.

8. **Aldosterone:** Aldosterone regulates electrolyte balance and fluid status. Athletes may experience changes in electrolyte levels due to sweating, requiring proper hydration strategies.

9. **Adiponectin:** Adiponectin plays a role in fat metabolism and insulin sensitivity. It can influence body composition and how the body handles energy stores.

10. **Leptin:** Leptin continues to regulate appetite and energy expenditure. Changes in body composition and activity levels may influence leptin levels.

11. **Melatonin:** Melatonin remains vital for sleep regulation, recovery, and maintaining circadian rhythms. Athletes need proper sleep to support growth, muscle recovery, and overall performance.

In Stage 4 (16-19 years old), athletes experience significant physical changes driven by hormonal shifts, especially during the late stages of puberty. These hormonal changes lead to increases in muscle mass, strength, and physical capabilities. Proper nutrition, training, and recovery strategies are essential to support these developmental changes while ensuring athletes' overall well-being. Coaches, parents, and athletes should be aware of the unique challenges and opportunities associated with this stage.

Technical Skills – Ebf Main Checklist Of Stage 4 Bowlers

The pursuit of excellence is an endeavor deeply rooted in the precise orchestration of multiple intricate components at this stage. Among these elements, perhaps none is as nuanced and fundamental as timing. This guide aims to dissect the technical intricacies of timing in bowling, an often underestimated aspect of the sport, which plays an indispensable role in achieving consistent and successful shots.

Bowling is not merely a matter of chance or raw talent; it is a complex interplay of technique, precision, and skill. For both amateur enthusiasts and seasoned professionals, perfecting the game hinges on mastering the subtleties of timing. A precisely timed shot can be the difference between a triumphant strike and a missed opportunity.

This comprehensive exploration seeks to unravel the multifaceted layers that encompass timing. From recognizing the pivotal role it plays to understanding its far-reaching influence on shot execution, this guide will equip bowlers with an in-depth understanding of timing's significance. Furthermore, it will empower them with the knowledge and strategies necessary to hone their timing skills to perfection.

As we venture deeper into the labyrinth of timing intricacies, bowlers of all skill levels will uncover the profound impact of impeccable timing on the pursuit of a flawless shot. The significance of timing resonates throughout every aspect of the game, from the very first step to the precise release of the bowling ball. Additionally, we will delve into the biomechanical fundamentals of the sport and how precise timing contributes to the generation of power, accuracy, and consistency.

Mastering the Bowler's Technique at stage 4: A Deep Dive into Timing and Biomechanics

Coaches working with bowlers at this stage should consider several key aspects highlighted below to facilitate effective skill development:

1. **Timing Awareness:** Coaches must emphasize the pivotal role of timing in bowling. Bowlers should be made aware that the precise moment the ball starts to swing significantly influences the outcome of their shots. Coaches should encourage bowlers to develop a heightened sense of timing and recognize its significance in their performance.

2. **Shot Execution and Consistency:** Coaches should emphasize that timing is the linchpin for consistent shot execution. They should help bowlers understand how timing directly correlates with the outcome of their shots. Coaches can work with bowlers to correct any timing issues, whether early or late, and help them achieve a more consistent performance.

3. **Motivation and Technique Revamping:** Coaches should discuss the potential need for a complete overhaul of a bowler's technique if timing adjustments are required. This discussion should emphasize the dedication and motivation needed for such changes. Coaches should support bowlers in making informed decisions regarding their training and coaching priorities.

4. **Swing and Release Impact:** Coaches should stress the ripple effect of timing on subsequent phases of a shot, especially the swing and release positions. Coaches should work with bowlers to ensure that timing corrections result in optimal swing trajectories and release points.

5. **Timing Complexity:** Coaches should explain the intricate nature of timing adjustments, focusing on different timing points and their implications. Bowlers should be made aware that early or late timing at these points can lead to various challenges, such as an ineffective release or loss of ball speed. Coaches can help bowlers identify specific areas that require adjustment.

6. **Practical Timing Techniques:** Coaches should provide practical guidance and drills to address timing issues. Whether it's emphasizing following the backswing with the hips and upper body or adjusting the speed of steps, coaches should offer actionable advice for improving timing. These techniques are valuable tools for bowlers looking to refine their skills.

7. **Biomechanics Emphasis:** Coaches should delve into the biomechanical aspects of bowling, stressing the importance of precise body movements. This knowledge forms a strong foundation for bowlers seeking to master their technique and understand how their upper body contributes to the downswing.

8. **Release Motion:** Coaches should underline the critical role of timing in the release motion. They should explain the significance of a foot halt before the release and the role of centrifugal force in the wrist. Coaches should assist bowlers aiming for precision and power in their release.

9. **Slide Length and Balance:** Coaches should address the relationship between the final step and slide length, which impacts overall performance. By helping bowlers optimize their approach to the lane and achieve better balance, coaches contribute to improved performance.

In essence, coaches should use the knowledge and insights provided in this overview to equip bowlers with a comprehensive understanding of timing and its intricate connections to various aspects of the game. By focusing on these key elements, coaches can empower bowlers to make informed decisions, refine their techniques, and ultimately enhance their performance on the bowling lane.

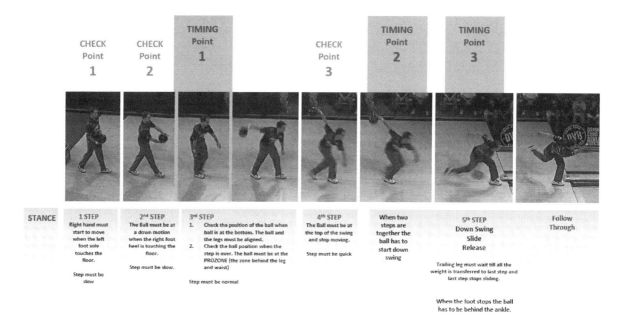

The Crucial Role of Timing in Bowling

Timing is crucial in the game of bowling. The exact second the ball starts to swing can have a big impact on how well the shot goes. The ball should ideally begin to move as soon as the initial step's toes make contact with the approach. However, bowlers frequently struggle to respond to this signal quickly enough, resulting in timing that is either too early or too late. Late timing can cause bowlers to send the ball towards their body rather than up and forward, with the swing beginning as early as the first stride. However, early timing may cause the swing to begin at the commencement of the second stride. Because it has the greatest impact on the swing and release position, which in turn impacts the release itself, timing correction at the initial point is vital.

Timing's Influence on Swing and Execution

It is crucial to remember that altering the time at the initial step is a big undertaking because it necessitates a total revamp of the method. This should only be done if bowlers have the motivation, drive, and time to devote to learning a new method and if the coach has the time to devote to them. Otherwise, concentrating on enhancing little specifics is a better course of action. The rest of the shot is significantly influenced by the timing at the first point. It is crucial to focus on timing correction if bowlers need to use their muscles during the swing or are accelerating the downswing owing to late timing. The swing and release position define the release itself. Additionally, late timing can hinder the bowler from altering the ball's reaction, such as speed or line. The timing at the first point can also be impacted by the earlier components of the method, such as the swing, beginning posture, and swing start. For instance, accelerating results in early timing whereas decelerating results in late timing. The initial steps may become excessively quick if the upper body is inclined in the starting posture, which will delay timing. Achieving ideal timing also depends heavily on the action utilized to initiate the swing. The shot's other components can benefit from the first point's timing being perfect. It can assist the bowler in developing proper body mechanics, a better release position, and quicker body speed—all of which are necessary for a successful shot. However, because of their natural gait, foot direction, swing direction, and body positioning, various bowlers take their steps in varying ways.

Adjusting Timing: When and How

Each timing point must be executed exactly for the proper release, with timing point 2 being especially important. Timing point 2 is challenging to identify without video analysis, but it has a big impact on timing point 3. Timing point 3 is crucial for a successful release, and timing point 2 early or late can provide considerable difficulties. Early timing at Timing point 3 can be brought on by early timing at Timing point 2, which is frequently brought on by high swing tension and too-fast or too-slow steps. This makes it practically impossible to perform an effective release. On the other hand, a bowler may be forced to bring the ball down rapidly, which will slow down the ball's speed, due to a late timing at timing point 2, which is frequently brought on by a late timing at timing point 1. Finding the core reason is important while addressing Timing point 2. Teaching bowlers to follow the backswing with their hips and upper body can be helpful if they have early timing due to too much swing tension. Slowing down the final two steps or cutting the fourth step short may be helpful if the steps are moving too quickly. By emphasizing Timing point 1 and obtaining earlier timing, late timing is frequently remedied.

Fine-Tuning Timing Across the Approach

There are various ways to implement Timing Point 2, such as a short or lengthy period at the top of the swing, and the impact of hand position may also have an effect on the technique. At the top of the swing, keeping the hand straight can help keep the bowling shoulder relaxed, whereas opening the hand counterclockwise (for right-handers) can produce elastic tension and cause the bowler to carry the ball. For right-handed bowlers, closing the hand in the opposite direction can similarly increase elastic tension and speed up the downswing, but for more seasoned bowlers, it may result in a full-roller release.

A thorough understanding of biomechanics and close attention to the body's movements are prerequisites for mastering the art of bowling. To ensure a powerful and precise throw, the motion of the upper body during the downswing is especially important.

Biomechanics and the Upper Body in Bowling

The spine angle should remain consistent during the final two stages, with the upper body turning around the bowlers' spine as they move into the release position in the third step. The bowler will either bounce the ball off the approach or use excessive energy to change the downswing's direction as a result of a downward movement of the spine angle during the last two steps. In contrast, a downward shift in the spine angle during the final two steps causes an earlier timing point, which impairs the bowler's capacity to carry out the proper release motion. For the purpose of generating force and guaranteeing a good throw, the inner abdominal muscles are crucial for setting up and maintaining upper body positions. According to biomechanical rules, power must originate from the ground and must be produced in a precise sequence: support (foot), balancing line of the body (body), and object (ball).

Timing's Key Role in the Release

The ability of the bowler to perform the proper release action and the style of release depends heavily on the timing of point 3. A foot halt prior to the release is crucial to creating the proper release action, as the body's stopping motion creates a centrifugal force at the wrist that helps it open up during the release. It is difficult to establish a proper release motion with early timing, and it takes outstanding separation skills to carry out the right release motion from a support that is still moving. The bowler's ability to generate ball speed is hampered by late timing, with body speed having little bearing on ball speed. In situations when the bowler wants to improve the number of revolutions or accuracy, or if the timing is too late and the bowler loses the advantages of body speed in creating ball speed, correcting timing point 3 is necessary. With the toes-first technique, the bowler slips with the toes and stops with the heel, which is essential for a successful throw. The length of the slide is influenced by the body's balance line, interchangeable heels, and soles, while the body's posture determines its center of gravity. A thorough knowledge of the body's mechanics and a mastery of timing are necessary to master the complex movements of bowling. Bowlers can only succeed on the lane by having a thorough awareness of how their bodies operate.

Motion of the Upper Body During Downswing: A Biomechanical Analysis

The position of the upper body becomes increasingly important to the success of the downswing as the bowler moves toward the release position during the third step. The upper body only rotates around its own axis, the spine, during the final two movements, hence it is crucial that the spine angle stay the same throughout. It often results in the downswing being overly vertical, forcing the bowler to bounce the ball to the approach or exert a lot of muscles to modify the downswing's direction if the spine angle is still traveling downhill during the final two steps. On the other hand, if the spine angle increases during the final two steps, it may result in an earlier time for Steps 2 and 3.

In order to execute the downswing properly, the inner abs must be engaged because these are the muscles that create and sustain the upper body positions. The force required to move an object comes from the earth, according to biomechanical laws. The chain of power production must go in the following order when powering a moving object: support (foot), balance line of the body (body), and object (ball). The item should be brought past the support as the last step in creating power, with the body's balance line on top of the support.

Timing 3, and Its Impact on the Entire Technique

Timing point 3 is crucial in defining how the bowler executes the release motion and the kind of release that is possible. If the foot stops before the release, performing the proper release motion is significantly simpler. In order to get the bowler's fingers to the top of the ball at the conclusion of the release action, the body's halting motion creates a centrifugal force at the wrist, which aids in the wrist opening up during the release. Early timing makes it exceedingly difficult to develop a proper release action, and the bowler must actively make the release. To execute the proper release motion from a support that is still moving, one must have exceptional separation talent. If the timing is off, however, the bowler forfeits the ability to use body speed to generate ball speed. The body speed that the bowler developed has very little impact on the ball speed if it takes too long from the stop of the foot to the release.

The Last Step and Its Effect on Slide Length

The execution of the downswing depends on the approach's final step. In order to slide with the toes and stop with the heel, the bowler should take the final step with the toes first. The length of the slide is also influenced by the body's equilibrium line. The slide is quite short and puts a lot of strain on the knee if the balancing line is in front of the support. The slide lengthens because there is less weight on the foot if the balance line is too far behind. The length of the slide is also influenced by the choice of heels and soles. Bowlers frequently employ excessive amounts of slide in their heels and soles, which causes balance problems. There are a few steps that must be taken in a certain order to generate the most power when producing power to a moving object, like a bowling ball, including optimal body positioning and stability. The body transfers power in a certain order from the ground up, in accordance with the rules of biomechanics. Creating a support, represented by the foot, is the first step. In order to stay balanced, the ball should be placed first, then the body's balance line should be on top of the support. The ball is pushed past the support to complete the move. This sequence can be likened to other competitions like the long jump or the javelin.

Mastering Timing Point 3: Key to Bowler's Technique and Performance

Bowlers' entire technique is greatly influenced by how well they time point 3. Bowlers' ability to execute the release motion and the sort of release they can execute is primarily determined by this. If the foot comes to a stop before the release, it is simpler to execute the proper motion. The bowler can get the fingers to the top of the ball at the conclusion of the release action because of the centrifugal force that the body's stopping motion exerts on the wrist, which aids in the wrist opening up during the release. Early timing makes it difficult to achieve the proper release action, forcing the bowler to actively make the release. To correctly release a support that is still moving, one must have exceptional separation talent. When timing is early, the bowler frequently delays the release point and releases the ball significantly or slightly upwards.

To increase the number of revolutions the ball makes, the bowler must correct time point 3. Additionally, accuracy suffers with early timing since the bowler must use a lot of muscles to release the ball. Timing that is too far behind prevents the bowler from using body speed to generate ball speed. The body speed that the bowler developed will no longer have much of an impact on the ball speed if it takes too long from the stop of the foot to the release. Although it's not often, this issue could arise. Correct timing point 3 if the bowler is releasing upwards as a result of the sliding support.

Balancing Elements for Bowling Success

In order to slide with the toes and stop with the heel, the bowler should take the final stride of the approach with the toes first. The length of the slide is influenced by the body's balancing line. The knee is put under a lot of strain if the balancing line is in front of the support and the slide is short. The slide lengthens if the balance line is too far behind since there is less weight on the foot. The length of the slide may also vary depending on the heels and sole. Bowlers frequently overslip their heels and soles, which can be fixed by switching them. The last step's position is influenced by the body's center of gravity, which is determined by the body's position. The length of the slide is influenced by body positioning as well. The slide will be quite brief if the balancing line is in front of the support, which will put a lot of strain on the knee. The slide will be longer if the balancing line is too far behind because there won't be any weight on the foot. The length of the slide can also be impacted by the heels and soles of bowling shoes. The excessive usage of slides by many bowlers in their heels and soles can hurt their performance. To achieve ideal slide length and performance, it is crucial to strike the proper balance.

In conclusion, developing the proper technique and timing is essential for a good bowling game. Each step must be carefully thought out and done correctly, from the upper body action during the downswing to the generation of power to the object. Any bowler may develop his ability and become a better bowler with practice and close attention to detail.

Tactical Education

Mastering the art extends far beyond simply knocking down pins. It entails a profound understanding of the dynamic interplay between the bowler, the ball, and the ever-changing conditions of the bowling lane. This introduction sets the stage for a comprehensive exploration of essential skills and techniques that bowlers of all levels can harness to enhance their game. From deciphering the subtle cues of ball transition to optimizing pin carry, and from refining equipment choices to fine-tuning release techniques, these fundamental aspects provide the tools needed to navigate the intricate landscape of modern bowling. Whether you're an aspiring novice or a seasoned pro, this guide equips you with the knowledge and insights to adapt, excel, and score those coveted strikes.

Understanding ball transition involves observing how the ball responds as the oil pattern on the lane changes over time and adapting your approach and release to accommodate these shifts. In certain situations, such as when the ball hooks earlier than usual, you may need to switch to a ball with a different surface or make adjustments to your release to account for the evolving oil pattern.

Reading ball transition means tracking the ball's movement down the lane and interpreting what it reveals about the condition of the oil pattern. If the ball hooks too early or too late, it might indicate uneven wear on the oil pattern in specific areas, requiring you to modify your technique or equipment.

Understanding pin carry is about recognizing how pins react when hit by the ball and how to position your shot for optimal pin carry. To increase your strikes or spares, you might need to adjust your speed or entry angle.

Charting equipment involves maintaining detailed records of each ball's characteristics, such as surface, weight, and drilling pattern, to aid in selecting the most suitable ball for each lane condition and making necessary strategy adjustments.

Advanced ball drilling analysis is a more complex method of assessing each ball's attributes and tailoring the drilling layout to match your individual playing style and the lane conditions you're facing.

Utilizing different release techniques refers to the various ways you can modify your release to create different ball motions and enhance your performance. For example, you might use a "full roller" release on dry lanes to reduce hook and enhance accuracy or a "fingertip" release on oily lanes to increase hook and power.

Line variation involves adjusting your stroke based on the ball's characteristics and your specific target on the lane. Depending on your goal, you may employ a "down and in" shot for a straighter trajectory or a "swing" shot for increased hook and power.

Lane adjustments entail altering your approach in response to the lane conditions, which could involve shifting your starting position, changing your ball speed, or adjusting your release. For instance, to compensate for the oil pattern, you might need to shift your starting position left or right if you're consistently leaving 10 pins.

Adjusting systems:

Below are some adjustment systems examples with numerical representations bowlers should learn at this stage:

2-1 Left Adjustment:

Shift the starting position two boards to the left.

Adjust the target one board to the left.

Ideal for minor lane corrections.

3-2 Left Adjustment:

Move the starting position three boards to the left.

Shift the target two boards to the left.

Suited for moderately challenging lane conditions.

6-4 Left Adjustment:

Make a substantial six-board shift to the left in the starting position.

Adjust the target four boards to the left.

Reserved for more extreme lane conditions or significant corrections.

2-2 Left Adjustment:

Lateral move of two boards to the left in both the starting position and target.

Offers flexibility for adapting to changing lane patterns.

2-2 Right Adjustment:

Lateral move of two boards to the right in both the starting position and target.

Provides a versatile option for adjusting to varying lane conditions.

These adjustments empower bowlers with a numerical framework for precise modifications to their starting positions and targets, allowing them to fine-tune their approach based on the unique challenges presented by different lane conditions during tournaments.

Example of Stage 4 Tactical education:

Table 1: Understanding Ball Transition		
Examples	**Level of Importance**	**Strategies**
Observe ball motion on the lane	High	Keep a watchful eye on the motion of the ball and make notes of any changes that occur over time.
Experiment with different balls during practice	High	Test the performance of different balls during practice sessions to determine which ones work best for you.

Table 2: Reading Ball Transition		
Examples	**Level of Importance**	**Strategies**
Track ball reaction after multiple shots	High	Pay attention to how the ball behaves after multiple shots in order to identify any patterns in its motion.
Pay attention to ball motion when lane oil starts to break down	High	Observe how the ball reacts to changing lane conditions, such as when the oil on the lane starts to break down.

Table 3: Understanding Pin Carry		
Examples	**Level of Importance**	**Strategies**
Observe pin carry after each shot	High	Pay attention to how the pins fall after each shot to gain a better understanding of how your ball is interacting with the lane.
Study lane conditions to anticipate pin carry	Medium	Analyze the lane conditions and make predictions about how the pins are likely to fall based on the ball motion and the layout of the pins.

Table 4: Charting Equipment		
Examples	**Level of Importance**	**Strategies**
Keep records of ball performance after each practice and competition	High	Make detailed notes on how each ball performs during practice and competition, including the lane conditions, the ball reaction, and the pin carry.
Experiment with different drilling layouts	High	Test out different drilling layouts to see how they affect the ball's performance on the lane.

Table 5: Advanced Ball Drilling Analysis		
Examples	**Level of Importance**	**Strategies**
Work with a professional to analyze ball performance	High	Seek the guidance of a professional to help analyze the performance of your ball and recommend adjustments to improve its performance.
Experiment with different ball surfaces and finishes	Medium	Test the performance of different ball surfaces and finishes to determine how they affect the ball's reaction on the lane.

Table 6: Release Uses		
Examples	**Level of Importance**	**Strategies**
Experiment with different release techniques	High	Test out different release techniques to see how they affect the ball's motion on the lane.
Work on developing a consistent release	High	Practice your release technique to develop a consistent release that produces the desired ball motion.

Table 7: Line Variation		
Examples	Level of Importance	Strategies
Experiment with different starting positions	High	Test out different starting positions on the approach to see how they affect your ball motion.
Work on developing multiple lines of attack	High	Practice developing multiple lines of attack to be able to adjust to changing lane conditions.

Table 8: Lane Adjustments		
Examples	Level of Importance	Strategies to Use
Changing target on lane to adjust for different lane conditions	High	Practice moving target during practice sessions
Adjusting ball speed to adapt to different lane conditions	High	Experiment with different ball speeds during practice sessions
Adjusting ball rotation to adapt to different lane conditions	Medium	Practice drills to develop ability to change ball rotation
Switching to different bowling balls or surface preparation to optimize performance on different lane conditions	High	Work with coach to determine best equipment and surface preparation for different lane conditions
Changing lines to adjust to different lane conditions and optimize pin carry	High	Experiment with different lines during practice sessions
Using different areas of the lane to optimize ball path and pin carry, including inside, outside, and down the middle of the lane	Medium	Practice drills to develop ability to use different areas of the lane

Table 14 – Example of Stage 4 Tactical education

Mental Skills And Training

For bowlers who have just begun to compete locally, using a mental questionnaire at this point can be quite helpful. First off, the questionnaire aids in establishing a baseline evaluation of the bowlers' mental skills and offers insightful information about their psychological strengths and limitations. Bowlers can use this self-evaluation to identify areas that need work, and they can then start to come up with solutions. For instance, bowlers can discover that they have trouble focusing and concentrating during competition. In this situation, individuals can concentrate on creating techniques to increase their attention, such as visualization, meditation, or a pre-shot ritual.

The questionnaire can also assist bowlers in identifying any unfavorable thought patterns, constricting beliefs, or emotional difficulties that can be influencing their performance. They can attempt to change their negative thought patterns into positive ones, boost their self-confidence, and become more resilient in the face of failures by recognizing these difficulties.

Mental Questionnaire Worksheet for Bowlers Who Compete Locally

Instructions: Please answer the following questions honestly and to the best of your ability. This questionnaire is designed to help you assess your mental game and identify areas for improvement.

HOW DO YOU TYPICALLY FEEL BEFORE A COMPETITION?

Confident

Nervous

Excited

Other (please specify): _____

HOW DO YOU HANDLE PRESSURE SITUATIONS DURING A COMPETITION?

I thrive under pressure

I struggle with pressure situations

I try to stay calm and focused

Other (please specify): _____

HOW DO YOU DEAL WITH MISTAKES OR SETBACKS DURING A COMPETITION?

I quickly move on and focus on the next shot

I dwell on my mistakes and it affects my performance

I try to stay positive and learn from my mistakes

Other (please specify): _____

HOW DO YOU STAY MOTIVATED AND FOCUSED DURING A LONG COMPETITION DAY?

I stay focused on my goals and stay positive

I get tired and lose focus as the day goes on

I take breaks and use mental techniques to recharge

Other (please specify): _____

HOW DO YOU DEAL WITH DISTRACTIONS DURING A COMPETITION?

I am able to tune out distractions and stay focused

I struggle to stay focused when there are distractions

I try to stay focused on my game and not let distractions affect me

Other (please specify): _____

HOW DO YOU MENTALLY PREPARE FOR A COMPETITION?

I have a routine that helps me stay focused and calm

I don't have a specific routine, but I try to stay calm and focused

I struggle to mentally prepare for competitions

Other (please specify): _____

HOW DO YOU HANDLE EMOTIONS DURING A COMPETITION?

I am able to control my emotions and stay focused

I sometimes let my emotions get the best of me and it affects my performance

I try to stay positive and use mental techniques to control my emotions

Other (please specify): _____

HOW DO YOU MENTALLY PREPARE FOR SPECIFIC LANE CONDITIONS OR OPPONENTS?

I have a plan and mental preparation for different lane conditions and opponents

I try to adapt and make adjustments during the competition

I struggle to mentally prepare for specific lane conditions or opponents

Other (please specify): _____

HOW DO YOU STAY MOTIVATED AND FOCUSED DURING PRACTICE SESSIONS?

I set goals and focus on improving specific aspects of my game

I sometimes struggle to stay motivated and focused during practice sessions

I try to stay positive and use mental techniques to stay motivated and focused

Other (please specify): _____

HOW DO YOU MENTALLY RECOVER FROM A BAD PERFORMANCE OR COMPETITION?

I reflect on my performance and identify areas for improvement

I sometimes dwell on my mistakes and it affects my future performance

I try to stay positive and learn from my mistakes

Other (please specify): _____

Methodology & Tools Used By Coaches:

Brain Dominance Assessment: The use of this technique can help identify a person's dominant brain hemisphere, which can have an impact on learning preferences and the development of motor abilities. For instance, persons who use their right brain more often could choose creative and visual learning techniques, whereas persons who use their left brain more often might favor logical and analytical techniques. Coaches can modify lessons to fit bowlers' learning styles if they are aware of the bowler's brain dominance.

Method of Communication Assessment: This instrument determines whether a bowler prefers verbal, visual, or tactile communication. For instance, a visual learner who plays bowling would prefer to watch instructional videos or diagrams, but a kinesthetic learner could favor hands-on training. Using this knowledge, coaches can modify their communication methods to best fit each bowler.

Sensory Process Teaching Methodology: This approach entails instructing bowlers on how to use their senses, including sight, touch, and sound, to enhance their performance and technique. To improve bowlers' feel for the ball or train their eyes to focus on certain targets on the lane, for instance, trainers may utilize sensory drills.

Sequential Teaching Method: To make learning more approachable, this technique includes breaking complex skills down into smaller, sequential steps. Coaches may instruct bowlers to concentrate on their footwork first before moving on to arm swing, release, and follow-through, for instance.

Whole-Part-Whole Teaching Methodology: This approach entails teaching a skill in its entirety, breaking it down into smaller pieces to concentrate on particular elements, and then putting it back together as a whole. Coaches may instruct bowlers on the complete approach and release, then concentrate on particulars like time or release technique before putting the whole thing back together.

Skill Evaluation Assessment: This program evaluates a bowler's current level of proficiency and points up potential improvement areas. For instance, coaches might employ a video analysis program to assess a bowler's footwork or release technique.

Learning Style Questionnaire: This tool determines whether a bowler prefers a visual, aural, or kinesthetic learning approach. For instance, a visual learner who plays bowling would prefer to watch instructional videos or diagrams, but a kinesthetic learner could favor hands-on training. Coaches can use this knowledge to customize their training to each bowler's unique learning style.

Coaches can provide individualized instruction and training by evaluating a bowler's abilities, learning preferences, and developmental needs using these technique tools. This could result in the development of skills that are more effective and efficient, which would ultimately boost performance on the lanes.

STAGE 5 (OPEN CHAMPIONSHIPS AND ZONE STANDARDS)

Bowlers who practice winning consistently place in the top three at National Championships. These bowlers diligently practice and adhere to a schedule, with the National Championships serving as the year's most important competition. They participate in physical training throughout the year that is specially designed to enhance performance in the listed competitions. These bowlers advance through this stage, becoming more consistent and capable of handling the stress of competitive events. Additionally, they are capable of practicing and competing in a variety of environments, receive extensive technical coaching from skilled coaches, and with time, gradually increase their consistency. Programs are being tailored depending on performance analysis and identified improvement areas. Annual fitness testing and monitoring are the foundation of physical training. The bowlers have now fully developed their technical, tactical, physical, and psychological skills and capacities. The goal of their training is to perform consistently and optimally in stressful competition scenarios.

All facets of these bowlers' preparation come together for their finest performance at national competitions since they have been trained to perform at their very best. When it comes to bowling, some bowlers may show talent that suggests world-class skill and could be selected as future national team contenders."

Role Structure

To ensure that they are certified to train bowlers at the Train to Win stage, coaches must fulfill a number of prerequisites. This entails having certification in both the competition introduction coach education and the competition growth coach education. In order to increase consistency and proficiency, coaches should constantly endeavor to improve their own abilities. They should also perfect the advanced techniques and drills listed on the bowling matrix. Additionally, they ought to continue their strength, flexibility, and endurance training regimens, which they can perform both inside and outside of the bowling center. As bowlers become more skilled and competitive and as personal equipment changes, coaches should evaluate it. In addition to league play, they ought to encourage bowlers to practice on their own for skill improvement without scoring. Coaches can employ cross-training and take part in other physical or sporting activities to supplement their bowling-specific training regimen. Coaches should construct a periodized program that highlights important tournaments in addition to league play and place equal emphasis on the growth process and bowler's score. Coaches should also advocate for and encourage psychological training for advanced performance in practice and competition, and they should be available to address bowlers' and parents' worries.

Parents and the bowler's support system should make sure that the program they are engaging in offers competent coaching. In order to maintain a balanced lifestyle, they should recognize the coach's role in the bowler's growth and success in the sport and encourage them to pursue hobbies outside of bowling. In order to make sure the bowler is still having fun, parents and the bowler's support system should talk to and listen to them. They should also support their involvement in a bowling program by respecting the rules and the bowler's long-term growth. While bowlers are competing, they should also maintain composure and exhibit neutral body language.

Bowlers themselves should work to promote bowling as a sport and serve as role models for aspiring young bowlers. They should work hard to prepare themselves physically and psychologically for training and competition, and they should be aware of how outside factors like sleep, nutrition, and other life concerns might affect their preparation and performance. Bowlers should collaborate with their coaches to seek advice from other professionals with knowledge in sports preparation, such as psychologists and nutritionists. They should look for training and competition environments that will resemble those at a national tournament, and they should dress, act, and behave like ambassadors for their clubs and provinces, exhibiting champion-like traits.

Depending on the overall program's priority for training, practice volume, frequency, and intensity will change. Other physical pursuits and involvement in different sports should rise during the regeneration period of training to give the bowlers more mental respite.

Initiatives from National Sport Organizations should establish and uphold the minimum coaching standards for a National Championship, collaborate with bowling center owners to encourage the employment of certified and experienced coaches, provide and publicize coach education seminars, and uphold the standards and specification requirements for National Competitions.

A bowler must hit the head pin 90-95% of the time, keep the ball on the lane 100% of the time, complete 20 to 40 games per week, make 90% of spares, and have a strike rate of 50% in order to advance to the Train to Win (International) stage.

Cognitive And Psychological Changes:

In **Stage 5 - Open Championships and Zone Standards**, bowlers focus on further improving their cognitive and psychological aspects to consistently perform at the national level and aspire to compete in renowned open championships. Here are the changes and improvements in cognitive and psychological aspects for bowlers at this stage:

1. **Mental Toughness and Resilience:**
   - Bowlers at this stage exhibit advanced levels of mental toughness and resilience. They can cope with high-stress situations and maintain focus and composure during open championships and other elite competitions.

2. **Strategic Mastery:**
   - Strategic thinking and game planning reach a higher level of complexity. Bowlers become experts in reading lane conditions, making real-time adjustments, and developing comprehensive strategies for various competition scenarios.

3. **Performance Consistency:**
   - Maintaining consistent performance becomes a hallmark of bowlers at this stage. They can consistently deliver their best performance under diverse conditions.

4. **Visualization and Mental Rehearsal:**
   - Bowlers engage in advanced visualization and mental rehearsal techniques, preparing themselves for the unique challenges presented by open championships and international competitions.

5. **Adaptability and Flexibility:**
   - These bowlers can adapt quickly to changing conditions, from lane oil patterns to competition formats. Their flexibility ensures that they can excel in different settings.

6. **Goal Setting and Achievement:**

   - Goal setting remains integral to their training. Bowlers set high-level performance goals and work systematically to achieve them, focusing on specific milestones within open championships.

7. **Emotional Control and Distraction Management:**

   - Advanced emotional control allows bowlers to manage their reactions to both successes and failures. They become adept at avoiding distractions and maintaining a laser-like focus.

8. **Teamwork and Leadership:**

   - Bowlers in team events exhibit strong leadership qualities and contribute to the success of their teams. They are excellent team bowlers, inspiring and supporting their teammates.

9. **Self-Analysis and Continuous Improvement:**

   - Rigorous self-analysis and performance review continue, with a focus on fine-tuning every aspect of their game. They are always seeking areas for improvement.

10. **Mental Preparation Routines:**

    - Bowlers develop specialized mental preparation routines for each competition, ensuring they are psychologically ready to perform at their best.

11. **Review of High-Pressure Scenarios:**

    - They engage in systematic exposure to high-pressure scenarios during practice to build a high resistance to stress and anxiety.

12. **Motivation and Self-Drive:**

    - Bowlers are intrinsically motivated and self-driven to excel on the national and international stage. They understand the effort required and willingly invest in their development.

13. **Elite Coaching and Support:**

    - They seek and value elite coaching and support from professionals who can provide specialized guidance and psychological preparation.

14. **Professionalism and Sportsmanship:**

    - Professionalism and sportsmanship are paramount. They represent their country and sport with distinction and adhere to the highest ethical standards.

15. **Adaptation to International Competitions:**

    - Bowlers prepare to compete on the international stage, where multi-sport events like the Asian Games or European Championships present unique mental challenges. Their mental preparation extends to global competitions.

16. **Balanced Lifestyle:**

    - Bowlers maintain a balanced lifestyle by managing their time effectively and ensuring adequate rest, nutrition, and overall well-being.

17. **Learning from Experiences:**

    - Every experience, including victories and losses, contributes to their growth and learning. They extract valuable lessons from each competition.

In Stage 5, bowlers demonstrate exceptional cognitive and psychological development as they aim for consistent success in open championships and at the national level. They exhibit advanced mental toughness, strategic mastery, and emotional control. With a strong commitment to self-improvement and professionalism, they are prepared to represent their country at international competitions. Their well-rounded and adaptable approach to the sport sets them apart as elite bowlers, ready to compete at the highest levels of the sport.

Neurological Development:

In **Stage 5 - Open Championships and Zone Standards**, bowlers have achieved an advanced level of neurological development, which plays a pivotal role in their success in open championships and zone-level competitions. Here are the key changes and improvements in neurological factors that occur during Stage 5:

1. **Exceptional Muscle Coordination:**
   - Bowlers have honed their muscle coordination to an exceptional level. They can precisely control their movements to deliver shots with maximum accuracy and consistency, even in challenging lane conditions.

2. **Enhanced Spatial Awareness:**
   - Spatial awareness is highly advanced, allowing bowlers to read complex lane patterns and make minute adjustments to optimize their shots.

3. **Peak Proprioception:**
   - Proprioception reaches its peak, giving bowlers an unparalleled sense of body position and movement. This is crucial for executing consistent, repeatable deliveries.

4. **Lightning-Fast Reaction Time:**
   - Bowlers exhibit extremely quick reaction times, enabling them to adapt instantaneously to changing lane conditions or any unexpected challenges during competitions.

5. **Mastery of Muscle Memory and Kinesthetic Sensitivity:**
   - Bowlers have mastered muscle memory and kinesthetic sensitivity, making it second nature to reproduce their desired shots and identify any deviations.

6. **Advanced Cognitive Flexibility:**
   - Cognitive flexibility is highly developed, allowing bowlers to seamlessly switch strategies and tactics during competitions, adapting to various scenarios as needed.

7. **Unshakable Mental Toughness and Resilience:**
   - Bowlers have cultivated unwavering mental toughness and resilience, making them exceptionally equipped to handle the immense stress and pressure of top-level competitions.

8. **Pinpoint Focus and Concentration:**
   - Focus and concentration have reached peak levels, ensuring bowlers can maintain their mental acuity throughout long and demanding competitive events.

9. **Expert Tactical Decision-Making:**
   - Bowlers make expert-level tactical decisions, including equipment choices and shot adjustments, based on their extensive knowledge of lane conditions and the competitive context.

10. **Laser-Sharp Visual Processing and Targeting Skills:**
    - Visual processing and targeting skills are highly refined, enabling bowlers to dissect intricate lane patterns and make micro-adjustments for consistently exceptional performance.

11. **Master Pattern Recognition:**
    - Bowlers are masters of recognizing and deciphering a wide range of lane patterns, allowing them to anticipate and respond to evolving conditions with precision.

12. **Deepened Memory and Learning Retention:**
    - Memory and learning capabilities are further enhanced, enabling bowlers to accumulate vast experience and knowledge to draw from in their competitions.

13. **Elite Stress and Pressure Management:**
    - Bowlers excel in managing stress and pressure, remaining composed and focused even in the most intense competitive environments.

14. **Exceptional Adaptability to Lane Conditions:**
    - Bowlers have unmatched adaptability to diverse lane conditions, demonstrating the ability to quickly assess and adjust to ever-changing oil patterns.

In Stage 5, bowlers are at the peak of their neurological development, which is crucial for their success in open championships and zone standards competitions. Their superior neurological enhancements set them apart as top-tier competitors, capable of consistently performing at an elite level. These neurological improvements, combined with their extensive experience and training, position them as strong contenders in national and international bowling events.

Brain Regions And Cognitive Functions Development:

1. **Spatial Information:**
    - Spatial information processing reaches its peak as bowlers aim for pinpoint precision and adaptability in high-stakes competitions.
    - They excel at reading complex lane conditions and strategic maneuvers by opponents.

2. **White Matter (WM):**
    - White matter connectivity becomes highly efficient, facilitating rapid sensory-motor integration and complex decision-making.
    - Bowlers fine-tune their neural pathways to execute advanced strategies with speed and precision.

3. **Motor Cortex:**
    - The motor cortex becomes exceptionally specialized, allowing for nuanced and precise motor control in response to varying lane conditions.
    - Bowlers demonstrate exceptional composure under pressure, delivering consistent performances in demanding competitions.

4. **Somatosensory Cortex:**
    - Enhanced somatosensory processing enables flawless body control, empowering bowlers to make minute adjustments during critical shots.
    - Bowlers maintain an acute awareness of muscle control and body positioning in high-stakes situations.

5. **Superior Parietal Lobule (SPL):**
    - The SPL is heavily involved in spatial orientation, decision-making, and sensory-motor integration in complex, high-pressure competitions.
    - Bowlers exhibit exceptional spatial awareness, making strategic decisions swiftly and accurately.

6. **Inferior Occipitofrontal Fasciculus (IOFF):**
    - Visual processing skills reach an elite level as bowlers adapt to ever-changing lane conditions and diverse competition styles.
    - Bowlers excel at deciphering the subtleties of lane patterns and making precise adjustments.

7. **Intraparietal Sulcus (IPS):**
    - The IPS plays a pivotal role in advanced spatial and numerical processing, essential for strategic planning and rapid decision-making in prestigious events.

- Bowlers demonstrate unmatched expertise in data-driven decision-making under extreme pressure.

8. **Precuneus:**

- The precuneus continues to drive self-awareness, mental imagery, and strategic planning, which are paramount in high-stakes competitions.
- Bowlers master mental visualization and tactical planning, positioning themselves as top contenders in national championships.

In **Stage 5**, bowlers diligently practice and adhere to a rigorous schedule, with national championships as the pinnacle of their competitive year. The cognitive functions and neural adaptations achieved during this stage allow them to perform optimally under intense competitive conditions, demonstrating consistency, precision, and adaptability. These developments position them as potential national team contenders and set the stage for the world elite level in their bowling journey.

Hormones Development:

Stage 5 (20 to 24 years old) represents the transition from late adolescence to early adulthood, and it is a critical period for athletes as they reach their physical prime. During this stage, there are specific hormonal changes and developments that influence an athlete's performance and body composition:

1. **Testosterone and Estrogen:** Testosterone levels in men remain relatively stable, promoting muscle maintenance and the development of male secondary sexual characteristics. In women, estrogen levels also stabilize, affecting menstrual regularity and bone health.

2. **Cortisol:** Cortisol levels can be influenced by factors like stress and exercise intensity. Proper stress management is essential to keep cortisol levels in check.

3. **Growth Hormone (GH):** GH continues to play a role in tissue growth, repair, and recovery. It remains important for muscle development and repair.

4. **Insulin:** Insulin sensitivity is influenced by factors like diet and physical activity. Maintaining healthy insulin sensitivity is important for energy metabolism and overall health.

5. **Epinephrine (Adrenaline) and Norepinephrine:** These stress hormones are crucial for maintaining heart rate, blood flow, and focus during high-intensity physical activities and competitions.

6. **Thyroid Hormones (T3 and T4):** Thyroid hormones continue to regulate metabolism and energy production, sustaining energy levels for athletes.

7. **Insulin-like Growth Factor-1 (IGF-1):** IGF-1 remains important for muscle maintenance and repair, especially following intense training or competition.

8. **Aldosterone:** Aldosterone plays a role in electrolyte balance, affecting an athlete's fluid and sodium balance, especially during periods of heavy sweating.

9. **Adiponectin:** Adiponectin continues to influence fat metabolism and insulin sensitivity, impacting an athlete's body composition.

10. **Leptin:** Leptin remains critical for regulating appetite and energy expenditure, influencing body weight and composition.

11. **Melatonin:** Melatonin continues to regulate sleep patterns and recovery, ensuring athletes maintain healthy sleep habits for optimal performance and recovery.

Stage 5 athletes often experience stability in hormonal levels, which can benefit their athletic performance. However, they must continue to focus on proper nutrition, training, and recovery strategies to maximize their potential. Coaching and support systems should adapt to athletes' changing needs as they move into the early stages of adulthood.

It's important to note that individual variations and lifestyle factors can influence these hormonal changes, and athletes should work closely with their coaches, sports nutritionists, and healthcare professionals to optimize their training and performance during this stage.

Technical Skills To Be Used:

For expert bowlers to enhance their game and win contests, they must possess advanced technical skills. Here are a few highly developed technical abilities that experienced bowlers frequently employ:

Technical Skill	Description	Drills to Practice
Lane Reading	Reading and understanding oil patterns and lane conditions.	- Bowl on different patterns regularly to gain experience. - Analyze the changing oil patterns during practice. - "Pattern Awareness" Drill: Predict the lane pattern before each shot.
Adjustment Mastery	Making quick and effective adjustments to changing conditions.	- Practice targeting adjustments with a consistent line. - Experiment with different angles and launch points. - "Adjustment Challenge" Drill: Randomly change your target and adjust accordingly with each frame.
Spare Shooting Accuracy	Consistently picking up single-pin spares and splits.	- Focus on specific spare target drills. - Work on corner pin conversions. - "Spare Shooting Challenge" Drill: Set up common spare combinations and aim to convert them with precision.
Advanced Ball Control	Precisely controlling the ball's trajectory and rotation.	- Work on spare shooting with specific ball motions. - Experiment with different ball layouts. - "Ball Control Variability" Drill: Use different balls and target specific pin positions to develop ball control.
Advanced Release Techniques	Mastering various release techniques to control the ball.	- Drill specific release techniques for different shots. - Record and analyze the ball's reaction for each release. - "Release Variation" Drill: Practice and compare different release styles to see their effects on ball motion.
Rev Rate Management	Controlling and adjusting your rev rate for different shots.	- Practice altering rev rate with the same delivery. - Analyze the impact of rev rate on the ball motion. - "Rev Rate Adjustment" Drill: Focus on changing rev rate while maintaining the same initial release.
Consistent Ball Speed	Achieving a consistent ball speed across varying conditions.	- Focus on maintaining a consistent approach and release. - Practice adjusting speed while keeping accuracy. - "Speed Control Challenge" Drill: Attempt to hit a specific speed target for each shot.
Balance and Posture	Maintaining balance throughout the approach and release.	- Balance drills focusing on finishing in a stable position. - Incorporate posture checks during your practice sessions. - "Balance Beam" Drill: Bowl on a straight line, focusing on maintaining balance throughout the approach.
Footwork Precision	Ensuring precise and well-timed footwork throughout.	- Work on maintaining consistent step patterns. - Practice adjusting footwork to accommodate lane conditions. - "Footwork Rhythm" Drill: Bowl with an emphasis on consistent and rhythmic footwork.
Pattern Recognition	Recognizing and strategizing for different lane patterns.	- Study past championship patterns and results. - Adjust your practice sessions to match specific patterns. - "Pattern Simulation" Drill: Create a practice environment that mimics championship lane conditions.
Equipment Maintenance	Properly maintaining and caring for bowling equipment.	- Regularly clean and resurface your bowling balls. - Learn to make minor grip adjustments as needed.
Mental Toughness	Developing focus, composure, and strategic decision-making.	- Work on breathing and visualization exercises.

Technical Skill	Description	Drills to Practice
		- Practice in high-pressure situations to build resilience. - "Pressure Situations" Drill: Simulate tournament pressure during practice sessions.
Implement Variations during Competition	Adjusting and implementing variations in response to competition conditions.	- Participate in competitive events to gain practical experience.
Speed Variation	Varying ball speed for strategic advantages during competition.	- "Speed Control Challenges" Drill: Practice adjusting speed under pressure and varying lane conditions.
Loft Variation	Altering the ball's loft to adapt to changing lane conditions.	- "Loft Precision" Drill: Work on lofting the ball with accuracy and consistency.
Release Variation	Implementing different release techniques for varied ball motion.	- "Release Strategy Scenarios" Drill: Practice implementing different releases based on competition conditions.
Stance Variation	Adapting your stance for different shots and lane conditions.	- "Stance Adjustment" Drill: Work on quick stance adjustments between shots.
Pointing the Shot Technique	Using the "pointing" technique to fine-tune your aim during competition.	- "Pointing Drill" Practice aligning your shot through the pointing technique under competition pressure.
Down the Boards Technique	Implementing the "down the boards" approach for precision shots.	- "Down the Boards Practice" Drill: Bowl with a specific down-the-boards approach to master the technique.
Boards Adjustments	Adjusting your target based on lane conditions and pin positioning.	- "Board Targeting Challenge" Drill: Practice targeting specific boards to match competition scenarios.
Box Technique	Implementing the "box" technique for lane management.	- "Box Technique Scenario" Drill: Simulate competition lane conditions and implement the box technique.
Implement Variations during Competition	Adjusting and implementing variations in response to competition conditions.	- Participate in competitive events to gain practical experience.

Table 15– These example drills provide practical ways to develop and refine the specified technical skills, as well as implement variations during competition for Stage 5 bowlers in open championships.

Tactical Education:

Develop a lane condition chart illustrating how to play a series of sport oiling patterns:

Advanced bowlers must gain a thorough awareness of the effects that various lane conditions have on ball motion and overall strategy. They ought to create a diagram that lists different fundamental oiling patterns and the related play alternatives. For instance, a "house shot" (standard house oil pattern) typically necessitates playing the ball further towards the pocket, but a "sport shot" (difficult oil pattern) frequently necessitates playing the ball in a straighter line with less hook.

Choosing the correct ball for the environment for the tournament:

Bowlers with more experience should know how to choose the best ball for the particular lane conditions. The ball motion can be influenced by elements including oil viscosity, oil pattern length, and lane surface texture. The surface, weight, and core of the ball that bowlers select must be appropriate for the lane conditions. A ball with a high surface friction (i.e., a dull surface) is optimal on a heavily oiled pattern, whereas a ball with a smooth surface (i.e., a polished surface) is preferable on a dry lane.

Skid manipulation techniques:

Skid manipulation strategies assist the bowler in changing the trajectory of the ball to account for changing lane conditions. Advanced bowlers develop their ability to control skid length by altering the ball's speed, release method, or surface. For instance, a bowler can raise the ball speed, employ a cleaner release, or polish the ball surface to reduce friction to make the ball skid farther down the lane.

Sensory aiming systems (SPECTO): In order to increase their accuracy, advanced bowlers use sensory aiming systems. These techniques entail aiming the ball towards the intended target by using visual or tactile clues. For instance, bowlers might aim their shot using a certain arrow or board on the lane.

Shadow technique: A certain amount of hook can be created on the ball using the shadow technique, which is a technique utilized by skilled bowlers. The ball can hook more easily if they release the ball in a precise method to build a wall in the oil pattern on the lane.

Ball surface & dynamics education:

The mechanics of bowling ball dynamics, including surface roughness, core design, and axis rotation, are understood by advanced bowlers. They are also aware of how these elements influence the ball's potential hook and general lane motion. They can improve their ball performance in various lane circumstances by comprehending these mechanics.

Recognizing what portion of the lane to play:

Advanced bowlers are able to identify the optimal spots to play on the lane for scoring possibilities. They have to take into account things like pin placement, lane topography, and ball motion. Bowlers can select the ideal starting position on the approach and modify their alignment and goal by being aware of these parameters.

Mapping friction differences across the lane surface:

Advanced bowlers are able to map out and determine the variations in friction across the lane surface. To maximize the motion of the ball, they can use this information to modify their ball speed, release technique, or target.

Mapping the oiling distribution across and down the lane:

The distribution of oil across and down the lane can be mapped by experienced bowlers. They can make use of this information to spot changes in the oil pattern, alter the surface or speed of their ball, and alter their shot to take into account the shifting lane conditions.

Design a traveling arsenal:

A well-designed arsenal of balls that can accommodate various lane conditions is essential for advanced bowlers. To fit certain lane circumstances, they should take into account each ball's coverstock, core, and drilling arrangement.

Choosing the ball for the environment:

Advanced bowlers are aware of the proper ball to select based on the lane circumstances. To choose the appropriate ball, they can consider elements like the length of the oil pattern, the viscosity of the oil, and the texture of the lane surface. They can choose the best ball from their portable armory using this knowledge.

Adjusting systems:

In the dynamic realm of bowling, where lane conditions are as diverse as the players themselves, the ability to adapt and fine-tune one's approach is paramount. Bowlers navigate the challenges of tournaments with strategic precision, and numerical adjustment systems serve as invaluable tools in their arsenal. Below are some examples of adjustment systems with numerical representations bowlers should learn:

2-2-1 Adjustment System:

Description: This system involves shifting your starting position by two boards, adjusting your target by two boards, and altering your ball speed by one mile per hour. It's a balanced approach to address minor changes in lane conditions.

4-3-2 Adjustment System:

Description: In this system, bowlers modify their starting position by four boards, their target by three boards, and their ball speed by two miles per hour. This adjustment is typically employed for more substantial changes in response to evolving lane conditions.

1-2-1 Speed Adjustment System:

Description: Bowlers using this system make nuanced adjustments by changing their ball speed. The starting position is adjusted by one board, the target by two boards, and the ball speed by one mile per hour. It's a precise approach for fine-tuning shot execution.

5-4-3 Zone Adjustment System:

Description: This system divides the lane into zones, and adjustments are made by shifting the starting position by five boards, the target by four boards, and the ball speed by three miles per hour. It provides bowlers with a systematic method to adapt to specific lane areas.

1-1-3 Timing Adjustment System:

Description: Focused on timing corrections, this system involves changing the starting position by one board, the target by one board, and the ball speed by three miles per hour. It's particularly useful for bowlers seeking precision in their timing adjustments.

3-2-2 Release Adjustment System:

Description: Bowlers using this system make adjustments to their release dynamics. The starting position is altered by three boards, the target by two boards, and the ball speed by two miles per hour. It's effective for refining the release phase of the shot.

2-1-1 Breakpoint Adjustment System:

Description: This system focuses on the breakpoint, where the ball makes its move toward the pocket. Adjustments involve shifting the starting position by two boards, the target by one board, and the ball speed by one mile per hour to optimize the breakpoint for improved pin action.

4-2-3 Sweep Adjustment System:

Description: Bowlers employing this system make adjustments to the sweeping motion of the ball. The starting position is shifted by four boards, the target by two boards, and the ball speed by three miles per hour, allowing for strategic changes in ball path.

1-3-1 Approach Adjustment System:

Description: This system centers on the approach to the foul line. Adjustments involve changing the starting position by one board, the target by three boards, and the ball speed by one mile per hour, providing a balanced approach to refining the bowler's movement towards release.

2-2-2 Rev Rate Adjustment System:

Description: This system is geared towards modifying the revolutions of the ball. Adjustments consist of shifting the starting position by two boards, the target by two boards, and the ball speed by two miles per hour, allowing bowlers to control the ball's revolutions for desired lane reaction.

Example of Tactical education in table:

Tactical Education Topics	Examples	Level of Importance	Strategies
Develop a lane condition chart illustrating how to play a series of basic oiling patterns	PBA Shark oil patterns	High	Analyze oil pattern characteristics, practice different lines and speeds
	House shot patterns	High	Study ball motion, adjust speed and rev rate, consider ball layout
Choosing the correct ball for the environment	Storm Phaze III	High	Analyze oil pattern, match ball characteristics to lane conditions
	Motiv Venom Shock	High	Adjust surface of ball to match oil pattern, consider ball layout
Skid manipulation techniques	Lofting the ball	Medium	Control skid distance, vary launch angle
	Changing ball surface	Medium	Adjust surface texture and grit to control skid and hook
Ball surface & dynamics education	Understanding RG and Differential	High	Match ball characteristics to lane conditions, adjust surface texture
	Ball reaction to different surfaces	High	Analyze ball reaction to different surface types, adjust surface texture

Tactical Education Topics	Examples	Level of Importance	Strategies
Recognizing what portion of the lane to play	Playing the outside portion of the lane	High	Observe the ball motion and pin carry during practice sessions. Try different starting positions
	Playing the inside portion of the lane	High	Observe the ball motion and pin carry during practice sessions. Try different starting positions
Mapping friction differences across the lane surface	Finding and playing the dry boards down lane	High	Observe the ball motion and pin carry during practice sessions. Adjust starting position and target accordingly
	Adjusting for a wet/dry condition	High	Observe the ball motion and pin carry during practice sessions. Adjust target and speed accordingly
Mapping the oiling distribution across and down the lane	Adjusting for a heavy oil pattern	High	Observe the ball motion and pin carry during practice sessions. Adjust ball surface, speed, and loft
	Adjusting for a light oil pattern	High	Observe the ball motion and pin carry during practice sessions. Adjust ball surface, speed, and loft
Design a traveling arsenal	Packing a versatile arsenal for a tournament	High	Research the oiling pattern and lane surface characteristics beforehand. Pack a variety of balls for different oiling patterns and lane conditions.

Table 16 – Examples of Stage 5 Tactical education

Competition Skills:

Design and implement a Peaking Program:

A peaking program is created to assist advanced bowlers in achieving their highest level of performance prior to a significant competition. Over the course of many weeks, the program often entails adjusting training loads and intensities, ending in a tapering phase that gives bowlers time to rest and recover before competition. For instance, a peaking program might include a few weeks of gradually increasing training loads and intensity, followed by a two-week tapering phase where training volume and intensity are reduced to allow for the best possible recovery.

Here is a sample of a 5-week peaking program for an experienced bowler prior championship:

Week 1: Base training

- *Increase training volume by 10% and concentrate on laying a firm foundation through regular practice.*
- *2 hours every practice session, 4 times per week*
- *Concentrate on enhancing your form and approach*
- *Include both flexibility and strength training activities.*

Week 2: Build-up phase

- *Boost training intensity by an additional 10%*
- *Practice four times a week for 2.5 hours each time, and keep your attention on enhancing your form and technique.*
- *Utilize drills and workouts specifically designed for competition settings.*

- *Start visualizing yourself winning to psychologically prepare for the competition.*

Week 3: Specific preparation

- *20% less training is required to accommodate rest and adaptation.*
- *Practice for two hours each, three times per week.*
- *Concentrate on particular competition circumstances, such as lane conditions and equipment choice.*
- *Include mental training methods like visualization and encouraging self-talk.*
- *Include tapering measures to improve performance.*

Week 4: Peaking phase

- *20% lessen the training volume.*
- *Practice twice a week for 1.5 hours at a time Pay attention to preserving form and technique while maximizing rest and recovery*
- *Embrace last-minute mental practices like goal-setting and confidence-boosting*
- *Choose your competition's equipment and make any necessary alterations.*

Week 5: Competition phase

- *Implement the pre-competition strategy and routine.*
- *Participate in upcoming competitions or events*
- *Utilize coping mechanisms in situations involving matchplay and step-ladder competitions.*
- *Conduct a post-competition analysis and make any required program adjustments.*

Designing and implementing a Simulation Training:

Advanced bowlers can get ready for upcoming tournaments by simulating the competition environment through simulation training. Setting up specific lane conditions or imitating tournament play may be part of this training. A simulation training program might, for instance, involve practicing on lanes with conditions similar to those anticipated for an upcoming competition, like changing oil patterns and pin placements. A match-play or step-ladder style in which you compete against other bowlers is another way to simulate tournament competition.

Here is a sample of a 5-day simulation training schedule for experienced bowlers:

Day 1: Warm-up & Drills

- *Warm-up: Start with 10 minutes of easy exercise to get your blood pumping, then do some dynamic stretches.*
- *Work on your release variations for 30 minutes, including variation of areas to play (i.e. Zone 1 , 2 and 3) . Roll the ball for 30 minutes at various speeds and angles to practice striking your target regularly.*
- *Spare Shooting: Practice various spare shots, such as single-pin spares and split conversions, for the next 20 minutes.*
- *Challenge: Finish the lesson with a 30-frame challenge in which you try to hit each spare and striking shot you worked on earlier.*

Day 2: Strategy & Cool-down

- *Warm-up: To get your blood flowing, start with 10 minutes of easy exercise. Next, do some dynamic stretches.*
- *Strategy: Develop a game plan for each of the various lane conditions and oil patterns you will be evaluating for the next 30 minutes. Spend 30 minutes practicing putting your plans into action.*
- *Drills: Spend the next 40 minutes practicing your skid manipulation techniques.*
- *Cool-down: Finish the workout with 10 minutes of foam rolling and mild stretches.*

Day 3: Warm-up & Spare Shooting

- *Warm-up: To get your blood flowing, start with 10 minutes of easy exercise. Next, do some dynamic stretches.*
- *Spare Shooting: Spend the next 60 minutes practicing various spare shots, such as split conversions and single-pin spares.*
- *Challenge: Finish the session with a 30-frame challenge in which you must attempt to make each practiced spare shot.*

Day 4: Warm-up & Drills

- *Warm-up: To get your blood flowing, start with 10 minutes of easy exercise. Next, do some dynamic stretches.*
- *Drills: Spend 30 minutes practicing your knowledge of ball dynamics and surface. Then spend 30 minutes practicing identifying which part of the lane to play for various oil patterns.*
- *Spare Shooting: Spend the next 20 minutes practicing various spare shots, such as split conversions and single-pin spares.*
- *Challenge: Finish the lesson with a 30-frame challenge in which you must attempt to complete each spare and strike shot you have been practicing.*

Day 5: Pre-event Preparation & Cool-down

- *Warm-up: To get your blood flowing, start with 10 minutes of easy exercise. Next, do some dynamic stretches.*
- *Pre-event Planning: Create a game plan and spend the next 30 minutes analyzing the lane conditions and oil patterns for your forthcoming event. Spend 30 minutes practicing putting your plans into action.*
- *Cool-down: Spend the final 10 minutes of the workout foam rolling and doing some light stretching.*
- *It should be noted that this is but one example of a simulation training plan that can be modified in accordance with unique demands and objectives.*

Competition strategy worksheet:

The particular tactics and plans to be used during a competition are laid out in a competition strategy worksheet. It contains details about the state of the lanes, the strengths and weaknesses of the opposition, and shot selection tactics. For instance, a competition strategy worksheet might have notes on which ball to use for each lane situation, how to adjust for shifting lane circumstances, and what kinds of shots to employ while facing particular opponents.

Here is an example of an advanced bowler's pre-competition strategy plan:

Mental Preparation:

- Positive Self-talk - Speaking kindly to yourself will help you perform better both before and during the tournament. Concentrate on your advantages and picture yourself making effective shots.
- Breathing exercises - Deep breathing exercises might help you stay cool under pressure and minimize anxiety.
- Goal Setting - Set attainable objectives for the tournament, both for the individual games and the entire series.
- Mental Practice - Picture yourself making accurate shots and maintaining concentration throughout the competition.
- Concentrate on the Process - Don't let other bowlers or other variables divert your attention from your own game.

Physical Preparation:

- Warm-up Routine - Develop a regular warm-up schedule that consists of stretching, bowling-specific exercises, and time spent on the lanes honing your approach and release.

- Nutrition - Prior to the tournament, follow a balanced diet and feed your body with nourishing foods and lots of water.

- Rest and recovery - Get plenty of rest before the competition, and give stretching, massages, and foam rolling first priority.

- Fitness Training - Add fitness training to your daily regimen to increase your overall physical stamina and fitness.

- Visualization - Envision yourself making accurate shots and maintaining your physical concentration throughout the competition.

Equipment Preparation:

- Ball Selection - Select the best balls for the particular oil pattern you will be bowling on after researching the lane conditions. Think about balls with a medium to high RG and a medium to high difference for the Scorpion PBA oil pattern.

- Layout Selection – Based on your playing style and the lane conditions, collaborate with your pro shop to choose the optimal layout for your chosen balls.

- Ball Maintenance - Keep your balls clean, ready to use, and with the appropriate surface changes and resurfacing as necessary.

- Spare Ball - Have a spare ball with a layout that is suited for the lane conditions, and regularly work on your spare shot.

- Accessories - Ensure you have all required accessories, including wrist supports, tape, and bowling shoes.

Technical Preparation:

- Lane Analysis - Conduct a thorough analysis of the lane conditions, including the oil pattern, to determine the optimal line and adjustments needed during the competition.

- Equipment Familiarity - Practice with the specific balls you plan to use during the tournament to familiarize yourself with their reactions to different lane conditions.

- Lane Play Strategies - Develop specific strategies for each lane, considering factors such as break points, angles, and adjustments for changing conditions.

Tactical Preparation:

- Opponent Analysis - Study the strengths and weaknesses of your opponents, focusing on their playing style, preferred equipment, and historical performance in similar conditions.

- Shot Selection Tactics - Plan shot selections based on the analysis of opponents and lane conditions. Consider adjustments for spares and strikes, adapting to the evolving game dynamics.

- Lane Adjustment Plan - Have a clear plan for adjusting to any unexpected changes in lane conditions, including ball changes, target adjustments, and overall game strategy modifications.

Knowledge Preparation:

- Rulebook Review - Familiarize yourself with the rules and regulations of the competition to ensure you are aware of any specific guidelines or penalties.

- Trend Analysis - Stay updated on current trends in bowling strategies, equipment, and techniques. Incorporate relevant trends into your game plan.

- Communication Plan - Establish a communication plan with your coach or team members to share insights, observations, and strategies during the competition.

- Mental Toughness Training - Enhance mental resilience through specific training exercises, ensuring you can maintain focus and composure in high-pressure situations.

Mastery Strategic Plan for Pre-Competition Preparation (Intensive):

Week 1: Comprehensive Foundation Building

Daily Focus: Integrated Mental and Physical Mastery with Fundamental Skills Drills

Morning Session (2 hours):

- *Positive self-talk and goal setting.*
- *Dynamic warm-up routine, including agility drills and visualization exercises.*
- *Fundamental skill drills: Target practice - focus on consistent targeting.*

Afternoon Session (30 minutes):

- *Breathing exercises integrated into the warm-up, with deep breathing during physical exercises.*

Evening Session (1.5 hour):

- *Review goals with visualization exercises.*
- *Nutrition plan discussion.*
- *Fundamental skill drills: Spare shooting - concentrate on accuracy.*
- *Fundamental skill drills: Release variations - experiment with different releases.*

Week 2: Skill Synergy Development

Daily Focus: Integrated Physical and Technical Proficiency with Skill-Specific Drills

Morning Session (2 hours):

- *Extended warm-up, including bowling-specific exercises and visualization exercises.*
- *Technical skill drills: Lane analysis practice, focusing on reading oil patterns.*
- *Physical conditioning drills: Strengthening exercises for specific bowling movements.*

Afternoon Session (1.5 hours):

- *Incorporate rest and recovery techniques.*
- *Technical skill drills: Ball selection practice - choosing the right ball for different lane conditions.*
- *Tactical skill drills: Simulated game scenarios with varying lane conditions.*

Evening Session (1 hour):

- *Mental visualization during rest and recovery.*
- *Fundamental skill drills: Release consistency - refine and maintain a consistent release.*

Week 3: Tactical Synthesis and Mental Resilience

Daily Focus: Integrated Technical and Tactical Acumen with Advanced Skill Drills

Morning Session (2 hours):

- *Combine lane and opponent analysis.*
- *Technical skill drills: Layout selection - work with the pro shop to optimize ball layouts.*
- *Tactical skill drills: Strategic spare shooting - plan for different spare scenarios.*

Afternoon Session (1.5 hours):

- *Tactical skill drills: Shot selection tactics - adapting based on opponent analysis.*

- *Technical skill drills: Adjustments for changing conditions - practice quick adaptability.*

Evening Session (1 hour):

- *Rulebook review integrated with mental toughness training.*

- *Tactical skill drills: Team communication scenarios - ensure effective communication under pressure.*

Week 4: Finalization and Unified Mastery

Daily Focus: Integration of All Aspects with Game Play Simulations

Morning Session (2.5 hours):

- *Comprehensive practice session covering mental, physical, technical, and tactical aspects.*

- *Game play simulation: Full-game scenarios with strategic adjustments.*

- *Visualization exercises integrated into mental preparation.*

Afternoon Session (1.5 hours):

- *Finalize communication plans with the team.*

- *Game play simulation: Team-based drills - practice collaborative strategies.*

- *Deep breathing during physical exercises.*

Evening Session (1 hour):

- *Mock competition integrating all elements.*

- *Game play simulation: High-pressure scenarios - practice maintaining composure in critical moments.*

Competition Week: Fine-Tuning and Cohesive Readiness

Daily Focus: Last-Minute Adjustments and Unified Team Approach with Game Play Drills

Morning Session (2 hours):

- *Implement lane adjustment plan collaboratively.*

- *Game play simulation: Tactical decision-making under various competition scenarios.*

- *Visualization exercises for mental focus.*

Afternoon Session (1.5 hours):

- *Review and reinforce communication plans with the team.*

- *Game play simulation: Team-based drills with rapid strategy adjustments.*

- *Deep breathing during physical exercises.*

Evening Session (1 hour):

- *Concentrate on mental toughness training.*

- *Game play simulation: High-pressure scenarios - practice maintaining composure in critical moments.*

- *Visualization exercises for mental resilience.*

This comprehensive approach ensures that all elements of preparation are seamlessly integrated, creating a unified and cohesive strategy for a professional bowler competing in regional and continental zone championships.

Pre-competition Technical and Tactical plan:

The steps that need to be taken in order to prepare for a competition are outlined in a pre-competition plan combining technical and tactical into one schedule. It covers tactics like workout and relaxation routines, travel arrangements, and meal preparations. For instance, a pre-competition strategy can include reducing training loads and intensities in the weeks before the event, planning enough time for rest and recovery, and adhering to a diet strategy to maintain optimum energy levels.

Here is an example of a pre-competition schedule for advanced bowlers that includes warm-up, drills, spare shooting, challenges, strategy, versatility on oil condition, simulation, and cool-down for every day over the course of five days per week for four weeks before a competition:

Week 1:	Week 2:	Week 3
Sunday:	**Sunday:**	**Sunday:**
Warm-up: 10 minutes of light cardio, followed by dynamic stretches	Warm-up: 10 minutes of light cardio and stretching	Warm-up: 10 minutes of cardio, dynamic stretching, and arm swings.
Drills: 5-7-10 spare drill, 3-6-9 drill, and 2-4-6 drill	Drills: Work on hitting the 10-pin from various angles and positions, using different release and loft variations	Drills: Work on targeting spares, with a focus on 10 pins and 7 pins. Do 5 sets of 5 shots each.
Spare shooting: 2-4-6-10 and 3-6-9-10 spare shooting	Spare Shooting: Focus on converting the 6-7-10 and 4-6-7-10 splits	Spare Shooting: Bowl 2 games of 10 frames, aiming to hit spares only.
Challenge: Bowl 10 strikes in a row	Challenge: Play a game of "strike or spare" where each shot must either result in a strike or a spare to move on to the next frame	Challenge: Bowl 3 games of 10 frames each, trying to score 200+ on each game.
Strategy: Practice playing different lines on the lane	Strategy: Work on playing the 3rd arrow on a medium-heavy oil pattern	Strategy: Focus on playing the middle of the lane, using a straight shot.
Versatility on oil condition: Bowl on a medium oil pattern	Versatile on Oil Condition: Bowl 3 games on a medium-heavy oil pattern, adjusting your line and ball speed as needed	Versatile on Oil Condition: Bowl 2 games on a medium-difficulty oil pattern, focusing on finding the right ball and technique to handle the conditions.
Simulation: Bowl 3 games at competition pace	Simulation: Play a 3-game series on the upcoming tournament pattern	Simulation: Bowl 3 games of 10 frames each, trying to simulate the competition environment as much as possible.
Cool-down: Static stretching for 10 minutes	Cool-down: Stretching and foam rolling	Cool-down: 10 minutes of static stretching and foam rolling.
Monday:	**Monday:**	**Monday:**
Warm-up: 10 minutes of light cardio, followed by dynamic stretches	Warm-up: 10 minutes of light cardio and stretching	Warm-up: 10 minutes of cardio, dynamic stretching, and arm swings.
Drills: Strike pocket drill, single pin spare drill, and 10 pin spare drill	Drills: Work on hitting the pocket consistently from the 2nd arrow, using different release and speed variations	Drills: Work on targeting strikes, with a focus on the 1-3 pocket. Do 5 sets of 5 shots each.
Spare shooting: 7-10 and 4-7-10 spare shooting	Spare Shooting: Focus on converting the 3-6-10 and 2-4-7-10 splits	Spare Shooting: Bowl 2 games of 10 frames, aiming to hit spares only.
Challenge: Bowl 2 games using a different ball in each frame and setting a target to achieve (i.e. total strikes atleast 14 out of 20 shots)	Challenge: Play a game of "pick your poison" where you choose a challenging spare to shoot each frame	Challenge: Bowl 3 games of 10 frames each, trying to score 220+ on each game.
Strategy: Focus on adjusting to lane transitions	Strategy: Work on playing the 2nd arrow on a medium-light oil pattern	Strategy: Focus on playing the outside of the lane, using a hook shot.
Versatility on oil condition: Bowl on a long oil pattern	Versatile on Oil Condition: Bowl 3 games on a medium-light oil pattern, adjusting your line and ball selection as needed	Versatile on Oil Condition: Bowl 2 games on a heavily-oiled pattern, focusing on finding the right ball and technique to handle the conditions.

Week 1:	Week 2:	Week 3:
Simulation: Bowl 4 games at competition pace	Simulation: Play a 3-game series on the upcoming tournament pattern	Simulation: Bowl 3 games of 10 frames each, trying to simulate the competition environment as much as possible.
Cool-down: Static stretching for 10 minutes	Cool-down: Stretching and foam rolling	Cool-down: 10 minutes of static stretching and foam rolling.

Tuesday:	Tuesday:	Tuesday:
Warm-up: 10 minutes of light cardio, followed by dynamic stretches	Warm-up: 10 minutes of light cardio and stretching	Warm-up: 10 minutes of cardio, dynamic stretching, and arm swings.
Drills: Slider drill, speed control drill, and rev rate drill	Drills: Work on hitting the pocket from the 4th arrow, using different release and ball surface variations	Drills: Work on targeting spares, with a focus on the 4-6-7-10 split. Do 5 sets of 5 shots each.
Spare shooting: 6-7-10 and 4-9 spare shooting	Spare Shooting: Focus on converting the 3-10 and 6-7 splits	Spare Shooting: Bowl 2 games of 10 frames, aiming to hit spares only.
Challenge: Bowl a game using only plastic spare ball	Challenge: Play a game of "strike or gutter" where each shot must either result in a strike or a gutter ball to move on to the next frame	Challenge: Bowl 3 games of 10 frames each, trying to score 200+ on each game.
Strategy: Practice playing different angles to the pocket	Strategy: Work on playing the 4th arrow on a heavy oil pattern	Strategy: Focus on playing the middle of the lane, using a hook shot.
Versatility on oil condition: Bowl on a short oil pattern	Versatile on Oil Condition: Bowl 3 games on a heavy oil pattern, adjusting your line and ball surface as needed	Versatile on Oil Condition: Bowl 2 games on a light-oiled pattern, focusing on finding the right ball and technique to handle the conditions.
Simulation: Bowl 5 games at competition pace	Simulation: Play a 3-game series on the upcoming tournament pattern	Simulation: Bowl 3 games of 10 frames each, trying to simulate the competition environment as much as possible.
Cool-down: Static stretching for 10 minutes	Cool-down: Stretching and foam rolling	Cool-down: 10 minutes of static stretching and foam rolling.

Wednesday:	Wednesday:	Wednesday:
Warm-up: 10 minutes of light cardio, followed by dynamic stretches	Warm-up: 10 minutes of light cardio and stretching	Warm-up: 10 minutes of cardio, dynamic stretching, and arm swings.
Drills: 3-6-9-10 spare drill, 4-6-7-10 drill, and 1-3-6-7-10 drill	Drills: Work on hitting the pocket from the 1st arrow, using different release and ball speed variations	Drills: Work on targeting strikes, with a focus on the 1-2-4-10 split. Do 5 sets of 5 shots each.
Spare shooting: 2-8-10 and 2-7 spare shooting	Spare Shooting: Focus on converting the 4-7 and 2-7 splits	Spare Shooting: Bowl 2 games of 10 frames, aiming to hit spares only.
Challenge: Bowl 10 strikes in a row using only a plastic spare ball	Challenge: Play a game of "all spares" where each shot must be a spare to move on to the next frame	Challenge: Bowl 3 games of 10 frames each, trying to score 220+ on each game.
Strategy: Practice playing different break points on the lane	Strategy: Work on playing the 1st arrow on a medium oil pattern	Strategy: Focus on playing the outside of the lane, using a straight shot.
Versatility on oil condition: Bowl on a custom pattern designed for the competition	Versatile on Oil Condition: Bowl 3 games on a medium oil pattern, adjusting your line and ball speed as needed	Versatile on Oil Condition: Bowl 2 games on a medium-difficulty oil pattern, focusing on finding the right ball and technique to handle the conditions.

Week 1:	Week 2:	Week 3
Simulation: Bowl 6 games at competition pace	Simulation: Play a 3-game series on the upcoming tournament pattern	Simulation: Bowl 3 games of 10 frames each, trying to simulate the competition environment as much as possible.
Cool-down: Static stretching for 10 minutes	Cool-down: Stretching and foam rolling	Cool-down: 10 minutes of static stretching and foam rolling.
Thursday:	Thursday:	Thursday:
Warm-up: 10 minutes of light cardio, followed by dynamic stretches	Warm-up: 10 minutes of light cardio and stretching	Warm-up: 10 minutes of stretching, followed by 15 minutes of light cardio (jogging or biking).
Drills: 10-pin drill, 7-pin drill, and 4-pin drill	Drills: Work on hitting the pocket consistently from the 3rd arrow, using different release and loft variations	Drills: 30 minutes of focus on hitting the same target repeatedly with the ball, moving between different areas of the lane to simulate changing oil conditions.
Spare shooting: 2-4-10 and 1-2-10 spare shooting	Spare Shooting: Focus on converting the 3-4-6-7-10 and 2-4-10 splits	Spare shooting: Focus on 7-10 splits, with 10 attempts.
Challenge: Bowl a game using only urethane ball	Challenge: Play a game of "strike or split" where each shot must either result in a strike or a split to move on to the next frame	Challenge: Bowl 10 frames with a specific target score in mind, adjusting strategy and ball selection as needed to reach the target.
Strategy: Focus on mental game and maintaining a positive attitude	Strategy: Work on playing the 3rd	Strategy: Focus on hitting the pocket consistently, adjusting ball speed and hand position to find the optimal line.
Versatility on oil condition: Bowl on a dual oil pattern	Versatility on oil condition: Bowl on a custom pattern designed for the competition	Versatile on oil condition: Bowl on a variety of oil patterns, adjusting ball selection and approach as needed to adapt to each pattern.
Simulation: Bowl 7 games at competition pace	Simulation: Bowl 6 games at competition pace	Simulation: Bowl three games as if in a competition setting, focusing on maintaining consistency and composure under pressure.
Cool-down: Static stretching for 10 minutes	Cool-down: Static stretching for 10 minutes	Cool-down: 10 minutes of stretching and relaxation techniques.

Table 17 – an example of a pre-competition schedule for advanced bowlers that includes warm-up, drills, spare shooting, challenges, strategy, versatility on oil condition, simulation, and cool-down for every day over the course of five days per week for four weeks before a competition

Game Strategy:

Game strategy in bowling during competition is a critical aspect of achieving success on the lanes. A well-thought-out game strategy is akin to a roadmap that guides bowlers through the different stages of a competition. Here, we outline the importance of game strategy, as illustrated example by the provided game-by-game approach:

Example

Game 1 - Start with a steady and reliable ball, concentrating on hitting your marks and maintaining possession of the ball. Aim for spares and make any necessary modifications.

Game 2 - In order to discover the ideal response, start to be more aggressive in your movements dependent on the lane conditions.

Game 3 - To retain your score, make any necessary adjustments while concentrating on accuracy and consistency.

Game 4 - Pay attention to maintaining your rhythm and timing while adjusting to any lane circumstances changes. Utilize all opportunities for strikes.

Game 5 - Concentrate on putting a strong end to the game and making any required modifications to optimize your score and momentum going into the championship game.

Game 6 - Evaluate your performance and standing in the match, and modify your approach as necessary. Keep your attention on your own game, and finish with assurance and tenacity.

The importance of a game strategy lies in its ability to provide structure, purpose, and adaptability throughout a competition. It helps bowlers stay focused on their goals, react to changing conditions, and make data-driven decisions to enhance their performance. Moreover, a well-crafted game strategy fosters mental resilience and allows bowlers to maintain a competitive edge even in the face of challenges. In the end, it's not just about rolling the ball; it's about navigating the complex and ever-changing environment of a competitive bowling tournament with skill and confidence.

Ball Brand	Coverstock	Dual Angle Layout	Game #	Axis Tilt	Axis Rotation	Ball Speed	Laydown	Arrow	Breakpoint
Storm	Hybrid	50 x 4.5 x 30	game 1-2	17 degrees	60 degrees	19 mph	15	12	6
Motiv	Pearl	65 x 4 x 35	game 3-4	16 degrees	50 degrees	19.5 mph	19	14	7
Brunswick	Solid	45 x 4.75 x 50	game 5-6	18 degrees	45 degrees	19 mph	22	16	7
Ebonite	Pearl	65 x 3.5 x 35	game 7-8	17 degrees	70 degrees	19.5 mph	26	19	8
Roto Grip	Pearl	55 x 5 x 45	game 8	19 degrees	40 degrees	19 mph	31	22	9

Table 18 – Example of Game Strategy for 6 game block

Match-play and stepladder coping strategies:

Developing effective match-play coping strategies is crucial for advanced bowlers as it addresses the unique challenges posed by competitive environments. Unlike practice sessions, tournaments involve heightened stress, the pressure of head-to-head competition, and the need for immediate adaptation to varying lane conditions. While practice allows bowlers to hone technical skills, the psychological aspects of match play demand specialized coping mechanisms. The intense focus, resilience to setbacks, and mental composure required during a match often differ significantly from the controlled environment of a practice session. The unpredictability of opponents, the dynamic nature of scores, and the stakes involved necessitate mental strategies that extend beyond the technical aspects of the game.

Attempting to simulate the exact conditions of match play in practice is challenging, as the psychological elements are inherently different when faced with the unpredictability and pressure of a tournament setting. Nevertheless, bowlers can enhance their readiness by incorporating simulated match scenarios into their training routines. This may involve practicing under time constraints, introducing competitive elements within the practice sessions, and deliberately creating an environment that challenges mental composure. By simulating match-play conditions, bowlers can develop and refine coping strategies, allowing them to cultivate a mindset that seamlessly transitions from practice to tournament situations. The mental methods outlined in the match-play coping strategy plan serve as valuable tools for bowlers seeking to master the psychological demands of competitive play, contributing to a holistic and well-rounded approach to elite-level bowling.

Match-play coping mechanisms are specialized mental and physical methods used to deal with the stress and difficulties that match-play contests present. As an illustration, breathing exercises, positive self-talk, and visualization exercises are some match-play coping tactics.

Here is an illustration of a match-play coping strategies plan for advanced bowlers, complete with ten mental methods and instructions for putting them into practice:

Focus on the present moment: *Keep your attention on the current moment and your breathing. Observe success while taking deep breaths. Avoid considering results from the past or the future. Pay attention to the shooting procedure.*

Develop a pre-shot ritual: *Create a regular ritual that will help you relax and prepare mentally for each shot. This regimen might incorporate physical exercises, deep breathing, and visualization.*

Positive self-talk: *Talking positively to yourself might help you feel more confident and self-assured. Use expressions like "I got this" or "I can make this shot." Refrain from criticizing or pushing oneself down.*

Reframe negative thinking: *When doubts or negative thoughts creep in, change them to positive ones. For instance, "I'm not good enough" may be rephrased as "I'm prepared and capable of making this shot."*

Accept the challenge: *Consider each game as a test of your mettle and an opportunity to advance. Setbacks and errors should not be used as motivation to give up; rather, they should be viewed as chances to improve.*

Set attainable targets: *Set attainable objectives for each game, such as a predetermined amount of strikes or spares. When you accomplish these goals, rejoice.*

Visualize success: *Envision yourself winning the match by employing strategies based on visualization. Imagine yourself making every shot with confidence and ease.*

Practice relaxation techniques: *To handle stress and anxiety during match play, incorporate strategies like progressive muscle relaxation, deep breathing, or meditation.*

Self-visualization: *Use your imagination to conjure up a vision of achievement. Consider the ball neatly striking the pocket as it rolls down the lane.*

Stay in control: *Maintain control over your feelings and responses. After each shot or frame, try to avoid getting too high or too low. Keep a level mind and remain committed to your objectives.*

Keep in mind that these are only a few instances of mental tactics that can be beneficial during match play. Every bowler is different; therefore, He may discover various approaches that suit him best. Find what works best for you by experimenting and trying different things.

1-Month Match-Play Coping Strategy Practice Plan for National Team Bowlers

Week 1: Establishing Foundations

Day 1-2: Self-Reflection and Goal Setting

- *Each bowler identifies personal strengths and areas for improvement in match-play scenarios.*
- *Set individualized, achievable goals for the month, focusing on mental aspects of performance.*

Day 3-4: Visualization Techniques

- *Introduce visualization exercises, emphasizing the importance of picturing success.*
- *Bowlers practice creating mental images of successful shots, maintaining focus, and handling pressure.*

Day 5-7: Pre-shot Ritual Development

- *Work on creating personalized pre-shot rituals to enhance mental readiness.*
- *Bowlers experiment with different routines and select the one that promotes relaxation and concentration.*

Week 2-3: Simulating Pressure Environments and Tactical Coping Strategies

Day 8-10: Competitive Practice Drills

- **Drill 1: Time Crunch Challenges**
  - *Bowlers practice under time constraints, simulating the pressure of a shot clock.*
  - *Focus on maintaining composure while executing precise shots within a limited timeframe.*
- **Drill 2: Team-based Pressure Rounds**
  - *Create a team competition where every member must perform under heightened pressure.*
  - *Encourage support and camaraderie to replicate tournament team dynamics.*
- **Drill 3: Head-to-Head Duels**
  - *Pair up bowlers for one-on-one duels during practice games.*
  - *Emphasize the psychological aspect of directly competing against a teammate, enhancing focus and determination.*

- *Drill 4: Blindfolded Bowling*
  - Bowlers take turns bowling blindfolded, relying solely on muscle memory and mental composure.
  - Enhance focus and adaptability under unexpected conditions.
- *Drill 5: Focus Zone Training*
  - Implement drills where bowlers consciously create a "focus zone" during practice, blocking out external distractions.
  - Enhance the ability to maintain concentration on individual performance rather than opponent scores.

Day 11-13: Psychological Stress Drills

- *Drill 6: Opponent Score Diversion*
  - Bowlers practice strategies to avoid getting distracted by the opponent's score during matches.
  - Emphasize staying mentally focused on personal game plans and routines.
- *Drill 7: Neutralizing External Pressure*
  - Introduce external distractions during practice, such as simulated crowd noise or spectators moving around.
  - Train bowlers to maintain mental composure despite external pressures.
- *Drill 8: Countering Scoreboard Watching*
  - Create scenarios where bowlers deliberately avoid looking at the opponent's scores on the scoreboard.
  - Develop mental habits to stay focused on their game rather than getting influenced by others.

Day 14-16: Adapting to Lane Conditions

- *Drill 9: Dynamic Lane Patterns*
  - Simulate dynamic changes in lane patterns during a single game, challenging adaptability.
  - Bowlers adjust strategies on-the-fly to changing conditions.
- *Drill 10: Spare Conversion Challenge*
  - Introduce a scenario where spare targets randomly shift during practice.
  - Enhance the ability to adapt to unexpected changes in spare shooting conditions.
- *Drill 11: Lane Condition Elimination*
  - Gradually eliminate certain lane conditions during practice games, forcing strategic adjustments.
  - Bowlers refine their adaptability skills by navigating through progressively challenging conditions.
- *Drill 12: Mental Trigger Analysis*
  - Bowlers analyze potential mental triggers opponents may use.
  - Develop strategies to remain focused and unfazed by opponents' attempts to disrupt concentration.

Day 17-19: Scenario-Based Training

- *Drill 13: Crisis Reaction Relay*
  - Create relay-style scenarios where bowlers respond to sudden crises, testing team coordination.
  - Emphasize quick thinking and communication under pressure.
- *Drill 14: Avoidance Techniques*
  - Bowlers practice techniques to avoid being mentally triggered by opponents, maintaining focus on their game.

- *Develop mental resilience to external provocations.*
- ***Drill 15: Mental Reset Strategies***
  - *Introduce exercises where bowlers quickly reset their mental state after potential opponent-triggering incidents.*
  - *Enhance the ability to regain focus and composure during matches.*

Day 21: Team Meeting - Mental Toughness

- *Guest speaker or sports psychologist discusses mental toughness and its role in elite-level competition.*
- *Team shares experiences and strategies for maintaining mental composure.*

Week 4: Fine-Tuning and Feedback

Day 22-24: Review and Refinement

- *Analyze the past weeks' performances, focusing on mental aspects.*
- *Refine coping strategies based on individual and team feedback.*

Day 25-27: Final Simulations

- ***Drill 16: Match Point Pressure Test***
  - *Simulate scenarios where bowlers must make specific shots to secure a match victory.*
  - *Evaluate mental resilience and performance under high-pressure situations.*
- ***Drill 17: Unexpected Lane Condition Challenge***
  - *Introduce a surprise change in lane conditions during a critical moment in practice matches.*
  - *Train bowlers to adapt swiftly to unforeseen challenges.*
- ***Drill 18: Mindful Opponent Interaction***
  - *Incorporate scenarios where bowlers engage with opponents in a friendly manner to maintain focus.*
  - *Emphasize the importance of positive interactions without letting them affect individual performance.*

Day 28: Team Debrief and Visualization

- *Team discusses learnings and experiences from the month.*
- *Engage in a final visualization session, focusing on upcoming tournaments.*

Day 29-30: Rest and Mental Preparation

- ***Drill 19: Visualization and Positive Affirmations***
  - *Bowlers engage in a final visualization session, mentally rehearsing successful performances.*
  - *Emphasize positive affirmations to boost confidence and maintain a positive mindset.*
- ***Drill 20: Team Unity Exercise***
  - *Foster a sense of unity within the team through collaborative activities.*
  - *Strengthening team bonds contributes to a supportive environment during the upcoming tournaments.*

This comprehensive one-month plan systematically develops advanced coping strategies for national team bowlers, ensuring they are mentally prepared and resilient in the face of the unique challenges presented by match-play scenarios.

Post-competition evaluation:

Stepping off the lanes after a challenging bowling competition doesn't mark the end of a bowler's journey; rather, it signifies the beginning of a critical phase – the post-competition evaluation. In the realm of advanced bowling, where precision and strategy can make all the difference, taking the time to reflect on one's performance becomes a crucial step toward continuous improvement. This introspective process goes beyond merely acknowledging the score on the board; it delves into the intricate details of physical and mental preparation, equipment choices, shot-making finesse, and strategic decisions that shape the outcome of each game.

Post-competition evaluation is akin to a personalized coaching session, an opportunity for advanced bowlers to dissect their performance and identify the nuanced aspects that warrant refinement. It involves a meticulous examination of every facet of the game, ranging from the effectiveness of warm-up routines to the intricacies of lane play and spare shooting accuracy. This reflective journey is not just about recognizing strengths but, more importantly, acknowledging and addressing weaknesses.

The advanced bowler's arsenal extends beyond the physical act of throwing a ball down the lane. It encompasses mental resilience, strategic acumen, and the ability to adapt to varying lane conditions. In the pursuit of excellence, post-competition evaluation serves as the compass, guiding bowlers towards targeted areas for enhancement. It involves watching video footage, scrutinizing performance data, and delving into the intricacies of mental and physical preparation methods.

Each section of the post-competition evaluation contributes to the tapestry of improvement. From the intricacies of physical endurance to the fine-tuning of spare shooting accuracy, this process is a roadmap to a more polished and formidable competitor. Advanced bowlers are not content with mere participation; they aspire to mastery, and this begins with an honest evaluation of their performance on the lanes.

Area of Evaluation	Steps to Take	Results
Physical Preparation	Review warm-up routine and stretching techniques	Warm-up routine and stretches were effective in preparing for competition
Mental Preparation	Reflect on pre-competition mental preparation strategies	Felt calm and focused during competition
Equipment	Review ball selection and layout	Ball selection and layout were effective for the oil pattern
Shot Making	Analyze shot accuracy and consistency	Struggled with accuracy on left side spares
Lane Play	Analyze performance on different lane conditions	Struggled with transition on fresh oil pattern
Spare Shooting	Review spare shooting accuracy	Missed several single pin spares
Game Strategy	Reflect on strategic decisions made during competition	Made good decisions in games 1-3 but struggled in games 4-6
Emotional Control	Reflect on ability to control emotions during competition	Struggled with frustration after missed spares
Physical Endurance	Assess physical stamina during competition	Felt fatigued towards the end of the 8-game block
Overall Performance	Evaluate overall performance and identify areas of improvement	Overall performance was average, need to focus on spare shooting and mental preparation for future competitions

Advanced bowlers can pinpoint particular areas for improvement and create winning competition tactics by using a thorough post-competition evaluation process.

Table 19 – Example of Post- competition evaluation sheet - Basic

Post competition Trauma:

Before the first ball is rolled down the lane, anticipation builds like a crescendo. For the advanced bowler, particularly in tournaments of personal significance, the emotional stakes are high. Dreams of triumph, visions of success, and the desire to prove oneself intensify as the competition date approaches.

However, not every tournament concludes with the sweet taste of victory. When the outcomes don't align with the aspirations, disappointment can be a heavy burden to bear. The emotional investment in the competition, coupled with the tangible effort put forth, can amplify the sense of defeat.

For some bowlers, the aftermath of a less-than-ideal performance can stir up questions about self-worth. Thoughts like, "Did I train hard enough?" or "Am I truly as skilled as I thought?" may linger, creating an internal struggle that transcends the boundaries of the bowling alley.

The immediate aftermath often involves a deep dive into personal performance. Bowlers may replay each frame in their minds, scrutinizing every choice and execution. While this reflection is a vital aspect of improvement, it can also become a double-edged sword, potentially magnifying errors and planting seeds of self-doubt.

For those who are deeply passionate about their sport, frustration can be a constant companion. Missed spares, strategic missteps, or a series of unexpected challenges may evoke a sense of frustration that lingers long after the tournament's conclusion.

In extreme cases, especially when the tournament held profound personal importance, the emotional aftermath can be likened to a form of trauma. The emotional investment, coupled with the perceived failure, can create a lasting impact on a bowler's psyche, influencing future performances and the overall relationship with the sport.

Post-event Coping Strategies and Moving Forward:

Seek Support: *Acknowledging the emotional toll and seeking support from friends, family, or even a sports psychologist can provide a valuable outlet. Talking about the experience and expressing emotions can be a cathartic process.*

Set Realistic Expectations: *Reassessing and adjusting expectations for future competitions can be crucial. Recognizing that not every tournament will yield success helps in cultivating resilience and mental fortitude.*

Learn and Grow: *Every setback is an opportunity for growth. Instead of viewing it as a failure, see it as a lesson. Analyze the performance objectively, identify areas for improvement, and use the experience as a stepping stone for future success.*

Mental Preparation: *Devoting time to mental preparation is not only essential before a tournament but also in the aftermath. Techniques such as visualization, mindfulness, and positive self-talk can contribute to a healthier mental state.*

Mental Skills

Advanced bowlers who compete in international competitions must have strong mental preparation in order to perform well. How some of these abilities may impact a bowler's performance is as follows:

How the brain works: Bowlers can improve their mental performance by being aware of how the brain works. For instance, bowlers can concentrate on the job at hand and make better decisions during competition if they are aware that the prefrontal cortex is in charge of decision-making and attentional control.

Switching hemispheres: The left hemisphere of the brain is in charge of logical reasoning and analysis, whereas the right hemisphere is in charge of imaginative reasoning and intuition. Advanced bowlers can develop the ability to alternate between these hemispheres depending on the scenario, such as intellectually analyzing lane conditions before using intuition to make shots.

Brain dominance: Everyone's left or right side of the brain is dominant in some way. Bowlers' mental preparation can be tailored to their capabilities by being aware of which parts of their brains they use most frequently. A right-brained bowler, for instance, might be more imaginative and visual, and visualization exercises might help.

Storing & retrieving information: Memory plays a critical part in bowling since bowlers must recall lane conditions, ball reflexes, and previous performances. Advanced bowlers might develop memory tricks like mnemonics or visualization to better retain and recall this information.

Concentration: Retaining your attention throughout a competition is essential for success. Advanced bowlers can improve their ability to concentrate by engaging in mindfulness exercises or employing mental signals to refocus their attention when they become distracted.

Dealing with distractions: During competition, there may be a variety of distractions, such as lane breakdowns and crowd noise. Advanced bowlers might develop coping mechanisms for these interruptions like breathing exercises or self-talk to maintain focus.

Visualization & mental rehearsal: Visualization, which is mentally practicing shots or scenarios beforehand, can be a highly effective method for raising performance. Advanced bowlers can practice specific areas of their game using visualization techniques, such as envisioning the desired ball reaction.

Relaxation & controlled breathing exercises: Exercises for relaxation and controlled breathing can assist bowlers in controlling their tension and anxiety during competition. Advanced bowlers might utilize strategies like progressive muscular relaxation or deep breathing to remain composed and focused under duress.

How to quiet the mind: To quiet the mind, one must learn to let go of obtrusive thoughts and feelings and concentrate on the here and now. Advanced bowlers can quiet their minds and sharpen their attention by practicing mindfulness techniques like meditation or body scanning.

Energy dispersement: Maintaining optimum performance throughout a competition depends on managing energy levels. Advanced bowlers can develop effective energy management techniques, such as pace between games or visualizing energy savings during breaks.

Stress & anxiety: These factors can hinder performance and are particularly difficult for bowlers who compete internationally. Advanced bowlers can regulate these emotions and perform at their best by using a range of strategies, including cognitive restructuring or relaxation exercises.

Arousal control: Finding the ideal amount of vigor and excitement to perform at one's best is known as arousal control. Advanced bowlers can regulate their arousal levels and keep their focus during the tournament by using strategies like visualization or positive self-talk.

Mental Skill	Impact on Bowler's Performance	Example
How the Brain Works	Awareness of brain functions aids in decision-making.	Using prefrontal cortex knowledge to focus on shots.
Switching Hemispheres	Alternating between logical analysis and intuition.	Analyzing lane conditions then trusting gut for shots.
Brain Dominance	Tailoring mental prep based on the dominant brain hemisphere.	Visualizing shots for right-brained, imaginative bowler.
Storing & Retrieving Info	Effective memory aids in recalling past experiences.	Using mnemonic techniques to remember lane patterns.
Concentration	Sustained focus throughout the competition.	Practicing mindfulness to stay attentive during play.
Dealing with Distractions	Coping strategies to handle interruptions.	Using breathing exercises to refocus after distractions.
Visualization & Rehearsal	Mentally practicing shots and scenarios.	Visualizing the desired ball reaction before throwing.
Relaxation & Controlled Breathing	Managing tension and anxiety during play.	Deep breathing to remain composed under pressure.
Quiet the Mind	Letting go of intrusive thoughts for better focus.	Practicing meditation to clear the mind before a shot.
Energy Dispersement	Managing energy levels for consistent performance.	Visualizing conserving energy during breaks.
Stress & Anxiety	Regulating emotions to perform well under pressure.	Using cognitive restructuring to manage anxiety.
Arousal Control	Finding optimal excitement levels for peak performance.	Using positive self-talk to maintain focus.

Table 20 – Example of Mental Skills abilities of Stage 5 bowlers

Physical Development:

Bowlers' physical development is an important part of their game and can have a big impact on how they prepare for and perform in international competitions. Physical growth may have the following effects on advanced bowlers:

Strength Training Assessment – This entails determining athletes' present level of strength using a variety of tests, such as the one-rep maximum or a functional movement screening. This might help identify any imbalances or weaknesses that their strength training program needs to address. For instance, a skilled bowler would have his upper body strength assessed to check for any imbalances that might interfere with his ability to deliver the ball accurately and consistently.

Example of Strength Training Assessment

Below is a table for a 4-day workout regimen aimed towards bowler muscle growth, fat loss, general strength, balance, and power. It features stretching, mobility, and flexibility exercises, exercises for the abs, cardio alternatives, and rest periods.

Day 1: Chest, Shoulders, Triceps, Abs, Balance, Power, and Cardio

Exercise	Sets x Reps	PRE*	Rest Time
Barbell Bench Press	3-4 x 8-10	8-9	60-90 seconds
Dumbbell Shoulder Press	3 x 10-12	8-9	45-60 seconds
Triceps Dips	3 x 12-15	8-9	45-60 seconds
Cable Crunches	3 x 15-20	8-9	30-45 seconds
Plank	3 x 30-45 seconds	N/A	30-45 seconds
Single-Leg Romanian Deadlifts	3 x 8-10 (each leg)	8-9	60-90 seconds
Medicine Ball Woodchoppers	3 x 12-15 (each side)	8-9	45-60 seconds
Treadmill Running	20-30 minutes	N/A	Moderate pace

Stretching, Mobility, and Flexibility Exercises

Day 2: Back, Biceps, Legs, Abs, Balance, Power, and Cardio

Exercise	Sets x Reps	PRE*	Rest Time
Deadlifts	3-4 x 6-8	8-9	60-90 seconds
Pull-ups	3 x 8-10	8-9	45-60 seconds
Barbell Squats	3 x 10-12	8-9	45-60 seconds
Russian Twists	3 x 15-20	8-9	30-45 seconds
Reverse Crunches	3 x 15-20	8-9	30-45 seconds
Swiss Ball Squats	3 x 12-15	8-9	45-60 seconds
Bosu Ball Lunges	3 x 10-12 (each leg)	8-9	45-60 seconds
Stationary Bike	20-30 minutes	N/A	Interval training

Stretching, Mobility, and Flexibility Exercises

Day 3: Chest, Shoulders, Triceps, Abs, Balance, Power, and Cardio

Exercise	Sets x Reps	PRE*	Rest Time
Incline Dumbbell Press	3-4 x 8-10	8-9	60-90 seconds
Seated Dumbbell Press	3 x 10-12	8-9	45-60 seconds
Skull Crushers	3 x 12-15	8-9	45-60 seconds
Bicycle Crunches	3 x 15-20	8-9	30-45 seconds
Side Plank	3 x 30-45 seconds	N/A	30-45 seconds
Swiss Ball Russian Twists	3 x 15-20 (each side)	8-9	30-45 seconds
Dumbbell Step-ups	3 x 10-12 (each leg)	8-9	45-60 seconds
Elliptical Training	20-30 minutes	N/A	Moderate intensity

Stretching, Mobility, and Flexibility Exercises

Day 4: Legs, Back, Biceps, Abs, Balance, Power, and Cardio

Exercise	Sets x Reps	PRE*	Rest Time
Barbell Squats	3-4 x 8-10	8-9	60-90 seconds
Romanian Deadlifts	3 x 10-12	8-96	45-60 seconds
Bent-Over Rows	3 x 10-12	8-9	45-60 seconds
Hanging Leg Raises	3 x 12-15	8-9	30-45 seconds
Reverse Plank	3 x 30-45 seconds	N/A	30-45 seconds
Single-Leg Calf Raises	3 x 10-12 (each leg)	8-9	45-60 seconds
Medicine Ball Slams	3 x 12-15	8-9	45-60 seconds
Stair Climbing	20-30 minutes	N/A	Moderate pace

Stretching, Mobility, and Flexibility Exercises

Table 21 – Example of Workout Plan for advanced bowler

Strength Training Development - The athlete might create a strength training program to correct any deficits or imbalances when the exam is finished. This program will often contain both general strength-building workouts and sports-specific activities. For instance, an experienced bowler may include arm and shoulder strengthening workouts like bench presses and bicep curls to enhance his capacity for powerful and precise delivery of the ball.

Cardiovascular Development - Cardiovascular development is crucial for enhancing endurance and general fitness. Running, cycling, or swimming are just a few examples of the activities that can be used to accomplish this. For instance, an experienced bowler can include routine jogging or cycling workouts in his training regimen to increase his general fitness and stamina on the lanes.

Increased Flexibility - A greater range of motion is possible thanks to increased flexibility, which is also beneficial for injury prevention. A skilled bowler may include yoga or stretching practices in his training regimen to increase flexibility and avoid problems like back or shoulder strains.

Biomechanical Analysis - Biomechanical analysis is the process of analyzing an athlete's movement patterns to spot any weak points or inefficiencies. Video analysis or other techniques can be used to do this. For instance, a skilled bowler might undertake biomechanical testing to spot any difficulties with approach or release that might impair performance as a whole.

BIO-MECHANICAL ASPECT	MEASUREMENT	IDEAL RANGE	BOWLER'S RESULTS
Stance Width	16-20 inches	15-18 inches	16 inches
Approach Length	12-14 feet	13-14 feet	13.5 feet
Swing Path	Straight	Straight	Straight
Backward Lean	8-10 degrees	10-12 degrees	14 degrees
Knee Bend	45-60 degrees	50-55 degrees	52 degrees
Release Point	Foul line	Foul line	Foul line
Follow-Through	Smooth and relaxed	Smooth and relaxed	Smooth and relaxed

The bio-mechanical elements indicated in this table are crucial elements of bowlers' technique that might affect their performance. Based on the most effective approach for an experienced bowler, the measurement column displays the recommended range for each component. The results column for bowlers displays the precise measurements for each element that was noted during the comprehensive bio-mechanical study. Based on a comparison between the optimum range and the bowler's outcomes, the bowler's coach or trainer can utilize this table to pinpoint any areas of the bowler's technique that may need work or adjustment. For instance, the coach might advise bowlers to expand their stance a little bit to encourage improved balance and stability during their approach if their current stance width is only 15 inches, which is at the lower end of the optimal range. Additionally, to enhance bowlers' general posture and balance, the coach might advise practicing maintaining their upper body more straight throughout their approach if their backward lean is 14 degrees, which is a little bit higher than the recommended range.

Table 22 – Example of Bio-Mechanical elements assessment

Nutritional Assessment - A nutritional evaluation looks at an athlete's current diet to find any deficits or room for improvement. A sports nutritionist consultation or blood tests can be used to determine this. To find out if an experienced bowler is consuming enough protein and other nutrients to support his training and recovery, for instance, He could have his diet evaluated.

Example:

NUTRITIONAL ASPECT	IDEAL RANGE	BOWLER'S RESULTS
Calories	2,500-3,000 per day	2,700
Protein	1.2-1.6 grams per kilogram of body weight	110 grams
Carbohydrates	5-7 grams per kilogram of body weight	350 grams
Fat	20-30% of total calories	70 grams
Fiber	25-30 grams per day	28 grams
Hydration	8-10 cups of water per day	9 cups

NUTRITIONAL ASPECT	IDEAL RANGE	BOWLER'S RESULTS

The nutritional factors stated in this table are essential parts of bowlers' diet that can affect their performance. Based on the best nutrition for an experienced bowler, the recommended range for each factor is displayed in the optimum range column. The bowler's results column displays the actual intake for each finding from the comprehensive nutritional evaluation. Based on a comparison between the recommended range and the bowler's performance, the bowler's coach or nutritionist can utilize this chart to pinpoint any areas of the bowler's diet that may need improvement or correction. For instance, the nutritionist might advise increasing the bowler's protein intake if it is only 110 grams (which is at the lower end of the recommended range) to support muscle growth and recovery. Additionally, the coach might advise bowlers to drink more water throughout the day to encourage improved overall hydration and athletic performance if they only consume 9 cups of water per day (which is significantly less than the recommended range).

Table 23 – Example of Nutrition assessment

Nutritional Education - Athletes who want to support their training and performance should receive nutritional education on how to choose appropriate foods. For instance, a skilled bowler might receive nutritional instruction on how to feed his body appropriately before and after competition as well as how to make smart food decisions when traveling to competitions.

NUTRITIONAL TOPIC	KEY INFORMATION
Pre-Competition Fueling	Aim to eat a meal containing carbohydrates, protein, and a small amount of fat about 3-4 hours before competition. • Consider a small, easily digestible snack (such as a banana or a protein bar) 30-60 minutes before competition if needed.
Post-Competition Recovery	Aim to eat a meal containing carbohydrates and protein within 30-60 minutes after competition to aid in muscle recovery. • Consider a recovery drink or snack that contains both carbohydrates and protein if a meal is not immediately available.
Healthy Eating on the Road	Plan ahead and pack healthy snacks such as fresh fruit, nuts, and whole-grain crackers to avoid relying on vending machines or fast food options. • Choose grilled or baked options instead of fried, and opt for lean protein sources such as chicken or fish.
Hydration	Aim to drink water throughout the day, and consume sports drinks only during prolonged or intense exercise. • Monitor urine color as an indicator of hydration status; aim for a light yellow color.
Supplements	Be cautious of supplement use, as some are not regulated and can contain harmful ingredients especially for bowlers. • Consult with a registered dietitian or sports medicine professional before starting any supplement regimen.

The dietary subjects included in this table are important ones that an experienced bowler might learn about to support his practice and performance. According to the most recent dietary recommendations and industry best practices, the important information column offers helpful advice and insights for each issue. This table can be used by the bowlers' coach or nutritionist to offer educational resources and advice to the bowler, assisting them in making wise and healthy eating decisions that benefit their athletic performance. For instance, if the bowler is preparing to travel for a competition, the coach may remind him of the value of bringing wholesome snacks and making wise food decisions while traveling, and He might offer recommendations for suitable options.

Table 24 – Example of Nutrition education sheet

WORLD ELITE CLASS

STAGE 6 (WORLD ELITE LEVEL)

In order to place on the podium in renowned competitions like the World Championships or the World Games, international bowlers are committed to developing their abilities and skills. These bowlers strive for consistency in their performances, being able to execute shots precisely, hit pins reliably, and adjust to testing lane oil patterns and other situations. For these high-stress and intensive tournament conditions, preparation that goes beyond physical training is essential. Multi-sport events like the IBF World Championships are known to be more mentally demanding than events for just one sport. Therefore, bowlers at this level need to practice mental preparation routines long before important competitions to make sure they can perform effectively under pressure. The bowlers and their support staff should establish a thorough training, competition, and rehabilitation program to correct any performance disparities. To make sure that these top bowlers are prepared in every way possible, it is important to assemble an integrated support team with high levels of competence.

Role Structure:

In order to achieve bowlers' training goals and overall performance objectives, coaches are essential. To ensure bowlers' buy-in, participation, comprehension, and responsibility for their success, they should keep an eye on every area of training and include bowlers in the planning process. To stay current on new advancements in the sport, coaches should aggressively pursue professional development opportunities in both formal and informal settings.

Recognizing that the long-term success of the bowler depends on the support of the training, competition, and recovery plan, parents and the bowler's support system should respect the bowler and the national coach. For the advantage of the bowler who is winning-focused, He should promote interaction and cooperation between the local personal coach and the national coach. Additionally, parents and the bowler's support system must be aware that during international competitions, bowlers are expected to adhere to the bowler code of conduct, which includes all directives and guidelines provided by the national coach and management.

Bowlers must take responsibility for their actions throughout both practice and competition. As ambassadors and role models for their Federation, bowling centers, and on the world stage, they should set performance goals and work to accomplish them, controlling distractions to ensure strong performances in the demanding and complicated tournament environment. Additionally, important is effective communication with all parties engaged in their preparation, including coaches, medical teams, managers, and the National Federation(s). The pursuit of leisurely outdoor pursuits besides bowling is also encouraged.

Bowlers who complete six games, make 90-95% of spares, hit the head pin 95% of the time, keep the ball in the lane 100% of the time, and have a strike rate of 50% to 60% are considered to be competitive on the world stage.

To build a stronger base of bowlers and coaches along with National Sport Organization should deliver high-quality programs, provide information for bowlers of all levels, and implement a coach mentoring system. Increasing the quantity of national team training camps, raising awareness of national bowlers in local communities, training and certifying coaches for the high-performance context, showcasing and successfully marketing Team members to inform the public about bowling beyond recreational experiences, and collaborating with owners of bowling centers to encourage the use of certified and qualified coaches are other crucial strategies to support the development of the sport.

Cognitive And Psychological Changes:

In **Stage 6 - World Elite Level,** bowlers are at the pinnacle of their careers, striving to achieve success in renowned international competitions such as the IBF World Championships. At this stage, their cognitive and psychological aspects have evolved to a remarkable degree to meet the high demands of elite competition. Here are the changes and improvements in these aspects for bowlers at this stage:

1. **Exceptional Mental Toughness:**
    - Bowlers at this level exhibit unparalleled mental toughness. They can handle the intense pressure and stress of world-class competitions, staying focused and composed even in the most challenging situations.

2. **Precise Shot Execution:**
    - They possess extraordinary mental precision in executing shots. Their ability to hit pins with exactitude and make adjustments to various lane conditions is unmatched.

3. **Adaptability to Lane Conditions:**
    - These elite bowlers can adapt swiftly and effectively to changing lane conditions and challenging oil patterns found at international competitions.

4. **Advanced Mental Preparation:**
    - Bowlers engage in rigorous and systematic mental preparation routines long before important competitions. They have developed a highly structured approach to mental readiness.

5. **Competing in Multi-Sport Events:**
    - Competitions like the IBF World Championships require an even higher level of mental preparation, given the intense nature of multi-sport events. They are prepared for the unique mental challenges these events present.

6. **Specialized Mental Training:**
    - Elite bowlers seek the guidance of specialized mental training professionals to ensure they are fully prepared to perform under the most demanding conditions.

7. **Integrated Support Team:**
    - They assemble an integrated support team with unparalleled expertise in sports psychology, physiologists, nutritionists, and other fields to leave no aspect of their preparation to chance.

8. **High-Level Goal Setting:**
    - Goals at this stage are at the highest level of competition. Bowlers set ambitious performance targets and work relentlessly to achieve them.

9. **Exceptional Emotional Control:**
    - Their ability to control emotions, both in times of success and adversity, is exceptional. They maintain a laser-like focus during competition.

10. **Elite Leadership:**
    - Elite bowlers take on leadership roles within their teams and inspire their fellow athletes. They contribute to the success of their teams on and off the lanes.

11. **Adaptation to a Global Stage:**
    - These bowlers are equipped to represent their countries on the world stage, adapting seamlessly to different countries, cultures, and international competition formats.

12. **Self-Analysis and Continuous Improvement:**
    - The pursuit of improvement is a never-ending journey. Bowlers continuously analyze their game, seeking any area for improvement, no matter how minor.

13. **Balanced Lifestyle:**
    - Maintaining a balanced lifestyle remains paramount, with a focus on time management, nutrition, rest, and overall well-being.

14. **Professionalism and Sportsmanship:**
    - They adhere to the highest ethical standards and uphold the values of professionalism and sportsmanship, serving as role models for their sport.

15. **Reflecting on International Experiences:**
    - Every international experience, whether a triumph or a setback, is an opportunity for growth and learning. They draw valuable insights from their global competition.

16. **Passion and Self-Drive:**
    - The passion for the sport and self-drive are undiminished. They understand the level of commitment required and willingly invest in their development.

17. **Learning from the Best:**
    - They continually seek inspiration and learning from the best in their field, both within and outside the sport of bowling.

Bowlers in Stage 6 have achieved the highest level of cognitive and psychological development, positioning themselves as some of the world's best athletes in their sport. Their exceptional mental toughness, precision, and adaptability make them formidable competitors on the global stage. With unwavering dedication to their sport and unparalleled mental preparation, they are ready to stand on the podium at renowned international competitions.

Neurological Development:

In **Stage 6 - World Elite Level**, athletes have reached the pinnacle of their neurological development, enabling them to excel in renowned competitions like the World Championships Here are the key changes and improvements in neurological factors that occur during Stage 6:

1. **Supreme Muscle Coordination:**
    - Athletes exhibit supreme muscle coordination, allowing them to execute their shots with unparalleled precision and consistency, regardless of the complexities of lane conditions.

2. **Enhanced Spatial Processing:**
    - Spatial processing abilities are advanced to an exceptional level. Athletes can read and analyze intricate lane patterns quickly, making micro-adjustments to optimize their shots.

3. **Peak Proprioception and Kinesthetic Awareness:**
    - Proprioception and kinesthetic awareness reach their peak, granting athletes an extraordinary sense of body position and movement. This precision is crucial for executing highly consistent and repeatable deliveries.

4. **Lightning-Fast Reaction Time and Decision-Making:**

   - Athletes display lightning-fast reaction times and make rapid, astute decisions during high-stress competitive situations, ensuring they can adapt instantly to changing conditions.

5. **Mastery of Advanced Muscle Memory:**

   - Athletes have achieved mastery of advanced muscle memory, enabling them to effortlessly reproduce their preferred shots consistently, even under the most challenging circumstances.

6. **Enhanced Cognitive Flexibility:**

   - Cognitive flexibility is highly advanced, enabling athletes to fluidly adapt their strategies and tactics during competitions, ensuring they can respond to a variety of scenarios effectively.

7. **Indomitable Mental Toughness and Resilience:**

   - Athletes possess indomitable mental toughness and resilience, allowing them to handle extreme levels of stress and pressure that are characteristic of elite international competitions.

8. **Pinpoint Focus and Concentration:**

   - Focus and concentration have reached their zenith, ensuring that athletes maintain a laser-like mental acuity throughout prolonged and demanding international competitive events.

9. **Masterful Tactical Decision-Making:**

   - Athletes exhibit masterful tactical decision-making, with the ability to make expert-level choices related to equipment, shot adjustments, and overall game strategy based on their deep understanding of lane conditions and the global competitive context.

10. **Eagle-Eyed Visual Processing and Precision Targeting:**

    - Visual processing and targeting skills have been refined to an extraordinary degree, allowing athletes to scrutinize complex lane patterns and execute precise micro-adjustments for consistent peak performance.

11. **World-Class Pattern Recognition:**

    - Athletes are world-class in recognizing, interpreting, and responding to a broad spectrum of lane patterns, giving them the ability to anticipate and adapt to evolving conditions with remarkable precision.

12. **Enhanced Memory and Rapid Learning Retention:**

    - Memory and learning capabilities are heightened, allowing athletes to accumulate extensive experience and knowledge, capitalizing on their vast reservoir of bowling insights.

13. **Elite Stress and Pressure Management:**

    - Athletes excel in managing stress and pressure, maintaining unwavering composure and focus in the most demanding and high-stakes international competitive environments.

14. **Adaptability to the Most Challenging Lane Conditions:**

    - Athletes demonstrate unparalleled adaptability to the most challenging lane conditions, consistently assessing and adjusting to evolving oil patterns with a high level of precision.

In Stage 6, athletes have reached the zenith of their neurological development, which is indispensable for their success at the world elite level. Their remarkable neurological enhancements set them apart as top-tier competitors, capable of consistently performing at a level that can secure podium positions in renowned international competitions. These neurological improvements, combined with their extensive experience and training, establish them as world-class bowlers who can compete at the highest echelons of the sport.

Brain Regions And Cognitive Functions Development:

1. **Spatial Information:**
   - Spatial information processing becomes finely honed to adapt to the most challenging and varied lane conditions in global competitions.
   - Bowlers demonstrate unmatched spatial intelligence and the ability to adapt quickly to unpredictable situations.

2. **White Matter (WM):**
   - White matter connectivity reaches an optimal state, facilitating rapid information processing, sensory-motor integration, and real-time decision-making under extreme pressure.
   - Bowlers display exceptional mental resilience and agility, enabling them to react to unpredictable lane conditions and formidable opponents.

3. **Motor Cortex:**
   - The motor cortex becomes highly specialized, allowing for unprecedented motor control and precision in the face of dynamic and unpredictable conditions.
   - Bowlers maintain extraordinary composure and execution in high-pressure, high-stakes international competitions.

4. **Somatosensory Cortex:**
   - Superior somatosensory processing empowers bowlers to execute flawless adjustments in response to ever-changing, challenging conditions.
   - Bowlers maintain an unwavering awareness of their body's feedback, ensuring exceptional precision in every shot.

5. **Superior Parietal Lobule (SPL):**
   - The SPL plays a central role in dynamic spatial orientation, strategic decision-making, and sensory-motor integration in the most demanding international competitions.
   - Bowlers exhibit exceptional spatial acumen, making swift and precise decisions in high-pressure situations.

6. **Inferior Occipitofrontal Fasciculus (IOFF):**
   - Advanced visual processing skills allow bowlers to decipher complex lane patterns and competitors' strategies at the international level.
   - Bowlers excel at reading and reacting to the nuances of international competition, making precise adjustments.

7. **Intraparietal Sulcus (IPS):**
   - The IPS reaches its zenith, facilitating advanced spatial and numerical processing, crucial for data-driven decision-making in international tournaments.
   - Bowlers demonstrate unparalleled expertise in tactical planning and decision-making under the most intense competitive circumstances.

8. **Precuneus:**
   - The precuneus remains crucial for self-awareness, mental imagery, and strategic planning, becoming paramount in high-pressure international competitions.
   - Bowlers master mental visualization and tactical planning, positioning themselves as world-class competitors in global events.

At **Stage 6**, bowlers prepare rigorously and adhere to a meticulous training, competition, and recovery program. This stage demands not only physical excellence but also unwavering mental fortitude to perform at the highest level in the most mentally and emotionally demanding tournaments. The cognitive and neurological enhancements achieved during this stage are instrumental in helping bowlers secure podium positions in prestigious international competitions. They become international icons and potential representatives of their countries in bowling's world elite level.

Hormones Development:

Stage 6 (25 and above) represents adulthood for athletes, and it comes with its own set of hormonal changes and considerations. During this stage, athletes may experience the following hormonal dynamics:

1. **Sex Hormones (Testosterone and Estrogen):** These sex hormones play a role in maintaining sexual characteristics, regulating the menstrual cycle in females, and influencing fertility. In early adulthood, these hormone levels tend to be stable, with testosterone levels typically at their peak in males and estrogen levels stable in females. However, hormone levels can vary among individuals.

2. **Cortisol:** Cortisol, the "stress hormone," remains important in regulating energy metabolism and responding to stress. It continues to play a role in the body's daily functions. Cortisol levels may vary depending on an individual's stress levels and lifestyle.

3. **Growth Hormone (GH):** GH levels decline as individuals reach adulthood. During early adulthood, GH is primarily involved in tissue repair and maintenance rather than significant growth.

4. **Insulin:** Insulin still regulates blood sugar levels and nutrient uptake by cells. It continues to be important for overall energy metabolism. However, insulin sensitivity can change with age and lifestyle factors.

5. **Thyroid Hormones (T3 and T4):** Thyroid hormone levels remain stable but can be influenced by factors like diet, exercise, and overall health. They continue to play a role in regulating metabolism and energy production.

6. **Leptin and Adiponectin:** These hormones play roles in appetite regulation and fat metabolism. Hormone levels can vary depending on an individual's body composition, diet, and physical activity levels.

7. **Melatonin:** Melatonin continues to regulate sleep patterns, ensuring that individuals get restful and restorative sleep, which is essential for overall health and well-being.

8. **Reproductive Hormones (Follicle-Stimulating Hormone and Luteinizing Hormone):** These hormones regulate the menstrual cycle in females and influence fertility in both males and females. In early adulthood, reproductive hormones are typically stable, but fertility can vary among individuals.

9. **Pregnancy-Related Hormones (if applicable):** In females who become pregnant during this age range, there are additional hormonal changes associated with pregnancy and breastfeeding.

It's important to note that individual variations in hormone levels and responses to lifestyle factors are common. Factors such as diet, exercise, stress, and overall health can influence hormonal balance during early adulthood. For specific concerns or to better understand your own hormonal profile, consulting with a healthcare provider or endocrinologist is advisable.

Tactical Education

Analyzing prior performance data to determine strengths and weaknesses and creating a strategic plan for upcoming competitions are required when creating a tactical portfolio based on data from previous competitions. World-class bowlers can use this to better plan for events, anticipate opponents' methods, and make wise tactical choices while competing. Here are four instances of how this tactical education subject might influence a bowler's performance in the here and now and in the future:

Example 1: When a bowler examines his historical competition data, He sees that He frequently fails to convert spares in pressure-filled circumstances. He creates a tactical portfolio that focuses on honing his spare conversion techniques, and He creates a strategy for dealing with these circumstances in competition. He can manage high-pressure circumstances better in the future and can convert more spares as a result.

Example 2: When a bowler examines his prior competition data, He discovers that certain lane conditions—like oily lanes—tend to improve his performance more than others. He uses this data to create a tactical portfolio that includes training in similar lane situations and creating plans for adjusting to changing circumstances while competing. This gives him a tactical advantage over rivals who might find it difficult to adjust to varied conditions and helps him perform consistently well on a range of lane conditions.

Example 3: When a bowler examines the data from previous matches, He discovers that He frequently struggles against particular opponents (such as left-handed bowlers). He creates a tactical repertoire that involves training against opponents who are similar to him and creating methods for going up against him. He will be better equipped to deal with these foes in the future and will be able to modify his strategy accordingly.

Example 4: When a bowler examines the results of previous competitions, He discovers that certain sorts of locations (such as indoor locations with air conditioning) tend to yield better results than others. With the use of this data, He creates a tactical portfolio that involves modifying his hydration and dietary plans in order to cope with various environmental factors. This gives him a competitive advantage over rivals who might struggle with these aspects by enabling him to perform consistently well regardless of the setting or environmental factors.

Tactical Portfolio Topic	Key Information
Strengths and Weaknesses Analysis	• Review past performance data to identify strengths and weaknesses. • Analyze data on scoring average, strike percentage, spare conversion rate, etc. to identify areas for improvement.
Lane Condition Analysis	• Analyze past performance data to identify patterns in lane conditions (e.g. oily lanes, dry lanes). • Develop strategies for adapting to different lane conditions during competition.
Opponent Analysis	• Analyze past performance data to identify patterns in opponent strengths and weaknesses (e.g. left-handed bowlers, aggressive bowlers). • Develop strategies for competing against different types of opponents.
Venue and Environmental Condition Analysis	• Analyze past performance data to identify patterns in performance based on venue and environmental conditions (e.g. indoor vs. outdoor, air conditioning vs. no air conditioning). • Develop strategies for adjusting hydration and nutrition strategies based on environmental conditions.
Tactical Plan Development	• Develop a tactical plan based on analysis of past performance data. • Set goals for improvement in identified areas of weakness. • Develop specific strategies for approaching different opponents and lane conditions.
Implementation and Evaluation	• Implement a tactical plan during training and competition. • Monitor progress and adjust tactics as needed. • Continuously evaluate and adjust tactical plan based on new performance data.

The tactical portfolio issues covered in this table are important areas that an experienced bowler may concentrate on when creating a strategic plan based on his historical performance data. Using current tactical standards and best practices, the key information column offers helpful advice on each topic.

This table can be used by the bowler's coach or a tactical specialist to give the bowler information and advice so He can create a strategy that will support his practice and performance. To detect patterns in lane circumstances or opponent strengths and weaknesses, for instance, the coach may assist the bowler in analyzing historical performance statistics. Together, He would then design specialized methods for dealing with these situations during competition. Along with setting goals for growth in the bowler's weak areas, the coach may also regularly evaluate and modify the game plan in light of fresh performance information.

Table 25 – Example of Tactical Education sheet

Mental Skills

A bowler of the highest caliber in the world must possess exceptional mental abilities to function well. Making them a part of the ongoing performance assessment and improvement process is crucial. The following are some of the important mental skills subjects that might be covered during this process:

Peak Performance Acquisition Chart: This chart aids bowlers in determining the mental abilities they must master to perform at their very best. Bowlers can rate their degree of proficiency in each category on the chart, which is divided into sections like attention, confidence, motivation, and emotional control. Bowlers and their coaches can then construct a plan to cultivate the mental abilities required to achieve at their highest level based on the results of this exam.

Mental Skill	Current Level of Ability	Target Level of Ability	Development Plan
Focus	70%	90%	- Practice mindfulness meditation for 10 minutes per day - Use a pre-shot routine to focus on each shot
Confidence	80%	90%	- Review past successes and achievements - Focus on positive self-talk and affirmations
Motivation	90%	90%	- Set challenging but achievable goals - Visualize successful performance
Emotional Control	60%	90%	- Practice deep breathing exercises - Learn to recognize and manage negative thoughts
Goal Setting	60%	90%	- Create SMART goals for each competition and training session - Review progress towards goals regularly with the coach
Visualization	70%	90%	- Create a visualization routine for competition and practice - Practice visualizing successful performances in different scenarios
Positive Self-Talk	80%	90%	- Create a list of positive self-talk phrases - Practice using positive self-talk in competition and training
Resilience	70%	90%	- Practice mental toughness exercises, such as visualization of challenging situations - Reframe setbacks as opportunities for growth and learning

Focus, assurance, drive, and emotional control are the mental abilities being tested in this instance. The chart offers a development plan for each skill as well as the skill's current level of proficiency and objective level of proficiency. Bowlers could employ a pre-shot ritual and mindfulness meditation, for instance, to increase focus. They could concentrate on using affirmations and constructive self-talk to boost their confidence. They could learn to notice and regulate their negative thoughts and do deep breathing techniques to increase emotional control. As progress is achieved toward the desired levels of skill, the coach and bowler will frequently evaluate and update the chart.

Table 26 – Example of Peak Performance Chart

Peak Performance Evaluation Worksheet: The bowler can assess his mental performance during competition using this worksheet. Such inquiries as "How well did I focus during the competition?" "Did I maintain confidence throughout the competition?" and "How well did I control my emotions during the competition?" can be found on the worksheet. The bowler can identify areas of strength and weakness and try to hone his mental abilities by assessing his mental performance after each match.

Example 1:			
Performance Area	Pre-Competition	During Competition	Post-Competition
Focus	- Review mental preparation checklist - Visualize successful performance	- Use a pre-shot routine to focus on each shot - Stay present in the moment	- Reflect on areas of focus during competition - Identify areas for improvement
Confidence	- Review past successes and achievements - Use positive self-talk and affirmations	- Believe in the ability to execute shots - Focus on strengths	- Celebrate successes and achievements - Identify areas for improvement
Motivation	- Set challenging but achievable goals - Practice visualization exercises	- Focus on intrinsic motivation and love of the game - Stay engaged and energized	- Reflect on progress towards goals - Identify areas for improvement
Emotional Control	- Practice relaxation and deep breathing exercises - Identify triggers for negative emotions	- Recognize and manage negative emotions - Stay composed under pressure	- Reflect on emotional response during competition - Identify areas for improvement

Performance Area	Pre-Competition	During Competition	Post-Competition
		Example 1:	
This worksheet would be used by the bowler's coach to assess each area of performance before, during, and after competition. The worksheet can also be used to pinpoint problem areas and create a strategy for ongoing mental skill improvement. The bowler may perform at his best and realize his full potential on the lanes by routinely assessing and enhancing mental skills.			
		Example 2:	
Emotional Control	- Practice relaxation and deep breathing exercises - Identify potential triggers for negative emotions	- Recognize and manage negative emotions - Stay composed under pressure	- Reflect on emotional response during competition - Identify areas for improvement
Strategy	- Review competition plan and goals - Identify key opponents and strategies	- Stay adaptable and make adjustments as needed - Execute shots with purpose and strategy	- Reflect on strategic decisions during competition - Identify areas for improvement
Physical Conditioning	- Develop a training plan with a certified strength and conditioning coach - Incorporate recovery techniques, such as stretching and foam rolling	- Maintain physical stamina and strength throughout competition - Use recovery techniques between games	- Reflect on physical performance during competition - Identify areas for improvement
Mental Toughness	- Practice visualization exercises to prepare for competition - Identify potential mental obstacles for competition	- Stay resilient and focused under pressure - Stay composed after mistakes	- Reflect on moments of mental toughness during competition - Identify areas for improvement
		Example 3:	
Goal Setting	- Set SMART goals for competition - Review past successes and areas for improvement	- Focus on achieving goals for each game - Make adjustments as needed	- Reflect on progress towards goals - Identify areas for improvement
Visualization	- Practice visualization exercises to prepare for competition - Review competition plan and strategies	- Use visualization to stay focused and mentally prepared - Visualize successful shots and outcomes	- Reflect on moments of successful visualization during competition - Identify areas for improvement
Team Dynamics	- Review team goals and strategies - Identify individual strengths and roles	- Communicate effectively with team members - Support and encourage team members	- Reflect on team dynamics during competition - Identify areas for improvement
Adversity	- Identify potential setbacks and obstacles for competition - Develop a plan for overcoming setbacks	- Stay composed and focused after setbacks - Learn from mistakes	- Reflect on moments of resilience and overcoming adversity during competition - Identify areas for improvement

Table 27 – Example of Peak Performance Evaluation Chart

Mental Traps: Negative ideas or preconceptions that impair performance are known as mental traps. A bowler, for instance, might think that He consistently performs poorly in instances of extreme pressure. If the bowler doesn't learn how to control him, these unfavorable beliefs could become a reality. The bowler can enhance his mental game and perform at a higher level by becoming aware of and avoiding certain mental pitfalls.

Fight or Flight Syndrome: The body's physiological response to stress is known as the "fight-or-flight" syndrome. Stress causes the body to release hormones like cortisol and adrenaline, which can raise blood pressure, heart rate, and breathing rate. This response, however useful in some circumstances, can also hinder performance if it is not adequately controlled. The bowler can perform better under pressure if He learns to identify and control the symptoms of fight or flight syndrome.

Fight or Flight Recovery Plan: This is a strategy to aid the bowler in recovering from the physical and psychological side effects of FRS. The strategy could call for deep breathing, visualization, or meditation, among other relaxation methods. A recovery strategy can help the bowler go back to a calm and concentrated condition, which can enhance performance.

Aspect	Strategy	Implementation
Physical Recovery	Rest and Relaxation	Take a day off from training after a competition. Schedule regular massage or physiotherapy sessions.
Nutrition	Replenishment of essential nutrients	Consume a post-workout meal within 30 minutes of training. Incorporate healthy fats, carbohydrates, and proteins into meals.
Sleep	Adequate rest and sleep	Aim for 7-9 hours of sleep per night. Establish a consistent sleep schedule. Create a relaxing bedtime routine.

Aspect	Strategy	Implementation
Stress Management	Mindfulness and relaxation techniques	Practice deep breathing, meditation, or yoga. Engage in hobbies or activities that promote relaxation.
Social Support	Connection with family and friends	Spend quality time with loved ones. Join a support group or community organization.
Mental Skills	Visualization and positive self-talk	Use visualization techniques to imagine success. Practice positive self-talk to boost confidence and reduce anxiety.
Active Recovery	Light exercise and movement	Incorporate low-intensity activities such as walking or yoga into recovery days.
Hydration	Proper fluid intake	Aim to drink 8-10 glasses of water per day. Avoid sugary drinks or alcohol.
Time Management	Prioritization and goal-setting	Use a planner or calendar to schedule activities and prioritize tasks. Set realistic goals and deadlines.
Recovery Modalities	Alternative recovery methods	Explore the use of ice baths, sauna, or foam rolling for muscle recovery.
Professional Support	Seek guidance from professionals	Consult with a sports psychologist or mental skills coach. Work with a strength and conditioning coach to optimize training.

Table 27 – Example of Fight or Flight Recovery Plan

Development Plan

The development of an athlete's personal brand and image, as well as the image of his sport, is the subject of this topic. Creating a distinct and recognizable personal brand that distinguishes a world-class elite bowler from other competitors in the sport may be necessary to achieve this. Public speaking engagements, participation in the community, and use of social media are examples of this.

Example: An elite world-class bowler might collaborate with a branding and marketing company to create a personal brand that highlights his particular skills and character. To enhance his reputation and image, He might also work with groups and charities that share his beliefs and objectives.

Sponsorship Deals: For athletes to have resources and financial support, sponsorship agreements are essential. Creating a plan for locating and getting sponsorship agreements that support an athlete's personal brand and values is the focus of this topic.

Example: A world-class professional bowler, for instance, might collaborate with a marketing team or agent to find sponsors that share his beliefs and personal brand. He can also create a portfolio of his prior achievements to present prospective sponsors.

Building a Success Mechanism: This topic focuses on creating a game plan, encompassing training, competition, and recovery tactics, for obtaining and maintaining success in the sport.

Example: A team of coaches, trainers, and medical experts may collaborate with world-class elite bowlers to create a detailed training and recovery plan that maximizes both their physical and mental performance. To stay motivated and focused on their long-term goals, they could also use goal-setting and visualization strategies. To make sure they are moving toward accomplishing their objectives, they may also frequently examine and improve their success mechanism.

Topic	Strategies	Tactics	Steps	Opportunities	Examples
Individual/ Sport Image Building	Develop a unique personal brand	Social media presence, community involvement, public speaking engagements	1. Define personal brand 2. Create a social media presence 3. Identify community involvement opportunities 4. Develop public speaking skills	1. Increased visibility and recognition 2. Improved reputation and credibility	Bowlers may work with a branding and marketing team to develop a personal brand that emphasizes their unique strengths and personality. They may also collaborate with organizations and charities that align with their values and interests to build a positive reputation and image.
Sponsorship Deals	Identify potential sponsors	Develop a portfolio of past successes and accomplishments	1. Identify potential sponsors that align with personal brand and values 2. Develop a sponsorship proposal 3. Negotiate terms and conditions	1. Financial support and resources 2. Exposure to a wider audience	Bowlers may work with an agent or marketing team to identify potential sponsors that align with their personal brand and values. They may also develop a portfolio of past successes and accomplishments to showcase to potential sponsors.

Topic	Strategies	Tactics	Steps	Opportunities	Examples
Building a Success Mechanism	Develop a comprehensive training and recovery plan	Incorporate goal-setting and visualization techniques	1. Define goals and objectives 2. Develop a training plan 3. Incorporate recovery and rest strategies 4. Implement goal-setting and visualization techniques	1. Improved physical and mental performance 2. Increased likelihood of achieving long-term goals	Bowlers may work with a team of coaches, trainers, and healthcare professionals to develop a comprehensive training and recovery plan that optimizes their physical and mental performance. They may also incorporate goal-setting and visualization techniques to maintain focus and motivation towards their long-term goals.

Table 28 – Example of bowler personal brand and image development plan

METHODOLOGY APPLIED TO SPORT PERIODIZATION TRAINING FOR SPORT *By Pedro Merani*

My understanding of methodology was one of the instruments that enabled me in my job as a coach to write down the training programs and have a clear perspective of what has to be done to achieve. Learning "periodization training for sport" made it easier for me to organize my efforts to accomplish the objectives I've set for each nation I've coached. Is where you will break down each aspect of the sport, starting with the long-term objective and working your way down to the first day of work, in "Periodization Training for Sport"?

A. The Strategic Plan

When a STRATEGIC PLAN is effective, we will identify the factors that contributed to how you planned the path to the objective as soon as the process got underway. This plan must outline the stages you'll take, the key duties, the scheduling of each stage, and other details.

It is important to know where you want to go, or what the program's ultimate goal is, in order to create an effective and successful strategy plan. You should also thoroughly analyze where the program is at the beginning of the process, with planning to serve as the engine that will take us from the present to the desired goal.

Considering these factors is necessary for good planning

A thorough examination of the sport's "reality" at the point where the procedure begins. For instance, the organizational structure, the training facilities, the operation of the development programs, and the caliber and ability of the athletes

A specific long-term objective with a deadline, one that is realistic, quantifiable, and ambitious and that can be assessed over time using a progressive evaluation system.

A tool that allows you to complete all the steps, outlining each one from the start to the end aim.

The program needs controls so that users may monitor results and make adjustments as necessary to reach the desired outcome.

Finally, the overall program will be evaluated to determine whether all of its objectives have been met.

B. How the training is

The training process must be carried out methodically in accordance with a written program to raise athletes' performance levels to reach their peak in all areas of the sport at the time to accomplish the goal, from the technical side, tactical, mental, and fitness.

As a result of this methodical training, changes will occur in all the areas that have been trained, which is why you must regularly track the program's development and make the necessary adjustments to meet the program's initial goals.

Once you've decided on your goals, you can specify how you'll work toward achieving those goals. By using this method, you can, for example, specify who will be in charge and the general direction to be taken.

You must create a broad and detailed program for each area you wish to work in after deciding on the work philosophy and who will be in charge of each area. What, for instance, needs to change in terms of the physical game, such as footwork and swinging, the theory, such as ball motion and reading lanes, the game plan and stress management techniques, and the fitness aspect, such as how to improve an athlete's strength and endurance?

Finally, the program must contain review periods where you can reflect on your performance, draw from your experience, and make the necessary adjustments to reach the predetermined goals for the following period.

C. The planning

The training Cycles

C.1 Mega-Cycle

Inside the Planning Program, is the largest structure. is the process by which the program develops over time, from the start until it reaches its highest aim. Planning to reach the goals you established when you started the program is necessary because they can be accomplished in 4 to 8 years (between one and two Olympic Cycles) after the program's start. This structure, which can be called a MEGA-CYCLE or PLURI-CYCLE because it consists of between 4 and 8 CYCLES, encompasses all the work that needs to be done from the start to the finish.

It's critical to have a clear understanding of the Mega Cycle's objectives since, for each Annual Cycle, every sport's training plan will be in line with the Mega Cycle's overall purpose.

C.2 Annual Cycles (CYCLE)

Is the structure that houses a 12-month calendar. It is typically adjusted to the fiscal year of the organization that gives the Federation the funding, which in most circumstances runs from April 1 to March 31 of the following year. Periods called Macro-Cycles are used to separate the Annual Cycle.

C.3 Macro Cycles

These structures, known as macro cycles, have working intervals of 4 to 16 weeks. The more significant aspect of this structure is that it takes into account the four phases of training: preparatory, where general training components are developed; pre-competition, where forms learned during the preparatory period are improved; competitive, where skills are fine-tuned and the athlete competes; and transition, where the athlete rests and recovers.

C.4 Month-Cycle (Period)

This structure counts in 3- to 5-week cycles that are part of the macro-cycles.

C.5 Micro-Cycles

This framework uses periods ranging from 3 to 15 days, but the most prevalent is 7 days, which corresponds to one week of training.

This cycle displays the precise labor that went into writing the program. Weeks of proficiency, times of hard labor (load), rest, general or specific preparation, etc.

C.6 Mini-Cycle (Session)

What they will perform at each training session is the smallest structure of the entire Planning program. The smallest one, however, is the most crucial because it includes a warm-up, a main portion (certain duties), and a conclusion (fun, relaxation, and recovery).

Conclusion

This is an overview of how to organize your training so that you can reach the objectives you established at the start of the program. In other words, you list every action you must take to accomplish the result in white and black. These objectives must always be in line with the ones you've defined for the Mega Cycle and any associated objectives for each Cycle. All aspects of the sport must function together in order to accomplish the established goal, hence work must be done in every area.

D. Priorities

The decision of the priorities for the Mega Cycle and each Cycle within the planning program is a further subject that is of utmost importance. The competitions must be prioritized at the start of the year by ranking them according to priority, and the training schedule must reflect these priorities. This will assist in choosing the phases of the training program, as well as the load, pre-competition, competition, and rest and recuperation times.

E. The path we walked

2009 saw the beginning of the Qatar National Youth Program. Athletes and coaches worked together to establish long-term goals, with the ultimate objective being to win at least a medal at the 2016 World Youth Championship. This aim was achieved, and the World Youth was celebrated in Nebraska, USA. We divided the strategic plan into two separate, four-year Mega Cycles. As the MEGA CYCLE 1 from 2009 to 2012 and the MEGA CYCLE 2 from 2013 to 2016, respectively.

The goal was to instruct them in the fundamentals of every facet of our sport during MEGA CYCLE 1. As an illustration, in the physical game, we concentrated on timing, balance, swing, and release. The "look" of the world's best athletes was imparted upon them. The foundations of the theory and a general understanding of the mental game have been taught to them through lectures. During this Mega Cycle 1, no outcomes were pursued.

In preparation for the MEGACYCLE 2, we started imparting athletes additional technical information, particularly about ball motion and lane play. Additionally, we have supported their technical skill development by increasing and reducing axis rotations, revolutions, loft, and speed. We have helped them mentally prepare for competition, and we are now focusing on their belief system. We were looking for outcomes at this time.

E.1 The Physical game or mechanics

We created and wrote our "curricula" for the MEGA CYCLE 1 in accordance with the game we often play. Based on how the "brain" interprets information, we have developed drills and rigorous, systematic training. Athletes who quit the program and later returned found that the form they had learned had been mostly assimilated. The training occasionally grew difficult and monotonous.

We have improved the forms we gained during the Mega Cycle 1 over this second 4-year period (MEGA CYCLE 2). We have adapted to their game and applied the best drills. After incorporating the principles, we could begin to focus on more intensive training that was tailored to each tournament. Each competition's "Peaking Program" (pre-competition time), which we have dubbed the intense and difficult training, including "load and unload" periods. The athletes were able to perform to the best of their abilities in accordance with their skill level thanks to this training system.

E.2 The mental game

The "mental game" was introduced to them through lectures twice a week throughout the MEGA CYCLE 1. We discussed the various components of the mental game (attitude, desire, focus, awareness, etc.) and taught them the fundamental mental techniques, such as "breathing, relaxation, and visualization", "self-positive talk," and cognitive restructuring. We used a variety of evaluation tools to assist students in comprehending the mentality required for top performance.

We continued using this method for the MEGA CYCLE 2, but we also added some private sessions to assist the participants in preparing mentally for the competition more quickly. Through these one-on-one sessions, we were able to track their development and continued assisting them in being more self-aware in order to better control their emotions under pressure. As a result, they became more self-aware, task-oriented, and connected to the "spirit" of the game and how to play it to go closer to what we refer to as the "zone" (bompu zen).

E.3 The fitness preparation

We exposed them to the fitness preparation throughout MEGA CYCLE 1. Physical training is unquestionably essential for the modern game we play in order to build strength, and stamina, and avoid injuries. However, as we have previously stated, they use the extra time they have between training sessions to complete their schoolwork and revise for their exams; as a result, asking them for more time than what we had planned for them proved to be somewhat challenging.

Due to the heavy study load that the young athletes were subjected to throughout the MEGA CYCLE 2, it was regrettably not possible to intensify the fitness training. To make up for this, we developed a set of unique workouts that the athletes performed both before and during the warm-up; these drills were designed to improve the strength of the core. They were able to improve their aiming system and release consistency with the help of these exercises, which also offered them a more stable finishing posture and excellent balance at the foul line.

E.4 The theory

During the MEGA CYCLE 1, we went over game theory, including how to recognize patterns, how to interpret and use the lanes, and ball motion. We went over the material in a very smooth manner because we were aware from the start that it was a really difficult issue to understand.

We covered the same topics in further detail in the MEGA CYCLE 2. To assist them in comprehending how the theory worked, we began training on the lanes in a very specific method. Sessions for special training in this area were planned.

Pedro Merani, Qatar National Team Head Coach

A UNIQUE APPROACH: REDEFINING THE CORE CHALLENGE AND OPTIMIZING BOWLING PERFORMANCE THROUGH PHYSICAL AND MENTAL ADJUSTMENTS *By Coach Ulf*

By utilizing conscious and unconscious proprioception senses to improve essential aspects of the game, the Core Balance Approach (C.B.A.) offers a novel perspective on bowling. This method, which was created in conjunction with biomechanics and physical therapy experts, aims to enhance balance, accuracy, repeatability, ball speed, revolutions, release control, awareness, and attention. Bowlers can improve the effectiveness and quality of their training drills by including the Core Balance Approach, which will result in quicker feedback and better outcomes. This system promotes injury avoidance and general performance development for bowlers of all styles and levels of expertise.

Introduction

The truth is that there is a wealth of information regarding bowling available. Writers offer pearls of wisdom that might be applied at particular times by sharing their viewpoints and beliefs. We all have our own perspectives, therefore coaches, trainers, and pro shop owners occasionally encounter this.

My quest for this "different approach" to bowling started when I was pressured by academicians, medical professionals, and physiotherapists to defend and explain the history of my beloved sport. I was forced to reevaluate the biomechanics of bowling after having knee surgery in the early 1990s and seeing bowler injuries in the early 2000s. The discussion took an unexpected turn at a meeting with the top biomechanist and chief physiotherapist at the Olympic training facility in Oslo, Norway. We asked for their assistance on behalf of our players, little realizing that this would spark an entirely new way of thinking that is still developing.

What if there were straightforward physical methods to improve:

- *Balance*
- *Consistency*
- *Accuracy*
- *Ball speed*

- *Revolutions*
- *Release control*
- *Awareness and focus*

Were we able to improve our bowling game by utilizing both our conscious and unconscious proprioception senses? Unanimously, the response is yes! We can improve about 70% of our technical training away from the bowling lane by integrating these senses.

Our technical workouts while working on the approach will be of a higher caliber thanks to this strategy. We perform exercises that provide better, more accurate, and quicker feedback, giving us better working tools as a result. Let's get some background information:

The Swedish national team's physiotherapist, who came from a different athletic background, raised concerns about the women's national team's training methods in the early 1990s and took action as a result.

The necessity for additional power without sacrificing precision and consistency became clear, especially with the advent of short oil conditions and the introduction of reactive resin.

Regardless of their bowling technique, athletes in the late 1990s and early 2000s suffered from a variety of injuries, including hip, back, knee, shoulder, wrist, and ankle issues.

I began to doubt the conventional approach to training and athletics after hearing from biomechanics and physiotherapy experts who had no preconceived beliefs about bowling technique.

These events established the groundwork for the project that is now known as the "Core Balance Approach." When I think back on this difficult path, I can't imagine ever wanting to be without the experiences we went through.

The difficulties we ran with included:

- *Developing a pedagogical approach that all coaches, trainers, and bowlers could understand and use successfully.*
- *Compiling enough data and verification that the method is effective for bowlers of all skill levels.*
- *Creating a system that is simple to recognize and understand.*
- *Making sure that it assists bowlers of all styles and levels of proficiency.*
- *Developing a method that enhances the bowler's abilities.*
- *Avoiding the requirement for extra equipment to put the method into practice.*
- *Giving experienced bowlers a challenge that piques their interest and activates their intuition in order to improve their game.*
- *Giving players fast feedback on their growth gives them the impression that they can advance and get better at any skill level.*
- *Reducing accidents in contemporary bowling.*

We created a philosophy to improve bowlers' performance in order to overcome these difficulties. This philosophy relies on using conscious and unconscious behavior, reflexes, and reactions. With the T.E.F.C.A.S. (Thought, Emotion, Focus, Conscious Awareness, and Sensory Perception) as the cornerstone of our system, we use routine tasks to draw attention to necessary alterations.

To improve performance in bowling, the "Core Balance Approach" (CBA) emphasizes the integration of Thought, Emotion, Focus, Conscious Awareness, and Sensory Perception (TEFCAS) as the essential building blocks. We intended to develop a comprehensive approach that covers not only the physical parts of the game but also the mental and emotional aspects by concentrating on these interconnected components.

The bowler's thinking and belief system are referred to as thought, the first element of TEFCAS. We underlined the value of encouraging self-talk, visualization, and goal-setting. Bowlers overcame obstacles and produced their finest work by developing a confident and concentrated mindset.

The second element, emotion, acknowledges that feelings have a big impact on performance. As part of our training, learning how to control emotions like enthusiasm, impatience, and worry became essential. Bowlers were able to control their emotions and have a level head while on the lanes with the aid of methods like deep breathing, relaxation exercises, and mindfulness.

The third element, focus, entails focusing attention and concentration on particular objectives. By removing distractions and focusing on shot execution, we taught bowlers to build a laser-like focus on their desired objective. Focus and attentional control were improved through mental exercises like visualization exercises and concentration drills.

The fourth element, conscious awareness, includes being completely present and conscious of one's environment and behaviors. It entails being aware of one's posture, motions, and how the bowling ball feels. Bowlers could improve their technique and make in-the-moment corrections by being more cognizant of their actions.

The last TEFCAS component, Sensory Perception, includes using the senses to obtain data and provide accurate judgments. We urged bowlers to use all of their senses throughout practice and competition in order to improve their sensory perception. This involved paying attention to visual clues offered by the lane conditions, the feel of the lane surface, and the sound of the ball striking the pins.

The Core Balance Approach combines these five components to enhance a bowler's potential by producing a synergistic result. We believed that bowlers could create a state of flow, where everything falls into place and performance becomes effortless, by addressing the physical, mental, and emotional aspects of the game.

We saw amazing changes as we used the Core Balance Approach with bowlers of all ability levels. Bowlers claimed better accuracy, more self-assurance, and greater enjoyment of their activity. The strategy helped recreational bowlers who wanted to improve their skills as well as competitive bowlers.

Our desire to push the limits of bowling performance was further motivated by our success and the encouraging comments we received. We kept enhancing and broadening the Core Balance Approach, taking into account knowledge from disciplines like sports psychology, neuroscience, and mindfulness exercises.

The Core Balance Approach is still in use today as a thorough framework for addressing the intricacies of bowling. We are committed to sharing our expertise and experiences with coaches, trainers, and players all around the world because it has acquired recognition and approval within the bowling community.

To sum up, the Core Balance Approach, which has its roots in TEFCAS, presents a paradigm shift in how we view bowling. The actual potential of bowlers is unlocked, and a road to mastery and fulfillment in the sport is created by integrating cognition, emotion, focus, conscious awareness, and sensory experience.

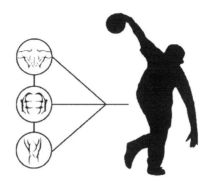

POWER BOWLING: BEYOND STRENGTH, TIMING, AND COORDINATION

The genetic make-up of bowlers dictates their innate potential, but how near they are to reach their top performance depends on how carefully these abilities are developed and in what order. It's essential to follow the First-Things-First philosophy to ensure long-term growth.

There are key stages for developing fundamental movement and general athleticism, just as there are for learning language and motor abilities. Prioritizing athletic development over the specialized development of bowling abilities is crucial before entering puberty.

Young bowlers miss an exceptional opportunity to develop neuromuscular trends that will ultimately render them quicker, stronger, streamlined, and exceptionally proficient when they focus excessively on technical skills too early and neglect the development of fundamental movement and athleticism. Once this chance has been lost, it cannot be recovered.

A bowler who lacks general athleticism before adolescence will likely struggle to compete against faster, stronger, and more athletic competitors, similar to a baseball player with excellent hand-eye coordination but restricted lateral agility or a soccer player with flashy footwork but lacking in strength and speed.

But What About Muscle Memory?

The majority of kids who learn basic movement patterns through unstructured play and involvement in a variety of sports do so spontaneously as they grow physically. Striking a balance between structured instruction and enabling kids to explore and adapt on their own is crucial.

In addition to perfecting their sport-specific talents, kids can concentrate on improving their overall athleticism. However, according to the age, physical capabilities, and mental maturity of each individual bowler, the amount of time devoted to each and the level of technical skill emphasis should be modified.

The Significance of Physical Training in Bowling

A key component of human existence, physical exercise, along with mental activity, has helped to make our species unique throughout evolution. Enhancing the bowler's physical potential and increasing the unique biomotor skills necessary for the sport are the two main goals of physical training in bowling.

Bowler practice includes both physical and psychological components, including bodily preparation to increase morpho-functional indices and mental conditioning to maintain constant effort and intensity. Physical training can be interpreted as a structured, hierarchical series of activities intended to make use of and enhance the bowler's physical attributes, according to some definitions found in the literature. It ought to be constantly implemented at various stages of athletic training, with an emphasis on the technical and tactical elements of the sport.

For young bowlers, making physical fitness a priority sets a strong basis for their future athletic aspirations. Junior bowlers must be treated as individuals with unique needs and talents rather than as little adults, thus it is crucial to have a thorough awareness of their psychomotor traits. To effectively lead the development of young bowlers, it is helpful to take into account the structure and traits of competitive efforts.

Effectiveness in bowling depends heavily on quickness, flexibility, and coordination. Traditional thinking claimed that sprinters were more naturally endowed than trained, but more current consensus acknowledges that speed abilities can be trained for. The ability to quickly and effectively change the direction of the body is agility. In bowling, agility is achieved by the use of balance, coordination, strength, and speed.

The conventional method of instructing young bowlers emphasizes the establishment of a fundamental bowling technique and the gradual acquisition of skills over the course of their motor skill development. The biomechanical structure of the bowler has an impact on the ball's speed and revolutions, as was previously mentioned. However, as their motor skills mature, young bowlers may find it challenging to achieve the speed and torque necessary to provide additional spin to the ball inside the specified release window. Changing the release or ball speed becomes challenging as abilities are almost fully developed because of the existing motor skill structure, which is very different from that of high-revolution bowlers. It could be difficult for someone who has mostly learned to play with straighter angles, such as strokers (250 to 380 RPM), to switch to becoming a high-revolution bowler (above 420 RPM).

Breakdown of the muscle involvement and the types of muscle fibers utilized in bowling:

1. *Leg Muscles (Quadriceps, Hamstrings, Calves):*
   - *Involvement: These muscles play a significant role in generating power and stability during the approach and slide.*
   - *Muscle Fiber Types: Both fast-twitch (Type II) and slow-twitch (Type I) muscle fibers are involved. Fast-twitch fibers contribute to explosive movements, while slow-twitch fibers provide endurance and stability.*

2. *Gluteal Muscles (Gluteus Maximus, Gluteus Medius):*
   - *Involvement: The gluteal muscles are essential for hip extension and stability during the slide and release.*
   - *Muscle Fiber Types: They primarily consist of fast-twitch muscle fibers, which provide the power required for hip extension and propulsion.*

3. *Core Muscles (Abdominals, Obliques, Lower Back):*
   - *Involvement: Core muscles help with balance, energy transfer, and posture maintenance.*
   - *Muscle Fiber Types: These muscles consist of both fast-twitch and slow-twitch fibers to provide stability and power while maintaining posture.*

4. *Back and Shoulder Muscles (Deltoids, Trapezius, Latissimus Dorsi):*
   - *Involvement: These muscles contribute to arm swing and follow-through.*
   - *Muscle Fiber Types: They primarily involve fast-twitch fibers for generating power during the arm swing and release.*

5. *Forearm and Hand Muscles (Wrist Flexors and Extensors, Finger Flexors):*
   - *Involvement: These muscles control wrist position and grip on the ball.*
   - *Muscle Fiber Types: They mainly consist of slow-twitch fibers for fine control and precision.*

6. **Quadratus Lumborum:**
   - **Involvement:** This muscle helps maintain spinal alignment and balance.
   - **Muscle Fiber Types:** It has a mix of both fast-twitch and slow-twitch fibers to provide stability and support.

7. **Tibialis Anterior:**
   - **Involvement:** The tibialis anterior muscle aids in lifting the toes during the slide and controlling footwork.
   - **Muscle Fiber Types:** It primarily consists of slow-twitch fibers for endurance and control.

8. **Triceps:**
   - **Involvement:** Triceps muscles control arm extension and the release.
   - **Muscle Fiber Types:** They predominantly involve fast-twitch fibers for the explosiveness required in the release.

The Formula of Torque x Distance = Rev

In bowling, the term "rev rate" refers to the number of revolutions a bowling ball makes as it travels down the lane before reaching the pins. Rev rate is a critical factor in a bowler's technique because it affects the ball's performance and the way it interacts with the pins.

The formula "Torque x Distance = Rev" represents a simplified way to understand how rev rate is influenced by a bowler's technique:

Torque: Torque is the rotational force applied to the ball. It's generated by the bowler's hand and wrist action during the release. The more torque you apply, the greater the rotational force on the ball.

Distance: Distance in this context refers to the distance the fingers and thumb travel on the inside of the ball's coverstock during the release. A longer distance of travel allows for a longer duration of contact with the ball, which can result in more revolutions.

Rev: Rev represents the number of revolutions the ball makes as it travels down the lane. It's measured in revolutions per minute (RPM).

Here's how these factors work together to influence rev rate:

- When a bowler applies more torque by turning their wrist and fingers, they impart a greater rotational force to the ball. This increased torque leads to more revolutions on the ball.
- A longer distance of travel for the fingers and thumb means that they have more time to grip and rotate the ball. This extended contact results in a higher rev rate.
- By maximizing both torque and distance, a bowler can increase the rev rate, making the ball spin more rapidly as it travels down the lane.

Techniques to enhance torque speed

Strengthening Exercises:

1. **Wrist Curls:**
   - Hold a light dumbbell in your hand, palm facing up.
   - Rest your forearm on a flat surface, allowing your hand and wrist to extend beyond the edge.
   - Curl your wrist upward, bringing the weight towards your forearm.
   - Slowly lower the weight back down.

2. **Reverse Wrist Curls:**
   - Hold a light dumbbell in your hand, palm facing down.

- *Rest your forearm on a flat surface, allowing your hand and wrist to extend beyond the edge.*
- *Curl your wrist upward, bringing the weight towards your forearm.*
- *Slowly lower the weight back down.*

3. **Grip Strengthening:**
   - *Use a grip strengthener or a stress ball to improve your hand and finger strength. A strong grip can help you control the ball and generate more torque.*

Bowling-Specific Drills:

4. **Wrist Flexion and Extension Drills:**
   - *Practice flexing and extending your wrist during your release. Concentrate on making the motion as smooth and controlled as possible. You can do this without a bowling ball in your hand to focus solely on your wrist action.*

5. **Balance Drill:**
   - *Stand with your feet shoulder-width apart and hold a bowling ball in your dominant hand.*
   - *Try to balance the ball on the fingertips of your bowling hand while keeping your wrist in a slightly flexed position.*
   - *This drill helps you develop wrist and forearm stability, which is essential for applying torque effectively.*

6. **Release Technique Drills:**
   - *Work with a coach or experienced bowler to fine-tune your release technique. Ensure that your hand remains behind the ball and your wrist is in a strong position during the release. Correct hand and wrist positioning will maximize your ability to apply torque.*

7. **Weighted Bowling Ball Drills:**
   - *Use a weighted training ball (a ball with added weight) during practice. This extra weight can help strengthen your wrist and forearm muscles and improve your ability to apply torque.*

8. **Practice with Increasing Speed:**
   - *Gradually increase the speed of your release while maintaining proper technique. This will help you develop the ability to generate torque quickly during the release.*

9. **Video Analysis:**
   - *Record your release with a video camera and review it to identify areas where you can improve your wrist and hand positioning and action.*

The Impact Of Increasing Rev Rate In Bowling

The toughest task in bowling is improving the bowler's rev rate. High rev rates have advantages and disadvantages, although they typically result in more pins being knocked down. A higher rev rate makes the bowling ball contact the pins with greater power, resulting in increased pin action, similar to how adding spin to a football or baseball increases its distance and lessens the impact of wind. High rev rates are a common characteristic of professional bowlers, which helps explain their amazing pin action. There are disadvantages to this method, though.

Below table summarizing the reasons why high-rev-rate bowlers have more impact on the pins compared to straighter or lower-rev-rate bowlers, along with explanations of the technical and physics-related aspects:

Reason	Technical Explanation	Physics Explanation	Mathematical Explanation
Increased Pin Action	Higher revolutions lead to greater ball motion, creating more pin action.	Increased angular momentum results in more kinetic energy being transferred to the pins upon impact.	Higher revolutions increase angular momentum, directly proportional to kinetic energy, resulting in improved pin action.

Reason	Technical Explanation	Physics Explanation	Mathematical Explanation
Greater Entry Angle	The steep entry angle results from the ball's high rev rate and rotation.	A steeper entry angle allows the ball to contact more pins at different angles, increasing pin action.	Entry angle is expressed in terms of rev rate and rotation, with higher values creating a steeper entry angle, modeled using trigonometric functions.
Carry Percentage	The ball retains energy due to high revs, increasing the likelihood of a strike.	Greater kinetic energy results in pins moving with more force, increasing pin carry.	Conservation of energy principles; high revs contribute to greater kinetic energy, leading to increased pin carry.
Increased Strike Potential	High revs help in hitting corner pins, such as the 10-pin (for right-handed bowlers).	The increased rev rate and entry angle improve pin action and reduce deflection, making it easier to knock down corner pins.	Strike potential as a function of rev rate, entry angle, and deflection; higher revs and steeper entry angles reduce deflection, increasing strike potential.
Pin Action Variability	High-rev bowlers can manipulate ball motion, creating a wider range of pin action.	Variations in ball motion lead to diverse pin reactions, increasing the chance of favorable pin carry.	Modeling the relationship between ball motion adjustments and pin action variability for high-rev bowlers.
Less Deflection	The ball deflects less upon impact due to high revs.	Reduced deflection results in a more direct transfer of kinetic energy to the pins, increasing pin action.	Deflection expressed as a function of rev rate and impact angle; higher revs contribute to less deflection.
Accuracy in Hook Shots	High-rev bowlers can control hook shots more precisely.	Better control of ball rotation allows for targeted hits on specific pin areas.	Mathematical expression of ball rotation control in terms of angular displacement and speed.
Adjustment Flexibility	High-rev bowlers can adjust to lane conditions with minor changes in release and target.	Adaptability enables optimal ball motion on different oil patterns, maximizing pin carry.	Describing adjustment flexibility as the ability to adapt release parameters for optimal ball motion on various oil patterns.
Strike Potential on Light/ Heavy Hits	High-rev bowlers can achieve strikes on light or heavy pocket hits.	Increased pin action compensates for minor off-target shots, increasing the chances of strikes.	Relationship between pin action and strike potential on off-target shots.
Ball Selection	High-rev bowlers choose equipment that complements their style, enhancing pin carry.	Proper ball selection maximizes the ball's interaction with the pins, increasing pin action.	Consideration of ball characteristics and their impact on pin action.
Mental Toughness	High-rev bowlers are mentally strong and adaptable in challenging conditions.	Mental resilience helps maintain focus and shot consistency, leading to effective pin impact.	Quantifying mental toughness through factors like focus and emotional resilience, expressing its impact on shot consistency and pin impact statistically.

Table 29 – These explanations showcase how technical aspects, such as ball motion control and adaptability, as well as physics principles like angular momentum and kinetic energy, contribute to the greater impact high-rev-rate bowlers have on the pins.

High revolution can improve the bowler's game, but before using them as his main tactic, it's important to weigh its benefits and drawbacks.

Many bowlers feel that having some rev rate is essential to their game, despite the disadvantages. For example, two-handed bowlers largely rely on a high rev rate to produce significant pin action, making use of their particular style that allows for higher speed and power. Even some one-handed bowlers who use a more traditional stance will up their rev rate to boost their striking force and get more pin action.

A number of crucial approaches can be used to improve the rev rate. A good strategy is to concentrate on where the wrists are during the release. Using a more forceful wrist snap might give the ball more revs and spin. Making improvements to your timing and footwork will also help you approach with more speed and force.

RPM Range	Estimated Strike Percentage	Example Bowlers
200-250	40-50%	Amateur or casual bowlers, or bowlers with a slower, more deliberate style
300-350	50-60%	Norm Duke, Walter R William, Parker Bohn
400-450	60-70%	Chris Barnes, Sean Rash
500-550	70-80%	Jason Belmonte, Anthony Simonsen
550-580	80-83%	EJ Tackett
580-600	81-85%	Robert Smith , Osku Palerrma

RPM Range	Estimated Strike Percentage	Example Bowlers
600+	82-88%	Jimmy Keith, Jesper Svensson

Table 30 – Example of bowlers RPM and percentage of strikes

Developing A Powerful Player - Strike Strong

In the world of bowling, power is a crucial asset, capable of elevating a player's performance to new heights. Precision, coupled with strength, becomes the cornerstone of success on the lanes. The training guide should be crafted to equip bowlers with the skills necessary for commanding and accurate shots. Recognizing the strategic importance of commencing this developmental journey early in an athlete's life, this guide focuses on building a robust foundation that directly influences future success. Developing a total bowler into an athletic and powerful player involves a comprehensive training that targets various aspects of their physical and technical abilities. Here's a structured plan covering key areas:

1. Powerful Snap Wrist:

Drills:

Wrist Snap Exercises: Use wrist weights or resistance bands to strengthen wrist muscles. Perform controlled snapping motions to mimic the release in bowling.

Targeted Release Drills: Focus on releasing the ball with a strong snap at the bottom of the swing.

Tactics:

Engage in regular wrist strengthening exercises to enhance flexibility and power.

Utilize wrist supports and grips for better control during releases.

Snap Speed and Consistency:

Goal: Increase Snap Speed by 3 mph in Four Weeks

Measurement: Use a speed radar to record baseline snap speed.

Target: Achieve a consistent increase in snap speed to 3 mph higher than the baseline within the next four weeks.

Frequency: Measure snap speed during designated drills and actual gameplay weekly.

Wrist Flexibility:

Goal: Improve Wrist Range of Motion by 15 Degrees in Six Weeks

Measurement: Utilize a flexibility assessment tool to measure baseline wrist range of motion.

Target: Increase wrist flexibility by 15 degrees within the next six weeks.

Frequency: Conduct flexibility assessments bi-weekly to track improvements.

2. Strong Wrist:

Drills:

Wrist Curls: Use dumbbells to perform wrist curls for overall wrist strength.

Plate Pinches: Hold weight plates with your fingers and thumb, promoting wrist stability.

Tactics:

Include wrist-strengthening exercises in your regular strength training routine.

Ensure proper wrist alignment and hand position during the release.

Wrist Strength Endurance:

Goal: Maintain Strong Wrist Position for 30 Seconds Longer in Three Weeks

Measurement: Record the duration of maintaining a strong wrist position during drills.

Target: Increase the duration of maintaining wrist strength by 30 seconds within the next three weeks.

Frequency: Monitor wrist strength endurance during strength training exercises twice a week.

Stability during Release:

Goal: Achieve 90% Consistency in Wrist Stability during Release in One Month

Measurement: Use video analysis to assess stability during ball release.

Target: Achieve a consistent 90% stability during the ball release within the next month.

Frequency: Regularly review video footage after each training session.

3. Lower Body Stability and Muscle Thickness:

Drills:

Squats: Develop leg strength and stability with various squat variations.

Lunges: Enhance balance and leg strength with forward and lateral lunges.

Tactics:

Focus on building muscle mass in the lower body through weight training.

Incorporate balance exercises, such as single-leg squats, to improve stability.

Leg Strength:

Goal: Increase Squat Weight by 10% in Five Weeks

Measurement: Record the amount of weight lifted during squat variations.

Target: Achieve a 10% increase in squat weight within the next five weeks.

Frequency: Measure leg strength during regular strength training sessions.

4. Endurance for Longer Games:

Drills:

High-Intensity Interval Training (HIIT): Mimic the demands of a game with short bursts of intense exercise followed by rest.

Long-Duration Cardio: Build overall stamina with activities like running or cycling.

Tactics:

Gradually increase training duration to build endurance over time.

Include sport-specific drills, like bowling with heavier balls, for extended periods.

HIIT Performance:

Goal: Reduce Recovery Time by 10% in Three Weeks

Measurement: Track the intensity and recovery times during HIIT sessions.

Target: Improve the ability to recover quickly by reducing recovery time by 10% within the next three weeks.

Frequency: Assess HIIT performance regularly, at least twice a week.

5. Strong Upper Body with Flexibility:

Drills:

Shoulder Press: Strengthen shoulder muscles for a powerful swing.

Yoga or Pilates: Improve flexibility and core strength.

Tactics:

Focus on a balanced upper body workout that targets both strength and flexibility.

Regularly stretch and perform dynamic warm-ups to maintain flexibility.

Shoulder Strength:

Goal: Increase Shoulder Press Weight by 5 lbs in Four Weeks

Measurement: Measure the maximum weight lifted in shoulder press exercises.

Target: Achieve a 5 lbs increase in shoulder press weight within the next four weeks.

Frequency: Include shoulder strength assessments in upper body workouts.

Flexibility Improvement:

Goal: Enhance Shoulder Flexibility by 10 Degrees in Five Weeks

Measurement: Use flexibility assessments to measure improvements in shoulder flexibility.

Target: Increase shoulder flexibility by 10 degrees within the next five weeks.

Frequency: Regularly assess and track improvements in shoulder flexibility.

6. Strong Lower Back:

Drills:

Hyperextensions: Strengthen lower back muscles with controlled back extensions.

Planks: Develop core strength to support the lower back.

Tactics:

Ensure proper form during all exercises to prevent lower back injuries.

Include exercises that target the entire core for overall stability.

Core Strength:

Goal: Extend Hyperextension Duration by 20 Seconds in Six Weeks

Measurement: Record the duration of controlled hyperextensions during training.

Target: Increase the duration of hyperextensions by 20 seconds within the next six weeks.

Frequency: Regularly assess core strength during specific exercises.

BRIDGING THE GAP BETWEEN CLASSIC SIMPLICITY AND MODERN POWER

Understanding the traditional approach to teaching bowling and its limitations in fostering a powerful and modern style is a common concern among aspiring bowlers. While numerous bowling resources emphasize the basics of footwork, swing, and fundamental skills, crucial for establishing a foundation, especially for beginners, these fundamentals may not always translate into the development of a powerful and modern style.

The advantages of embracing the basic simple style are evident, making it an attractive starting point for beginners. Firstly, the basic simple style provides a straightforward and easy-to-understand foundation, allowing individuals to grasp the fundamental mechanics of the game without overwhelming complexity. This simplicity aids beginners in navigating the early stages of their bowling journey. Additionally, a simpler style contributes to consistency, enabling bowlers to achieve predictable results and pick up spares with greater ease. The lower physical demands of the basic style make it accessible to a wider range of individuals, fostering inclusivity within the sport.

However, as with any approach, there are drawbacks to the basic simple style. The limited power generated by this style can hinder a bowler's ability to achieve high scores and optimal pin action, a crucial factor in bowling success. Furthermore, bowlers with a basic style may struggle to adapt to changing lane conditions and various oil patterns, limiting their versatility. In the landscape of modern competitive bowling, the basic style might not be as effective, potentially putting bowlers at a disadvantage against opponents with more powerful and dynamic approaches.

On the flip side, transitioning to the modern power style introduces a set of challenges. Firstly, the modern power style demands a higher level of physical fitness, strength, and flexibility, requiring individuals to invest time in building these necessary attributes. Learning this style involves mastering intricate techniques such as advanced ball rotation, timing adjustments, and explosive footwork, presenting a complex learning curve that can be particularly challenging for beginners. Shifting from a basic style to a modern power style is a daunting task, involving the relearning and unlearning of certain habits. This process can be frustrating and time-consuming, as individuals navigate the difficulties of adapting to a new approach.

Consistency becomes a struggle when attempting to achieve a modern power style, with bowlers facing periods of inconsistency during the transition. The mental adaptation required is not to be underestimated, as developing a modern style not only involves physical adjustments but also demands mental adaptability to handle the increased pressure and expectations associated with this style. Balancing the physical and mental aspects of the modern power style is crucial for long-term success on the lanes. In navigating these intricacies, aspiring bowlers must weigh the advantages and disadvantages of each style, considering their individual goals, preferences, and commitment to the sport.

Advantages of Learning the Basic Simple Style:

1. **Easy to Grasp**: *The basic simple style provides a straightforward and easy-to-understand foundation for beginners. It helps individuals learn the fundamental mechanics of the game without overwhelming complexity.*

2. **Consistency**: *A simpler style can lead to more consistency in a bowler's game, making it easier to achieve predictable results and pick up spares.*

3. **Lower Physical Demands**: *The basic style places fewer physical demands on bowlers, making it accessible to a wider range of individuals.*

Disadvantages of Learning the Basic Simple Style:

1. **Limited Power**: *The basic style may not generate the same power and pin action as the modern style, which can hinder a bowler's ability to achieve high scores.*

2. **Less Versatility**: *Bowlers with a basic style may struggle to adapt to changing lane conditions and various oil patterns.*

3. **Reduced Competitive Edge**: *In modern competitive bowling, the basic style might not be as effective, potentially putting the bowler at a disadvantage.*

Obstacles Faced When Learning the Modern Power Style:

1. **Physical Demands**: *The modern power style requires a higher level of physical fitness, strength, and flexibility. Individuals may need time to build the necessary physical attributes.*

2. **Complex Technique**: *Learning the modern power style involves mastering intricate techniques such as advanced ball rotation, timing adjustments, and explosive footwork. This complexity can be challenging for beginners.*

3. **Transition Difficulty**: *Shifting from a basic style to a modern power style can be a daunting task, as it involves relearning and unlearning certain habits. It can be frustrating and time-consuming.*

4. **Consistency Struggles**: *Achieving a consistent modern power style can be elusive, and individuals might face periods of inconsistency while making the transition.*

5. **Mental Adaptation**: *Developing a modern style not only involves physical adjustments but also requires mental adaptability to handle the increased pressure and expectations that come with this style.*

To address this issue, a more comprehensive and systematic approach to coaching young bowlers can be beneficial. This approach should integrate the development of both physical and technical skills, with a focus on building a powerful and modern style from the early stages of learning. By introducing key elements of a modern style early on, bowlers can gradually incorporate these skills into their game, ensuring a smoother transition as they progress.

One way to achieve this is by breaking down the components of a powerful and modern style into manageable and teachable units. This could involve isolating specific elements such as footwork, timing, release, and ball rotation, and teaching them individually. By doing so, bowlers can learn and master these elements one by one, gradually integrating them into their overall technique. Emphasizing the importance of these specific skills, while still ensuring a solid foundation, will help individuals develop a powerful and modern style more efficiently.

Additionally, providing ample opportunities for practice and repetition can be beneficial. Allowing bowlers to execute hundreds of shots over time enables them to gradually refine their technique and develop muscle memory. This repetitive practice, combined with a focus on the key elements of a modern style, will enable them to improve both mentally and physically over the course of a few years.

However, it's essential to acknowledge that transitioning from a basic bowling style to a powerful and modern style is challenging and requires dedication. Not all bowlers will be able to achieve this level of skill, as it requires a unique combination of physical abilities, coordination, and practice. Nonetheless, by implementing a systematic and targeted coaching approach, the chances of individuals developing a powerful and modern style, thus enhancing their overall bowling performance, can be increased.

Master Plan: Transitioning to a Modern Powerful Bowling Style

Phase 1: Foundation Building (Weeks 1-2)

Action 1: Evaluate Current Style • Task: Record your current bowling style, emphasizing footwork, release, and ball rotation. • Example: Record several games and analyze videos to identify areas for improvement.

Action 2: Set Clear Objectives • Task: Define specific goals for transitioning to a modern style, e.g., increase rev rate, improve accuracy, and achieve higher pin carry. • Example: "Increase rev rate by 20%, maintain a pin carry percentage rate to 80% "

Action 3: Learn Modern Style Basics • Task: Study videos and materials on modern bowling styles, focusing on ball rotation, footwork, and timing. • Example: Watch tutorials, read books, and attend workshops on modern bowling techniques.

Action 4: Wrist Torque and Strength Drills (Weekly) • Task: Begin exercises to speed up wrist torque and strengthen the wrist for improved ball rotation. • Example: Practice wrist curls and use wrist devices; increase torque by 15% each week.

Phase 2: Technical Development (Weeks 3-4) – Add up to Phase 1

Action 5: Footwork Drills (Continuous) • Task: Practice modern footwork techniques, like a four-step or five-step approach, for improved balance and timing. • Example: Work with a coach on a five-step approach, ensuring precise and consistent steps.

Action 6: Ball Rotation Training (Weekly) • Task: Develop a strong wrist action for increased ball rotation. • Example: Utilize wrist snap drills, like the towel drill; increase rotation by 15% each week.

Action 7: Timing Practice (Continuous) • Task: Focus on timing adjustments to match the modern style. • Example: Practice releasing the ball when your sliding foot reaches a specific mark on the approach.

Phase 3: Strength and Conditioning (Weeks 5-7) Add up to Phase 2

Action 8: Physical Fitness (Continuous) • Task: Develop strength and flexibility through a tailored fitness regimen. • Example: Perform squats, lunges, core workouts, and wrist strengthening routines regularly.

Phase 4: Mental Toughness and Adaptation (Weeks 8-11) Add up to Phase 2 and 3

Action 9: Mental Conditioning (Continuous) • Task: Develop mental resilience to handle the pressure of a modern style. • Example: Engage in visualization exercises and practice maintaining focus during challenging situations.

Phase 5: Game Integration (Weeks 12-15) Add up to Phase 2, 3 and 4

Action 10: Adaptation to Competitive Settings (Continuous) • Task: Transition acquired skills into competitive games or league play. • Example: Participate in league competitions, applying the modern style consciously.

Phase 6: Continuous Improvement (Ongoing)

Action 11: Regular Self-Analysis (Continuous) • Task: Continuously record and analyze performances to identify areas for improvement. • Example: Review video footage after each game and make notes for self-improvement.

Action 12: Coaching and Feedback (Continuous) • Task: Seek guidance and feedback from a coach or experienced bowlers. • Example: Regularly schedule coaching sessions for personalized guidance and feedback.

Action 13: Tournament Participation (Continuous) • Task: Join local tournaments to test the modern style under various conditions. • Example: Participate in open tournaments for valuable experience in competitive settings.

Note: This master plan is a guideline and can be adjusted based on individual progress and needs. The key to success is consistency and dedication to the process, continuous practice, and a willingness to adapt to the demands of the modern powerful bowling style.

The Theory of Speed at early Stage in Sport

Speed and agility, when harnessed effectively, offer a multifaceted advantage to athletes, and this holds true not only for bowlers but across the spectrum of sports. Physically, the incorporation of speed into training routines enhances cardiovascular fitness, muscle strength, and overall endurance. The dynamic and rapid movements required in sports demand a high level of cardiovascular conditioning, allowing athletes to sustain peak performance throughout the duration of a game or competition. Moreover, the explosive power generated through speed training contributes to the development of fast-twitch muscle fibers, crucial for swift and powerful actions in various sporting maneuvers.

From a technical standpoint, speed serves as a catalyst for refining motor skills and coordination. Athletes with heightened speed capabilities exhibit a heightened ability to execute precise movements with efficiency.

Power and Speed in Bowling

In the context of bowling, a swift and controlled approach to the lane, coupled with a rapid release, can significantly impact accuracy and strike rates. The integration of speed in the early stages of bowling development may thus serve as a crucial component in shaping a bowler's technical prowess.

Neurologically, the cultivation of speed fosters enhanced cognitive processing and decision-making. Rapid response times become second nature to athletes who have undergone speed-focused training, enabling them to adapt swiftly to changing game scenarios. In bowling, the ability to make split-second decisions regarding adjustments in approach or target can be the differentiating factor between a spare and a strike.

In essence, the philosophy of introducing speed and power elements early on in a bowler's journey is rooted in the recognition of the holistic advantages it brings. It transcends the immediate gains in accuracy and strikes, extending its influence to the physical, technical, and neurological dimensions of athletic performance. While a foundational style is crucial, the strategic infusion of speed and agility lays the groundwork for a well-rounded and competitive athlete, capable of navigating the complexities of sport with finesse and effectiveness.

Speed Component

The "speed component" in a bowler's body refers to the ability to generate and control speed during the various phases of a bowling delivery, from the approach to the release of the ball. This speed component primarily involves the coordinated movement of specific body parts, and harnessing it can provide several benefits in the sport of bowling.

1. **Leg Speed**: The legs play a crucial role in generating speed in bowling. A powerful and explosive leg drive during the approach provides momentum, which translates into ball speed. This leg speed allows bowlers to cover the distance from the foul line to the pins rapidly. By developing strong and agile leg muscles, bowlers can achieve a brisk approach and, subsequently, generate greater ball speed.

2. **Arm Speed**: The speed at which a bowler swings their arm and releases the ball impacts the overall delivery speed. A faster arm swing contributes to higher ball velocity, making it challenging for the pins to settle. By developing wrist and forearm strength and practicing a swift arm swing, bowlers can increase their arm speed, ultimately leading to faster ball deliveries.

3. **Release Speed**: The speed at which a bowler releases the ball is a critical component of the overall speed. A quicker and well-timed release results in a snappier and more potent roll. By honing their release techniques and practicing efficient timing, bowlers can achieve a faster and more controlled release speed.

4. **Consistency of Speed**: Maintaining consistent speed throughout the delivery is equally important. Speed fluctuations can affect accuracy and the ball's reaction down the lane. Bowlers aim to develop a consistent and repeatable speed component that optimizes their shot-making capabilities.

Physical Advantages: Starting young bowlers on the path to speed and power from the outset endows them with a range of physical advantages. Speed training enhances muscle strength and coordination, particularly in the legs, arms, and core. The explosive power generated by swift and precise movements contributes to a more robust and versatile physical foundation. This, in turn, leads to better endurance, allowing young bowlers to maintain their performance levels consistently throughout lengthy competitions. Additionally, an early focus on speed development helps reduce the risk of injuries by promoting better body mechanics and muscular balance.

Technical Advantages: From a technical perspective, instilling speed elements early helps young bowlers develop a modern and dynamic bowling style. The ability to execute a quick and controlled approach, a powerful swing, and a snappy release is integral to modern bowling techniques. Early exposure to these technical aspects allows bowlers to refine their mechanics over time, resulting in more accurate and potent shots. Moreover, a faster tempo in the approach and release minimizes the influence of external factors, making it easier for young bowlers to adapt to changing lane conditions and challenges as they progress.

Neurological Advantages: The neurological benefits of introducing speed in early bowling development are equally significant. Rapid and synchronized movements necessitate exceptional hand-eye coordination and decision-making abilities. Young bowlers who adapt to high-speed and well-timed repetitions early on tend to exhibit enhanced mental agility, allowing them to respond swiftly to various challenges during competitions. This heightened neurological conditioning not only boosts performance but also contributes to greater self-confidence and resilience in high-pressure situations.

Advantages in Adaptation and Longevity: Furthermore, the early introduction of speed-oriented training in bowling brings with it long-term advantages. Speed tends to diminish with age, but young bowlers who have adapted to higher speeds from the start gain a valuable advantage. They can effectively manage power and speed as they mature, thereby extending the longevity of their competitive careers. This adaptability ensures that they remain competitive even as their physical attributes evolve.

Muscle Type and Athletic Performance: Exploring Factors for Power Bowlers and Explosive Athletes

In the world of bowling, power bowlers are a unique breed with the capacity to produce a staggering amount of revolutions and a fast ball. This maneuver calls for a blend of physical strength, ability, and a strong wrist snap that pushes the ball down the lane with intense rotation. Increased ball movement and hook possibilities follow, dramatically increasing the likelihood of getting strikes. However, learning this bowling technique has its difficulties, especially in terms of wrist and finger fatigue.

According to research, athletes who have a higher percentage of fast twitch muscle fibers typically do better in turning the bowling ball. Faster ground contact times, made possible by these muscle fibers, are essential for generating speed and reaching high rev rates. Even though some people might have a natural tendency toward high revs, everyone can, to some extent, increase their rev rate and speed. However, a person's potential starting point and total advancement are affected by things like his neurotype and the composition of his muscle fibers.

Using a variety of muscles and requiring precise motions, bowling is a physically demanding game. Bowling uses the stretch-shortening cycle (SSC), which includes eccentric, isometric, and concentric phases, just as in other physical sports. Bowlers can exert greater force and move more quickly by using a pre-stretch or countermovement. Power bowlers might concentrate on honing particular nodes or sections of their bowling action to improve performance. They can store more energy in their upper bodies by prolonging the arm pull, which will boost momentum transfer in the final two steps of their approach. Using this "whip-like" motion, the delivery is sincere and potent.

The body prefers to go toward its flaws or dysfunctions, which is important to comprehend. Therefore, for bowlers looking to compete at their top level, thorough training that covers all facets of physical ability is essential. Targeting power, flexibility, strength, and coordination falls under this category. Bowlers can build the well-rounded physical skills necessary for power bowling and explosive athleticism by exercising each component separately and together.

DECODING THE MYELINATED MOTOR PATTERN OF POWER STYLE

People who enjoy bowling are aware of the need for power in their technique. Power, however, is more than just physical strength; it centers on a finely tuned motor pattern that develops through time. The neuronal connections in bowlers' brains that are responsible for coordinating motions grow as they improve and hone their skills, creating a recognizable and effective motor pattern.

Concentrating on particular actions that involve exact muscle coordination is necessary for improving technique. A myelinated motor pattern that is deeply embedded in muscle memory can be established by using high-volume or slow-speed training to achieve this. Every time, a bowler enters the lane, he strengthens and improves his myelinated circuit, establishing an altogether individual neuromuscular pattern. While physical characteristics like body proportions certainly have an impact on this pattern, it is ultimately the bowler's responsibility to embrace his talent and use it to his fullest advantage. Therefore, with each ball delivered, continual practice and technical improvement result in a more effective and potent neuromuscular pattern.

Key elements of a modern powerful release style with a focus on the neuromuscular patterns:

1. **Balance and Stability**: *The foundation of a powerful release begins with balance and stability. Neuromuscular patterns ensure that the bowler maintains a solid base during the approach, enabling a controlled and explosive delivery.*

2. **Efficient Footwork**: *Modern bowlers exhibit efficient footwork patterns. Neuromuscular coordination allows for a quick and coordinated approach, ensuring that the bowler reaches the foul line with precise timing to optimize energy transfer.*

3. **Fluid Arm Swing**: *The neuromuscular patterns in the arm swing emphasize a fluid motion. This involves a relaxed, yet controlled, arm movement, with the wrist in a strong position for maximum revs on the ball.*

4. **Wrist Snap**: *A modern release style relies on the neuromuscular pattern of a strong wrist snap. The bowler's hand and wrist are finely tuned to impart the desired axis rotation and rev rate on the ball, maximizing hook potential.*

5. *Timing and Coordination*: *Timing is critical in a powerful release. Neuromuscular patterns ensure that the legs, hips, shoulders, and arm work in perfect coordination, creating a seamless and efficient motion from start to finish.*

6. *Muscle Engagement*: *Neuromuscular patterns activate specific muscle groups at the right moments. This involves engaging the core muscles for stability, utilizing the leg muscles for power in the approach, and coordinating the forearm and hand muscles for a dynamic release.*

7. *Precision and Consistency*: *The neuromuscular patterns emphasize precision and consistency in the release. Bowlers with a modern powerful style exhibit a repeatable motion, ensuring that each shot is consistent in terms of speed, rev rate, and accuracy.*

8. *Mental Preparedness*: *Neuromuscular patterns also encompass mental aspects. Bowlers with a modern powerful release style develop mental toughness, which enables them to stay focused, confident, and composed under competitive pressure.*

Bowlers develop the capacity to create force in a precise way that complements their unique talents during adolescence. These movement patterns become hard to change because they become so firmly established. Wired movement patterns indicate strong resistance to change, even though technological modifications can and should be done. Therefore, it is essential to establish the right pattern early on in the developing process.

Factors at Play: Several elements, including speed and force, can affect the ball release in bowling:

- **Fast Twitch Fiber Proportion:** Movement speed and explosiveness are influenced by the proportion of fast-twitch to slow-twitch muscle fibers. The delivery of bowlers who have a higher percentage of fast-twitch fibers is usually quicker and more explosive.

- **Muscle Fascicle Lengths:** The ability to generate force is directly influenced by the length of the muscle fibers. Shorter fibers enable more rapid force creation, while longer fibers generate more force. For instance, bowlers with longer upper body muscle fascicles can swing their arms with more force and speed.

- **Tendon Length and Flexibility:** These factors affect how much force can be generated. Stronger ball releases are produced as a result of longer, more flexible tendons that store more energy.

- **Tendon Insertion and Joint Moment Arm:** During ball release, force is generated depending on the sites at which tendons attach to bones and the moment arms of important joints like the elbow and wrist. For instance, bowlers with a longer moment arm at the elbow joint will be able to swing their arm with more force.

- **Strength and Speed of the Nervous System:** The nervous system's strength and speed influence the movement's velocities and accuracy. Strong core drives enable bowlers to produce more power and show greater control over their actions.

- **Skeletal Structure Aspects:** Body leverage and angles during ball delivery are influenced by bone length and shape. For instance, bowlers with longer arms are able to swing their arms with more force and speed.

Hypothetical Examples:

Fast Twitch Fiber Proportion: Bowler X has a higher proportion of fast-twitch fibers than bowlers with a lesser proportion, enabling him to deliver the ball with outstanding speed and explosive force.

Muscular Fascicle Lengths: Bowler Y has longer muscular fascicles in his upper body, allowing him to swing his arms with more speed and strength and release the ball with more force.

Tendon Length and Pliability: Bowler Z has tendons that are longer and more pliable, allowing him to store more energy and release it with greater force, providing him an advantage in producing force.

Tendon insertion and joint moment arm: Bowler W has a larger moment arm at the elbow joint, which, in comparison to bowlers with shorter moment arms, enables him to produce more force in his arm swing and create a strong ball release.

Strength and Speed of Nervous System: Bowler V has a powerful and quick nervous system, which enables him to exert more force and demonstrate better control over his motions, increasing ball speed and improving accuracy.

Skeletal Structure: Bowler U's longer arms provide him a leverage advantage and enable him to swing his arms with higher speed and power, resulting in a strong ball release.

When considering these elements, it's crucial to keep in mind that some of them are determined by DNA and cannot be changed by training. Others, however, can be enhanced with the use of suitable practice techniques and training methods. Bowlers can unleash more power and accuracy in their deliveries by refining their skills depending on these variables.

Power Bowling: More Than Just Strength Power bowling involves more than just physical strength; it also requires exact timing and coordination, along with the capacity to withstand and channel forces. It is not dependent on attaining remarkable gym results. Unbelievably, there are bowlers as little as 59 kg who find it difficult to squat their own weight but display an outstanding RPM of over 500! These rare cases defy assumptions and are proof of the incredible strength of the human body in the game of bowling. These bowlers are in the top 10% of bowlers in terms of speed, demonstrating that power is a complex quality. However, it is crucial to determine if these occurrences are actual representations of the great potential our bodies contain in the sport of bowling or rare outliers.

Muscle Fiber Type Fatigue Rate and its Impact on Bowling Performance

Understanding the function of different muscle fiber types is essential in the world of bowling, where strength, accuracy, and endurance are critical. While there is no clear consensus on the ideal fast-twitch fiber distribution in bowlers, scientific evidence points to a critical function for these fibers in producing the power and speed necessary for effective bowling performances.

Professional bowlers are found to have more fast-twitch fibers in their upper body muscles than amateur bowlers, according to studies. This research suggests that a higher proportion of these fibers may be favorable for producing the speed and power required for successful bowling. It's crucial to remember, though, that most people are born with roughly equal amounts of fast and slow twitch fibers, with fast-oxidative glycolytic (FTa) fibers often predominating.

Although it's commonly believed that rapid twitch fibers are used for high-intensity activity and slow twitch fibers are used for low-intensity work, this oversimplification isn't accurate. In actuality, slow twitch fibers, which are more aerobically efficient, do the majority of sub-maximal work, while fast twitch fibers are gradually recruited as the intensity of the effort approaches its maximum.

There are different groups of muscle fibers that make up muscles like the biceps femoris, and each group is supplied by a separate motor neuron. These units, often referred to as motor units, are made up of fibers of the same kind. The fibers inside a particular motor unit will therefore be of the same kind, either slow twitch (ST), fast-oxidative glycolytic (FTa), or fast glycolytic (FTx), despite the fact that a muscle has a variety of fiber types.

The "size" idea is used to recruit motor units. For low to moderate-intensity labor, slow twitch fibers are recruited first because their motor neurons are smaller and require less stimulation to activate. To produce the most force and power, the largest motor units associated with FTx fibers are ultimately activated after larger motor units connected with FTa fibers have been recruited as the work's intensity increases.

Exploring cutting-edge training methods that can improve a bowler's skills requires an understanding of the effects of different muscle fiber types on performance. By limiting the oxygen supply, blood flow restriction (BFR) bands, for instance, can be used to pre-fatigue slow-twitch muscle fibers. This pre-fatiguation sets up the fast twitch fibers to react to exercise loads more quickly and effectively, which accelerates the building of lean muscle and improves overall performance in bowling.

Bowlers can modify their training programs to maximize performance by understanding the intricate interactions between different muscle fiber types and their patterns of recruitment. A well-rounded training program can maximize a bowler's muscle fiber composition, whether it be by strengthening slow twitch fibers with endurance-focused activities or by stimulating rapid twitch fibers using BFR bands. Therefore, embrace science, try out various training techniques, and watch as your bowling performance soars to new heights.

The effects of different muscle fiber types, particularly slow-twitch (ST) and fast-twitch (FT) fibers, on the speed and strength of a bowler are as follows:

Slow-Twitch (ST) Muscle Fibers:

Speed: Slow-twitch fibers are more fatigue-resistant and designed for endurance. They are less involved in generating explosive speed. Therefore, an emphasis on these fibers might not directly contribute to increased bowling speed.

Strength: ST fibers provide good muscular endurance but have limited capacity for generating high levels of strength and power. Training them extensively might improve a bowler's ability to maintain form and control throughout a long bowling session, but it may not significantly enhance their strength.

Fast-Twitch (FT) Muscle Fibers:

Speed: Fast-twitch fibers are responsible for explosive movements and high-speed actions. Training these fibers can directly impact a bowler's speed, allowing for more explosive movements during the delivery.

Strength: FT fibers have a higher potential for generating strength and power. Focusing on these fibers can lead to increased strength, which is crucial for generating ball speed and accuracy in bowling.

Streamline plan for transitioning from Low-Twitch Fiber to Fast-Twitch Fiber composition in bowlers

Phase 1: Baseline Assessment

1. *Muscle Fiber Analysis: Begin by assessing the muscle fiber composition in the wrist. This can be done through specialized tests to understand the distribution of fast-twitch (FT) and slow-twitch (ST) muscle fibers in this area.*

Phase 2: Skill-Specific Training - Wrist Strength Exercises

In this phase, your focus is on strengthening the wrist muscles with an emphasis on transitioning to fast-twitch (FT) muscle recruitment. Here's a detailed explanation of how to perform the exercises, including speed, reps, sets, and intensity.

Wrist Strength Exercises: (Continuous)

1. *Wrist Curls:*
   - *Exercise: Sit on a bench or chair with your forearm resting on your thigh, palm facing up, and the wrist hanging off the edge.*
   - *Speed: Perform wrist curls in a controlled manner, emphasizing the upward (flexion) movement.*
   - *Reps: Start with 3 sets of 12-15 repetitions per wrist.*
   - *Sets: Gradually progress to 4 sets as your wrist strength improves.*
   - *Intensity/Weight: Begin with a light dumbbell (1-2 pounds) or a wrist curler device. As you advance, increase the weight in small increments.*

2. *Reverse Wrist Curls: (Continuous – weight to be increased by 5% every week)*
   - *Exercise: Sit in the same position as for wrist curls but with your palm facing down.*
   - *Speed: Execute the reverse wrist curls with controlled movements, emphasizing the upward (extension) phase.*
   - *Reps: Begin with 3 sets of 12-15 repetitions per wrist.*
   - *Sets: As you progress, increase to 4 sets.*
   - *Intensity/Weight: Use a light dumbbell or wrist curler with a weight appropriate for your current strength level, gradually increasing the weight as you get stronger.*

Progress Monitoring and KPIs:
   - *Duration: Perform wrist strength exercises 2-3 times per week to allow for proper recovery and muscle adaptation.*

- *Intensity*: Increase the weight or resistance incrementally, ensuring that each set remains challenging but manageable.

- *KPIs (Key Performance Indicators)*: Focus on the following KPIs to move to the next level of wrist strength and transition toward optimal FT muscle recruitment:

- *Increased weight*: Gradually lift heavier weights for wrist curls and reverse wrist curls.

- *Improved muscle endurance*: Observe the ability to maintain form and strength throughout the sets and repetitions.

- *Enhanced wrist stability*: Look for reduced fatigue and better control during bowling practice.

- *Decreased discomfort or pain*: Ensure that the exercises are performed without causing discomfort or pain.

Phase 3: Bowling Skill Practice

During Phase 3, you will integrate your improved wrist strength into your bowling skills. This is a crucial step in transitioning your wrist muscle fiber composition and maximizing your bowling performance.

Bowling Skill Practice:

1. **Release Technique**:
   - Focus on wrist position and movement during the release.
   - Pay attention to the timing and coordination of your wrist snap with the release point.
   - Drills: Use release drills that emphasize wrist action, such as releasing the ball with a sharp snap while maintaining accuracy and balance.

2. **Rev Rate Development**: *(Continuous – Speed or torque to be increased by 10% every week)*
   - Gradually increase your rev rate by applying more wrist action.
   - Practice generating a higher rev rate while maintaining control.
   - Drills: Engage in rev rate-specific drills, where you focus on increasing the number of revolutions while hitting your target consistently.

3. **Accuracy and Control**:
   - Work on manipulating the ball's trajectory and spin with precision.
   - Concentrate on hitting specific target areas consistently.
   - Drills: Implement accuracy drills that challenge your ability to control the ball's path while incorporating wrist action for fine adjustments.

Duration and KPIs for Skill Practice:

- *Duration*: Dedicate regular practice sessions to skill development. Ideally, practice your release, rev rate, and accuracy for at least 1-2 hours a few times per week.

- *KPIs (Key Performance Indicators)*: To transition your wrist muscle composition effectively and optimize bowling skills, monitor the following KPIs:

- *Improved wrist snap*: Observe a more powerful and controlled wrist snap during the release.

- *Increased rev rate*: Track the number of revolutions and ensure it is gradually on the rise.

- *Enhanced accuracy and control*: Assess your ability to consistently hit the desired target areas with the desired ball reaction.

Phase 4: Progress Monitoring

Regular Assessment: Periodically assess your wrist muscle composition and strength to track progress. This will help you adjust your training plan and technique accordingly.

Factor	Role in Bowler	How it Affects Performance	Advantages	Disadvantages	Effect on Speed/ Strength and Power
Fast Twitch Fiber Proportion	Speed and explosiveness	Higher proportion = faster, more explosive delivery	Greater ball speed and power	Lower endurance	Speed
Muscle Fascicle Lengths	Force generation capability	Longer fibers = greater force, shorter fibers = speed	Higher speed and power in arm swing	Lower force generation capability	Speed and power
Tendon Length and Pliability	Force production	Longer and more flexible tendons store more energy	Powerful ball release	Potential for injury with excessive force	Power
Tendon Insertion and Joint Moment Arm	Force generation during ball release	Longer moment arm = greater force in arm swing	Increased force in arm swing	Potential for joint stress or injury	Power
Nervous System Strength and Speed	Speed and precision of movements	A strong and fast nervous system = more force and control	Increased force and better control	Potential for overexertion or fatigue	Speed and precision
Skeletal Structure Aspects	Body leverages and angles	Longer arms = greater speed and power in arm swing	Increased speed and power in arm swing	Potential for reduced maneuverability	Speed and power
Recruitment of Motor Units	Force and Power Generation	Activation of larger motor units = greater force and power generation	Increased force output and power	Potential for increased muscle fatigue	Power
Blood Flow Restriction (BFR) Training	Muscle Fiber Stimulation and Growth	Pre-fatiguing slow twitch fibers = enhanced response of fast twitch	Accelerated lean muscle growth and improved performance	Potential for overtraining or injury	Endurance

Table 31 – Factors and elements for powerful styles

THE SCIENCE OF BIOMECHANICS FOR POWER AND REVOLUTIONS IN TWO-HANDED BOWLING

Bowling, as a sport, extends its inclusive embrace to individuals of diverse physical attributes and athletic capacities. It stands out as a game where towering height and superlative athleticism are not prerequisites for participation. However, delving into the intricacies of two-handed bowling introduces a nuanced layer that warrants careful consideration, enhancing the overall depth of the bowling experience.

The decision to employ a two-handed bowling technique is underpinned by a range of strategic advantages. Embracing this approach unlocks the potential for a more versatile selection of bowling balls and, perhaps more significantly, affords the bowler greater control over the trajectory of the thrown ball. This heightened control, in turn, not only augments accuracy but also elevates the scoring potential. For those actively seeking optimal equipment for two-handed bowling, comprehensive recommendations are available to meet specific needs and preferences.

The rationale behind opting for a two-handed approach in bowling extends beyond a mere quest for increased power. Rather, it serves as a methodological refinement to smoothen the transition between forms, thereby fostering a more balanced and effective striking mechanism. Traditional barriers that would typically require extensive practice and honed technique are circumvented in two-handed bowling, where the simultaneous use of both hands expedites the acquisition of a potent spin toss, resulting in accelerated skill development.

Mastering the technique of two-handed bowling, however, is not an instantaneous process but a journey characterized by dedication, persistent practice, and unwavering patience. The pursuit of proficiency necessitates an investment of time and resources beyond mere league participation. The dividends, though delayed, prove rewarding as the two-handed approach engenders a substantially increased hook and the ability to execute curving shots, often sparking spirited discourse among fellow bowlers.

At its fundamental level, bowling entails the competitive act of strategically propelling a ball down an alley with the primary goal of knocking over ten pins in a single throw. The versatility of executing this maneuver with either the dominant or non-dominant hand adds an additional layer of complexity, requiring precision and finesse as the ball hurtles down the lane at speeds approximating 20 miles per hour.

An exploration of two-handed bowling unveils a myriad of complexities, surpassing initial perceptions. This exploration delves into the nuances of both one-handed and two-handed techniques, providing invaluable insights for individuals keen on refining their skills. Subsequent sections of this discourse offer concise yet comprehensive tips on the distinctive facets of two-handed bowling, encompassing the stance, approach, grip, swing, and release.

Within the realm of two-handed bowling, the stance occupies a pivotal position. The bowler leverages the non-dominant hand to cradle the front of the ball during the backswing, providing essential stability and support. As the ball propels forward, the supporting hand guides it, not only intensifying the spin during execution but also endowing an additional layer of control crucial for optimal performance across diverse lane conditions.

The approach in two-handed bowling introduces initial challenges, particularly for novices. However, the maintenance of a consistent pace and the meticulous refinement of technique become paramount. A measured approach typically involves four or five steps, the length of which is contingent upon the individual bowler's stride. The initial steps mirror those of a one-handed bowler, establishing a rhythmic cadence that lays the foundation for subsequent stages of the approach.

During the second step, the strategic redistribution of weight becomes critical, compensating for the dominant hand and aligning with the intended direction of the throw. An intricate adjustment involves three or four steps interspersed with skip steps to preserve momentum before executing a slide on an "outstep." The final step, a slide-skip combination, assumes a pivotal role in maintaining alignment, generating momentum, and infusing power into the throw.

The grip, an elemental aspect of a bowler's technique, interlaces with the release to shape the outcome of every throw. Two-handed bowlers adopt various gripping styles—some incorporating the thumb, while others embrace a cradle-all-around approach, enveloping the ball entirely in one hand. The positioning of the non-dominant hand on the ball before release dictates the ensuing reactions upon contact with the surface.

The swing in bowling orchestrates a delicate equilibrium between power and control. The bowler bears the responsibility of generating momentum during the backswing, with the positioning of the swing influencing the power and potential control issues of the subsequent throw. Striking an optimal balance is paramount, as a swing closer to the shoulder blades or above yields a more forceful throw but may compromise control.

Rolling a bowling ball metamorphoses into an intricate art, demanding meticulous attention to technique, power, and accuracy for the desired trajectory. The extensive practice invested in perfecting throws refines the ability to execute potent tosses with precision, particularly in the context of two-handed bowling. Maintaining the non-dominant hand on the ball until release is crucial, unleashing the elbow right before release to enhance speed and ball revolutions.

The release in two-handed bowling emerges as a nuanced maneuver, ideally occurring next to the ankle to leverage maximum power. Attempting to artificially induce more spin using the non-dominant hand at this stage is cautioned against; instead, a well-executed stance and throw naturally produce the desired spin. In essence, mastering the multifaceted technique of two-handed bowling evolves into a journey of exploration and refinement, promising enhanced power, control, and a heightened level of enjoyment on the bowling alley.

Why 2 Hand Bowlers Have More Rev And Power

The landscape of bowling has undergone a transformative shift with the emergence of two-handed bowling, a technique that has redefined the conventional norms of the sport. Beyond its visually distinctive form, this approach stands out for its unparalleled ability to generate heightened revolutions and power on the bowling ball. Delving into the mechanics of two-handed bowling unveils a tapestry of biomechanical intricacies that distinguishes it from traditional one-handed styles. At the heart of this evolution lies the deliberate departure from the use of the thumb in the grip, a departure that extends beyond mere aesthetics to fundamentally alter the dynamics of the release. As we unravel the complexities of this technique, exploring the synchronized movements, enhanced core engagement, and the intricate interplay of both hands, a compelling narrative emerges—one that positions two-handed bowling as a revolutionary force in the world of competitive bowling.

1. **Dual Power Sources:**
   - *Execution:* Initiating the backswing involves a synchronized movement of both arms, with the non-dominant arm actively supporting the ball. As the bowler transitions into the release, both arms contribute simultaneously to the forward motion.
   - *Biomechanics:* The kinetic chain starts from the legs, transferring energy through the core and shoulders to both arms. The simultaneous engagement of both arms optimizes the transfer of energy to the ball, resulting in increased revs and speed.

2. **Extended Finger Placement and Longer Release Window:**
   - *Execution: In the two-handed technique, the absence of thumb insertion allows the fingers to be positioned further down and under the ball during the entire approach.*
   - *Biomechanics: The extended finger placement creates a longer release window, meaning that the fingers remain in* contact with the ball for an extended duration—from the initial part of the backswing to the point of release. This extended interaction contributes to increased revolutions as the fingers have a more extended period to influence the ball's spin.

3. **Enhanced Angular Release Chain:**
   - *Execution*: In the two-handed bowling style, the release chain encompasses the shoulder, elbow, wrist, and fingers, forming a sequence that imparts spin to the ball. Notably, the absence of the thumb alters the dynamics of this chain.
   - *Biomechanics:* The two-handed technique introduces a more extreme angular release chain, as each point in the chain—shoulder, elbow, wrist, and fingers—experiences a heightened degree angle. This extreme angular configuration, coupled with the quick transition between these points, results in a more rapid and forceful release. The amplified angular momentum contributes significantly to the generation of additional revolutions on the ball.

4. **Unrestricted Release due to Absence of Thumb Constraint:**
   - *Execution:* Traditional one-handed bowling styles involve gripping the ball with fingers and thumb coming together in the center, creating a point of convergence that demands a synchronized release.
   - *Biomechanics:* The presence of the thumb in traditional styles necessitates that both the thumb and fingers work together, potentially causing a minor constraint during the release. In contrast, the two-handed approach, void of the thumb, eliminates this constraint, allowing for a more aggressive and unhindered release. The absence of thumb interference results in a cleaner release, enabling the fingers to exert maximum influence on the ball's spin without any constraint from the thumb. This contributes to a more aggressive and efficient release, fostering increased revolutions on the ball.

5. **Enhanced Core Engagement:**
   - *Execution:* Maintaining a tight core throughout the approach involves controlled abdominal and oblique muscle engagement. The core remains stable during the backswing and dynamically activates during the release.
   - *Biomechanics:* A strong core acts as the fulcrum of the body's rotational forces, ensuring efficient energy transfer from the lower body to the upper body, amplifying the power generated.

6. **Leverage from Non-Dominant Arm:**
   - *Execution:* The non-dominant arm provides crucial support during the backswing and guides the ball during the release, actively contributing to the overall motion.

- *Biomechanics:* Leveraging the non-dominant arm creates an additional pivot point, enhancing the bowler's ability to generate torque and speed, especially during the transition from the backswing to the release.

7. **Wider Shoulder Rotation:**

   - *Execution:* Achieving a broader range of shoulder rotation involves a deliberate emphasis on a wide backswing, allowing both shoulders to rotate freely.
   - *Biomechanics:* Wider shoulder rotation increases the angular momentum, creating a more forceful release and translating to higher ball speed.

8. **Increased Hip Flexibility:**

   - *Execution:* Incorporating hip flexibility in the approach requires a deliberate focus on hip rotation during the backswing and transition.
   - *Biomechanics:* Improved hip flexibility facilitates a more significant rotational movement, allowing for a smoother transfer of energy, which contributes to increased revs and speed.

9. **Optimized Timing and Synchronization:**

   - *Execution:* Achieving optimal timing and synchronization involves a precise coordination of both arms throughout the entire approach.
   - *Biomechanics:* A well-coordinated motion minimizes energy loss, ensuring that the force generated by the legs is efficiently transferred through the core to both arms, resulting in a more powerful release.

10. **Extended Arm Reach:**

    - *Execution:* A more extended reach during the release is facilitated by a deliberate extension of both arms forward.
    - *Biomechanics:* The longer lever arm increases the distance over which force is applied to the ball, resulting in heightened ball speed.

11. **Efficient Weight Transfer:**

    - *Execution:* Efficient weight transfer involves a powerful transition of weight from the back foot to the front foot during the approach.
    - *Biomechanics:* Proper weight transfer ensures that the kinetic energy generated by the lower body is effectively transferred to the upper body, enhancing the overall delivery speed.

12. **Balanced Biomechanics:**

    - *Execution:* Maintaining a balanced stance requires a conscious effort to distribute weight evenly between both feet.
    - *Biomechanics:* A balanced stance minimizes strain on specific muscle groups, reducing the risk of injury and allowing for consistent, repeatable motions.

13. **Greater Spin Potential:**

    - *Execution:* Cupping the wrist with both hands involves a controlled rotation during the release.
    - *Biomechanics:* A strong wrist position with coordinated movements of both hands optimizes the spin potential, contributing to increased angular momentum and overall ball speed.

14. **Optimal Release Point Control:**

    - *Execution:* Refining control over the release point necessitates meticulous hand positioning and wrist control.
    - *Biomechanics:* Precise control over the release point allows for fine-tuning of the delivery, ensuring maximum speed and revs with accuracy.

15. **Consistent Ball Path and Trajectory:**

   - *Execution:* The biomechanical advantages contribute to a consistent ball path.

   - *Biomechanics:* A repeatable motion, facilitated by the two-handed technique, results in a more predictable and consistent ball path across different shots.

16. **Reduced Arm Strain:**

   - *Execution:* Distributing the load between both arms lessens strain on the dominant arm.

   - *Biomechanics:* Reduced strain allows bowlers to sustain a higher level of performance without succumbing to fatigue or discomfort.

Neruological And Psychological Elements Are Builts Differently Using 2 Hands Style

Bowling, as a sport, encompasses a rich tapestry of styles, each demanding a harmonious blend of physical prowess and mental acuity. Among the diverse techniques, the two-handed bowling style has emerged as a distinctive and strategically potent approach employed by skilled bowlers. Beyond its visual appeal, this dual-handed method offers a spectrum of advantages that transcend the mere execution of the game. The two-handed bowler benefits neurologically from enhanced brain activation, sensory integration, and proprioceptive finesse, orchestrating a symphony of refined coordination and cognitive prowess. Simultaneously, from a psychological standpoint, practitioners of the two-handed style often cultivate a profound sense of confidence, adaptability, and a strategic edge over their one-handed counterparts. The intricacies of this technique weave together a unique combination of neurological and psychological attributes that contribute to the success and allure of the two-handed bowling style, positioning it as a captivating and strategically masterful approach in the world of competitive bowling.

Neurologically, the two-handed bowler engages in a symphony of enhanced brain activation, propelling the sport into a realm of refined coordination and communication between hemispheres. This stems from the simultaneous involvement of both hands in the intricate process of delivering a powerful shot. The resulting bilateral brain activation is a neurological symphony that contributes to improved motor coordination and cognitive prowess. Moreover, the multi-directional cognitive processing demanded by the two-handed style sets it apart neurologically. Coordinating movements for both hands and simultaneously assessing lane conditions require a higher level of cognitive processing. This not only sharpens cognitive abilities but also enhances overall neurological processing speed.

Furthermore, the adoption of the two-handed technique triggers an evolution in sensory integration, as the bowler processes information from multiple sources concurrently. This heightened sensory integration not only sharpens awareness but also fosters adaptability on the lane, allowing the bowler to make split-second adjustments based on a comprehensive understanding of their surroundings. The precise control required over the movements of both hands fosters finely tuned proprioceptive abilities, contributing to enhanced shot accuracy. In this way, the two-handed bowler embarks on a journey of neuromuscular refinement, enhancing proprioception and fine-tuning sensory integration to a degree unparalleled in traditional one-handed bowling.

The two-handed approach also induces a paradigm shift in the development of motor skills. The repetition and refinement of this technique lead to the nuanced development of complex motor skills as both hands synchronize their movements seamlessly. This not only contributes to enhanced neurological dexterity but also instills a sense of precision in the execution of each shot. The intricacies of the two-handed technique stimulate neural plasticity, allowing the bowler's brain to adapt to new challenges and refine motor patterns over time. This continuous adaptation and refinement characterize the neurological journey of a two-handed bowler, leading to a level of mastery that transcends the conventional boundaries of the sport.

Beyond the neurological realm, the two-handed bowler ascends to new heights in the psychological arena, navigating the intricate landscape of confidence, adaptability, and strategic prowess. The adoption of a unique and visually impressive style becomes a psychological catalyst, instilling a profound sense of confidence in the bowler. This newfound confidence transcends the physical execution of the game, influencing decision-making, composure, and the ability to handle pressure situations with grace.

The journey to mastering the two-handed technique often involves overcoming challenges, fostering adaptability and resilience. Bowlers undertaking this unique approach develop a psychological resilience that sets them apart in the face of setbacks. The ability to adapt to different lane conditions and opponents becomes a hallmark of the two-handed bowler's psychological repertoire, adding a layer of strategic versatility to their game.

The psychological edge over opponents is a notable aspect of the two-handed style. The uniqueness of this technique introduces an element of unpredictability that may unsettle competitors, providing a strategic advantage in the psychological chess match of the game. Opponents find themselves facing not just a bowler but a strategist who employs a unique and unpredictable style, creating a mental challenge that transcends the physical act of knocking down pins.

Achieving proficiency in the two-handed technique becomes a source of motivation through mastery. Bowlers set and achieve incremental goals, fostering a continuous cycle of improvement. This sense of achievement, coupled with the motivation to refine and perfect their technique, propels the two-handed bowler forward in their quest for excellence. The journey becomes as much a psychological endeavor as a physical one, intertwining the development of skill with a profound sense of purpose and dedication to the craft.

The intricacies of the two-handed style also cultivate strong visualization skills. The bowler learns to mentally rehearse and visualize their movements, contributing to improved performance. This enhanced ability to visualize shots and anticipate outcomes adds a layer of strategic depth to the psychological toolkit of the two-handed bowler. It becomes a mental chess game, where each shot is not just a physical act but a meticulously planned move in the broader strategy.

In terms of competitive versatility, two-handed bowlers often exhibit a greater ability to adapt to different lane conditions and opponents. This adaptability contributes to a more confident and strategically flexible mindset. The intricacies of two-handed bowling demand mental toughness and focus. Bowlers develop the ability to maintain composure and concentration in high-pressure situations, contributing to overall psychological resilience. The two-handed bowler becomes a symbol of adaptability, mental fortitude, and strategic prowess, navigating the challenges of the game with a level of sophistication that sets them apart.

Advantages of Two-Handed Bowler (Neurological)	Description
1. Enhanced Bilateral Brain Activation	Engaging both hands in the bowling motion stimulates bilateral brain activation, fostering improved coordination and communication between the brain hemispheres. This can enhance overall neurological function.
2. Increased Sensory Integration	The use of both hands in the bowling process enhances sensory integration, as the brain processes information from multiple sources simultaneously. This heightened integration can lead to better adaptability on the lane.
3. Fine-Tuned Proprioception	The two-handed style requires precise control over hand movements, leading to the development of finely tuned proprioceptive abilities. This heightened sense of body awareness contributes to improved shot accuracy.
4. Dual-Handed Motor Skill Development	Practicing and perfecting the unique movements of both hands in two-handed bowling contribute to the development of complex motor skills, enhancing the bowler's overall neurological dexterity.
5. Multi-Directional Cognitive Processing	Two-handed bowlers often engage in multi-directional cognitive processing, coordinating movements for both hands and assessing lane conditions simultaneously. This cognitive demand can enhance overall neurological processing speed.
6. Improved Neural Plasticity	The continuous adaptation and refinement of the two-handed technique stimulate neural plasticity, allowing the bowler's brain to adapt to new challenges and refine motor patterns over time.
7. Efficient Cross-Lateral Brain Connectivity	The coordinated movements of both hands in two-handed bowling foster efficient cross-lateral brain connectivity, promoting seamless communication between different areas of the brain involved in motor control.
8. Enhanced Hand-Eye Coordination	The use of both hands requires heightened hand-eye coordination, as each hand contributes to the precise release of the ball. This can lead to superior hand-eye coordination compared to one-handed bowlers.

Advantages of Two-Handed Bowler (Psychological)	Description
1. Unique Style Confidence Boost	The distinctive and visually impressive two-handed style can provide a confidence boost, instilling a sense of uniqueness and mastery that positively influences the bowler's psychological state.
2. Adaptability and Resilience	Learning and mastering the two-handed approach often involves overcoming challenges, fostering adaptability and resilience. This psychological fortitude can positively impact a bowler's ability to handle pressure situations.
3. Psychological Edge over Opponents	The uniqueness of the two-handed style can create a psychological edge over opponents, introducing an element of unpredictability that may unsettle competitors and provide a strategic advantage.
4. Motivation through Mastery	Achieving proficiency in the two-handed technique provides a source of motivation through mastery, encouraging bowlers to set and achieve goals for continuous improvement.

Advantages of Two-Hand-ed Bowler (Psychological)	Description
5. Enhanced Visu-alization Skills	The complexity of the two-handed style encourages the development of strong visualization skills, allowing bowlers to mentally rehearse and visualize their movements for improved performance.
6. Competitive Versatility	Two-handed bowlers often exhibit greater versatility in their approach, adapting to different lane conditions and opponents. This adaptability contributes to a more confident and strategically flexible mindset.
7. Mental Tough-ness and Focus	The intricate nature of two-handed bowling demands mental toughness and focus. Bowlers develop the ability to maintain composure and concentration in high-pressure situations, contributing to overall psychological resilience.
8. Sense of Achieve-ment and Motivation	The journey of mastering the two-handed style involves setting and achieving incremental goals, fostering a sense of achievement and motivation for continuous improvement in the psychological aspect of the game.

Table 32 – Advantages of 2 handed bowler neurologically and psychologically

THE SIGNIFICANCE OF TIMING IN BOWLING: TAILORING APPROACHES FOR DIFFERENT STYLES *By Ruben Ghiragossian*

Abstract: In this article, the significance of timing in bowling is examined, along with the necessity of adapting coaching strategies to different bowling styles. Coaches may maximize timing for both one-handed and two-handed bowlers by knowing how several factors, such as footwork, swing length, and release, interact with one another. Bowlers of various styles and ages can succeed under the same conditions thanks to the sport's inclusion, highlighting its innovative nature as a performance-driven activity.

The introduction of "Two Hand Bowling" has inspired a variety of discussions and comparisons among bowlers. Certain parts of bowling's general concept are immediately obvious, and among fans, the benefits and drawbacks of various bowling techniques frequently come up for discussion. However, timing is a factor in the physical game that must be carefully taken into account.

In order to explore this topic, we must first accept that each bowling style demands a unique set of basics and options. While the physical game and release considerations have historically been governed by the idea that all bowlers or styles should conform to the same rules, reality reveals that various styles should be handled differently in this situation.

Different time sequences and qualities must be taken into account for diverse groups, including one-handed and two-handed bowlers, women, and kids. What distinguishes them, and how should we handle these distinctions, are the crucial questions.

How does time work exactly? It basically refers to how much longer it takes the bowling ball to get to the foul line than it does for the bowler's body to get there. We actually take into account two additional factors when looking at timing: distance and velocity. Timing, to put it simply, includes everything like footwork spacing, tempo, the placement and form of the ball during the swing, as well as the total distance traveled by the ball during the entire action.

The permissible swing length and the pressures the system can endure are the main factors to take into account when thinking about timing for a specific style—not in absolute terms, but rather with a personalized approach for each style.

The following are some general timing considerations:

1. *The distance from the bowler's stance to the foul line depends on his height.*

2. *The footwork pace depends on the bowler's age and physical strength.*

3. *Specific physical restrictions dictate the swing's height and range of motion.*

4. *The allowable swing height range will depend on whether the bowler uses a one-handed or two-handed method.*

What is the best way to handle these questions now? It takes more than simply adhering to a predetermined script to decide how to mix all of these components. Understanding how these components interact is essential for effective coaching, which entails creativity. After spending a lot of time with different two-handed bowlers, it becomes clear that comprehending their timing requirements is not difficult at all. In actuality, there isn't much of a distinction between instructing one-handed bowlers and this situation. In actuality, the list of fundamentals stays the same when examining the most successful trends across various types.

Here are some crucial foundations for bowlers who use one or two hands:

- *The bowling ball should be placed straight ahead or just inside the vertical headline pointing down.*

- *At the end of the swing, the hand needs to be straight or just slightly open.*

- *The arms must move in a plane that follows the play line.*

To be honest, the pins themselves do not distinguish between one-handed and two-handed deliveries or whether bowlers utilized their thumb during the approach to the foul line, thus these principles are the same. The timing system utilized for the release is determined by the interval between when the feet cross the foul line and when the ball does. What is the proper timing profile, and how much time disparity should be incorporated into our system, is the question that therefore emerges?

The system's strongest point, which is located underneath its center of gravity, should line up with the neutral point for release time. The bowler's slide length and foot separation distance decide this particular area. The complexity of the release makes additional time differential necessary. In the modern game, the system must unload such situations while the ball is still descending due to factors including the position of the ball in the hand, wrist cupping, and other bowling tactics used by both one-handed and two-handed bowlers.

Ruben Ghiragossian, Author of the Kegel Coaching Master's Programs

PEL LEARNING RATIOS IN BOWLING

The popular and difficult sport of bowling calls for a combination of physical prowess, mental concentration, and tactical judgment. Learning and perfecting the art of bowling requires a dynamic interplay between distinct cognitive, perceptual, and motor processes, just like learning and mastering any physical ability. Performance Engaging Experience Learning (PEL), a cutting-edge strategy for improving motor skills in sports like bowling, has gained popularity in recent years. In order to encourage optimal performance and improve the overall learning experience, PEL highlights the value of building a rich, interesting, and contextually appropriate learning environment.

Early Learning Stage:

The early learning stage in bowling is a foundational period where bowlers, whether children or adults, focus on developing fundamental motor abilities. This encompasses essential aspects like grip, stance, approach, and release. During this phase, the emphasis is on building a robust technical foundation and gaining a basic understanding of the rules and tactics involved in the sport. Applying principles from the Player Engagement and Learning (PEL) model is particularly effective at this level. Instructors use strategies such as storytelling, gamification, and visual aids to create a positive and engaging learning environment, promoting skill acquisition and motivation. Rapid feedback and positive reinforcement play a vital role in boosting the confidence and self-esteem of beginners, thereby accelerating their skill development.

Distinguishing between children and adults at the early stage of PEL learning reveals nuanced differences in priorities. For children, immediate positive reinforcement holds significant importance, with celebrations of small achievements aimed at building confidence and motivation. Engaging young learners through gamification, storytelling, and visual aids is crucial, as is maintaining a focus on creating an enjoyable environment for initial skill acquisition. In contrast, adult beginners benefit from positive reinforcement and acknowledgment of early successes, fostering confidence for continued participation. An engaging learning environment remains essential, with the introduction of basics in an interesting way to keep adults motivated and committed. Foundational learning is a shared priority, but adults receive a slightly greater emphasis on clear explanations and practical experiences to kickstart their understanding of the sport.

Considering the basic beginners learning stage, certain key considerations come to the forefront. Fundamental skill development is paramount, whether focusing on children or adults. For children, this involves honing basic motor skills with age-appropriate equipment to ensure a positive early experience. In contrast, adult beginners are introduced to fundamental techniques such as the correct grip, basic stance, and a simple approach to the foul line. Creating an engaging learning environment is crucial for both age groups. Children benefit from interactive methods like storytelling, gamification, and visual aids, while adults appreciate a balance between structured learning and engaging activities. Positive reinforcement plays a vital role in both scenarios, celebrating small achievements for children and recognizing early successes for adults, fostering motivation and enjoyment in the learning process. Introducing beginners to the basic rules of bowling is also essential. For children, this involves simplifying concepts like scoring, foul lines, and frames, using visual aids to enhance understanding. Adults receive a brief overview of bowling rules to ensure a basic understanding of scoring and fundamental game mechanics. Overall, a balanced approach to structured learning and enjoyable engagement is key in the early learning stage, laying the foundation for a lifelong appreciation of the sport for both children and adults.

Difference Between Children And Adults At The Early Stage Of Pel Learning

1. **Children:**
   - Performance: 30%
   - Engagement: 40%
   - Learning: 30%

2. **Adults:**
   - Performance: 25%
   - Engagement: 35%
   - Learning: 40%

Rationale for Basic Beginners Learning Stage:

1. **Children:**
   - **Performance (30%):** At the basic stage, children benefit from immediate positive reinforcement, celebrating small achievements to boost confidence and motivation.
   - **Engagement (40%):** Engagement is crucial for young learners. Utilizing gamification, storytelling, and visual aids in the learning process enhances participation and enthusiasm.
   - **Learning (30%):** While foundational learning is important, the majority of emphasis remains on creating an enjoyable and stimulating environment for initial skill acquisition.

2. **Adults:**
   - **Performance (25%):** Beginners, including adults, benefit from positive reinforcement and acknowledgment of early successes. It helps build confidence and encourages continued participation.
   - **Engagement (35%):** Adult beginners appreciate an engaging learning environment. Introducing the basics in an interesting and interactive way keeps them motivated and committed.
   - **Learning (40%):** While foundational learning is a key focus, there is a balanced emphasis on providing adults with clear explanations and practical experiences to kickstart their understanding of the sport.

Considerations for Basic Beginners Learning Stage:

1. **Fundamental Skill Development:**
   - **Children:** Focus on developing basic motor skills such as grip, stance, approach, and release. Use age-appropriate equipment and ensure a positive early experience.

- **Adults:** Introduce adults to the fundamental techniques of bowling, emphasizing the correct grip, basic stance, and a simple approach to the foul line.

2. **Engaging Learning Environment:**

   - **Children:** Utilize interactive methods like storytelling, gamification, and visual aids. Keep learning sessions short, engaging, and varied to maintain children's interest.

   - **Adults:** Balance structured learning with engaging activities. Incorporate relatable examples and demonstrations to help adults connect with the basics of the sport.

3. **Positive Reinforcement:**

   - **Children:** Celebrate small achievements and provide positive reinforcement to boost confidence. Create a supportive atmosphere that encourages children to enjoy the learning process.

   - **Adults:** Recognize and acknowledge early successes, providing positive feedback to motivate adults in their initial bowling journey.

4. **Introduction to Bowling Rules:**

   - **Children:** Introduce basic rules such as scoring, foul lines, and the concept of frames. Keep explanations simple and use visual aids to enhance understanding.

   - **Adults:** Provide a brief overview of bowling rules, ensuring adults have a basic understanding of scoring and fundamental game mechanics.

5. **Balanced Structured Learning:**

   - **Children:** Offer a mix of structured learning activities and unstructured play. Allow children to explore the basics in a fun and enjoyable manner.

   - **Adults:** Provide a structured introduction to bowling fundamentals, balancing explanations with practical exercises to help adults grasp the basics effectively.

Week 1: Introduction to Bowling Basics

Day 1: Children (1 hour)

1. *Performance (30%): Celebrate successful attempts, provide positive feedback on grip and stance.*

2. *Engagement (40%): Use storytelling to introduce the concept of bowling. Use age-appropriate visuals to explain grip and stance.*

3. *Learning (30%): Focus on basic motor skills - grip and stance. Use interactive games to reinforce learning.*

Day 2: Adults (1 hour)

1. *Performance (25%): Acknowledge successful attempts, reinforcing correct grip and stance.*

2. *Engagement (35%): Use relatable examples to explain the basics. Incorporate a short video demonstration of proper technique.*

3. *Learning (40%): Emphasize correct grip, basic stance, and a simple approach. Provide clear explanations and allow practical exercises.*

Day 3: Children (1 hour)

1. *Performance (30%): Celebrate successful releases, reinforcing positive outcomes.*

2. *Engagement (40%): Gamify learning by introducing a friendly competition. Simplify and visually explain scoring concepts.*

3. *Learning (30%): Continue working on motor skills. Introduce basic rules like scoring and foul lines using visual aids.*

Day 4: Adults (1 hour)

1. *Performance (25%): Acknowledge proper releases, providing positive reinforcement.*

2. *Engagement (35%): Incorporate a mini-competition to make learning fun. Relate scoring concepts to common experiences.*

3. *Learning (40%): Review basic rules and scoring. Clarify any questions and ensure a basic understanding of game mechanics.*

Week 2: Skill Refinement and Engagement

Day 1: Children (1 hour)

1. *Performance (30%): Encourage consistent performance, celebrate progress.*

2. *Engagement (40%): Introduce a bowling-related story. Use gamified drills to enhance skill development.*

3. *Learning (30%): Focus on refining grip, stance, and approach. Keep sessions engaging with varied activities.*

Day 2: Adults (1 hour)

1. *Performance (25%): Recognize improved consistency, providing positive feedback.*

2. *Engagement (35%): Introduce a relatable story about bowling experiences. Incorporate interactive drills for skill refinement.*

3. *Learning (40%): Emphasize the importance of consistent technique. Provide practical exercises to reinforce learning.*

Day 3: Children (1 hour)

1. *Performance (30%): Celebrate improved performance, host a friendly mini-competition.*

2. *Engagement (40%): Continue storytelling and gamified activities. Make learning a positive and enjoyable experience.*

3. *Learning (30%): Assess and reinforce fundamental skills. Answer questions and provide additional guidance.*

Day 4: Adults (1 hour)

1. *Performance (25%): Acknowledge progress, organize a fun and low-pressure competition.*

2. *Engagement (35%): Conclude with a bowling-related anecdote. Foster a social atmosphere and encourage participants to enjoy the game.*

3. *Learning (40%): Review key techniques and address any lingering questions. Provide resources for continued learning.*

Week 3: Skill Refinement and Engagement

Day 1: Children (1 hour)

1. *Performance (30%): Encourage consistent performance, celebrate progress.*

2. *Engagement (40%): Introduce a new aspect of bowling using a creative story. Incorporate gamified drills for continued skill development.*

3. *Learning (30%): Focus on refining grip, stance, and approach. Keep sessions engaging with varied activities.*

Day 2: Adults (1 hour)

1. *Performance (25%): Recognize improved consistency, providing positive feedback.*

2. *Engagement (35%): Share a relatable story about bowling experiences. Implement interactive drills to refine skills.*

3. *Learning (40%): Emphasize the importance of consistent technique. Provide practical exercises to reinforce learning.*

Day 3: Children (1 hour)

1. *Performance (30%): Celebrate improved performance, host a friendly mini-competition.*

2. *Engagement (40%): Continue storytelling and gamified activities. Make learning a positive and enjoyable experience.*

3. *Learning (30%): Assess and reinforce fundamental skills. Answer questions and provide additional guidance.*

Day 4: Adults (1 hour)

1. *Performance (25%): Acknowledge progress, organize a fun and low-pressure competition.*

2. *Engagement (35%): Conclude with a bowling-related anecdote. Foster a social atmosphere and encourage participants to enjoy the game.*

3. *Learning (40%): Review key techniques and address any lingering questions. Provide resources for continued learning.*

Week 4: Skill Mastery and Fun Competition

Day 1: Children (1 hour)

1. *Performance (30%): Celebrate mastery of basic skills, host a friendly mini-competition.*

2. *Engagement (40%): Continue storytelling and gamified activities. Ensure a positive and enjoyable learning experience.*

3. *Learning (30%): Assess and reinforce fundamental skills. Address any specific questions or concerns.*

Day 2: Adults (1 hour)

1. *Performance (25%): Acknowledge progress and mastery of foundational techniques.*

2. *Engagement (35%): Conclude with a memorable bowling-related story. Encourage social interaction and camaraderie.*

3. *Learning (40%): Review key techniques, emphasize continuous improvement, and provide resources for further exploration.*

Day 3: Children (1 hour)

1. *Performance (30%): Celebrate improvement and individual achievements. Host a fun and inclusive mini-competition.*

2. *Engagement (40%): Incorporate storytelling and interactive elements. Maintain a positive and dynamic learning environment.*

3. *Learning (30%): Encourage children to reflect on their progress. Address any specific concerns and provide additional guidance.*

Day 4: Adults (1 hour)

1. *Performance (25%): Acknowledge progress and individual achievements. Organize a friendly competition to celebrate improvement.*

2. *Engagement (35%): Share anecdotes and encourage a sense of community among adult learners. Foster a positive and enjoyable atmosphere.*

3. *Learning (40%): Review key techniques, answer questions, and provide resources for continuous learning.*

Intermediate Learning Stage:

The intermediate learning phase in bowling marks a critical stage where athletes, having solidified their foundational skills, now progress towards more intricate tactics and strategies. This stage encompasses the refinement of motor skills and the introduction of advanced game mechanics, such as lane play, ball speed management, and spare shooting. Coaches often employ principles from the Player Engagement and Learning (PEL) model to enhance the learning process during this phase. By creating challenging and realistic practice scenarios, coaches aim to elevate players' decision-making abilities and strategic thinking. Furthermore, encouraging self-reflection and self-evaluation empowers bowlers to actively participate in their own learning journey and take ownership of their performance.

Distinguishing between children and adults at the intermediate stage of PEL learning sheds light on the evolving priorities and needs of each group. For children, the focus shifts from basic skill acquisition to refining and showcasing these skills. Performance, while still important, takes a back seat to a more patient and skill-focused approach. Engagement remains crucial, and activities should continue to be stimulating, introducing new challenges to maintain interest. The emphasis on learning intensifies as young bowlers refine techniques, understand game strategies, and delve deeper into the nuances of bowling.

Conversely, adults at the intermediate stage also witness a slight decrease in the emphasis on performance. Mastery and consistency become focal points, with refined goal-setting and a pursuit of sustained excellence. Engagement remains vital to keep adult learners motivated, and activities should strike a balance between challenge and enjoyment to sustain interest. The majority of emphasis, however, shifts towards learning, reflecting the ongoing need for skill development, strategy refinement, and a deeper understanding of the sport.

Considering the intermediate stage in bowling learning, certain key considerations come to the forefront. The refinement of techniques becomes paramount, with children encouraged to fine-tune their grip, stance, approach, and release. Adults, on the other hand, focus on fine-tuning technical aspects and addressing specific challenges, often benefiting from individualized coaching tailored to their unique areas of improvement.

The introduction of advanced strategies is another crucial aspect of the intermediate stage. For children, this involves the gradual introduction of basic strategic concepts like lane positioning and spare shooting. Conversely, adults delve into more intricate strategies, such as adjusting to lane conditions, reading oil patterns, and developing a consistent pre-shot routine.

Goal-setting and feedback mechanisms play a pivotal role in both age groups. Children are involved in setting achievable performance goals, with positive reinforcement and constructive feedback serving as motivational tools. Adults, meanwhile, collaborate with coaches to set realistic performance goals, with detailed feedback aiding in continuous improvement.

Maintaining balanced engagement is a universal consideration for both children and adults in the intermediate stage. For children, this entails incorporating a mix of skill-focused activities and enjoyable challenges, fostering a supportive and positive atmosphere. Adults benefit from a balance between structured skill development and engaging activities, ensuring sustained interest and investment in the learning process.

Difference Between Children And Adults At Intermediate Stage Of Pel Learning

Children:

It is challenging to estimate a precise percentage because the significance of each factor might change based on the person and his unique learning demands. However, in general, the emphasis may be distributed as follows for a young starting bowler at the intermediate level of PEL learning:

1. **Children:**
   - Performance: 25%
   - Engagement: 30%
   - Learning: 45%

2. **Adults:**
   - Performance: 20%
   - Engagement: 25%
   - Learning: 55%

Rationale for Adjusted Ratios:

1. **Children:**
   - **Performance (25%):** While performance remains important, the focus shifts toward refining and showcasing learned skills rather than immediate outcomes. This allows for a more patient and skill-focused approach.
   - **Engagement (30%):** Continued engagement is crucial as learners progress. Activities should remain stimulating, and new challenges can be introduced to maintain interest.
   - **Learning (45%):** The emphasis on learning increases as learners refine techniques, understand game strategies, and delve deeper into the nuances of bowling.

2. **Adults:**
   - **Performance (20%):** Similar to children, the emphasis on performance decreases slightly as the focus shifts towards mastery and consistency. Goal-setting becomes more refined, and learners aim for sustained excellence.
   - **Engagement (25%):** Engagement remains important to keep adult learners motivated. Activities should offer a mix of challenge and enjoyment to sustain interest.
   - **Learning (55%):** The majority of emphasis is on learning, reflecting the need for ongoing skill development, strategy refinement, and a deeper understanding of the sport.

Considerations for the Intermediate Stage:

1. **Refinement of Techniques:**
   - **Children:** Provide opportunities for refining grip, stance, approach, and release. Encourage the application of learned techniques in different scenarios.
   - **Adults:** Focus on fine-tuning technical aspects and addressing specific challenges. Individualized coaching can address personalized areas of improvement.

2. **Introduction of Advanced Strategies:**
   - **Children:** Introduce basic strategic concepts such as lane positioning and spare shooting. Keep it simple and gradually progress as they become more comfortable.
   - **Adults:** Explore more advanced strategies, including adjusting to lane conditions, reading oil patterns, and developing a consistent pre-shot routine.

3. **Goal-Setting and Feedback:**
   - **Children:** Involve children in setting achievable performance goals. Offer positive reinforcement and constructive feedback to maintain motivation.
   - **Adults:** Collaborate with adult learners to set realistic performance goals. Provide detailed feedback to aid in continuous improvement.

4. **Balanced Engagement:**
   - **Children:** Incorporate a mix of skill-focused activities and enjoyable challenges. Foster a supportive and positive atmosphere.
   - **Adults:** Balance structured skill development with engaging activities to keep adults invested in the learning process.

Week 1: Refinement of Techniques

Day 1: Children (1 hour)

1. *Performance (25%): Encourage the application of refined techniques. Celebrate successful execution.*

2. *Engagement (30%): Introduce a creative challenge related to technique refinement. Keep activities stimulating to maintain interest.*

3. *Learning (45%): Focus on refining grip, stance, approach, and release. Provide opportunities for children to actively apply and showcase their learned skills.*

Day 2: Adults (1 hour)

1. *Performance (20%): Acknowledge the application of refined techniques. Emphasize consistency and mastery.*

2. *Engagement (25%): Introduce a specific challenge to address individual technical aspects. Keep the session enjoyable to sustain interest.*

3. *Learning (55%): Focus on fine-tuning technical aspects and addressing specific challenges. Provide individualized coaching to address unique areas of improvement.*

Day 3: Children (1 hour)

1. *Performance (25%): Reinforce the previous day's learning, encouraging continued improvement. Introduce a friendly competition to make it engaging.*

2. *Engagement (30%): Incorporate a mix of skill-focused games and enjoyable challenges. Foster a positive atmosphere to keep children excited.*

3. *Learning (45%): Assess and reinforce fundamental skills. Address any specific questions or concerns from the children.*

Day 4: Adults (1 hour)

1. *Performance (20%): Acknowledge the progress made in the previous sessions. Introduce a fun and low-pressure competition for enjoyment.*

2. *Engagement (25%): Share bowling-related stories or experiences to maintain interest. Incorporate engaging activities to break the routine.*

3. *Learning (55%): Review key techniques and strategies. Provide resources for continuous learning and deeper understanding of the sport.*

Week 2: Introduction of Advanced Strategies

Day 1: Children (1 hour)

1. *Performance (25%): Celebrate successful application of basic strategic concepts. Encourage children to showcase their understanding.*

2. *Engagement (30%): Gradually introduce more advanced concepts like lane positioning and spare shooting. Keep it simple and enjoyable.*

3. *Learning (45%): Explore basic strategic concepts and gradually progress. Allow children to apply these concepts in a supportive environment.*

Day 2: Adults (1 hour)

1. *Performance (20%): Acknowledge successful application of advanced strategies. Emphasize the importance of adapting to different lane conditions.*

2. *Engagement (25%): Introduce advanced strategies like adjusting to lane conditions and reading oil patterns. Keep the session challenging and enjoyable.*

3. *Learning (55%): Delve into more intricate strategies. Focus on developing a consistent pre-shot routine and refining overall game strategy.*

Day 3: Children (1 hour)

1. *Performance (25%): Reinforce the previous day's learning, celebrating achievements. Include a mini-competition to maintain engagement.*

2. *Engagement (30%): Incorporate storytelling related to bowling experiences. Keep activities varied and interesting to sustain interest.*

3. *Learning (45%): Address any specific questions or concerns from the children. Provide additional guidance on advanced strategies.*

Day 4: Adults (1 hour)

1. *Performance (20%): Acknowledge progress and sustained excellence. Organize a fun and low-pressure competition.*

2. *Engagement (25%): Share anecdotes and encourage social interaction among adult learners. Balance structured skill development with engaging activities.*

3. *Learning (55%): Review key techniques and strategies. Provide resources for continuous learning and deeper understanding of the sport.*

Week 3: Goal-Setting and Feedback

Day 1: Children (1 hour)

1. *Performance (25%): Set achievable performance goals for children. Celebrate milestones and progress.*

2. *Engagement (30%): Incorporate a goal-oriented game or challenge. Provide positive reinforcement and constructive feedback.*

3. *Learning (45%): Emphasize continuous improvement. Engage children in self-reflection and self-evaluation.*

Day 2: Adults (1 hour)

1. *Performance (20%): Collaborate with adults to set realistic performance goals. Acknowledge achievements and milestones.*

2. *Engagement (25%): Integrate goal-setting into the session. Balance challenge and enjoyment to sustain motivation.*

3. *Learning (55%): Provide detailed feedback to aid in continuous improvement. Encourage self-reflection and active participation in their learning journey.*

Day 3: Children (1 hour)

1. *Performance (25%): Celebrate overall progress and achievements. Host a friendly mini-competition.*

2. *Engagement (30%): Incorporate a mix of skill-focused activities and enjoyable challenges. Foster a supportive and positive atmosphere.*

3. *Learning (45%): Assess and reinforce fundamental skills. Address any specific questions or concerns from the children.*

Day 4: Adults (1 hour)

1. *Performance (20%): Acknowledge progress and sustained excellence. Organize a fun and low-pressure competition.*

2. *Engagement (25%): Share anecdotes and encourage social interaction among adult learners. Balance structured skill development with engaging activities.*

3. *Learning (55%): Review key techniques and strategies. Provide resources for continuous learning and deeper understanding of the sport.*

Week 4: Balanced Engagement

Day 1: Children (1 hour)

1. *Performance (25%): Celebrate overall progress and achievements. Host a friendly mini-competition.*

2. *Engagement (30%): Incorporate a mix of skill-focused activities and enjoyable challenges. Foster a supportive and positive atmosphere.*

3. *Learning (45%): Assess and reinforce fundamental skills. Address any specific questions or concerns from the children.*

Day 2: Adults (1 hour)

1. *Performance (20%): Acknowledge progress and sustained excellence. Organize a fun and low-pressure competition.*

2. *Engagement (25%): Share anecdotes and encourage social interaction among adult learners. Balance structured skill development with engaging activities.*

3. *Learning (55%): Review key techniques and strategies. Provide resources for continuous learning and deeper understanding of the sport.*

Day 3: Children (1 hour)

1. *Performance (25%): Reinforce the achievements from the previous days. Host a mini-tournament to encourage friendly competition.*

2. *Engagement (30%): Include a storytelling session related to bowling experiences. Keep activities varied and interesting to maintain interest.*

3. *Learning (45%): Address any specific questions or concerns from the children. Provide additional guidance on advanced strategies.*

Day 4: Adults (1 hour)

1. *Performance (20%): Acknowledge progress and sustained excellence. Organize a fun and low-pressure competition.*

2. *Engagement (25%): Share anecdotes and encourage social interaction among adult learners. Balance structured skill development with engaging activities.*

3. *Learning (55%): Review key techniques and strategies. Provide resources for continuous learning and deeper understanding of the sport.*

Advanced Learning Stage:

The advanced learning stage in bowling represents the pinnacle of skill development, characterized by the mastery of intricate motor skills, a high degree of proficiency, and the ability to perform consistently under pressure. Typically inhabited by competitive athletes striving for excellence in competitive contexts, this stage relies on the application of Player Engagement and Learning (PEL) principles to optimize performance and sustain motivation and engagement. Coaches leverage cutting-edge technologies like video analysis and virtual reality to enhance skill development, while mental skills training, including goal setting, visualization, and arousal management, becomes essential to help bowlers navigate performance anxiety and maintain focus in high-pressure situations (Ericsson et al., 1993).

In the advanced stage, the distinction between children and adults at the PEL learning level introduces nuanced differences in priorities. For young bowlers, the emphasis on immediate performance outcomes slightly decreases as they shift towards mastering and showcasing well-honed skills. Engagement remains vital, fostering a love for the sport through activities that provide both challenge and enjoyment. However, the majority of emphasis lies in continuous learning, allowing advanced learners to explore nuances, refine techniques, and deepen their understanding of bowling.

In contrast, advanced adult learners at this stage place a further decreased emphasis on immediate performance outcomes. The focus shifts towards sustained excellence and mastery, where high-level performance becomes a natural outcome of refined skills. While engagement remains important, advanced learners are often self-motivated, seeking activities that cater to their desire for challenge and improvement. The majority of emphasis is on ongoing learning, concentrating on advanced techniques, strategic decision-making, and the mental aspects of the game.

Considerations for the advanced stage include the introduction of specialized skill development. For children, this involves exploring advanced spare shooting techniques and lane play strategies, coupled with encouraging experimentation using different ball types and releases. Adult learners delve into more complex skills, including adjusting to challenging lane conditions, mastering multiple release variations, and cultivating a consistent mental game. Strategic decision-making evolves with the introduction of more advanced concepts, such as playing different parts of the lane and adapting to changing conditions. This necessitates fostering critical thinking about shot selection for both children and adults.

Goal-setting and self-assessment become crucial aspects of the advanced stage. For children, fostering independence involves involving them in setting and assessing their goals, encouraging self-reflection, and providing guidance on areas of improvement. Adult learners collaborate closely with coaches to set ambitious yet achievable performance goals, actively engaging in self-assessment and reflection after each session. The development of mental toughness and focus is introduced at the advanced level, encompassing handling pressure situations and maintaining focus during competitions for children. Advanced adults, on the other hand, delve into advanced mental toughness strategies, including visualization, pre-shot routines, and techniques to manage competition-related stress.

Encouraging competitive experience becomes an integral part of the advanced stage, with children actively participating in age-appropriate competitive settings to promote a positive and supportive experience. Advanced adult learners immerse themselves in competitive leagues, tournaments, and events, applying and refining their advanced skills in a real-world context.

Difference Between Children And Adults At Advance Stage Of Pel Learning

Children:

As previously established, the relative relevance of performance, engagement, and learning will vary depending on the player in question, his objectives, and his level of expertise. However, in general, the percentages for a young beginner bowler in the advanced level of PEL learning can be as follows:

1. **Children:**

   - **Performance:** 20%
   - **Engagement:** 25%
   - **Learning:** 55%

2. **Adults:**

   - **Performance:** 15%
   - **Engagement:** 20%
   - **Learning:** 65%

Rationale for Adjusted Ratios:

1. **Children:**

   - **Performance (20%):** At the advanced stage, the focus on immediate performance outcomes slightly decreases as learners shift towards mastering and showcasing well-honed skills.
   - **Engagement (25%):** Engagement remains vital, fostering a love for the sport. Activities should provide both challenge and enjoyment to sustain interest.
   - **Learning (55%):** The majority of emphasis is on continuous learning, as advanced learners explore nuances, refine techniques, and deepen their understanding of bowling.

2. **Adults:**

   - **Performance (15%):** The emphasis on performance decreases further, as advanced adult learners focus on sustained excellence and mastery. High-level performance becomes a byproduct of refined skills.
   - **Engagement (20%):** While engagement remains important, advanced learners are often self-motivated. Activities should cater to their desire for challenge and improvement.

- **Learning (65%):** The majority of emphasis is on ongoing learning, with a focus on advanced techniques, strategic decision-making, and mental aspects of the game.

Considerations for the Advanced Stage:

1. **Specialized Skill Development:**
   - **Children:** Introduce specialized skills such as advanced spare shooting techniques and lane play strategies. Encourage experimentation with different ball types and releases.
   - **Adults:** Dive into specialized skills like adjusting to challenging lane conditions, mastering multiple release variations, and developing a consistent mental game.

2. **Strategic Decision-Making:**
   - **Children:** Introduce more advanced strategic concepts, such as playing different parts of the lane and adapting to changing conditions. Encourage critical thinking about shot selection.
   - **Adults:** Emphasize strategic decision-making based on lane patterns, opponent analysis, and adjusting to unforeseen challenges during competitions.

3. **Goal-Setting and Self-Assessment:**
   - **Children:** Foster independence by involving children in setting and assessing their goals. Encourage self-reflection and provide guidance on areas of improvement.
   - **Adults:** Collaborate closely with adult learners in setting ambitious but achievable performance goals. Encourage self-assessment and reflection after each session.

4. **Mental Toughness and Focus:**
   - **Children:** Introduce basic mental toughness concepts, such as handling pressure situations and maintaining focus during competitions.
   - **Adults:** Emphasize advanced mental toughness strategies, including visualization, pre-shot routines, and techniques to manage competition-related stress.

5. **Competitive Experience:**
   - **Children:** Encourage participation in age-appropriate competitive settings, promoting a positive and supportive competitive experience.
   - **Adults:** Actively engage in competitive leagues, tournaments, and events to apply and refine advanced skills in a real-world context.

Week 1: Specialized Skill Development

Day 1: Children (1 hour)

1. *Performance (20%): Emphasize mastery and showcase of well-honed skills. Introduce a mini-competition to showcase advanced techniques.*
2. *Engagement (25%): Incorporate enjoyable challenges that provide both excitement and skill improvement.*
3. *Learning (55%): Focus on specialized skill development, such as advanced spare shooting techniques and lane play strategies. Encourage experimentation with different ball types and releases.*

Day 2: Adults (1 hour)

1. *Performance (15%): Acknowledge the showcase of refined skills. Emphasize sustained excellence and mastery.*
2. *Engagement (20%): Provide self-motivated challenges that cater to their desire for improvement.*
3. *Learning (65%): Dive into specialized skills like adjusting to challenging lane conditions, mastering multiple release variations, and developing a consistent mental game.*

Day 3: Children (1 hour)

1. *Performance (20%): Reinforce the mastery of advanced techniques. Host a friendly competition to maintain engagement.*

2. *Engagement (25%): Introduce storytelling sessions related to advanced skill development experiences. Keep activities varied and interesting.*

3. *Learning (55%): Address any specific questions or concerns from the children. Provide additional guidance on strategic decision-making.*

Day 4: Adults (1 hour)

1. *Performance (15%): Acknowledge progress and sustained excellence. Organize a challenging but enjoyable competition.*

2. *Engagement (20%): Share anecdotes and encourage social interaction among adult learners. Balance structured skill development with engaging activities.*

3. *Learning (65%): Focus on advanced techniques, strategic decision-making, and mental aspects of the game. Provide resources for continuous learning.*

Week 2: Strategic Decision-Making

Day 1: Children (1 hour)

1. *Performance (20%): Celebrate achievements from the previous days. Host a mini-tournament to encourage friendly competition.*

2. *Engagement (25%): Incorporate a mix of skill-focused activities and enjoyable challenges. Foster a supportive and positive atmosphere.*

3. *Learning (55%): Introduce more advanced strategic concepts like playing different parts of the lane and adapting to changing conditions. Encourage critical thinking about shot selection.*

Day 2: Adults (1 hour)

1. *Performance (15%): Acknowledge progress and sustained excellence. Organize a fun and challenging competition.*

2. *Engagement (20%): Share anecdotes and encourage social interaction among adult learners. Balance structured skill development with engaging activities.*

3. *Learning (65%): Emphasize strategic decision-making based on lane patterns, opponent analysis, and adjusting to unforeseen challenges during competitions.*

Day 3: Children (1 hour)

1. *Performance (20%): Reinforce achievements from the previous days. Host a mini-tournament to maintain engagement.*

2. *Engagement (25%): Introduce storytelling sessions related to strategic decision-making experiences. Keep activities varied and interesting.*

3. *Learning (55%): Address any specific questions or concerns from the children. Provide additional guidance on goal-setting and self-assessment.*

Day 4: Adults (1 hour)

1. *Performance (15%): Acknowledge progress and sustained excellence. Organize a challenging but enjoyable competition.*

2. *Engagement (20%): Share anecdotes and encourage social interaction among adult learners. Balance structured skill development with engaging activities.*

3. *Learning (65%): Collaborate closely with adult learners in setting ambitious but achievable performance goals. Encourage self-assessment and reflection after each session.*

Week 3: Goal-Setting and Self-Assessment

Day 1: Children (1 hour)

1. *Performance (20%): Set and celebrate performance goals. Host a friendly competition to encourage goal-oriented play.*

2. *Engagement (25%): Incorporate enjoyable challenges related to goal-setting. Foster a positive atmosphere for continuous improvement.*

3. *Learning (55%): Encourage self-reflection and self-assessment. Provide guidance on areas of improvement.*

Day 2: Adults (1 hour)

1. *Performance (15%): Acknowledge achievements and set ambitious performance goals. Organize a challenging competition.*

2. *Engagement (20%): Integrate goal-setting into the session. Balance challenge and enjoyment to sustain motivation.*

3. *Learning (65%): Provide detailed feedback to aid in continuous improvement. Encourage self-assessment and reflection after each session.*

Day 3: Children (1 hour)

1. *Performance (20%): Celebrate overall progress and achievements. Host a friendly mini-competition.*

2. *Engagement (25%): Incorporate a mix of skill-focused activities and enjoyable challenges. Foster a supportive and positive atmosphere.*

3. *Learning (55%): Assess and reinforce fundamental skills. Address any specific questions or concerns from the children.*

Day 4: Adults (1 hour)

1. *Performance (15%): Acknowledge progress and sustained excellence. Organize a fun and low-pressure competition.*

2. *Engagement (20%): Share anecdotes and encourage social interaction among adult learners. Balance structured skill development with engaging activities.*

3. *Learning (65%): Review key techniques and strategies. Provide resources for continuous learning and deeper understanding of the sport.*

Week 4: Competitive Experience

Day 1: Children (1 hour)

1. *Performance (20%): Celebrate achievements and set the stage for a friendly competition. Encourage positive competition experiences.*

2. *Engagement (25%): Introduce age-appropriate competitive settings to promote a positive and supportive experience.*

3. *Learning (55%): Provide feedback on competitive experiences. Reinforce mental toughness and focus concepts.*

Day 2: Adults (1 hour)

1. *Performance (15%): Acknowledge progress and sustained excellence. Organize a competitive session with a focus on applying advanced skills.*

2. *Engagement (20%): Actively engage in competitive leagues, tournaments, and events to apply and refine advanced skills.*

3. *Learning (65%): Provide feedback on competitive experiences. Emphasize continuous learning in real-world contexts.*

Day 3: Children (1 hour)

1. *Performance (20%): Celebrate overall progress and achievements. Host a friendly mini-competition.*

2. *Engagement (25%): Incorporate a mix of skill-focused activities and enjoyable challenges. Foster a supportive and positive atmosphere.*

3. *Learning (55%): Assess and reinforce fundamental skills. Address any specific questions or concerns from the children.*

Day 4: Adults (1 hour)

1. *Performance (15%): Acknowledge progress and sustained excellence. Organize a fun and low-pressure competition.*

2. *Engagement (20%): Share anecdotes and encourage social interaction among adult learners. Balance structured skill development with engaging activities.*

3. *Learning (65%): Review the performance from competitive experiences. Focus on advanced techniques, strategic decision-making, and mental aspects of the game. Provide resources for continuous learning and deeper understanding..*

CRUCIAL ELEMENTS FOR DEVELOPMENT

1- Building a Strong Foundation

The key to gaining physical literacy and dominating bowling is the knowledge of fundamental abilities. Balance, coordination, flexibility, and hand-eye coordination are among the basic movement abilities that are necessary for bowling. Bowlers may find it difficult to attain their greatest potential without a strong foundation in these abilities. It is essential to introduce basic motions and abilities through engaging activities and games. As bowlers advance, they should concentrate on mastering fundamental sports fundamentals that complement the unique demands of bowling. Participating in a variety of sports activities promotes the growth of basic movement abilities. The optimal time to develop physical literacy, which includes movement proficiency and sports skills, is before the adolescent growth spurt, however, it can be improved at any stage of life. Programs for older persons should place a high priority on preserving flexibility, balance, and coordination. Bowlers should always endeavor to improve their basic athletic movements and skills because these are the cornerstones of a better bowling experience. Bowlers with physical disabilities might need to relearn certain basic movement techniques, whilst those with intellectual disabilities would need more time and perseverance to master particular bowling techniques. Some skills might not ever be fully mastered, requiring constant guidance and adaption.

2- Specialization in Bowling

In contrast to early specialization sports like gymnastics, figure skating, and diving, bowling is classified as a late specialization sport. Sports requiring late specialization demand extremely complex motor abilities, which are harder to master if introduced later in development. National champions in bowling range in age from 25 to 50, with the top bowlers frequently reaching their optimum performance between the ages of 30 and 40. Because early specialization in bowling can result in injuries and fatigue, it is imperative to avoid it. Instead, to foster physical literacy in youngsters, a variety of sports should be encouraged. Coaches, parents, and support systems should encourage multisport participation rather than concentrating primarily on a late-specialization sport, such as bowling. 64% of bowlers started bowling before the age of 10, according to interviews. 66% percent of the top athletes who finished on the podium at national competitions had also begun bowling before the age of ten. These successful bowlers also participated in a variety of other sports, with over 60% of them playing basketball, soccer, and baseball, and 80% of them playing gymnastics. The fact that 50% of the best bowlers, both domestically and worldwide, began bowling before the age of five was an important discovery. They had also played other sports before the age of ten, which allowed them to hone their basic athletic abilities before focusing on bowling. The fact that many young bowlers had the chance to try out other sports before turning ten, such as baseball, gymnastics, basketball, hockey, and track and field, is noteworthy. While bowling can be marketed as a great sport for kids to attempt, it's crucial to underline that bowling proficiency can be attained by anyone, regardless of age or disability.

3- Holistic Approach to Bowler Development: Maximizing Potential, Performance, and Enjoyment

A thorough strategy that considers bowlers' physical, mental, cognitive, and emotional health is necessary for their development. When creating training, competition, and recovery regimens, these elements must be taken into account. Technical ability alone may not be a reliable indicator of a bowler's capacity to withstand the stress of regional or worldwide contests. Young bowlers could endure scholastic or peer pressure, whereas adults might deal with pressures from a family or a job. Older bowlers' physical limitations must also be taken into account in order to create a comprehensive program that meets their unique requirements.

Hypothetical Examples

Alex Thompson, a bowler whose journey in the sport is a testament to the holistic approach to development, maximizing potential, performance, and enjoyment.

Background: Alex, currently in their late twenties, discovered a passion for bowling during their early teens. Starting as a casual bowler, Alex's natural talent and enthusiasm quickly propelled them into a more serious pursuit of the sport.

Physical Development: Understanding the importance of physical health in bowling, Alex engages in a well-rounded fitness routine. Regular strength training not only enhances their ability to deliver powerful shots but also helps prevent injuries. Flexibility exercises and targeted workouts address the specific demands of the sport, ensuring optimal performance on the lanes.

Mental and Cognitive Health: Recognizing the mental and cognitive aspects of bowling, Alex actively participates in mindfulness and visualization exercises. Mental resilience is a crucial component of their training regimen, helping them navigate the pressure of competitions. Cognitive training involves strategic decision-making, understanding lane patterns, and adapting to varying conditions, giving Alex a competitive edge.

Emotional Well-being: Emotional health is prioritized in Alex's holistic development plan. The sport's enjoyment is at the forefront, ensuring that the love for bowling remains a driving force. Alex actively engages in team-building activities with fellow bowlers, fostering a supportive and enjoyable bowling community.

Life Balance: Balancing bowling with other life commitments is essential for Alex. Whether juggling academic responsibilities during college or managing work and family commitments as an adult, the training and competition schedule is designed to align with their life stage. This approach prevents burnout and ensures a sustainable, lifelong connection with the sport.

Adaptability to Age: As Alex progresses in age, the development plan adapts accordingly. Special attention is given to addressing any physical limitations that may arise with age. Modifications to the training routine cater to the changing needs, ensuring that Alex's bowling journey remains fulfilling and injury-free.

Comprehensive Support System: Alex benefits from a comprehensive support system that includes coaches, sports psychologists, and fellow bowlers. Regular check-ins and open communication ensure that all aspects of their well-being are considered in the development plan.

Results: This holistic approach has not only elevated Alex's technical skills but has also translated into consistent high-level performances in regional and even international contests. Beyond the scores and trophies, Alex's joy for the sport has remained intact, making bowling a lifelong pursuit that continues to bring fulfillment and satisfaction.

In essence, Alex Thompson exemplifies the success that comes from a holistic approach to bowler development, where physical, mental, cognitive, and emotional well-being are all integral parts of the journey toward maximizing potential, performance, and enjoyment in the sport of bowling.

4- The Ten S's of Training for Bowler Development

A bowler's annual plan should include these ten critical training components to the fullest extent possible to maximize his potential, performance, and enjoyment:

1. **Stamina (Endurance):** While it may not be necessary for bowling itself, stamina is important during competitions. Stamina training should be done during the peak height velocity (PHV) period, which

denotes the maximal growth rate. To improve endurance, aerobic capacity exercise should be implemented gradually before PHV.

2. **Strength:** Depending on developmental age, strength training has distinct sensitive times. Boys typically experience it 12 to 18 months after PHV, while girls typically experience it just after PHV or at the start of menarche. Bodyweight exercises, lesser loads, medicine balls, and Swiss balls can all be used during training.

3. **Speed:** Although it is not the main goal of bowling, children and young people should nevertheless be trained in it for general development. Age-appropriate speed training windows exist, highlighting the significance of timing in speed development.

4. **Skill:** For boys and girls, respectively, the best ages for skill training are between 9 and 12 and 8 and 11 years old. The time should be used to improve technical bowling ability.

5. **Suppleness (Flexibility):** For both sexes, the best time to practice suppleness is between the ages of 6 and 10. Extra consideration should be given to flexibility during PHV. Bowlers are aware that flexibility is an important physical skill to master.

6. **Sustenance:** Depending on the bowler's stage of development, proper diet, hydration, sleep, and regeneration are essential elements. Missing meals might cause weight gain or make it more difficult to train and compete effectively.

7. **Strengthening the Mind:** Concentration, relaxation, and confidence are skills that are essential for both bowling and daily life. For bowlers to improve their focus and performance, mental training should be incorporated at all stages to help them deal with success and failure.

8. **Scholarly Balance:** It's crucial to strike a balance between the responsibilities of the classroom, tests, and extracurricular activities. By taking into account academic requirements, a well-designed program supports the all-encompassing approach to bowler development.

9. **Stature/Structure:** Coaches can successfully address the five S's within the overall sports program by keeping track of stature measurements and developmental age.

10. **Socio-Cultural:** Bowlers who compete in tournaments have the chance to experience various cultures, geographies, cuisines, and architectural styles, which helps them to extend their perspectives. Bowlers should benefit from these opportunities by venturing outside of the hotel and competition venue.

Coaches, teachers, owners, and parents may promote a holistic approach that maximizes the potential, performance, and enjoyment of bowlers at every stage of their journey by including these ten factors in bowler development programs.

5- Early Developers and Late Developers

Since everyone develops at a different rate, some bowlers are early developers while others are late developers. Physical, mental, cognitive, and emotional maturity are all parts of development age.

There is diversity in the length of time it takes to finish the maturation process, normally lasting 3 to 4 years, during adolescence, which commonly starts around 10 or 11 for girls and a few years later for boys. But depending on the person, this time frame can vary by two to four years. For bowlers, these disparities in developmental ages might bring benefits and drawbacks, posing problems and opening up possibilities within the sporting system.

Physical literacy, fundamental motor skills, and sport-specific skills take longer to develop in late developers. Children have a developmental window before puberty that is perfect for learning and honing sports skills. But because of their greater size, strength, speed, and ability, early developers are frequently given the advantage in the sport system. As a result, young children frequently receive more and better sporting experiences than their counterparts who mature later in life. Coaches, administrators, and program coordinators must therefore make sure that all kids have plenty of opportunities to practice and play while also taking into account their developmental stage as bowlers.

Does bowling draw those who have given up on other sports because of this problem? Do bowlers who are improving quickly have an advantage over those who are progressing more slowly during practice or competitions?

These factors have an impact on creating suitable training regimens and choosing who will compete. According to this, bowlers who are the same age chronologically may require different developmental support. The social and recreational sides of the game may be impacted by this disparity.

Coaches must take into account each player's physical, mental, cognitive, and emotional maturity while creating programs and assembling teams to ensure a fulfilling and joyful experience, whether they are dealing with bowlers who have impairments or not.

Hypothetical Examples:

Example: Sarah and Michael are both 12 years old and passionate about bowling. However, Sarah experienced an early growth spurt and is physically more mature than Michael. Due to her early development, Sarah has better coordination and strength, giving her an advantage in bowling technique and power. On the other hand, Michael is a late maturer and is still catching up with his physical development. He requires additional time to improve his motor skills and overall athleticism. Coaches and trainers must consider these differences in their training programs and provide appropriate challenges to accommodate each bowler's developmental age.

6- Training Periodization

Periodization is the process of developing a tactical plan to assist bowlers in achieving their performance goals. This schedule sets out and organizes competition, recovery, and training (volume, intensity, and frequency) in a methodical and controlled manner. Its goal is to maximize performance at the appropriate moment. The characteristics of each bowler, including his stage of growth, trainability, sport age, training age, and performance gaps connected to the demands of the sport, are taken into consideration while creating a periodization plan.

Hypothetical Example:

Example: Alex is a competitive bowler who wants to perform at his best at a significant competition. His trainer develops a periodized training schedule that, over a predetermined period of time, steadily raises the volume and intensity of his training sessions. The strategy takes into account Alex's age at the time of training, his developmental stage, and the particular skills he needs to learn. Alex can maximize his training by adhering to the periodized schedule, which enables him to peak at the appropriate time and give his best performance during the competition.

7- Competition Structure and Planning

"The competition system makes or breaks a bowler," according to Balyi et al. (2005). Competition format and frequency are key factors in the growth of bowlers. The tournament framework should focus on skill development, tactical competencies, and physical capacities in accordance with the Long-Term Athlete Development (LTAD) strategy and the requirements for effective bowling.

At some points, improving one's skills takes precedence over competing, winning, and participating in official competitions. During practice, concentrating on winning can prevent a bowler from improving his technique. Bowlers frequently overemphasize competition and ignore training, as was noted in the previous section on weaknesses. As a result, many essential sports abilities are not adequately taught.

Hypothetical Example

Young bowler Emily recently joined a neighborhood bowling league. The club places a strong emphasis on skill development and offers bowlers chances to hone his craft without the stress of official contests. Since Emily is still developing her skills, Emily's coach is more concerned with improving her bowling technique than with winning contests. This strategy enables Emily to develop a solid base of abilities before moving on to tournaments with higher levels of competition in the future.

8- Alignment of the System

With the help of the LTAD concept, the entire sport system may be brought into alignment and agreement with all parties. In order to effectively develop and deliver sports programs, it is recommended by LTAD that parents, teachers, schools, coaches, clubs, leisure facilities, and governments work together. This is because sports programs are developed and delivered by a variety of organizations, government levels, and people. It is important to coordinate all areas of programming, including bowler development programs, competition structures, competition schedules, and even the federation's plans.

Do the present governance frameworks impede bowlers' growth and development? Are coach education programs designed to fulfill the needs of bowlers according to his LTAD stage? Does the system offer a clear development path for bowlers with compatible competition structures? Does the choice of bowlers for international teams support the LTAD model's ideas?

Example: In a certain area, the local bowling association works along with coaching groups, and educational institutions, to coordinate their efforts and build a thorough growth route for bowlers. To ensure a uniform approach to bowler development, they establish clear communication paths, pool resources, and coordinate coaching activities. As bowlers advance through various stages, this alignment promotes a smooth transition, ensuring they get the assistance and chances they need to realize their greatest potential.

9- The Ten-Year Rule

The "ten-year rule," which states that becoming an expert in sports, music, or any other field requiring considerable knowledge requires 10,000 hours of focused practice or serious training, has been identified through research in a number of different fields (Gladwell, 2008). Effective programs can help participants accrue those "10,000 hours," whether they are outside or in a bowling center. Consideration should be given to the proper number of hours at each LTAD stage as well as the particular skills that must be practiced and mastered there. It's crucial to recognize that producing elite bowlers has accompanying costs. As a result, all parties participating in the "bowler development process" should be aware of the difficulties associated with completing the "10,000 hours" and be ready to deal with them.

Imagine if a bowler had to put in 10,000 hours of practice before becoming an adult because He had to specialize in bowling at a young age. Such a strategy is to be prevented because it could result in athletes quitting his sport. The quantity and quality of training and competition must be properly planned if you want to become the best. A world-class contender or a national champion cannot be accomplished easily. To ensure the bowler receives the appropriate training, all individuals involved in his support must be prepared.

Hypothetical Example:

Example: Jason, a gifted bowler, begins his training when he is ten years old. He enrolls in a bowling academy that offers a planned training schedule created to help him build up the necessary amount of practice time throughout his development. A thoughtful combination of technical drills, physical conditioning, and competition experience is included in Jason's training schedule. Jason gradually improves and develops into a highly skilled bowler by regularly devoting himself to practice and accruing the requisite hours, finally representing his country in international championships.

10- Continuous Improvement:

The core concept of the LTAD (Long-Term Athlete Development) framework is heavily influenced by the widely recognized Japanese manufacturing concept known as Kaizen. The LTAD framework is under constant evaluation and remains adaptable to new scientific discoveries, sport-specific advancements, and observations. It acknowledges the multitude of approaches available for athlete development, including optimizing existing processes and structures, forging collaborations, fostering innovative thinking, and engaging with various stakeholders within the sporting system. The commitment to long-term athlete growth should persist, with a dedication to ongoing improvement and a rejection of complacency, even when it may appear to be the easier path. Tailored programs should be offered to diverse communities within bowling centers, and coaching should be of the highest quality, keeping pace with advancements in training methodologies and equipment innovations for individuals striving for excellence in competitive endeavors. The overarching goal is to consistently enhance every aspect of the sport while adhering to a proactive "Can do, must do" approach.

Stages of LTAD in Bowling:

The capacity of a bowler to continuously exhibit particular skills and advance in accordance with the recognized "stage indicators" is the basis for progression through the LTAD stages. This step-by-step strategy motivates bowlers to concentrate on developing essential abilities while allowing instructors to focus their instructional efforts appropriately. The following elements affect a bowler's development:

1. Possessing the necessary foundational motor skills, including balance, coordination, agility, and hand-eye coordination, for bowling.

2. Engaging in complementary sports; athletes who have previously competed in activities requiring agility, balance, and coordination may advance more quickly.

3. Coaching - A bowler's development can be greatly aided by effective coaching techniques that take into account technical, tactical, physiological, and psychological factors.

4. Equipment fit - Depending on their physical characteristics and degree of expertise, bowlers must have equipment that is sized and suited adequately. Poorly fitting or overly hefty equipment can make it difficult to perform a skill.

5. Practice time - Bowlers who can regularly practice under optimal circumstances and devote more time to training are likely to advance more quickly.

Learning and Development Continuum:

The talents and aptitudes that are prioritized at each LTAD level are described in the accompanying matrix. The growth, improvement, perfection, and maintenance stages of the bowling technique should be considered as a progressive learning continuum. Based on a bowler's developmental stage, each talent and aptitude is given a specific stage, suggesting the best timing for its inclusion in the overall training program. Bowlers and coaches should evaluate these techniques while keeping in mind that an integrated training program is essential for successfully implementing these competencies in practice and competitive settings.

Understanding the Terms:

Introducing: A bowler who is in the introduction stage of his game is aware of the basic bowling motions needed to perform a certain talent or strategy. He is given a conceptual knowledge of the skill's performance as well as an introduction to its fundamental components. This stage lays the groundwork for the following phases of development.

Example: A young bowler is taught how to grip the bowling ball properly and release it. He learns how to aim the pins, how to position his hands correctly, and the value of a flawless delivery.

Developing: The bowler concentrates on frequent practice to hone and enhance the skill's execution during the developing period. He focuses on maintaining performance, making sure that the fundamental application of the skill improves in accuracy and dependability. Coach feedback is really important in directing his development.

Example: An aspiring bowler practices his approach and release mechanics for hours, for instance. His instructor provides comments, which He uses to improve his timing, arm swing, and footwork. He strives to execute the technique consistently and create muscle memory through diligent repetition.

Refining: The bowler has advanced to the refining stage when He can combine his skill with other elements of the game. He begins by incorporating his own distinctive styles, then modify the talent to fit his own physical, technical, tactical, and psychological prowess. The bowler may combine several techniques and execute himself or herself skillfully in both practice and game settings.

Example: A bowler who is improving has honed his delivery style and established his unique bowling style. He competently carries out complex bowling techniques including hook shots and spare conversions. He can modify his strategy throughout competitions because He has a thorough understanding of how to shift his approach dependent on lane conditions.

Perfecting: The bowler has thoroughly adapted the skills to his capabilities and has grown comfortable with his own bowling technique during the perfecting stage. Even under the strain of highly competitive competitions, He can preserve proper technique. He consistently performs well and aims to do the skill as well as possible.

Example: At the national level, a bowler who is perfecting his craft competes and routinely posts high scores. He is an expert at accurate bowling, constantly hitting his mark and producing the greatest amount of pin carry. Because his ability is instinctive to him, He can perform at his peak in crucial competitions.

Maintaining: The maintenance stage highlights how crucial it is to practice and play bowling regularly in order to retain one's technical, tactical, and physical skills. Even skilled bowlers must train frequently and remain active in the sport to maintain their performance levels over time.

Example: A seasoned bowler with a lot of success still practices and takes part in Bowling for Life events. Practice helps him keep up his skills, improve his technique, and stay involved in the sport. By remaining active and involved, kids keep their skills honed and prepared for competitions in the future.

FROM MOTOR SKILLS TO MASTERY: UNDERSTANDING THE PATH TO ELITE BOWLING *By*
Coach Mark Heathorn

I think it is impossible to determine which bowlers will become elite (professional, rather than (only) a world championship medalist), until they do.

There are a multitude of factors which in my opinion can and will affect the chances of an individual achieving a performance in no particular order of importance or chronology.

- *Physical literacy, motor skills development. If the core movements (running, jumping, throwing, gripping, balance, coordination, catching) are not maximized during the first 6 to 7 years then it can be too late to maximize performance in many athletic pursuits. Does this apply to bowling? It should, especially as we have seen the development in technique to a far more athletic motion, and of course with the now rampant appearance of the thumb-out method(s), which is more bio-mechanically sound and safe but uses more muscle than the most efficient thumb-in swings and approach.*

- *Upbringing. This aspect has a big impact on the first topic in terms of the exposure and encouragement to develop movement capabilities, through play and other sports, particularly the early specialist activities like gymnastics, dance, and swimming. In England, we are seeing much more that kids only really play sports where one or more parents are active enough to make that happen. In bowling, there is still quite a large percentage of kids with "bowling parent(s)" who play. Discipline, positive environments, schooling, routines, other siblings (or not), parental expectations, all these things are variable and impactful.*

- *Access and Finances. How much time and money players have afforded them in their formative years (in the sport), 12-15, will have a huge impact on the potential performance peak and sustainability of said peak. Access to bowling lanes, the quality of the facility, access to a coach or coaches, and the level and ability of said coaches will direct the journey of the development, either deliberately or randomly. There are, and certainly have been, many examples that I have seen of talented players who happen to be with the wrong coach.*

- *Competition. The standard of competition, the volume of competition in teenage years will either slow, or speed up development, whilst also helping to build mental fortitude, and exposing players to other necessary skills, like planning, goal-setting, routine, learning to lose, learning to win, as well as bowling specific scoring skills and capabilities (within the mind).*

- *Opportunities. Linked to finances as well, but opportunities to play higher level tournaments, such as Zonal Champs and World Champs (but not a necessity), train perhaps with other (hopefully better) players.*

- *Equipment. Obviously financial again but being able to have access to enough equipment to help performance as often as is necessary at the level they are at is sadly more important than perhaps it should be.*

- *Determination and Drive. Internal factors. Does the individual have the necessary driving factors and determination to succeed? Where does this come from, is it innate or learned from the home during formative years? There are certainly some professionals who are definitely not the best in terms of technique (in theory) but have certainly maximized performance – WRW is the most obvious example I would suggest.*

- *Technical Factors. In today's game and for the foreseeable future, the value of the combination of Spin (rev) Rate and Velocity are number 1 importance. So if these are not developed to a certain level, the factor of repeatability is lessened the further up the pyramid you go.*

- *Fitness*. *The fitness required for our game is different from more anaerobic activities, but elite players need endurance muscle fitness, and cardiovascular. More than ever players need to be fit to bowl rather than bowl to be bowling-fit.*

- *Luck*. *This will rear its head along the way (or not in many cases) and provide one or more aspects as listed above with the boost it might need to help.*

- *Randomization and Combination*. *All of the above will either work or not work. Each element where decisions need to be made rely on the information at hand at the time to make the best decision for the long term, which even for the most experienced (coaches) will not always work.*

As a professional coach, I can now (nearly) guarantee a certain progression for each individual I work with, at whatever standard He is at when we begin working together. However, there are many factors outside of my control that can reduce the impact of my coaching and knock it back.

Additionally, players in each country come into contact with NGB development/ pathway/ performance programs and so depend on the quality of that.

In England, we have examples of players who have become professional within the system, and outside of the system, and a combination of both.

Coach Mark Heathorn, EBF L3 Coach, Team England Coach

NURTURING YOUNG BOWLERS FOR SUCCESS By Coach Khalifa Khalfan

My career as a junior bowling coach with young bowlers has been a fantastic one filled with growth, difficulties, and successes. I've had the opportunity to see directly how these aspiring athletes change and improve while coaching bowlers of various age groups, from pre-teens to teenagers. I have worked hard to establish a supportive environment where kids can thrive both on and off the lanes because of my commitment to and love for the sport.

My coaching philosophy has been built on an understanding of the particular traits and requirements of each age group. Pre-teens who are eager to start bowling need hands-on coaching to perfect their core abilities and technique. I serve as their coach, giving them the encouragement and one-on-one care they require to lay a solid foundation. I assist them in realizing their capabilities and create a strong love for the game through meticulous training and close observation.

As I made the switch to working with teenagers, I noticed that they were prepared for advanced methods and mental game training. These young bowlers have a fierce ambition to perfect the game and win matches. I modify my coaching techniques to push their limits and teach them the skills of strategy, mental toughness, and the capacity to retain focus in the face of fierce competition. Together, we master the game's complexities while advancing their abilities and assisting them in attaining new heights.

Young bowlers must develop in a setting that is encouraging and supportive. I recognize the value of promoting a positive environment throughout practices and competitions. They gain important life skills in this environment of companionship and cooperation. I place a strong emphasis on the virtues of sportsmanship, recognizing one another's accomplishments, and standing by one another in trying circumstances. I enable my junior bowlers to develop their confidence and create lifetime friendships by giving honest feedback and keeping lines of communication open.

I plan competitions that are suitable for young bowlers' needs in order to make sure they have a meaningful and pleasurable experience. They have a venue to compete against their peers in these leagues and tournaments, encouraging healthy competition and developing their development. I cultivate their passion for bowling while igniting their ambition to excel by striking a balance between the competitive spirit and the social sides of the game.

Physical changes have a significant role in the development of young bowlers. Their bodies change as they get older, which may affect their technique. In light of this, I collaborate closely with them to figure out these modifications and create them. I concentrate on keeping balance and coordination during growth spurts to make sure that their technique fits their changing bodies. Additionally, I teach them the value of appropriate warm-up exercises and injury prevention techniques, placing a high priority on their health.

Bowling is a game that requires both mental and physical toughness. As a result, I spend a lot of time teaching my younger bowlers how to handle stress, stay in the moment, and maintain confidence in the face of adversity. By using goal-setting techniques, visualization exercises, and positive reinforcement, I give them the resilience to bounce back from setbacks and grow stronger. Together, we develop a mindset that views hardship as a chance for growth, putting them in a position to succeed both on and off the lanes.

Young bowlers have excellent possibilities to grow their social skills and sense of togetherness by joining a bowling team. I take an active role in planning team-building exercises to promote productive communication and cooperation among coworkers. In order to foster strong relationships and enduring friendships, I emphasize the value of support and encouragement. Beyond just playing the sport, these young athletes understand the value of teamwork and the incomparable joy that comes from working together to achieve a common objective.

It is crucial to take care of my junior bowlers' emotional needs. They can openly express their emotions in the secure environment I establish for them. I am aware that the road to success in competitive bowling can be paved with highs and lows, successes and setbacks. As a result, I offer advice on how to handle stress, deal with disappointment, and get beyond challenges both on and off the lanes.

In my coaching philosophies, open communication is essential. I encourage my junior bowlers to express their ideas and worries because I understand how crucial it is for them to grow emotionally as well as physically and technically. I provide a sympathetic ear and support anytime they encounter difficulties or stumbling blocks in their bowling adventure. By fostering their emotional resilience, I equip them to handle the emotional rollercoaster that frequently goes along with the quest for excellence.

Diversity is a lovely feature that enhances bowling as a sport. I am adamant about promoting an accepting environment where each and every young bowler feels respected and valued. I advocate for an accepting and understanding culture by recognizing the distinctive backgrounds and characteristics of each individual. My junior bowlers' personal development as athletes and people is accelerated when they are encouraged to value and learn from one another. In this way, we create a melting pot of various experiences and viewpoints.

Although I agree that competitiveness is an essential component of bowling, I also see the need to achieve a balance between intense competition and unadulterated fun. During practice sessions, I plan entertaining games and activities to put a smile on everyone's face. These times allow my junior bowlers to unwind, have fun, and develop a passion for the game that will last a lifetime. I make sure that bowling is an activity they appreciate for years to come by fostering their passion and maintaining the spirit of play.

My ultimate goal as a junior bowling coach goes beyond the walls of the bowling center. I want to leave a lasting impression on my young bowlers, giving them not just the technical know-how but also the morals and lessons that go beyond the boundaries of the sport. I teach them the value of self-control, tenacity, and goal-setting, traits that will be pillars of strength in all facets of their lives.

Goal-setting is a crucial component of human development, therefore I push my young bowlers to make both short- and long-term goals. I teach them the skill of setting realistic objectives and working assiduously to attain them, whether it's raising their average score, competing in regional contests, or getting college scholarships. As a result, I help them develop a growth mentality and a solid work ethic that will help them succeed in all of their future activities.

Values like cooperation and sportsmanship go well beyond the lanes. Teamwork and collaboration are essential for success in the sport of bowling. I stress the value of encouraging one another, whether in times of collective success or failure. I develop my junior bowlers' character in addition to their athletic prowess by teaching them the value of teamwork and the satisfaction that comes from working together toward a common objective.

The sport of bowling encourages individuality and inventiveness. I urge my youth bowlers to discover their own distinctive styles and let their creativity run wild on the lanes in addition to the technical parts of the sport. I create an atmosphere where people are encouraged to accept their uniqueness, experiment, and try new things. I assist them in learning the delight that comes from totally immersing themselves in the game and developing their own voice by fostering their artistic expression.

Finally, I am aware of the significant impact I have on the lives of my junior bowlers as a coach and mentor. I make an effort to set a good example by exhibiting compassion, accountability, and honesty. As they manage the difficulties they encounter both inside and outside of the sport, I pay attention to their worries, offer direction, and provide steadfast support. My goal is to motivate them to develop not only as good bowlers but also as kind, responsible, and civic-minded people who enrich their neighborhoods. I believe that my duty as a coach goes well beyond simply imparting bowling technique; it also includes forming the personalities and futures of these young athletes.

The best part of being a coach is seeing my junior bowlers improve and progress. I take great delight in watching them develop throughout their journey into self-assured, tenacious, and well-rounded people. Their accomplishments serve as a monument to their perseverance, commitment, and the advice they have gotten along the road. My heart is filled with excitement knowing that I have contributed to their athletic and personal growth, which motivates my own commitment to the sport.

I set out on a goal to make a lasting impression with each new team of junior bowlers I had the honor to coach. Along with teaching them the fundamentals of bowling, I also try to inculcate in them the morals and life lessons that will guide them in the future. The bowling club serves as a learning environment for life, teaching the players self-control, tenacity, and the value of setting goals. These characteristics serve as the foundation for success in any venture individuals decide to undertake.

I place a strong emphasis on the value of sportsmanship and teamwork in addition to the technical skills. Bowling involves teamwork and coordination; it is not merely a solitary activity. I foster my junior bowlers' capacity to function effectively as a team by encouraging them to encourage and lift one another up. They get an appreciation for unity and understand that their combined effort is greater than the sum of their individual successes. These priceless lessons encourage a feeling of community and establish the groundwork for enduring friendships.

I like the idea of embracing diversity in the bowling community. Each junior bowler brings to the sport a special combination of experiences and viewpoints. I urge my bowlers to respect and honor people from all backgrounds, creating an atmosphere where everyone feels comfortable. My junior bowlers gain a deeper perspective of the world by embracing the variety that diversity gives, and they also become ambassadors of inclusion and understanding.

Even though competition can be fierce, I think it's important to combine the serious quest of perfection with the simple joy of playing the game. I am aware that a junior bowler's path should be full of amusing incidents, friendly competition, and enjoyment. To maintain a fun and engaging environment throughout our practice sessions, I include playful activities and games. I ensure that my students not only improve their abilities but also build a passion for bowling that lasts a lifetime by bringing joy to their bowling experience.

My objective as a coach is to motivate each junior bowler to realize his greatest potential by igniting the fire of desire within him. I am aware of the influence I have as a role model, and I work hard to set the best possible example. I serve as an example of the value of honesty, toughness, and compassion in both success and failure. I enable my junior bowlers to overcome difficulties, take on problems head-on, and develop into the greatest versions of themselves by providing a consistent source of support and direction.

In conclusion, my experience coaching junior bowling has been rewarding and motivating. As I mentor young bowlers through their early years, I get to see how they develop as people and athletes. I want to make a significant difference in their lives by using a holistic approach that incorporates technical skill development, emotional support, teamwork, and personal growth. I am thrilled to be a part of their bowling journey, developing their passion and preparing the road for future strike champions as Khalifa Khalfan, the Bahrain Federation Junior Development Coach.

Coach Khalifa Khalfan, Bahrain Federation Junior Development Coach

TRANSFER SKILL TRAINING:
VERSATILITY AND ADAPTABILITY

Transfer skill training stands at the forefront of contemporary strategies, garnering significant attention for its transformative potential in various sports, with a particular focus on bowling. This comprehensive guide navigates through the theoretical foundations and practical applications of transfer skill training, unveiling its capacity to revolutionize the sport. The overarching goal is to provide bowlers of diverse proficiency levels, ranging from novices taking their initial steps to seasoned professionals honing their craft, with invaluable insights into seamlessly integrating transfer skill training into their practice regimens.

Transfer skills training in bowling refers to a method of practice and skill development that focuses on transferring learned skills from one context or setting to another. The idea is to enhance a bowler's ability to apply and adapt their skills in different situations, improving overall performance on the lanes. This training approach recognizes that the skills acquired during practice should seamlessly translate into real-game scenarios, competitions, and varying lane conditions.

Key aspects of transfer skills training in bowling include:

1. Contextual Relevance: The training emphasizes the importance of practicing skills in contexts that closely resemble actual gameplay. This involves replicating the conditions, challenges, and strategic decisions that bowlers face during competitions.

2. Variability in Practice: Rather than repetitive drills, transfer skills training introduces variability in practice. This helps bowlers adapt their techniques to different situations, such as adjusting to changing lane conditions, facing diverse opponents, or encountering varying oil patterns.

3. Cognitive Engagement: The approach considers the cognitive aspects of bowling, encouraging bowlers to think strategically, make quick decisions, and adapt to unforeseen challenges. This mental engagement is crucial for success in competitive settings.

4. Integration of Technical and Psychological Elements: Transfer skills training recognizes the interconnectedness of technical and psychological aspects of bowling. It aims to develop both the physical techniques (such as grip, stance, and release) and the mental resilience needed for effective performance under pressure.

5. Real-time Decision Making: Bowlers practicing transfer skills training are exposed to scenarios that require real-time decision-making. This could involve adjusting their approach, targeting specific areas on the lane, or adapting to unexpected changes in the game environment.

6. Adaptability: The training cultivates adaptability, enabling bowlers to perform well in a variety of situations. Whether it's facing different lane conditions, competing against various opponents, or adjusting to the demands of a tournament, bowlers trained in transfer skills can navigate these challenges more effectively.

7. Progressive Complexity: The training program often follows a progression from simpler to more complex scenarios. This allows bowlers to gradually build their skills and confidence, ensuring a smooth transition from practice to actual gameplay.

Holistic Journey Guide Through Transfer Skill Training In Bowling

The essence of this guide lies in its exploration of both the technical and psychological dimensions inherent in the methodology of transfer skill training. By dissecting these facets, the aim is to empower individuals with the knowledge and tools necessary to enhance their performance on the bowling lanes. Whether one is navigating the early stages of their bowling journey or aiming to refine the intricacies of a well-established skill set, the guide seeks to offer universal guidance that transcends skill levels.

At its core, transfer skill training serves as a dynamic approach, recognizing that the acquisition and refinement of skills extend beyond mere repetition. Instead, it delves into the nuanced interplay between technical precision and psychological fortitude. Through a deep dive into this methodology, bowlers can unlock new avenues for growth, tapping into the reservoir of potential within themselves.

This guide invites bowlers to embrace a holistic perspective, acknowledging that success in the sport is not solely determined by physical prowess but also by a keen understanding of the mental and strategic components. As we navigate the multifaceted landscape of transfer skill training, the aspiration is to equip bowlers with the insights needed to navigate their unique journey, fostering a continuous evolution in their skill sets and elevating their performance to new heights on the lanes.

Part I: The Technical Skills Of Transfer Skill Training

Mastering Versatile Release Techniques

The release affects the trajectory and behavior of the ball on the lane, making it a crucial component of bowling technique. Training in transfer skills places a focus on the development of adaptable release techniques that can accommodate various lane conditions. To respond to diverse lane surfaces, bowlers are advised to practice alternative releases, such as straight, hook, or loft. To increase the hook on oily lanes or decreasing the hook on dry lanes, respectively, can have a significant impact on scoring potential. Bowlers improve their adaptability and maximize performance on a variety of lanes by becoming experts in a variety of release techniques.

BIBOY RIVERA

Nurturing Resilience through Pressure Shots

In essence, my daily routine revolved around extensive bowling and training sessions lasting three to four hours. I would engage in various drills, focus on mastering specific skills, practice different lines and angles, and simulate match situations by matching equipment with different lane conditions. Additionally, I dedicated six months to a sports psychology program before major tournaments, ensuring that I could apply the mental skills I had acquired in high-pressure situations. While I didn't have any particular rituals or habits, right before stepping onto the lanes, I would condition my mind to remain calm and focused.

Hypothetical Examples:

Example: Developing Flexible Release Techniques John has been diligently working on transfer skill training to improve his technical abilities. John is a bowler. He understands the value of developing adaptable release tactics to accommodate various lane situations. John works on a variety of release techniques, including the straight, hook, and loft. He gains the power to modify his release depending on the lane surface he meets by doing this. For instance, John modifies his release to increase hook potential on oily lanes so that he can obtain stronger pin action and increase his scoring potential. On the other hand, he adjusts his release to be more aggressive to hook on oily lanes, giving him better control over his shots. John has developed into a well-rounded bowler who can easily adjust to various lane conditions through constant practice and the development of his release skills.

Adapting to Diverse Equipment

There are many different coverstocks, and layouts available for bowling balls, and each one has a different effect on how they perform on the lane. To improve their adaptability and versatility, bowlers who participate in transfer skill training are encouraged to become familiar with a variety of equipment. To achieve the best performance possible with the equipment selected, this calls for practicing with various ball types and altering ball speed, rev rate, or axis rotation. Bowlers can optimize their methods and produce better results on the lanes by becoming proficient with a variety of bowling balls.

ARTURO QUINTERO

Precision and Consistency: The Cornerstones of Effective Bowling

To maintain my edge, I follow a rigorous practice routine. Five days a week, I devote myself to honing my skills and pushing my physical and mental limits to new heights. My practice sessions involve repetitive releases, meticulously fine-tuning my technique to achieve consistency. I engage in focused exercises, both on and off the lanes, to stay in peak physical condition. This comprehensive approach ensures that I am always prepared to face any challenge that comes my way.

Hypothetical Examples:

Example: Getting Used to Different Equipment Sarah, a devoted bowler, is aware of the value of equipment adaptation in the sport. She spends time getting acquainted with a variety of bowling balls as part of her transfer skill training. Sarah tests various coverstocks, and layouts while closely analyzing how each ball performs on the lane. Sarah maximizes her performance and scoring potential by modifying her ball speed, rev rate, or axis rotation depending on the equipment she has selected. For instance, she modifies her approach to generate a more acute entrance angle into the pocket while using a ball with higher hook potential (Low RG/High Diff). In contrast, Sarah uses a more straight shot with a ball that has a lower hook potential (High RG/Low Diff). Sarah gains a competitive edge by making wise judgments that result in better results thanks to her thorough understanding of various bowling balls and her aptitude for modifying her technique accordingly.

Cultivating Strategic Shot-Making

Strategic shot-making is heavily emphasized in transfer skill training, which sharpens bowlers' decision-making skills while playing. In order to adjust to changing lane conditions and competition formats, bowlers deliberately create practice scenarios that involve spare shooting tactics, strategic shot placements, and various approaches. For instance, according to lane conditions or competition rules, changing target points or ball speed to accommodate outside or inside lines. Bowlers develop flexibility and adaptation through smart shot-making, which enables them to succeed in a variety of competitive environments.

Hypothetical Example:

Example: Building a Strategic Shot-Making Mindset Michael, an aspiring bowler, is aware of the value of making smart shots on his path to becoming a proficient player. He concentrates on honing his gameplay decision-making skills through transfer skill training. Michael participates in a variety of circumstances that call for calculated shot selection during practice sessions. In order to adjust to shifting lane circumstances and tournament formats, he trains several spare shooting tactics, strategically putting shots on the lane, and experimenting with various lines. For instance, Michael modifies his target points and ball speed to play either outside or inside lines according to the demands of the game when faced with difficult lane conditions. Michael gains adaptability and versatility by regularly incorporating strategic shot-making into his training program, which enables him to succeed in a variety of competitive environments.

Nurturing Resilience through Pressure Shots

The pressure cooker that is competitive bowling frequently puts bowlers under extreme stress. Transfer skill training includes pressure shot practice sessions to bolster confidence and mental resilience. Bowlers create difficult spare shooting circumstances or play high-stakes games with penalties for missed shots to imitate these frantic times. This focused training enables bowlers to strengthen their focus, resilience, and unshakable concentration under pressure, all of which are essential skills for excelling in competitive settings.

Hypothetical Example:

Example: Resilience Building Using Pressure Shots Emily, a bowler who wants to compete at a high level, is aware of the need to have resilience under pressure. She dedicates particular practice sessions to mimicking high-pressure circumstances as part of her transfer skill training. Emily creates extremely difficult practice shooting scenarios to test her ability to function under pressure. She also plays high-stakes games in which missed shots have consequences, which requires her to stay focused and composed. Through these pressure shot practice sessions, Emily strengthens her mental toughness, cultivates resilience, and improves her ability to maintain focus under duress. When she participates in competitions or league play, these abilities come in handy because they enable her to maintain composure, make judgments with confidence, and provide her best effort when it counts.

Precision and Consistency: The Cornerstones of Effective Bowling

Precision and consistency are regarded as the foundational elements of a great bowling performance in transfer skill training. Bowlers practice drills that place a strong emphasis on accuracy and consistency in order to maximize these qualities. Bowlers accomplish astounding outcomes by ingraining muscle memory, perfecting techniques, and honing performance. Targeting particular pins, hitting precise boards down the lane, or attempting to maintain a constant ball speed and rev rate are all examples of specific practice routines. Bowlers improve the accuracy and repetition required for great performance in competitive settings by relentlessly focusing on accuracy and consistency in practice.

Hypothetical Example:

Example: The foundations of successful bowling are accuracy and consistency. Alex, a committed bowler, is aware that accuracy and reliability are necessary for outstanding performance. He concentrates on exercises that emphasize accuracy and consistency as he trains transfer skills. Alex devotes time to practicing hitting exact boards in the lane, honing his ability to target specific pins, and aiming for constant ball speed and rev rate. He strengthens his techniques and builds muscle memory with these activities, which help him produce amazing outcomes. During practice, Alex maintains a laser-like focus on accuracy and consistency, which shows in his competitive performance. He routinely hits his target and achieves the best pin carry with each shot thanks to his accuracy and repetition. Alex builds a solid base for success in competitive settings by making accuracy and consistency the cornerstones of his bowling game. He stands out as a fierce opponent in the world of bowling thanks to his capacity to produce shots with pinpoint accuracy and maintain a constant performance level.

Part Ii: Psychological Skills In Transfer Skill Training

Unleashing the Power of the Mind

It is impossible to emphasize the importance of psychological abilities in the sport of bowling. A bowler's mental toughness, attention, concentration, confidence, and capacity for managing pressure play crucial roles in maximizing success in addition to technical proficiency. We go into the theoretical foundations and real-world applications of transfer skill training for psychological skills in this part. We provide bowlers of all skill levels with the resources they need to succeed on the lanes by highlighting the psychological components of bowling and revealing techniques to harness the power of the mind.

Hypothetical Example:

Alex is a committed bowler who recognizes the critical importance of psychological abilities in improving performance. Alex develops his mental toughness, attention, and capacity for handling pressure through transfer skill training. Alex excels on the lanes by using his mental strength and displaying outstanding performance and fortitude under pressure.

Focus and Laser-Sharp Concentration:

As sustaining mental acuity during a game or competition is crucial, bowling calls for unshakable attention and razor-sharp concentration. In order to improve performance under pressure, transfer skill training incorporates specialized strategies during practice sessions. Bowlers can use mindfulness techniques to improve their attention and concentration, such as conscious breathing or visualization. Bowlers who master these techniques are better able to control their attention spans, stay completely present in the moment, and make wise decisions while on the lanes.

Hypothetical Example:

Aspired bowler Rachel has embraced transfer skill training to improve her mental focus and concentration. Rachel practices mindfulness techniques throughout her practice sessions. She practices mindful breathing and visualization to train her mind to be present and block off distractions. Rachel maintains a high level of awareness throughout her games with constant focus and laser-sharp concentration, enabling her to make accurate shots and tactical choices on the lanes.

Confidence and Self-Belief:

The cornerstone on which remarkable bowling performances are constructed is confidence. Training in transfer skills encompasses a variety of strategies to develop and nurture steadfast self-belief. Bowlers are urged to use encouraging self-talk, make realistic goals, and evaluate their performance. Bowlers increase their confidence and self-belief by setting reasonable goals, monitoring their progress, and celebrating their victories. With this optimistic outlook at their disposal, bowlers overcome difficulties with unshakable tenacity.

Hypothetical Example:

Mark, a committed bowler, is aware of how important confidence is to his performance. Training in transfer skills helps Mark actively build his confidence. He talks to himself well, praising his strengths and skills. Mark diligently monitors his development and sets reasonable goals for himself. In order to face each tournament with strength and optimism, Mark feeds his confidence and self-belief by acknowledging and enjoying his victories along the route.

Managing Pressure and Anxiety:

In order to perform at your best, pressure and anxiety are rampant in the intense environment of competitive bowling. A variety of tactics are taught in transfer skill training to aid bowlers in taming the beast of pressure. Bowlers develop pressure-management skills that increase resilience and mental toughness via deliberate practice. To properly handle stress and anxiety, one can use breathing exercises, thought-stopping methods, and cognitive restructuring. By learning these strategies, bowlers remain calm and collected even under extreme strain.

Hypothetical Example:

The difficulties caused by pressure and anxiety in competitive situations are ones that Stephanie, an experienced bowler, is aware of. Through training in transfer skills, Stephanie has created efficient coping mechanisms for these psychological challenges. She uses breathing techniques to manage her emotions and quiet her mind. In order to break negative thought patterns and replace them with uplifting, empowering thoughts, Stephanie also employs mind-stopping strategies. By using these pressure-reduction strategies, Stephanie remains composed and gives her best effort even in high-stress circumstances.

Developing Unyielding Mental Toughness:

A key component of success in bowling is mental toughness, which equips bowlers to overcome challenges, disappointments, and adversity. Through exposure to difficult circumstances, adversity training, and self-reflection, transfer skill training helps bowlers develop mental toughness. Mental toughness is developed by accepting difficult lane conditions, taking part in competitive simulations, and practicing reflection. With this tenacity at their disposal, bowlers bounce back from failures, exhibit unflinching perseverance, and continuously perform at their best under the most trying conditions.

Hypothetical Example:

On the lanes, Michael is renowned for his unrelenting mental tenacity. He credits the transfer skill training he has embraced for his perseverance. Michael exposes himself voluntarily to difficult lane conditions, testing his limits and skills. He also takes part in competitive simulations where he faces challenging competition and high pressure. Michael also evaluates his performances, identifying areas for development, and taking lessons from failures. Through this approach, Michael develops his mental toughness, which enables him to overcome challenges and constantly give excellent performances.

Visualization and Mental Rehearsal Techniques:

Strong approaches used in transfer skill training to improve performance include visualization and mental rehearsal. Bowlers practice visualization techniques, vividly visualizing themselves executing the ideal shot while also mentally practicing their strategy. These methods encourage mental visualization, boost concentration, and focus, and create unwavering faith in bowlers' abilities. Pre-shot rituals and practice sessions include visualization and mental rehearsal, which helps bowlers perform at their best in competitive settings.

Hypothetical Example:

Amy, a serious bowler, is aware of the need for mental preparation and visualization. Amy includes these strategies into her practice regimen as a component of her transfer skill training. She vividly sees herself making the perfect shot before each shot, picturing the ball's trajectory and the pins falling in her head. Amy also runs over her strategy in her head, visualizing each tactical move she will make on the lanes. Amy improves her focus, concentration, and confidence via visualization and mental practice, which paves the road for her success in challenging situations.

Table: Transfer Skill Training in Bowling		
Part I: Technical Skills		
Skill	Description	Example
Versatile Release Techniques	Practicing different release techniques to adapt to varying lane conditions	Adjusting release to control the amount of hook on dry lanes or to increase rev rate on oily lanes
Adapting to Different Equipment	Practicing with different types of equipment to develop versatility and adaptability	Adjusting ball speed, rev rate, or axis rotation based on the ball used
Strategic Shot-Making	Practicing strategic shot-making to develop decision-making skills on the lanes	Adjusting target or ball speed to play outside or inside lines
Pressure Shots	Practicing pressure shots in practice sessions to develop mental toughness and confidence	Setting up challenging spare shooting scenarios or practicing high-pressure games
Accuracy and Consistency	Practicing accuracy and consistency drills to develop muscle memory and fine-tune techniques	Practicing targeting specific pins, hitting specific boards on the lane, or achieving consistent ball speed and rev rate
Part II: Psychological Skills		
Skill	Description	Example
Mental Focus and Concentration	Practicing mental focus and concentration techniques to improve performance under pressure	Practicing mindfulness techniques, such as breathing exercises or visualization
Confidence and Self-Belief	Building confidence and self-belief through positive self-talk, goal-setting, and performance analysis	Setting realistic goals, tracking progress, and celebrating successes
Pressure and Anxiety Management	Practicing pressure management techniques to build resilience and mental toughness	Practicing breathing exercises, thought-stopping techniques, or cognitive restructuring
Mental Toughness	Developing mental toughness through exposure to challenging situations, adversity training, and self-reflection	Practicing challenging lane conditions, participating in competitive simulations, or reflecting on performance

Table: Transfer Skill Training in Bowling		
Visualization and Mental Rehearsal	Practicing visualization and mental rehearsal to enhance performance	Visualizing shots, imagining executing the perfect shot, and mentally rehearsing the game plan

Table 33 - The above table shows various technical and psychological skills that can be enhanced through transfer skill training in bowling, along with examples of how these skills can be developed. By practicing and mastering these skills, bowlers can improve their performance and adapt to different lane conditions, equipment, and competition formats.

BALANCING THE BOWLING EQUATION: THE BALANCE OF PHYSICAL, TECHNICAL, AND MENTAL SKILLS *By Coach Bettina Lund*

Bowling coaching is like a fascinating balancing act between main ingredients: the physical and technical skills, and the mental abilities. As a coach, blending these parts in a way that helps the individual athlete improve is an important task.

In coaching, we often see that athletes developing into top bowlers manage to blend these two parts really well: The careful work on physical and technical aspects, and the strong mindset. Imagine this: One bowler becomes great by mixing 65% of his success from how He practices and does things physically, and 35% from how strong He is mentally. Now, there's another bowler just as good, but He does it a bit differently. He gets to the top with 65% mental strength and 35% very good technical skills. The challenge for a coach is understanding and detecting the differences in his bowlers and focus the coaching accordingly. Coaches who succeed in this will be on track to help develop the next group of champions.

Hypothetical Examples

Scenario 1: The Precision Maestro

Imagine a bowler named Alex, renowned for his exceptional accuracy and technical finesse. Alex's approach to the game reflects a meticulous fusion of 65% physical/technical mastery and 35% mental prowess. His physical game is strong and versatile – every movement, from his approach to his release, is a symphony of precision. Alex spends hours refining his techniques, scrutinizing his stance, grip, and release to achieve optimal results.

The mental aspect adds the final touches to Alex's performance. His mental resilience serves as the bedrock of consistency. When faced with challenging lane conditions or high-pressure situations, Alex's unwavering focus and calm demeanor keep him steady. Mental mindset including visualization techniques and breathing exercises form a crucial 35% of his overall success equation. This balanced blend of meticulous physical technique and unflinching mental strength propels Alex to championship victories.

Scenario 2: The Strategic Strategist

Now, meet Emily, an equally remarkable bowler who takes a different route to excellence. Emily is renowned for her strategic prowess and mental agility. Her prowess is defined by a distinctive formula: 65% mental brilliance intertwined with 35% refined physical execution. Emily might not have the textbook-perfect technique, but her mental toolkit more than compensates for that fact.

Emily's game is a showcase of strategic acumen. She studies lane patterns meticulously and adapts her game plan accordingly, exploiting her opponent's weaknesses. The majority of her success (65%) comes from the astute reading of the game, coupled with an uncanny ability to maintain a calm demeanor in high-stakes scenarios. While her physical execution is important for the overall result (35%), her mastery over mental facets like focus, determination, and adaptability provides the edge that decides championship matches.

In these fictional tales, Alex exemplifies a physical/technical specialist with a strong mental foundation, while Emily is a mental strategist backed by solid physical execution. The beauty of bowling coaching lies in understanding and harnessing these intricate proportions, molding athletes into elite bowlers based on their unique blend of skills.

Evolving and adapting

Over the years, a lot of things have changed in the sport of bowling. I think we will see this more clearly when looking back over the last few decades. What I think looking back is that male vs female bowlers back then in general did have a different focus. Male bowlers would tend to make more of a difference with their physical game like strength and how they throw the ball, and would look at making improvements on these parameters first. At the same time, female bowlers would be more level in their physical game but would shine and make a difference based on their mental game, making this the area of first looking for further improvements.

In today's sport, I do believe that tactical game and understanding, together with versatility in executing the technique that the "in the moment" situation demands, is the first and equal focus for both male and female bowlers in their practice road to success.

That does take away from the fact that even if elements and skill sets needed to excel may have changed over the years, coaching can still be explained as helping the athlete improve in practice and helping the athlete get and stay in flow during competition.

Finding talented bowlers who could become great is a bit like trying to catch a cloud. It's not easy and needs a lot of care because it's not always as simple as it looks. Sometimes, players who are really good at the technical parts of bowling don't do as well in important matches if they're not feeling mentally strong. On the other hand, there's something interesting – some people are really mentally sharp, and even if they're not the best at the technical stuff, they can use their mental strength to do better than people who are technically better than them, but not as strong mentally. This mix of skills means more than just what you see on the surface.

For coaches, understanding and being able to help improve on both the technical and mental parts can make a big difference, and it can shape how far a player goes in his journey to becoming great. Finding the right combination of the elements involved is what can help players reach their highest potential. This is what becoming excellent in bowling is all about, and at the same time what makes coaching in bowling equally challenging and rewarding.

By Coach Bettina Lund, Denmark Women National Team Coach

TRADITIONAL TRAINING IN BOWLING VS TRANSFER TRAINING

Progressive Traditional Training Approaches in Bowling: Expanding the Boundaries of Technical Skill Development

The foundation of skill development in the sport of bowling has traditionally been traditional training, which emphasizes target precision and the repetition of basic motions like grip, approach, and release. This methodical approach is successful in promoting technical proficiency, improving focus and discipline, permitting gradual advancement, and encouraging equipment familiarity. In this thorough investigation, we dig into the theoretical foundations and practical implementations of conventional training, highlighting the benefits of successful bowlers who have benefited from this tried-and-true method.

The Power of Repetition

The strength of repetition, which serves as the foundation for helping bowlers acquire superior technical skills, is at the heart of conventional instruction. Bowlers improve their grip, approach, release, and target accuracy through repetitive practice, which eventually results in reliable and accurate shots. Through conscious repetition, the complex interaction between the mind and body required to carry out these motions is polished, leading to improved muscle memory and accuracy.

Discipline and Focus: Bowlers must maintain consistent focus and discipline during practice sessions according to traditional instruction. Drills and exercises' repetitive nature demands sustained focus and attention to detail, which provides a favorable environment for skill improvement. In competitive settings, the capacity to stay focused when practicing translates naturally, enabling bowlers to play with outstanding consistency and precision under pressure.

Progressive Mastery: The systematic progression of traditional training, in which bowlers proceed consistently through a series of drills and exercises of escalating difficulty, is one of its distinguishing features. Before attempting more advanced tactics, bowlers build a strong foundation thanks to this gradual approach to skill development. Bowlers can master every facet of their game gradually by building on previously gained talents, which results in a well-rounded and complete skill set.

The Equipment Advantage: Traditional instruction provides a detailed grasp of the bowling equipment in addition to concentrating on technical proficiency. In order to make wise selections during contests, bowlers get intimately familiar with the nuances of their bowling balls, shoes, and other accessories. This equipment familiarity improves adaptation to changing lane circumstances, enabling bowlers to successfully modify their strategies and techniques.

Exemplifying Success: Two well-known individuals in the field of conventional training stand out as models of achievement, demonstrating the effectiveness of this tried-and-true strategy.

Challenges Inherent In Traditional Training Approaches: Expanding The Boundaries Of Skill Transfer In Bowling

NORM DUKE

He is a legendary figure in the world of professional bowling and exemplifies the benefits of conventional instruction. Duke continually astonishes audiences with his performances thanks to his silky-smooth and controlled delivery. His strategy is based on conventional training tenets and places emphasis on the creation of a repeatable and reliable physical technique. Duke has had a very successful career on the PBA Tour as a result of embracing the power of repetition and achieving an admirable degree of accuracy and dependability

Traditional training, which emphasizes the repetition of key motions including grip, approach, release, and target accuracy, has long been the cornerstone of talent development in the world of bowling. This methodical approach has been successful in fostering technical competence, discipline, gradual advancement, and equipment familiarity. To investigate alternate strategies that promote improved skill transferability and performance optimization, it is necessary to be aware of the shortcomings of conventional training. We explore the theoretical foundations and practical applications of transfer training in this in-depth analysis, highlighting its benefits and exhibiting cutting-edge techniques that bridge the gap between practice and competition.

Understanding the Limitations: Overcoming Transfer Obstacles

Limited Transferability: As a result of its focus on solitary exercises, traditional training may not be as effective in transferring knowledge to a competitive setting. When faced with various lane conditions, varied oil patterns, and high-pressure scenarios, bowlers may find it difficult to apply their learned techniques, which ultimately affects how well they perform in contests.

Lack of Contextual Training: In traditional training, drills and exercises alone frequently fall short of accurately simulating the nuances and complexity of real-world bowling circumstances. Bowlers may not have experienced genuine game scenarios, which limits their capacity to apply abilities to competitive settings where flexibility and judgment are essential.

Overemphasis on Technique: The heavy emphasis on technique in traditional training may unintentionally overshadow other crucial facets of bowling, like strategic decision-making, mental toughness, and flexibility in various lane conditions. As a result, bowlers may be exceptionally skilled technically but suffer in competitive situations where a variety of circumstances are at play.

Risk of Overuse Injuries: Traditional training has a high risk of overuse injuries due to its repeated nature. Due to the repetitive actions involved in practice, bowlers may develop muscle imbalances, incur joint tension, and face other physical illnesses. These wounds may have a negative impact on performance over the long run and general health.

Revolutionizing Skill Transfer: The Transfer Training Paradigm

Transfer training, which emphasizes the direct application of abilities inside the competitive context, provides a cutting-edge alternative to conventional methodologies. Transfer training tries to close the gap between practice and competition by emphasizing contextually appropriate practice, allowing bowlers to more easily apply their knowledge for improved performance.

Implementing Effective Transfer Training Methods:

Competitive Practice: Bowlers gain priceless experience by participating in practice sessions that closely resemble actual competitive situations. This involves playing practice games with teammates or rivals, practicing in a variety of lane settings, and introducing strategic components into training sessions. Such competitive training improves situational awareness, adaptability, and decision-making skills, facilitating skill transfer to actual competitions.

WALTER RAY WILLIAMS JR.

Mental Training: The vital part that the mind plays in bowling performance is acknowledged by transfer training. Bowlers are given the mental toughness, attention, and concentration needed to excel under duress during tournaments via mental training techniques like visualization, mindfulness, and self-regulation techniques.

He has won multiple championships on the Professional Bowlers Association (PBA) Tour thanks to his outstanding accuracy and consistency. His dedication to classical training, which has never wavered, has contributed to his success. Williams Jr. has spent numerous hours perfecting his physical skills and immersing himself in endless practice sessions to become an expert in his field. His position as one of the best bowlers in the history of the sport has been cemented by this relentless pursuit of technical mastery.

Video Analysis: Bowlers are given the ability to rigorously study and assess their performances in both practice and competitive environments by using video analysis as a transfer training tool. Bowlers can identify areas for growth by analyzing their technique, form, and strategic decisions on video. With increased self-awareness, one can make targeted adjustments and perform better in actual competitions.

Simulation Training: The use of technology-driven simulation training, such as virtual reality or bowling simulators, gives bowlers the chance to practice in extremely lifelike game scenarios. These virtual environments mimic various lanes, scoring schemes, and tournament forms. Bowlers acquire abilities that more successfully transition to actual tournaments by practicing in a controlled yet realistic environment.

Practicing Traditional Training:

1. **Repetitive Drills:** *Traditional training emphasizes the power of repetition. Bowlers practice fundamental motions such as their grip, approach, and release repeatedly to enhance muscle memory and precision.*

2. **Disciplined Practice:** *Discipline and focus are essential in traditional training. Bowlers must maintain consistent focus during practice sessions to develop a heightened level of concentration and attention to detail.*

3. **Progressive Mastery:** *The training involves a systematic progression. Bowlers start with basic drills and gradually advance to more challenging exercises as they build a strong foundation of skills.*

4. **Equipment Familiarity:** *In addition to technical skills, traditional training ensures that bowlers become intimately familiar with their bowling equipment, including balls, shoes, and accessories. This familiarity enables them to adapt to changing lane conditions.*

Practicing Transfer Training:

1. **Context-Specific Scenarios:** *Transfer training seeks to create practice scenarios that closely mimic real-world bowling circumstances. Bowlers engage in exercises and drills that replicate genuine game scenarios, allowing them to apply their skills effectively in competitive settings.*

2. **Skill Integration:** *Transfer training aims to balance technical skills with strategic decision-making, mental fortitude, and adaptability to diverse lane conditions. Practice sessions focus on developing well-rounded bowlers who excel both technically and competitively.*

3. **Injury Prevention:** *Transfer training incorporates a variety of training methods and techniques to reduce the risk of overuse injuries. By using a more diverse set of training exercises, it minimizes strain on specific muscle groups and promotes overall health.*

4. ***Performance Analysis:*** *In transfer training, performance analysis is crucial. Video analysis, tracking statistics, and feedback from coaches and peers help bowlers identify areas for improvement and make necessary adjustments.*

Both traditional and transfer training have their distinct approaches to practice. The choice between these methods depends on individual goals, preferences, and the desired balance between technical proficiency and competitive performance. Bowlers can benefit from a combination of both training approaches to develop a comprehensive skill set that excels in all aspects of the sport.

For coaches and bowlers alike, the ongoing argument over whether traditional training or transfer training is preferable in the sport of bowling has significant ramifications. To successfully navigate this debate, one must carefully evaluate the information that is currently available and have a thorough awareness of the many different factors that go into the best possible training and performance. Here, we look at the theoretical foundations and practical tips that coaches and bowlers can use to design training plans that make the most of both traditional and transfer training approaches.

The adoption of a comprehensive strategy by coaches that smoothly incorporates both conventional and transfer training techniques is advised. Coaches can supplement these efforts by utilizing transfer training strategies, while still recognizing the intrinsic value of traditional training in the development of technical abilities and fundamentals. Bowlers can develop mental toughness, improve their ability to use their polished abilities in realistic game circumstances and adjust to the numerous challenges faced in various environments by doing this. A comprehensive training regimen that successfully integrates the advantages of both strategies promotes the growth of a well-rounded skill set, which translates into superior performance in high-stakes competitions.

The value of realistic practice, which aims to as nearly resemble competition situations as possible, must be stressed by coaches. To do this, different lane conditions must be presented to bowlers, practice sessions must incorporate strategic elements and challenging competition scenarios must be developed. Bowlers are prepared to translate their skills and techniques into a competitive setting by engaging in such intentional and contextually pertinent practice. The degree to which training replicates the intricacies and strains present in such contexts determines one's capacity to adapt and do well in real-world competitions.

In order to provide bowlers with the skills they need to develop steadfast mental fortitude, focus, and attention, coaches are advised to add mental training approaches into their programs. Bowlers are given the psychological fortitude required to succeed under the severe strain of competitive circumstances via methods including visualization, mindfulness, and self-regulation skills. Coaches help bowlers reach their full potential and perform at their best when it counts most by developing a solid mental base.

Coaches should use video analysis as a powerful tool for giving specific feedback and promoting continual progress. Bowlers can learn a great deal about areas that need improvement by carefully examining technique, form, and strategic decisions in video footage of both practice sessions and competitive activities. Bowlers are better able to adapt their game as a result of their increased self-awareness, which improves performance outcomes.

By introducing simulation training into their programs, coaches can increase the effectiveness of their training. Bowlers can immerse themselves in incredibly realistic game scenarios by utilizing cutting-edge technology such as virtual reality or bowling simulators. These computer-generated environments accurately reproduce various lane conditions, scoring schemes, and competition forms. Bowlers can hone their abilities and adaptability by deliberately practicing in these regulated yet genuine situations, ensuring smooth transitions to real-world tournaments.

Each bowler is a diverse individual with distinctive skills, weaknesses, and learning preferences, and coaches must understand this. Unlocking each bowler's maximum potential requires tailoring training regimens based on unique profiles. While some bowlers may benefit from using traditional training techniques, others might perform better when using transfer training strategies. In order to maximize their training programs, coaches should employ a fluid and adaptive strategy, regularly evaluating and monitoring the progress of each bowler.

2-Month Master Plan for National Team Bowling

Traditional Training Focus:

Week 1: Foundation Building

- *Technical Training:*
    - *Grip refinement: Focus on consistent grip pressure and hand position.*
    - *Repetition: 50 grips per session.*
    - *Additional Drill 1: Grip Strength Exercises*
    - *Additional Drill 2: Perfect Release Drill*
    - *Additional Drill 3: Balance Board Training*

- *Psychological Training:*
    - *Discipline and focus exercise: Maintain concentration during repetitive drills.*
    - *To-Do: Stay fully focused for 30 minutes of continuous practice.*
    - *Additional Drill 1: Visualization Techniques*
    - *Additional Drill 2: Controlled Breathing Exercises*
    - *Additional Drill 3: Positive Self-Talk*

- *Tactical Training:*
    - *Basic accuracy: Target a specific pin repeatedly.*
    - *Simulation: Simple lane conditions with a straight shot.*
    - *Additional Drill 1: Pin-Point Accuracy Challenge*
    - *Additional Drill 2: Spare Shooting Drill*
    - *Additional Drill 3: Precision Lane Adjustment Practice*

- *Simulation Training:*
    - *Virtual lane practice: Introduce bowlers to basic virtual simulations.*
    - *Simulation: Straightforward lane conditions.*
    - *Additional Drill 1: Virtual Bowling Mini-Games*
    - *Additional Drill 2: Lane Pattern Recognition Exercise*
    - *Additional Drill 3: Virtual Spare Challenge*

Week 2-4: Progressive Mastery

- *Technical Training:*
    - *Advanced approach refinement: Work on foot placement and timing.*
    - *Repetition: 75 approaches per session.*
    - *Additional Drill 1: Advanced Footwork Drills*
    - *Additional Drill 2: Timing and Rhythm Exercises*
    - *Additional Drill 3: Target Pin Drill*

- *Psychological Training:*
    - *Focus under pressure: Increase intensity during drills to test concentration.*
    - *To-Do: Maintain focus during challenging simulated scenarios.*

- *Additional Drill 1: Pressure Simulation Games*
- *Additional Drill 2: Competitive Mindset Visualization*
- *Additional Drill 3: Adversity Response Training*
- **Tactical Training:**
  - *Lane condition adaptation: Adjust tactics based on changing conditions.*
  - *Simulation: Varied lane conditions in virtual scenarios.*
  - *Additional Drill 1: Lane Pattern Transition Drill*
  - *Additional Drill 2: Tactical Decision Games*
  - *Additional Drill 3: Dynamic Lane Adjustment Practice*
- **Simulation Training:**
  - *Realistic competition simulations: Mimic tournament pressure.*
  - *Simulation: Virtual tournaments with different opponents.*
  - *Additional Drill 1: Virtual Tournament Final Round*
  - *Additional Drill 2: Opponent Simulation Challenges*
  - *Additional Drill 3: Pressure-Packed Virtual Matches*

Week 5-6: Equipment Familiarity

- **Technical Training:**
  - *Equipment adjustments: Practice adapting to different bowling balls.*
  - *Repetition: 60 shots with various bowling balls.*
  - *Additional Drill 1: Ball Change Drills*
  - *Additional Drill 2: Spare Ball Precision Practice*
  - *Additional Drill 3: Multi-Ball Switching Exercise*
- **Psychological Training:**
  - *Pressure situations: Create scenarios to simulate tournament pressures.*
  - *To-Do: Successfully execute under simulated high-pressure situations.*
  - *Additional Drill 1: High-Pressure Simulation with Equipment Changes*
  - *Additional Drill 2: Equipment Decision Visualization*
  - *Additional Drill 3: Quick Decision-Making Challenges*
- **Tactical Training:**
  - *Strategic decision-making: Incorporate strategic elements into practice.*
  - *Simulation: Virtual games with strategic challenges.*
  - *Additional Drill 1: Strategy Integration Games*
  - *Additional Drill 2: Quick Decision Tactical Challenges*
  - *Additional Drill 3: Team Strategic Session*
- **Simulation Training:**
  - *Tournament-style scenarios: Simulate final rounds of tournaments.*
  - *Simulation: Intense virtual championships.*
  - *Additional Drill 1: Virtual Championship Finals*

- *Additional Drill 2: Multi-Game Virtual Tournament*
- *Additional Drill 3: Virtual Masters Challenge*

Week 7-8: Review and Intensity Increase

- *Technical Training:*
  - *Intensity boost: Increase speed and power in drills.*
  - *Repetition: 80 shots with increased intensity.*
  - *Additional Drill 1: Power and Speed Training*
  - *Additional Drill 2: Dynamic Approach Speed Drill*
  - *Additional Drill 3: Controlled Power Shots*
- *Psychological Training:*
  - *Final pressure simulations: Prepare for the highest pressure scenarios.*
  - *To-Do: Maintain composure and focus during intense simulations.*
  - *Additional Drill 1: Extreme Pressure Simulation Games*
  - *Additional Drill 2: Visualization under Extreme Stress*
  - *Additional Drill 3: Focus Endurance Challenges*
- *Tactical Training:*
  - *Combine tactics: Integrate various tactics into simulated games.*
  - *Simulation: Complex virtual scenarios with strategic challenges.*
  - *Additional Drill 1: Multi-Tactic Integration Games*
  - *Additional Drill 2: Tactical Decision Speed Rounds*
  - *Additional Drill 3: Team Strategic Marathon*
- *Simulation Training:*
  - *Championship simulations: Simulate final rounds of tournaments.*
  - *Simulation: Intense virtual championships.*
  - *Additional Drill 1: Virtual Championship Finals*
  - *Additional Drill 2: High-Stakes Virtual Showdown*
  - *Additional Drill 3: Virtual All-Star Challenge*

Transfer Training Focus:

Week 1: Context-Specific Scenarios

- *Technical Training:*
  - *Combine technical drills with specific scenarios: e.g., adjusting grip under pressure.*
  - *Repetition: 40 scenario-based shots.*
  - *Additional Drill 1: Realistic Spare Conversion Challenges*
  - *Additional Drill 2: Pressure-Packed Strike Shots*
  - *Additional Drill 3: Quick Adjustment Drill*
- *Psychological Training:*
  - *Visualization exercises: Imagine specific scenarios and execute shots mentally.*

- *To-Do: Visualize and execute shots under simulated game pressure.*
- *Additional Drill 1: Mental Toughness Marathon*
- *Additional Drill 2: Pressure Visualization Challenge*
- *Additional Drill 3: Controlled Breathing during Simulation*

- **Tactical Training:**
  - *Decision-making in practice games: Introduce strategic decisions in friendly matches.*
  - *Simulation: Simulated games with strategic challenges.*
  - *Additional Drill 1: Tactical Decision Speed Rounds*
  - *Additional Drill 2: Quick Decision-Making Challenges*
  - *Additional Drill 3: Team Tactical Marathon*

- **Simulation Training:**
  - *Specific challenge scenarios: e.g., simulating a difficult spare conversion.*
  - *Simulation: Virtual scenarios replicating real-world challenges.*
  - *Additional Drill 1: Complex Scenario Virtual Challenges*
  - *Additional Drill 2: High-Pressure Virtual Scenarios*
  - *Additional Drill 3: Virtual Masters Challenge*

Week 2 -4: Skill Integration

- **Technical Training:**
  - *Balanced practice: Combine technical drills with strategic decision-making.*
  - *Repetition: 50 shots with integrated tactics.*
  - *Additional Drill 1: Tactical Integration Marathon*
  - *Additional Drill 2: Decision-Driven Approach Shots*
  - *Additional Drill 3: Mixed Challenge Drills*

- **Psychological Training:**
  - *Adaptability under pressure: Introduce unexpected elements during mental training.*
  - *To-Do: Stay adaptable during unpredictable scenarios.*
  - *Additional Drill 1: Adaptive Visualization Games*
  - *Additional Drill 2: Dynamic Pressure Simulation*
  - *Additional Drill 3: Quick Adjustment Mental Challenges*

- **Tactical Training:**
  - *Adapting to lane conditions: Integrate changing lane conditions into tactical practice.*
  - *Simulation: Virtual scenarios with dynamic lane conditions.*
  - *Additional Drill 1: Dynamic Lane Adjustment Challenges*
  - *Additional Drill 2: Tactical Decision Speed Rounds*
  - *Additional Drill 3: Adaptive Strategic Games*

- **Simulation Training:**
  - *Integrate tactics: Execute strategic decisions in virtual scenarios.*
  - *Simulation: Virtual games with strategic challenges.*

- *Additional Drill 1: Virtual Team Strategic Session*
- *Additional Drill 2: Tactical Decision Marathon*
- *Additional Drill 3: Complex Scenario Virtual Challenges*

Week 5-6: Injury Prevention and Performance Analysis

- *Technical Training:*
  - *Diversified training: Incorporate a variety of shots to prevent overuse injuries.*
  - *Repetition: 60 shots with diverse challenges.*
  - *Additional Drill 1: Mixed Challenge Drills*
  - *Additional Drill 2: Controlled Power Shots*
  - *Additional Drill 3: Balanced Approach Drills*

- *Psychological Training:*
  - *Stress management exercises: Implement mindfulness techniques.*
  - *To-Do: Use stress management techniques during intense simulations.*
  - *Additional Drill 1: Mindfulness and Controlled Breathing Session*
  - *Additional Drill 2: Stress Simulation with Relaxation Techniques*
  - *Additional Drill 3: Controlled Breathing during Simulation*

- *Tactical Training:*
  - *Analyzing performance in practice games: Review and strategize after each game.*
  - *Simulation: Video analysis of virtual games.*
  - *Additional Drill 1: Tactical Decision Review Session*
  - *Additional Drill 2: Team Tactical Analysis Session*
  - *Additional Drill 3: Strategic Decision Statistical Review*

- *Simulation Training:*
  - *Virtual analysis: Review and analyze virtual performances.*
  - *Simulation: Video analysis of virtual scenarios.*
  - *Additional Drill 1: Scenario Review and Adjustment Session*
  - *Additional Drill 2: Virtual Performance Statistical Analysis*
  - *Additional Drill 3: Virtual Scenarios Breakdown*

Week 7-8: Performance Optimization

- *Technical Training:*
  - *Fine-tuning techniques: Address specific technical aspects identified in performance analysis.*
  - *Repetition: 70 shots with targeted adjustments.*
  - *Additional Drill 1: Precision Lane Adjustment Practice*
  - *Additional Drill 2: Targeted Equipment Adjustment Drills*
  - *Additional Drill 3: Technical Perfection Marathon*

- *Psychological Training:*
  - *Advanced mental toughness exercises: Simulate high-stakes scenarios.*

- *To-Do: Visualize and execute shots under simulated game pressure.*
- *Additional Drill 1: Extreme Pressure Simulation Games*
- *Additional Drill 2: Visualization under Extreme Stress*
- *Additional Drill 3: High-Stakes Virtual Showdown*

- ***Tactical Training:***
  - *Combine tactics: Integrate various tactics into simulated games.*
  - *Simulation: Complex virtual scenarios with strategic challenges.*
  - *Additional Drill 1: Virtual Tournament Final Round*
  - *Additional Drill 2: Multi-Tactic Integration Games*
  - *Additional Drill 3: Advanced Strategic Decision Games*

- ***Simulation Training:***
  - *Championship simulations: Simulate final rounds of tournaments.*
  - *Simulation: Intense virtual championships.*
  - *Additional Drill 1: Virtual Championship Finals*
  - *Additional Drill 2: High-Stakes Virtual Showdown*
  - *Additional Drill 3: Virtual All-Star Challenge*

LEARN TO UNLEARN: ALTERING AUTOMATED MOVEMENT PATTERNS

B owlers must modify their current motor skills and tactics to account for the changes brought about by the development of innovative training tools. It is not just the addition of new equipment, though, that necessitates alterations to traditional movement patterns.

It is crucial to consider how changing automated mobility patterns may affect daily life. In this sense, automaticity is the execution of a skill "with minimal demands on attention capacity" (Magill & Anderson, 2016). Despite its importance, there hasn't been much research done on this topic (Carson et al., 2017). Therefore, it is difficult for bowlers and instructors to improve established movement skills because there are so few evidence-based guidelines available. By offering a thorough explanation of the definition of modifying movement patterns and detailing the causes, goals, and difficulties involved with such modifications, this chapter seeks to allay these worries.

It may be difficult for a bowler to switch to a new technique if He has been using the same one for a long time, especially if it is largely automated. A bowler who has been employing the End-over-End or stroke style, for example, would find it challenging to adapt to the huge hook-ball technique, which calls for a different approach and release. It may be difficult for the bowler to move to the new method because He will have to relearn his old one from scratch, but with practice and perseverance, it is doable.

Defining The Transformation Of Automatized Movement Patterns:

It refers to the process of understanding, analyzing, and reshaping the ingrained and automatic movement patterns that bowlers develop over time. These patterns are typically the result of extensive practice and repetition, and they become deeply ingrained in a bowler's muscle memory and motor skills.

The term suggests a deliberate and strategic approach to altering or optimizing these established movement patterns to enhance a bowler's performance. This transformation could involve adjustments to various aspects of the bowling technique, including the approach, stance, grip, release, and follow-through.

Significant difficulties arise when attempting to change current movement patterns, particularly for seasoned bowlers whose movements have undergone substantial practice. There are numerous ways to tackle this issue, each of which has specific drawbacks and characteristics.

1. **Relearning: Reacquiring Previously Automatized Skills**

    -   After becoming hurt or having to take a long vacation from bowling, relearning is required.
    -   A player who has been injured and returns after a period of time may need to retrain his old movement habits.

- Bowling fundamentals may need to be reintegrated by athletes who have been away from the sport for a while.

2. **Skill Transfer: Transferring Proficiencies across Tasks**

- Skill transfer is the process of transferring abilities from one bowling style to another.
- Straight bowling proficiency can be translated to curved bowling, and vice versa.
- Accurate aiming can be applied to many shot kinds, such as spare pickups.

3. **Adaptation Learning: Gradually Shifting Motor Skill Execution**

- Trial-and-error gradual improvements to motor abilities are part of adaptation learning.
- In bowling, it could entail changing the player's posture or strategy in response to criticism or film analysis.
- Weight distribution changes throughout the approach can improve precision and force.

4. **Error Correction: Rectifying Erroneous Movement Patterns**

- Error correction entails changing problematic movement patterns in response to criticism.
- It might be difficult to correct persistent technical mistakes in bowling.
- By correcting habitual wrist tilting during ball release, compensating mistakes are kept from developing.
- Error correction is aided by coach feedback, video analysis, or training aids like wrist braces or elbow supports.

A thorough investigation of the many strategies mentioned above is necessary to comprehend the complexities of changing automatized movement patterns. Players and coaches can traverse the challenges of improving established movement skills by examining the theoretical underpinnings, practical considerations, and potential consequences linked to each strategy. With the aid of this theoretical framework, they can direct athletes toward enhanced performance and flexibility, enabling them to flourish in the challenging world of bowling.

Exploring The Distinctions Between Changing Automatized Movement Patterns And Motor Learning In Bowling

In the realm of bowling, it's essential to understand the differences between altering automatized movement patterns and the process of motor learning. These distinctions play a crucial role in skill development and improvement.

Foundation of Change:

Changing Automatized Movement Patterns: This concept revolves around the long-term refinement of a previously acquired skill. It differs from learning a completely new motor skill since it builds upon existing knowledge. Unlike the cognitive phase of motor learning where new skills are acquired, altering automatized movement patterns begins with an established skill set (Carson & Collins, 2016, 2017; Panzer, 2002).

Task Objectives:

When modifying these patterns in bowling, the primary objective is to retain the same overall task goals while employing a different movement pattern. This ensures that the fundamental purpose of the skill remains unchanged.

The terminology used in discussing alterations to movement patterns in bowling can sometimes be unclear. However, the term "changing movement patterns" offers a more precise and transparent description of the process. It encompasses various scenarios, such as transitioning between techniques or adjusting specific aspects of a movement or technique.

Challenges and Considerations:

Injury Risk: One significant challenge when altering movement patterns in bowling is the potential risk of injury. Changes in technique can subject the body to new stresses, particularly if they involve different muscle activation patterns or ranges of motion. Additionally, mastering a new technique demands dedication and effort.

Expert Guidance: Collaborating with experienced coaches or trainers who can provide guidance and feedback is crucial for effective movement pattern adjustments in bowling. This process may involve breaking down the movement into smaller components and focusing on each element before integrating them into the overall pattern. Additionally, incorporating flexibility and strength training into the training regimen can help prepare the body for the physical demands of the new technique.

Distinguishing Motor Learning from Altering Movement Patterns:

Motor Learning: According to Schmidt and Lee (2011), motor learning encompasses the acquisition of a motor skill through practice, resulting in a change that is not immediately apparent and is largely permanent. However, one key difference lies in the starting point. Motor learning often begins in the cognitive phase, as stated by Fitts and Posner (1967), where learners are in the process of acquiring new skills.

Understanding these distinctions between altering automatized movement patterns and motor learning is essential for comprehending the intricate nature of skill enhancement. Recognizing the unique characteristics and starting points of each process empowers practitioners to develop tailored interventions to optimize the transformation of ingrained movement patterns in the context of bowling and other sports.

Hypothetical Examples

Examples of Bowlers:

Since she had been bowling for a while, Sarah had honed an automated movement style. But she understood that her approach wasn't producing consistent outcomes. She decided to alter her movement style while keeping her overall work objectives in mind under the advice of her coach. Together, they dissected her movement into smaller parts, honed each component, and then combined them into a fresh, more efficient movement pattern. Sarah was able to successfully change her automated movement pattern and raise her performance on the lanes after putting a lot of time and work into it.

James was an accomplished bowler with years of experience who had mastered his craft. However, he believed that his current movement style was overtaxing his body and raising the possibility of damage. He looked for a capable coach who specialized in technical improvement. James' movements were closely examined by the coach, who noted places that required adjusting to ease the strain on his body. He experimented with new muscle activation patterns and fluid motion ranges to create a new movement pattern. James was able to alter his movement pattern, lower the possibility of injury, and enhance his overall performance through constant practice and the use of strength and flexibility training.

Examples of Coaches:

Lisa, a student of Coach Mark, was having trouble with her bowling movement patterns. Due to Lisa's inconsistent method, she was unable to effectively keep her task goals. Coach Mark used a thorough strategy to assist Lisa in altering her movement habits. He divided her technique into smaller parts and concentrated on refining each part with deliberate drills and exercises. Coach Mark helped Lisa combine the improved parts into a fresh, more efficient movement pattern by offering advice and comments. With consistent practice and the coach's encouragement, Lisa was able to alter her movement patterns and improve her performance on the lanes.

Tom, a junior bowler, addressed Coach Emily about changing his movement patterns to improve his performance. Tom had already established a strong basis in the sport, but he felt the need to improve his technique. Tom and Coach Emily extensively examined Tom's present movement patterns and pinpointed areas for development. They concentrated on particular elements including body alignment, release technique, and footwork. Coach Emily gave Tom detailed directions, demonstrated the appropriate motions, and offered criticism to help him make the necessary corrections. Tom gradually altered his movement patterns under the coach's direction, developed his abilities, and saw a noticeable improvement in his total performance.

Exploring The Rationale, Goals, And Obstacles Of Changing Automatized Movement Patterns

Reasons necessitating the modification of automatized movement patterns

The desire to alter an existing movement pattern might be brought on by a variety of circumstances. According to Newell's constraint-led method, a change in performance conditions is one common cause. These conditions may be present in the activity being performed, the person doing the movement, or the environment. The possibilities for action are shaped by constraints, which can also have a positive or negative impact on how movement patterns emerge. Timing, body angles, and other taught abilities may need to be adjusted as a result of task-related changes. Physical modifications or limits brought on by developmental processes or injuries might lead to individual differences. The environment includes all exterior factors, such as the terrain, the climate, or the make-up of the team. Any change in these variables may make the prior motor behavior less useful or appropriate, necessitating a change in the movement pattern.

For bowlers, sustaining or improving performance requires the capacity to adjust to new circumstances. It could be necessary to learn a new technique again or modify an existing one to better suit the altered situation. Finding the precise modifications needed and making them while maintaining the technique's core principles is the difficult part. It is significant to emphasize that altering a long-established movement pattern requires patience and persistence throughout a challenging and time-consuming procedure. However, bowlers may successfully adjust to new performance conditions and improve their overall performance with the right direction and instruction.

Additionally, it may be necessary to modify current motor abilities even in the absence of modifications to the performance environment. For instance, a bowler who uses a poor technique could nonetheless succeed. However, the technique may prove constricting as the bowler advances to higher skill levels or age groups, or when competing under pressure. A shift in approach may be useful in such circumstances.

Furthermore, as noted by Walter and Swinnen (1994), the appearance of automatized errors can be problematic and can solidify as parts of a person's motor repertoire. These mistakes, sometimes known as "bad habits," emerge when a bowler can effectively carry out the movement by including compensating behaviors that lessen the error's immediate effects. Such automated mistakes, however, can impair performance and raise the danger of damage. Coaches should therefore be aware of these fault kinds and take action as soon as possible to stop them in order to avoid long-term effects that the bowler might not be aware of.

Hypothetical Examples

Example of a Bowler: John, an expert bowler, realized that his game was getting worse under specific circumstances. Despite years of training, he found it difficult to adjust to shifting lane circumstances and retain his consistency. He sought the advice of an experienced coach who examined his technique and pointed out potential areas for development. He collaborated to change John's automated movement pattern to better fit the altered performance requirements. John was assisted by the coach in fine-tuning his timing, body angles, and other technical elements. John successfully altered his movement style via persistent practice, which enabled him to adjust to various situations and improve his overall performance on the lanes.

Example of a Tenpin Coach: Emma, a young bowler under Coach Megan, experienced some unintentional automatized faults in her movement pattern. Despite her skill, Emma's performance was being hampered by these mistakes. Coach Megan saw the value of getting involved early to stop these mistakes from becoming set habits. Through targeted drills and feedback, she worked with Emma to identify the specific issues and fix them. The necessity of performing the right movements without resorting to compensatory actions was underlined by Coach Megan. Emma was able to successfully remove the automatized faults from her movement pattern through constant practice and the coach's direction, which increased her performance and decreased the chance of injury.

Objectives underlying the need for change

If existing movement patterns are to be changed, a key consideration is whether the new technique should completely replace the old one or if both motor programs can coexist in the future. These processes are referred to as shift (replacement) and bifurcation (coexistence) by Carson and Collins (2011). When the original movement pattern is no longer useful (which frequently occurs when changing a method or correcting an error), replacement is desirable. Keeping the initial movement pattern can be useful in circumstances where limits or conditions temporarily change.

During practice, a player can decide to try out a different release method, such as switching to a backhand release from the standard forward release. He may choose to switch to the new method and abandon his old release in favor of the backhand release if He discovers that it increases his accuracy and ball speed. He might decide to keep his previous release and employ the new approach solely in specific circumstances, such as when confronted with a particular lane condition if He is not consistently effective with it. As a result, both the old and new procedures would coexist in his motor repertoire as He used the technique in a bifurcation process.

What happens neurologically and psychologically to the bowler

The process of changing automated movement patterns in bowling involves intricate neurological and psychological adjustments. Here's a breakdown of the key aspects:

Neurological Changes:

Neurological adaptations during the process of altering automated movement patterns in bowling are intricately linked to synaptic plasticity, motor cortex activation, and muscle memory rewiring. Firstly, the phenomenon of synaptic plasticity comes to the forefront, whereby modifying movement patterns serves as a catalyst for the brain's remarkable ability to undergo synaptic changes. This process involves the formation of new neural connections and the strengthening of existing ones, a dynamic response to the evolving demands imposed by the updated motor skills. As bowlers engage in the intentional reshaping of their techniques, synaptic plasticity enables the brain to intricately adapt, facilitating the establishment of more efficient neural pathways.

Secondly, the motor cortex, a critical hub responsible for voluntary muscle control, undergoes significant shifts in activation patterns during the adjustment of movement patterns. The meticulous modifications to elements such as grip, stance, and other facets necessitate precise signals from the motor cortex. This heightened cortical involvement reflects the intricate coordination required to execute the refined motor skills. The adaptability of the motor cortex showcases the brain's ability to orchestrate and fine-tune voluntary movements in response to the nuanced adjustments demanded by the altered bowling techniques.

Thirdly, the concept of muscle memory rewiring takes center stage in the neurological transformations associated with changing movement patterns. Muscle memory, the repository of automated movement patterns, undergoes rewiring as a result of repetitive practice. The neural connections linked to the newly adopted techniques are reinforced through this iterative process, solidifying the integration of the updated motor skills into the bowler's muscle memory. The rewiring of muscle memory is a testament to the brain's capacity for plasticity and adaptation, as it systematically incorporates the learned adjustments into the automated repertoire of motor skills.

Psychological Changes:

Psychological Changes in the context of altering automated movement patterns in bowling encompass a multifaceted landscape that significantly influences both cognitive and emotional aspects of a bowler's performance. Initially, when bowlers embark on adapting to new movement patterns, they encounter an increased cognitive load. This surge in mental effort stems from the need to consciously focus on implementing the changes, demanding heightened attention to the nuances of the adjusted techniques. This cognitive load, while targeted at the immediate alterations, may also have ripple effects on other facets of performance, requiring a comprehensive recalibration of mental processes.

The process of learning new movement patterns introduces a dynamic interplay of frustration and patience. As bowlers strive to incorporate unfamiliar techniques, disruptions in proficiency can lead to frustration. The challenge lies in maintaining composure and resilience during this phase, making patience a crucial virtue. Breaking old habits and adjusting ingrained muscle memory is inherently challenging, necessitating a sustained and patient approach to navigate through the complexities of skill transformation.

Confidence, a cornerstone of athletic performance, undergoes fluctuations during the adaptation process. Successes in implementing the new techniques provide boosts to confidence levels, validating the efforts made. Conversely, setbacks may cast doubts on the efficacy of the changes, requiring bowlers to navigate uncertainties with a resilient mindset. The journey of overcoming these challenges contributes significantly to the development of mental resilience, forging a more robust mental game.

Adapting to new movement patterns not only demands technical adjustments but also fosters mental adaptability and resilience. Bowlers learn to navigate errors as integral parts of the learning process, embracing a mindset of continuous improvement. This adaptive resilience contributes to a holistic development of the bowler's mental fortitude, enhancing their ability to face challenges with poise and determination.

The incorporation of new techniques into one's bowling repertoire is intricately linked with self-efficacy, the belief in one's ability to successfully adapt. Successfully implementing and executing these changes enhances a bowler's self-efficacy, fostering a positive influence on overall psychological well-being. This mental fortification becomes a cornerstone for sustained motivation and dedication to the arduous process of skill enhancement.

Changing movement patterns necessitates heightened focus and concentration from bowlers. The cognitive demands of adjusting techniques require sustained mental clarity amidst the technical intricacies. This enhanced focus positively impacts overall game awareness, sharpening the bowler's ability to make informed decisions and execute precise maneuvers on the lanes.

Monitoring and Assessment:

The meticulous monitoring and assessment of bowlers undergoing the transformation of automated movement patterns encompass a comprehensive range of strategies aimed at gauging performance, technical implementation, and psychological well-being. These methods play a crucial role in offering valuable insights into the effectiveness of the adaptation process and guiding further refinement.

Firstly, performance metrics serve as quantitative indicators of progress. Tracking scoring averages, spare conversion rates, and the consistency in executing modified techniques provides tangible data on the impact of the altered movement patterns on overall game performance. These metrics offer a clear picture of the direct correlations between skill adaptation and on-lane success, guiding the adjustment process with empirical evidence.

Secondly, video analysis emerges as a powerful tool for a nuanced understanding of the implementation of new movement patterns. Regularly analyzing videos allows for a visual assessment of the techniques in action. Side-by-side comparisons between the previous and modified patterns facilitate a comprehensive evaluation, offering a detailed perspective on the nuances of the adjustments. This visual feedback aids both bowlers and coaches in identifying specific areas for improvement and fine-tuning.

Thirdly, coaching feedback forms an integral part of the assessment process. Frequent and constructive feedback from coaches provides invaluable insights into the technical aspects of the adapted movement patterns. Coaches, with their expertise, can offer corrections, encouragement, and strategic guidance, fostering a collaborative environment that supports the bowlers throughout the adaptation journey. This real-time feedback loop is essential for refining the techniques and ensuring a continuous and adaptive learning process.

Lastly, incorporating psychological assessments into the monitoring framework adds a layer of understanding regarding the mental aspects of skill adaptation. Periodic assessments gauge factors such as mental resilience, confidence levels, and adaptability to change. These assessments provide a holistic view of the psychological impact of the adaptation process, aiding in tailoring interventions to support the bowler's mental well-being. Understanding the psychological dimensions ensures a more balanced and resilient approach to the challenges posed by the transformative journey.

In conclusion, the process of changing automated movement patterns involves a complex interplay of neurological and psychological factors. Effective monitoring and assessment strategies are crucial for understanding progress and ensuring a balanced approach to skill enhancement.

INTERVENTION APPROACHES - ALTERING AUTOMATIZED MOVEMENT PATTERNS

As far as we know, four approaches have been put forth to aid in and direct the process of altering automatized movement patterns. These methods consist of:

Approach 1- The Method Of Amplification Of Error (Mae):

MAE is a motor learning strategy that focuses on internal feedback mechanisms in an effort to improve a person's capacity for correct movement self-detection. Coaches can direct the bowler in amplifying the error and detecting the necessary alterations in motor activity by identifying the main error in the movement pattern that directly influences the outcome. Subpar bowling methods and automated mistakes can be addressed with this recurrent movement pattern correction process.

The Method of Amplification of Error (MAE) has been extensively studied for its efficacy in a variety of motor learning and sporting contexts. For instance, Milanese et al. (2016) examined the effectiveness of MAE, direct verbal teaching, and a control group in enhancing golfers' swings at various ability levels. The findings showed that both MAE and direct verbal instruction significantly improved performance metrics, although MAE had steeper learning curves and more pronounced overall improvements. However, it's crucial for instructors and bowlers to carefully examine any hazards posed by amplifying errors, including the potential for injuries. To determine the viability and dependability of this strategy in the specific context of bowling, more research is required.

Amplification of Error in Bowling

A practical example of how the Method of Amplification of Error (MAE) can be applied to bowling to enhance a bowler's performance.

Scenario: *Imagine a bowler who consistently struggles with maintaining a straight delivery path. His ball often veers off course, leading to inconsistent results and lower scores. The primary error in this case is the deviation from the desired straight path, which significantly affects the outcome of each throw.*

Application of MAE:

Identifying the Error: *The coach carefully observes the bowler's technique and identifies the main error, which is the deviation from the straight path. This is the critical movement pattern that requires correction to improve the bowler's performance.*

Amplification of Error: With the error pinpointed, the coach utilizes the MAE strategy. He instructs the bowler to deliberately exaggerate this error during practice sessions. This means that the bowler intentionally makes his shots veer even further from the desired straight path.

Immediate Self-Detection: As the bowler amplifies the error, He becomes acutely aware of the deviations in his shots. This heightened self-detection allows him to recognize the specific moments and movements that lead to the error.

Motor Activity Adjustment: With each practice session, the bowler focuses on making corrections to his motor activity. He experiments with different adjustments to his stance, approach, release, or follow-through to bring the ball closer to the desired straight path.

Progress and Results: Over time, through consistent practice using the MAE approach, the bowler experiences significant improvements in his accuracy and consistency. He gradually refines his technique and develops a heightened sense of control over his shots. The amplified error serves as a powerful learning tool, enabling the bowler to make precise adjustments to his movements and achieve the desired straight delivery path.

Cautions and Considerations: While MAE has shown promise in improving motor skills, it's essential to approach this strategy with caution, just as Milanese et al. (2016) pointed out. Bowlers and coaches should be mindful of potential risks, such as overexertion or injury when deliberately amplifying errors. Therefore, ongoing research and evaluation are necessary to determine the suitability of MAE within the specific context of bowling.

Monitoring and assessment:

1. *Video Analysis:*
   - *Record the bowler's practice sessions and games.*
   - *Use video analysis tools to review the footage, paying close attention to the specific error identified in the MAE process (deviation from the straight delivery path).*
   - *Evaluate whether the bowler is consistently amplifying the error during practice sessions.*

2. *Error Measurement:*
   - *Implement a measurement system to quantify the deviation from the desired straight path. This could involve tracking the angle of deviation or the distance from the target.*
   - *Compare error measurements before and after the application of MAE to assess improvements over time.*

3. *Self-Reflection and Awareness:*
   - *Engage in regular communication with the bowler to understand their perception of the error and the effectiveness of the MAE process.*
   - *Encourage the bowler to keep a journal or log detailing their experiences and insights during practice sessions.*

4. *Consistency in Error Amplification:*
   - *Monitor if the bowler consistently amplifies the identified error during practice sessions. Inconsistencies may indicate a need for further clarification or adjustment in the application of MAE.*

5. *Performance Metrics:*
   - *Track key performance metrics such as accuracy, consistency, and overall scores.*
   - *Compare performance metrics before and after the implementation of MAE to assess improvements in the bowler's overall game.*

6. *Coaching Feedback:*
   - *Obtain feedback from the coach regarding the bowler's progress and the effectiveness of MAE.*
   - *The coach should assess whether the bowler is making appropriate motor activity adjustments and refining their technique as intended.*

7. *Physical Well-being:*

- *Monitor the bowler's physical condition to ensure that deliberate amplification of errors does not lead to overexertion or injury.*

- *If there are signs of overexertion or discomfort, adjustments to the intensity or frequency of MAE practice may be necessary.*

8. ***Long-Term Progression:***

- *Assess the bowler's long-term progression to determine if improvements in accuracy and consistency are sustained over time.*

- *Evaluate whether the bowler continues to refine their technique and maintain control over their shots.*

9. ***Adaptability and Transferability:***

- *Evaluate the bowler's ability to transfer the corrections made through MAE to actual game situations.*

- *Test the bowler's adaptability by introducing variations in lane conditions or target placements.*

Approach 2- The Old Way New Way Method:

OWNW is another method for error correction that was created by Lyndon (1989) has been used in a variety of contexts, such as sports and skill-based instruction. This approach specifically targets habit errors, which happen when improper execution becomes a routine or automatic behavior. The Old Way New Way technique, like MAE, puts the bowler's intentional concentration toward the fault.

The proactive interference problem is directly addressed by the Old Way New Way methodology. The existing habits and associated memory contents prevent the learning of new movement patterns when established movement patterns are changed. Performance frequently relies largely on signals, which causes people to return to the predetermined movement pattern that has been repeatedly performed. The Old Way New Way technique places a strong emphasis on the bowlers' knowledge of their faulty performance and their capacity to distinguish between correct and incorrect executions in order to settle this conflict and reduce proactive interference. The guidance of this procedure is greatly aided by coaches.

Three phases make up the intervention for the Old Way New Way. The bowler gains the ability to distinguish between the new and old versions of a movement during the practice phase, referring to the original as the "old way." Specific areas that need to be corrected are found by dividing the action into little pieces. During the mediation stage, bowlers contrast the old and new approaches numerous times while considering their similarities and differences. The person is told to perform this step numerous times because it is crucial for skill development. The newly learned approach is then performed, repeated, stabilized, and solidified through continuing training, mimicking other learning processes, in the final generalization and application phase.

Bowling players can successfully fix their movement patterns by using the Old Way New Way approach and the approach of Amplification of Error (MAE). These strategies offer coaches and athletes methodical and organized frameworks for dealing with subpar techniques, automated mistakes, and habitual movements. Bowlers can change their current movement patterns and improve their overall performance in the sport through focused practice, feedback, and increased self-awareness.

In order to implement the Old Way New Way approach, the coach and the bowler must work together. Together, they must navigate a complex process of identifying technical mistakes and creating a unique protocol for the intervention session. This session consists of a thorough set of four phases that have been painstakingly created to improve the bowler's physical and mental acuity in relation to both conventional and novel approaches. These steps help to gradually distinguish between the two methods while also giving plenty of opportunities to put the new strategy into practice and reinforce its adoption.

The bowler's self-reports provide a vital source of data during the training session, illuminating the gradual development of error awareness and the parallel growth of a profound comprehension of the proper movement. This increased awareness fosters the bowler's greater self-confidence while also igniting a flurry of enthusiasm. The large performance improvement, however, is the most important result. The Old Way New Way methodology successfully eliminates ingrained bad habits by acting as a catalyst for quick and long-lasting transformation.

An example in changing the Swing Shape of a player

Phase	Steps to Do	Tactics	Challenges	Duration
Preparation Phase	1. Learn to distinguish between the old and new ways of performing the swing shape. 2. Label the original version as the "old way". 3. Break down the action into its minimal units to identify the specific areas that require correction.	a. Observe and analyze videos of the bowler's swing shape to identify areas for improvement. b. Use mirrors to provide real-time feedback to the bowler during practice sessions.	Identifying and recognizing specific areas of the swing that need correction, breaking down the action into its minimal units	A few days to a week
Mediation Phase	1. Practice contrasting the old way with the new way by repeatedly switching between the two techniques. 2. Reflect on the similarities and differences between the old and new ways. 3. Repeat the process five times.	a. Use drills and exercises that isolate the specific areas requiring correction. b. Provide verbal feedback to the bowler to reinforce the correct technique.	Adapting to the new technique, reflecting on similarities and differences between the two techniques	One to two weeks
Generalization and Application Phase	1. Practice, repeat, stabilize, and consolidate the newly learned technique through continued practice. 2. Gradually increase the difficulty level of practice drills and exercises.	a. Provide positive reinforcement to the bowler for correct technique. b. Use video feedback to allow the bowler to see their progress over time.	Consolidating the new technique in actual gameplay situations	Several weeks to months

Table 34 – An example of changing swing shape of a player using Old Way / New Way approach

Example of Old Way/ New Way plan for a bowler:

Old Way New Way Method Practical Plan for Correcting Player's Swing Shape

Phase 1: Preparation

Step 1: Technical analysis: *A thorough examination of the player's swing shape is conducted by the coach and player to pinpoint the precise areas that need improvement.*

Step 2: Labeling: *Participants refer to their standard swing shape as the "old way."*

Step 3: Breaking down the action: *To pinpoint the precise regions that need improvement, players break down their swing structure into its smallest components.*

Phase 2: Mediation

Step 4: Contrasting the old way with the new way: *By alternately using the two strategies and comparing their likenesses and dissimilarities, players learn to contrast their previous swing shape with the new swing shape.*

Step 5: Repetition: *The gamer must carry out this procedure at least five more times.*

Phase 3: Generalization and Application

Step 6: Practice and consolidation: *Identical to other learning techniques, repetition is used to repeatedly rehearse, maintain, and consolidate the newly taught swing shape.*

Step 7: Self-report and performance assessment: *In order to track their development, players submit self-reports following each training session and performance evaluations following each competition.*

Monitoring and Assessment:

1. **Video Analysis:**
   - *Record the player's swings during practice sessions and games.*
   - *Use video analysis tools to compare the "old way" and "new way" swings.*
   - *Assess whether the player is successfully implementing the changes in their swing shape.*

2. **Technical Analysis:**
   - *Regularly conduct technical analyses to evaluate the player's swing shape.*
   - *Compare the initial analysis (before implementing the "New Way") with subsequent analyses to identify improvements and areas that still need attention.*

3. **Contrast and Comparison:**

- *During practice sessions, have the player deliberately switch between the "old way" and "new way."*
- *Observe and document the differences in performance, focusing on how well the player can transition between the two swing shapes.*

4. ***Repetition and Consistency:***
   - *Monitor the player's ability to consistently repeat the "new way" swing.*
   - *Track the number of repetitions performed during practice sessions and assess the player's ability to maintain the desired changes over time.*

5. ***Self-Reports:***
   - *Implement a self-reporting system where players document their experiences and perceptions after each training session.*
   - *Use the self-reports to gain insights into the player's understanding of the changes, any challenges faced, and areas where they feel progress has been made.*

6. ***Performance Assessments:***
   - *Conduct regular performance assessments during competitions.*
   - *Compare performance data before and after implementing the "New Way" to measure improvements in actual game situations.*

7. ***Feedback Loop:***
   - *Establish a feedback loop between the player and the coach.*
   - *Encourage open communication for the player to express any difficulties or successes in implementing the changes to their swing shape.*

8. ***Long-Term Progression:***
   - *Evaluate the player's long-term progression by comparing swing shapes over an extended period.*
   - *Assess whether the improvements are sustained and whether any additional adjustments or refinements are needed.*

9. ***Adaptability in Competition:***
   - *Assess the player's ability to apply the "new way" in various competitive scenarios.*
   - *Introduce pressure situations during practice to simulate game conditions and evaluate how well the player adapts their swing shape.*

10. ***Performance Metrics:***
    - *Track specific performance metrics related to accuracy, consistency, and overall scores.*
    - *Use these metrics to measure the impact of the swing shape changes on the player's overall bowling performance.*

Approach 3 - The Five-A Approach

Understanding the two areas of technical change, as outlined by Carson and Collins (2011), is crucial for improving a player's competency. Regaining requires correcting an incorrect or suboptimal approach, frequently by going back to an earlier level of learning, while refinement involves acquiring a unique technique. There are two ways to change a previously learned technique: either build a new movement pattern (bifurcation) or shift gradually from the old to the new. The researchers found that while bifurcation is more durable over time, the shift may produce better initial accuracy.

The Five-A strategy was developed by Carson and Collins (2016) to control the process of change in an established motor skill. To do this, bowlers must first recognize the need for change and distinguish between the intended new technique and the current one (Analysis). The next step is for them to become conscious of their existing movement pattern (Awareness) and adjust the necessary parts of their current technique (Adjustment). Finally, for the development of resilient and independent motor skills (Assurance), bowlers must integrate the modified elements (Automation).

PHASE	CONTENT
1) ANALYSIS	For bowlers, the analysis phase involves identifying the specific aspect of their current technique that needs to be changed. For example, it could be the release of the ball or the angle of approach. The bowler's intention to change and improve in that particular area is also secured during this phase.
2) AWARENESS	In the awareness phase, bowlers focus on de-automating the erroneous or to-be-adjusted technique. They consciously bring their attention to the specific movement pattern that needs adjustment. For example, they may become aware of their incorrect arm swing or foot placement during the approach.
3) ADJUSTMENT	During the adjustment phase, bowlers make modifications to the erroneous or to-be-adjusted technique. They work on correcting the identified issues and improving their skill. For instance, they may adjust their grip on the ball or work on maintaining a more consistent release.
4) (RE)AUTOMATION	In the (re)automation phase, bowlers focus on internalizing the changed aspects of their technique. They practice the modified technique repeatedly until it becomes automatic and ingrained in their muscle memory. This ensures consistent execution of the corrected technique.
5) ASSURANCE	The assurance phase aims to promote the development of automaticity even under pressure conditions such as competition. Bowlers practice their corrected technique in various competitive situations, learning to execute it confidently and effectively when faced with challenging circumstances. They build assurance in their ability to perform at their best under pressure.

Table 35 – The Five-A Model according to Carson and Collins (2016) on Bowling

Below example of how the Five-A method could be applied to correct footwork in a bowler:

Analysis: *This analysis looks at the issue with the existing footwork pattern. To pinpoint the bowler's footwork faults, video analysis is used. The data can, for instance, show that the bowler is not receiving enough slides, which might affect his accuracy and power.*

Awareness: *To demonstrate the kinesthetic differences between proper and improper stepping patterns, the bowler is given instructions. While the coach offers direction and comments, the bowler is encouraged to test out various strategies.*

Adjustment: *To achieve the necessary technical change, the bowler trains his mental abilities. For instance, the bowler can utilize visualization and self-talk strategies to visualize oneself effectively executing the right footwork pattern. To assist the bowler in improving his technique, the coach may also offer criticism through the use of video analysis or other techniques.*

(Re)Automation: *The bowler eventually incorporates the new footwork pattern into his stroke. The bowler steadily increases the number of repetitions after introducing the new pattern into practice sessions. The visualization script includes this procedure to make the bowler more at ease with the shift.*

Assurance: *To increase self-assurance and act as pre-event training, the bowler exhibits the new footwork pattern during competition simulations. To assist the bowler feel and readiness in his new technique, the coach offers comments and encouragement. In order to assess development and pinpoint any areas that require additional improvement, follow-up examinations are performed.*

The bowler can significantly increase his footwork and improve his entire game performance by employing this technique.

Monitoring and Assessment:

1. **Analysis:**

   - **Video Analysis:** *Regularly record the bowler's footwork during practice sessions and games. Use video analysis tools to identify specific faults and measure relevant metrics.*

- **Data Tracking:** *Quantify key parameters such as the number of slides, accuracy, and power. Keep a record of this data for comparison over time.*

2. **Awareness:**

   - **Observation and Feedback:** *Observe the bowler during practice to ensure they are applying the awareness gained from instructional methods. Provide immediate feedback on their recognition and correction of footwork issues.*

   - **Quiz and Discussion:** *Engage in discussions with the bowler to assess their understanding of kinesthetic differences. Quiz them on proper footwork techniques to reinforce their knowledge.*

3. **Adjustment:**

   - **Mental Training Evaluation:** *Assess the effectiveness of mental training techniques (visualization, self-talk) by engaging in conversations with the bowler. Evaluate their ability to visualize and self-talk during practice sessions.*

   - **Feedback Loop:** *Provide ongoing feedback on the bowler's progress. Use video analysis to highlight areas for improvement and guide mental adjustments.*

4. **(Re)Automation:**

   - **Repetition Monitoring:** *Track the number of repetitions performed with the new footwork pattern during practice sessions. Ensure that the bowler is gradually increasing the volume of practice while maintaining accuracy.*

   - **Comfort Assessment:** *Assess the bowler's comfort level with the corrected footwork. Ask for feedback on any challenges faced during the (re)automation process.*

5. **Assurance:**

   - **Simulation Evaluation:** *Conduct simulated competitive scenarios and evaluate the bowler's application of the new footwork pattern under pressure. Provide feedback on their performance and identify areas for improvement.*

   - **Confidence Check:** *Gauge the bowler's confidence in their ability to apply the corrected footwork in actual game situations.*

6. **Follow-up Examinations:**

   - **Regular Check-ins:** *Schedule follow-up examinations at predetermined intervals to assess continued development. Use video analysis and quantitative data to measure progress.*

   - **Feedback Sessions:** *Encourage the bowler to share their experiences and insights during follow-up examinations. Use their feedback to make any necessary adjustments to the training plan.*

7. **Overall Game Performance:**

   - **Performance Metrics:** *Continuously track performance metrics such as accuracy, consistency, and scores during actual games.*

   - **Comparison Analysis:** *Compare the bowler's performance before and after implementing the Five-A method to identify improvements and areas that may still need attention.*

8. *Feedback Loop:*

   - *Open Communication:* *Maintain an open and transparent communication channel with the bowler. Encourage them to share thoughts, concerns, and feedback on the effectiveness of the Five-A method.*

   - *Collaborative Problem-Solving:* *Work collaboratively with the bowler to address any challenges or obstacles encountered during the correction process.*

Stage	Description	Activities	Tools/Resources	Expected Outcomes
Analysis	Identify the problem and its impact on the bowler's game.	Observe and analyze the bowler's footwork during play.	Video recording equipment, notebook, pen/pencil	A clear understanding of the current movement pattern, and areas of improvement identified.
Awareness	Develop an awareness of proper footwork and the kinaesthetic differences between correct and incorrect movements.	Demonstrate proper footwork technique, have the bowler practice different footwork techniques, and provide feedback.	Cones, markers, video recording equipment, notebook, pen/pencil	The bowler can accurately identify the difference between correct and incorrect footwork, and increased awareness of body position during movement.
Adjustment	Develop mental skills to reinforce the new movement pattern.	Use visualization and mental imagery techniques to reinforce the new movement pattern, have the bowler practice the new footwork technique, and provide feedback.	Audio recording equipment, visualization prompts, notebook, pen/pencil	Improved confidence, comfort, and consistency in the new footwork technique.
(Re)Auto-mation	Gradually increase the difficulty of the drill, working towards the game situation.	Gradually increase the speed and complexity of the footwork drill, simulate game situations, and provide feedback.	Cones, markers, video recording equipment, notebook, pen/pencil	The bowler's new footwork technique is gradually becoming automatic, and it can be applied in game situations.
Assurance	Provide opportunities for the bowler to practice the new footwork technique under pressure.	Create game-like situations where the bowler can practice the new footwork technique under pressure, provide feedback, and monitor performance.	Video recording equipment, simulation equipment, notebook, pen/pencil	The bowler has gained confidence in the new footwork technique, can apply it in game situations, and achieves improved performance.

Table 36 – The Five-A Model monitoring and assessment of a bowler

Approach 4 - Directed Forgetting: An Effective Approach For Skill Correction In Bowling

Sports performance is greatly improved by skill correction, especially in bowling. A useful strategy for skill improvement is provided by the method of directed forgetting, which is based on the value of precise memory retrieval. Movements may be unsuccessfully carried out due to interference, which happens when conflicting memory contents make retrieval or encoding difficult. Directed Forgetting instructs participants to purposefully forget previously learned topics in order to reduce distraction.

Although Directed Forgetting has been thoroughly researched in verbal learning situations, it has received very little attention when applied to motor activities. Tempel and Frings' (2016) recent research, however, has shown its effectiveness in motor sequence tasks, particularly in lowering interference for recently acquired material. Notably, forgetting deliberate acts can be more difficult than forgetting word information. Directed Forgetting can be used to reduce distraction and promote performance improvement in skill correction interventions for bowlers. This may entail encouraging bowlers to give up their old movement patterns and focus on learning new ones in order to reduce the possibility of conflict between the old and new techniques.

Example of how Directed Forgetting can be used in skill correction for a bowler who needs to make a major timing change:

Analysis: The bowler's current timing is analyzed, and it is determined that a major change is necessary for optimal performance.

Awareness: The bowler is taught to repeatedly practice his former timing while emphasizing the feeling and stance that go along with it. He is then told to repeatedly execute the new timing, emphasizing the kinaesthetic variations between the two timings.

Adjustment: The bowler is then told to put his old timing out of his mind and concentrate only on mastering the new timing. Visual cues and mental pictures are used to reinforce the new timing.

(Re)Automation: As the bowler gets used to the new time, the emphasis changes to gradually boost movement speed and intensity while keeping the timing accurate.

Assurance: To get the bowler ready for competition, competitive simulations are incorporated into the imaging script. Video and kinematic feedback are also provided to make sure the new time is being applied properly.

The bowler can eliminate interference from his old timing and concentrate completely on learning the new timing by employing Directed Forgetting in this manner, which can ultimately increase performance.

Monitoring and Assessment:

1. ***Baseline Analysis:***
   - ***Initial Performance Assessment:*** *Conduct a detailed analysis of the bowler's current timing and overall performance.*
   - ***Identify Necessity for Change:*** *Determine if a major timing change is necessary for optimal performance.*

2. ***Awareness:***
   - ***Practice Observations:*** *Monitor the bowler's practice sessions where they repeatedly practice their former timing and then execute the new timing.*
   - ***Feedback Sessions:*** *Engage in regular feedback sessions to assess the bowler's awareness of kinesthetic differences between the old and new timings.*

3. ***Adjustment:***
   - ***Mental Training Assessment:*** *Evaluate the effectiveness of directed forgetting in instructing the bowler to put the old timing out of their mind and focus on mastering the new timing.*
   - ***Use of Visual Cues:*** *Assess the bowler's response to visual cues and mental pictures used to reinforce the new timing.*

4. ***(Re)Automation:***
   - ***Progression Tracking:*** *Monitor the bowler's progression as they get used to the new timing. Track movement speed and intensity while keeping the timing accurate.*
   - ***Consistency Check:*** *Evaluate the consistency in applying the new timing across various practice sessions.*

5. ***Assurance:***
   - ***Competitive Simulations:*** *Assess the bowler's performance in competitive simulations that are incorporated into the imaging script.*
   - ***Feedback Analysis:*** *Use video and kinematic feedback to ensure the new timing is being applied properly during competitive simulations.*
   - ***Confidence Levels:*** *Gauge the bowler's confidence levels in applying the new timing during simulated competitions.*

6. ***Follow-up Examinations:***
   - ***Scheduled Check-ins:*** *Conduct regular follow-up examinations to assess continued development and identify any areas that may require additional attention.*
   - ***Feedback Loop:*** *Encourage the bowler to provide feedback on their experience with directed forgetting and its impact on skill correction.*

7. ***Overall Performance Metrics:***
   - ***Performance Metrics:*** *Continuously track overall performance metrics such as accuracy, consistency, and scores during actual games.*
   - ***Comparison Analysis:*** *Compare the bowler's performance before and after employing the Directed Forgetting approach to measure improvements.*

8. ***Research and Practicality:***
   - ***Literature Review:*** *Stay informed about any new research on the practicality and effectiveness of Directed Forgetting in sports, especially in motor sequence learning.*
   - ***Experimentation:*** *Consider conducting controlled experiments or case studies to assess the viability of directed forgetting as a complementary approach to other methods for changing movement patterns.*

9. ***Qualitative Assessment:***
   - ***Bowler's Perception:*** *Regularly inquire about the bowler's perception of the directed forgetting process. Ask about the ease or difficulty of putting the old timing out of their mind.*

10. ***Long-Term Impact:***
   - ***Sustainability:*** *Evaluate whether the changes in timing are sustained over the long term.*
   - ***Adaptability:*** *Assess the bowler's ability to adapt the directed forgetting approach to address other aspects of their game.*

At this time, there is not enough data to say with certainty whether Directed Forgetting helps to change automated complicated motor skills in sports. However, in light of the encouraging preliminary results in motor sequence learning, it is essential for researchers to look into the practicality of directed forgetting in sports and investigate whether it could act as a viable alternative or complementary approach to other methods for successfully changing previously learned movement patterns. When bowlers actively identify "bad habits" or mistakes while attempting to alter an automated movement pattern, directed forgetting may prove to be especially helpful.

The following table lists the benefits and drawbacks of four various methods for modifying automatized movement patterns for coaches and bowlers:

Approach	Advantage for Coaches	Advantage for Bowlers	Disadvantage for Coaches	Disadvantage for Bowlers
Method of Amplification of Error (MAE)	Provides immediate feedback and error detection.	Helps bowlers develop better movement patterns and technique.	Requires coaches to accurately identify and amplify errors.	May be challenging for bowlers to adapt to amplified errors initially.
Old Way New Way method	Allows coaches to break down the movement into simpler steps.	Helps bowlers understand and learn new movement patterns effectively.	May take time and patience for coaches to guide bowlers through the transition process.	Requires bowlers to unlearn old habits and adjust to new movement patterns.
Five-A Approach	Provides a systematic framework for skill modification.	Helps bowlers develop a clear plan for changing their movement patterns.	Coaches need to thoroughly understand and apply the five steps in the approach.	Bowlers may find it difficult to execute all five steps consistently.
Directed Forgetting	Allows coaches to help bowlers forget automatized errors and focus on correct movements.	Helps bowlers eliminate ingrained errors and improve performance.	Coaches need to effectively guide bowlers in forgetting the automatized errors.	Bowlers may struggle to let go of familiar movement patterns and embrace the new ones.

Table 37 – list of benefits and drawbacks of four various methods for modifying automatized movement patterns for coaches and bowlers.

More research is needed to better understand how to alter automated movement patterns, and instructors and bowlers alike would benefit from evidence-based recommendations to help them adapt their techniques and improve their game. Although the Five-A Method, the Old Way New Way approach, and the Method of Amplification of Error have shown promising applications in sports, more randomized controlled research is required to evaluate the validity, reliability, and generalizability of each methodology. Nevertheless, for practitioners, such as coaches, instructors, and bowlers who seek or confront the task of altering programmed movement patterns, all three approaches provide helpful inspiration, direction, and a strong basis.

The Psychological Struggle With Old And New Habits In Competitions

Entering a crucial competition, a bowler finds themselves at a crossroads, grappling with the decision of whether to adhere to the newly adopted movement patterns or fall back on the familiar territory of their old habits. This dilemma is not just a physical challenge but a psychological conundrum, exposing the intricate relationship between trust, belief, and performance on the bowling lanes.

The transition from well-established movement patterns to new, refined techniques is a journey fraught with uncertainties. As the bowler steps into the competitive arena, the weight of this decision becomes palpable. The allure of familiarity, the comfort of knowing how one will perform with the old habits, tugs at the bowler's resolve to embrace change. On the other hand, the promise of enhanced performance and the potential for greater success beckons from the realm of the newly adopted patterns.

In such a situation, trust emerges as a linchpin. Trust in the coaching process, trust in the hours of deliberate practice, and perhaps most importantly, trust in oneself. The bowler must grapple with questions that extend beyond the technical nuances of movement patterns. Can they trust that the new techniques will hold up under the pressure of competition? Can they trust that the hours of practice will translate into a seamless performance when it matters the most?

The bowler's internal dialogue becomes a battleground of conflicting thoughts. The known, the comfort of the old habits, whispers promises of predictability. It says, "You've been here before; you know how it goes." Yet, the unknown, the uncharted territory of the new patterns, speaks of growth and potential. It says, "This is your chance to transcend, to reach new heights."

In this mental tug-of-war, the role of the coach becomes pivotal. Coaches are not just instructors; they are mentors, guides navigating the bowler through uncharted waters. The coach's ability to instill confidence, to reinforce the belief that the adopted changes are not just experimental but purposeful, is paramount. It's a delicate dance of encouragement and assurance, assuring the bowler that the journey of change, though challenging, is a path toward improvement and success.

The bowler, amidst the cacophony of doubt and certainty, must also confront the external expectations – the expectations of teammates, fans, and perhaps even their own past performances. The fear of judgment, the fear of failure, looms large. The decision to stick with the new patterns is not merely a technical choice; it's a declaration of belief, a declaration that the process of transformation is valid, and that the potential for success lies in embracing the unknown.

There's a paradoxical beauty in this struggle. It's a testament to the complexity of the human mind and the intricate nature of athletic performance. The bowler, in this crucible of decision-making, confronts not just the physical demands of the sport but the vulnerability that comes with change. It's a vulnerable space where the bowler confronts their own insecurities, their fear of the unfamiliar, and their desire for validation.

Is there a quick solution to this dilemma? Unfortunately, the nature of such decisions resists quick fixes. It's a process that requires reflection, communication, and a deep understanding of the individual athlete's psyche. However, there are strategies to navigate this juncture more effectively.

Firstly, open communication between the bowler and the coach is essential. The coach must create an environment where the bowler feels comfortable expressing their concerns, doubts, and fears. Honest conversations about the pros and cons of each choice can help clarify the path forward.

THE TECHNICAL MASTERY OF BOWLING PROGRESSION

Secondly, simulations and mock competitions during practice sessions can provide a bridge between the comfort of routine and the demands of competition. These simulated scenarios allow the bowler to test the new patterns under conditions that mimic the pressure of a real competition, fostering a sense of readiness and familiarity.

Additionally, mental preparedness techniques, such as visualization and positive self-talk, can equip the bowler with the tools to manage the psychological challenges of decision-making during competitions. Visualization, in particular, allows the bowler to mentally rehearse success with the new patterns, instilling a sense of confidence and familiarity.

Ultimately, the decision to stick with the new patterns or revert to old habits is a deeply personal one. It requires a delicate balance of trust in the coaching process, belief in one's capabilities, and the courage to confront the unknown. The bowler stands at the intersection of tradition and evolution, where the past meets the future, and the decision made reverberates not only through the competition but through the broader journey of skill development and personal growth. In the end, the bowler's ability to navigate this pivotal moment lies in their resilience, self-awareness, and the unwavering belief that, whether old or new, their chosen path is a step towards mastery and excellence in the sport of bowling.

Hypothetical Examples of sustain Flow state with new pattern during competition

As Sarah engages in the championship, she encounters an additional layer of complexity: the elusive flow state. The first few frames bring a palpable struggle as she grapples with the integration of her modified techniques. The familiarity of her old habits, coupled with the pressure of the competition, momentarily disrupts the flow state she seeks.

As the championship progresses, Sarah's adaptability shines through. Through intentional breathing, refocusing rituals, and adaptive mindfulness, she gradually finds her rhythm. The coach's collaborative approach becomes a catalyst for identifying personalized techniques to reignite the flow state.

In a pivotal moment, Sarah, fully immersed in the competition, seamlessly transitions into the flow state. The rhythmic dance of her movements aligns with the synchronicity of her thoughts, creating a harmonious fusion of skill and mindset. The struggle transforms into a triumph, and Sarah bowls with a sense of effortlessness and precision.

Overcoming the Flow State Challenge:

1. ***Awareness and Acceptance:***

    - ***Action:*** *Acknowledge the initial struggle to find the flow state, recognizing it as a natural part of the adaptation process.*

    - ***Purpose:*** *This awareness allows Sarah to accept the temporary disruption, preventing frustration and maintaining a positive mindset.*

    - ***Trusting the New Habit:*** *Internal Dialogue: "It's okay to face challenges initially. This is part of the*

The Inspiring Journey Of Diandra: Specialization In Bowling

My journey towards greatness demanded sacrifices from an early age. While other kids my age enjoyed parties and football games, my evenings were consumed by late-night practice sessions. From 9:30 p.m. until midnight, I honed my skills, relentlessly striving for perfection. Looking back now as a mother, I realize how extraordinary it was for my parents to support my passion and allow me to pursue my dreams. But my determination was unwavering. After coming home from school, I would nap and complete my homework, eagerly waiting for my father to return from work so we could have dinner together before heading off to practice. Those late-night practices became my norm, and the sacrifices continued to pile up. I missed out on social events and typical teenage experiences, fully aware that greatness demanded unwavering dedication. It was during this time that my older sister, Kassy, emerged as a serious bowler. Seeing her dedication and success fueled my competitive spirit even more. I realized that if I wanted to win, I had to match her commitment and push myself further. At the age of 12, I began working with Coach Dick Tucker, who became my mentor until I left for college in 1998. Many expected me to follow in my sister's footsteps and attend Wichita State University, a collegiate bowling powerhouse. However, I made a tough decision to forge my own path and establish my own identity as "Diandra," not just "Kassy's little sister." This decision marked a turning point in my life. People barely knew my name then; I was merely the shadow of my sister. Opting for the University of Nebraska surprised everyone. But looking back, it was the best decision I could have made.

journey towards improvement. I trust that adapting to the new techniques is a process, and challenges are stepping stones to success."

2. **Breathing Techniques:**

   - **Action:** *Incorporate intentional breathing exercises between shots, focusing on deep and rhythmic breaths.*

   - **Purpose:** *Controlled breathing promotes relaxation, helping Sarah manage the heightened stress of competition and facilitating a smoother transition into the flow state.*

   - **Trusting the New Habit:** *Internal Dialogue: "Deep breaths. This is my anchor. It's not just about the breath; it's a cue that I'm in control. I trust that this deliberate breathing aligns with the new techniques and sets the stage for my optimal performance."*

3. **Refocusing Rituals:**

   - **Action:** *Develop refocusing rituals, such as a specific visualization or a brief mantra, to re-center attention during challenging moments.*

   - **Purpose:** *These rituals serve as anchors, redirecting Sarah's focus back to the present moment and fostering the conditions for the flow state to reemerge.*

   - **Trusting the New Habit:** *Internal Dialogue: "Visualize the perfect shot. 'Smooth and steady.' This mantra brings me back. These rituals are my reminders that the new techniques are not just physical; they are ingrained in my mindset."*

4. **Adaptive Mindfulness:**

   - **Action:** *Adapt mindfulness techniques to be dynamic, incorporating them seamlessly into the bowling routine.*

   - **Purpose:** *By maintaining mindfulness in motion, ensure a continuous state of awareness, allowing Sarah to navigate challenges while staying attuned to the rhythmic flow of the competition.*

   - **Trusting the New Habit:** *Internal Dialogue: "Stay present. Mindfulness is not a pause; it's a continuous flow. This constant awareness aligns perfectly with the new techniques. I trust that this dynamic mindfulness is enhancing my adaptability."*

5. **Coach Collaboration:**

   - **Action:** *Collaborate closely with the coach during the competition, discussing the nuances of the flow state and seeking guidance on reestablishing it.*

   - **Purpose:** *The coach's insights provide tailored strategies for Sarah to reconnect with the flow state, ensuring that she taps into her optimal performance zone.*

   - **Trusting the New Habit:** *Internal Dialogue: "Communicate with the coach. They understand the intricacies. Their guidance is a valuable resource. By involving them, I'm reaffirming my trust in the process. Together, we navigate the journey of integrating these new techniques successfully."*

COACHING IN BOWLING

A definition of a complete coach should encompass the following:

Physical Skill Development	Mental Skill Development	Fitness & Strength Development	Tactical Knowledge	Knowledge of Equipment Considerations	Program Development
From beginner to elite	*Life skill development*	*Basic understanding of fitness/ strength principals*	*Develop an understanding of competition skills*	*Grip assessment capabilities*	*Designing a bowler development plan*
Acquisition of coaching drills	*Competition skill development*	*Analyzing the requirements specific to bowling*	*Lane pattern analysis*	*An understanding of equipment terms & nomenclature*	*Designing a team development plan*
Acquiring the ability to identify errors	*Mental coping strategies*	*Energy systems*	*Understanding ball shape requirements*	*Education in ball drilling fundamentals*	*Designing a training camp*
Acquisition of error correction windows	*Mental tool acquisition*	*Energy sources*	*Reading a lane expertise*	*An understanding of generic ball dynamic considerations*	*Designing and understanding the principals of a youth development program*
	Mental tool application	*Nutrition requirements prior to and during competition*	*Mapping a lane expertise*	*An ability to match up ball surface requirements*	*Designing a youth curriculum sequence*
	Avoiding mental traps	*Acknowledging the principles of a balanced diet to the bowlers' well-being*	*Application of equipment match-up*		*Design and implement competition plans including; peaking programs, simulation training & competition coping strategies.*
		Designing a bowler warm-up routine			*Designing & implementation of an overall country development plan*

Table 38 – A definition of a complete coach in a table

Reaching the coveted state of flow in bowling is a theoretical and psychological phenomenon that holds immense significance for bowlers seeking peak performance. This optimal state of consciousness, where individuals feel fully immersed and deeply focused in their activity, can be achieved through the quality of coaching and guidance provided. A skilled coach plays a vital role in creating an environment that nurtures a bowler's growth and minimizes concerns about technical errors. By offering expertise, constructive feedback, and tailored training plans, coaches enable bowlers to refine their skills and develop a solid foundation, instilling a sense of confidence and trust in their own capabilities. Moreover, a skilled coach understands the importance of addressing psychological aspects alongside technical proficiency, providing the necessary tools to help bowlers overcome mental obstacles and maintain focus under pressure. When bowlers receive exceptional coaching, they enter the flow state with a profound sense of freedom from worries about technical errors. The coach's guidance and expertise create a supportive atmosphere where bowlers can fully immerse themselves in the present moment, effortlessly adapting to the ever-changing dynamics of the game. This state of flow allows bowlers to tap into their full potential, unlocking their innate talent and experiencing the sheer joy of the sport.

Obtaining certification as a coach in the sport of bowling has unquestionably difficult standards that call for a high degree of knowledge and ability. However, it may be claimed that the aforementioned requirements contain a broader range of qualities as well, which are essential for a qualified national coach to continuously succeed. They are not just restricted to technical abilities. Although having strong physical skills is frequently connected with the title of coach, it is important to understand that developing such skills can be a lifelong endeavor because they are vital for seeing problems and coming up with workable solutions. As a result, these abilities are held in the greatest regard by the bowling community, which recognizes their importance in determining a bowler's advancement. Despite the fact that my goal is not to downplay the value or significance of these abilities, it is worthwhile to think about a different title that would be more appropriate: master instructor.

Choosing whether to serve as a competition coach or an instructor is one of the toughest choices a coach must make. When the development of various age groups is taken into account, this conundrum becomes much more difficult to solve. We are faced with decisions that primarily take into account our productivity and personal interests. When considering our interests, we must decide whether to support complex biomechanics of movement or complex physics guiding the bowling ball's metamorphosis as it travels down the lane. By determining whether we are interested in elements before or after the foul line, we can further define this interest. In the end, this choice affects our concentration and, as a result, the particular talents we should prioritize. As a result, we must decide whether to position ourselves primarily as coaches or instructors, each of which has its own implications and duties. The responsibility of an instructor includes emphasizing the educational component of bowling while concentrating on teaching bowlers new information and abilities. In this role, the instructor is charged with creating a profound awareness of the intricate biomechanics behind the movement or the intricate physics dictating the behavior of the ball. By exploring these topics, teachers provide bowlers with the underlying information and technical know-how they need to improve their game. The pedagogical aspect of teaching comprises a thorough strategy, catering to the mental growth and skill learning of bowlers at different levels.

Contrarily, a coach's responsibilities extend beyond academics to include a more all-encompassing approach to a bowler's growth. In addition to offering technical advice, coaches take on a multidimensional role, addressing the psychological and tactical factors that affect performance. A coach has an interest in the total development and well-being of the bowlers He is in charge of, developing their mental fortitude, sharpening their strategic reasoning, and cultivating a positive and encouraging training environment. Coaches are accountable for developing a close bond with their players, comprehending their unique needs and goals, and adjusting their instruction accordingly. Beyond the lanes, they also serve as mentors, motivators, and cultivators of a winning mindset.

Then what do the Coach's Capabilities Metrics look like?

1) Experience

Regardless of the degree of competence one has gained, the pursuit of knowledge and experience is a crucial component of coaching. Coaches in training must understand that their journey is a continual process marked by an unquenchable desire for information and a firm dedication to lifelong learning. Being a veritable storehouse of knowledge needs a deep comprehension of the philosophical foundations and psychological complexities of coaching. Experience is more than just the total number of years spent in the coaching industry. It includes a comprehensive understanding of bowling that takes into account its tactical, psychological, and technical aspects. Coaches must always work to expand their expertise while staying current with the most recent studies, innovations, and achievements in their profession. By constantly updating their methods and methodologies in response to new trends and best practices, coaches may stay at the cutting edge of their profession thanks to this never-ending quest for knowledge.

Additionally, coaching experience includes assimilating the knowledge and ideas of other coaches, academics, and industry professionals in addition to personal interactions and observations. The coach's grasp of various coaching philosophies and practices is widened through participating in meaningful conversation and collaboration with colleagues. This encourages a rich exchange of ideas and viewpoints. Coaches can benefit from a richness of collective knowledge by accepting collective wisdom and incorporating a variety of insights into their own coaching toolkit. The term "experience" in the context of coaching refers to more than just gaining technical know-how. It includes developing a profound psychological grasp of bowlers as well as the nuances of human behavior. Given that bowlers' psychological health has a significant impact on their performance on the lanes, coaches need to explore the areas of motivation, self-belief, resilience, and mental toughness. Coaches may effectively nurture and improve the mental states of their bowlers, facilitating optimal performance and general well-being, by having a thorough understanding of psychological principles and approaches.

The capacity to translate theoretical information into real-world applications is a key component of experience. Coaches must be able to modify their methods, interventions, and coaching styles to fit the particular requirements and traits of different bowlers. This necessitates having a thorough understanding of the various learning styles, personalities, and skill levels of bowlers and the ability to adapt coaching tactics accordingly. Coaches with experience can traverse the challenges of bowler development by using a specialized strategy to optimize each bowler's potential. Coaches must understand that experience is not a static concept. Instead, it is a dynamic and ever-evolving process that demands a dedication to introspection, self-reflection, and constant progress. Coaches should regularly examine their own coaching practices, find areas for improvement, and look for chances to further their professional careers. Coaches can actively seek out new challenges, welcome constructive criticism, and improve their coaching methods by adopting a growth mindset.

Hypothetical Examples

a) With more than 15 years of coaching experience, Coach Smith has worked with bowlers of all ages and abilities. Through years of actual play, he has gained a profound understanding of the technical elements, tactics, and nuances of the game. Based on his vast experience, he is able to accurately assess bowlers' performances, pinpoint areas that require work, and offer personalized feedback and direction.

b) Coach Johnson is a relatively new coach in the bowling community having just earned his coaching certification. He has little previous coaching expertise, and he hasn't yet had the chance to deal with a variety of bowlers. Although he may have a theoretical understanding of the sport, his lack of actual experience may limit his capacity to recognize and effectively respond to the various demands of bowlers.

2) Communicative abilities

It's common to undervalue the importance of communication abilities as a crucial tool for determining how competent coaches are. In reality, as "efficacy" covers a wider range of coaches' ability to communicate their expertise, it could be more acceptable to use that word in place of "communication." Even if coaches have vast knowledge, sharp judgment, and a variety of error-correction techniques, these skills are useless if they are unable to properly convey their expertise to the bowlers they are coaching. Because bowlers need a variety of communication channels to digest and internalize their instruction, coaches must actively look for ways to improve their communication abilities.

It is crucial to comprehend the different ways that bowlers learn in order to facilitate successful communication. Bowlers have unique preferences and tendencies when it comes to absorbing and processing information, which coaches must be aware of. For accurate comprehension and replication of processes, visual learners rely on witnessing demonstrations and other visual aids. Aural learners flourish in a setting that prioritizes verbal directions and explanations because it helps them hear concepts through their ears. On the other hand, kinesthetic learners learn better through hands-on activities and physical activity. Coaches can adjust their communication tactics in order to ensure that each bowler receives instruction in a way that fits with his chosen mode of learning by understanding and accommodating these various learning styles. A diverse strategy is needed to improve communication abilities. In order to identify their own communication strengths and potential areas for development, coaches should actively engage in self-reflection and introspection. Asking for feedback from bowlers, other coaches, and dependable mentors can give you important insights into how to improve your communication. Coaches should also investigate numerous methods and tools intended to develop their communication skills. These could consist of talks, classes, and specialist training courses that concentrate on coaching communication in particular. Coaches who put in the time and effort to improve their communication abilities can close the information-to-application gap, successfully imparting their knowledge to bowlers, and enabling them to realize their full potential.

The ability to express intricate ideas and technical information in a way that bowlers can understand is a crucial component of effective communication. Coaches must work to simplify complex concepts into more manageable parts and use analogies, metaphors, and visual aids to aid with understanding. This not only improves bowlers' comprehension but also strengthens the bond between coaches and players because bowlers feel supported and in control as a result of clear and concise communication. Communication also includes active listening and empathic understanding in addition to the transfer of information. In order to foster a secure and encouraging environment where bowlers feel heard and appreciated, coaches must learn how to actually listen to their players. Bowlers' problems, motives, and obstacles can be better understood by coaches through active listening, which enables them to offer individualized advice and support. As coaches must be sensitive to the emotional situations of their bowlers and transmit understanding and support in a sympathetic manner, empathy is essential to effective communication.

Hypothetical examples

a)   Coach Lee is a gifted communicator who excels at breaking down difficult technical ideas into easily digestible terms. To encourage and inspire his bowlers, he actively listens to them, offers helpful criticism, and communicates with them in a positive manner. His interpersonal skills promote mutual respect, open dialogue, and trust, which improves coaching relationships.

b)   Coach Brown has trouble communicating with his players and frequently fails to provide them with the guidance and criticism they need to improve. He could employ difficult-to-understand technical jargon or give feedback in an unfavorable or critical manner, which might demoralize and discourage his bowlers. His ineffective communication skills can make it difficult for him to build strong bonds with his bowlers and inhibit their growth.

3) Competitive outcomes

Whether they accept this reality or not, coaches are evaluated in large part based on their performance in competition. But the idea of results involves two separate parts that demand careful thought. The first factor, sometimes known as the outcome, relates to measurable indicators like grades, awards, and rankings. These tangible metrics are frequently used as the main barometer for assessing a coach's effectiveness. However, the second factor, which was determined through a performance-based review, is more concerned with the improvement and development of bowlers' abilities. When a coach asks a bowler, "How do you think you performed today?" the answer should address both the outcome and the performance element. Bowlers are better understood by instructors who train them to think about both aspects of their performance. A bowler might confess, for example, "I felt that my bowling technique was solid, but my scores did not reflect my efforts," or "Although I achieved a high score, my concentration wavered throughout the game." These comments reveal an increased understanding of the two-fold nature of performance evaluation, which takes into account both the result and the caliber of execution.

Results for coaches should act as a crucial yardstick for evaluating their work and a gauge of their current skill levels. A coach's competence and efficacy are demonstrated by his capacity to produce the intended outcomes, whether those outcomes are victories, championships, or other competitive objectives. But it's crucial to understand that coaching abilities are developed over time through ongoing development and improvement. Therefore, rather than serving as indisputable evidence of coaches' skills, the results they obtain should be seen as indicators of their progress along their developmental trajectory. In order to achieve success, coaches must develop a growth-oriented attitude that goes beyond just concentrating on the here and now. While competitive outcomes are insightful, they only represent coaches' experience and a small portion of their coaching expertise. Results should be viewed by coaches as insightful feedback that highlights their players' strengths and areas in need of improvement. Coaches improve their abilities, strengthen their plans, and lead their bowlers to peak performance via ongoing learning, introspection, and adaptation. A thorough assessment of a coach's performance ought to include a complex analysis that goes beyond only looking at the numbers. Considerations should be made for elements including the improvement of bowlers' abilities, the promotion of a supportive team environment, the use of efficient training techniques, and the promotion of mental and psychological toughness. A coach's genuine proficiency may be shown in his capacity to foster bowlers' development both on and off the field and to instill in them a sense of motivation, tenacity, and self-belief.

Hypothetical examples

a)   Bowlers that Coach Miller has coached consistently place first in regional and international events and have a successful track record. His coaching techniques, plans, and training regimens have helped his bowlers perform significantly better, as seen by their competitive outcomes. His ability to coach is acknowledged and appreciated in the bowling community, and he has a track record of producing high-performing bowlers.

b)   Coach Patel has had trouble getting his bowlers to consistently perform well in competition. His bowlers' performance has plateaued and they haven't been able to place highly in regional or national championships. In order to pinpoint areas for growth and aid his bowlers in achieving better competitive outcomes, Coach Patel may need to reevaluate his coaching techniques, approaches, and training regimens.

4) Development of Life Skills in their Bowlers

An enormous obligation that goes beyond coaching is the development of life skills in bowlers. We have a significant impact on how our bowlers' value systems are developed as parents, educators, and coaches because we help mold their personalities and direct them along the road to success. It is up to us to fully commit to fulfilling this duty and to doing so by emulating the highest possible standards of decency, morality, and sportsmanship.

While improving physical performance and accomplishing measurable goals are frequently the emphasis of coaching, the importance of developing life skills should not be disregarded. In reality, our influence on the total growth of our pupils can set us apart as excellent coaches. The development of life skills must be incorporated into our coaching development plans in light of this significant influence, aligning our methods and approaches with the overarching objective of fostering well-rounded persons. Life skills include a wide range of fundamental traits and abilities that go beyond the boundaries of the bowling alley. They include virtues like cooperation, fortitude, self-control, empathy, and adaptability. The development of these talents in our bowlers is facilitated by the incorporation of these ideas into our coaching philosophy and methodology. By using focused and intentional coaching techniques, we can encourage our bowlers to take on difficulties, improve their communication abilities, and establish a strong work ethic that goes beyond bowling. Life skill improvement in bowlers has enormous long-term advantages. We prepare our bowlers for success not only in their sporting aspirations but also in their personal and professional endeavors by providing them with the tools to handle the difficulties of life. The lifelong lessons they acquire on the field transcend the boundaries of competition, forming their character and giving them a sense of moral courage that will direct their actions and choices.

The ideals and ideas we want to instill in our bowlers must be modeled by us as coaches, thus we must lead by example. We want to teach our bowlers values of integrity, respect, and sportsmanship, and we want our words, actions, and relationships to consistently represent those values. We foster an ethical culture and encourage our bowlers to uphold these values both on and off the pitch by demonstrating these actions. A holistic strategy that incorporates psychological and social factors into our coaching tactics is necessary for the development of life skills. Each bowler has different personalities, strengths, and challenges, so we can customize our teaching techniques to support his own development. We establish a climate that supports self-awareness and personal growth by encouraging open conversation, encouraging self-reflection, and offering helpful criticism. The influence we have on our bowlers is increased as a result of including life skills development in our coaching development plans, which also benefits our own professional development as coaches. It forces us to continuously hone our strategy, look for fresh information and ideas, and adjust our operating procedures in order to satisfy our customers' changing needs. We engage on a voyage of self-improvement and self-discovery as we devote ourselves to the total development of our bowlers, expanding our knowledge of human psychology, motivation, and behavior.

Hypothetical examples

a)   Coach Thompson places a high priority on his bowlers' overall development and stresses the value of developing life skills outside of bowling. His coaching curriculum includes team-building exercises, leadership development lessons, and personal growth activities. In order to help his bowlers succeed outside of the bowling alley, he urges them to develop self-control, fortitude, cooperation, and time management abilities.

b)   Coach Nguyen places less emphasis on the development of his bowlers' life skills and instead concentrates completely on the technical aspects of bowling. He doesn't give his bowlers the chance to gain other crucial life skills; instead, he only concentrates on how well they bowl. His bowlers could not have the required life skills to overcome obstacles, control stress, and achieve success in other aspects of their lives as a result.

5) Bowler's Skill Development Acquisition

Within the bowling industry and coaching community, the acquisition and development of skills in bowlers form a vital part of evaluation. Technical proficiency, tactical awareness, and mental toughness are just a few of the characteristics that instructors and coaches are frequently judged on. In order to promote continual progress and mastery, coaches must pay precise attention to and dedication to these talents, which span a wide range of areas. Coaches spend a large amount of their time helping bowlers develop their technical abilities. This includes the development of bowling-specific biomechanical movements, body placement, and execution strategies. Coaches are able to pinpoint areas for growth and offer focused advice to increase bowlers' technical skills by carefully dissecting and evaluating the complex mechanics of the sport of bowling. Due to the ongoing evolution of bowling and the emergence of new insights and techniques, the pursuit of technical excellence is a lifetime endeavor for both teachers and bowlers. Coaches place a high priority on helping bowlers develop their tactical skills in addition to their technical capabilities. This calls for improving situational awareness, game analysis, and strategic decision-making. Coaches provide bowlers with the cognitive tools required to make educated decisions and modify their methods to varied competitive settings by providing a thorough understanding of the game and its dynamics. Coaches assist bowlers in their pursuit of tactical mastery through precise planning, good communication, and critical thinking.

MYTH: "A DISCIPLINARIAN APPROACH IS BEST FOR YOUNG BOWLERS WHO ASPIRE TO PLAY AT THE NEXT LEVEL."

Reality: The belief that a strict disciplinarian approach is the most effective coaching method for young bowlers aiming to reach higher levels in bowling is a misconception. Different individuals respond differently to coaching styles, and a one-size-fits-all approach may not be optimal. While some young bowlers may thrive under a structured and disciplined environment, others may require a more nurturing and supportive approach.

Coaches should consider the individual needs and preferences of each young bowler. Establishing high standards and holding young athletes accountable for their actions and performance can be more effective than relying solely on discipline. By emphasizing personal responsibility and fostering a supportive and inclusive atmosphere, coaches can instill a sense of ownership in young bowlers. Encouragement, positive reinforcement, and open communication are key elements in nurturing their development and helping them reach their potential.

The focus should be on developing well-rounded athletes who not only excel in the sport but also grow as individuals. By understanding and catering to the unique needs of young bowlers, coaches can create an environment that promotes motivation, self-discipline, and personal growth, enabling them to thrive on their journey to higher levels in bowling.

Another crucial area in the growth of bowlers is the area of mental abilities. Coaches devote a lot of time and energy to developing bowlers' mental toughness, attention, and emotional regulation because they understand how important psychological variables are to performance. They help bowlers build powerful goal-setting tactics, visualization exercises, and techniques to get over performance anxiety and keep a positive outlook in stressful circumstances. Coaches equip bowlers with the mental toughness and growth-oriented mindset they need to face challenges, get past failures, and reach their best potential. The process of developing abilities is dynamic and multidimensional, going much beyond the technical, tactical, and mental domains. Additionally, coaches are very important in developing bowlers' interpersonal and social abilities. Another crucial area in the growth of bowlers is the area of mental abilities.

Hypothetical examples

a)   Coach Davis builds skills in a systematic and progressive manner, beginning with basic methods and working his way up to more complex ones. He uses personalized drills, exercises, and training plans for each of his bowlers while also giving frequent feedback and encouragement. His bowlers consistently perform better on the lanes, demonstrating a considerable improvement in their technical abilities.

b)   Coach Wilson lacks a disciplined approach to skill development and frequently gives his bowlers general advice without taking into account their unique demands. He doesn't offer reinforcement or comments on a regular basis, which may hinder the growth of his bowlers' skills. They could find it difficult to develop their technical abilities, and they might not play to their full bowling ability.

6) Reputation/Ethics

Everyday life presents people with the enormous challenge of juggling the fine line between reputation and integrity. The steadfast values of honesty and moral rectitude that characterize our integrity frequently clash with our reputation, which is built on the impressions and opinions of others. We occasionally find ourselves in a position where we must decide whether to uphold our integrity or maintain our reputation. Unfortunately, it's frequently impossible to uphold our reputation without sacrificing our ethics. Integrity is the cornerstone of trust, covering both our own and other people's confidence in us. It is a deeply ingrained value that, once tarnished, cannot be restored. The repercussions of betraying one's integrity might last a lifetime and bring about unimaginable suffering and regret. As they progress through their careers, coaches regularly come upon turning points where moral judgments must take center stage. These choices can entail showing favor to a pupil or giving in to selection bias temptation. Coaches' self-perception and reputation within the bowling community will be shaped by how they respond to these moral conundrums.

For coaches, the tug-of-war between reputation and integrity frequently poses a complex and difficult quandary. On the one hand, a coach's reputation can be a significant commodity that opens doors to chances, wins them respect, and establishes credibility in the field. However, reputation is an ephemeral and changeable construct that is prone to the whims of the public and is open to distortion and misunderstanding. On the other hand, integrity is a constant trait that transcends temporary views and stands the test of time. Trust and respect are built on the fundamental base of sincerity and moral integrity. Making morally challenging decisions that can conflict with other people's expectations and preferences is necessary for upholding integrity. It necessitates steadfast adherence to moral standards even in the face of hardship or temptation. Coaches who uphold their moral principles serve as moral role models for their players, their teammates, and the larger bowling community, earning their respect and affection. Coaches who uphold moral principles with tenacity not only develop a strong sense of self-worth but also serve as a compelling example for others to follow. There are several ways that ethical conundrums can appear in the coaching world. For instance, coaches could feel pressured to influence game results or compromise the selection process for their own benefit or to appease outside forces. Those who value integrity, however, resist these pressures because they are aware of the long-term consequences of sacrificing their moral compass. They recognize that doing what is right, even when it is difficult or unpopular, is what defines success in the ultimate sense, not in flashy awards or momentary triumphs. Integrity in coaching encompasses all aspects of the coaching philosophy and methodology, not just individual actions. Teams with ethical coaches cultivate an environment that values truthfulness, justice, and openness. They establish in their bowlers a solid sense of morality and a profound respect for the virtues of honesty and sportsmanship. Coaches support the development of not only skilled bowlers but also moral people who bring these ideals into their personal and professional lives by creating an environment that upholds these values.

Hypothetical examples

a)   The bowling world holds Coach Thompson in high regard for his moral coaching methods. In his teaching style, he places a high value on integrity, fair play, and good sportsmanship. He emphasizes the significance of upholding the bowling's ideals and sets a good example for his bowlers. Talented bowlers are drawn to him because of his reputation as a trustworthy and moral instructor, and he also enjoys the respect of his peers and the bowling community.

b)   Due to his unscrupulous coaching methods, Coach Adams has a damaged reputation. His bowlers have suffered as a result of accusations against him of favoritism, cheating, and other unethical actions. Because of his unethical actions, he has lost the respect and trust of his bowlers and peers, which has had a severe influence on his teaching talents and efficacy.

7) Effort

In the field of bowling, coaching extends much beyond technical proficiency and talent. It goes in-depth on the levels of commitment and attention that a coach gives to his bowlers. Any flaws or mistakes made along the road are easily overlooked when coaches exhibit steadfast dedication to the growth and success of their bowlers. In actuality, the coaches' unrelenting effort becomes the determining factor in how effective they are. Coaching is a difficult and demanding career, frequently recognized as one of the most difficult tasks ever attempted by humankind. Coaches often shoulder a heavy burden of obligation. The unwavering love and dedication to their trade, however, is what distinguishes excellent instructors from others. They are driven to go above and beyond no matter the challenges they encounter because of this innate sense of purpose and real love for their bowling.

Coaching effort goes beyond the physical effort needed to conduct practice sessions or create tactical game plans. It includes emotional engagement, endless hours spent evaluating and perfecting tactics, and a never-ending desire to learn and get better. The coaches' unwavering faith in their bowlers' ability and unrelenting desire to see them achieve is reflected in their effort.

Coaches' effort is seen when their heart is fully committed to their role. Every encounter they have with their bowlers is permeated by it, producing a nurturing and encouraging environment that fosters growth and development. Coaches work tirelessly to inspire and encourage their bowlers to push past their comfort zones, endure hardship, and pursue achievement. The effects of a coach's work go well beyond bowling's technical features. It has significant psychological ramifications for the bowlers they are coaching.

Bowlers develop a sense of trust, security, and confidence in their own skills when they see their coach's consistent commitment to action. Knowing that their coach is entirely committed to their journey and honestly cares about their development and well-being gives them a sense of value and support. Bowlers can learn a lot from coaches' patience, discipline, and steadfast dedication to their goals by watching how hard He works. It shows that success is something that must be worked for and achieved by tenacity and a relentless pursuit of greatness.

High-effort coaches serve as catalysts for personal development and transformation, encouraging their bowlers to pursue excellence in all facets of their lives as well as in bowling. An ongoing dedication to self-reflection and constant progress constitutes effort rather than a one-time act of devotion. The best teachers are always looking for ways to improve their techniques, comprehend their bowlers' requirements more thoroughly, and hone their own abilities and knowledge. They view difficulties and failures as chances for learning and development, using each one as a springboard to advance in their position.

Hypothetical examples

a)   *Coach Garcia consistently puts a lot of effort into his instruction. He makes the time and effort to learn about and keep up with the most recent bowling methods, strategies, and tools. He meticulously organizes and carries out training sessions, keeps tabs on the development of his bowlers, and offers regular comments. His relentless commitment to teaching results in his bowlers' success and ongoing progress.*

b)   *In his coaching style, Coach Thompson shows a lack of effort. He doesn't spend enough time arranging and planning training sessions, giving regular feedback, or actively looking for ways to enhance his teaching techniques. His lack of effort can prevent his bowlers from developing fully and moving forward at all.*

8) Effectivity

Hypothetical examples

a)   *Coach Johnson has a very successful coaching style. He is aware of the unique requirements of each of his bowlers, and he adapts his coaching strategies accordingly. He employs a range of coaching methods and approaches to speak with, inspire, and lead his bowlers in an effective manner. His bowlers consequently consistently exhibit progress in their performance and succeed in their objectives.*

b)   *Coach Williams has trouble making his coaching methods effective. He does not modify his coaching strategies to fit the various learning preferences and ability levels of his bowlers. His bowlers might not be able to understand his instructions or respond to his feedback, which would hinder their ability to advance and perform better.*

Effectiveness is a crucial characteristic of a coach in Bowling, as exemplified by the comparison between Coach Johnson and Coach Williams. Coach Johnson demonstrates a highly successful coaching style by acknowledging the unique requirements of each of his bowlers and adapting his coaching strategies accordingly. He recognizes that different individuals possess distinct learning preferences and ability levels, and thus employs a diverse range of coaching methods and approaches to effectively communicate, inspire, and lead his bowlers. As a result, Coach Johnson's bowlers consistently exhibit progress in their performance and successfully achieve their objectives. On the other hand, Coach Williams encounters difficulties in achieving coaching effectiveness. He fails to modify his coaching strategies to align with the various learning preferences and ability levels of his bowlers. This limitation impedes his bowlers' ability to comprehend his instructions or respond adequately to his feedback, ultimately hindering their advancement and diminishing their performance potential.

9) Planning

A bowling coach's job description includes planning, which necessitates a good working relationship with bowlers in order to facilitate growth and eventual success. Coaches create a framework that not only directs decision-making but also paints a clear image of the future by creating thorough and rigorous development plans and competitive tactics for each individual bowler or team. The proverb "success is where preparation meets opportunity" has a particularly strong resonance in this situation. Unwavering confidence is fostered by being well-prepared, and planning is the essential component of truly excellent preparation. Participants can stay focused and poised, prepared with preplanned solutions to handle any difficulties that may arise, rather than having their plans wrecked by unforeseen situations. In order to effectively teach your bowlers, you must have a thorough awareness of the many factors, including mental, physical, fitness, strength, tactical, and equipment considerations, that go into their performance. Additionally, one of the most challenging tasks in a coach's life is handling egos. Establishing a support network made up of both familial and mentor-based relationships will help coaches maintain their composure while navigating this perilous route. This will prevent them from becoming overwhelmed by the demands of their job.

Both the early phases of a bowler's development and the fine-tuning period at the elite level are important, but the bowling community and industry give the elite coach more credit. Individuals can determine which area of the growth continuum best fits their particular goals by understanding the driving forces behind coaching. People can determine the best station to occupy within the field of development by evaluating their hobbies and how they interact with coaching skills. Last but not least, an unquenchable appetite for knowledge becomes crucial because everything in the world is constantly changing, including expertise. Knowledge's half-life is getting shorter and shorter in today's digitally connected culture as information travels great distances at breakneck speed. Coaches who want to retain their effectiveness and make sure that their knowledge is up-to-date and applicable must therefore make a firm commitment to lifelong learning and staying informed of the most recent trends and developments.

Hypothetical examples

a) *Coach Thompson is renowned for his careful preparation when it comes to his coaching style. He creates thorough training schedules, establishes clear objectives for his bowlers, and routinely assesses their development. He makes sure that his bowlers participate in systematic practice sessions that include a range of topics related to the game, such as technique, tactics, and mental preparation. His preparation guarantees that his bowlers have a clear development plan and are well-prepared for competitions.*

b) *Effective planning is missing from Coach Davis' coaching style. He might not have a well-defined training schedule or fail to provide his bowlers with clear objectives. His practice regimen could be unorganized and might not cover all essential game-related topics. His bowlers could fail to reach their full potential as a result of not having a clear path for their growth.*

A thorough evaluation of a coach's ability is necessary given the complex nature of guiding elite bowlers. A variety of important indicators, including experience, communicative skills, competitive results, the development of life skills in bowlers, skill acquisition, reputation/ethics, effort, effectivity, and planning, can be used to assess their proficiency. These factors serve as the cornerstone on which coaches' influence over the growth and performance of their bowlers is constructed. The path and accomplishments of the bowlers under their direction may be significantly impacted by their capacity to succeed or suffer in these areas. As a result, it is necessary for coaches to embrace an attitude of continuous growth and work hard to improve their skills in each of these important areas. Coaches can enhance their influence in guiding their bowlers toward unmatched success by doing this in order to realize their full potential.

The Defilement Of Innocence - A Coach's Journey Through The Pitfalls Of Bowling Development

In directing and forming their bowlers' development, coaches are essential. But there are obstacles on the way to being an accomplished and successful coach. Coaches may run into obstacles along the way that will impede their growth and make it more difficult for them to effectively coach their bowlers. One such difficulty is the defiling of innocence, in which coaches can fall into the ego-suffocating trap, advance from the developing stage to champion status, experience a waning drive for knowledge, or give in to hubris. We will go into these perilous routes in this literature and investigate how coaches should avoid them in order to maintain their development and have a beneficial effect on their bowlers.

Receptivity to Ego Suffocation:

The qualities of innocence and humility are ornaments on the path to brilliance. As aspiring coaches set out on their transformative journey, their openness to picking up tips from others and welcoming criticism paves the way for their development. Dangerous phenomena called ego suffocation, however, threatens to tarnish their once-humble spirit as the winds of experience and achievement blow through their sails. Coaches become trapped in a psychological web of arrogance and narrow-mindedness as a result of this psychological entanglement, making them blind to the knowledge of others, including their own bowlers. What is the result? A significant effect on their ability to instruct and the health of their bowlers.

The rich ground of success is frequently where the seeds of ego suffocation are spread. As coaches climb the success ladder, recognition and victories mount, feeding a sense of invincibility and infallibility. The mask of humility gradually gives way to an all-consuming conviction that they are infallible and have the solutions. This egotistical worldview creates insurmountable obstacles, making coaches hesitant to innovate and change. Previously enthusiastically adopted new methods and approaches are now seen as unnecessary or irrelevant. The coaches' ability to change is limited by the firm grasp of ego suffocation, which inhibits their ability to advance and give their bowlers the greatest instruction. The disregard for criticism is just as harmful, especially when it comes from the bowlers themselves, whose growth and development coaches are charged with fostering. The once-appreciated conversations between the coach and the bowler turn into monologues as the coach's voice drowns out the important viewpoints of those who are on the front lines of competition. Bowlers lose motivation and perform worse because they feel ignored, undervalued, and unloved. The resulting toxic environment fosters mediocrity and stagnation, restricting the potential of both the coach and the bowler. Coaches must develop self-awareness and embrace the power of vulnerability in order to avoid the perilous plunge into ego suffocation. The first step in recovering humility is to acknowledge the attraction of success and how it can taint judgment. Coaches who often reflect on themselves can peel back the layers of their ego to uncover its motivations and prejudices. Coaches can encourage an openness to novel concepts, strategies, and viewpoints by encouraging a growth mindset. Curiosity can be reawakened, creating a quest for information that leads people ahead on the path of unending growth. In addition, coaches need to rebuild the holy relationship of open communication and trust with their bowlers. The flame of cooperation is rekindled by sincere collaboration, which is characterized by attentive listening and sincere affirmation of their bowlers' experiences. By valuing the bowler's voice, coaches establish a culture that supports development, encourages creativity, and improves performance. Bowlers who feel appreciated and respected take an active role in their personal growth, which helps them reach new levels of success. The path from innocence to ego-suffocation is not predetermined; coaches make this decision as they go along. Coaches can maintain their intrinsic humility and stay open to other people's advice by cultivating a thorough understanding of their own vulnerabilities. Coaches may protect their bowlers' well-being and help them reach their greatest potential by regularly reflecting on their own behavior and committing to encouraging open communication.

Ego Suffocation: An egotistical coach could be unable to accept criticism from his bowlers or from other coaches. For instance, a coach who has had success in the past and has a firm trust in his coaching techniques may ignore advice or criticism from his bowlers because He believes they are right. This might prevent the coach and his bowlers from working together and communicating openly, which would impede their growth as players.

Hypothetical Scenario

In the early stages of his coaching career, Coach Anderson was known for his humility and openness to learning. As he guided his bowlers through various challenges, he embraced new ideas and welcomed constructive criticism, recognizing that continuous growth was essential for both him and his team. His coaching philosophy was rooted in the belief that success was not an endpoint but a journey of perpetual improvement.

However, as victories and accolades began to accumulate, a subtle shift took place within Coach Anderson. The very success that once fueled his passion for coaching started to cast a shadow on his humility. The seeds of ego suffocation began to sprout in the rich ground of his achievements. The more recognition he received, the more he found himself succumbing to a sense of invincibility and an unwavering belief that he had all the answers.

This transformation in Coach Anderson's mindset had a profound impact on his coaching approach. Once receptive to innovative methods and open to change, he now viewed established practices as sacrosanct, dismissing any need for adaptation. The once-cherished dialogues with his bowlers, where ideas flowed freely, turned into one-sided monologues dominated by Coach Anderson's unwavering opinions.

The negative consequences of this shift became evident in the bowling alley. Bowlers, who once felt valued and heard, now experienced a sense of neglect and undervaluation. Motivation waned, and performance suffered as the toxic environment of ego suffocation took root. Coach Anderson's coaching style, once a source of inspiration, now became a hindrance to progress.

Recognizing the downward spiral, Coach Anderson embarked on a journey of self-reflection. He acknowledged the allure of success and how it had subtly altered his judgment. Regular introspection allowed him to peel back the layers of his ego, revealing its motivations and biases. Coach Anderson embraced vulnerability, acknowledging that continuous learning was a lifelong commitment.

To break free from the clutches of ego suffocation, Coach Anderson actively worked to rekindle the flames of cooperation with his bowlers. Open communication and trust became the cornerstones of his renewed coaching philosophy. He listened attentively to his bowlers' experiences, affirming their perspectives and fostering an environment that encouraged creativity and growth.

By valuing the voices of his bowlers, Coach Anderson created a culture that prioritized development over stagnation. The once-toxic atmosphere transformed into one of collaboration and support. Bowlers, feeling appreciated and respected, re-engaged with their personal growth, reaching new levels of success.

The journey from innocence to ego suffocation, Coach Anderson realized, was not predetermined; it was a conscious decision made along the coaching path. By cultivating a deep understanding of his vulnerabilities and committing to ongoing self-reflection, Coach Anderson not only protected his bowlers' well-being but also reignited the spark of genuine collaboration. Through humility and openness, he rediscovered the essence of coaching as a dynamic and reciprocal process, ensuring that success remained a journey of perpetual growth for both coach and bowler alike.

The Transformation from Novice to Champion: Avoiding the Pitfalls of Coaching Transition

In one's coaching career, becoming a champion coach is a revolutionary turning point. It represents an amazing progression as trainers move from being inexperienced to respected authorities in the industry. But this change also presents its own difficulties. Coaches run the risk of becoming complacent or haughty as they gain success and experience, believing they have attained the summit of their capabilities. The risk comes from ignoring personal development and depending only on accumulated knowledge. This course might result in a lack of innovation and stagnation. Coaches must accept the notion that development is an ongoing process that goes beyond prior successes in order to avoid these errors. They must constantly update their knowledge, hone their abilities, and adjust to the bowling industry's constant change.

Regardless of their accomplishments, champion coaches exhibit a humble and curious mindset and are constantly willing to learn. Self-awareness, resilience, and an unrelenting dedication to improvement are necessary for the shift from a developing coach to a champion status. Coaches must face their presumptions, biases, and limitations at this crucial juncture. Their growth may be hampered by the impulse to celebrate prior success. Champion coaches practice a growth mentality as a result, viewing their accomplishments as stepping stones rather than goals. They carve a road of unending progress.

Champion coaches are aware that their skill is based on curiosity, adaptability, and a relentless quest of mastery in order to prevent stagnation. They are aware of the depth of knowledge and the necessity of constant learning and research. They are exposed to various viewpoints and cutting-edge methods through interaction with other coaches, business professionals, and new research. Because of their collaborative nature, they are able to think outside the box when it comes to coaching and offer fresh ideas for the growth of bowlers.

In addition, successful coaches show humility by admitting that they are still developing and improving. They don't let praise alone influence them; instead, they see their successes as motivation for continued advancement. They foster a climate of improvement by acknowledging that there is always more to learn, which motivates its bowlers to follow suit. The coach and bowler's mutually beneficial relationship serves as a catalyst for transformational growth, advancing both to previously unheard-of levels of success.

Beyond personal accomplishment, champion status is sought. It entails a strong dedication to enhancing the game, the bowlers, and the coaching profession as a whole. Champion coaches use their enhanced stature as change agents to advance inclusion, sportsmanship, and moral behavior. They are aware of how their influence affects their bowlers' lives and the development of the sport outside of the bowling alley.

A coach who has successfully led his team or individual bowlers from a developmental stage to a champion status may become complacent. For instance, if a coach has guided a bowler to numerous championships, He can begin to take his success for granted and lose interest in continuing his own education and development. This may lead to a plateau in teaching strategies and a failure to adopt new tactics or plans, which would lower the performance of his bowlers.

The Oscillation of the Coaching Mind: From Unceasing Desire for Knowledge to the Abyss of Declining Quest

A coach who is truly effective has a passion for knowledge, according to the coaching industry. Bowlers can achieve incredible feats if their coaches use a powerful tool to encourage their tireless pursuit of knowledge and skill improvement. However, there is a hidden threat—a hazard that coaches must avoid—in this admirable endeavor: the waning of their desire for knowledge.

Beginning their coaching careers, coaches are motivated by an unquenchable quest for knowledge. They are aware that the road to greatness calls for constant inquiry as they submerge themselves in the enormous body of information that surrounds their industry. Coaches can find novel approaches, apply cutting-edge research, and draw on the collective knowledge of the coaching community thanks to this dedicated quest. Their uncompromising dedication to personal development informs their coaching strategies and guarantees the ongoing improvement of their trade.

Coaches, though, could unwittingly find themselves teetering on the verge of complacency as time goes on and victories mount. Success itself can slowly stifle a person's need for knowledge, resulting in feelings of self-satisfaction and a lessened desire to grow. The appeal of routine and familiarity starts to trump the anticipation of the unknown. As curiosity dwindles, so does the spark of invention.

Subtle changes in a coach's mentality and actions reflect a waning interest in learning. Coaches who formerly avidly absorbed new information may develop complacency, become content with their current expertise, and become hesitant to step outside of their comfort zone. The thrill of exploring new terrain is overshadowed by the enticing familiarity of the familiar. Coaches who follow this path could also show resistance to change. They cling to antiquated ideas and behaviors rather than embracing new fashions, scientific discoveries, and evolving practices. Their coaching philosophies become stale, making it difficult for them to adjust to the bowling industry's constant change. Coaches run the risk of being outmoded, unconnected to modern technology, and unprepared for the changing demands of their bowlers in this condition of stasis.

The coach-bowler connection is affected throughout by a diminished desire for information. Coaches unintentionally restrict the development and potential of their bowlers when they become entrenched in their established practices. A static landscape devoid of new ideas and viewpoints replaces the once-fertile ground for creativity and innovation. Bowlers may see the coach's waning excitement as a lack of interest in their personal growth since they long for direction and motivation. As performance plateaus, motivation wanes, and the once-vibrant relationship between coach and bowler dwindles.

Coaches must engage in a voyage of self-reflection and spark the flames of intellectual curiosity in order to overcome the abyss of a waning quest for knowledge. They must rekindle the surprise and awe that sparked their coaching careers and stoked their insatiable hunger for knowledge. As coaches are reminded that mastery is a journey rather than a destination, adopting a development mindset becomes crucial. They need to break down the boundaries of complacency and actively look for learning opportunities, whether through collaboration with other coaches, professional development courses, or mentorship. Coaches revive their own enthusiasm and unleash a fresh sense of purpose in their coaching undertakings by reigniting their intellectual fervor.

Declining Interest in Learning: A coach may get uninterested in learning new things and have a stale coaching style. For instance, if a coach stops going to workshops and seminars and stops keeping up with the most recent developments in bowling technique, his coaching skills may become outdated. Because of this, his ability to innovate and adapt to the changing needs of his bowlers may suffer, which would lower his performance.

Beware the Snare of Conceit: Unraveling the Paradox of Coaching Success

Success and grandeur can sometimes lead coaches into the perilous trap of hubris. Hubris shows itself as an inflated ego, an exaggerated belief in one's brilliance, and a cloud that hinders clear vision, ultimately reducing the effectiveness of coaching. As coaches climb the ladder of success, they become more susceptible to the seductive allure of superiority, thinking that their coaching style is the only effective one. Consequently, they ignore suggestions, dismiss comments, and reject different viewpoints from their own bowlers. They resist change, and this unwanted companion hampers their growth, creating a toxic coaching atmosphere where bowlers feel unappreciated, demoralized, and lacking in enthusiasm, negatively impacting their performance.

To escape the grip of hubris, coaches must engage in serious self-reflection and nurture humility. They need to recognize that their coaching abilities, while admirable, are not flawless. There is always room for improvement and new discoveries. Coaches should commit themselves to active listening, valuing the opinions of their bowlers, fellow coaches, and others involved in the bowling industry. By adopting an open mindset, coaches can welcome different perspectives into their coaching environment, weaving together a dynamic tapestry of concepts and methods. They should remain receptive to fresh ideas and approaches, swiftly adapting their teaching strategies to meet the evolving needs of their bowlers and the ever-changing landscape of the sport.

The seductive allure of hubris may tempt coaches with claims of invincibility, overshadowing their inherent humility and jeopardizing their coaching abilities. Coaches can only avoid its pitfalls by developing self-awareness, maintaining an unwavering commitment to improvement, and embracing humility. This approach fosters an atmosphere of empowerment, trust, and unwavering encouragement, safeguarding their own personal journey. Let coaches embrace the lesson of humility as their guiding compass on the path to greatness. By overcoming the traps of hubris, they can create a lasting legacy that resonates with future generations, leaving behind a positive impact on the sport.

"**Marshall Kent's Motivations**

Among the many influential figures in my life, former Team USA member Harry Mickelson stood out as a role model and confidant. With his wealth of experience and mental game strategies, he not only helped me elevate my performance to new heights but also ignited a burning motivation within me. However, it wasn't just the guidance of these exceptional individuals that propelled me forward; it was the unwavering support of the bowling community around me. Their unwavering belief in my potential fueled my confidence and provided the boundless motivation to passionately chase my dreams. Throughout my journey, I eagerly embraced the wisdom of multiple coaches and mentors, each offering a unique perspective on both the game of bowling and life itself. My father remained a constant pillar of support, while Harry Mickelson's insights from his time on the PBA Tour continued to shape my fiercely competitive mindset.

Conceit: When a coach exhibits arrogance, He might believe He is better than others and ignore criticism or suggestions from him. For instance, if a coach rejects alternative suggestions or feedback from his bowlers or fellow coaches because He doesn't agree with his coaching method, it may foster a toxic coaching atmosphere. This may make bowlers feel undervalued and disheartened, which would ultimately affect their performance and drive.

MYTH: "A KID MUST BE IN A SPORT'S DEVELOPMENT PROGRAM FROM AN EARLY AGE TO MAKE IT."

Reality: The belief that early involvement in a sport's development program is the sole path to success is a myth. The journey to success in bowling, and sports in general, is non-linear and varies for each individual. Longitudinal studies have shown that early recruitment into development programs does not guarantee long-term success at the senior level. In fact, some of the most accomplished athletes are recruited into programs at a later age than their peers. It is not the early involvement in development programs but rather a combination of factors such as talent, dedication, diverse sporting experiences, and the right training approach that contribute to long-term success. Engaging in multiple sports during childhood and adolescence can enhance overall development and increase the likelihood of achieving high levels of performance. It is important for parents and young bowlers to understand that success is not solely dependent on early involvement in development programs, but rather on a comprehensive approach that includes a range of experiences and opportunities for growth.

The journey of coaches in the world of bowling development is a challenging one, filled with obstacles that test their strength and determination. They face a lurking danger known as ego suffocation, the tricky transition from being a beginner to becoming a champion, a waning thirst for knowledge, and the tempting trap of conceit. These formidable foes can hinder coaches' ability to effectively mentor and guide their bowlers, stunting their own personal growth in the process. However, coaches can navigate this treacherous path and forge a path of continuous growth by employing certain strategies. These strategies involve developing specific qualities that will serve as their guiding compass and help them overcome these challenges.

The foremost quality for coaches is to remain open to criticism. By embracing constructive feedback and valuable insights from others, coaches can push past their own limitations and elevate their coaching skills to new heights. This receptive mindset fosters a dynamic and mutually beneficial coach-bowler relationship, creating an environment that is conducive to growth and development. Additionally, the transition from being a beginner to a champion is a critical crossroad that requires caution. The temptation to become complacent can be strong as coaches bask in the rewards of success, but they can overcome this trap by staying committed to lifelong learning. By embarking on a constant quest for knowledge, actively seeking new approaches, staying updated on recent advancements, and staying abreast of cutting-edge studies, coaches can fuel their intellectual curiosity, propel themselves forward, and provide the resources necessary to motivate and develop their bowlers. As time goes on, coaches may find their once fervent desire for learning dwindling. To reignite this flame, coaches must revive their thirst for self-improvement and discovery. This can be accomplished through introspection, acknowledging their areas of weakness, and actively seeking opportunities for growth. By breaking free from the chains of inertia, coaches can rekindle their pursuit of greatness. Finally, and perhaps most importantly, coaches must confront the arrogance that threatens to undermine their effectiveness. It is crucial to recognize that no coach is an expert in all aspects of bowling. Humility becomes their defense against the allure of an inflated ego. By respectfully appreciating the viewpoints and ideas of others, coaches foster an environment of cooperation and inclusivity. This open-minded approach empowers bowlers, nurtures their development, and paves the way for collective success.

Navigating the Labyrinth of Ego Suffocation: A Coach's Triumph over Self-Deception

We set out on a path as coaches where our ego can serve as both a motivator and a potential roadblock. Maintaining this fine balance is essential, especially as the reputation of our coaching improves. Conceit can seduce us, clouding our judgment and taking our attention away from our genuine goal. Nowhere is this conflict more evident than in coaching, where the development of our bowlers and our coaching skills are directly impacted by our capacity to preserve humility. We must set out on a journey of self-discovery and reflection in order to avoid being suffocated by ego.

It takes more than just technical know-how and strategic insight to become a master coach. Self-awareness and emotional intelligence are crucial in forming our coaching identities. We discover vulnerabilities, insecurities, and ego-driven inclinations by probing the depths of our psyche. This process of self-disclosure enables us to face our prejudices, phobias, and propensity to look for approval from others. Creating a support network is essential for this process. When our judgment becomes obscured, mentors, peers, and confidants act as our anchors by offering insightful advice and critical criticism. They protect our reputation and serve as a constant reminder of our actual calling as coaches, which is to empower and encourage our athletes rather than pursue personal glory.

Which period of growth—the early stages of development or the emergence of elite performance—holds higher value when assessing bowler development? Both eras have influenced bowlers' overall development. However, champion-guiding elite coaches frequently receive the most attention. It is crucial to defy social norms and connect with the fundamental goal of coaching, which is a persistent dedication to the development and well-being of our bowlers, regardless of their stage of development. Our passions and natural talents must be matched with the many demands of coaching in order for us to successfully traverse this dynamic environment. Knowing our own interests, passions, and strengths enables us to use them as a compass to steer us in the direction of coaching domains that strongly resonate with our true selves. By establishing this symbiotic connection between our particular interests and our coaching abilities, we are able to reach our full potential and design a coaching journey that is entirely individual to us.

The pursuit of coaching excellence, however, goes beyond ego management and self-discovery. An unquenchable appetite for knowledge becomes essential in a time of rapid technological advancement and plenty of information. Expertise changes quickly, therefore we must embrace intellectual curiosity if we want to stay on top. Our guiding principles are to question accepted beliefs, challenge social norms, and modify our teaching approaches to the constantly evolving world of bowling.

However, mere knowledge is insufficient. We must put our theories and principles into practice by developing detailed competition and development plans for each bowler or team under our direction. These plans serve as compass points, pointing us in the direction of greatness and giving us a clear picture of the future. Technical competence, competition proficiency, mental toughness, tactical prowess, and physical conditioning are all aspects of athletic development that must be addressed in order to achieve holistic growth and success. A clear completion model walks us through bowlers' development, outlining their own developmental trajectory and final destination.

Success is built on a foundation of readiness. Our bowlers gain confidence as a result of our emphasis on planning and preparation because we provide them with the tools and tactics they need to deal with obstacles during competition. Our bowlers are protected from distractions and uncertainties by well-designed competition and development plans, which promote resilience, adaptation, and unshakeable focus. We equip ourselves to help bowlers reach their greatest potential by embracing humility, pursuing knowledge, and developing comprehensive programs.

In order to transcend the limitations of conceit, let us as coaches embrace the harmony of humility and empowerment. By clearly outlining our course and our goals, we foster the development of our bowlers and foster a culture where they are valued, inspired, and given the tools to succeed. It is an ongoing process that calls for self-awareness, flexibility, and a sincere desire for their success.

We must give up self-promotion in order to build humility, and we must let our deeds and the good we do in the lives of our bowlers do the talking. True differentiation may be found in the important connections we create and the changes we enable, not in the lofty assertions we make about ourselves. We demonstrate the spirit of humility in our coaching approach by concentrating on the requirements of our bowlers and giving priority to their growth.

Creating a personal coaching philosophy serves as a compass that guides all of our decisions and deeds. This philosophy, which is based on our values, principles, and beliefs, serves as the guide for staying on track with our goals. We must immerse ourselves in the huge sea of coaching literature and absorb the knowledge of our forebears if we are to develop a philosophy that endures. We can unearth hidden truths and improve our coaching methodology by participating in critical conversations and challenging preconceived notions.

To provide a path for each bowler's or team's development, a thorough competition strategy and development plan must be created. These strategies ought to include every facet of their athletic development, including technical prowess, psychological fortitude, and physical condition. By taking care of each aspect, we establish the groundwork for their holistic development and give them the resources they need to succeed in the competition.

A clear completion model also makes it easier to follow bowlers' progress and find their particular path to success. We can then adjust our coaching selections and techniques as necessary to make sure their journey is in line with their ultimate objectives. We can fine-tune our strategy and promote their continual improvement by conducting regular assessments and modifications based on their progress.

As coaches, readiness becomes our guiding principle. We build a sense of confidence and resiliency in our bowlers by meticulously planning and preparing them. They are prepared for the difficulties and ambiguities they face during competition because they have a strong foundation and a clear strategic plan to follow. They are better equipped to face hardship, grow from failures, and overcome it because of their readiness.

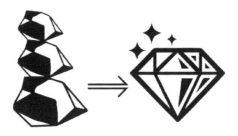

QUALITY OF TRAINING

Redefining Performance Enhancement

Sports performance is influenced by a variety of variables, but two important ones are natural selection and the adaptations that come through training for a particular sport. Genetics and the idea of selection are closely related, and the latter is essentially immune to outside influence. On the other hand, a variety of stimuli offered during the training process are necessary for the manifestation of genetic potential that results in certain adaptations. The overall goal of this procedure, which consists of several steps, is to close the gap between the desired performance level and the current performance level. These phases include setting goals, learning about the specific demands of the sport, evaluating the bowler's skills and areas for improvement, applying training principles, orchestrating training load factors (such as exercises, modes of locomotion, volume, intensity, and frequency), and incorporating recovery strategies (such as rest and nutrition).

Example: Jason Belmonte

Belmonte's commitment to the training regimen is responsible for his achievement. He establishes clear objectives for himself, concentrating on both short- and long-term aims. Additionally, he has an extensive understanding of the criteria unique to his sport, continuously reviewing his own performance and getting advice from trainers and other professionals.

Belmonte uses a variety of practice objectives and several training modalities to imitate game-like scenarios in order to optimize his training load factors. Additionally, he pays great attention to his recuperation techniques, making sure to obtain adequate sleep and keep up a balanced diet.

The quantitative features of training characteristics in elite athletes across several sports have been widely studied and documented. These elements have undergone in-depth examination, and subsequent experimental studies have assessed the training models built from the routines of elite athletes. However, when asked to elaborate on the variables influencing their performance, successful bowlers regularly highlight the need for high-quality training. Curiously, the discipline of sport science has paid little attention to this feature, and a number of fundamental questions about it need investigation.

What really makes for high-quality training? According to Oxford Languages, the word "quality" comes from the Latin word "qualis," which means "how" or "what kind." Quality is concerned with the level of quality in something or the way activities are carried out. Unexpectedly, the sport science community has not yet reached an agreement on a clear definition of training quality, with the majority of practitioners claiming that it depends on one's perspective. These viewpoints might be either holistic, looking at the overall training process, or atomistic, looking only at the individual training sessions.

What elements affect how training quality is modulated? Many different contextual factors have an impact on the complex web of the training process. The most important of these are bowler-dependent traits and propensities, which include factors like age, gender, training background, drive, maturity, proficiency with training techniques, recovery/training status, as well as the demands of their job, studies, and familial obligations. The coach, who brings a wealth of knowledge, experience, and pedagogical abilities to the table together with the dynamic interaction between training peers, support staff, training facilities, weather conditions, and equipment, however, also has a significant impact on the quality of training.

The idea of training quality digs deeply into thorough comprehension, covering assessments, choices, and fine-tuning. Each of these dimensions, whether physiological, technical, tactical, or psychological, has its roots in observations, perceptions, and analyses across several training areas. Without the issue of training quality, coaching would be unnecessary and bowlers could all adopt a uniform, one-size-fits-all method. The bowlers themselves are ultimately responsible for achieving a high level of training quality, although coaches and supporting staff can have an indirect impact by acting in a way that targets the bowlers. This helps to explain why bowlers, coaches, and support personnel may have slightly different opinions about the quality of training since their mindsets and training methods are formed by their assigned positions. Coaches frequently place a strong emphasis on pre-training dose planning, active supervision and feedback during training execution, and post-training analysis. Contrarily, bowlers often put emphasis on preparation, making sure they have enough rest and recovery after the previous session, carrying out their allotted tasks while training with a focused attitude, then catering to their nutritional needs, cleansing routines, and quickly changing into dry clothing.

Hypothetical Examples

Example 1: Sarah has had years of coaching expertise as a bowler. She is incredibly driven and adamant about raising her performance level. Sarah is aware that her coach, who possesses vast sport-specific knowledge, experience, and pedagogical skills, has a significant impact on the quality of her training. As a result, she actively asks her coach for input during training sessions and evaluates the session afterward to pinpoint areas that need to be improved. In order to ensure that she can train at a high level, Sarah also monitors her recuperation and training status and modifies her training load factors accordingly.

Example 2: John is a young bowler who has only recently begun his training. Although he is very determined, he lacks experience and is unaware of the needs particular to his sport. The quality of John's training is greatly influenced by his coach, who offers advice on the right workouts, volume, intensity, and frequency. In order to help John effectively raise his performance level, the coach also concentrates on dose planning before the session, supervision and feedback during training execution, and session analysis afterward. John regularly monitors his training and recuperation progress to make sure he is refreshed and ready for each training session.

Who has the power to decide whether or not the training process is of a satisfactory caliber? In real-world circumstances common in the world of elite or top-tier sports, the assessment of training effectiveness primarily depends on the results obtained from the process itself. These results often have a quantitative nature and are operationalized through performance indicators that are objectively specified, where the quality of an outcome is inextricably related to how far it deviates from a predetermined goal. The bowler may not be selected for upcoming teams, the coach may be fired by the organization in charge of regulating the sport, and financial assistance may be withdrawn if the results consistently fall short of the intended objective. However, it is crucial that assessments concentrate more attention on the effectiveness of the steps taken to promote long-term development within the particular sport discipline. Since the holistic nature of training quality cannot be fully judged using objective criteria alone, this endeavor provides a far more difficult issue. Seasoned coaches' ability to evaluate training quality may be enhanced by their track record of success with several bowlers over time. All parties concerned in the training process must, however, actively participate in evaluation procedures that gauge the quality of the instruction. This accomplishes two key goals: first, it facilitates in-depth discussions about the effects of the numerous factors at play; and second, it builds a strong basis for all stakeholders to work together to improve training quality.

The use of specialized training methods is required by professional bowlers' pursuit of perfection. These top-notch training techniques are essential conduits for the growth of the athletes' physical, technical, and mental skills.

We will discuss the key components of a quality training program for elite players.

Expert Coaching:

In order to improve their abilities and realize their full potential, elite athletes need professional coaching. Skilled coaches should be fully aware of the sport's physical and technical demands as well as the mental skills necessary for success. Additionally, they should be able to create and carry out training plans that are customized for the requirements of each player. Drills, games, and simulations are just a few of the coaching techniques that skilled coaches should have at their disposal. They must be able to offer suggestions and corrections to players so they may refine their technique.

Hypothetical Examples

John, a bowler, works with a knowledgeable instructor who has a wealth of knowledge about the game. His coach offers him individualized criticism and guidance to enhance his performance since he has a thorough understanding of the technical, tactical, physical, and mental components of bowling.

Periodization:

Periodization refers to the technique of breaking the training year up into various phases, each having a distinct objective. Periodization is a crucial part of a top-notch training plan for elite athletes. The preseason, in-season, and off-season are frequently included in the periodization phases. Building strength, endurance, and technical skills are the main priorities during the preseason phase. The emphasis changes to maintaining physical condition and enhancing game-specific skills during the in-season period. The off-season period is when rest and recovery are prioritized.

Hypothetical Examples

A periodized training schedule that Rachel, a professional bowler, follows is carefully planned and created to assist her in performing at her best during contests. She divides her training into stages, each with distinct priorities and goals, and modifies the number and intensity of her workouts in accordance with her competition schedule.

Sports-Specific Training:

Sports-specific training is necessary for elite athletes to acquire the technical abilities needed in their sport. Sports-specific training involves honing the particular abilities and methods needed for the sport. Soccer players, for instance, need to work on their passing, ball handling, and shot accuracy. Tennis players should work on their forehand, backhand, and serving mechanics. A component of sport-specific training is simulating game situations. Players can improve their game awareness and decision-making abilities thanks to this.

The technical, tactical, physical, and mental qualities necessary for bowling are being developed in Mark, a junior bowler, as part of a training regimen tailored to his sport. In order to get ready for various competition circumstances, he practices exercises and drills that replicate the movements and demands of the sport.

Mental Conditioning:

A good training regimen for elite athletes must include mental conditioning. Elite athletes must possess mental fortitude, tenacity, and the capacity to perform well under duress. Techniques for mental conditioning may include visualization, relaxation, and encouraging self-talk. Techniques for managing stress can also be a part of mental conditioning. Elite athletes must be able to handle stress and anxiety, and mental conditioning can aid athletes in acquiring these coping mechanisms.

Hypothetical Example

A mental coach works with Sarah, a professional bowler, to help her build the mental abilities necessary for peak performance. She gains skills in goal-setting, visualization, encouraging self-talk, and relaxation to help her cope with stress, maintain her concentration, and perform well under pressure.

MYTH: "A BOWLER MUST SPECIALIZE IN THE SPORT AS EARLY AS POSSIBLE OR HE/ SHE WILL NEVER BE PHYSICALLY OR PSYCHOLOGICALLY SUCCESSFUL."

Reality: It is crucial to dispel the myth that early specialization is the only path to success in bowling, particularly in youth sports. This belief overlooks important factors that contribute to overall athletic development and can negatively impact young bowlers' mentality and enjoyment of the sport. The amount of time dedicated to training is just one aspect of athletic performance, with coaching, passion, enjoyment, and natural talent also playing significant roles. There is no conclusive evidence to support the notion that early specialization guarantees long-term, high-level success in bowling.

What truly matters in becoming successful bowlers the dedication, determination, and work ethic individuals bring to their training and development? Regardless of when one starts their bowling journey or how far behind their peers they may feel, it is their passion and hard work that will propel them forward. Embrace the journey, stay focused on goals, and trust that dedication and perseverance will lead to desired outcomes. Becoming a champion in bowling is not solely determined by the timing of one's start, but rather by the commitment and effort invested in the sport.

Recovery:

A top-notch training regimen for elite athletes must include recovery. Stretching, massages, and ice baths are some recovery methods. Recovery strategies aid in both injury prevention and athlete recovery following practice and competition. The importance of nutrition in rehabilitation cannot be overstated. A particular diet is necessary for elite athletes to maintain peak physical condition. The diet ought to be heavy in protein and carbohydrates and created to supply the body with the resources it needs to heal.

In order to maintain his performance and avoid injuries, Tom, a competitive bowler, understands the value of rehabilitation. He integrates several recuperation techniques into his training routine, such as getting enough sleep, staying hydrated, eating well, stretching, and taking breaks when his body requires them.

Quality of training – Early Stage

For young bowlers to lay a solid technical and physical basis, early bowler development is essential. The success and long-term growth of a bowler can be significantly impacted by effective training techniques used during this period. In this essay, we'll talk about how to use effective training techniques for developing young bowlers.

Hypothetical Example

Young bowler Lisa takes part in a training regimen that prioritizes quality training over quantity. Her instructor concentrates on structured, gradual technique and foundation development to make sure she learns the right motions and shuns negative habits.

Multi-Sport Participation:

Young bowlers ought to play different sports from an early age. Bowlers can gain a wide variety of physical and technical skills by playing multiple sports. Additionally, this method aids bowlers in avoiding overuse injuries and burnout. Bowlers benefit from well-rounded growth through multisport participation. The physical and technical demands of other sports vary, which enables bowlers to develop a wide variety of talents. Due to the fact that they are not continuously using the same actions, bowlers are also better able to avoid overuse problems.

Hypothetical Example

In order to improve his overall athleticism and physical literacy, Jack, a junior bowler, takes part in a range of sports and activities. He understands that participating in several sports aids in the development of a variety of coordination, agility, and movement qualities that are transferrable to bowling.

Developmentally Appropriate Training:

Young bowlers should receive training that is developmentally appropriate. This means that the development of the bowler's skills should take into account both his physical and mental capabilities. Young bowlers, for instance, might not be able to execute difficult technical maneuvers or intense physical training. Age-appropriate training also means that it should be developmentally suitable. Young bowlers shouldn't be trained harshly or pushed too hard. Burnout, which can result from this and affect both the body and the mind, can lower motivation and performance.

Hypothetical Example

Emma, a young bowler, takes part in a training regimen that is specific to her age, skill level, and developmental stage. Her trainer creates exercises and drills that are suitable for her physical and mental capabilities and gradually increases the level of difficulty and intensity.

Emphasis on Fundamentals:

Young bowlers should concentrate on honing key techniques at a young age. Balance, coordination, and agility are a few of these. Young bowlers who master these techniques can subsequently accomplish more complicated maneuvers. Fundamental abilities aid bowlers in avoiding injuries as well. Bowlers can lower their risk of injury as they advance to more sophisticated skills by building a solid base of fundamental skills.

Hypothetical Example

The importance of understanding the sport's foundations is something that professional bowler Alex is aware of. To be able to repeat his motions repeatedly and precisely, he spends a lot of time honing his technique, footwork, and release.

Small-Sided Games:

For the early growth of bowlers, small-sided games are a crucial part of effective teaching techniques. Young bowlers have more chances to touch the ball, make choices, and use their technical skills in small-sided games. Additionally, this method aids in the decision-making and game-awareness development of bowlers. For young bowlers, small-sided games offer a pleasant and interesting setting. Bowlers can enjoy the game without the stress of performing well in a competitive setting by participating in small-sided games.

Hypothetical Example

Ben, a bowler, takes part in small-sided games that mimic competition situations and aid in the development of his tactical abilities. He gains the ability to read the state of the lanes, modify his strategy, and choose wisely when under duress.

Positive Reinforcement:

In order to improve young bowlers, proper training techniques must include positive reinforcement. Praise and encouragement for young bowlers' efforts and advancement are examples of positive reinforcement. Young bowlers' self-esteem and confidence are boosted by positive reinforcement. This strategy aids bowlers in cultivating a positive outlook on practice and competition.

Hypothetical Example

When Olivia, a junior bowler, performs well in practice and competition, her coach and parents encourage her. She gains motivation, self-assurance, and a good outlook on the sport as a result.

Quality of Psychological training - Early stage

In order to develop a bowler early on, psychological training is crucial. Young bowlers who get high-quality psychological training methods can improve their confidence, resilience, and mental toughness. In this essay, we'll talk about how to use effective psychological training techniques for developing young bowlers.

Hypothetical Example

A young bowler named Jake takes part in a psychological training program that aims to improve his mental abilities and resilience. To reduce stress and perform at his best, he learns strategies like goal-setting, visualization, and positive self-talk.

Positive Self-Talk:

Young bowlers can benefit psychologically from practicing positive self-talk. It entails speaking and thinking positively about oneself in order to uplift and inspire oneself. Young bowlers can boost their self-confidence and create a good mindset by using positive self-talk. Young bowlers can learn from coaches and parents how to talk to themselves positively during practice and competition. Before a game, for instance, instructors might advise bowlers to repeat affirmations like "I am strong" or "I am confident." This strategy can assist young bowlers in cultivating a good outlook and a confident approach to competition.

When confronting a challenging shot or after a less-than-ideal frame, a player may employ self-talk to tell themselves to remain cool and confident. Norm Duke, one of the best bowlers in the world, who frequently employs positive self-talk while competing, is one example.

Goal-Setting:

Another good psychological training technique for young bowlers is goal-setting. Setting goals entails choosing SMART (specific, measurable, attainable, relevant, and time-bound) objectives. Young bowlers who create goals can concentrate on particular aspects of their game and monitor their development over time. Young bowlers can develop SMART goals with the aid of their parents and coaches. For instance, young bowlers might decide to increase their dribbling abilities by a given percentage over a certain amount of time. This strategy can assist young bowlers in concentrating on particular aspects of their game and cultivating a sense of satisfaction when they reach their objectives.

For instance, a player may decide to focus on increasing his strike percentage or honing a particular talent, such as refining his release technique. EJ Tackett of the United States, who has set and attained a number of objectives throughout his career, is one example of a great athlete who uses goal-setting well.

Visualization:

Young bowlers who want to enhance their game can benefit from the psychological training technique of visualization. Visualization is the process of mentally practicing a skill or performance. Young bowlers can gain confidence and get ready for competition with the aid of this strategy. Young bowlers can do visualization exercises prior to competition with the help of their coaches and parents. Young bowlers, for instance, can picture themselves scoring a goal or making a crucial save. This strategy can assist young bowlers in creating an image of success in their minds and approaching competition with confidence.

It's possible for players to see themselves making a flawless strike or scooping up a challenging spare. Danielle McEwan, a top athlete from the United States, has commented about how visualization helps her maintain her composure and focus when competing.

Relaxation Techniques:

A good psychological training tool for young bowlers is relaxation techniques. Young bowlers can better control their stress and anxiety by practicing relaxation techniques like deep breathing, progressive muscle relaxation, or meditation. Young bowlers can learn calming techniques from coaches and parents that they can employ both before and during the competition. For instance, a young bowler might practice deep breathing prior to a match in order to relax and get ready for competition.

Jesper Svensson from Sweden is one example of a great athlete who makes use of these strategies. He has spoken about how meditation and other relaxing methods help him maintain his composure and attention while playing.

Positive Reinforcement:

In the early stages of bowler development, positive reinforcement is a crucial part of psychological training techniques. Praise and encouragement for young bowlers' efforts and advancement are examples of positive reinforcement. Young bowlers can develop a positive attitude toward practice and competition with the use of positive reinforcement. Young bowlers may benefit from it by developing their self-esteem and confidence.

A coach might commend players for improving their overall score or making a challenging shot, for instance. Shannon O'Keefe of the United States is a great athlete who has benefited from positive reinforcement. She has talked about how her coaches' and teammates' support and encouragement have contributed to her success.

THE ART OF COACHING: BALANCING SELFLESSNESS AND EXPERTISE IN SPORTS *by Peter Somoff*

Abstract: To successfully lead athletes and teams to success, coaching is a multifaceted position that calls for selflessness and skill. This article examines the various coaching levels, from amateur to professional, and highlights the significance of realizing that coaches are not teammates but rather the team's leaders and voice-setters. It explores the difficulties coaches confront, including balancing individual and team dynamics, taking age, culture, and outside influences into account, and communicating effectively in a way that inspires players. The article also emphasizes the value of accurate evaluation, individualized coaching strategies, and the necessity of overcoming self-doubt and fear of failure in athletics. It ends by going over the special abilities needed to make the transition from player to successful coach as well as the significance of a coach in analyzing, foreseeing, and communicating successful methods to players.

By Somoff - Coaching. Most people who hear this word immediately develop a variety of preconceptions. Descriptors like expert, strict, know-it-all, guru, leader, psychologist, father figure, idol, idiot, teacher, winner, loser, and genius spring to mind. You may hear all of this by simply watching your favorite sports program.

Particularly in team sports, the coach is frequently questioned, acts as the team's spokesperson, and sets the tone. This is undoubtedly a crucial role, and the best coaches know how to make use of it. Additionally, there are many different levels of coaching, including coaching for kids, amateur coaching, professional coaching, coaching for groups or teams, and even coaching for individuals on teams. While coaching differs in each category, people who are successful in this role share one trait. That exhibits selflessness. Let's define coaching in more detail.

The definition makes no reference to the coach being a member of the team. Who is the last person introduced at a professional sporting event? Where does the coach live, exactly? The margins.

Does the director's name appear first when you watch a movie? the stars, or both? Is the director listed among the final credits?

This is so for a reason—neither the player nor the coach is the star. This very crucial guideline must be understood and upheld if you want to be a good coach. In a lot of instances, people who coach themselves want to be the center of attention, or they even want to play out their fantasies through coaching or get rid of grievances. This is not the appropriate setting or time for this, as the coach risks doing more harm than good to the players.

It's important to realize that coaching comes with a lot of responsibility because you are entrusted with someone's or a team's performance. Coaches occasionally participate substantially in some areas while not participating at all in others. As a coach, you must operate almost like a judge, constantly assessing your own actions and those of those around you to see if what you are saying, doing, or instructing is fair and beneficial to everyone. Additionally, you must be able to draw on that person's past experiences—both positive and negative—to predict what might occur as a result of your coaching. Of course, there are various levels of expertise and experience that must be taken into account when deciding how and what to apply. There is a lot to balance when you add this to factors like age, culture, outside influences, and the ongoing commentary on social media. The coach's instructions must be so clear and effectively conveyed that the player is forced to comply. Additionally, this varies depending on who, where, how, and when.

The idea of team bowling is particularly focused on a support network as bowling is a solitary sport. There is no assist or passing of the ball when you bowl as a team. The players are exposed and standing alone on the approach, under pressure to produce on their own. The only teamwork that exists, then, is support, strategy, the sharing of ideas for lane play and ball play, joy and sympathy, and most importantly, not having a bad influence on your teammates. But how about actually doing it? The decision is ultimately up to the person and no one else. Why discuss these topics? It's because we can't succeed if we lose sight of the collaboration, the genuine difficulty, and the work required. There isn't much time for the player or coach to think about anything aside from the task at hand. The most effective athletes in any discipline frequently utilize the word "concentration." Due to the swiftness of the activity, focus and instinctive motions are blended in fast-moving sports. However, in sports like bowling or golf where there is no set amount of time and the player must take the initiative, the silence can be deafening. When we play, self-doubt is without a doubt the biggest battle we face since it permeates all elements of our performances. Simply put, thinking of "butterflies" is another way of feeling anxious, which, when broken down, is another way of conveying self-doubt. Why do we actually feel anxious? I don't have any problems and will probably breeze through if I'm standing on a short beam that's six inches off the ground. However, if I lift that exact same beam 50 feet, everything changes. Why, even if the distance and beam are both the same, my imagination is racing with potential outcomes. My attention is not on winning, but rather on what can be lost. Failure is something that we all fear. The same thing happens while taking a written test; you worry about failing, you check the clock, you go back to questions you couldn't answer in the hopes that an answer would miraculously appear, and you finally fail. How can this be avoided? When you prepare and study, you put more emphasis on the subject matter than your end aim. The same is true with artistic performances; everything is choreographed and there are no surprises. The more skilled and seasoned artists correct mistakes and resume their performance in such a way that the audience is unaware of them. The less experienced performers, who obviously lack experience, have memories that they may either use to their advantage or destroy them. Additionally, during artistic performances, the crowd is hidden from view by darkness. In sports, none of this occurs since it is not preplanned or choreographed; athletes simply have a general concept of what is in front of them. They must respond to their own actions, those of others, and the physical changes in the environment that occur when bowling. Another aspect is that the audience is plainly seen and audible, though not always in a favorable or bad way. Success cannot be guaranteed because there are so many diverse factors at play; it can only be predicted.

The discipline required to become a coach necessitates letting go of any prejudice you may have toward your accomplishments as a player, thus it is important to note this while discussing coaching at a higher level. Coaching requires the ability to swiftly assess, access what is occurring, identify trends, and then be able to communicate that message to the player. In reality, the message must be delivered in a way that the player is fully persuaded and determined to follow through. In a perfect world, you wouldn't blame the coach when other factors enter the picture and affect the outcome. The question is, how do you overcome that challenge? Based on his experience with various personalities, cultures, languages, and trends, a better coach is able to communicate those ideas. The cacophony that constantly surrounds players—including videos, the internet, uninformed critics, and well-intentioned but uneducated casual players seeking to change or assist—can also be silenced by a competent coach. Your participant, pupil, or protégé must be completely convinced that you are on the right track. A good evaluation example. A female bowler with a 150 average once struggled with sticking at the foul line. She experimented with various slide soles and slide socks, which helped her stop the sticking. Her ball's accuracy and speed were now highly erratic and low. So what was the issue? It was the fit of her ball, but why was this place unnoticed? Because you have to delve beyond the obvious, consider other explanations, and determine how this path came to be, you must search beyond the obvious. In other words, because the ball could not fit in her hand, she had to compress it, which brought the ball closer to her spine. As a result of the subconscious brain's adjustment, the body is then tilted forward, placing 80% of the wearer's weight over the slide foot. Now it is almost hard to slip because of this. However, if the fit is improved, good posture develops, and the ball moves away from the spine, the weight is distributed evenly, allowing the player to slide without the aid of a sock while maintaining ball speed and accuracy, which is what actually happened.

By accurate judgment, this is exactly what we mine, but that I for the typical casual gamer. How about the best athletes?

Before continuing, we must accept the fact that not everyone who plays this sport, regardless of all the coaching He receives, will be successful at any level. He either doesn't have the physical characteristics, talent, drive, or intelligence needed to achieve. To believe that from the standpoint of a coach is a little off-target. For instance, if the other intangibles are missing, you cannot train someone to write wonderful music or have an artist make an original work of art. Coaching for bowling is similar to ball drilling in that it can only improve a ball that has already been rolled well; it cannot build a ball from scratch.

Along with passion, drive, ego, and heart, as one Hall-of-Famer told me, these qualities cannot be measured or discounted. Additionally, there are several levels of coaching's emphasis and intensity. Because this is a personal game, the requirements and strategies of each player vary greatly. Others are very technical or detail-oriented, while others need organization. Naturally, the exact opposite can also be asserted. Each player obviously needs extra assistance with a certain component of the game. Irrespective of the player, we constantly seek out better solutions, and sometimes it is the most difficult to make that individual aware of all the factors that can affect one's performance, including expectations, fear of failure, expectations from family and friends, travel, weather, food, the immediate environment, and biorhythms. Everything has to line up perfectly at the highest level for it to all work. I have worked with several players, spoken with them frequently, and faced off against them personally. Pete Weber, Brian Voss, Dave Husted, Hugh Miller, and Marshall Holman are examples of contemporaries. I'm from the bowling-friendly Pacific Northwest region of the US. Gary Mage, Johnny Guenther, and Earl Anthony all signed my PBA application, but I don't recall ever having them lecture me. I only wish I had paid closer attention back then. I obviously failed because I was so eager to demonstrate a better approach. At the time, information was not easily accessible. I mistakenly believed that the PBA bowling community was large, and I spent a lot of time watching others bowl in order to learn how to do it myself. Earl once came across me feeling defeated and said something I'll never forget, "Peter, no one out here is going to teach you how to beat them." I had such naive ideas about what was possible. At the time, it was also clear to me that I was not only relying on my athletic abilities. I would consider the risk and the balance instead. Additionally, I was more interested in what other people did and how they could get better. Being a voice for individuals who, at whatever level, just wanted to understand what they were doing was also extremely important to me. The distinction between sports selfishness and selflessness became clear at that point, and you had to make a decision. Sports selfishness is not what it first appears to be; to perform at the best level, one must be totally focused on the present, and therefore one must follow his body's and mind's instincts. If that means getting enough rest, then getting enough rest; practicing; practicing; not communicating well with anyone; you get the idea. The best sportsmen, actors in screenplays, or CEOs, for that matter, probably don't do his own laundry or stress out over dinner or hotel reservations. This brings me back to my original argument when I was talking about the great players because these folks only have one task to complete. They are all firmly devoted to the mission they are about to complete, have no question that what they intend to do is the right thing to do, and have a solid basis for what they want to do. They don't think negatively, and they have basic, calm thoughts in their heads.

Do you want to discover what it takes to succeed? I'll give you an illustration. A high school bowler came up to me around 25 years ago and begged for assistance. When I asked him what his objective was, he replied, "To play on the PBA tour." Okay, let's see; find a lane and warm up, I replied. He did, and as I down to discuss the task at hand with him, he was completely confident in his abilities. I followed up by asking what his favorite target on the lane was. He said, "14 at the arrows." Then, all I requested was that he roll the ball across the tape at the arrows as I instructed him to fire 12 shots. The rest of what it did was unimportant. Given his enthusiasm and drive, I accidentally gave him aboard. Anything else would be an open space, so one board outside of that would be a spare. After adding up the shots, I informed him that his average player rating on tour was around 165. He then yelled at me and walked away, never to be seen or heard from again. A few months later, he came up to me when I was bowling and inquired about a weight combination that really didn't matter. I could tell he wanted to talk to me because he had just shot 299 that evening without also shooting a 700 series. We had a conversation, and I assured him that I hadn't meant to offend him, but he had informed me that in order to succeed he needed to understand that if he wanted to compete with the greatest players in the game, they don't make those errors. I enquire about his willingness, to which he replies, "Whatever it takes." Since you cannot coach a lousy fit, we began by improving his fit. The most important aspect of a player's game is how well the ball fits in relation to the hand. I can't stress this enough; it's the biggest error I see everywhere, from players failing to maintain adequate texturing and hole tightness to the ball being drilled at the wrong angles and spans. I also find it challenging to imagine how somebody could instruct at the highest level without having a thorough understanding of fitness and bowling. This also brings up various skin and body types, where an understanding of physiology and kinesiology is quite helpful.

Additionally, traditional fingertips come in a range of sensitivity levels, depending on how sensitive the hand is. The professionals want a fit that will provide them with exact feedback; the beginner needs a fit that will allow for significant errors. Better players don't make costly errors; they need to recognize if it's me, the ball, or the lane that's in trouble. This level of bowling comes with the knowledge that your opponents will make accurate shots and a finite amount of frames. You need to make a decision quickly, but you also need to stick with it.

Beyond this, we needed to create a solid physical game that would work well under pressure, was based on leverage, and allowed everything to develop naturally. This player put in a lot of effort while, unavoidably, maturing. We faced numerous challenges, challenges in competitions, and difficulties. Then his game was destroyed by his peers, who kept pushing him to go somewhere else. This player stuck with the program despite all the interruptions. All of a sudden, I was doing the listening and responding rather than the talking. We collaborated as a team toward a similar objective *and solved the problem when I occasionally lacked the answer. There was no room for ego in this voyage between us. Success came slowly; there were still failures, but they weren't as severe or damaging as they had been. The player's emotional attitude decreased and was replaced by a more pragmatist mindset. It resembled going to work exactly. Years later, this player began to learn how to succeed; the elusive fire or heart was still present, but we also had the necessary physical resources and the courage to carry on. The best skill that this player acquired from his practice sessions was how to correct oneself when things go wrong. Remember that your brain seeks to return to its previous state whenever you change one of its "bad habits" rather than creating new ones. After a few minutes of exercises that were previously utilized to realign these inconsistent problems, we can go forward. What was the specific remedy? Whatever happens, the important thing is that we had a very reasonable and tried procedure for getting back in sync. What transpired to this high school bowler who had a bad attitude, a lot of fire, but little knowledge? As the tournament's leader, he took home the 1995 PBA National Championship under the name Scott Alexander. I also discovered something: Scott, not me, was ultimately the one who adopted that strategy; Scott had to exercise self-control and deal with his issues, not me. I don't mind at all that he won the title instead of me. If we are truly committed to our work as coaches, the fact that someone relied on us, believed in what we had to say, and was successful as a result of it should be enough of a reward.*

This is not to say that a coach should exclusively coach for free. Coaches should be recognized and hold players and teams accountable by speaking the truth to them. In my opinion, everyone needs to pay on all sides. A reliable single voice is priceless in today's world of social media assassinations and constant cacophony. It's 2019, so let's upgrade that to platinum.

Peter Somoff, USBC Gold Coach and IBPSIA President

QUALITY CHECKLIST OF A GOOD COACH

The caliber of coaching a bowler receives has a profound impact on the quality of his sporting experience. A lifelong interest in the sport and physical exercise can be fostered by good instruction, which can assist bowlers in realizing their full potential. On the other hand, poor coaching can result in detrimental effects like fatigue, dropout, injuries, and a lack of passion. As a result, it is crucial that all bowlers adopt high-quality teaching as the norm.

With a better understanding of bowler development and the transmission of cutting-edge research and efficient teaching techniques via academic publications, coaching newsletters, social media, and digital sports programming, the coaching profession in bowling has made great strides. Nevertheless, despite these initiatives, there is still a substantial gap between the theoretical understanding of excellent coaching and its actual day-to-day execution.

The initiative to define core values and best practices that should direct and coordinate coaching techniques in bowling has been taken to close this gap. A well-created and research-based resource, The Quality Coaching - Principles & Structure creates a common vocabulary for individuals working in Team and/or Bowling Academies. It tries to educate coaches on the most successful coaching techniques without imposing strict rules.

In order to improve a bowler's competence, confidence, connection, and character in certain coaching settings, this coaching strategy places an emphasis on the consistent use of integrated professional, interpersonal, and intrapersonal knowledge. Leading sporting and coaching organizations all around the world have embraced this integrative definition of coaching effectiveness. It is the outcome of a thorough assessment of the coaching, teaching, expertise, positive psychology, and bowler development literature as well as considerable applied research. To verify its validity and applicability, the definition underwent a rigorous review by coaches, coaching educators, and significant sport organizations.

MYTH: THE COACH KNOWS BEST.

Reality: The belief that coaches possess all-encompassing knowledge and can single-handedly correct errors in bowlers is a myth. Research emphasizes the importance of a collaborative approach to error correction, where bowlers actively participate in the process. Studies have shown that bowlers who take ownership of their development, set goals, and provide self-feedback experience greater improvement in performance.

Real-life examples further debunk the myth. Emily, Jason, and Alex, all bowlers in different stages of their development, showcased the significance of collaboration in error correction. By initiating open dialogues with their coaches, sharing their observations, and proposing alternative strategies, they actively contributed to their own improvement. Through this collaborative effort, they achieved significant progress and disproved the notion that the coach knows best.

In conclusion, a collaborative approach between coaches and bowlers is vital for effective error correction. Bowlers should take an active role in their development, providing self-feedback, initiating conversations with their coaches, and offering their perspectives. By fostering a collaborative environment, coaches and bowlers can combine their knowledge and expertise to devise personalized plans that lead to enhanced performance. Dispelling the myth of the coach as the sole authority empowers bowlers to become active participants in their own growth and development.

Three separate elements make up high-quality coaching:

Coaching expertise, bowler results, and the coaching atmosphere.

Acquiring and using evidence-based coaching practices, tactics, and procedures constitutes coaching expertise. The development of the bowlers themselves, including their abilities, performance, personal development, and general well-being, is the emphasis of bowler outcomes. The term "coaching environment" describes the setting in which coaching occurs and includes elements like organizational support, athlete-centered strategies, empowering and supportive coaching relationships, and the creation of a welcoming atmosphere for growth and learning.

The bowling community can guarantee that players have the best coaching experiences possible by adhering to these principles and fostering a culture of quality teaching, which will result in ideal results and a long-lasting passion for the game.

Developing Crucial Coaching Skills

Given the complex nature of teaching and the variety of roles they play, the significance of gaining fundamental coaching knowledge cannot be overstated for bowling coaches. There are three basic types of coaching knowledge that all coaches need to have:

Expertise in the Field: This includes having a thorough knowledge of the sport of bowling and employing efficient teaching techniques. Coaches must have a thorough understanding of the history, customs, rules, and culture of bowling. They should also be knowledgeable about a wide range of athletic abilities, strategies, training techniques, and safety factors. In order for coaches to use their information effectively and customize it to specific bowlers, they should also investigate the learning requirements and developmental processes of bowlers.

1. **Interpersonal Connections:** Within the context of sports, coaches must be able to build trusting relationships and exercise effective leadership. This requires building trusting relationships and effective communication skills with bowlers as well as other stakeholders like officials, administrators, parents, and program coordinators. Additionally, coaches should exhibit emotional intelligence by keeping an eye on and controlling their own emotions while creating healthy and fruitful connections. To lead and motivate individuals and teams to success, one must have strong leadership abilities.

2. **Inward Reflection and Growth:** Coaches must be self-aware and have a firm commitment to their own development. They ought to have a distinct sense of purpose and core beliefs that operate as directives for their coaching work. As coaches negotiate the different highs and lows of their coaching experience, it is essential

Qualities that a coach must possess in order to achieve greatness.

1) Leadership- A great coach must guide, inspire and empower an athlete or team to achieve full potential.

2) Knowledge- a great coach must have in depth knowledge, must Know the fundamental skills and tactics .Must answer every question .

3) Motivation- must convey passion to the players, must have a positive attitude and enthusiasm for the game and pass it on to the players. Must make practice fun and challenging.

4) Knows the athlete- needs to pay attention to emotions, strengths and weaknesses. Needs to be a mentor and a counsellor.

5) Consistency - must teach the same message constantly and consistently

6) Effective communication skills- must set goals that are clear to the players, give feedback and acknowledge success. Must listen to players.

Coach Frank Buffa

to have perspective and balance in the face of difficulties. Recognizing their skills and weaknesses as coaches enables coaches to increase their efficiency and favorably influence the development of their bowlers.

Bowling coaches can better prepare themselves to handle the varied demands of their position by acquiring thorough coaching expertise throughout these three categories. This information provides a strong foundation for their coaching methods and helps create a supportive atmosphere for the development and success of their bowlers.

Coaches can continuously improve their performance by identifying their strengths and areas for development. Reflection is crucial because it enables coaches to assess their methods objectively and make the necessary changes to support continuous improvement.

Bowling coaches may increase their effectiveness and give their bowlers the best support by owning and continuously developing five critical coaching knowledge domains. This theoretical and psychological paradigm encourages a holistic approach to coach development by acknowledging the value of both interpersonal and technical abilities in coaching.

Professional expertise: New bowlers may look to a coach for advice who is educated in various bowling methods and styles, such as spin, hook, or straight bowling, and who can instruct them on how to develop their abilities properly. In order to better predict the trajectory and speed of the ball, a coach might, for instance, demonstrate to young bowlers how to change their grip, stance, or approach to the lane or how to read oil patterns on the lane surface.

Interpersonal skills: Young bowlers may benefit from a coach who can establish positive and encouraging team dynamics and who can interact with them and their teammates successfully. For instance, a coach might encourage young bowlers to voice their opinions and concerns, pay close attention to their criticism, and promote trust and respect among the entire team.

A young bowler may look up to a coach who is an excellent role model for self-control, resiliency, and constant growth. For instance, a coach might advise rookie bowlers to set reasonable objectives, monitor their development, and recognize their accomplishments along the way. Additionally, a coach can assist young bowlers in adopting healthy behaviors and attitudes by serving as an example, such as remaining focused, positive, and open-minded.

Bowler-Centered Outcomes

Bowler-centered outcomes, which include the growth and performance of the bowlers themselves, are the essential markers of high-quality coaching in the sport of bowling. The goal of holistic bowler development is to mold not only better bowlers but also better people; quality coaching goes beyond developing competent athletes and competitive persons. The Four C's of the bowler development framework, which serves as a road map to identify and foster important aspects of a bowler's progress beyond technical bowling skills, is in line with this quest for holistic bowler outcomes.

1. **Competence:** The mastery of technical and tactical bowling skills is the foundation of competence. It includes all of the sport's complex technical elements, such as grip, stance, approach, release, and follow-through. Additionally, tactical awareness is stressed, including the capacity to assess the playing environment, modify line and length, and formulate successful strategies. Competent bowlers place a high priority on their physical well-being, which includes strength, stamina, flexibility, and agility. Fostering competency requires the development of healthy training habits, such as appropriate hydration, nutrition, rest, and recovery.

2. **Self-belief:** Self-belief, resilience, mental toughness, and a positive self-perception are all components of confidence. A self-assured bowler loves risk-taking, exhibits coolness under pressure, and has an optimistic outlook on their talents. A friendly environment, constructive criticism, and opportunities for both success and failure are necessary for a bowler to develop confidence. Bowlers who exude confidence are more likely to deliver their best effort and enjoy the game.

3. **Connection:** Connection is the development of enduring friendships and social ties with people both inside and beyond the context of sport. Bowlers' drive, engagement, and devotion to the game are increased when they feel a connection to their teammates, coaches, and the larger bowling community. Positive social connections also support mental health, which in turn improves a bowler's performance as a whole.

4. **Character:** A bowler's morally upright and ethical conduct is reflected in his character. It encompasses the principles of fair play, integrity, empathy, and respect for the game. Bowlers with good character understand the value of sportsmanship, play by the rules, and show respect for the opposition. Additionally, they are aware of their impact on the game and make an effort to set an example for others both on and off the field. A good and inclusive culture is fostered within the squad and the larger bowling community by developing strong character qualities.

Quality coaching in bowling can holistically nurture the growth and development of bowlers by recognizing and emphasizing these four bowler-centered outcomes. This will give bowlers the mental toughness, social connections, and ethical foundation they need to succeed in the sport over the long term. This theoretical and psychological viewpoint emphasizes the need for an all-inclusive coaching strategy that concentrates on the entire development of bowlers as individuals.

Contextual Fit

Even though there are a ton of coaching resources online, it's crucial for bowling coaches to use caution and take the context into account before putting any suggested coaching techniques or training methods into practice. The capacity to modify one's teaching expertise in order to meet the unique demands of the bowlers while taking into account the unique characteristics of the coaching environment is a prerequisite for providing quality coaching in the sport of bowling.

The concept of quality coaching can be usefully examined within four different situations that have things in common, despite the fact that each coaching situation has its own particular qualities. Coaches can obtain a better understanding of the dynamic nature of coaching and adjust their style by looking at how coaching environments and bowlers' growth stages interact.

Effective coaching requires an understanding of the specifics and requirements of each coaching context. The four recognized coaching environments offer a framework that helps trainers deal with the difficulties that come with developing bowlers. Coaches may maximize their coaching tactics and develop environments that support growth and advancement by taking into account the unique requirements and features connected with each location.

It is crucial to understand that coaches' capacity to adapt to and match their coaching method with the particular context in which they operate also plays a role in how effective their coaching is. This necessitates a thorough comprehension of the bowler's current developmental stage, their unique requirements, and ambitions, as well as the contextual circumstances that might affect their development.

Coaches can better satisfy the unique requirements of bowlers in a variety of settings by embracing the concept of contextual fit. This method highlights the necessity of customizing coaching tactics to meet the unique requirements of each coaching situation while acknowledging the dynamic nature of coaching. Coaches can better understand the contextual aspects that affect their efficacy as teachers and foster an environment that promotes the growth of bowlers via the use of theoretical and psychological lenses.

Foundational Coaching Knowledge: Unlocking The Path To Excellence

One must build a solid foundation of thorough knowledge embracing numerous fields in order to become a top-notch bowling instructor. Each coach sets out on his coaching journey with a unique combination of educational experience and theoretical knowledge. In the early phases of coaching, newly learned information exists as disjointed bits of knowledge. However, when coaches develop more expertise and engage in reflective activities, patterns start to emerge and knowledge is structured into a structure that is simple to access. Top-tier coaches exhibit this cognitive process, referred to as the creation of mental representations. The amount and caliber of their mental representations are how expert trainers differ from novices.

It is widely accepted that professional knowledge, interpersonal knowledge, and intrapersonal information make up the core of fundamental coaching knowledge.

Professional Knowledge: Unleashing the Power Within

Two fundamental coaching functions constitute the core of professional expertise:

Preparing training programs of the highest caliber. Aiding bowlers in achieving their best performance in competitive settings.

A thorough understanding of bowling's historical backdrop, rules, and special requirements is essential for properly educating and guiding bowlers. As a result, coaches' expertise in the following three areas is used to determine how knowledgeable they are:

A. Bowling Experience and Expertise: Mastering the Craft

In every setting, coaches must at the very least have a firm understanding of safety rules and bowling restrictions. Additionally, it is helpful to get knowledge about the sport's distinctive customs and culture by research and observation, in part. However, active participation in the activity itself is the greatest way to fully understand various nuances and cultural complexities. Thus, although it is not required, having some prior experience as a bowler gives an advantage in the world of performance sports. Direct involvement makes it easier for instructors to understand the difficulties faced by bowlers, ultimately creating trust and confidence. The fact that excellent bowlers do not necessarily make for exceptional coaches must be acknowledged, though.

B. Teaching and Learning Abilities: Nurturing Growth and Flourishing

Coaches who lead practice sessions that maximize bowler growth have a number of critical traits:

- Facilitating the development of demanding and precise practice objectives, either by the bowlers themselves or by encouraging them to do so.

- Keeping bowlers' attention and focus throughout practice sessions.

- Giving bowlers options and actively soliciting their advice on practice design can empower them.

- Incorporating competition and game-like features into drills.

These guidelines enable coaches to create a learning environment that promotes skill development and improves overall performance.

Deliberate practice is the term used to describe these traits collectively. This type of practice is motivated by aim, purpose, and a concentration on skill development. Understanding the four guiding concepts for bowler learning is necessary for creating intentional practice training sessions.

Bowler Learning Principle	Sample Coaching Strategy
Influence of Prior Knowledge on Bowler Learning	Assess bowlers' readiness by eliciting their explanation or demonstration of the skill to evaluate their cognitive preparedness
The Impact of Bowler Motivation on the Learning Process	Seek bowlers' feedback on the perceived difficulty of learning activities to achieve an optimal challenge-skill equilibrium
Skill Mastery through Component Skill Acquisition	Facilitate skill acquisition by sequentially describing and demonstrating the essential steps required for proficient performance
Integration of Deliberate Bowling Practice with Targeted Feedback	Pre-identify feedback cues and establish feedback bandwidths to guide bowlers towards meeting learning and performance standards

Table 39 -Principles of Bowler Learning and Sample Coaching Strategies

The core of coaching is teaching. The four bowler learning concepts serve as a strong foundation for improving as a teacher. Effective teaching skills are something that top coaches take great satisfaction in acquiring.

C. Aptitude for Competition Coaching

A careful plan must be followed before, during, and after the competition in order to perform at one's best. Skilled coaches prioritize their bowlers' relaxation and timing prior to competitions to make sure they attain their best performance at the appropriate time. Additionally, they help bowlers enter their unique zones of peak psychological and emotional states by facilitating pre-competition rituals. Coaches make sure their bowlers are well-fueled just before the competition starts to match the energy requirements of the occasion.

Competent coaches closely monitor bowler performance throughout the competition and take action as needed. Depending on the individual rules and peculiarities of the sport, instructors may be able to direct bowlers directly during contests to a different level. Effective coaches, however, focus on the three E's of competitive coaching as a general rule to help their bowlers towards peak performance:

- Examine: Throughout contests, coaches closely examine and evaluate bowler efficiency.

- Encourage: Coaches help bowlers stay focused and confident by offering encouragement and support.

- Encourage: Coaches help bowlers stay focused and confident by offering encouragement and support.

Beyond the actual performance, competitive coaching plays a larger significance. Coaches have an excellent chance to get bowlers ready for the next matches or practice sessions right after a match. Regardless of whether success or failure is an overwhelming emotion, good coaches urge bowlers to take advantage of this post-competition period for relaxation, healing, self-reflection, and emotional processing.

Interpersonal Knowledge

The ability of a coach to build beneficial and productive relationships with others is referred to as interpersonal knowledge. Interpersonal knowledge gives coaches insight into how to coach each unique bowler and communicate effectively within the sporting setting, while professional knowledge provides the framework for understanding what to coach.

There are two key skills related to interpersonal knowledge in coaching:

Emotional Intelligence: Coaches who have emotional intelligence are able to recognize, make use of, comprehend, and control their emotions. This enables students to appreciate the sources and influences of emotions, identify and empathize with their own emotions as well as the emotions of others, harness emotions to improve focus and decision-making, and control their own emotions as well as the emotions of their bowlers.

CHOI BOK EUM

Interpersonal knowledge

My role model in the world of bowling was my mentor, the person who taught me the game. His words carried a sense of trust that inspired belief in others. Moreover, he possessed extensive knowledge and expertise in the sport. Living together and learning bowling theory during our training camp was not easy, but his passion and dedication were evident.

As for someone who recognized my potential abilities, I cannot be entirely certain. However, if I had to name someone, it would be James Kim.

Example on Coach - Emotional Intelligence: Coach A's method of instruction exhibits great emotional intelligence. He is capable of sensing and comprehending both his own and his bowlers' emotions. Coach A can empathize with a bowler who is feeling upset or disheartened and offer support and encouragement to help him get through his difficulties. As well as managing his own emotions well, Coach A maintains composure under pressure, which has a favorable effect on the team's emotional climate. Coach A fosters a positive and emotionally balanced coaching atmosphere that enables his bowlers to succeed by recognizing and managing emotions.

Transformational Leadership: Coaching bowlers effectively requires helping them to become capable leaders by fostering transformational leadership skills in them. Shared and transformational leadership techniques are emphasized in modern leadership frameworks. Therefore, bowling instructors ought to divide up the leadership roles and duties among their players and throughout their programs. Giving bowlers and other participants in the coaching environment the opportunity to assume leadership roles builds confidence, ownership, and a sense of group efficacy, which improves cohesion and results in better performance.

Example on Coach - Transformational Leadership: Inspiring his bowlers to become capable leaders themselves, Coach B exemplifies transformational leadership qualities. Each team member is given the opportunity to contribute and make decisions through his active distribution of leadership positions and duties. By giving his bowlers leadership responsibilities both on and off the bowling lane, Coach B cultivates a sense of pride and confidence in his team. Because bowlers feel appreciated and invested in the team's performance, this strategy strengthens team togetherness. Coach B fosters a culture of cooperation, group efficacy, and continual improvement through the instillation of transformational leadership skills, which enhances the performance and development of his bowlers.

Positive role models and transformational coaches encourage and support bowlers' ideas and continuously act in their bowlers' best interests. They inspire people via a compelling vision. Transformational coaching concentrates on supporting bowlers in attaining their goals, as opposed to transactional leadership, which revolves around coaches exploiting bowlers to achieve their own needs. According to research, shared and transformational leadership improves the bowler-coach relationship, fosters bowler fun, and eventually results in better performance.

Enhancing Emotional Intelligence

Astute observational abilities are essential for high-caliber instruction since bowling instructors spend a lot of time studying their bowlers and thinking about the ideal circumstances for bowler development. While tracking the development of a bowler's skills is important, coaches must also evaluate the bowler's motivation, emotions, and moods. It can be quite difficult to determine a bowler's emotive state, in contrast to spotting technical or tactical skill deficiencies. Coaches with high emotional intelligence exhibit exceptional performance by:

- Emotion Perception: Effectively recognizing the emotions of others and appropriately identifying their own sentiments.
- Emotion Utilization: Producing impulses to improve the ability to concentrate, make decisions, and solve problems.
- Emotion Understanding: Understanding the basic causes of emotions and how emotions affect other people's conduct.
- Emotion Management: Demonstrating emotional control and educating bowlers on how to recognize and manage their own emotions.
- Transformational Leadership

A complicated and well-studied aspect of coaching is leadership in the field of sports. Bowlers look to their coaches for leadership, but the best coaches also develop their players' leadership skills.

Modern leadership styles emphasize the value of transformational and shared leadership. Therefore, bowling instructors should assign leadership roles and tasks to different bowlers and groups within their programs. Giving bowlers and other coaching staff members the tools they need to lead builds their confidence and cultivates a feeling of pride in the sport. Enhanced cohesion, also known as collective efficacy, follows from this.

Inspiring others with a compelling vision, actively promoting and supporting bowlers' input, and constantly working in their bowlers' best interests are just a few of the ways that transformational coaches serve as great role models. They commit themselves to helping bowlers and supporting them as they pursue their objectives. This contrasts sharply with transactional leadership, in which coaches only use bowlers to meet their own needs. According to research, shared and transformational leadership strengthens the bonds between coaches and bowlers, increases bowlers' satisfaction, and has a considerable positive impact on performance.

Young bowlers who play on teams with transformational coaches may be encouraged to take on leadership roles, such as planning team outings or arranging pre-game warm-up activities. This can enhance the young bowler's self-assurance and sense of ownership in his sporting endeavors, as well as help him become a more cohesive and successful team.

Another young bowler might be motivated by a transformative coach who acts as a good example and aids him in creating a compelling vision for his future in the sport. The coach could advise the young bowler to set ambitious but doable objectives and offer encouragement and direction along the way. This can strengthen the bond between the coach and the bowler, increase the player's pleasure in the game, and boost his performance.

Self-Exploration: Unveiling Intrapersonal Knowledge

Quality coaching is built on a foundation of intrapersonal knowledge, which goes beyond professional and interpersonal expertise. Intrapersonal knowledge focuses on a deep understanding of oneself, while the first two focus on what and how to coach. This self-awareness is essential for helping coaches define their basic principles, develop their coaching skills, and cultivate a long-lasting coaching profession. The following are among the crucial abilities linked to intrapersonal knowledge:

Unveiling Self-Awareness

Coaches start their coaching careers for a variety of reasons, including the desire to give back to the sport, to assist others in developing and achieving their goals, to make a living, or to volunteer. But the best coaches embrace a mission rather than just a justification. Inspiring coaches to work toward their vision and goals while also forcing them to hold themselves to the same high standards they set for their bowlers, a strong sense of coaching purpose functions as both a pull and a push for coaches.

This coaching objective is comparable to a coach's "why." Astute coaches increasingly recognize and explain their mission through regular reflection, even though it may not be obvious or clearly defined at the beginning of a coaching career.

The Power of Reflection

The regular and methodical practice of reflection—a profound process of introspection on coaching—helps to improve intrapersonal knowledge. Effective trainers use two types of reflection:

- Reflective practice
- Critical reflection

The coaching dilemmas inspire both types of reflection.

When coaches attempt to address coaching issues, reflective practice is utilized. Because solving problems is a fundamental component of coaching, excellent coaches look for potential answers from a variety of sources. The best coaches test these answers through experiments, frequently getting input from other coaches or bowlers before putting them into practice.

However, top-notch coaches spend some time delving into problem analysis through critical reflection in addition to problem-solving. Before coming up with alternative solutions, this entails asking hard questions of oneself, such as why a certain problem has emerged.

Although the quick-paced nature of coaching frequently stresses reflective practice, from time to time resisting the need to solve issues quickly and putting aside some time for inquiry and contemplation shows to be extremely beneficial. With the help of this purposeful approach, coaches can review and improve their coaching mission while recognizing opportunities for ongoing development.

The Pursuit of Continuous Improvement

A good coach exudes confidence while also being modest enough to understand that learning is a lifelong process. John Wooden, a great college basketball coach, once said, "It's what you learn after you know it all that counts." This is sound advice. Coaches that adopt a growth mindset look for possibilities for self-improvement constantly in order to hone their trade and stay informed of new trends and research. They continuously improve their teaching abilities while giving their bowlers the best possible instruction.

Unleashing the Coaching Potential: Embracing Continuous Growth in Bowling

The saying reads, "True growth begins when you acknowledge that there is always more to learn." While many bowling coaches typically wait until the end of the season to reflect, excellent coaches are constantly alert in identifying areas where their coaching practice can be improved.

Although small learning gains can be made throughout the bowling season, instructors should focus on self-directed study during the off-season when national championships are less of a priority. For coaches, this period of reflection offers a favorable environment for exploring their potential. For the best learning results, instructors should focus their studies on particular bowling-related subjects or delve into the knowledge shared by successful bowling coaches. A thorough analysis of the performance of both bowlers and coaches from the previous season can be used to pinpoint high-impact areas. Coaches can read well-known coaching memoirs or ask for suggestions from peers in other sports disciplines when choosing a coach to study.

When coaches collaborate with the larger learning networks of other coaches, the advantages of consistent and rigorous self-guided study are greatly enhanced. Establishing and maintaining a strong learning network is made possible by active involvement in coaching clinics and social media sites devoted to bowling. Making solid contacts within the bowling community encourages constant progress and offers a wider viewpoint on coaching methods. Coaches can promote coaching in bowling while also fostering their own growth by drawing on the pooled wisdom and experiences of like-minded people.

The search for expertise in the field of bowling instruction goes far beyond the idea of having all the answers. Effective coaches understand that genuine growth results from a lifetime commitment to learning. Coaches can reach their full potential and usher in a new age of excellence in bowling coaching by embracing continual growth.

Self-Awareness: By probing into their reasons for playing the sport and inspiring them to reflect on their beliefs and objectives, coaches can aid young bowlers in growing a strong sense of purpose. Bowlers can better concentrate on their strengths and overcome any obstacles they may encounter by understanding their personal motivations for playing.

Reflection: By requesting that young bowlers reflect on their performance during a game or practice, coaches can motivate their athletes to engage in reflective practice. Then they can collaborate with the bowlers to find opportunities for development and test out potential remedies.

Continuous Improvement: Coaches can assist young bowlers in creating clear learning objectives and locating tools to help them reach those objectives. This could entail deciding on a particular subject to research, such as a specific tactic or plan, or choosing a coach to observe and learn from.

AMLETO MONACELLI

The Essence of a Bowler-Centered, Coach-Driven Approach

My dad, my biggest supporter and coach, played an instrumental role in shaping the bowler and person I am today. Together, we competed in numerous tournaments, including representing Venezuela on the national team. His unwavering belief in my abilities and his words of encouragement over countless phone calls during my early days on the Professional Bowlers Association (PBA) Tour strengthened my resolve and made me feel invincible.

Throughout my journey, I was fortunate to have incredible mentors and coaches who shaped my game and guided me towards success. Ruben Cardenas, a close friend and confidant, played multiple roles in my life—friend, coach, and at times, even a father figure. His guidance and unwavering belief in my abilities propelled me forward. I also had the privilege of working with esteemed coaches like John Jowdy, Fred Borden, Bob Learn, and Ruben Shiragossian, who each contributed their expertise to my development as a bowler.

Putting Bowlers At The Heart: A Holistic Approach To Achieving Bowler-Centered Outcomes

Every great journey sets off with its destination in mind. For coaches, this entails defining the goals they have for their bowlers during their supervision. These results are the main objectives; they are important, attainable goals that will maintain the bowlers' progress. When properly chosen and established, such aim outcomes also assist in energizing and inspiring bowlers, encouraging their continued engagement in sport.

Every extraordinary journey starts with a specific objective in mind. This involves imagining what bowlers will discover, develop into, and achieve while under your coach's tutelage. These objectives form the cornerstone of coaching, acting as realistic goals that direct the growth of the bowlers in a directed manner. These aim outcomes can engage and motivate bowlers while also fostering their long-term dedication to the sport when carefully chosen and established with purpose.

The substantial benefits of adopting a bowler-centered, coach-driven strategy that prioritizes the overall development and well-being of bowlers are highlighted in this chapter. Such a strategy is successful because it bases desired results on the particular requirements of the bowlers and is supported by moral coaching judgments and behaviors.

AUMI GUERRA:

Coach Competence

The Essence of a Bowler-Centered, Coach-Driven Approach

Selflessness and unshakable commitment to assisting bowlers in realizing their goals are essential components of a bowler-centered, coach-driven approach. The unrelenting commitment to acting in the bowlers' best interests rather than their own is a defining characteristic of outstanding instructors.

The coach and bowler work together to determine the desired outcomes at the beginning of the journey. Although coaches may have broad aims in mind, giving bowlers a voice in goal setting increases their enthusiasm and dedication to these targets. The coach's job is to facilitate and guide this conversation, making sure that the goals are challenging yet doable with the help of the coach. This calls for a precise evaluation of the bowler's current skills, assets, and weaknesses.

Goal objectives include both more subjective process indicators (such as effort, attitude, and work ethic) and more objective performance measures (such as average,

My family served as my role models. My mom's work ethic, my dad's courage, Karina's competitive spirit, Alexandra's resourcefulness, and Niccole's charisma inspired and shaped me. I developed these strengths as I progressed. Wearing the national team uniform was no longer enough; I yearned for monumental victories on a grand scale.

Dave Caplan, our pro shop operator, played a pivotal role in my development. A lifelong bowler and Spanish speaker, he mentored me both in bowling and language. His unwavering belief in my potential continues to guide me.

Then, in 1997, I met Craig Woodhouse during the FIQ Championships. He became our head coach, starting in 2000. Craig's straightforward coaching, high standards, and technical knowledge transformed my game. We've remained a team, constantly striving for improvement.

spare and strike percentages, rankings, and triumphs). This strategy adheres to the well-known SMART framework for goal formulation, where the objectives are:

- Specific: Distinctly stated and delineated.
- Measurable: Progress indicators that are visible and trackable.
- Attainable: Aided by adequate training materials and coaching help.
- Realistic: Given their present performance level, within the bowlers' ability.
- Time-bound: Stipulated by a certain time limit or deadline.

Bowler Example - Good Application: Bowler A successfully uses the SMART framework under the direction of his coach. By the end of the bowling season, He specifically sets out to increase his spare conversion rate from 60% to 80%. This objective is quantifiable because He may monitor his development by keeping track of how many spares He converts both during practice and competition. Bowler A discusses his aim with his coach to make sure it is attainable, and the coach offers the proper training materials and coaching support, such as drills for shooting spares and technique improvement. The objective is reasonable since it allows for progressive improvement and takes into consideration Bowler A's existing performance level. Last but not least, Bowler A provides a precise timescale for his efforts by setting a time-bound target of three months to accomplish his goal.

Coach Example - Bad Application: When he sets goals for his bowlers, Coach B uses the SMART framework incorrectly. Coach B simply encourages its bowlers to "improve their overall performance" without giving any specific objectives. The bowlers find it challenging to comprehend what aspects of their game they should concentrate on due to the lack of specificity. The lack of defined observable and trackable progress indicators renders the goals immeasurable. Coach B fails to support the goals' ability to be attained by not offering the proper coaching or training resources. The objectives are unattainable since they do not take into account the bowlers' present skill levels or offer a clear route for progress. Last but not least, there is no time-bound component, thus the bowlers have no target date or time to aim for.

After setting acceptable target outcomes, a good coach provides a setting that will help bowlers reach their objectives. As bowlers work to achieve their goals, providing feedback and support becomes more important than just planning workouts and delivering direction during tournaments. Authentic, encouraging, and constructive criticism is skillfully used to maintain bowlers' attention on their targets while also strengthening their will to put forth the necessary effort.

Bowlers' progress should be closely monitored by coaches, who should work with them to adapt their objectives as needed. It is essential to closely monitor the results of practice and competition while keeping an eye out for outside influences that can limit the bowlers' capacity to succeed.

Coaches create an environment where bowlers feel comfortable giving information and insights that can drive tailored coaching recommendations by regularly demonstrating genuine interest in the bowlers' lives outside of sports and showing concern for their general well-being.

Coaches must adhere to the following principles in order to improve bowlers' enjoyment, happiness, motivation, and performance:

- Agree on difficult but achievable goals that are appropriate for the bowlers' experience and age.

- Throughout the coaching process, reward the initiative and contribution of the bowlers.

- Explain the reasoning behind coaching decisions to encourage comprehension and buy-in.

BIBOY RIVERA

Targeting critical performance deficiencies

Throughout my journey, I've been fortunate to have incredible role models who inspired me to push beyond my limits. Paeng Nepomuceno and Bong Coo, both legends in the world of bowling, have exemplified discipline, work ethic, and unwavering dedication to the sport. Despite their remarkable achievements, they remain humble and approachable. Their influence on me is immeasurable, as I strive to embody the same principles, beliefs, and actions that have guided their successful careers.

Various coaches have played vital roles in different stages of my bowling journey. Orly Gan, Caloy De Leon, and Pete Ayala were patient mentors who taught me the fundamentals and nurtured my skills from the very beginning. It was crucial to establish a solid foundation and develop habits that would propel me to the next level. Mastering the basics proved to be a pivotal factor in my growth as a bowler.

As I advanced to higher levels, I had the privilege of being trained by Coach Madoka Amano, a renowned foreign coach with an impressive track record of producing international bowling champions. Bong Coo introduced me to Coach Madoka, and under his strict guidance, I underwent rigorous training for three to four hours a day. We focused on various aspects of the game, including drills, improving my physical game, enhancing versatility, and ensuring shot repeatability. Endurance and stamina were vital to withstand the demands of bowling for an entire day. Thanks to Coach Madoka's tutelage, my career took a turning point, and I began to taste victory both domestically and internationally.

- To support bowlers' development, congratulate them on both performance improvements and goal progress.

- Offer bowlers encouraging, constructive criticism that helps them improve.

- Provide coaching based on the individual learning and development requirements of each bowler.

- Incorporating the bowler's role as an athlete, take into consideration outside elements in life that could affect goal achievement.

Example 1:

When dealing with a young bowler, a coach could start by setting goals together, such as raising the bowler's average score and spare %. The coach can create practice plans to help the bowler reach his objectives by getting the bowler's feedback on his perceived strengths and weaknesses.

Example 2:

Young bowlers may be given SMART goals by their coaches, such as raising their attitude and work ethic in practice or reaching a certain average score by the end of the season. The coach can keep tabs on the bowlers' development and modify their objectives as necessary, offering encouraging and constructive criticism all along the way.

Example 3:

A coach may consider non-sporting elements that might limit a young bowler's capacity to succeed. The coach might assist bowlers in establishing techniques to deal with problems while still advancing toward their bowling objectives, for instance, if they are having trouble with their studies or coping with personal concerns. Additionally, the coach can take an interest in the bowler's activities outside of bowling, forging a strong bond with the player.

The Holistic Development And Psychological Well-Being Of Bowlers

Deep concern for the total development of bowlers should be the driving force behind coaching goals and strategies. Adopting a coaching philosophy that puts the holistic growth and well-being of bowlers first necessitates recognizing their individual, emotional, cultural, and social identities and understanding the influence these identities have on their athletic development and performance. This rule applies to bowlers of all skill levels, from novices to seasoned pros. The Four C's approach, which was covered in the first chapter, is a popular paradigm for determining comprehensive bowler results.

Competence.

Coaches frequently state that their primary motivation for getting involved is the desire to help bowlers improve their abilities. In a similar vein, bowlers usually cite improving their skills as a major driving force for playing the sport. A strong foundation of general health, fitness, and physical well-being is required for proficiency in executing the methods involved in bowling. Thus, superior instructors go beyond only imparting sport-specific techniques and strategies to work on their bowlers' overall skill development. Additionally, they inform bowlers of the value of healthy training and lifestyle practices, emphasizing matters like nutrition, sufficient rest and recuperation, and

AJ JOHNSON:

Matching Coaching Philosophy to Coaching Context

I've played sports since childhood. My father played fast-pitch softball competitively and took me to many ballparks to watch. I always watched my dad and grandfather bowl. I always wanted to play sports. Bowling was always there, but I wanted to play Division 1 college football like my cousin at Illinois. From age 5, I played football, baseball, and basketball. I stopped playing basketball my sophomore year to bowl. In my senior year, bowling became more important than football, even though I was a varsity quarterback. As a kid, I was driven to improve at whatever I did. I was the one dragging my parents around to do everything. I put school first so I could focus on all my sports. Going through all of that at a young age and still having that drive from being an athlete my whole life has made me who I am today, both as a bowler and as a person.

I loved many sports as a kid. I had several bowling role models because I liked different things about them. I always wanted to watch Tommy Jones on TV and throw like him. His power inspired me to have a high back swing and rev rate as a kid. Because he got excited and got into every shot on shows. Chris Barnes is another role model because of his desire to improve and be a threat each week. As I got older and bowled with Chris on Team USA, he became a mentor.

injury avoidance. This strategy gives bowlers the ability to realize their full potential and take charge of the abilities needed to succeed.

Competence Example: Coach A is aware that bowlers' growth must take competency into account. He creates extensive training plans that give equal attention to general health and well-being as well as sport-specific skills and tactics. Coach A stresses to his bowlers the value of eating a healthy, balanced diet, obtaining enough sleep and recuperation time, and avoiding injuries. Coach A helps his bowlers realize their full potential and succeed on the bowling lane by focusing on the overall development of skills and encouraging them to take charge of their training and lifestyle habits.

Confidence.

Bowlers must have constant confidence in their ability to use tactics efficiently, especially under duress, in order to achieve the zenith of their development or performance. Bowlers must develop the capacity to perform in competitive settings and maintain motivation despite setbacks they suffer while learning intricate sports techniques. The holistic growth of bowlers and the fulfillment of results focused on the bowler depend heavily on effective teaching practices that address self-doubt and dissatisfaction while encouraging confidence through methods like positive self-talk and visualization.

Confidence Example: Coach B is aware of how crucial confidence is to a bowler's performance. He employs efficient instructional techniques that handle self-doubt and frustration while encouraging his bowlers to have a strong sense of self-belief. In order to help bowlers overcome obstacles and perform under pressure, Coach B promotes positive self-talk and visualization tactics. Coach B promotes the all-around growth of his bowlers and enables them to accomplish desired results by instilling confidence in them and giving them essential mental skills.

Connection.

Strong-willed and independent qualities are common among elite bowlers. These qualities are helpful in fostering a competitive attitude, but unless bowlers learn to train and compete alongside other bowlers as well as against them, their progress may be hampered. Whether a sport is individual or team-oriented, it generally calls for some level of collaboration and support among teammates. Teams that have a high level of trust and a shared commitment to similar goals perform and develop at their best. Bowlers need to develop the ability to accept and efficiently utilize input from others, as well as actively interact with fellow bowlers, even when training and competing independently. Gaining the respect and trust of people in one's bowling network is an essential part of a bowler's development.

Connection Example: In order to succeed at bowling, Coach C emphasizes the value of cooperation and teamwork. He fosters a welcoming and inclusive environment where bowlers may practice and compete alongside other people as well as against them. Coach C fosters camaraderie and a sense of shared goals among bowlers by encouraging cooperation, trust, and mutual support. He urges bowlers to interact with their other players, actively seek out and use feedback, and build solid connections within their network of bowling friends. Coach C's method promotes bowlers' overall development and enables them to flourish both on their own and as members of a team.

Character.

A single incidence of unethical behavior can diminish the success of an entire bowling career. The holistic development and welfare of bowlers depend on coaches' methodical and intentional efforts to create bowler character. The coach has the capacity to influence whether an athletic experience helps develop character or just creates character. Simply playing a sport does not automatically impart character. The first stage in developing a bowler's character is to create fundamental principles and standards that express expectations and proper conduct in a straightforward manner. The best way to transmit these beliefs and standards is by modeling, in which the coach takes on the role of a live example of the ideas they want to instill.

Character Example: Coach D is aware that a bowler's journey must include character development as a key component. He defines expectations and appropriate actions, establishing distinct core values and norms. Coach D sets an exemplary example by upholding the values of morality, sportsmanship, and ethics. He promotes a climate of respect, accountability, and justice by highlighting the value of character both on and off the bowling alley. Coach D prioritizes character development to make sure that the sporting experience helps his bowlers develop strong characters, which has a favorable impact on their overall growth.

Bowler Outcome	Description
Competence	Mastery of bowling technical, tactical, and performance skills; attainment of optimal health, fitness, and physical well-being.
Confidence	Development of unwavering self-belief, resilience, mental toughness, and a strong sense of positive self-worth.
Connection	Acquisition of proficient interpersonal skills, fostering the ability to establish and maintain meaningful, positive relationships.
Character	Cultivation of profound respect for the sport and others, adherence to principles of integrity, self-discipline, and ethical and moral decision-making.

Table 40 - The Four C's Model of Comprehensive Bowler Outcomes

Contextual Fit

The coaches' shared goal is to give neighborhood kids and teenagers the chance to bowl, hone their abilities, and possibly represent their town and area in competitive and advanced levels of play. Young bowlers frequently experience the excitement of competition for the first time or score their first goal before developing a passion for the sport. In order to enhance and channel that passion, talented and committed instructors are essential. Successful coaches recognize the importance of tailoring their strategy to the bowlers, environments, and circumstances because they know that efficient coaching depends on the particular context. These coaches also recognize that individualized teaching is necessary at different stages of a bowler's development in order to achieve holistic bowler development. They make an effort to tailor their behaviors, conversations, and advice in order to have a positive influence on young bowlers and motivate bowlers to pursue their goals.

Types of Coaching Contexts

In bowling, coaching is a process of directed development and improvement that takes place at distinct growth stages. A youngster just starting out in bowling has very different needs than a three-time world champion in the prime of his career. The fundamentals of good instruction, however, never change. However, whether bowlers continue to improve and enjoy their bowling experience depends on the coach's capacity to translate these ideas into coaching techniques. The two widely acknowledged categories that include bowlers' involvement in the sport are participation bowling and performance bowling. Performance bowling places more of an emphasis on competitiveness and achievement than participation bowling, which promotes involvement and fun.

Bowlers' development differs and is personal to each person. At various points in their lives, different people may join or leave these groups. For instance, young performance bowlers might opt to change sports, which would cause them to interact with a different sports group. From one season to the next, coaches frequently change. While some bowlers may continue to train with the same instructor throughout their careers, the majority change coaches when they begin a new season or stage of development. Sporting pathways are personalized, context-specific, and nonlinear due to the numerous variables involved. Because of this, it's critical for each coach to modify his strategy in light of the specific conditions and surroundings as well as the bowlers' sports group.

Developmental Model of Sport Participation

The Long-Term Athlete Development (LTAD) framework is complemented by the developmental model of sport participation (DMSP). In order to take into account the distinct requirements of each sport as well as the substantial differences in individual bowler profiles, it divides bowler development into three stages. Each phase is not given a definite age or length of time.

- **Sampling Phase**
  In a setting that emphasizes enjoyment and fun, bowlers participate in different sports activities and develop well-rounded fundamental movement abilities. Skill level shouldn't be a factor in limiting participation at this stage because the main goal is to increase involvement and expose bowlers to different sports.

- **Specializing Phase**
  As training demands rise, bowlers start to concentrate on very few sports and the main one is Bowling, sometimes favoring one in particular. Bowlers are often grouped according to ability level throughout this stage, and participation chances may decrease.

- **Investment Phase**
  Bowlers pledge to perform at a high level in bowling. This stage is often reserved for a small number of bowlers who have been identified as showing potential for high-level performance.

Phase Name	Description	Role of the Coach	Strategies	KPI	Examples
Sampling Phase	Bowlers participate in multiple sports beside bowling and develop foundational movement skills	Introduce bowlers to various sports and promote enjoyment of physical activity	Encourage fun, exploration, and variety in activities	Participation rates	Offering different sports, organizing fun games and activities
Specializing Phase	Bowlers focus on a few sports but mainly bowling, possibly favoring one as training demands increase	Guide bowlers to identify a primary sport and improve specific skills	Provide opportunities for targeted training and competition	Skill development, performance improvement	Grouping bowlers by skill level, providing specialized coaching and training
Investment Phase	Bowlers commit to achieving high-level performance Bowling	Support bowlers in developing skills, strategies, and mental toughness to achieve high-performance goals	Provide access to high-level coaching, training, and competition	Achievement of high-level performance goals	Identifying and nurturing bowlers with high potential, providing access to elite training and competition opportunities

Table 40 – Phases of developmental model of sport participation (DMSP)

The DMSP Phases and Coaching Implications

The DMSP's phases provide a general framework for comprehending bowlers' development and the kind of coaching necessary as they advance through these stages. There are important implications for coaching from two main DMSP points:

A. **Unstructured Play** - According to research, skilled bowlers frequently develop in surroundings with lots of opportunities for unstructured play. Deliberate practice is essential for skill development, but it's also critical to balance it out with activities that include spontaneous play. Failure to do so increases the risk of overuse injuries and emotional and physical exhaustion. Bowlers can take the initiative and manage activities during free play, which maximizes enjoyment and intrinsic drive.

B **Sport Diversification** - The DMSP promotes sport diversification or sampling in order to solve the issue of early sport specialization. A young person who participates in several activities will be active in sports longer and more successfully. Early specialization frequently impairs later career success for bowlers. High-performance bowlers may have played a variety of sports up through high school, and college coaches favor signing athletes with wide experience in sports.

Matching Coaching Philosophy to Coaching Context

Every coach has particular talents, personalities, and viewpoints that are influenced by his life experiences. His coaching philosophy, which directs his judgments and actions in day-to-day coaching, is influenced by these factors. The quality coaching structure's principles and ideals must be in line with the coaches' coaching philosophy.

Coaches must adapt their teaching philosophies to retain a bowler-centered, coach-driven approach that offers developmentally appropriate instruction and support as bowlers move through various stages and phases of their growth.

Example 1 (Good Practice): Coach A is aware of how crucial it is to adapt his coaching philosophies to the coaching environment. He understands that different phases and stages in a bowler's growth call for varied tactics. Coach A employs a loving and supportive coaching attitude for young and inexperienced bowlers that places an emphasis on skill development and laying a solid foundation. Coach A modifies his coaching philosophy to place greater emphasis on strategic thinking, competition readiness, and skill development as bowlers go to more advanced levels. Coach A guarantees a thorough and efficient development experience for its bowlers by matching their coaching philosophy with the unique requirements of each level.

Example 2 (Bad Practice): Coach B doesn't change his coaching philosophies to fit the coaching environment. Regardless of the bowler's stage of growth, he continues to use a rigorous, one-size-fits-all method. Coach B follows the same coaching philosophy whether working with young novices or experienced competitors, ignoring the significance of adapting his strategy to each student's demands. As a result, the bowlers' progress is hampered by a lack of training and support that is developmentally appropriate. Coach B loses possibilities for personal development and underutilizes the potential of his bowlers by ignoring the requirement of aligning coaching philosophy to the coaching setting.

Long-Term Program Development

Coach development gains from adopting a holistic and long-term program development approach, much like bowler development is optimized through a bowler-centered, holistic approach. This strategy works best when administrators of sports programs and coaches:

- Possess a distinct sense of mission.

- Be mindful of the particular context and features of the program.

- Run as a learning community, encouraging ongoing development and improvement.

The LTPD approach, in contrast to the conventional sports program approach, keeps coaches and program administrators concentrated on continual growth while unified around a common goal and open communication. The objective is long-term growth and success, not quick victories.

Targeting Critical Performance Deficiencies

When performing long-term program evaluations, it becomes clear that there are many areas that need to be improved. However, aiming to close every performance gap might be difficult and ineffective.

Prioritizing a small number of critical performance flaws with the potential to produce significant improvements in both development and performance is a more efficient approach. These critical concerns with high-impact performance gaps have a direct impact on other system components. Significant results can be attained with even a small improvement in these areas.

Characteristic	Traditional bowling program (Example)	LTPD-oriented bowling program (Example)
Shared purpose	Winning championships as the ultimate goal, with little emphasis on overall development	Fostering a lifelong love for the sport and prioritizing the holistic development of bowlers
Bowler	A highly competitive bowler focused solely on achieving tournament victories	A young bowler passionate about the sport, seeking personal growth and skill development
Coach	A coach solely focused on winning championships, prioritizing short-term results over long-term development	A coach dedicated to creating a positive and supportive environment, nurturing the bowler's holistic growth
Mindset	Short-term focus on immediate tournament success, overlooking long-term growth	Long-term commitment to continuous improvement and holistic development

Characteristic	Traditional bowling program (Example)	LTPD-oriented bowling program (Example)
Bowler	A bowler obsessed with winning individual matches or tournaments, often neglecting skill refinement and personal growth	A bowler who values consistent progress, sets long-term goals, and embraces challenges as opportunities for improvement
Coach	A coach pushing the bowler to win at any cost, neglecting the bowler's long-term development	A coach instilling a growth mindset, encouraging the bowler to embrace challenges and focus on personal improvement
Methods	Sporadic practice sessions without clear objectives or progressive training plans	Structured training programs encompassing technical skills, physical conditioning, and mental preparation
Bowler	A bowler practicing irregularly and without a specific training plan, focusing solely on game performance	A bowler following a well-structured training regimen, including skill-specific drills, strength and conditioning exercises, and mental skills training
Coach	A coach conducting practice sessions without a clear focus or long-term development plan, emphasizing tournament results	A coach designing comprehensive training programs, including technical, physical, and mental components, tailored to the bowler's individual needs
Techniques	Extrinsic motivators like rewards and punishments, creating fear-driven performance	Setting mutually agreed upon targets and nurturing intrinsic motivation for self-improvement
Bowler	A bowler driven by external rewards, such as trophies or financial incentives, often leading to performance anxiety	A bowler motivated by personal growth and intrinsic rewards, finding joy in the process of skill development and self-improvement
Coach	A coach relying on punishments or negative reinforcement to push the bowler towards desired outcomes	A coach fostering intrinsic motivation, setting challenging yet achievable goals, and providing constructive feedback to inspire self-improvement
Collaboration	Limited knowledge sharing and individual focus, resulting in isolated efforts	Promoting systems thinking, open communication, and collaboration among coaches, bowlers, and support staff
Bowler	A bowler primarily focusing on individual performance and rarely seeking guidance or support from peers	A bowler actively participating in team activities, sharing knowledge, and seeking input from coaches and teammates
Coach	A coach with limited collaboration, failing to create a supportive team environment for bowlers	A coach fostering teamwork, encouraging bowlers to support and learn from each other, and facilitating open communication among all stakeholders
Leadership	Charismatic hero-leader approach emphasizing individual achievements	Servant-leadership style focusing on the growth and well-being of bowlers
Bowler	Bowlers looking up to a coach solely for their own success and often relying heavily on the coach's guidance	Bowlers who sees the coach as a mentor, valuing their guidance and support in personal and athletic development
Coach	A coach using a directive leadership style, focusing on his own accomplishments and dictating all aspects of the bowler's development	A coach adopting a servant-leadership approach, prioritizing the bowler's growth, well-being, and long-term development over personal achievements
Decision making	Decisions made with little consensus, often influenced by politics and manipulation	Collaborative decision-making by a team of problem solvers, using shared power and collaboration
Bowler	Bowler: John, a talented bowler, feels frustrated because decisions regarding his training and competition opportunities are made without considering his input or preferences.	Bowler: Sarah, a young bowler, actively participates in decision-making processes. Her coach seeks input from Sarah and other team members to make informed decisions that benefit development and progression.
Coach	Coach: Coach Smith, who holds a position of authority, makes decisions based on personal interests and uses manipulation to maintain control.	Coach: Coach Thompson facilitates collaborative discussions, encourages open dialogue, and empowers bowlers to be involved in decision-making.
Communication	Limited and controlled communication channels, restricting information flow and collaboration	Open and shared communication, promoting transparency and fostering a culture of collaboration
Bowler	Bowler: Alex, an aspiring bowler, finds it challenging to access important information about training schedules, competitions, and team updates.	Bowler: Emily, an enthusiastic bowler, benefits from open and shared communication within the program. Important information, such as training plans, performance feedback, and upcoming events, is readily accessible to all bowlers and coaches.
Coach	Coach: Coach Brown communicates sparingly, keeping most information confidential and shared only on a need-to-know basis.	Coach: Coach Anderson establishes clear communication channels, encourages open dialogue, and fosters a culture of transparency and collaboration.

Characteristic	Traditional bowling program (Example)	LTPD-oriented bowling program (Example)
Processes	Inconsistent tools and programs with sporadic implementation and variable results, causing resistance to change	Consistent tools and processes used to improve and standardize instruction, methods, and relations
Bowler	Bowler: Michael, a dedicated bowler, faces challenges due to the lack of standardized training programs and inconsistent coaching methods within the program.	Bowler: Olivia, an aspiring bowler, benefits from the LTPD-oriented program's consistent and standardized training processes. The program utilizes proven methodologies, well-defined training programs, and standardized coaching methods to ensure all bowlers receive quality instruction and support.
Coach	Coach: Coach Johnson often implements new techniques sporadically, leading to confusion and resistance from bowlers.	Coach: Coach Davis follows established processes, implements consistent training methods, and continually evaluates and improves the program based on best practices.
Results	Variable results based on the capabilities of individual bowlers and coaches	Program excellence sustained over time across all sports
Bowler	Bowler: Mark, a talented bowler, achieves success despite limited resources and inconsistent coaching.	Bowler: Sophia, a bowler in the LTPD-oriented program, benefits from the program's sustained excellence. She experiences consistent progress and achieves her goals due to the program's comprehensive support and high-quality coaching.
Coach	Coach: Coach Wilson's coaching skills and dedication play a significant role in Mark's accomplishments.	Coach: Coach Garcia, along with the coaching staff, ensures program excellence is maintained over time, resulting in a track record of successful bowlers.

Table 11 – Characteristics of Traditional Versus LTPD-Oriented Sport Programs

Identifying High-Impact Performance Gaps

The emphasis on individual performance problems in different sports may obscure underlying high-impact gaps. For instance, in bowling, the emphasis on shooting skills may be present, but low levels of fitness may prevent individuals from having the tactical edge needed to position themselves for the shot. Dealing with fitness as a fundamental weakness is necessary to address shooting performance difficulties. Team trust is another important, high-impact performance issue. When teammates lack trust in one another and put themselves above the team's success, they may not carry out essential jobs like applying pressure to defenders to make the best scoring possibilities.

Engage several people who are familiar with the program to assess and rank the discovered performance gaps in order to determine their priority. The high-impact gaps that require quick repair will be highlighted by adding up the ratings and comparing the rankings. The best return on investment for ongoing program and coaching improvements comes from carefully addressing these shortcomings.

Building on Coaching Strengths

While identifying performance gaps is essential, a new strategy emphasizes the need to build on strengths to achieve continuous progress. It is known as the strengths-based approach and places more emphasis on strengths than on weaknesses.

The term "coaching strengths" refers to intrinsic qualities that are real and improve performance. These qualities include behaviors, emotions, and cognitive habits. Coaches act in accordance with their mission and fundamental values by matching their coaching with their abilities. Making use of one's strengths promotes greater engagement, greater satisfaction, greater energy and performance, and greater optimism. Additionally, highlighting strengths fosters coaching confidence and resilience, both of which are necessary for maintaining effort and energy.

The five guiding concepts of the strengths-based approach are as follows:

A. Put the focus on what is strong, right, and effective.

B. Recognize that each person has qualities that merit respect.

C. Our strengths hold the key to realizing our full potential.

D. It is important to use our strengths to address our weaknesses.

E. Using our strengths produces the biggest impact.

Even though it may not be obvious at first, excellent coaches eventually identify the coaching specialties that play to their strengths. A straightforward method can be used by coaches to determine their natural strengths. For instance, at the conclusion of each coaching month, asking yourself the following three questions can help you identify their strengths:

- Which of my coaching sessions was the most successful this month, and why?

- Which particular coaching circumstance did I excel in this month?

- Which coaching-related activities energized me the most last month?

A coach who naturally interacts well with young bowlers may decide to concentrate on this skill by including more interactive and fun activities in their practice sessions. Games or tasks that promote communication between bowlers and the coach as well as opportunities for the coach to offer praise and constructive criticism are examples of this.

A coach who excels at giving feedback and technique analysis may decide to concentrate on this area of training by including more video analysis and one-on-one coaching sessions. This may entail establishing precise technical objectives for every bowler, using video analysis to assess how He performed, and giving him detailed feedback to help him advance his technique. Additionally, the coach could work with bowlers to create individualized training schedules that are concentrated on their unique strengths and shortcomings.

Acknowledging the Influence of Quality Coaches

Since they are committed to fostering bowlers' passion for the sport while supporting their success, the recognition of excellent coaching is extremely important to them. All coaches who are involved in the bowler's growth path should ideally strive to become excellent coaches who continuously maximize the bowler's potential. Actively looking for new ways to recognize coaches' contributions to bowler development and performance in order to highlight the impact they make on those areas.

A full review of coaching growth and influence, going beyond the simple results of a season, is made possible by using an evaluation process that focuses on important indications of quality coaching. While many coaches are frequently judged or praised based just on victories or championships, it is important to understand that effective coaching transcends these purely material indicators and takes many different forms at all levels. The is dedicated to recognizing both activities and results in ways that have real significance for coaches. Table 5.2 offers additional possibilities that can be taken into consideration to recognize and value high-quality coaching in addition to the instances of coach recognition currently provided by the.

CAROLINE LAGRANGE

Acknowledging
the Influence of
Quality Coaches

I have been fortunate to have two incredible coaches, Mark Lewis and Gordon Vadakin, during my time at Wichita State University (WSU). They shaped my skills and helped me develop both my physical and mental game. Coach Lewis focused on refining my physical technique, working on my approach, release, and overall form. He emphasized the importance of consistency and repetition, ensuring that every movement was deliberate and precise. Coach Vadakin, on the other hand, honed my mental game, teaching me how to stay focused, handle pressure, and maintain a positive mindset even in challenging situations.

My time at WSU was transformative. Not only did I excel in my bowling skills, but I also grew as a person. I learned the value of discipline, perseverance, and teamwork. The camaraderie among my teammates and the support from the coaching staff created a nurturing environment where we could push each other to reach new heights.

Program	Description	Additional Suggestions
Coach of the Year awards	This program acknowledges and presents annual coaching recognition plaques across various categories, such as Physical Game Coach, Competition Coach, Conditioning Coach.	Introduce an annual coaching awards program that allows coaches to join a distinguished list of previously recognized peers. Incorporate criteria based on quality coaching principles, evaluation results, and feedback from bowlers and the organization.
Newsletters and publications	A regular newsletter is published, featuring articles from esteemed coaches in the Club. This serves as a platform to recognize and celebrate innovative coaches who serve as positive role models for bowlers.	Encourage coaches who exemplify quality principles to contribute articles, participate in podcasts, or share videos discussing best practices and concepts that would interest the community.
Speaking events	The program conducts coaching workshops annually to enhance the professional development of club coaches. It identifies coaches within the club system who showcase innovative approaches to coaching.	Showcase the expertise of exceptional coaches by inviting them to speak at town hall meetings, deliver keynote addresses at banquets, or engage with the membership, shedding light on the intricacies of quality coaching.

Table 12 – Coach Recognition Examples and Suggestions

In order to make sure coaches feel valued and compensated for their contributions, it is essential to recognize and acknowledge the worth of high-quality coaching. It promotes a culture of excellence by showcasing people who exhibit excellent coaching, and it ought to be a primary goal for every administration.

Enhancing Coach Well-Being

Ironically, instructors frequently overlook their own health despite their best attempts to give their bowlers a fun and positive experience that will help them improve and perform at their best. Coaches suffer from common problems like high stress, poor diet, sleep deprivation, family issues, and social isolation. These self-destructive practices should be discouraged because they are neither desirable nor sustainable.

During competitive events, coaches, who are devoted servants to their bowlers, get physically and emotionally exhausted. If left unchecked, exhaustion and anxiety can sap their enthusiasm and passion. In extreme circumstances, these challenges could result in mental health issues or even result in coaches quitting their jobs.

When a coach's health is damaged, it has an impact on both the coach and the growth and performance of the bowlers. Relationships with family and friends may also sustain permanent harm. Unfortunately, a lot of bowling organizations don't prioritize coaches' health.

By making coach well-being a top priority and a core component of our Quality Coaching Principles, we hope to foster a culture in which recognizing and addressing coach well-being is commonplace. We encourage coaches to take preventative action to avoid such circumstances rather than letting them passively suffer the repercussions. Quality coaching ultimately equates to coaches who are mentally and emotionally balanced.

Hypothetical Examples

Example 1: Coach X is a committed bowling coach who recognizes the value of looking after his own health in order to mentor his bowlers in an effective manner. He puts self-care first by using stress management techniques, making sure he keeps a balanced and healthy diet, and placing a high priority on getting enough relaxation and sleep. To maintain a healthy work-life balance, Coach X actively seeks support from his social network and participates in activities outside of coaching. Coach X fosters a supportive coaching atmosphere and sets a good example for his bowlers by taking care of their own well-being.

Example 2: Within the bowling community, Coach Y actively promotes coach wellbeing. He actively interacts with bowling associations to promote understanding of the significance of assisting coaches' mental and emotional well-being. Coach Y works with other coaches to create materials and initiatives that speak to the particular issues that coaches encounter, such as offering stress management classes and promoting healthy lifestyles. Additionally, he promotes open communication and builds a community where coaches may connect, exchange experiences, and seek support. The dedication of Coach Y to improving the coach's well-being helps the development and success of the bowling coaching industry as a whole.

Effective Task Management

Recognizing that not all jobs are equally important and urgent, effective coaches organize their workload. Tasks can be divided into four different types using the framework developed by leadership expert Steven Covey:

Critical and urgent: Needing quick attention for tasks of the utmost importance.

1. Important but not urgent tasks can wait till later without sacrificing their effectiveness.

2. Not urgent but not critical: jobs that are of little importance but must be completed quickly (delegating these jobs is advised).

3. Activities that provide little or no value to work or personal life and should be limited or eliminated are not vital or urgent.

By transferring less important or urgent coaching obligations, coaches can better manage their work and personal lives. It is essential that coaches surround themselves with capable friends, encouraging coworkers, and dependable assistants.

Hypothetical Examples

Example of Coach: Coach Rebecca Adams - Task Management Expert

Coach Adams is exceptional at planning and setting priorities so that urgent and important tasks get the attention they require right away. She fosters a productive and well-balanced work-life environment by handling her coaching obligations well.

Example of Coach: Coach Brian Thompson - Delegation Specialist

Coach Thompson is aware of the value of assigning assignments that are urgent but not essential. He maximizes his coaching efficiency while keeping a good work-life balance by delegating these duties to qualified assistant coaches.

Eventually, unwavering support from the organizations and programs they work with is the best approach to encourage coaches to maintain a healthy work-life balance. In addition to actively monitoring and ensuring that coaches prioritize self-care, this support should go beyond simply mentioning the need for balance in job descriptions and objectives.

Ensuring a Fulfilling Experience

The unique difficulties that bowling provides to both players and instructors are what make it so appealing. Nevertheless, neither party can be certain that they will get the intended results, despite their best efforts.

While winning championships and receiving honors cannot be guaranteed, they can be pursued with great satisfaction. Our league is lucky to have a large number of outstanding coaches who give bowlers incredibly great experiences. The guidelines presented in this paper are meant to guarantee that our bowlers receive the instruction they need to realize their full potential and enjoy each stage of their bowling journey. Coaches will feel more fulfilled in their duty as mentors both on and off the playing field if they follow these guidelines.

Hypothetical Examples

Example 1: Coach A is a well-known bowling instructor who emphasizes his bowlers' mental and emotional growth. He is well-versed with the psychological facets of the sport and works closely with his athletes to develop their concentration, resiliency, and confidence. Coach A uses mindfulness exercises and visualization techniques to assist bowlers in controlling performance anxiety and staying focused while competing. He establishes a constructive training environment that encourages individual development and peak performance.

Example 2: Coach B is renowned for his technical proficiency and meticulousness when coaching. He is devoted to helping his bowlers improve their physical technique and technical prowess and has a thorough understanding of the biomechanics of bowling. Coach B offers custom drills and exercises to target particular technical issues and uses video analysis to pinpoint areas for growth. To maximize the power, accuracy, and consistency of his bowlers' performances, he places a high priority on optimal body alignment, footwork, and release mechanics. The comprehensive growth and accomplishment of his players are facilitated by Coach B's analytical approach and dedication to technical excellence.

"The Coach's Playbook: Empowering Athletes for Success"

Abstract 2: Beyond Xs and Os, coaching is a complicated skill. This article explores the many facets of coaching and identifies the attributes that make a great coach. A coach molds athletes into well-rounded people through motivation, strategic thinking, leadership, and effective communication. It looks at the value of encouraging a good team dynamic and persistently pursuing personal and professional development. Learn about coaching's transforming power and the tremendous effects it has on athletes' lives, both on and off the field.

MY COACHING JOURNEY: A PATHWAY TO EXCELLENCE *By Frank Buffa*

Frank Buffa

Don Johnson

Carmen Salvino

Bill Taylor

John Rowdy

Fred Borden

I had no idea that when I took the crucial decision to give up teaching in order to concentrate entirely on my bowling pro shop, it would kindle a fierce desire in me to work as a coach. I set out on a quest to learn from the top experts in the area because I was determined to understand everything I could about the game. These famous coaches—Fred Borden, Bill Taylor, John Jowdy, Carmen Salvino, and Don Johnson—became my role models, and I eagerly sought out their guidance.

I took the initiative to arrange a number of clinics across the province in the 1980s and 1990s, inviting these renowned trainers to impart their knowledge to aspiring bowlers. The feedback was overwhelmingly positive, and the bowlers loved having the chance to work with these master coaches. This experience gave me a distinct advantage in addition to improving my coaching abilities. I painstakingly cataloged each coach's strengths in my coaching toolbox after closely studying them. I would distinguish myself from other coaches through the integration of many specialties.

My mentor was a particular coach named Fred Borden. I was greatly inspired by his unbridled enthusiasm and energy for the game. His contagious enthusiasm for bowling inspired my own commitment to coaching.

I started my first coaching job in Italy in 2000, using my proficiency in the language to establish a stronger connection with the bowlers. I had just six months to choose a team to represent us at the European Championships, which were being hosted in Israel. I was filled with grit, so I did all possible to get my team ready. We beat the odds by giving them fresh balls and honing their talents, and we won a fantastic bronze medal. My coaching career officially began with this victory, leaving an everlasting memory in my heart.

I was approached by the UAE Federation in 2002 with an alluring offer to lead their squad. This proved to be the most memorable part of my coaching career, without a doubt. We had a pool of twelve outstanding players to pick from, but we still excelled in every competition. The greatest coaching fulfillment, though, came in 2004, when Mohd Al Qubaisi won the world ranking masters in Moscow. The enthralling finals were televised live, and a whopping 8,000 spectators packed the Olympic Arena to see them. When we returned to Dubai and were recognized as champions, the pure ecstasy of our victory was magnified. We were treated as special guests of the Royal Family the next day, which was a genuinely remarkable experience that will forever be recorded in the annals of my coaching career.

I served as the Qatar national team's coach from 2006 until 2008. This time period produced a great deal of cherished memories, and I still keep in touch with many of the people I had the honor of working with.

I decided to stop coaching clients overseas in 2008 so that I could focus more on my company. In Canada, I started a training facility and carried on coaching, using my enthusiasm for the game to develop young athletes. A moment of great honor occurred in 2009 when I earned the USBC's prestigious Gold Coach accreditation. This honor, given to just a select group of active gold coaches, marked the highest level of accomplishment in my coaching career.

As I look back on my 20 years of coaching, I have discovered many attributes that a coach needs to excel:

Leadership: An excellent coach acts as a motivator, enabling individuals or teams to reach their maximum potential.

Knowledge: It is essential to have in-depth knowledge of the core abilities and strategies. Every question should be able to be answered, and a competent coach should have extensive knowledge of the sport.

Motivation: A great coach must have the capacity to fuel players' passion. He should have a positive outlook, radiate passion for the sport, and transmit that passion to his athletes. For the team to remain motivated, practices need to be fun and demanding.

Understanding the Athlete: Each player's emotional state, strengths, and shortcomings must be carefully observed by a coach. He should act as a counselor as well as a mentor, offering advice and assistance when required.

Consistency: Delivering messages and teachings consistently is crucial. To ensure clarity and success, a skilled coach must continuously emphasize important concepts and methods.

Effective Communication Skills: For a coach, having strong communication skills is crucial. He ought to provide his athletes with specific objectives, constructive criticism, and praise for accomplishments. A great coach must also be a good listener who values the opinions and ideas of his athletes.

Over the course of my coaching career, these traits have served as the cornerstone of my philosophy. I have been able to mentor and mold athletes by adhering to these ideals, fostering their abilities, and assisting them in achieving great success both on and off the lanes.

As I reflect on my coaching career, I feel a great sense of appreciation and pride. My life has been forever changed by the encounters I've had, the friendships I've made, and the victories we've shared. In addition to being my vocation, coaching has allowed me to contribute to the expansion and advancement of the sport I adore.

Mohd Al Qubaisi

Going forward, I'm excited to keep having a good influence on athletes' lives by imparting my knowledge and skills to the upcoming champions. Every day that goes by serves as a reminder to me of the power of coaching, and its capacity to influence, transform, and leave a long-lasting mark on the sports world. Additionally, a coach's responsibilities go beyond the technical skills of his sport. It also includes character development and mentoring. In addition to emphasizing talent development, a skilled coach instills values like perseverance, sportsmanship, and discipline. He acts as a role models, inspiring athletes to develop into better people as well as better sportsmen.

A coach must be able to strategize and adapt in the competitive world of sports. He should research his opponents, find their weak points, and create strategies to take advantage of those shortcomings. Flexibility is essential because the coach must be ready to modify strategies in response to evolving conditions during a game or competition.

A coach must also foster a favorable learning atmosphere. He should encourage the players to support one another and work together, fostering a sense of friendship and togetherness. A healthy team chemistry is necessary for athletes to realize their full potential and contribute to the team's success.

An excellent coach needs to keep up with the newest innovations in the sport because coaching is a lifelong process of learning and development. To improve his expertise and coaching methods, he should participate in ongoing professional development activities such as conferences, seminars, workshops, and workshops. This commitment to ongoing development guarantees that the coach can give his athletes the greatest advice and mentoring possible.

In the end, a coach's influence goes well beyond the accomplishments and recognition. The athletes he is guiding experience personal development, which is where success is truly measured. A great coach takes pride in seeing his players succeed in all facets of life, not just on the field.

To sum up, coaching is a significant and transforming journey that calls for a special fusion of leadership, expertise, drive, understanding, consistency, and good communication. To be entrusted with an athlete's growth and to help a sport advance is both an honor and a duty. In my role as a coach, I'm dedicated to embracing these values, growing personally and professionally, and leaving a lasting impression on the people I have the privilege of mentoring.

Frank Buffa, USBC Gold Coach and Owner of Buffa Distribution

COACH PATHWAY TO ATHLETE JOURNEY

Numerous nations have realized the critical importance of giving aspiring young bowlers a trajectory that nurtures their talent, paving the way for the development of victorious bowlers in the future. In recent years, there has been an increase in the establishment of meticulously designed and strategically tailored pathways for youth sports. Coaches are given enormous responsibilities because they must expertly guide junior bowlers through the transition to the senior level, where their skills will be put to the ultimate test. The best trainers have an unwavering dedication and an unmatched talent for bringing out the hidden potential in their bowlers, with the specific goal of improving their chances of experiencing resounding success.

The foundation of creating ideal coach-bowler dynamics is what is known as "relational coaching," which experts have highlighted as a crucial component of excellent young sports coaching. This idea captures the complex interpersonal dynamics that allow instructors to interact with bowlers in a way that has a significant impact. The formation of skill and competence perceptions occurs through effective interactions between instructors and bowlers, which also boosts self-confidence and general well-being. Additionally, the quality of the coach-bowler relationship is a highly effective predictor of the growth of a variety of personal, social, and cognitive abilities.

It is crucial to delve further into the philosophical underpinnings and developmental experiences of pathway coaches given the significant financial investments made in talent pathways over the past ten years and the undeniable role that excellent coaching plays in developing young bowlers. In order to unravel the complex web of talent development and maximize the potential of upcoming bowlers along these pathways, it is essential to comprehend their special position and the transformative journeys they take with their bowlers.

Hypothetical Examples

Example 1: Michael, a promising bowler, begins a talent path with big aspirations. Coach Thompson, though, lacks the dedication and aptitude required to maximize Michael's potential. Coach Thompson fails to build a solid rapport with the bowler, which results in little engagement and direction. As a result, Michael's opinion of his abilities and competence is unchanged, which harms his self-confidence and general well-being. Michael's overall development as a bowler is eventually hampered by the absence of a helpful and transformative coaching approach.

Example 2: The goal of Emma, a gifted bowler, is to get to the senior level. She starts on a talent pathway. Unfortunately, her coach, Coach Wilson, does not place a high priority on building a strong coach-bowler relationship. Emma feels distant and unsupported because of the lack of open communication and individuality in their relationship. Emma's conviction in her own abilities is subsequently challenged, which impairs her feeling of self-worth and hinders the development of her personal, social, and cognitive skills. Emma's development down the talent pathway is ultimately hampered by Coach Wilson's poor coaching strategy, which lowers her chances of success.

Coaching young athletes involves more than just providing instructions; it also serves as an educator, a moral compass, and a knowledge base for both coaches and players. Young bowlers' total personal development is prioritized by effective youth coaches, who exhibit traits like sincere concern, high standards, and transformative coaching methods. Young bowlers encounter increased demands as they advance in their sport, necessitating the acquisition and use of psychological skills as the cornerstone of their advancement.

Young bowlers have unequaled chances for optimal growth that promotes positive youth development (PYD) in structured activities, particularly in sports. Coaching interventions consciously create and foster social and personal qualities in bowlers as well as in their overall lives. Particularly in competitive young sports, it is acknowledged that PYD outcomes, such as perseverance, respect, teamwork, and leadership, flourish. According to empirical data, acquiring psychological skills improves learning capacity and gives people the resilience they need to overcome obstacles and achieve their potential. Scholars have also seen skill transfer, which is when psychological and behavioral abilities acquired through sports pathways continue to be useful outside of sports even after leaving those pathways.

While having the potential to revolutionize, talent routes can also carry inherent hazards and have a negative impact on the development of young bowlers. A sophisticated understanding of the psychological, social, and contextual aspects that influence the pathway experience is necessary to strike a balance between developing potential and ensuring well-being. This guarantees that paths foster growth and flourishing instead of impeding holistic development.

Hypothetical Examples

Example 1: Young bowler, James, joins a talent route with high expectations for professional and personal growth. However, James' holistic development is not given priority by his coach, Coach Smith, who is exclusively concerned with winning at any cost. James is subjected to enormous pressure from Coach Smith, who also sets unattainable standards for him while disregarding his mental health. James experiences increased stress and anxiety as a result of the demanding and rigorous coaching approach that produces a poisonous environment. As a result of the poor coaching style, James's passion for the game wanes and his overall growth as a bowler and person is impeded.

Example 2: Fostering the growth of young bowlers is the responsibility of Coach Johnson, an accomplished coach working within a talent pipeline. Coach Johnson, however, doesn't show true concern for the development and welfare of the bowlers under his supervision. Coach Johnson places more importance on immediate success and winning individual awards than on the bowlers' overall growth. This strategy discourages cooperation and teamwork by pitting bowlers against one another in a competitive and ruthless setting. The absence of emphasis on social and personal skill development denies bowlers many opportunities to develop qualities like persistence, leadership, and respect. The bowlers' long-term growth and flourishing are hampered as a result, and the talent pipeline falls short of creating the ideal environment for healthy young development.

Issues of the Coach on his Athletes	Potential Negative Outcomes for Athletes in the Future
Lack of Dedication and Aptitude	Reduced self-confidence and skill development
Inadequate Skill Development	Limited growth in sports skills and competitiveness
Poor Communication	Misunderstandings, frustration, and lack of trust
Neglecting Personal Development	Limited holistic development and life skills
Excessive Pressure	Burnout, stress, and potential physical/mental health issues
Inadequate Mental Coaching	Lack of mental resilience and emotional well-being
Favoritism or Bias	Demotivation and feelings of unfair treatment
Lack of Feedback and Guidance	Stagnation in skill improvement and performance
Ineffective Pathway Planning	Uncertain transition to higher levels and reduced future prospects
Lack of Individualized Attention	Reduced skill development, slower progress, and lack of personal focus
Poor Sportsmanship and Ethics	Adoption of unsportsmanlike behavior and a negative reputation
Inadequate Training Facilities	Limited access to proper resources for skill development
Overemphasis on Winning	High stress levels, reduced enjoyment, and burnout
Inadequate Injury Management	Increased risk of injuries, potentially career-ending injuries
Lack of Inclusivity and Diversity	Limited opportunities and diversity in the sport
Inconsistent Pathway Support	Uncertainty in career progression and future prospects

Table 43– Coach's Impact on Athletes: Potential Negative Outcomes, from reduced self-confidence to limited career prospects, stemming from issues like inadequate skill development, poor communication, excessive pressure, and more

THE TRANSITION FROM BOWLER TO COACH

The process of transitioning from a bowler to a coach has gotten a lot of attention in prior studies, along with the complex journey of young bowlers. The transition from being an "almost" elite bowler to being a junior bowling coach is an important alternative path to take, even if elite bowlers receive the most attention in this regard. "Almost" is a term used in sports psychology to describe young bowlers with exceptional skill who may not have advanced to the top of senior sport but still have a ton of untapped potential. Talent pathway coaches are in a perfect position to engage with this group, using a transformational approach that promotes their entire development since they have first-hand knowledge and a thorough grasp of the demands and challenges experienced by young bowlers.

MYTH: "COACHES WHO HAVE PLAYED AT A HIGH LEVEL MAKE THE BEST COACHES."

Reality: The assumption that coaches who have achieved high levels of play make the best coaches is incorrect. Effective coaching in bowling is not solely determined by personal achievements as a player. Exceptional coaches excel in teaching and communication, tailoring their approach to meet the needs of individual athletes. They possess a deep understanding of the game, can break down complex techniques into understandable steps, and create a positive learning environment. Great coaches recognize the diverse abilities of their athletes and utilize various teaching methods, visual aids, and constructive feedback to foster skill development. They also focus on building strong interpersonal relationships, providing emotional support, and instilling a love for the game. Coaching proficiency is about teaching, connecting, and supporting athletes rather than personal achievements as a player.

How coaches gain this profound awareness via their own personal journeys and put it to use in their coaching practice is a crucial topic of discussion. A foundation for developing a more significant and lasting learning experience for the present generation of young bowlers is provided by the adoption of integrative coaching concepts by talent pathway coaches who have traveled the pathway as young bowlers themselves. It is proposed, based on the principles of experiential learning, that past experiences give instructors invaluable knowledge to aid in the development and advancement of young bowlers. By fostering emotional, behavioral, and perceptual complexity through supervised encounters, experiential learning fosters development. Coach education places a strong emphasis on active and critical reflection, which is at the center of the experiential learning process, in recognition of the significance of informal and experiential learning for coach growth.

It's crucial to note that abilities can transfer from one domain to another, for example, coaching inside a talent route, just as participation in a talent pathway as a young bowler can. It is logical to suppose that the abilities young bowlers acquire while participating in the sport can easily transfer to other fields after being deselected, such as the world of sports coaching. One of the most important variables in this complex equation is the coaches' capacity to draw on their earlier experiences and enable active and critical thought on the substance and goal of their coaching practice.

Hypothetical Examples

Example 1: Emily, a gifted bowler, came close to making it to the professional level despite constantly competing at a high level in several competitions. However, Emily's love for the game never wavered, and she made the decision to change careers from "almost" top bowler to young bowling coach. Emily adopted a transformative teaching style after drawing on her personal experiences and developing a thorough grasp of the demands and pressures placed on young bowlers in talent routes. She focused on fostering her young charges' overall growth because she was aware of her tremendous potential. Through her leadership, Emily fostered a culture in which her bowlers were encouraged to reach their full potential both on and off the lanes by being supported, inspired, and empowered. Her transformation from an "almost" top bowler to a successful junior bowling coach is a prime example of the transformational power of life experiences and the enduring effects they can have on the growth of young bowlers.

Example 2: Coach Michael has always had a strong enthusiasm for bowling and has firsthand knowledge of the highs and lows of pursuing a professional bowling career. Michael was aware that, although not reaching the peak of senior sport, his experience had given him invaluable knowledge and abilities that may be useful to ambitious young bowlers. Michael accepted the position of a talent pathway coach after being motivated by his own developmental journey. He led his bowlers through carefully crafted experiences that developed not just their technical abilities but also their emotional resilience and cognitive complexity, drawing on the concepts of experiential learning. Michael helped his bowlers comprehend the meaning and goal of their coaching practice through active and critical reflection, empowering them to apply the skills they learned on the lanes to other areas of their lives. Michael developed an environment that went beyond conventional coaching paradigms by embracing his personal trajectory and implementing experiential learning methods. This environment helped his young bowlers reach their full potential by encouraging holistic growth and self-discovery.

The expertise and insight that talent pathway coaches have gained during their journey from "almost" great bowlers to effective youth bowling coaches is invaluable to their young athletes. These coaches may create an environment that goes beyond conventional coaching techniques by reflecting on their own experiences and putting experiential learning principles to use. This environment will encourage young bowlers to grow holistically, discover themselves, and realize their full potential.

The Impact Of The Epistemological Chain

In particular, during the shift from youth bowler to coach, the epistemic chain (EC) is vital to the growth of coaches. The EC is a reflection of the coaches' knowledge and learning beliefs, which have been developed by their own experiences as athletes as well as the process of deriving meaning from their own experiences and coaching practice. Coaches can critically assess their preparation, practice, and reflections by using the EC as a tool for introspection and analysis, resulting in a more advanced coaching style. Experienced coaches have observed their EC change as a result of engaging learning environments and encouraging connections, enabling young bowlers to take charge of their education and develop a variety of personal abilities. It would be fascinating to investigate further how talent development experiences affect youth coaches' knowledge, abilities, and coaching philosophies. Recognizing that a coach's philosophy is woven together from many different aspects—personal experiences, introspection, and formal coach education—is key.

Based on the impact of the Epistemological Chain (EC) on coaching, here is a table explaining different coach issues:

Coach Issue	Explanation
Lack of Self-Reflection	Coaches who do not engage with their EC may lack the ability to reflect on their experiences and learning, hindering their growth and development.
Inadequate Learning Beliefs	Coaches with limited or rigid learning beliefs may resist new ideas and methods, preventing them from adapting to evolving coaching practices.
Limited Application of Knowledge	Coaches who do not apply knowledge derived from their own experiences and coaching practice may struggle to effectively guide their athletes.
Resistance to Change	Coaches who resist changing their coaching style in response to their evolving EC may hinder the development of their athletes.
Disconnect from Athlete Learning	Coaches who do not align their coaching with the epistemic growth of their athletes may fail to empower them to take charge of their education.
Narrow Coaching Philosophy	Coaches who do not embrace diverse aspects within their EC may have a narrow coaching philosophy, limiting their effectiveness.

Coach Issue	Explanation
Ineffective Coaching Style	Coaches who do not use their EC for introspection and analysis may lack the tools to develop an advanced coaching style.
Limited Integration of Coach Education	Coaches who do not recognize the value of formal coach education within their EC may miss out on opportunities to enhance their knowledge and skills.

Table 44– The Epistemological Chain is essential for coaches' growth, as it influences their beliefs, learning, and coaching style, which, in turn, impact their ability to guide and develop athletes effectively. Coaches who actively engage with their EC are more likely to adapt and evolve, resulting in a more comprehensive and effective coaching approach.

The Importance Of A Coaching Philosophy

Understanding coaches' behavioral patterns require understanding their coaching philosophy, which they must be able to define clearly and engage in reflective deliberation about. Although coaches frequently rely on their instinct and practical knowledge, developing a defined coaching philosophy can significantly increase coaching effectiveness. Coaches' coaching philosophy is molded by their basic ideas and values and is based on their practice, activities, and conduct. Experience, whether acquired as a coach or a bowler, is crucial to the coaching process because it enables coaches to navigate their interactions and obtain real knowledge. There is still much to learn about how instructors reflect on and use their experiences as bowlers to create new information, though. Last but not least, coaching is a diverse and organic process that extends beyond pedagogy, so while formal coach education is vital, it should not be considered the main driver of a coach's ideology.

Hypothetical Examples

Example 1: Former young bowler turned coach, Sarah, is a firm believer in the value of the epistemic chain (EC) as a tool for self-improvement. Sarah has seen her EC develop over time, drawing on her own experiences as well as introspective thought. She has improved her preparation, practice, and thoughts through introspection and critical assessment, resulting in a more complex and sophisticated coaching style. Sarah is aware of the influence her extensive work in talent development environments has had on her knowledge, abilities, and coaching philosophies. Young bowlers' complete growth both on and off the lanes is promoted by Sarah by embracing the EC and giving them the tools they need to be active participants in their own learning.

Example 2: Coach Mark, a seasoned coach with a thorough awareness of coaching's complexities, is aware of the critical need to have a clearly defined coaching philosophy. He thinks that the basis for successful coaching is a defined coaching philosophy. Mark develops a coaching philosophy that guides his practice, actions, and conduct by drawing on his intuitive insights and practical skills. His experiences as a coach and a bowler have influenced his coaching philosophy, which he has developed by carefully reflecting on and analyzing the tapestry of his interactions. Mark agrees that while formal coach education is crucial, it is not the only factor in a coach's ideology coming into being. He sees coaching as an organic, multilayered activity that goes beyond education and necessitates coaches to draw on their real-world experiences in order to expand their knowledge and understanding.

Amplifying Youth Bowler Development Through Transfer Of Experience

By drawing on their own athletic pasts inside the talent pathway, pathway coaches are in a powerful position to accommodate the different developmental needs of young bowlers. Applying knowledge and abilities from one setting to another by drawing on prior experiences is a crucial aspect of learning transfer. The congruence with current and future learning contexts, as well as the content, context, and complexity of the first experience, are all important considerations for successful transfer. Coaches should build a solid personal foundation, participate in reflective practices, and give themselves enough time to assimilate prior knowledge to enhance learning transfer. We can learn a great deal about coaches' coaching beliefs and how they develop and mentor young bowlers holistically by understanding how coaches incorporate their experiences as young bowlers into their coaching.

The task of coaching young bowlers involves many different complications and difficulties. In light of the fact that the majority of these athletes won't compete at the high-performance senior levels, it is essential to examine the transferable experiences, challenges, and learning opportunities they face during talent development. We can establish a setting that best supports the growth and development of all young bowlers in talent programs by comprehending the complex dynamics of their travels. This goes beyond limiting success and makes sure each bowler starts off on a trajectory full of rewarding encounters and successful outcomes.

Positive Effects of Transferring Experience:

1. ***Improved Bowling Techniques:*** Coaches who draw on their own experiences in bowling can provide valuable insights and practical knowledge to help athletes enhance their bowling techniques. This firsthand experience can lead to more effective and tailored coaching, accelerating the athletes' skill development.

2. ***Enhanced Motivation:*** Coaches who share their stories of overcoming challenges or achieving success in bowling can inspire and motivate their young bowlers. These stories can instill a strong work ethic, determination, and a desire for improvement in the athletes' bowling performances.

3. ***Resilience and Mental Toughness:*** Sharing personal experiences of dealing with challenging lane conditions or competitive pressures in bowling can help athletes develop resilience and mental toughness. Coaches can impart coping strategies and the mindset required to overcome obstacles on the lanes.

4. ***Holistic Development:*** Coaches who incorporate their experiences in bowling into coaching can provide guidance on not only bowling technique but also personal growth, character-building, and life skills, ensuring athletes are well-rounded individuals both on and off the lanes.

Negative Effects of Transferring Experience:

1. ***Biased Coaching:*** Coaches who excessively rely on their own bowling experiences may unintentionally impose their playing style or preferences on their athletes, limiting the individuality and creativity of the athletes' bowling techniques.

2. ***Lack of Adaptability:*** Coaches who solely rely on their past experiences in bowling might resist new coaching methods and fail to adapt to evolving lane conditions or strategies. This rigidity can hinder the athletes' development in a changing bowling landscape.

3. ***Burnout Risk:*** Coaches who push athletes to replicate their own high-intensity bowling experiences may inadvertently increase the risk of burnout. Athletes may feel pressure to match their coach's achievements, leading to physical and mental exhaustion from bowling.

4. ***Stagnation:*** Coaches who focus solely on their past experiences in bowling may overlook the evolving techniques and strategies needed by their athletes, potentially hindering their progress and skill development on the lanes.

Psychological Effects:

Positive psychological effects that can be transferred from coach to bowling athletes include:

1. ***Confidence:*** Coaches who share their experiences of overcoming self-doubt on the lanes can boost their athletes' self-confidence and belief in their bowling abilities.

2. ***Focus and Concentration:*** Coaches can impart effective mental strategies for maintaining focus and concentration during bowling competitions.

Negative psychological effects that can be transferred from coach to bowling athletes include:

1. ***Performance Anxiety:*** If a coach conveys their own anxieties or past performance pressures in bowling, it may lead to similar anxieties in their athletes when competing.

2. ***Overthinking:*** Coaches who emphasize the complexity of the game may inadvertently lead their athletes to overanalyze and overthink their actions, which can hinder their performance in bowling.

Hypothetical Examples

Example 1: Think about Sarah, a pathway coach. Although Sarah was a skilled young bowler with a lot of potential, she was unable to compete at the professional or international level. Sarah currently instructs young bowlers, drawing on her own experiences in the talent route and utilizing her knowledge and abilities to direct them toward holistic development and maximizing their potential. Sarah creates a setting that goes beyond conventional coaching techniques by reflecting on her experience as a bowler and utilizing experiential learning principles, enabling profound self-discovery and growth in her young charges.

Example 2: Coach Mark, who began his career as an "almost" top bowler, is another illustration. Despite not competing at the highest levels in adult sports, Mark had a lot of talent and potential. Mark now uses the epistemological chain and his personal experiences to further his coaching career as a route coach. In order to develop a more sophisticated strategy and obtain a deeper grasp of coaching, he critically assesses his preparation, practice, and reflections. The empowerment of young bowlers to take ownership of their learning and build a diverse range of personal abilities is a hallmark of Mark's coaching philosophy, which is reinforced by his personal experiences and introspection.

FROM WORLD CHAMPION BOWLER TO CHAMPIONSHIP COACH: EMBRACING CHANGE AND ADAPTING IN THE BOWLING WORLD *By Robert Anderson*

Abstract: This story focuses on the transition of a former world champion bowler into a teaching job that was difficult, questioning social conventions, and embracing scientific research. The coach obtained important knowledge and created novel strategies through coaching education, statistical research, and engagement with athletes from numerous sports. Leading a national team, helping a promising young bowler succeed, and having a big impact on Saudi Arabia's bowling scene are notable accomplishments. The coach places a strong emphasis on leadership, flexibility, lifelong learning, and meaningful interactions with other coaches. The coach considers the necessity to remain aware of changes and open-minded to new approaches and ideas in a field that is continually evolving. The story ends with the idea that coaches must adapt to these changes if they want to succeed in their coaching jobs because the bowling world is constantly evolving.

I had a rebellious mindset toward the federation and its prescribed coaching techniques when I first started my coaching career. I had seen the many bowling styles of the best players during my seven years of professional travel. I realized that assuming everyone would adopt the same strategy would lead to diverse outcomes, especially when taking into account variables like height variations. This insight made me wonder about the system.

"Despite being 30 cm shorter than Martin, why should I achieve the same results as Martin when I am doing the exact same thing?" I queried. The response was straightforward: "Just do it."

Another query was raised: "Why, when different bowling alleys have different lane markings, do I have to start at the same spot on the lane?" The reply was the same: "Just do it."

As my cynicism increased, I came to the conclusion that I no longer needed to follow the conventional coaching techniques. A chance did arise, though, when a new sports director joined the federation and requested me to help expand the educational system. I finished the federation's coaching education program in four years because I was eager to help others. Sports in Sweden adhere to EU regulations, which include four educational levels (levels 1-4) under the sport federation. After passing these stages, one can apply to the sports university for Elite Trainer Education, which is step 5. I got admitted to the program in 2010, and it turned out to be a great educational opportunity. I discovered that I was surrounded by elite athletes who were switching from active sports careers to coaching, so I could no longer rely simply on my position as a world-champion bowler. Our research covered a wide range of topics, such as biomechanics, physiology, and psychology. We had to write papers on each subject, concentrating on our particular sport, in order to apply what we had learned. My knowledge was greatly increased by interacting with professors, educators, and sportsmen from various sports.

Timing Angle and Ball Speed in Nordic Elite Bowlers is the name of a significant research project I started during the last six months of the program. The goal of this study was to disprove the idea that everyone can get the same results by ignoring physiological variance. Only half of our class ultimately obtained diplomas, and I am really proud to be one of them.

I started working with the youth squad while continuing to bowl for the national team. I went with them to the 2012 World Youth Championship in Bangkok, where we had outstanding success. We even set a new record in the team competition, and we took home the gold in the Masters category. We still enjoy thinking back on the time I told the last bowler he needed a strike to break the world record only to find out it was actually my record he beat.

I carried out another study called the "Down Swing Ratio" in an effort to comprehend the ethereal elements of the game. This study sought to categorize bowlers so that practical advice could be more easily given to them. Although I personally found this study to be fruitful, I began to believe that I had ventured too far into the scientific realm for most bowlers or instructors to properly understand.

The Down Swing Ratio examines the swing's highest point in relation to the remaining distance to the foul line.

There was a tall youngster named Jesper who wanted to play for the national team all of these years. He battled with his anger but thrived on the Junior team. He joined Pergamon and my team, and I started assisting him with his practice. Our interaction felt more like a partnership at first than like a coach-athlete connection. On oil patterns less than 35 feet, Jesper was virtually unstoppable because of his incredible ball speed. The problem materialized when patterns were longer than 38 feet, though. In order to improve his performance on patterns between 37 and 38 feet, we focused on lowering his swing and moving his hand closer to his foot.

When we went to the World Youth Championship in Hong Kong in 2014, Jesper was already a favorite at the age of 18. He had a rocky start in the first game, but we corrected it, and he advanced to the singles finals where he lost to a different skilled two-handed bowler. But Jesper's perseverance got him to the Masters final, where he failed to make a strike on one of the lanes and trailed by 20 pins with only two frames left to play. He came to me, frustrated, and asked, "What should I do?" I yelled out, "Change the ball," in an instant. I had internal doubts about what I had said, but I didn't want to make Jesper doubt himself. I gave him my unwavering assurance that the choice would be successful. Amazingly, it did. He moved to the opposite lane and fired three straight strikes to win the championship. The doubles competition saw two additional Swedish bowlers, Marcus and Pontus, win, making this year's Young World Championship our most successful to date.

As a result of these accomplishments, I took over as Team Pergamon's sports director and trainer. After two years, I left my job with the national team and was given the chance to work in Saudi Arabia with the famous Rick Benoit. In 2016, I moved, and that was the beginning of a journey that would teach me priceless lessons about being an international coach. I teamed up with an old friend to work for his company, Lanetalk, when I got back to Sweden. Our goal was to help bowlers and federations analyze pinfall statistics to improve training methods in the rapidly changing world of technology and information. I believe that the skill sets needed to be a coach and a trainer are distinct. I firmly feel that having experience playing competitive bowling gives one a greater comprehension of the nuances required to become a championship coach (albeit I could be wrong; this is just my own opinion). becoming a good role model is essential for becoming a successful coach. Everyone must abide by the guidelines established for the group. In addition, I've found that your bowlers will overlook whatever errors you make if you put in the effort and honestly care about their welfare. However, if they have any doubts about your dedication, one mistake -- and mistakes will happen -- could permanently harm your relationship with them. Let others interrogate you. Accepting their questions keeps you alert and motivates you to be cautious with your words. Before giving bowlers advice during a match or competition, consider whether you're actually trying to help them or just trying to demonstrate your expertise.

There is a big difference between being a boss and being a leader. Instead of just telling athletes what to do, your role as a leader should be to enable them to take responsibility for their own development. converse intelligently with other instructors. I've had the good fortune to study under many outstanding trainers, and their experiences have shown me how easily industry factors, such as reactive bowling balls, oil patterns, or lane circumstances, may cause our perception of the finest bowling tactics to change. You run the risk of being complacent and lagging behind the times if you are overconfident that you have all the answers. It's commonly believed that when learning ceases, coaching skills also stop. I currently work with young Swedish bowlers, and the prevalence of two-handed bowling has changed the game. My in-depth analysis of bowlers' timing and length is now five years old, making it no longer current. I must face this fact and apply the knowledge I learned from that research to my future endeavors. As bowling coaches, it is our responsibility

Jesper Svensson

to adapt to and embrace change, whether it be for the better or worse. As they say, we have to "roll with it," keeping an adaptable and positive attitude.

It gives me a lot of satisfaction to mentor and develop the upcoming generation of bowlers in my current position with the Swedish young squad. It's an opportunity for me to impart my expertise and love of the sport to others while also teaching them the virtues of commitment, tenacity, and sportsmanship. I am incredibly happy to see them grow and advance, and I am appreciative of the opportunity to support their success. In the end, coaching is a never-ending process of self-development. Humility, curiosity, and a thirst for knowledge are necessary. I am becoming more and more aware that there is always something new to learn, uncover, and explore in the coaching world. If we want to be the best coaches we possibly can be, stagnation is not an option. When I think back on my coaching career, I am happy with the accomplishments I have accomplished and the difference I have been able to make in the lives of the bowlers I have had the honor to work with. The relationships formed, the lessons discovered, and the personal development realized along the journey are more important than just the victories and records.

I am enthusiastic about bowling's future and the chances that lie ahead when I look ahead. The potential for innovation and development in our sport is boundless with advances in technology, improved access to data, and a growing international community of dedicated bowlers. As a coach, I'm dedicated to remaining on top of these advancements and always modifying my strategies to bring out the best in each bowler I deal with. In summary, coaching is more than just a job; it's a calling, a way of life, and a way of encouraging athletes to realize their greatest potential. It calls for a fusion of technological know-how, people abilities, and a profound comprehension of the dynamically shifting nature of the sport. I am thankful for the chances that have helped me develop as a coach as I continue on this road, and I am looking forward to the difficulties and successes that lie ahead. Together, let's embrace the spirit of competition, develop potential, and leave a lasting impression on the bowling community.

Robert Anderson

SUCCESSFUL TRAINING TRANSFER
THROUGH ECOLOGICAL DYNAMICS

Optimizing Training Transfer Through Ecological Dynamics

The drills and activities that coaches have their bowlers practice are meant to help them play better. Ecological dynamics offers coaches a useful perspective to address mobility issues and guarantee effective training transfer. These techniques are already being used by the best bowling teachers in the world, with spectacular results.

The key to implementing this principle is to design learning environments that encourage inquiry and "repetition without repetition." Coaches accomplish this by organizing timetables, creating training materials, and disseminating information in a way that motivates bowlers to solve problems on their own and adjust rapidly.

Bowling is seen as a sophisticated adaptive system in ecological dynamics. The state of the lanes, the bowling alley, the bowling ball, and the bowler themselves all come into play during a game of bowling. Bowlers can recognize and take advantage of advantageous action chances thanks to the interactions that produce information that they continuously adapt to.

A dynamic cycle of modifications results from the difficulties presented by the task, the environment, and the bowler combined. Due to the continual exchanges between perception and action, the information a bowler receives is constantly changing. These possibilities for action are referred to as affordances, and they indicate the possible actions that the bowler may do depending on the task, the surrounding environment, and their own capabilities.

The ultimate aim of coaching and performance is victory. Every bowler strives to achieve higher-order performance outcomes like more pinfalls, victories, improved league play, and better tournament finishes. A variety of lower-order events, such as skill execution, physical training, and decision-making, have an impact on achieving these objectives. The results of these lower-order events are determined by their combined impact on the higher-order events. The key to victory is evident: winning more games necessitates scoring more pins, which is necessary to win contests. Positive outcomes in the fundamental lower-order performance outcomes that support the sport must be attained in order to do this.

Practical Application Of Ecological Dynamics In Bowling - Creating Learning Environments Together

By jointly developing learning environments, ecological dynamics can be practically used to improve skill acquisition and performance in bowling. This entails developing training environments that follow the rules of ecological dynamics.

Based on bowlers' prior experience or their own skills, coaches need to pinpoint the key components of modifications. This makes it possible for coaches to choose the problems that will have the biggest impact on performance.

Cooperation between bowlers and instructors is essential for creating original and imaginative solutions to interrelated issues, and continually improving performance. Coaches and bowlers can get important knowledge and insights that will guide the construction of better environments in the future by designing learning environments that motivate bowlers to take on difficulties.

The prior knowledge and expertise of each bowler are key factors in the environment design. A deeper level of task engagement is possible thanks to the expert bowlers' in-depth insights into the environment's most pertinent task-related information. On the other hand, younger and less skilled bowlers can need streamlined challenges or assignments that highlight the most important details within a certain activity or circumstance.

The following are some real-world examples of ecological dynamics in bowling and how they can be applied to jointly construct successful learning environments:

To maximize skill development in bowling, representative learning design is essential. Coaches can maximize the transfer of abilities to actual bowling settings by designing training assignments and environments that closely resemble the difficulties of competitive play. This entails creating bowling lanes with certain pin locations, ball options, and lane conditions that precisely replicate the demands of competitive play. Bowlers can hone their perceptual, cognitive, and motor skills by practicing in these realistic settings. This will help them be better prepared for the game and be able to use their skills in a competitive context with ease.

> *In order to simulate the lane circumstances found in competitive tournaments, such as the oil patterns and pin placements, a coach sets up a training session at a bowling alley. The same kind of balls that bowlers would ordinarily use in tournaments are recommended. The training exercises entail practicing a variety of shots while adjusting to the lane circumstances, including strikes, spares, and various spare combo shots. This enables bowlers to develop perceptual skills for interpreting lane circumstances, cognitive abilities for making decisions, and motor skills for carrying out various shots in a realistic setting.*

YOUSIF FALAH:

Enhancing Skill Transfer with Realistic Training Environments

Being exposed to a competitive sporting environment from a young age nurtured my competitive spirit. Participating in different sports on a competitive level instilled in me a drive to excel in each one. While I knew it was impossible to master them all, I recognized the essence of striving to be the best and looked up to role models in each sport to understand their journey to greatness.

Among these role models, Tim Mack stands out as my ultimate inspiration. His impact on my life goes beyond bowling; his positive outlook, never-give-up attitude, and global influence have shaped me both as an athlete and as a person. Ron Hoppe was the first to recognize my potential and became my first real coach. We worked tirelessly together until his untimely departure. Another influential figure in my journey is Mohammed Janahi, who dedicated countless hours to coaching me upon his return to Bahrain.

Optimizing Skill Transfer through Manipulation of Bowling Constraints

By adjusting the numerous limitations that affect a bowler's motions and decision-making, coaches can improve skill acquisition and performance. These limitations, including lane characteristics, ball mass, and pin placements, have a big impact on ecological dynamics. Coaches can vary these limitations in training conditions to produce a variety of challenges that force bowlers to modify their methods and approaches, which ultimately helps them transfer their knowledge to competitive settings. During practice sessions, coaches might introduce various lane conditions, alter ball weights, or change the positioning of pins, giving bowlers the chance to improve their game's adaptability and versatility.

By modifying the pin positions or the oil patterns, the coach can alter the lane conditions during a practice session. Due to these shifting conditions, bowlers must modify their methods and approaches, such as ball speed, trajectory, and target points. Bowlers gain the ability to alter their actions and decision-making in response to various challenges by frequently changing the limitations, which helps them transfer their skills to competitive settings where lane conditions may change.

Modification	Explanation	Neurological Aspect Developed	Psychological Aspect Learned
Varying Lane Conditions	Change oil patterns, lane length, or surface friction for adaptability in different environments.	Sensory perception and adaptation	Adaptability and mental resilience
Moving Pin Placements	Rearrange pin positions to practice different spare pickups and strike targeting.	Visual-spatial awareness	Concentration and precision
Altering Footwork Patterns	Adjust the footwork approach, such as steps and timing, to refine balance and accuracy.	Kinesthetic awareness and coordination	Balance and stability
Modifying Ball Release Point	Practice different release points to control the ball's path and hook potential.	Fine motor skills and hand-eye coordination	Precision and consistency
Introducing Lane Transition Scenarios	Simulate lane transitions from oily to dry conditions for adapting to real game situations.	Cognitive flexibility and problem-solving	Adaptation and strategy
Using Different Bowling Balls	Switch between various types of bowling balls to understand their characteristics.	Sensorimotor coordination	Knowledge and ball selection
Incorporating Spares and Split Scenarios	Create scenarios for practicing challenging spare conversions and split pickups.	Visual perception and spatial awareness	Focus and composure
Experimenting with Approach Angles	Modify the angle of approach to the lane, enhancing versatility in shot selection.	Spatial orientation and perception	Strategy and versatility
Adjusting Ball Speed	Practice varying ball speeds to manage lane conditions effectively.	Timing and motor control	Speed control and decision-making
Implementing Mental Challenges	Introduce mental exercises to enhance focus and concentration under pressure.	Cognitive control and emotional regulation	Mental resilience and concentration
Simulating Competitive Pressure	Create competitive practice scenarios to prepare for actual tournaments.	Cognitive processing and decision-making	Confidence and competition mindset
Simulating Tournament Feeling and Environment	Replicate the ambiance, pressure, and environment of a tournament to acclimate bowlers to the competitive atmosphere.	Psychological preparedness	Tournament mindset and composure
Monitoring Biometric Data	Use technology to analyze biometric data like heart rate and breathing for stress management.	Self-awareness and stress regulation	Stress management and emotional control
Enhancing Video Analysis	Provide video feedback to bowlers for better self-assessment and improvement.	Visual-motor coordination and self-evaluation	Self-awareness and performance analysis

Table 45– These modifications not only enhance the physical aspects of bowling but also contribute to the neurological and psychological development of the athlete, improving their adaptability, focus, and overall performance.

Improving Performance through Smart Decision-Making Training

Making good decisions is essential to succeeding in the game. The importance of making wise decisions on the bowling lanes, such as choosing the right ball, aiming for particular pins and modifying approaches to match lane circumstances, is brought home by ecological dynamics. Coaches can design learning settings that focus on this skill in order to improve bowlers' decision-making abilities. Several techniques, like as video analysis, virtual simulations, and decision-making exercises that closely resemble real-game circumstances, can be used to do this. Bowlers can improve their decision-making abilities by participating in these training sessions, which will help them make quick decisions during competitive play.

Through the use of virtual simulations and video analysis, the coach integrates decision-making training into the learning environment. Bowlers assess their decision-making process, discuss potential plans with their teammates, and review video records of their performances to review how they performed. To develop realistic decision-making scenarios, virtual simulations like interactive bowling software can be employed. In these situations, bowlers choose which ball to use, what targets to aim for, and how to alter their strategy in response to shifting lane conditions. This fosters the growth of decision-making abilities in a secure and controlled setting for bowlers.

Here are more specific and realistic examples for each of the training sessions:

1. **Video Analysis Sessions:**

   - *Example: Review a video of a recent league game where the bowler had to make a critical decision in the 10th frame, such as choosing a hybrid pin down ball or making a lane adjustment. Discuss the decision's impact on the game's outcome.*

2. **The future of Virtual Reality Decision-Making Simulations**

   - *Example: Bowlers use VR to simulate a high-pressure tournament final frame. They must decide between a reactive resin ball and a urethane ball for the final strike. The VR environment replicates the tension and crowd noise.*

3. **Lane Condition Adaptation Workshops:**

   - *Example: Bowlers practice on lanes with different oil patterns, ranging from heavy oil to dry conditions. They must adapt their ball choice and approach to excel in each scenario.*

4. **Real-Time Decision Challenges:**

   - *Example: During a practice session, the coach unexpectedly alters the oil pattern on a specific lane. Bowlers are required to make quick adjustments, such as choosing a different ball and changing their angle.*

5. **Mental Decision-Making Exercises:**

   - *Example: Bowlers participate in visualization exercises before a tournament. They imagine being in a close match, needing a huge game at the last game. They must decide which ball to use and visualize the perfect shots.*

6. **Interactive Decision Workbooks:**

   - *Example: Bowlers receive a workbook with scenarios like "You're facing a challenging split. Which ball do you choose and where do you aim?" They complete the workbook, discussing their choices afterward.*

7. **Coaching Drills with Decision Emphasis:**

   - *Example: In a strike-building drill, bowlers work on a sequence of shots. The coach randomly assigns different spares between strikes, forcing the bowlers to make on-the-fly decisions on ball choice and adjustments.*

8. **Team Decision Challenges:**

FREDERIK ØHRGAARD

Exploring challenges: a path to skill development

So, to all the aspiring athletes out there, I encourage you to embrace the power of your mind. Understand that success isn't solely determined by physical prowess but also by mental fortitude. Invest time and effort into developing your mental game, exploring techniques like focusing on performance, mastering the "register, accept, and react" process, and harnessing the power of visualization.

- *Example: Bowlers are divided into teams for a practice session. Each team must collectively decide on the best approach for a specific lane condition, fostering communication and shared decision-making.*

Social connection and information-movement coupling are crucial in the fast-paced environment of bowling. The important influence of contact with teammates, rivals, and coaches on athletic performance is acknowledged by ecological dynamics. Coaches can design learning environments that encourage social interaction among bowlers to maximize this component. Team-building exercises like friendly competitions, panel debates, and insightful feedback sessions might help with this. Bowlers can increase their capacity to interpret and respond to real-time information, which will improve their decision-making abilities and overall performance on the lanes, by actively participating in these social interactions.

By setting up team games or small-group conversations, the coach promotes social contact among the bowlers during the practice period. Bowlers exchange experiences, tips, and criticism with one another to learn from one another. Bowlers can use the coach's pertinent information regarding lane conditions, ball performance, and opponent analysis to instantly modify their methods and game plans. This improves information-movement coupling, which helps bowlers understand how to analyze and react to pertinent information from their social context, leading to better performance and decision-making.

Empowering Bowlers through Self-Regulated Learning: Self-regulated learning is a major idea supported by ecological dynamics in the realm of bowling. It emphasizes that athletes should actively participate in the improvement of their skills. Bowlers can set their own objectives, monitor their progress, and evaluate their performance in learning environments that coaches can design. This gives individuals the ability to better understand themselves, assess their own performance, and make the required adjustments. Bowlers can efficiently learn new skills and enhance their performance by adopting self-regulated learning.

By giving bowlers the freedom to define their own objectives, keep track of their progress, and evaluate their performance, the coaches encourage self-regulated learning. Bowlers are urged to think about their advantages, disadvantages, and opportunities for growth. They establish clear objectives for each training session, keep tabs on their progress, and modify their practice schedules in response to their own assessments. The development of self-awareness, self-evaluation, and self-correction skills as a result of this motivates bowlers to take charge of their learning process and enhance their performance.

Coaches can use a variety of ecological dynamics-based tactics to improve skill development and performance in bowling. These include self-regulated learning, decision-making training, manipulating limitations, representational learning design, and social interaction. Coaches may develop a useful and efficient training environment that enables bowlers to flourish and realize their full potential by co-designing learning environments that take these ideas into account.

Exploring Challenges: A Path To Skill Development

In bowling, representative task design entails developing obstacles that closely mirror the requirements of actual performance. Through this method, bowlers can improve their performance on the lanes and strengthen their talents.

Bowlers go through three crucial phases while controlling task problems: search, discovery, and environmental challenges.

SEARCH

Bowlers attack the problems of the game head-on in the search phase with a fierce resolve to succeed. They like the chance to test out numerous methods and strategies in order to explore a wide range of options. Bowlers bravely explore unfamiliar ground, whether it's experimenting with release techniques, perfecting their stance, or testing out various ball types. In this stage, the focus is on innovation, curiosity, and taking measured risks to identify the tactics that maximize their performance.

Example Task: Oil Pattern Exploration

In order to determine the best line for racking up strikes, bowlers are given a training exercise where they must investigate and adjust to various oil patterns on the lane. Utilizing a number of balls and modifying ball speed, trajectory, and target areas, the task requires you to examine the lane conditions and choose the best method for racking up strikes.

The first few frames are bowled by bowlers using a particular ball and stroke while concentrating on a particular section of the lane. Then they watch the ball's behavior, such as its trajectory, entry angle, and pin action, to learn more about the lane conditions and oil pattern. They decide whether to alter their technique, ball choice or aim point based on their observations in order to increase the likelihood that they will get strikes.

As an illustration, bowlers might decide to move their target point to the outside and change their ball speed in order to lessen the hook if they observe that the ball is hooking excessively as a result of thick oil in the center of the lane. To determine the one that plays best on the present oil pattern, they may also experiment with several balls with differing coverstocks, core designs, and weights.

In order to establish a more demanding and dynamic atmosphere, the instructor may introduce new oil patterns or alter the current one as the training session goes on. In order to maximize their chances of scoring, bowlers must constantly modify their skills and strategy to account for the shifting environmental factors.

Discovery: Mastering Strategies: Solidifying Solutions

The varied range of options convert into sound plans throughout the discovery phase. Bowlers begin to pinpoint the strategies that produce the best results through their constant experimenting. They hone their methods by choosing their balls carefully, improving their approach, and honing their release. The goal is to develop reliable, repeatable procedures that may be used in a variety of lane-related situations. This stage improves their capacity to modify and confidently carry out their strategies.

Example task: target Point Discovery

Bowlers are given a training job in which they must identify the best target areas on the lane for making strikes. Utilizing a single ball, they must change their technique and target areas to scout out the lane and find the best locations for repeatable strikes.

Beginning with a steady technique and a focus on a certain part of the lane, bowlers begin their game. In addition to observing how the ball behaves and how the pin moves, they also collect data on the lane's topography, the amount of oil, any dry patches, and other factors. They decide whether to alter their target points, ball speed, or rotation based on their observations in order to increase the likelihood that the ball will hit the pocket and result in strikes.

For instance, bowlers may elect to reposition their target point towards the center or edge of the lane or alter their ball speed and rotation to vary the ball's entry angle into the pocket if they detect that the ball is entering the pocket too high or too low. To find the best method for reliable strikes, they can experiment with various target points, ball speeds, and rotations.

In order to create a more demanding and dynamic environment, the coach may add various lane conditions as the training session goes on, such as altering the oil pattern or introducing dry sections. The best target points for scoring strikes must always be found, so bowlers must constantly modify their skills and strategies to account for the shifting environment.

This discovery assignment challenges bowlers to hone their motor abilities for completing a variety of shots with adaptation, their cognitive skills for making decisions about target points, ball speed, and rotation, and their perceptual skills for reading the lane circumstances. In order to improve skill learning and transferability to real contests where lane conditions can fluctuate, bowlers also learn to read and react to feedback from the ball's behavior and pin action.

Environmental Challenges

Implementing the developed techniques in practical situations is the goal of the third phase, environmental issues. Bowlers must overcome a variety of obstacles, such as adjusting to various lane conditions and fighting against opponents with various playing philosophies. Applying the knowledge and methods learned in earlier stages is the main goal in order to boost performance and succeed on the lanes.

Utilizing the knowledge, the bowler possesses to improve results is the focus of the exploitation phase. Let's think about a particular lane condition that complies with International Bowling Federation requirements. When a talent is first being developed, manipulating limitations might take the form of narrative, such as playing in the shadow and then slowly shifting left (3-2 every 7 frames) or changing hand and wrist postures as the lane wears out. The bowlers are encouraged to experiment with alternative lane-attack strategies by the coach, who offers them a variety of possibilities. As bowlers advance, they learn how to take advantage of particular circumstances.

Scenario-Based Coaching: Creating Realistic Training Environments

At this point, scenario-based coaching is quite successful. Coaches must, however, have a thorough understanding of performance dynamics in order to accurately mimic competition. The coach may see, for instance, that bowlers frequently shift too far back in later games in an effort to improve their margin and set up strikes. Coaches observe how bowlers respond to various situations and alter as needed to meet the demands of the tournament. The design of the training environment is heavily influenced by this knowledge, which incorporates certain obstacles that closely resemble real-life events.

For Beginners: The coach sets up various scenarios during a practice session with varying lane conditions, including dry, medium, and oily lanes. In accordance with the unique lane conditions, beginners are expected to modify their technique, ball speed, and targeting methods. For instance, they might need to utilize a slower ball speed and a target that is closer to the middle of the lane on dry lanes and a quicker ball speed and a target that is closer to the edges on oily lanes. In order to help them adjust their approach and release to the shifting circumstances, the coach gives them comments on their decision-making, ball release, and targeting accuracy.

For Elite Bowlers: In order to inform the professional bowler's tactical choices during a match, the coach uses scenario-based coaching to assess the lane conditions, pin placements, and competitor performance. Based on the lane circumstances and competition plans, the coach could advise modifying the starting position, ball choice, or aiming approach, for instance. The coach also stresses how crucial it is to recognize and take advantage of environmental opportunities, such as modifying the lane conditions to generate a more advantageous ball path or determining the ideal breakpoint for maximum pin carry.

Wayfinding : Mastering The Bowling Environment

Wayfinding is a key ability in bowling that entails utilizing the environment to your advantage. It is essential for bowlers to appropriately understand the lane conditions in order to get the greatest results.

The term "wayfinding," which was first used by James Gibson, describes the process of learning how to look for and recognize pertinent information in the environment in order to navigate and address performance-related issues. This pertains to bowling and includes analyzing the state of the lanes, determining the temperature and humidity, and studying the actions of other bowlers. In order to reach desired outcomes, effective wayfinding in bowling necessitates the capacity to recognize and negotiate contextual elements. Bowlers need to be adept at identifying oil patterns on the lane, using this knowledge to choose the best ball figuring out the best stance, and aiming points for their shots. Moreover, flexibility is necessary for effective navigation in bowling. The oil patterns might alter as the game goes on, and other elements like noise and distractions might also enter the picture. Competent bowlers adjust to these changes quickly and vary their tactics to maintain constant performance levels. Effective navigation in bowling requires the ability to adjust to shifting circumstances in addition to scanning the environment. Oil patterns on the lanes may change as the game goes on, and other environmental elements like noise and distractions may also come into play. Successful bowlers are able to adjust to these changes right away and shift their approach to maintain performance levels.

AJ JOHNSON:

Wayfinding

While practicing drills, I do a few things every time. I'll work on a specific thing until it feels natural. Each practice session ends with 30 minutes of shooting spares. I warm up and do a couple of timing drills like 4-steps, then I practice different things on the pattern and try to strike from all angles with different bowling balls to keep my game sharp.

For Beginners: To help newcomers improve their spatial awareness and navigational abilities on the bowling lanes, the coach integrates wayfinding drills into the practice sessions. The instructor might, for instance, place targets or markers at various spots along the lane and educate beginners to direct their balls toward those targets while modifying their technique and ball speed. This can assist new drivers in improving their lane awareness, spatial perception, and decision-making abilities while taking environmental factors into account.

For Elite Bowlers: To test the elite bowlers' decision-making and navigational abilities in competitive settings, the coach incorporates wayfinding drills into the training sessions. The coach might simulate situations in which the lane conditions vary during a game, such as going from dry to greasy, and educate the top bowlers to modify their targeting techniques in accordance with those scenarios. This can assist top bowlers in enhancing their capacity for environmental adaptation, attentional control, and decision-making.

Effective Feedback: Guiding Bowler's Performance

Feedback is essential for directing bowlers' performance because it can either reinforce their existing movement strategies or motivate them to look for new chances. It is an important component of skill development.

To help the bowler align with a particular movement template, coaches used to provide feedback by talking about movement mistakes. A nonlinear strategy, on the other hand, takes a different route by focusing the bowler's attention on a particular job goal. The bowlers can use their natural propensities for self-organization thanks to this external attentional focus.

Coaches should think about whether to give feedback with an internal or external reference depending on what they think is best for the bowler at that specific time. The bowlers should always be directed toward specific environmental knowledge as the main goal. This gives them the freedom to research and identify practical performance solutions on their own.

For Beginners: The coach offers feedback that is pertinent, precise, and in line with the training session's objectives, structure, and substance. For instance, the coach might comment on the novices' ball release, footwork, and targeting precision, highlighting the connection between these elements and the particular lane conditions, ball choice, and performance outcomes. The goal of the feedback is to make it easier for newcomers to comprehend the ecological dynamics of the activity and how their actions affect the results.

For Elite Bowlers: The coach gives input that is more focused on the strategic choices, lane circumstances, and performance results of the best bowlers. For instance, the coach might offer advice on how the top bowlers make decisions in various circumstances, such as spare shooting, lane transitions, and lane breakdowns, and how they might take advantage of available opportunities to improve their performance. Elite bowlers can improve their decision-making, perception, and action methods with the help of feedback.

Enhancing Attention Through Demonstrations

Demonstrations have historically been utilized to give bowlers a visual model to help them refine their movement strategies. Depending on their particular needs, these examples and other types of feedback might either limit or increase the bowler's search efforts.

A non-linear approach, however, contends that demonstrations ought to urge bowlers to focus more intently on the data at hand in the playing field. In order to challenge the bowler to combine new actions and reach a new performance objective, practitioners should vary task challenges based on the bowler's current ability. While mobility challenges can be used in conjunction with demonstrations to safely push the bowler to acquire new skills, demonstrations still serve a crucial role in the coaching process.

Coaches can successfully improve the bowler's attention to pertinent information in the environment by combining demonstrations with specific movement tasks. This strategy pushes the bowler to actively look for the best answers for a better performance.

For Beginners: In order to effectively educate beginners on how to shift their attention, use their peripheral vision, and gather information from their surroundings while bowling, the coach uses visual demonstrations. To demonstrate to beginners how to change their focus from the target to the ball, how to use their peripheral vision to keep an eye on the lane circumstances, and how to gather data from the pins and ball reaction to make modifications, for instance, the coach may use film analysis or live demonstrations. During bowling, novices' attentional focus, awareness, and perceptual skills improve thanks to the visual examples.

For Elite Bowlers: The coach uses examples to draw attention to attentional cues important for elite bowlers' performance under duress. For instance, the coach might give a demonstration of how to accurately analyze lane conditions, understand ball reaction, and keep track of competitors' strategies during a match. The demos are intended to improve the best bowlers' sensitivity to pertinent information in their environment, their ability to make wise decisions, and their ability to modify their plans as necessary.

The Role Of Ecological Dynamics In Enhancing Bowling Performance

Sports can be viewed as complex adaptive systems, which emphasize the vital role that people play in influencing performance outcomes. Athletes' cumulative experiences and interactions have a direct impact on how well they perform in both basic and advanced skills. Coaches can develop training environments that mimic the competitive environments faced by bowlers by utilizing constraint manipulation and representational task design. This method speeds up learning and gives bowlers the power to take responsibility for their results.

Future Perspectives For Bowling Coaches:

Bowling coaches should strive to create training environments that reflect the complexity and unpredictability of actual competition settings. Coaches can create realistic practice scenarios that call for real-time adaptation and decision-making by adjusting the lane conditions, oil patterns, and pin placements. Bowlers' capacity to adapt and perform at their best during contests is improved by exposing them to a variety of demanding environmental circumstances during training.

Implementing Scenario-Based Coaching and Wayfinding Drills: Bowlers of all skill levels benefit from using scenario-based coaching and wayfinding drills in their practice sessions to improve their decision-making, environmental awareness, and navigational skills. These exercises simulate actual bowling situations and provide bowlers the chance to hone their adaptability, attentional control, and spatial awareness—skills that are crucial in the fast-paced game of bowling.

Tailoring Specific and Targeted Feedback: Coaches should adapt their criticism to each training session's objectives, structure, and substance. Feedback for newcomers should emphasize method adaptation, decision-making, and identifying environmental clues. Advanced bowlers gain from feedback that is more focused and targeted and covers tactical choices, lane circumstances, and performance consequences. Feedback that is timely and pertinent increases learning and skill transfer to competitive settings, ultimately increasing bowlers' performance and outcomes.

Utilizing Demonstrations for Attentional Cues: In addition to instructing technical concepts, visual demonstrations can also be useful for directing attentional cues. Coaches can show how to effectively switch their focus, use their peripheral vision, and gather information from their surroundings. Coaches help bowlers acquire better attentional focus and awareness during performances by using visual demonstrations.

Individualizing Training Programs: It is essential for coaches to understand the particular skills, assets, and shortcomings of each bowler. As a result, training plans should be customized to meet the unique requirements and objectives of every bowler. This could entail altering the level of challenge in practice exercises, giving tailored feedback, and addressing unique difficulties and limitations. For both novice and professional bowlers, individualized training plans optimize the learning process and maximize improvement potential.

Bowling instructors can enable players to realize their full potential and produce great performance results by embracing the concepts of the ecological dynamic and incorporating their implications into their coaching methods.

Examples:

For beginners: A coach puts up various lane conditions during a practice session, including dry, medium, and greasy lanes, and instructs beginners on how to modify their technique, ball speed, and aiming techniques accordingly. The coach helps them learn how contextual cues affect their performance and offers comments on their decision-making, ball release, and targeting precision. The novices practice modifying their approach and release in accordance with the unique lane conditions, honing their adaptability and decision-making abilities in a practical setting.

For elite bowlers: An elite bowler receives coaching during a match to discuss his tactical choices, lane circumstances, and performance outcomes. With the aid of video analysis, the coach can demonstrate to the bowler how his choices were impacted by the shifting lane conditions and pin placements and how He might have improved his performance. Additionally, the coach provides attentional signals, such as how to successfully switch from the target to the ball and take in information from the surroundings. In order to make better decisions and pay more attention during following competitions, the expert bowler makes use of this feedback and examples.

The Importance Of Synergy Development Under Constraints In Bowling:

In order for a bowling synergy to occur, multiple components—including the bowler's body, the bowling ball, and the surrounding environment—need to work in harmony. The limitations present in the bowling environment, such as the lane characteristics, oil patterns, and pin placement, have a substantial impact on the bowler's range of movement options and have an immediate effect on the development of synergistic motions. For example, the quantity and distribution of oil on the lane have an impact on the friction between the ball and the lane, which in turn has an impact on the trajectory, speed, and spin of the ball. Therefore, in order to accomplish the desired trajectory and pin placement, bowlers must quickly adapt their movement patterns to these lane conditions. To do this, they must smoothly integrate their body movements with the ball.

The coordination of the many parts of the bowler's body is greatly aided by constraints. For the ball to roll optimally and hit the targeted target precisely, the bowler's arm, wrist, and fingers must precisely coordinate during the ball release. In order to take into consideration the unique constraints given by the environment, such as the lane conditions, ball weight, and desired outcome, bowlers must continuously alter their coordination patterns. Bowlers acquire higher levels of performance within the particular parameters of bowling by developing synergies that optimize their movement patterns via regular practice and experience.

Example 1: The oil pattern on the lane in a professional bowling match could be difficult, with thick oil in the middle and dry spaces on the sides. Because there is less friction in the center of the lane and more friction on the sides, the bowlers must adjust their movement pattern. To attain the required pin placement, they may need to modify their approach, release technique, and ball speed. In order to overcome the limitations of the oil pattern and record a high score, the bowlers must have perfect coordination between their body motions and ball release.

Example 2: A bowler may experience various lane conditions in a recreational bowling league from one alley to the next, including changes in oil patterns, lane surfaces, and pin placements. To bowl at his best, a bowler must swiftly adjust his movement patterns to the unique requirements of each lane. He must also coordinate his body motions and ball release. To find the best synergy for each lane circumstance, this may entail testing with various approaches, strategies, and ball choices.

Enhancing Performance Through Sensitivity To Environmental Cues In Bowling:

The ability to respond quickly to visual and aural contextual stimuli is crucial for effective bowling. Bowlers constantly observe their environment and use that information to modify their movement patterns and take prompt action. Bowlers can modify their approach, release, and targeting tactics by using visual cues such as pin locations, lane markers, and the bowling ball's trajectory. Bowlers can use auditory cues to improve their technique and overall performance. These cues include the sound of the ball striking the pins and the feedback they receive after releasing the ball.

The success of bowlers greatly depends on their capacity to be tuned in to their surroundings and quickly digest information to make essential adjustments to their movement patterns. Bowlers can improve their performance in real-time thanks to this increased sensitivity, which allows them to modify their methods and techniques based on the immediate feedback they receive from their surroundings.

Example 1: Due to a certain pin configuration, a bowler may see that the ball consistently hits the pocket but does not knock all of the pins down. Based on this knowledge, he might change his targeting approach to maximize his odds of getting a strike, such as using a different ball or going for a different pin. The bowler can quickly and efficiently modify his technique to maximize his performance due to his sensitivity to the information offered by the pin placement and the movement of the ball.

Example 2: A bowler may discover during a practice session that his ball routinely hooks too early or too late on the lane, leading to less ideal pin placement. The aural input he receives from the sound of the ball striking the pins may lead him to alter his release method, ball speed, or spin. Due to his sensitivity to the ball behavior on the lane, the bowler can alter his technique in real time for a better ball trajectory.

AJ JOHNSON

Feedback and Information Processing

I had a true coach in college who pushed me and got me where I am. My first coach, Dennis Knepper, is still McKendree University's men's head coach. We mostly looked at my swing and gave me visual feedback to see the differences. I worked with him all through college to clean up and create power more easily for tournaments. We had a unique player-coach bond that only grew over four years; we would butt heads all the time, but we were best friends trying to achieve a common goal. Teamwork wins. By working with me every day in college, he made me believe I could achieve everything I wanted and more.

Implications For Enhanced Learning Design In Bowling - Fostering Synergy Formation Under Constraints And Sensitivity To Environmental Cues:

Designing efficient learning strategies for the sport can be aided by viewing bowling as a complex adaptive system that is sensitive to environmental cues and synergy building under limitation. These ideas can help bowlers' performance be optimized and their learning process be sped up for coaches and trainers.

Practice Variability: The limitations of the bowling environment should be taken into account while designing practice sessions, which should include variations in lane conditions, oil patterns, pin positions, and ball choices. Bowlers can build flexible movement patterns and coordination tactics during practice that will improve their performance in a variety of bowling conditions. Bowlers improve their versatility and resilience by practicing under a variety of conditions and learning to modify their technique, strategy, and decision-making in response to the unique limits encountered.

Feedback and Information Processing: Coaches should educate bowlers on how important it is to be sensitive to environmental cues and teach them how to interpret and use environmental feedback efficiently. To improve the bowlers' perception-action coupling, this may entail giving fast feedback during practice sessions, using video analysis tools, or including aural signals. Bowlers can improve their technique and performance in real-time by being taught to actively seek out and use information from their environment, which will lead to more effective and efficient learning.

Individualized Coaching: Coaches should use a personalized instruction style in recognition of the distinctive movement patterns, coordination techniques, and perceptual motor talents that each bowler possesses. This entails carrying out tests to determine each bowler's skills, weaknesses, and limitations and devising tailored training regimens that maximize their performance in accordance with their unique traits. Coaches can customize their coaching techniques to improve the learning process and encourage the formation of efficient synergies in bowling by taking into account the unique restrictions and sensitivities of each bowler.

Constraints-Led Approach: By adjusting the restrictions available in the practice environment, coaches can push bowlers to consider various movement alternatives and create flexible coordination techniques. This strategy is known as a constraints-led approach to teaching. To encourage self-organization and the creation of fresh coordination patterns in bowlers, this can involve modifying the lane conditions, ball choices, or task limitations. This strategy develops a more fluid and adaptable performance by encouraging bowlers to actively examine and modify their movement patterns.

Practice Variability:

Example: During practice sessions, set up different lanes with varying oil patterns, such as heavy oil, medium oil, and dry conditions. Bowlers must adjust their ball choices, angles, and speed to excel in each environment. This variability in practice helps them adapt to different lane conditions encountered during tournaments.

Feedback and Information Processing:

Example: Use video analysis tools to record bowlers' performances during practice. After each shot, review the footage together, providing immediate feedback on their technique, balance, and ball reaction. This real-time feedback helps bowlers make quick adjustments and improve their performance.

Individualized Coaching:

Example: Conduct individual assessments for each bowler to identify their unique strengths and weaknesses. For a bowler who excels in spares but struggles with strikes, tailor a training regimen that emphasizes strike shots. For another bowler who has exceptional hook control, focus on refining their hook delivery further. Personalized coaching maximizes each bowler's potential.

Constraints-Led Approach:

Example: Implement a constraints-led approach by regularly altering the lane conditions during practice. For instance, introduce a sudden change in oil pattern or pin placements. Bowlers must adapt to these dynamic conditions, encouraging them to develop flexible movement patterns and coordination tactics. This approach promotes self-organization and adaptability.

The Significance Of Affordances In Bowling Performance:

Athletes' environmental opportunities for action are referred to as affordances in the world of sport. Athletes detect and make use of these possibilities to direct their actions and choices while carrying out a particular task, like bowling. It is significant to stress that affordances are relational and dependent on the individual's capabilities, intentions, and perceptions rather than intrinsic features of the environment. As a result, how players interpret and utilize these opportunities can have a significant impact on their effectiveness and success in a given sport.

A variety of approaches exist for affordances to appear in the context of bowling. For instance, the bowling lane provides affordances that bowlers can recognize and take advantage of. The amount of oil on the lane determines the frictional qualities, which in turn directly affect the ball's trajectory and speed. Bowlers who have a great understanding of these opportunities might modify their tactics and aiming plans to increase their chances of scoring. Bowlers can improve their accuracy and performance by sensibly recognizing and utilizing these affordances.

Furthermore, bowlers have target affordances thanks to the arrangement and placement of pins. To choose the best trajectory and angle for their ball delivery, bowlers must precisely see and comprehend the spatial relationship between the pins. Skilled bowlers use these target affordances to their advantage to improve their accuracy and raise their chances of reaching the intended targets.

Aspects of the bowling alley, oil patterns, pin locations, and interactions with the bowling ball are only a few examples of affordances in the context of bowling.

For example, different methods and techniques can be used by bowlers depending on the lane circumstances, such as the quantity and distribution of oil on the lane. While a dry alley may offer more hook possibilities, one with heavy oiling may allow for a straighter trajectory for the bowling ball. To perform at their best, bowlers must recognize these opportunities during competition and quickly adjust to them.

Pin placements are another example of an affordance in bowling. Different targeting methods and ball trajectories can be used by bowlers depending on how the pins are arranged on the pin deck. In order to maximize their chances of knocking down more pins, bowlers may need to modify their target and ball speed based on the pin placements. The affordances offered by the pin placements can affect how bowlers make decisions and carry them out when competing.

Practical Application of Learning Design in Ecological Dynamics - Examples for Beginners:

Enhancing Perceptual Skills: The development of perceptual abilities that enable bowlers, especially beginners, to more accurately perceive and interpret the affordances present in the bowling environment is a critical component of the learning design in ecological dynamics. Coaches can create training regimens that are expressly intended to improve newcomers' perception of the bowling lane's features, such as the distribution of oil patterns and the positioning of pins. Beginners can more skillfully adjust their actions and decision-making to maximize their performance by developing their perceptual abilities.

For example, to introduce newcomers to various lane conditions and oil patterns in simulated practice scenarios, instructors might employ scenario-based coaching techniques. This can assist new players in improving their capacity to recognize and respond to various affordances, such as changing their targeted approach or ball speed in response to lane conditions. Coaches can assist novices in strengthening their perceptual abilities and improving their decision-making during competition by giving them the opportunity to explore and experiment with various affordances.

Progressive Skill Development: Progressive skill development is a key tenet of learning design under the ecological dynamics paradigm. This entails gradually exposing novice bowlers to situations and tasks that are more difficult. Coaches can create training plans that introduce novices to various bowling environment affordances gradually, starting with easier activities. Beginners' abilities will advance in a planned and controllable way by being subjected to a variety of affordances and being gradually challenged.

For instance, beginners can begin by honing their fundamental skills, such as ball delivery technique and targeting, on a straight lane with a simple oil pattern. They can gradually advance to practicing on lanes with various oil patterns, pin placements, and lane conditions as they become adept in these tasks. This methodical technique enables new bowlers to gradually adjust to and learn from the affordances afforded by various bowling situations, aiding in their skill development in a way that is more ecological and flexible.

Adaptive Training Programs: Through the use of adaptive training methods, advanced bowlers who have already attained a high level of talent can gain knowledge of ecological dynamics. In these programs, the training tasks and environment are customized to the bowlers' unique demands and performance. Coaches help bowlers consistently adapt and advance their abilities by altering the training environment based on the bowlers' capabilities. Elite bowlers can maximize their performance potential by taking use of the unique affordances offered by the bowling environment by using this adaptive technique.

Incorporating various lane conditions, oil patterns, and pin placements, for instance, instructors can create training plans that can be adjusted in response to a bowler's performance. This may entail altering the pin placements to test a bowler's targeting and accuracy during practice sessions or changing the oil patterns on the fly. Coaches can assist elite bowlers in developing their flexibility and decision-making abilities, which are essential in competition, by regularly exposing them to various affordances and challenging them to adjust.

Emphasis on Self-Organization: Ecological dynamics' core idea of self-organization emphasizes how people naturally spontaneously adjust and order their motions in response to the affordances provided by their surroundings. Coaches might emphasize self-organization more during practice for elite bowlers. Coaches help the optimization of bowlers' performance by encouraging them to investigate and take advantage of the affordances within the bowling environment. Elite bowlers can creatively change their technique and strategy using this method, making use of the unique opportunities presented by each circumstance.

For example, during practice sessions, instructors can encourage top bowlers to experiment with various ball trajectories, release positions, and aiming techniques. This will enable them to modify and organize their motions in response to the affordances they notice. Elite bowlers may benefit from this as they work to improve their capacity for self-organizing their movements and tactics in the heat of battle, resulting in more adaptable and successful performances.

IMPLICATIONS FOR OPTIMAL LEARNING DESIGN IN SPORT: With an emphasis on affordances in sports, integrating ecological dynamics ideas into learning design might provide helpful insights for creating efficient training regimens and coaching strategies in the context of bowling. The following conclusions are drawn:

Personalized Training Programs: The need to adjust training regimens to the needs of certain athletes is highlighted by learning design in ecological dynamics. Each bowler has distinct perceptual talents, decision-making processes, and movement capabilities that coaches must carefully evaluate. Coaches can create extremely effective and specialized training experiences by offering tailored perceptual training, gradually improving skill development and adaptive training programs that match each bowler's perceived affordances.

Adaptability as a Key Skill: The ecological dynamics framework lays a strong emphasis on sports performance adaptation. Coaches should create training plans that consistently test bowlers' ability to adjust to the various affordances found in the bowling environment in order to develop this important talent. Bowlers' adaptability is cultivated by coaches by dynamically shifting training tasks, the training environment, and numerous limits. This prepares bowlers for a competition where conditions are continuously changing.

Decision-Making and Spontaneous Organization: Decision-making and spontaneous organization play a critical part in ecological dynamics learning design. In order to enable bowlers to coordinate their motions and make decisions based on perceived affordances, coaches should design training programs. Bowlers' decision-making abilities and capacity to adjust to the changing demands of the bowling environment are developed by including decision-making tasks, problem-solving exercises, and opportunities for bowlers to explore various movement options during practice sessions. Bowlers' decision-making and self-organization abilities are crucial for success in dynamic sports like bowling, so instructors encourage a more active and independent role for bowlers in their learning process.

Long-Term Skill Development: In contrast to short-term performance improvements, the ecological dynamics paradigm places a lot of emphasis on long-term skill development. Training plans should be created by coaches with the improvement of fundamental movement abilities, perceptual skills, and decision-making processes as their top priorities. Coaches aid in the development of strong, adaptable skills that can be used successfully in a variety of competitive situations by adopting a holistic and multidimensional approach to skill development, taking into account the interaction between perception, cognition, and action, and designing training tasks that facilitate the integration of these components.

Contextualized and Ecologically Valid Training: Ecological dynamics learning design emphasizes the significance of training challenges that appropriately reflect the competitive environment. Coaches should create training plans that are ecologically sound and contextualized so that bowlers are exposed to affordances that closely mirror those found in real competition. This entails implementing situational limitations, creating realistic and dynamic practice environments, and encouraging task diversity and unpredictability. Coaches enable bowlers to build abilities that effortlessly transfer to competition by matching training objectives with the ecological requirements of the bowling environment, leading to more effective and efficient skill acquisition.

Hypothetical Examples

Personalized Training Programs: Sarah, a novice bowler, participates in a tailored training regimen that aims to improve her awareness of the opportunities available to her at the bowling alley. To help her analyze the lane conditions, oil patterns, and pin placements, her coach creates particular exercises. Sarah gains a greater understanding of the bowling environment through targeted drills and feedback, empowering her to choose her shots more wisely.

Adaptability as a Key Skill: James, an intermediate bowler, takes part in a training regimen that places a strong emphasis on flexibility. His coach exposes him to both dry and greasy lanes, among other lane conditions. James gains the ability to modify his ball speed, rotation, and targeting approach to suit the particular circumstances he meets by training on several lanes with various oil patterns. This improves his capacity to change course quickly during competitions, providing him an advantage.

Decision-Making and Spontaneous Organization: Alex, a skilled bowler, participates in training sessions that emphasize judgment and impulsive planning. He challenges Alex to select the most advantageous approach and targeting method based on the affordances supplied by the pin locations by setting up situations with various pin arrangements. As a result, Alex is able to make better decisions and adjust his movements in real-time, which results in more effective shot execution.

Long-Term Skill Development: Emily, a committed young bowler, takes part in a long-term skill development program. The mastery of basic movement techniques, such as keeping the correct bowling stance, carrying out a consistent approach, releasing the ball with accuracy, and following through smoothly, is a priority for her coach. By concentrating on these fundamental abilities and offering purposeful practice opportunities, Emily develops a strong technical base that will assist her development and advancement as a bowler.

Contextualized and Ecologically Valid Training: Jason, a seasoned professional bowler, participates in practices that closely resemble the atmosphere of a match. His instructor plans practice sessions at various bowling alleys, each of which has a different set of lanes and pin positions. Even crowd noise and other distractions are added by the coach to replicate the strain of a tournament environment. Jason improves his capacity to modify his technique and decision-making to meet the unique requirements of each tournament he competes in by training in these ecologically realistic circumstances.

FINAL WORD

Bowling's Path to Mastery and Excellence

In the world of sports, few disciplines can rival the captivating blend of skill, strategy, and passion that defines the sport of bowling. As we prepare to close the final chapter of our journey through "The Technical Mastery of Bowling Progression: Path to Ultimate Motor Skills Development," it is fitting to reflect on the rich tapestry of knowledge and insights that we have woven together in this trilogy. This comprehensive exploration has taken us on a multifaceted journey through the art and science of bowling, and it has equipped us with a deeper understanding of why we learn these skills and how to adapt new motor skills.

The acquisition and refinement of motor skills extend far beyond the lanes of the bowling alley. The development of these skills is not exclusive to any one sport; rather, it's a fundamental aspect of human growth, personal achievement, and success in various disciplines.

Bowling, like many other sports, presents a unique opportunity to hone and showcase motor skills. The art of rolling a bowling ball down the lane, with precision, spin, and accuracy, demands the seamless coordination of various muscle groups and sensory inputs. These skills can be a source of immense satisfaction and accomplishment for athletes of all skill levels.

Moreover, the process of learning and improving motor skills has wide-ranging benefits that transcend the specific context in which they are acquired. It fosters discipline, patience, perseverance, and a deep understanding of the learning process. These skills are not confined to a bowling alley; they are transferable to various facets of life, including education, professional careers, and personal relationships.

As we've explored the intricacies of skill development within the realm of bowling, we have not only equipped you with the tools to excel in this sport but have also imparted valuable lessons that extend to other domains. The ability to set goals, adapt to feedback, and practice with dedication are attributes that serve individuals well in any pursuit.

In the pursuit of excellence, it is crucial to remember that the mastery of motor skills is not limited to a single sport or activity. The knowledge and insights shared within this trilogy are not only relevant to the world of bowling but can be applied to other endeavors, guiding individuals toward success and fulfillment.

This trilogy is not confined to theory; it's enriched with practical strategies for enhancing skill acquisition. It aims to transform not just your approach to bowling but your understanding of the broader landscape of athletics and competition.

As we conclude this trilogy, the keys to technical mastery and the wisdom to redefine your approach to this dynamic sport are within your reach. We invite you to embark on this transformative journey, one that transcends the boundaries of the sport itself, offering profound insights into human achievement and the relentless pursuit of greatness through the art of bowling.

The world of professional bowling is a captivating one, full of fascinating stories and remarkable individuals who influence the game. With every step onto the approach and every grip on the ball, we continue to discover the wonder of competitive bowling.

We are deeply honored and appreciative of the opportunity to educate and enlighten the bowling community. Our objective is that these publications serve as sources of knowledge and inspiration, illuminating the road to excellence for athletes of all skill levels.

As you turn the final pages of this trilogy, may you carry with you the wisdom and insights gathered along this enlightening journey. Let the knowledge and passion instilled within these words accompany you as you continue to navigate the intricate and captivating world of bowling. May your dedication, practice, and unwavering pursuit of excellence lead you to new levels of performance and fulfillment on the lanes. Thank you for allowing us to be part of your bowling journey, and may you find continued inspiration and success in this wonderful sport.

REFERENCES:

- Adams JA. Historical review and appraisal of research on the learning, retention, and transfer of human motor skills. Psychology Bull. 1987;101:41–74.

- Baldwin TT, Ford KJ. Transfer of training: a review and directions for future research. Pers Psychol. 2006;41:63–105.

- Bandura A. Social cognitive theory of self-regulation. Org Behav Hum Decis Process. 1986;50:248–87

- Carson, H. J., & Collins, D. (2011). Refining and regaining skills in fixation/diversification stage performers: The Five-A Model. International Review of Sport and Exercise Psychology,4, 146–167.doi:10.1080/175098 4x.2011.613682

- Chase, W. G., & Simon, H. A. (1973). Perception in chess. Cognitive Psychology, 4(1), 55-81.

- Cheng EW, Ho DC. A review of transfer of training studies in the past decade. Pers Rev. 2001;30:102–18.

- Colvin, G. (2010). Talent is overrated: What really separates world-class performers from everybody else. Penguin.

- Coyle, D. (2009). The talent code: Greatness isn't born. It's grown. Here's how. Bantam.

- Dryden, J. (1693/1885). Of dramatic poesy and other critical essays (Vol. 1). London, England: J. M. Dent & Sons.

- Ericsson KA, Krampe RT, Tesch-Römer C. 1993. The role of deliberate practice in the acquisition of expert performance. Psychol. Rev. 100, 363–406. (10.1037/0033-295X.100.3.363) - DOI

- Ericsson, K. A., Charness, N., Feltovich, P. J., & Hoffman, R. R. (2006). The Cambridge handbook of expertise and expert performance. Cambridge University Press.

- Ericsson, K. A., Krampe, R. T., & Tesch-Romer, C. (1993). The role of deliberate practice in the acquisition of expert performance. Psychological Review, 100(3), 363-406.

- Fitts, P. and Posner, M.I. (1967) Human Performance. Brooks/Cole Publishing, Belmont, CA.

- Galton, F. (1874). Hereditary genius: An inquiry into its laws and consequences. Macmillan.

- Gibson, J., The Ecological Approach to Visual Perception. 1979, Boston: Houghton Mifflin Company. 332.

- Guadagnoli MA., Lee T.D., Challenge Point: A Framework for Conceptualizing the Effects of Various Practice Conditions, Journal of Motor Behaviour, 2004, 36, 212–224.

- Kaufman, S. B. (2013). Ungifted: Intelligence redefined. Basic Books.

- Lyndon, E. H. & Dawson, C. J. (1995, June). The conceptual mediation program: A practical outcome from a novel perspective on conceptual change. Paper presented at the Australian Association of Science Education Annual Conference, Adelaide.

- Lyndon, E. H. (1989). I did it my way! An introduction to Old way/new way. Australasian Journal of Special Education, 13, 32-37.

- Lyndon, E. H. (2000). Conceptual mediation: A new theory and new method of conceptual change. Australia: University of Adelaide. Unpublished doctoral dissertation.

- Magill, R. A. & Hall, K.G. (1990). A review of the contextual interference effect in motor skill acquisition, Human Movement Science, 9, 241-289.

- Marcus, G. (2012). Guitar zero: The science of becoming musical at any age. Penguin.

- Milanese, C., Facci, G., Cesari, P., & Zancanaro, C. (2008). Amplification of error: A rapidly effective method for motor performance improvement. The Sport Psychologist, 22, 164–174

- Paradise A. State of the industry: ASTD's annual review of trends in workplace learning and performance. Alexandria: ASTD; 2007.

- Schmidt, R. A., and Lee, T. D. (2011). Motor Control and Learn-ing: A Behavioral Emphasis, 5th Edn. Champaign, IL: HumanKinetics

- Shenk, D. (2011). The genius in all of us: Why everything you've been told about genetics, talent, and IQ is wrong. Doubleday.

- Schmidt, R. A., and Lee, T. D. (2011). Motor Control and Learning: A Behavioral Emphasis, 5th Edn. Champaign, IL: Human Kinetics

- Simonton, D. K. (1976). Talent and its development: An emergenic and epigenetic model. Psychological Review, 83(6), 444-477.

- Simonton, D. K. (2000a). Creative productivity: A predictive and explanatory model of career trajectories and landmarks. Psychological Review, 107(3), 576-595.

- Syed, M. (2010). Bounce: Mozart, Federer, Picasso, Beckham, and the science of success. HarperCollins.

- Tziner A, Haccoun RR, Kadish A. Personal and situational characteristics influencing the effectiveness of transfer of training improvement strategies. J Occup Psychol. 1991;64:167–77.

- Williams, A. M. and Ford, P. R. (2009). Promoting a skills-based agenda in olympic sports: The role of skill-acquisition specialists, Journal of Sports Sciences, 27, 1381-1392.

Index

Q